ESSENTIAL CUBS

DOUG MYERS

**Chicago Cubs Facts,
Feats, and Firsts—
from the Batter's Box
to the Bullpen
to the Bleachers**

CB
CONTEMPORARY BOOKS

Library of Congress Cataloging-in-Publication Data

Myers, Doug, 1964–
     Essential Cubs : facts, feats & firsts—from the batter's box
  to the bullpen to the bleachers / Doug Myers.
          p.   cm.
     Includes bibliographical references (pp. 355–356) and index.
     ISBN 0-8092-2610-3
     1. Chicago Cubs (Baseball team)   2. Chicago Cubs (Baseball team)—
  History.   I. Title.
  GV875.C6M94   1999
  796.357'64'0977311—dc21   99-11603
                                                                CIP

Cover design by Todd Petersen
Interior design by Precision Graphics

Published by Contemporary Books
A division of NTC/Contemporary Publishing Group, Inc.
4255 West Touhy Avenue, Lincolnwood (Chicago), Illinois 60646-1975 U.S.A.
International Standard Book Number: 0-8092-2610-3

99 00 01 02 03 04 CU 15 14 13 12 11 10 9 8 7 6 5 4 3 2 1

contents

To "The Professor," who may yet realize that baseball exists to explain everything else

acknowledgments

A tip of the Cubs hat to Cindy and Penny . . . Mom and Dad . . . Tinker, Evers, and Chance . . . the Motel 6 Baseball League . . . Andre Dawson and Rick Sutcliffe . . . Debbie Crisfield and John Monteleone . . . Ernie Banks and Gene Baker . . . Barry Gifford and David Lynch . . . Mordecai Brown and Orvie Overall . . . Bill Murray and Carl . . . Stan Hack and Ron Santo . . . Bob Dylan and Catfish Hunter . . . Bill Hands and Billy Williams . . . Crash Davis and Nuke Laloosh . . . Dick Drott and Frank Ernaga . . . the Thompson Twins, Hunter and Jim . . . Ryne Sandberg and Billy Herman . . . Helen Warren and Frank Juiliano . . . Gabby Hartnett and Charlie Grimm . . . Carl Hiaasen and Warren Zevon . . . Lee Smith and Bruce Sutter . . . Thurman Munson and Ken Hubbs . . . Bill Lee and Lon Warneke . . . Zachary Taylor Davis and Charlie Weeghman . . . Jerome Walton and Dwight Smith . . . Harry Caray and Jack Brickhouse . . . Sammy Sosa, Kerry Wood, and the 1998 Cubs.

And 480', Waveland Avenue, tape-measure thanks to Randy Voorhees at Mountain Lion, Inc., in Princeton, New Jersey, for coming up with the idea for this book and selling it, and to Rob Taylor at NTC/Contemporary Publishing for buying it.

introduction

The first time I went to Wrigley Field was in a rented RV in the midst of a 10-game-10-day-10-city odyssey in the summer of 1989. Gondo, Flash, the Pig, Lucky, and Yitzhak were with me for a ride—with Wilbury, the Greek, Zeigler, and the Varmint there in spirit—that had taken us through Shea, the Big O, Three Rivers, Riverfront, Busch, and County Stadium. With that kind of antiseptic symmetry as a prelude, nothing could feel better than squeezing into the sweaty back row of Wrigley's right-field bleachers on a sweltering Friday afternoon.

It was July 28, 1989, and the Cubs won the first of three straight against the Mets that day, as Dwight Smith took Rick Aguilera deep and Shawon Dunston ended the game with an over-the-shoulder catch, spin, and throw to double Juan Samuel off first. Having been wandering teamless since Thurman Munson's death nearly 10 years before to the day, I converted to Cub-ism on the spot.

This is the book I wish someone had given me that day. It contains everything Cubs fans need to know, want to recount, or wish they'd clipped from the newspaper the day it happened. It's a scrapbook of stories, statistics, and observations—a history of the first 123 seasons of Chicago Cubs baseball in names and numbers, facts and legends, box scores and scorecards. Here's just a scratching of the playing surface:

- The top 50 hitters and top 25 pitchers in Cubs history, including their lifetime statistics in Chicago
- The most famous trades in team history, classified by Good, Bad, and Ugly—not for the faint of heart!
- The 100 wildest games ever played by the Cubs, from a 36–7 pasting of Louisville in 1897 to a 15–12 comeback victory over the Milwaukee Brewers in the heat of a pennant race in 1998
- The All-Name, All-Nickname, and All-Flash-in-the-Pan teams—a time to celebrate Abraham Lincoln "Sweetbreads" Bailey, Pickles Dillhoefer, and the briefly devastating Dick Drott (the Kerry Wood of 1957)
- The top 10 for all the major hitting, pitching, and baserunning categories—and a few new ones—as well as impressive achievements hidden in a player's statistics
- Dubious distinctions in the field, on the mound, or at the plate, from serving up three homers to the opposing pitcher, to the only man in history to make 50 errors and strike out 100 times in the same season
- A line score and game summary for every World Series game ever played by the Cubs

- An in-depth look at the greatness of not just Ernie Banks but also the vastly under-rated Ron Santo, Stan Hack, Jimmy Ryan, and Bruce Sutter
- The weirdest on-field moments, from the fire of 1894 to the blackout of 1977, from the team's arrest by the Sunday Observance League in 1895 to a drunk yuppie charging the mound 100 years later, from two balls in play to a 220′, game-winning home run
- A list, breakdown, analysis, and celebration of all 66 of Sammy Sosa's home runs, a day-by-day account of the 1998 season's highlights, and a comparison of Kerry Wood with the greatest rookie pitchers ever

I hope you enjoy roaming through it as much as I enjoyed building it. And may next year truly be one of these years.

abbreviations

A	assists
AB	at-bats
BA	batting average
BB	bases on balls
BK	balks
CG	complete games
DP	double plays
E	errors
ERA	earned-run average
FA	fielding average
G	games
GA	games ahead
GB	games behind
GS	games saved
H	hits
HBP	hit by pitch
HR	home runs
IP	innings pitched
L	losses
(L)	left-handed pitcher
LOB	left on base
OBA	on-base average
Pct.	percentage (winning)
Pos.	position
R	runs
(R)	right-handed pitcher
RBI	runs batted in
S	saves
SA	slugging average
SB	stolen bases
ShO	shutouts
SO	strikeouts
TC/G	total chances per game
W	wins
WP	wild pitches
2B	doubles
3B	triples

the clubhouse

Since 1876, a National League team has played in Chicago, the longest run of any professional baseball franchise. The Cubs will have played their 18,000th game in 1999—laid end to end, that's enough to last more than four years at 24 hours a day, seven days a week. In the process, more than 1,600 players will have worn the team's uniform, producing more than 1,250 shutouts and more than 10,000 home runs. Sometime in 1999, the pitching staff will have chalked up its 78,000th strikeout and the offense will have recorded its 84,000th run—a journey of more than 5,700 miles, or from Chicago to New York City seven times.

But there is more to the history of the Cubs than numbers. There are legends and folklore, dynasties and droughts, heroes and flakes, the famous and infamous, and feats glorious and obscure, sublime and ridiculous, from before Wrigley Field and before the team was even the Cubs. This story begins in the clubhouse, with the year-by-year results of the team and with the greatest players to ever wear the Chicago uniform.

Read on to discover:

- The 16 names other than "Cubs" by which Chicago's National League team has gone
- The 12 eras of the Cubs, including its two dynasties, spanning the seasons from Albert Goodwill Spalding and Cap Anson to Kerry Wood and Sammy Sosa
- How the winningest team in baseball history—the 116–36 Cubs of 1906—was built, piece by piece, beginning with the arrival of Frank Chance in 1898
- The team's 50 greatest hitters and 25 greatest pitchers, including a host of long-forgotten 19th-century stars, an unknown legend who is one of only nine players to have 200 hits and 100 walks in one season, and the Cubs' only Triple Crown winner (or is he? . . .)
- The nine Cubs who've won the league's MVP Award, the six who just missed, and the five who would have taken the award had it been given when they played—including one player who would have taken it home *seven* times
- The four pitchers who've won the Cy Young Award and the lucky 13 who would have taken the prize *20* times had it been awarded before 1956

It's right this way, under the third-base stands, down the hall and on the right.

THE TEAMS

The National League was born on April 22, 1876, and the Chicago Cubs were born three days later—debuting with a 4–0, Albert Spalding shutout in Louisville. Back then, they were the White Stockings, and the National League competition didn't sound so familiar either:

National League Titles

TEAM	NUMBER	YEARS
Brooklyn/Los Angeles Dodgers		
Early Championships	3	1890, 1899, 1900
Modern Championships	6	1955, 1959, 1963, 1965, 1981, 1988
Total Championships	9	
Pennants	12	1916, 1920, 1941, 1947, 1949, 1952–53, 1956, 1966, 1974, 1977, 1978
Division Titles	4	1983, 1985, 1994, 1995
Total	25	
Boston/Milwaukee/Atlanta Braves		
Early Championships	8	1877–78, 1883, 1891–93, 1897–98
Modern Championships	3	1914, 1957, 1995
Total Championships	11	
Pennants	4	1948, 1958, 1991, 1992
Division Titles	5	1969, 1982, 1993, 1997, 1998
Total	20	
New York/San Francisco Giants		
Early Championships	2	1888–89
Modern Championships	5	1905, 1921, 1922, 1933, 1954
Total Championships	7	
Pennants	12	1904, 1911–13, 1917, 1923–24, 1936–37, 1951, 1962, 1989
Division Titles	1	1987
Total	20	
Chicago Cubs		
Early Championships	6	1876, 1880–82, 1885–86
Modern Championships	2	1907, 1908
Total Championships	8	
Pennants	8	1906, 1910, 1918, 1929, 1932, 1935, 1938, 1945
Division Titles	2	1984, 1989
Total	18	
St. Louis Cardinals		
Early Championships	0	
Modern Championships	9	1926, 1931, 1934, 1942, 1944, 1946, 1964, 1967, 1982
Total Championships	9	
Pennants	6	1928, 1930, 1943, 1968, 1985, 1987
Division Titles	1	1996
Total	16	

continued

TEAM	NUMBER	YEARS
Pittsburgh Pirates		
Early Championships	2	1901–02
Modern Championships	5	1909, 1925, 1960, 1971, 1979
Total Championships	7	
Pennants	2	1903, 1927
Division Titles	7	1970, 1972, 1974–75, 1990–92
Total	16	
Cincinnati Reds		
Early Championships	0	
Modern Championships	5	1919, 1940, 1975–76, 1990
Total Championships	5	
Pennants	4	1939, 1961, 1970, 1972
Division Titles	4	1973, 1979, 1994–95
Total	13	
Philadelphia Phillies		
Early Championships	0	
Modern Championships	1	1980
Total Championships	1	
Pennants	4	1915, 1950, 1983, 1993
Division Titles	4	1976–78, 1981
Total	9	

National League in 1876 (by order of finish)

Chicago White Stockings   Later known as the Colts, Orphans, and Cubs.

St. Louis Brown Stockings   The National League's first St. Louis franchise lasted only two seasons. Today's Cardinals date back to 1892, when they joined the league as the Browns.

Hartford Dark Blues   Lasted two seasons.

Boston Red Caps   Later known as the Beaneaters, Doves, and Rustlers, before becoming the Braves in 1912, moving to Milwaukee in 1953, and then to Atlanta in 1966.

Louisville Grays   Lasted two seasons. The Louisville Colonels of the American Association were merged into the Pittsburgh Pirates in 1900.

New York Mutuals   This was the name of the National League's first New York entry. The team lasted one year, being kicked out of the league for skipping its last road trip of the season. Today's Giants date back to the Troy Trojans of 1879, which moved to New York in 1883 and to San Francisco in 1958.

Philadelphia Athletics   This was the name of the National League's first Philadelphia entry. It, too, was kicked out of the league for skipping its last western swing. Today's Phillies date back to the Worcester Ruby Legs of 1880, which moved to Philadelphia in 1883.

Cincinnati Red Stockings   In existence until 1880. Today's Reds date back to an
                                  American Association team that joined the National
                                  League in 1890.

Though six of 1901's "original eight" NL cities were represented, only the Cubs and Braves
date back to 1876. The Pirates debuted in the National League in 1887 as the Alleghenys. The
Brooklyn Bridegrooms joined the National League from the American Association in 1890.
Later they came to be known as the Superbas, the Robins, and Dodgers before moving to
Los Angeles in 1958.

The Names

Before they were Cubs, Chicago's National League ball club was the White Stockings—winning
six pennants under that name from 1876 to 1889. During 1890, the players formed their own
league—the Players League—the most extreme "labor action" the sport has seen. So many
young players were signed to replace the veterans who jumped to this new league that sportswriters began calling the White Stockings the Colts. When player-manager "Baby" "Cap"
and eventually "Pop" Anson was finally dismissed after 22 years with the team, the Colts
became known as the Orphans.

The team, at various times, was also referred to as the Black Stockings (they switched to
black socks in 1888), Ex-Colts, Rainmakers (when a number of games were rained out in
1898), Cowboys and Rough Riders and Desert Rangers (when they spent spring training in
New Mexico in 1899), and the Remnants (because so many of its best players had jumped to
the American League).

By 1902, the name White Stockings had already been snagged by Chicago's American
League team. The name Cubs had been used during the 1900 season by Charles Sensabaugh,
the sports editor of the *Chicago Daily News*. Its connotation was similar to that of Orphans,
and it was easier to fit into the headlines. The name Cubs began to appear regularly on
March 27, 1902, and has been used ever since.

Other names continued to pop up: Recruits, Panamas (for the straw hats a number of
players wore after a trip to Panama), Zephyrs, Nationals, Spuds (an odd tribute to the Irish
ancestry of owner Charlie Murphy), and Trojans (in 1913, when Johnny Evers, a native of
Troy, New York, managed the team).

In a sense, the Cubs did not officially become the Cubs until a cub first appeared on the
team's uniform—1908—the last time they won a World Championship.

The Results—by Era

With all the talk of the Cubs' inability to reach the World Series, some might conclude that
the team had played losing baseball for more than 100 years. Actually, only the Dodgers and
Giants have more championships and pennants than the Cubs in the National League. The
team has had two very impressive dynasties—1880 through 1886 and 1906 through 1910—
and one stretch of consistent, competitive baseball (1929 through 1938) that saw them win
four pennants in 10 years.

Cubs history can be broken into 12 eras, which are summarized in the following pages.

1876–86: The First Dynasty

The story of the White Stockings begins before the inaugural 1876 season with the raiding
of the National Association's Boston franchise. Four star players—catcher Deacon White,
first-baseman Cal McVey, second-baseman Ross Barnes, and star pitcher Albert Goodwill

1876–86

YEAR	W	L	Pct.	GB	FINISH	MANAGER
1876	52	14	.788	+6	1	Albert Spalding
1877	26	33	.441	15.5	5	Albert Spalding
1878	30	30	.500	11	4	Bob Ferguson
1879	46	33	.582	5.5	3	
	41	21	.661			Cap Anson
	5	12	.294			Silver Flint
1880	67	17	.798	+15	1	Cap Anson
1881	56	28	.667	+9	1	Cap Anson
1882	55	29	.655	+3	1	Cap Anson
1883	59	39	.602	4	2	Cap Anson
1884	62	50	.554	22	T4	Cap Anson
1885	87	25	.777	+2	1	Cap Anson
1886	90	34	.726	+2.5	1	Cap Anson

We shall no longer endure the criticism of the respectable people because of drunkenness in the Chicago nine.

Albert Goodwill Spalding, 1886

Spalding—were lured away to Chicago. In a much smaller deal that did not create nearly the ruckus, the White Stockings also coaxed a young third baseman named Cap Anson to jump to Chicago from his Philadelphia team. McVey hit .308, Barnes won the batting title (.429), White led the league in RBIs with 60 (in 66 games!), Spalding went 47–13, and Chicago ran away with the pennant.

The White Stockings won another five pennants by 1886, narrowly missing two others in 1879 and 1883. The teams of 1880, 1881, 1882, 1885, and 1886 were led by Hall of Famers Cap Anson (3,000 hits), John Clarkson (328 wins), and King Kelly, the Babe Ruth of the 19th century, who played hard, lived harder, and died young. This era came to an abrupt end after the 1886 season, when the White Stockings turned in their second consecutive subpar showing in a postseason exhibition series with the American Association–champion St. Louis Browns. Some players showed up hungover or drunk. Some may have taken payoffs to throw games in what they viewed as a meaningless series to pad their relatively meager paychecks. Spalding, the team's owner, didn't find it meaningless, and he decided to do something about the conduct of his players.

1887–97: Temperance and Mediocrity

If they played today, the Chicago sports pages would look more like a police blotter than they already do. In fact, in many ways, the 1886 champs made the *1986* champs look like choirboys. Much as Mets GM Frank Cashen tried to clean up the New York locker room, White Stockings management tried to do the same—and both ended up gutting their ball clubs.

After the 1886 season, team owner, former player, and fierce temperance advocate Albert Goodwill Spalding decided to run the drunkards off of his team—even though they were his best players. Thirty-one-game winner Jim McCormick went to Pittsburgh with left-fielder Abner Dalrymple. Center-fielder George Gore, a perennial .300 hitter, went to New York. King Kelly, the sport's biggest superstar and reigning batting champion (.388), was sold to Boston for the unheard-of sum of $10,000. Hall of Fame pitching ace John Clarkson followed before the 1888 season. The team finished third in 1887, second in 1888, and headed down from there.

The final blow came in 1890, when the players formed their own league—the Players League—and siphoned off more than half of the National League talent. The White Stockings suffered far more losses than most, as every regular but Cap Anson, Tommy Burns, and Wild Bill Hutchison jumped to the new league. The league lasted only one season, but the

1887–97

YEAR	W	L	Pct.	GB	FINISH	MANAGER
1887	71	50	.587	6.5	3	Cap Anson
1888	77	58	.570	9	2	Cap Anson
1889	67	65	.508	19	3	Cap Anson
1890	84	53	.613	6	2	Cap Anson
1891	82	53	.607	3.5	2	Cap Anson
1892	70	76	.479	29	7	Cap Anson
1893	56	71	.441	29	9	Cap Anson
1894	57	75	.432	34	8	Cap Anson
1895	72	58	.554	15	4	Cap Anson
1896	71	57	.555	18.5	5	Cap Anson
1897	59	73	.447	34	9	Cap Anson

damage to the White Stockings endured. Only Fred Pfeffer, Jimmy Ryan, and pitcher Ad Gumbert jumped back to Chicago. The Colts came close to a pennant in '91, then slipped into the middle of the pack for the rest of the decade.

After the 1897 season, Cap Anson—45, still the player-manager, and still one of the team's best hitters—was relieved of his duties and replaced with one of the few players who hadn't jumped in 1890: Tom Burns.

1898–1905: Rebuilding

On the surface, the eight seasons from 1898 to 1905 appear to show the Orphans (and by 1902, the Cubs) going nowhere. They came no closer to first place than eight games in 1903 and went through four managers. But in retrospect, things were looking up as early as 1898. Here's a time line of the key events in the formation of one of baseball's great dynasties:

Building a Dynasty

1898   A catcher named Frank Chance joins the team.

1900   Chance's frequent injuries and the arrival of catcher Johnny Kling push Chance to the outfield.

1902   New manager Frank Selee, who guided the Boston Beaneaters to five pennants in the 1890s, shifts Chance to first base. The 1902 season also saw the debuts of a converted third baseman (Joe Tinker) at shortstop and a converted shortstop (Johnny Evers) at second.

1898–1905

YEAR	W	L	Pct.	GB	FINISH	MANAGER
1898	85	65	.567	17.5	4	Tom Burns
1899	75	73	.507	26	8	Tom Burns
1900	65	75	.464	19	T5	Tom Loftus
1901	53	86	.381	37	6	Tom Loftus
1902	68	69	.496	34	5	Frank Selee
1903	82	56	.594	8	3	Frank Selee
1904	93	60	.608	13	2	Frank Selee
1905	92	61	.601	13	3	
	37	28	.569			Frank Selee
	55	33	.625			Frank Chance

1903   Tinker, Evers, and Chance are in place.

1904   Before the 1904 season, Mordecai Brown is acquired, a 21-year-old outfielder named Wildfire Schulte is discovered in upstate New York, and utility man Solly Hofman is found in St. Louis. The Cubs finish second.

1905   Frank Selee falls ill, and Frank Chance, though only 27, is elected manager by his teammates. The club plays .635 ball under Chance and finishes third. Rookie Ed Reulbach wins 18 games. In the off-season, Harry Steinfeldt and Jimmy Sheckard are acquired, at Chance's urging. All of it played a part in a 24-game jump in the standings in 1906.

1906–12: Tinker to Evers to Chance, Brown to Overall to Reulbach

The Cubs of 1906, 1907, 1908, and 1910 are best known for the double plays turned by Joe Tinker, Johnny Evers, and Frank Chance. Just as important a trio, if not more so, were pitchers Mordecai Brown, Orvie Overall, and Ed Reulbach.

These Cubs teams were built on pitching, defense, and smart, aggressive play. They won at least 90 games every season during this stretch and fell short of a fifth pennant in 1909 when they won *only* 104 games and lost 49. They denied Ty Cobb's Detroit Tigers a title in one-sided World Series victories in both 1907 and 1908—the only two Series the Cubs have ever won.

As the Cubs fell to the Philadelphia Athletics in five games in the 1910 Series, cracks in their armor were already beginning to show. Orvie Overall, coming off a disappointing season and Series, retired in a salary dispute. The high-strung Johnny Evers, who missed the 1910 World Series with a broken leg at the same time he was suffering huge investment losses, missed most of the 1911 season with a nervous breakdown. Injuries limited Frank Chance to 87 at bats in 1911, and frequent beanings drove him to the hospital for an operation to remove blood clots in his brain at the end of the 1912 season. Mordecai Brown had lost his effectiveness in 1912 and was banished to the minors.

That the club was able to even stay competitive is a tribute to their professionalism.

1906–12

YEAR	W	L	Pct.	GB	FINISH	WORLD SERIES	MANAGER
1906	116	36	.763	+20	1	White Sox 4 Cubs 2	Frank Chance
1907	107	45	.704	+17	1	Cubs 4 Tigers 0 (tie)*	Frank Chance
1908	99	55	.643	+1	1	Cubs 4 Tigers 1	Frank Chance
1909	104	49	.680	6.5	2		Frank Chance
1910	104	50	.675	+13	1	Athletics 4 Cubs 1	Frank Chance
1911	92	62	.597	7.5	2		Frank Chance
1912	91	59	.607	11.5	3		Frank Chance

*Game One was suspended, due to darkness, with the score tied, allowing the Cubs to sweep the Tigers in "five."

1913–25: Disarray

The 13 years following the departure of Frank Chance after the 1912 season saw the team go through nine managerial changes, including five in five years. It also saw ownership of the team pass from Charles Murphy (forced out by fellow owners due to his sheer obnoxiousness) to Charlie Weeghman to William Wrigley. Finally, it also saw the team move from West Side Grounds to Weeghman Park in 1916—a stadium that would later come to be called Wrigley Field. The Cubs did win the pennant in the war-shortened 1918 season, but they lost to the Red Sox and Babe Ruth despite a team ERA of 1.04 in the six-game Series. From there, they spiraled downward. On the last day of the 1925 season, catcher Gabby Hartnett dropped a foul pop, costing the Cubs the game and giving them their first last-place finish.

1913–25

YEAR	W	L	Pct.	GB	FINISH	WORLD SERIES	MANAGER
1913	88	65	.575	13.5	3		Johnny Evers
1914	78	76	.506	16.5	4		Hank O'Day
1915	73	80	.477	17.5	4		Roger Bresnahan
1916	67	86	.438	26.5	5		Joe Tinker
1917	74	80	.481	24	5		Fred Mitchell
1918	84	45	.651	+10.5	1	Red Sox 4 Cubs 2	Fred Mitchell
1919	75	65	.536	21	3		Fred Mitchell
1920	75	79	.487	18	T5		Fred Mitchell
1921	64	89	.418	30	7		
	41	55	.427				Johnny Evers
	23	34	.404				Bill Killefer
1922	80	74	.519	13	5		Bill Killefer
1923	83	71	.539	12.5	4		Bill Killefer
1924	81	72	.529	12	5		Bill Killefer
1925	68	86	.442	27.5	8		
	33	42	.440				Bill Killefer
	23	30	.434				Rabbit Maranville
	12	14	.462				George Gibson

1926–38: So Close

Hartnett's dropped pop-up also gave the Cubs first choice in the minor-league draft. New manager Joe McCarthy, a career minor leaguer, snagged outfielder Hack Wilson from the Giants. Later in the same draft, he plucked another outfielder, Riggs Stephenson, from the Indians. He was well on his way to building one of the great hitting teams in baseball history. A rookie shortstop named Woody English debuted in 1927. The Pirates' star outfielder, Kiki Cuyler, in his manager's doghouse, was practically stolen in a trade before the 1928 season.

1926–38

YEAR	W	L	Pct.	GB	FINISH	WORLD SERIES	MANAGER
1926	82	72	.532	7	4		Joe McCarthy
1927	85	68	.556	8.5	4		Joe McCarthy
1928	91	63	.591	4	3		Joe McCarthy
1929	98	54	.645	+10.5	1	Athletics 4 Cubs 1	Joe McCarthy
1930	90	64	.584	2	2		
	86	64	.573				Joe McCarthy
	4	0	1.000				Rogers Hornsby
1931	84	70	.545	17	3		Rogers Hornsby
1932	90	64	.584	+4	1	Yankees 4 Cubs 0	
	53	46	.535				Rogers Hornsby
	37	18	.673				Charlie Grimm
1933	86	68	.558	6	3		Charlie Grimm
1934	86	65	.570	8	3		Charlie Grimm
1935	100	54	.649	+4	1	Tigers 4 Cubs 2	Charlie Grimm
1936	87	67	.565	5	T2		Charlie Grimm
1937	93	61	.604	3	2		Charlie Grimm
1938	89	63	.586	+2	1	Yankees 4 Cubs 0	
	45	36	.556				Charlie Grimm
	44	27	.620				Gabby Hartnett

Finally, the greatest right-handed hitter in baseball history, second-baseman Rogers Hornsby, was bought from the Boston Braves.

A .303 team batting average helped carry the Cubs to the pennant in 1929, but they hit only .249 in the World Series, blowing an 8–0 lead in the seventh inning of Game Four and a 2–0 lead in the ninth inning of Game Five along the way. Despite four consecutive winning seasons, Joe McCarthy was let go as the 1930 season drew to a close. McCarthy went on to manage 20 more seasons in the big leagues without a single losing record; his successor, the decidedly unpleasant Rogers Hornsby, became the first manager to be fired in midseason and have his replacement take the team to the World Series. Unfortunately, the Yankees blew the Cubs out in four games. Three years later, the Cubs put together a 21-game winning streak to take the 1935 pennant, only to lose to the Tigers in six games. Another three years, another midseason managerial change—Gabby Hartnett for Charlie Grimm this time—another September charge to the pennant, and another four-game sweep at the hands of the Yankees in 1938.

The 1938 season ended on a thoroughly sour note, with player-manager Gabby Hartnett screaming at his defeated players on the train ride home to Chicago.

1939–53: The Decline and Fall

From 1939 to 1953, the Cubs managed only two winning seasons—a third-place finish in 1946 and a thoroughly unexpected pennant in 1945. With the defending-champion Cardinals decimated by the draft, the Cubs took the pennant by three games—due in large part to the midseason sale by the Yankees of their best pitcher, Hank Borowy, to the Cubs. Borowy went 11–2 and won two more games in the World Series, but the needle was on Empty when he started Game Seven after pitching a total of nine innings in Game Five and Game Six.

When the regulars came home from the war, the Cubs headed back into the second division and stayed there—done in by an owner who didn't really like baseball, an inferior farm

1939–53

YEAR	W	L	Pct.	GB	FINISH	WORLD SERIES	MANAGER
1939	84	70	.545	13	4		Gabby Hartnett
1940	75	79	.487	25.5	5		Gabby Hartnett
1941	70	84	.455	30	6		Jimmy Wilson
1942	68	86	.442	38	6		Jimmy Wilson
1943	74	79	.484	30.5	5		Jimmy Wilson
1944	75	79	.487	30	4		
	1	9	.100				Jimmy Wilson
	0	1	.000				Roy Johnson
	74	69	.517				Charlie Grimm
1945	98	56	.636	+3	1	Tigers 4 Cubs 3	Charlie Grimm
1946	82	71	.536	14.5	3		Charlie Grimm
1947	69	85	.448	25	6		Charlie Grimm
1948	64	90	.416	27.5	8		Charlie Grimm
1949	61	93	.396	36	8		
	19	31	.380				Charlie Grimm
	42	62	.404				Frankie Frisch
1950	64	89	.418	26.5	7		Frankie Frisch
1951	62	92	.403	34.5	8		
	35	45	.438				Frankie Frisch
	27	47	.365				Phil Cavarretta
1952	77	77	.500	19.5	5		Phil Cavarretta
1953	65	89	.422	40	7		Phil Cavarretta

system that wasn't producing pitching talent, and an overmatched general manager who was regularly fleeced by rival GMs. By 1953, attendance had dropped below 1 million for the first time since the war and would stay there until the Cubs climbed back into contention in 1968. If not for the signing of a young shortstop named Ernie Banks from the Kansas City Monarchs, who knows how much worse it might have gotten.

1954–65: Mr. Cub and the Second Division

From 1954 to 1965, the Cubs finished no closer to first than 13 games and never finished higher than fifth. In the late '50s, there was next to nothing to smile about in Wrigley Field but Ernie Banks. His best years were 1958 and 1959, when he was the first National Leaguer to win two consecutive MVP Awards (despite playing for a losing team) and firmly established himself as the greatest slugging shortstop the game had seen.

Unfortunately, he had absolutely no supporting cast until 1961 when Ron Santo and Billy Williams established themselves as everyday players. By then, his knees were beginning to give out, and the Cubs were in the middle of one of the most boneheaded innovations baseball has seen: revolving head coaches. The turmoil continued in 1962, short-circuiting the careers of the few talented young pitchers the farm system had produced in the past 15 years.

Perhaps if Dick Ellsworth, Bob Anderson, or Glen Hobbie had been handled differently during their formative years, the team might not have felt the need in 1964 to trade a young

1954–65

YEAR	W	L	Pct.	GB	FINISH	MANAGER
1954	64	90	.416	33	7	Stan Hack
1955	72	81	.471	26	6	Stan Hack
1956	60	94	.390	33	8	Stan Hack
1957	62	92	.403	33	T7	Bob Scheffing
1958	72	82	.468	20	T5	Bob Scheffing
1959	74	80	.481	13	T5	Bob Scheffing
1960	60	94	.390	35	7	
	6	11	.353			Charlie Grimm
	54	83	.394			Lou Boudreau
1961	64	90	.416	29	7	
	5	6	.455			Vedie Himsl
	4	8	.333			Harry Craft
	5	12	.294			Vedie Himsl
	2	0	1.000			El Tappe
	3	1	.750			Harry Craft
	0	3	.000			Vedie Himsl
	35	43	.449			El Tappe
	5	6	.455			Lou Klein
	5	11	.313			El Tappe
1962	59	103	.364	42.5	9	
	4	16	.200			El Tappe
	12	18	.400			Lou Klein
	43	69	.384			Charlie Metro
1963	82	80	.506	17	7	Bob Kennedy
1964	76	86	.469	17	8	Bob Kennedy
1965	72	90	.444	25	8	
	24	32	.429			Bob Kennedy
	48	58	.453			Lou Klein

outfielder named Lou Brock to the St. Louis Cardinals for a veteran pitcher, Ernie Broglio, who had nothing on the ball except his fingers. Things got bad enough after the 1965 season so that the Cubs hired a forceful personality to run the team for the first time since Joe McCarthy: Leo Durocher.

1966–72: The Lip

After a giant step backward and the team's sixth last-place finish (its fifth in 18 seasons), the abrasive and aggressive Durocher began to have some impact. The team improved by 28 games in the standings from 1966 to 1967, propelled by the development of three players acquired from other organizations—Glenn Beckert, Randy Hundley, and Fergie Jenkins; two products of the farm system—Don Kessinger and Ken Holtzman; and the continued excellence of Banks, Santo, and Williams. Bill Hands emerged in 1968, and veteran Phil Regan was brought in to handle the closer's duties. For a while in 1969, it looked as if the Cubs were going to finally return to the postseason, but they ran out of gas and coasted to a halt right in the path of divine intervention. They ended up as the most famous and most celebrated second-place team in the history of sports.

Durocher's act had already begun to wear thin as early as July 1969, and by 1971, the team was practically in open rebellion. He was finally fired midway through the 1972 season, and the breakup of his team—which had already begun with the trading of Ken Holtzman—continued through 1973 and 1974.

1966–72

YEAR	W	L	Pct.	GB	FINISH	MANAGER
1966	59	103	.364	36	10	Leo Durocher
1967	87	74	.540	14	3	Leo Durocher
1968	84	78	.519	13	3	Leo Durocher
1969	92	70	.568	8	2	Leo Durocher
1970	84	78	.519	5	2	Leo Durocher
1971	83	79	.512	14	3	Leo Durocher
1972	85	70	.548	11	2	
	46	44	.511			Leo Durocher
	39	26	.600			Whitey Lockman

1973–81: End of the Line

It didn't get any better than a .500 record and some brief tastes of first place in the eight seasons between the Leo Durocher and Dallas Green regimes. Durocher's Cubs departed one by one—with Don Kessinger the last to go, after the 1975 season to make way for Dave Rosello and Mick Kelleher.

In an odd twist of fate, Philip K. Wrigley—owner of the team since 1932—had passed away within days of the death of the reserve clause in 1977. The age of free agency had begun. The Cubs had two young superstars in Bill Madlock and Bruce Sutter, only to trade both of them away rather than meet their escalating salary demands. Days after the 1981 baseball strike began, Rick Reuschel was the last Cubs standout to be dealt away for economic reasons. A few days later, Philip Wrigley's heirs sold the ball club to the Tribune Company to pay the inheritance tax bill.

Only the strike saved the Cubs from what would have been the third 100-loss season in the club's history.

There's nothing wrong with this team that more pitching, more fielding, and more hitting couldn't help.

Bill Buckner, 1981

1973–81

YEAR	W	L	Pct.	GB	FINISH	MANAGER
1973	77	84	.478	5	5	Whitey Lockman
1974	66	96	.407	22	6	
	41	52	.441			Whitey Lockman
	25	44	.362			Jim Marshall
1975	75	87	.463	17.5	5	Jim Marshall
1976	75	87	.463	26	4	Jim Marshall
1977	81	81	.500	20	4	Herman Franks
1978	79	83	.488	11	3	Herman Franks
1979	80	82	.494	18	5	
	78	77	.503			Herman Franks
	2	5	.286			Joey Amalfitano
1980	64	98	.395	27	6	
	38	52	.422			Preston Gomez
	26	46	.361			Joey Amalfitano
1981	38	65	.369			Joey Amalfitano
	15	37	.288	17.5	6	
	23	28	.451	6	5	

1982–97

YEAR	W	L	Pct.	GB	FINISH	PLAY-OFFS	MANAGER
1982	73	89	.451	19	5		Lee Elia
1983	71	91	.438	19	5		
	54	69	.439				Lee Elia
	17	22	.436				Charlie Fox
1984	96	65	.596	+6.5	1	Padres 3 Cubs 2	Jim Frey
1985	77	84	.478	23.5	4		Jim Frey
1986	70	90	.438	37	5		
	23	33	.411				Jim Frey
	1	1	.500				John Vukovich
	46	56	.451				Gene Michael
1987	76	85	.472	18.5	6		
	68	68	.500				Gene Michael
	8	17	.320				Frank Lucchesi
1988	77	85	.475	24	4		Don Zimmer
1989	93	69	.574	+6	1	Giants 4 Cubs 1	Don Zimmer
1990	77	85	.475	18	4		Don Zimmer
1991	77	83	.481	20	4		
	18	19	.486				Don Zimmer
	0	1	.000				Joe Altobelli
	59	63	.484				Jim Essian
1992	78	84	.481	18	4		Jim Lefebvre
1993	84	78	.519	13	4		Jim Lefebvre
1994	49	64	.434	16.5	5		Tom Trebelhorn
1995	73	71	.507	12	3		Jim Riggleman
1996	76	86	.469	12	4		Jim Riggleman
1997	68	94	.420	16	5		Jim Riggleman

1982–97: Ryno and Harry

Fresh from bringing the only championship in Phillies history to Philadelphia, Dallas Green arrived in Chicago in 1982. The new GM didn't last five seasons, but two other new arrivals lasted a lot longer: Ryne Sandberg and Harry Caray. Caray came from the White Sox, of all places, to replace Jack Brickhouse, who had been the voice of the Cubs for nearly 40 years. Sandberg was an afterthought in the deal that sent Ivan DeJesus to the Phillies.

Jim Frey guided a veteran team filled with ex-Phillies to the Eastern Division pennant in 1984, while Don Zimmer took a much younger team to a division title in 1989. Thanks in large part to Ryno's heroics and Harry's histrionics, the Cubs saw their attendance top 2 million for the first time in 1984—and stay there nearly every season since, despite frequent managerial changes, devastating injuries, and disappointing finishes.

Harry suffered a stroke and Ryno retired, but both were back for more. Ryne Sandberg retired for good after the 1997 season, while Harry Caray passed away before the 1998 season—one that both of them would have loved to be there to see.

1998–: The Start of Something Good? . . .

Sammy Sosa's amazing season overshadowed possibly the most significant happening of the 1998 season: the emergence of Kerry Wood as the most overpowering strikeout pitcher in the team's history. Should the young right-hander bounce back from elbow surgery, the wild-card berth of 1998 could be just the first of many trips to the postseason . . . knock Wood.

1998

YEAR	W	L	Pct.	GB	FINISH	PLAY-OFFS	MANAGER
1998	90	73	.552	12	2*	Braves 3 Cubs 0	Jim Riggleman

*Wild card

Through the Years

Of the 15 opposing teams in the National League, the Cubs have a record of .500 or better against 10 of them.

Opponent	1st Game	W	L	Pct.
Diamondbacks	1998	7	5	.583
Padres	1969	199	148	.573
Braves	1876	1,179	971	.548
Brewers	1997	8	7	.533
Phillies	1883	1,174	1,036	.531
Cardinals	1892	1,064	998	.516
Reds	1890	996	966	.508
Mets	1962	307	301	.505
Dodgers	1890	982	974	.502
Marlins	1993	33	33	.500
Rockies	1993	34	35	.493
Giants	1883	1,008	1,075	.484
Expos	1969	230	249	.480
Pirates	1887	1,038	1,125	.480
Astros	1962	220	262	.456

THE PLAYERS

With a story as long and involved as that of the first 123 seasons of the Chicago Cubs, it's best to get to know the main characters as soon as possible—all 75 of them.

With more than 1,600 players having worn the team's uniform, finding locker-room space for the greatest ever becomes a tricky proposition. This section presents the top 25 pitchers and top 50 hitters, along with their career statistics as a Cub (through 1998). Note that since stolen bases weren't tabulated by today's scoring rules until 1898, pre-1898 SB totals aren't included for the 19th-century players.

All of these players meet at least one of the following criteria: (1) Hall of Famer; (2) winner of the MVP, Cy Young, or Rookie of the Year Award (or robbed of same); (3) accumulated a whole lot of wins, saves, hits, or home runs in a Cubs (or White Stockings or Orphans or Colts) uniform; or (4) simply came up big in the clutch.

The Top 75

PLAYER	Pos.	Ht./Wt.	B/T	BIRTHPLACE	SERVICE
Grover Alexander	SP	6'1''/185	R/R	Elba, Nebraska	1918–26
Cap Anson	1B	6'0''/225	R/R	Marshalltown, Iowa	1876–97
Ernie Banks	SS-1B	6'1''/180	R/R	Dallas, Texas	1953–71
Glenn Beckert	2B	6'1''/190	R/R	Pittsburgh, Pennsylvania	1965–73
Mordecai Brown	SP	5'10''/175	R/R	Nyesville, Indiana	1904–12, 1916
Bill Buckner	1B	6'0''/185	L/L	Vallejo, California	1977–84
Tommy Burns	SS-3B	5'7''/150	R/R	Honesdale, Pennsylvania	1880–91
Guy Bush	SP	6'0''/175	R/R	Aberdeen, Mississippi	1923–34
Phil Cavarretta	1B-OF	5'11''/175	L/L	Chicago, Illinois	1934–53
Frank Chance	1B	6'0''/190	R/R	Fresno, California	1898–1912
John Clarkson	SP	5'10''/155	R/R	Cambridge, Massachusetts	1884–87
Larry Corcoran	SP	5'2''/120	L/R	Brooklyn, New York	1880–85
Kiki Cuyler	OF	5'11''/180	R/R	Harrisville, Michigan	1928–35
Bill Dahlen	SS	5'9''/180	R/R	Nelliston, New York	1891–98
Abner Dalrymple	OF	5'10''/175	L/R	Warren, Illinois	1879–86
Jody Davis	C	6'4''/190	R/R	Gainesville, Georgia	1981–88
Andre Dawson	OF	6'3''/180	R/R	Miami, Florida	1987–92
Shawon Dunston	SS	6'1''/175	R/R	Brooklyn, New York	1985–95, 1997
Bull Durham	1B-OF	6'1''/185	L/L	Cincinnati, Ohio	1981–88
Woody English	SS-3B	5'10''/155	R/R	Fredonia, Ohio	1927–36
Johnny Evers	2B	5'9''/125	R/R	Troy, New York	1902–13
Larry French	SP	6'1''/195	R/L	Visalia, California	1935–41
George Gore	OF	5'11''/195	L/R	Saccarappa, Maine	1879–86
Mark Grace	1B	6'2''/190	L/L	Winston-Salem, North Carolina	1988–
Clark Griffith	SP	5'7''/155	R/R	Clear Creek, Missouri	1893–1900
Charlie Grimm	1B	5'11''/175	L/L	St. Louis, Missouri	1925–36
Stan Hack	3B	6'0''/175	L/R	Sacramento, California	1932–47
Bill Hands	SP	6'2''/185	R/R	Hackensack, New Jersey	1966–72
Gabby Hartnett	C	6'1''/195	R/R	Woonsocket, Rhode Island	1922–40
Billy Herman	2B	5'11''/180	R/R	New Albany, Indiana	1931–41
Solly Hofman	IF-OF	6'0''/160	R/R	St. Louis, Missouri	1904–12, 1916
Ken Holtzman	SP	6'2''/175	R/L	St. Louis, Missouri	1965–71, 1978–79
Rogers Hornsby	2B	5'11''/175	R/R	Winters, Texas	1929–32
Randy Hundley	C	5'11''/170	R/R	Martinsville, Virginia	1966–73, 1976–77
Bill Hutchison	SP	5'9''/175	R/R	New Haven, Connecticut	1889–95
Ferguson Jenkins	SP	6'5''/205	R/R	Chatham, Ontario	1966–73, 1982–83
Billy Jurges	SS	5'11''/175	R/R	Bronx, New York	1931–38, 1946–47
King Kelly	C-IF-OF	5'10''/170	R/R	Troy, New York	1880–86
Don Kessinger	SS	6'1''/170	B/R	Forrest City, Arkansas	1964–75
Johnny Kling	C	5'9''/160	R/R	Kansas City, Missouri	1900–08, 1910–11
Bill Lange	OF	6'1''/190	R/R	San Francisco, California	1893–99
Bill Lee	SP	6'3''/195	R/R	Plaquemine, Louisiana	1934–43, 1947
Greg Maddux	SP	6'0''/170	R/R	San Angelo, Texas	1986–92
Bill Madlock	3B	5'11''/185	R/R	Memphis, Tennessee	1974–76
Pat Malone	SP	6'0''/200	L/R	Altoona, Pennsylvania	1928–34
Rick Monday	OF	6'3''/195	L/L	Batesville, Arkansas	1972–76
Keith Moreland	C-OF-3B	6'0''/190	R/R	Dallas, Texas	1982–87
Bill Nicholson	OF	6'0''/205	L/R	Chestertown, Maryland	1939–48
Orvie Overall	SP	6'2''/215	B/R	Farmersville, California	1906–10, 1913
Andy Pafko	OF-3B	6'0''/190	R/R	Boyceville, Wisconsin	1943–51
Claude Passeau	SP	6'3''/200	R/R	Waynesboro, Mississippi	1939–47

continued

PLAYER	Pos.	Ht./Wt.	B/T	BIRTHPLACE	SERVICE
Fred Pfeffer	2B	5'10''/185	R/R	Louisville, Kentucky	1883–89, 1891, 1896–97
Ed Reulbach	SP	6'1''/190	R/R	Detroit, Michigan	1905–13
Rick Reuschel	SP	6'3''/230	R/R	Quincy, Illinois	1972–81, 1983–84
Charlie Root	SP	5'10''/190	R/R	Middletown, Ohio	1926–41
Jimmy Ryan	OF	5'9''/160	R/L	Clinton, Massachusetts	1885–89, 1891–1900
Ryne Sandberg	2B	6'1''/175	R/R	Spokane, Washington	1982–94, 1996–97
Ron Santo	3B	6'0''/190	R/R	Seattle, Washington	1960–73
Hank Sauer	OF	6'3''/200	R/R	Pittsburgh, Pennsylvania	1949–55
Wildfire Schulte	OF	5'11''/170	L/R	Cohocton, New York	1904–16
Jimmy Sheckard	OF	5'9''/175	L/R	Upper Chanceford, Pennsylvania	1906–12
Lee Smith	RP	6'5''/220	R/R	Jamestown, Louisiana	1980–87
Sammy Sosa	OF	6'0''/200	R/R	San Pedro de Macoris, Dominican Republic	1992–
Harry Steinfeldt	3B	5'9''/180	R/R	St. Louis, Missouri	1906–10
Riggs Stephenson	OF	5'10''/185	R/R	Akron, Alabama	1926–34
Rick Sutcliffe	SP	6'7''/215	R/R	Independence, Missouri	1984–91
Bruce Sutter	RP	6'2''/190	R/R	Lancaster, Pennsylvania	1976–80
Jack Taylor	SP	5'10''/170	R/R	New Straitsville, Ohio	1898–1903, 1906–07
Joe Tinker	SS	5'9''/175	R/R	Muscotah, Kansas	1902–12, 1916
Hippo Vaughn	SP	6'4''/215	B/L	Weatherford, Texas	1913–21
Lon Warneke	SP	6'2''/185	R/R	Mt. Ida, Arkansas	1930–36, 1942–43, 1945
Billy Williams	OF	6'1''/175	L/R	Whistler, Alabama	1959–74
Ned Williamson	SS-3B	5'11''/175	R/R	Philadelphia, Pennsylvania	1879–89
Hack Wilson	OF	5'6''/190	R/R	Ellwood City, Pennsylvania	1926–31
Heinie Zimmerman	3B	5'11''/175	R/R	New York, New York	1907–16

Their exploits will be covered in much greater detail throughout this book. Briefly, here's why these Hall of Famers (present and future), Cubs legends, unknown legends, clutch performers, 19th-century stars, and the rest merit a locker in the All-Time Cubs clubhouse. (Fans of Billy Sunday, Lou Novikoff, Adolfo Phillips, and Dickie Ray Noles: have no fear. We'll get to everyone eventually.)

Hall of Famers

For these players, it's easy enough to let their Hall of Fame plaques speak for them (with editing as appropriate and corrections as necessary).

Grover Cleveland Alexander (P)
"Great National League pitcher for two decades with Phillies, Cubs, and Cardinals starting in 1911."

W	L	S	G	GS	CG	IP	H	BB	SO	ShO	ERA	Pct.
128	83	10	242	224	159	1,884	1,919	268	614	24	2.84	.607

Q. Who was the first Cub inducted into the Hall of Fame?

A. Grover Cleveland Alexander

Cap Anson (1B)
"Greatest hitter and greatest National League player-manager of 19th century. Started with Chicago in National League's first year, 1876. Chicago manager from 1879 to 1897, winning five pennants. Was .300-class hitter 20 years, batting champion four times."

G	AB	R	H	2B	3B	HR	RBI	BB	SO	BA	SA
2,276	9,108	1,719	3,000	528	124	96	1,715	952	294	.329	.446

Ernie Banks (SS-1B)

"Hit 512 career homers, with more than 40 in a season five times. Had record five grand slams in 1955. First to be elected NL Most Valuable Player two successive years, 1958–59. Led league in home runs and runs batted in twice and slugging percentage once. Established records for most homers in season by shortstop (47 in 1958) and for fewest errors (12) and best fielding average (.985) by a shortstop in 1959."

G	AB	R	H	2B	3B	HR	RBI	BB	SO	SB	BA	SA
2,528	9,421	1,305	2,583	407	90	512	1,636	763	1,236	50	.274	.500

Mordecai Brown (P)

"Member of Chicago NL championship team of 1906, '07, '08, '10. A right-handed pitcher, won 239 games during major-league career. First major leaguer to pitch four consecutive shutouts, achieving this feat on June 13, June 25, July 2, and July 4 in 1908."

W	L	S	G	GS	CG	IP	H	BB	SO	ShO	ERA	Pct.
188	83	39	346	241	206	2,329	1,879	445	1,043	48	1.80	.694

Frank Chance (1B)

"Famous leader of Chicago Cubs. Won pennant with Cubs in first full season as manager in 1906—that team compiled 116 victories, unequaled in major-league history. Also won pennants in 1907, '08, and '10 and World Series winner in '07 and '08."

G	AB	R	H	2B	3B	HR	RBI	BB	SO	SB	BA	SA
1,274	4,269	795	1,266	200	79	20	590	546	28	404	.297	.394

Kiki Cuyler (OF)

"Led NL in stolen bases 1926, '28, '29, '30. Batted .354 in 1924, .357 in 1925, .360 in 1929, .355 in 1930. Lifetime total 2,299 hits, batting average .321."

G	AB	R	H	2B	3B	HR	RBI	BB	SO	SB	BA	SA
949	3,687	665	1,199	220	66	79	602	352	370	161	.325	.485

Johnny Evers (2B)

"Middle-man of the famous double-play combination of Tinker to Evers to Chance. With the pennant-winning Chicago Cubs of 1906, '07, '08, '10 and with the Boston Braves miracle team of 1914."

G	AB	R	H	2B	3B	HR	RBI	BB	SO	SB	BA	SA
1,408	4,855	742	1,339	183	64	9	448	556	60	291	.276	.345

Clark Griffith (P)

"Associated with major-league baseball for more than 50 years as a pitcher, manager, and executive. Served as a member of the Chicago and Cincinnati teams in the NL and the Chicago, New York, and Washington clubs in the AL. Compiled more than 200 victories as a pitcher."

W	L	S	G	GS	CG	IP	H	BB	SO	ShO	ERA	Pct.
152	96	1	265	253	240	2,189	2,445	517	573	9	3.40	.613

Gabby Hartnett (C)

"Caught 100 or more games per season for 12 years, 8 in succession, 1930 to 1937, for league record. Set mark for consecutive chances for catcher without error, 452 in 1933–34. Highest fielding average for catcher in 100 or more games in seven seasons; most putouts NL, 7,292; most chances accepted NL, 8,546. Lifetime batting average .297."

G	AB	R	H	2B	3B	HR	RBI	BB	SO	SB	BA	SA
1,926	6,282	847	1,867	391	64	231	1,153	691	683	28	.297	.490

Billy Herman (2B)

"Master of the hit-and-run play owned .304 lifetime batting average. Made 200 or more hits in season three times. Led league in hits (227) and doubles (57) in 1935. Set major-league records for second basemen with five seasons of handling 900 or more chances and NL mark of 466 putouts in 1933. Led loop keystoners in putouts seven times."

G	AB	R	H	2B	3B	HR	RBI	BB	SO	SB	BA	SA
1,344	5,532	875	1,710	346	69	37	577	470	282	53	.309	.417

Ferguson Jenkins (P)

"Canada's first Hall of Famer. 284–226 lifetime with 3,192 strikeouts and 3.34 ERA despite playing 12 seasons of his 19-year career in hitters' ballparks—Wrigley Field and Fenway Park. Won 20 games seven seasons, including six consecutive, 1967 to 1972. Cy Young Award winner, 1971. Trademarks were pinpoint control and changing speeds."

W	L	S	G	GS	CG	IP	H	BB	SO	ShO	ERA	Pct.
167	132	6	401	347	154	2,672	2,402	600	2,038	29	3.21	.559

King Kelly (C-IF-OF)

"Colorful player and audacious base runner. His sale (from Chicago to Boston) for $10,000 was one of the biggest deals of baseball's early history."

G	AB	R	H	2B	3B	HR	RBI	BB	SO	BA	SA
681	2,873	728	899	193	49	33	323	229	179	.313	.449

Joe Tinker (SS)

"Famous as a member of one of baseball's greatest double-play combinations—from Tinker to Evers to Chance. A big leaguer from 1902 through 1916 with the Chicago Cubs and Cincinnati Reds and the Chicago Feds. Manager Cincinnati 1913 and Chicago NL 1916. Shortstop on Cubs' team that won pennants in 1906, '07, '08, and '10."

G	AB	R	H	2B	3B	HR	RBI	BB	SO	SB	BA	SA
1,538	5,554	669	1,444	219	93	28	670	345	88	304	.260	.348

Billy Williams (OF)

"Soft-spoken, clutch performer was one of the most respected hitters of his day. Batted solid .290 over 18 seasons, socking 426 home runs. Hit 20 or more homers 13 straight seasons. 1961 NL Rookie of the Year, 1972 NL batting champion with .333. Held NL record for consecutive games played with 1,117."

G	AB	R	H	2B	3B	HR	RBI	BB	SO	SB	BA	SA
2,213	8,479	1,306	2,510	402	87	392	1,353	911	934	86	.296	.503

Hack Wilson (OF)

"Established major-league record of 190 runs batted in and National League high of 56 homers in 1930. Led or tied for NL homers title four times. Compiled lifetime .307 batting average and drove in 100 or more runs six years. Hit two homers in one inning in 1925 and three in one game in 1930."

G	AB	R	H	2B	3B	HR	RBI	BB	SO	SB	BA	SA
850	3,154	652	1,017	185	44	190	768	463	461	34	.322	.590

Hall of Famers with Cubs Service

There are 40 Hall of Famers who were Cubs at one time or another, as player, pitcher, or manager. The eventual inductions of Ryne Sandberg, Andre Dawson, Greg Maddux, Lee Smith, and Joe Carter will make it 45. Of these, 13 hitters and 6 pitchers spent at least five seasons in Chicago. In other words, you could practically fill a major-league locker room just with Cubs Hall of Famers.

Five or More Seasons

	Service	Seasons	Induction
Hitters			
Cap Anson	1876–97	22	1939
Gabby Hartnett	1922–40	19	1955
Ernie Banks	1953–71	19	1977
Billy Williams	1959–74	16	1987
Frank Chance	1898–1912	15	1946
Joe Tinker	1902–12, 1916	12	1946
Johnny Evers	1902–13	12	1946
Billy Herman	1931–41	11	1975
Kiki Cuyler	1928–35	8	1968
King Kelly	1880–86	7	1945
Hack Wilson	1926–31	6	1979
Pitchers			
Mordecai "Three-Finger" Brown	1904–12, 1916	10	1949
Ferguson Jenkins	1966–73, 1982–83	10	1991
Grover Cleveland Alexander	1918–26	9	1938
Clark Griffith	1893–1900	8	1946
Managers			
Leo Durocher	1966–72	7	1994
Joe McCarthy	1926–30	5	1957

Less than Five Seasons

	Service	Seasons	Induction
Hitters			
Rogers Hornsby	1929–32	4	1942
Roger Bresnahan	1900, 1913–15	4	1945
Lou Brock	1961–64	4	1985
Jimmie Foxx	1942–44	3	1951
Chuck Klein	1934–36	3	1980
Hugh Duffy	1888–89	2	1945
Ralph Kiner	1953–54	2	1975
Richie Ashburn	1960–61	2	1995
Rabbit Maranville	1925	1	1954
Monte Irvin	1956	1	1973
Highpockets Kelly	1930	1	1973
Fred Lindstrom	1935	1	1976
Tony Lazzeri	1938	1	1991
Pitchers			
Dizzy Dean	1938–41	4	1953
John Clarkson	1884–87	4	1963
Albert Goodwill Spalding	1876–77	2	1939
Burleigh Grimes	1932–33	2	1964
Rube Waddell	1901	1	1946
Robin Roberts	1966	1	1976
Hoyt Wilhelm	1970	1	1985
Managers			
Frankie Frisch	1949–51	3	1947
Lou Boudreau	1960	1	1970
Frank Selee	1902–05	4	1999

Future Hall of Famers

Here are four Cubs who should be in Cooperstown eventually and what their plaques might say when they get there.

Andre Dawson (OF)

"A complete player. Strong-armed, Gold Glove outfielder was one of only four players to hit 300 home runs and steal 300 bases. Hit 438 lifetime home runs, including league-leading 49 in 1987. Hit at least 10 home runs for 18 consecutive seasons. Only player to win MVP Award with last-place team."

G	AB	R	H	2B	3B	HR	RBI	BB	SO	SB	BA	SA
867	3,262	431	929	149	27	174	587	198	453	57	.285	.507

Greg Maddux (P)

"Expert at changing speeds and hitting spots, he was the greatest pitcher of his generation. Won a major-league record four Cy Young Awards in a row from 1992 through 1995. Outstanding fielding, hitting, and baserunning pitcher."

W	L	S	G	GS	CG	IP	H	BB	SO	ShO	ERA	Pct.
95	75	0	212	208	42	1,442	1,352	455	937	13	3.35	.559

Ryne Sandberg (2B)

"The greatest-fielding second baseman the game has seen, with .990 lifetime fielding percentage, nine consecutive Gold Gloves (1983–91), a record 123 consecutive games without an error, four other stretches of 50+ errorless games, and four seasons without a throwing error. Set major-league record for home runs by a second baseman. Won MVP in 1984."

G	AB	R	H	2B	3B	HR	RBI	BB	SO	SB	BA	SA
2,151	8,379	1,316	2,385	403	76	282	1,061	761	1,259	344	.285	.452

Lee Smith (RP)

"Tall, hard-throwing right-hander was first to reach 400 saves. Retired with major-league-record 478 saves, 180 recorded with Chicago Cubs. Recorded 25 saves or more for 13 consecutive seasons, 1983 through 1995. Led league four times with three different teams."

W	L	S	G	GS	CG	IP	H	BB	SO	ShO	ERA	Pct.
40	51	180	458	6	0	682	591	264	644	0	2.92	.440

Cubs Legends

These players aren't Hall of Famers, but they are great Cubs who racked up a lot of hits, home runs, wins, or saves in a Chicago uniform.

Glenn Beckert (2B)

Beckert was the Cubs' starting second baseman for nine years, from 1965 through 1973, hitting at least .280 for six consecutive seasons. A finger injury shortened Beckert's career year of 1971, robbing him of an almost-certain 200 hits. He hit .342 in 131 games, placing him third in the batting race behind Joe Torre and Ralph Garr, and just ahead of Roberto Clemente. Beckert was a four-time All-Star (1969–72).

G	AB	R	H	2B	3B	HR	RBI	BB	SO	SB	BA	SA
1,247	5,020	672	1,423	194	31	22	353	248	235	49	.283	.348

Bill Buckner (1B)

Before Buckner became a tragic figure, he was a terrific hitter who would have reached 3,000 hits if not for his bad wheels. He was the Cubs' first baseman from 1977 to 1983, hitting at least .280 each season. He won a batting title in 1980 with a .324 average (refusing to sit out the last game to protect his lead), and he knocked in 105 runs in 1982. Due to the stiff competition at first base, he made only one All-Star appearance as a Cub, in 1981.

G	AB	R	H	2B	3B	HR	RBI	BB	SO	SB	BA	SA
974	3,788	449	1,136	235	25	81	516	187	159	56	.300	.439

Guy Bush (P)

Bush was signed out of the Cotton States League for $1,200 and a jug of corn whiskey, was with the Cubs for 12 seasons, and was a prominent swingman for them from 1925 through 1934. He won 152 games in Chicago, 34 in relief. He also earned 27 saves (an impressive number for the time), including a league-leading 4 in 1925 and 8 in 1929. After winning at least 15 the previous five seasons, he finally won 20 in 1933, thanks in part to lucky four-leaf clovers mailed to him by Cubs fans.

W	L	S	G	GS	CG	IP	H	BB	SO	ShO	ERA	Pct.
152	101	27	428	252	127	2,201	2,354	734	712	14	3.81	.601

I never saw a ball hit so hard. He was fat and old, but he still had that great swing.

Guy Bush after surrendering Babe Ruth's final two home runs in 1935, when Bush was a Pirate and Ruth a Boston Brave

Phil Cavarretta (1B-OF)

A Chicago native, Cavarretta literally grew up with the Cubs, appearing in his first game for them at age 18 in 1934 and his last at age 37 in 1953 as player-manager—the longest tenure for anyone playing for his hometown team. He was a regular at 19 for the 1935 pennant-winner, hitting .275 with 82 RBIs. His best years were during World War II—he hit .321 with a league-leading 197 hits in 1944 and won the MVP Award in 1945 with a league-leading .355 average and 97 RBIs. He was a four-time All-Star (1944–47), and he hit .317 in postseason play.

G	AB	R	H	2B	3B	HR	RBI	BB	SO	SB	BA	SA
1,953	6,592	968	1,927	341	99	92	896	794	585	61	.292	.416

Eighteen years old? You should be in high school!

Boston Braves outfielder Babe Ruth to Phil Cavarretta before a game in 1935

Shawon Dunston (SS)

Dunston had a rifle arm as well as good power for a shortstop, stole 20 bases four times, and raised the level of his game when it mattered most. A bad back sidelined him for most of 1993 and 1994, but he bounced back with his best season in 1995. He returned from San Francisco in 1997 to give Cubs fans one more season to cheer Dunston to Sandberg to Grace.

G	AB	R	H	2B	3B	HR	RBI	BB	SO	SB	BA	SA
1,254	4,570	563	1,219	225	48	107	489	171	770	175	.267	.407

Mark Grace (1B)

Though never a batting champion as of 1998, Grace is an extremely consistent hitter who has been at .296 or above for 10 of his 11 seasons and in the league's top 10 in 9 of his first 11 seasons. His best seasons have been 1993 (.325 with 98 RBIS) and 1995 (.326 with 92 RBIS, 97 runs, and a league-leading 51 doubles in the strike-shortened season). In the field, he's a perennial Gold Glover who dug many a Shawon Dunston fastball out of the dirt and made it look easy.

G	AB	R	H	2B	3B	HR	RBI	BB	SO	SB	BA	SA
1,606	6,053	875	1,875	371	37	121	831	768	489	63	.310	.443

Charlie Grimm (1B)

Grimm was the Cubs' starting first baseman from 1925 through 1934 and served three terms as manager, in the '30s, '40s, and '60s. A singles and doubles hitter, he hit at least .289 in 8 of his 10 full-time seasons in Chicago, knocking in 91 runs in only 120 games for the 1929 offensive-powerhouse team. In 1932, he became the first to take over a team in midseason and manage it to a World Series—Jolly Cholly's easygoing nature having an immediate impact on players who'd been struggling under Rogers Hornsby's cold perfectionism.

G	AB	R	H	2B	3B	HR	RBI	BB	SO	SB	BA	SA
1,334	4,917	596	1,454	270	43	61	697	386	229	26	.296	.405

Stan Hack (3B)

Hack played 16 years for the Cubs and was their full-time third baseman from 1934 through 1945. A leadoff hitter, he scored 100 runs seven times—five years in a row—and led the league in stolen bases in 1938 and 1939 and in hits in 1940 and 1941. Hack was a five-time All-Star whose greatest gift was consistency—from 1934 through 1943, he hit no lower than .289 and no higher than .320. He became one of the top fielders in the game, reeling off a then-record streak of 54 consecutive games at third without an error in 1942. He batted .348 in four World Series.

G	AB	R	H	2B	3B	HR	RBI	BB	SO	SB	BA	SA
1,938	7,278	1,239	2,193	363	81	57	642	1,092	466	165	.301	.397

Don Kessinger (SS)

Kessinger took over the Cubs shortstop position in 1965 and kept it until 1975. An excellent glove man, he made himself into a good leadoff hitter—first by learning how to switch-hit in 1966, then by becoming more selective at the plate in 1969. He was rewarded with six All-Star appearances (1968–72, 1974). It was no coincidence that his best years—1969 and 1970, when he achieved career highs in extra-base hits, hits, and runs scored—were also the Cubs' best seasons.

G	AB	R	H	2B	3B	HR	RBI	BB	SO	SB	BA	SA
1,648	6,355	769	1,619	201	71	11	431	550	629	92	.255	.314

Bill Lee (P)

Lee's career numbers make him look like a .500 pitcher, but at the peak of his game, he was the best in the league. The ace of the Cubs' pennant-winning staffs of 1935 and 1938, he won 20 games both seasons and led the league in winning percentage each time. His career year was 1938, when he went 22–9, leading not just in winning percentage but also in wins, shutouts (9), and ERA (2.66). He was an All-Star in 1938 and in 1939, when he just missed winning 20 games for the third time.

W	L	S	G	GS	CG	IP	H	BB	SO	ShO	ERA	Pct.
139	123	9	364	297	153	2,270	2,317	704	874	25	3.51	.531

Bill Nicholson (OF)

Nicknamed "Swish" for his powerful swings and frequent misses, Nicholson was the most feared hitter in the major leagues during World War II. A five-time All-Star, he led the league in home runs and RBIs in both 1943 and 1944. He was one of the great Cubs power hitters, but his production began to decline in 1945 as diabetes sapped his strength and weakened his eyesight.

G	AB	R	H	2B	3B	HR	RBI	BB	SO	SB	BA	SA
1,349	4,827	738	1,313	245	53	205	833	696	684	26	.272	.472

Andy Pafko (OF-3B)

The Cubs center-field position has been unsettled since 1951 when Pafko, a five-time All-Star, was traded to the Brooklyn Dodgers. He knocked in 110 runs in 1945 despite hitting only 12 home runs. His best year was 1948, when he knocked in 101 runs and batted .312 while learning to play third base. He returned to the outfield and had one more big year in Chicago—a career-high 36 home runs, .304 batting average, and 92 RBIs in 1950.

G	AB	R	H	2B	3B	HR	RBI	BB	SO	SB	BA	SA
960	3,567	486	1,048	162	40	126	575	332	243	28	.294	.468

Charlie Root (P)

Though Root is most famous for being the pitcher who served up Babe Ruth's "called shot," no player has won more games in a Cubs uniform. He pitched for four Cubs pennant-winners, leading the league in wins with 26 in 1927 and in winning percentage in 1929, when he went 19–6. He appeared frequently in relief throughout his career, picking up 42 of his wins out of the bullpen, his last one at age 42.

W	L	S	G	GS	CG	IP	H	BB	SO	ShO	ERA	Pct.
201	156	40	605	339	177	3,137	3,184	871	1,432	21	3.54	.563

He has blinding speed, and his curve cracks like amplified static on a sultry night.

Sportswriter Irving Vaughn, on Charlie Root

Ron Santo (3B)

One of the Hall of Fame's most glaring omissions, Santo was a consistent run-producer with a great batting eye and an underrated fielder. He was the Cubs captain and cleanup hitter and a nine-time All-Star.

G	AB	R	H	2B	3B	HR	RBI	BB	SO	SB	BA	SA
2,126	7,768	1,109	2,171	353	66	337	1,290	1,071	1,271	35	.279	.472

Sammy Sosa (OF)

By the time he's through, Sosa may have more home runs than any Cub except Ernie Banks. Though he owns a strong right-field throwing arm and is the first Cub to hit 30 home runs and steal 30 bases, he'll be most remembered for his record-setting 1998 season, in which he hit 66 home runs, scored 134, and knocked in 158 in leading the Cubs into postseason play for the first time in nine years.

G	AB	R	H	2B	3B	HR	RBI	BB	SO	SB	BA	SA
920	3,633	589	998	138	22	244	684	292	903	165	.275	.526

Riggs Stephenson (OF)

Stephenson was a star football player at the University of Alabama, and his notoriously poor throwing arm stemmed from a gridiron injury. His defensive weaknesses kept him from winning a starting infield job with the Cleveland Indians, though he hit .336 for them over five seasons. The Cubs grabbed him and turned him into a left fielder, and he rewarded them with eight consecutive .300 seasons.

G	AB	R	H	2B	3B	HR	RBI	BB	SO	SB	BA	SA
978	3,474	533	1,167	237	40	49	589	395	176	39	.336	.469

Bruce Sutter (RP)

Sutter spent only five seasons with Chicago, but he was named to four All-Star teams. He led the league in saves in 1979, took the Cubs to arbitration, and won a then-stunning $700,000 salary. The Wrigley family, shedding high-priced players as their ownership neared its end, dealt him to St. Louis, where he led the league in saves three more times. He also led St. Louis to its 1982 World Series championship, winning two postseason games and saving another three.

W	L	S	G	GS	CG	IP	H	BB	SO	ShO	ERA	Pct.
32	30	133	300	0	0	492	371	149	494	0	2.40	.516

Hippo Vaughn (P)

Vaughn is most remembered as the losing pitcher in the famous "double no-hitter" of 1917, but he was also the greatest left-handed pitcher in Cubs history. He won at least 17 games seven years in a row, including 20+ five times. He was at his most dominant in 1918, when he led the league in wins, shutouts, innings, strikeouts, and ERA.

W	L	S	G	GS	CG	IP	H	BB	SO	ShO	ERA	Pct.
151	105	4	305	270	177	2,216	1,971	621	1,138	35	2.33	.590

Unknown Legends

These are some names that even serious baseball fans might not know. Several of them were key contributors to one of baseball's great dynasties, the Cubs of 1906 through 1910.

Woody English (SS-3B)

Woody English had 200 hits and 100 walks in the wild hitting year of 1930, when his on-base percentage was .430 and he scored 152 runs. He batted .319 the following season and had 200 hits again, but his walk totals declined and his home runs fell from 14 to 2. English was a good fielder who also saw action at third base, and he was pretty much a regular at either position from 1928 through 1934. He was also the only member of the team whom Rogers Hornsby was willing to have as a roommate. English was selected to the inaugural 1933 All-Star team.

G	AB	R	H	2B	3B	HR	RBI	BB	SO	SB	BA	SA
1,098	4,296	747	1,248	218	50	31	373	498	470	51	.291	.386

Larry French (P)

Between Hippo Vaughn (1914–20) and Ken Holtzman (1966–71), the only other consistent lefty winner the Cubs had was Larry French. He was in double figures in wins from 1935 to 1940, leading the league in shutouts with four in both 1935 and 1936.

W	L	S	G	GS	CG	IP	H	BB	SO	ShO	ERA	Pct.
95	84	8	272	185	87	1,486	1,586	382	642	21	3.54	.531

Solly Hofman (IF-OF)

One of the first and greatest utility players, Hofman filled in at every position except catcher and pitcher. During 1907 and 1908, Hofman came to bat more than 400 times without having a full-time position. In 1906 and 1908, he was the Cubs' starting center fielder in the World Series rather than Jimmy Slagle, hitting more than .300 both times. He also found himself in center field during the infamous "Merkle Boner" game, starting the final disputed and convoluted force-out by retrieving the ball and overthrowing Johnny Evers at second base.

G	AB	R	H	2B	3B	HR	RBI	BB	SO	SB	BA	SA
884	3,046	441	824	117	38	14	374	323	89	158	271	348

Billy Jurges (SS)

Playing alongside Hall of Famer Billy Herman, Billy Jurges was the other half of the Cubs' outstanding double-play combination of the 1930s. A sure-handed fielder with good range, Jurges led the league in fielding average three times as a Cub. His best season at the plate came in 1937 when he hit .298 with 10 triples and was named to the All-Star team.

G	AB	R	H	2B	3B	HR	RBI	BB	SO	SB	BA	SA
1,072	3,658	423	928	176	34	20	390	306	335	22	.254	.337

Johnny Kling (C)

Gabby Hartnett wasn't the only great catcher to wear a Cubs uniform. Arguably one of the most underrated backstops in baseball history, Kling caught one of the greatest pitching staffs of all time: the Cubs of 1906, 1907, 1908, and 1910 (he took a year off in 1909 to become a billiard champion, the only season in that stretch that the Cubs failed to win the pennant). He led the league in fielding percentage in 1906 and 1907 while contributing with the bat as well, hitting .284 and .312.

G	AB	R	H	2B	3B	HR	RBI	BB	SO	SB	BA	SA
1,024	3,539	396	958	151	54	16	436	222	41	116	.271	.357

Q. Only nine 20th-century players—among them Wade Boggs, Ty Cobb, Jimmie Foxx, Lou Gehrig, Stan Musial, Babe Ruth, and Hack Wilson—have accumulated 200 hits and 100 walks in the same season. What relatively obscure Cubs infielder also did it?

A. Woody English, 1930

Orvie Overall (P)

Mordecai Brown is the best known of the Cubs pitchers of 1906–10, but Overall was dominant as well. The big right-hander won 20 games twice, led the league in shutouts in 1907 and 1909, and was nearly untouchable in World Series play. In 1911 at age 33, he walked away from the game in a contract dispute, returning briefly in 1913.

W	L	S	G	GS	CG	IP	H	BB	SO	ShO	ERA	Pct.
86	44	9	162	133	95	1,132	863	358	727	28	1.92	.662

Claude Passeau (P)

Ask even a knowledgeable baseball fan what Cubs pitcher won 20 games and threw a one-hitter in the World Series, and you probably won't get Claude Passeau for an answer. During the 1939 season, the Cubs got the junk-ball-throwing Passeau from the Phillies for three players, including Kirby Higbe. Passeau went on to win 13 games for the Cubs that year and stayed in double figures through 1945, being named to five All-Star teams in the process.

W	L	S	G	GS	CG	IP	H	BB	SO	ShO	ERA	Pct.
124	94	15	292	234	143	1,915	1,919	474	754	23	2.96	.569

Ed Reulbach (P)

One of the great unknown legends in all of baseball, Reulbach went 60–15 for the 1906–08 pennant-winners, leading the league in winning percentage each season (a threepeat not yet duplicated). During the last days of the wild 1908 pennant race, he threw four consecutive shutouts, including two *in the same day*.

W	L	S	G	GS	CG	IP	H	BB	SO	ShO	ERA	Pct.
136	65	7	281	216	149	1,865	1,459	650	799	31	2.24	.677

Wildfire Schulte (OF)

Schulte was a regular in both left field and right field for the Cubs from 1905 until he was traded in 1916. He was a steady though not spectacular performer for the Cubs pennant-winners, raising his game in the postseason, where he batted 40 points above his lifetime average. He saved his best for 1911 as the Cubs dynasty began to fade, hitting .300 with a league-leading 21 home runs and 107 RBIs.

G	AB	R	H	2B	3B	HR	RBI	BB	SO	SB	BA	SA
1,563	5,835	827	1,590	254	117	92	712	455	421	214	.272	.403

Jimmy Sheckard (OF)

Sheckard was the Cubs' left fielder from 1906 through 1912, coming over from Brooklyn in a trade after the 1905 season. At different times in his career, he was a power hitter, an average hitter, and a patient hitter who drew walks. With the Cubs, it was the latter, especially in 1911, when he drew a then-record 147 walks and scored a league-leading 121 runs.

G	AB	R	H	2B	3B	HR	RBI	BB	SO	SB	BA	SA
1,001	3,530	589	907	172	46	17	294	629	192	163	.257	.346

Harry Steinfeldt (3B)

Steinfeldt is more than just the answer to a famous trivia question: Who filled out the Tinker-Evers-Chance infield at third base? The question could just as easily have been: Who was the leading hitter on the winningest team in baseball history? Steinfeldt paced the 116-win 1906 Cubs with a .327 batting average and a league-leading 176 hits and 83 RBIs. He played third base for the 1907, 1908, and 1910 pennant-winners as well but did not reach those levels again.

G	AB	R	H	2B	3B	HR	RBI	BB	SO	SB	BA	SA
733	2,596	339	696	120	28	9	332	213	29	92	.268	.346

Jack Taylor (P)

The "Brakeman" won 20 games for the Cubs in 1902 and 1903 and then was accused of dumping games in the first City Championship Series with the White Sox in 1903. He was traded to the St. Louis Cardinals for an uproven youngster named Mordecai Brown but returned to the Cubs in the middle of the 1906 season, going 12–3 for Chicago and 20–12 for the season.

W	L	S	G	GS	CG	IP	H	BB	SO	ShO	ERA	Pct.
108	90	3	215	196	188	1,801	1,770	368	425	14	2.66	.545

Clutch Performers

They're not Hall of Famers, they aren't legendary, and a number of them had only limited stretches of effectiveness. They are, however, players who "played big"—all of them key contributors to winning teams.

Jody Davis (C)

Catcher had been a very unsettled position in Chicago ever since Randy Hundley tore up his knee in a 1970 home-plate collision. Davis changed that when he arrived in 1981. He was the team's everyday catcher from 1982 through 1987, was named to two All-Star teams, hit at least 17 home runs five years in a row, and knocked in a career-high 94 runs during the Cubs' pennant-winning season of 1984.

G	AB	R	H	2B	3B	HR	RBI	BB	SO	SB	BA	SA
990	3,318	350	834	158	11	122	467	307	647	7	.251	.416

Bill Hands (P)

A career record of 111–110 belies Hands's status as a big-game pitcher. His emergence as a frontline starter in 1968 gave the Cubs their first Big Three since Wyse-Passeau-Derringer in 1945. He won 20 games in 1969 and was one of the few Cubs' pitchers able to win games during the final weeks of the pennant race.

W	L	S	G	GS	CG	IP	H	BB	SO	ShO	ERA	Pct.
92	86	9	276	213	64	1,564	1,485	389	900	14	3.18	.517

Ken Holtzman (P)

Holtzman, along with Bill Hands and Fergie Jenkins, rounded out the Cubs' Big Three of 1968 through 1971. At his best, he was a dominating left-hander who threw two no-hitters and narrowly missed two others. He had differences with manager Leo Durocher, and his demand for a trade after the 1971 season was granted, signaling the beginning of the breakup of the '69 Cubs.

W	L	S	G	GS	CG	IP	H	BB	SO	ShO	ERA	Pct.
80	81	3	237	209	57	1,427	1,399	530	988	15	3.81	.497

Randy Hundley (C)

In "Home Plate" (Chapter 8), you will find a list of all the catchers between Gabby Hartnett in 1940 and Randy Hundley in 1966. Hundley was a great defensive catcher and field leader, and before succumbing to overwork and injuries, he could hit, too. Hundley knocked in at least 60 runs in each of his first four seasons with the Cubs, hitting 19 home runs in 1966 and 18 in 1969.

G	AB	R	H	2B	3B	HR	RBI	BB	SO	SB	BA	SA
947	3,158	301	758	111	12	80	364	248	519	12	.240	.360

Pat Malone (P)

Malone was a frontline starter for the Cubs from 1928 through 1934 who came up big during pennant-winning seasons, leading the league in wins with 22 in 1929 and winning 15 in 1932. After losing eight of his first nine decisions as a rookie in 1928, he went 17–5. One of his best seasons was 1930, when he led the league in wins with 20 and complete games with 22.

W	L	S	G	GS	CG	IP	H	BB	SO	ShO	ERA	Pct.
115	79	8	265	200	107	1,632	1,628	577	878	16	2.18	.593

Keith Moreland (C-OF-3B)

Very quietly, Keith Moreland put up some impressive numbers for the Cubs from 1982 through 1987. He played regularly in right field, served a season at third base, filled in at first, and even caught a few games, while hitting at least 12 home runs and driving in at least 68 runs each season. He hit 30 doubles three times, batted .300 twice, drove in 100 runs once, hit a career-high 27 home runs in 1987, and even stole 12 bases in 1985. During the 1984 pennant drive, Moreland was NL Player of the Month in August, knocking in 32 runs.

G	AB	R	H	2B	3B	HR	RBI	BB	SO	SB	BA	SA
902	3,240	394	912	153	12	100	491	308	387	19	.281	.429

Rick Sutcliffe (P)

Perhaps no pitcher has meant more to a team than Sutcliffe did to the '84 Cubs. Though spending only four months with the team—after coming over from the Indians in a June trade—Sutcliffe still led the Cubs in victories and was dominant enough to win the Cy

Young Award based on a half season's worth of work. He went 16–1, won 14 in a row, and pitched the pennant-clincher. A Cub from 1984 through 1991, he was frequently hampered by injuries—though he was healthy enough to lead the league in wins in 1987 and win 16 games for the '89 pennant-winner.

W	L	S	G	GS	CG	IP	H	BB	SO	ShO	ERA	Pct.
82	65	0	193	190	40	1,267	1,186	481	909	11	3.74	.558

Lon Warneke (P)

With the Cubs, Warneke was one of the league's top pitchers from 1932 through 1936, winning at least 16 games each season. He led the league in wins with 22 for the 1932 pennant-winner, won 22 again in 1934, and won another 20 in 1935. In the '35 World Series against Detroit, Warneke earned the Cubs' only two victories—a four-hit shutout in Game One and another six scoreless innings in Game Five. He went on to spend seven seasons as an umpire in the National League.

W	L	S	G	GS	CG	IP	H	BB	SO	ShO	ERA	Pct.
109	72	11	262	190	122	1,625	1,549	413	706	17	2.84	.602

Nineteenth-Century Stars

Many of the exploits of the 19th-century ballplayers have been discounted, simply because the rules were so different that comparison with today's statistics is difficult if not impossible. These players were among the best of their time, and several were teammates of Hall of Famers Cap Anson and King Kelly on the pennant-winners of the 1880s.

Tom Burns (SS-3B)

Burns was the shortstop in the White Stockings' "Stonewall Infield" of Anson-Pfeffer-Burns-Williamson. He played for five pennant-winners, knocked in at least 65 runs six times, and batted .309 during his rookie season.

G	AB	R	H	2B	3B	HR	RBI	BB	SO	BA	SA
1,239	4,881	715	1,291	235	69	40	567	267	446	.264	.365

John Clarkson (P)

Clarkson was one of the first overhand pitchers and one of the first students of hitters. He recorded his 136 wins in only four seasons in Chicago, winning his three best—53, 35, and 38—from 1885 to 1887. After the 1887 season, he was sold to Boston for $10,000. He went on to win 326 games and was inducted into the Hall of Fame in 1963.

W	L	S	G	GS	CG	IP	H	BB	SO	ShO	ERA	Pct.
136	57	0	199	197	186	1,731	1,523	300	960	15	2.39	.705

Larry Corcoran (P)

Diminutive but deadly effective, Corcoran was part of baseball's first pitching rotation—the ace of a two-man staff with Fred Goldsmith. He was a star for five seasons, including the

Fast & Loose: 1876–1900

In 1876, baseball bore little resemblance to today's game. The pitcher stood 45' from home plate, threw underhand, and faced batters who could request high or low pitches. Foul balls weren't strikes, and balls bouncing over fences were home runs—even though some fences were less than 200' from home plate! Things weren't all bad for pitchers: foul balls caught on one bounce were an out, and it took nine balls to walk a batter.

During the first 25 years of the National League's history, tinkering with the rules was an annual event. Here are some of the highlights:

- *In 1880, a walk was issued after eight balls rather than nine.*
- *In 1881, the pitcher's mound was moved back from 45' to 50'.*
- *In 1882, it was ball seven, take your base.*
- *In 1883, a foul ball caught on one bounce was no longer an out.*
- *In 1884, a pitcher was allowed to pitch from as high as his shoulder, rather than underhand. That was the good news for the hurlers; the bad news was six balls now meant a free pass. This went back up to seven in 1886 but came right back down to five the following year.*
- *In 1887, batters could no longer call for a high or low pitch, but it required two called third strikes to be caught looking.*
- *In 1888, it was back to three strikes and you're out, and the ground-rule double was established for balls bouncing over fences less than 210' from home plate.*
- *In 1889, they finally arrived at ball four.*
- *In 1892, the ground-rule double was pushed back to fences less than 235' from home plate.*
- *In 1893, flat-sided bats were outlawed, but the mound was moved back to 60' 6" from home plate—marked by a new thing called a pitching rubber.*
- *It wasn't until 1895 that a foul tip was a strike, and it wasn't until 1900 that home plate was widened from a 12" square to a 17"-wide polygon.*

Comparing 20th-century and 19th-century statistics can often be a meaningless exercise. The rules that governed play—and the equipment used by the players—led to high-scoring, error-filled contests in which the objective was simply to put the ball in play. In 1876, the average game featured more than seven unearned runs (in most seasons since World War II, there has been an average of less than one unearned run per game). Few batters struck out, fewer still drew bases on balls, and batters often choked halfway up the bat. Home runs were rare—despite the short porches in many ballparks—yet, the typical game in 1894 was still an 8–7 affair.

In 1893, when the pitchers were moved back 10', runs went up by 3 per game and another 1½ the following year—to levels that have never been reached again in major-league baseball. Forced to innovate, the defense tightened up, and the pitchers got creative. By 1898, runs per game were fewer than they'd been before the mound was moved five years before—a remarkable accomplishment, aided in large part by trick pitches such as the spitball.

This cycle of the pitchers innovating and the hitters—or the rules-makers—responding continued for the next 100 years.

1880–82 pennant-winners, winning at least 27 games each season and 43 as a rookie in 1880. Corcoran threw three no-hitters, more than any other Cubs pitcher.

W	L	S	G	GS	CG	IP	H	BB	SO	ShO	ERA	Pct.
175	85	2	270	262	252	2,338	2,084	462	1,086	22	2.26	.673

Bill Dahlen (SS)

Dahlen was the team's shortstop from 1891 through 1898, producing more big-hitting moments than any other Cubs shortstop except for Ernie Banks. He hit .350 twice, drove in 100 runs once, and owns the longest hitting streak in club history and one of the longest ever (42 games in 1894). He played 21 seasons in the major leagues, accumulating nearly 2,500 hits.

G	AB	R	H	2B	3B	HR	RBI	BB	SO	SB	BA	SA
986	3,904	896	1,166	203	106	57	560	472	266	27	.299	.449

Abner Dalrymple (OF)

Dalrymple played left field and led off for the five White Stockings pennant-winners of the 1880s, hitting at least .290 in each of his first six seasons with the club. He led the league in hits with 126 in 1880 and runs scored with 91.

G	AB	R	H	2B	3B	HR	RBI	BB	SO	BA	SA
709	3,181	666	938	173	65	40	216	140	241	.295	.428

George Gore (OF)

Gore played alongside Dalrymple in center field from 1879 through 1886, leading the league in runs scored twice and walks three times. He hit .300 six times (and .298 once), leading the league in 1880 with a .360 mark.

G	AB	R	H	2B	3B	HR	RBI	BB	SO	BA	SA
719	2,963	772	933	162	60	24	288	343	176	.315	.434

Wild Bill Hutchison (P)

A graduate of Yale, Hutchison was a solid starter for seven seasons with Chicago from 1889 through 1895 and the league's best pitcher from 1890 to 1892. He led the league in wins, games, complete games, and innings each season, as he piled up 42, 44, and 37 victories. Hutchison walked many but struck out more—but his dominance ended in 1893 when the pitcher's mound was finally moved back to 60′6″.

W	L	S	G	GS	CG	IP	H	BB	SO	ShO	ERA	Pct.
182	158	3	367	339	317	3,026	3,055	1,106	1,226	21	3.56	.535

Bill Lange (OF)

Called Little Eva for his dancing ability, Lange was the graceful center fielder of the Colts and Orphans from 1893 through 1899. He hit .300 six times, knocked in 80 runs five times, and stole 41 bases in 1899. He married into wealth and walked away from the game at 28, possibly cutting short a Hall of Fame career. His bride's father wanted nothing to do with a ballplayer, so he gave it up—only to have his marriage end in divorce.

G	AB	R	H	2B	3B	HR	RBI	BB	SO	SB	BA	SA
811	3,195	689	1,055	133	79	40	578	350	86	63	.330	.459

Fred Pfeffer (2B)

Pfeffer is the only player to have three tours of duty with Chicago's National League franchise. He was a White Stocking from 1883 through 1889, jumped to the Players League with many of his teammates, then returned to what were then the Colts in 1891. After four seasons with Louisville and four games with the New York Giants, he returned to Chicago in 1896 and retired along with Cap Anson after the 1897 season (thus missing by one season the chance to be a White Stocking, Colt, *and* Orphan). He had a few big years at the plate, knocking in 95 runs for the 1886 pennant-winner, but earned his keep with the glove . . . so to speak. Pfeffer was a great fielder despite his insistence on fielding bare-handed for most of his career.

G	AB	R	H	2B	3B	HR	RBI	BB	SO	BA	SA
1,093	4,280	742	1,080	147	71	79	532	328	379	.252	.375

Jimmy Ryan (OF)

Cubs fans point to Ron Santo and Stan Hack as the most deserving among uninducted Hall of Famers, but Ryan may in fact be the most glaring omission. With 2,500 hits and a .306 average, he is one of only three players to achieve both levels without being inducted. He was a strong-armed right fielder and leadoff man from Holy Cross who broke in at the tail end of the 1880s dynasty. Playing regularly for Chicago for 14 seasons, he hit .300 nine times (along with .293 and .299), drew walks, hit for power, and stole bases (including 34 at the age of 34 in the first season they were tabulated by today's scoring rules). He missed by one home run being the first Cub to have 100 home runs, 2,000 hits, and a .300 batting average—an honor destined to fall to Mark Grace sometime during the 1999 season.

G	AB	R	H	2B	3B	HR	RBI	BB	SO	SB	BA	SA
1,660	6,757	1,409	2,073	362	142	99	914	683	325	57	.307	.446

Ned Williamson (SS-3B)

The final member of the Stonewall Infield, third-baseman—and occasional shortstop, second-baseman, first-baseman, catcher, and pitcher—Ned Williamson set a major-league home-run record of 27 in 1884 that lasted longer than Babe Ruth's 60. Williamson never hit 10 before or after, his 27 being in large part a function of a grounds rule change. In every season other than 1884, fly balls hit over the fence at Lakefront Park 180' from home plate were considered a double rather than a home run. Fluke record aside, Williamson was a solid player who lasted 11 seasons with the White Stockings and led third basemen in fielding percentage five times—four of those times, not coincidentally, with a pennant-winner.

G	AB	R	H	2B	3B	HR	RBI	BB	SO	BA	SA
1,065	4,042	744	1,050	211	80	61	478	465	482	.260	.397

. . . And the Rest

Let the arguments begin. The Top 75 is rounded out with these seven players, whose time with the club may have been brief, who never played with a winner, or whose tenure was checkered—or all of the above—but whose numbers rank high on the All-Time Cubs lists.

Bull Durham (1B-OF)

Durham's numbers are impressive, especially his rare combination of power and speed, which has been exceeded by only Sammy Sosa and Ryne Sandberg. Unfortunately, he will always be remembered as the guy who let the ground ball go through his legs in Game Five of the 1984 NLCS . . . the hyped prospect who came over from St. Louis for Bruce Sutter and never lived up to expectations . . . and whose development went backward after a career year at age 25 in 1982, perhaps due to off-the-field problems that finally came to light in 1988.

G	AB	R	H	2B	3B	HR	RBI	BB	SO	SB	BA	SA
921	3,215	474	898	173	36	138	485	419	608	98	.279	.484

Rogers Hornsby (2B)

Though a Hall of Famer, Hornsby belongs on the Cardinals' Cooperstown list. He has the fewest at bats of any player on the Top 75 list, having come to Chicago late in his career. Hornsby had only one big season left (1929)—but it was arguably the greatest offensive performance in Cubs history, propelling the Cubs to the pennant.

G	AB	R	H	2B	3B	HR	RBI	BB	SO	SB	BA	SA
317	1,121	245	392	91	10	58	264	165	104	3	.350	.604

Bill Madlock (3B)

Madlock lasted only three seasons in Chicago but won two consecutive batting titles before being dumped when his salary demands exceeded Phil Wrigley's level of comprehension. He could have been the one to finally replace Ron Santo. Instead, he remains the only player since World War II to bat .340 for two different teams.

G	AB	R	H	2B	3B	HR	RBI	BB	SO	SB	BA	SA
400	1,481	210	498	86	13	31	202	140	124	35	.336	.475

Rick Monday (OF)

Monday played five seasons for the Cubs during the often brutal mid-1970s. He hit 20 home runs three times, struck out an average of 108 times per season, and was only 37-for-79 in stolen-base attempts—and this was the team's *leadoff* hitter. Monday did, however, come the closest to stabilizing a center-field position that's been in flux ever since Andy Pafko was traded.

G	AB	R	H	2B	3B	HR	RBI	BB	SO	SB	BA	SA
702	2,551	441	690	114	26	106	293	383	540	37	.270	.460

Rick Reuschel (P)

Big Daddy was the Bob Rush of the '70s, a number-two or number-three starter asked to be the ace of a weak staff. He won at least 10 games every season from 1972 through 1980, almost exclusively for losing teams. Bruce Sutter got most of the credit in 1977 when the Cubs found themselves back in contention, but Reuschel's 20 wins, four shutouts, and 2.79 ERA had a lot to do with it. He left Chicago once by trade and then later via free agency, resurrecting his career in Pittsburgh and then returning as a Giant in 1989 to close out the Cubs in Game Five of the NLCS.

W	L	S	G	GS	CG	IP	H	BB	SO	ShO	ERA	Pct.
135	127	3	358	343	65	2,291	2,365	640	1,367	17	3.50	.515

Hank Sauer (OF)

"The Mayor of Wrigley Field," Sauer brightened the dreary early '50s with his power stroke. In 1952 in a controversial decision, he became the first member of a nonwinning team to take the MVP. It was his best season; he led the league in home runs (37) and RBIs (121) and even won the All-Star Game with a home run. Sauer hit 30 home runs for the Cubs three other times, and went deep 41 times in 1954.

I don't mind your hitting a home run off me, but, jeez, don't look at me as if you wanted to kill me.

A pitcher, on Hank Sauer's "game face"

G	AB	R	H	2B	3B	HR	RBI	BB	SO	SB	BA	SA
862	3,165	498	852	141	17	198	587	365	454	6	.269	.512

Heinie Zimmerman (3B)

Zimmerman may or may not have been the first to win the Triple Crown in 1912, depending on whose numbers you use. He definitely led the league in hits (207), doubles (41), home runs (14), batting average (.372), and slugging average (.571). Either he led the league with 103 RBIS, or he finished second to Honus Wagner with only 99 as some more recent calculations suggest. Zimmerman played every infield position with the Cubs and some outfield, but he was primarily a third baseman. He didn't play full-time until 1911 when he took over second base in place of Johnny Evers (who'd had a nervous breakdown) and enjoyed the first of three consecutive .300 seasons. He stayed in the lineup until he was dealt to the Giants during the 1916 season for Larry Doyle—a bad deal for the Cubs until they turned around and dealt Doyle for Lefty Tyler, whose 19 wins helped them capture the pennant in 1918.

G	AB	R	H	2B	3B	HR	RBI	BB	SO	SB	BA	SA
906	3,356	473	1,027	196	77	48	530*	181	298	122	.306	.453

*Includes 103 RBIs in 1912

THE AWARDS

Most Valuable Player—Winners

The Baseball Writers' Association of America has been selecting an MVP every year since 1931. Prior to that, the League Award was given to the best in the NL from 1924 to 1929. Before that, the Chalmers Automobile Company gave the Chalmers Award (and a new car) to the league's best from 1911 to 1914. A Cub has won each. Many Cubs would have won the award in the seasons that none were given. And finally, more than a few Cubs have been near misses who could have or should have won the award.

1911 Wildfire Schulte
Schulte batted .300 and led the league with 21 home runs and 107 RBIs, numbers that proved impressive enough to beat out Christy Mathewson by four votes. Mathewson had gone 26–13 with a 1.99 ERA for the pennant-winning Giants.

1929 Rogers Hornsby
It was a hitters' year, and Hornsby took an award that any four Cubs could have rightfully claimed. Hornsby hit .380 with 39 home runs and 149 RBIs, while every member of the Cubs' outfield hit at least .345 and knocked in at least 102 runs (Riggs Stephenson hit .362, Kiki Cuyler kicked in 43 steals, and Hack Wilson knocked in 159 runs!). For the Giants, a 20-year-old named Mel Ott hit 42 home runs, knocked in 151 runs, and batted .328. In Brooklyn, Babe Herman hit .381 and knocked in 113. Hornsby's closest competition turned out to be Lefty O'Doul, who led the league at .398 with 32 home runs and 122 RBIs.

1935 Gabby Hartnett
Most catchers lose their bat speed and, with it, their offensive production as they get older. Not Hartnett. At 34, he had his finest year since the wild 1930 season, hitting .344 with 91 RBIs in only 116 games. His closest competition was Dizzy Dean, who won 28 games for the second-place Cardinals. Hartnett just missed a second MVP in 1937 when he lost by only two votes to Joe Medwick (who'd won the Triple Crown!).

Nonslugging MVPs

YEAR	MVP	Pos.	HR
1931	Frankie Frisch	2B	4
1934	Mickey Cochrane	C	2
1944	Marty Marion	SS	6
1945	Phil Cavarretta	1B	6
1950	Phil Rizzuto	SS	7
1959	Nellie Fox	2B	2
1962	Maury Wills	SS	6
1973	Pete Rose	OF	5

1945 Phil Cavarretta

Phil Cavarretta earned an interesting distinction with his 1945 Most Valuable Player Award. He led the league at .355 and knocked in 97 runs, but his six home runs made him one of those rare nonsluggers to win the award (except for pitchers, of course). He beat out Tommy Holmes of the sixth-place Braves, who missed the Triple Crown by three hits and seven RBIs and had a 37-game hitting streak (so, perhaps Cavarretta should have shared the award with Cubs pitcher Hank Wyse, who snapped Holmes's streak on July 12 in a 6–1 win at Wrigley).

Above is the list of MVPs who haven't hit at least 10 home runs. Only two played a "power" position: Pete Rose and Phil Cavarretta.

1952 Hank Sauer

Sauer was the first player to win an MVP for a team without a winning record (the Cubs were 77–77, good enough for fifth place but 19½ games from the top). The pennant-winning Dodgers saw their votes being split among Jackie Robinson, Pee Wee Reese, Gil Hodges, Duke Snider, and Roy Campanella. Sauer outhomered all of them (37) and drove in more runs (121), both good enough to lead the league—thanks to a blazing start, in which he batted .349 and piled up 18 home runs and 58 RBIs in his first 50 games. Finishing a close second (15 votes) wasn't a Dodger at all, but Robin Roberts, who went 28–7 for a fourth-place Phillies team that went 59–60 without him.

1958 Ernie Banks

Though Banks's fielding slipped a bit in '58—he led the league in errors with 32, accomplishing a less desirable 30/30—he had his finest offensive season: a league-leading 47 home runs (in a year in which no one else hit even 36) and 129 RBIs (only one other player topped 100) while batting .313 and slugging .614 (also tops in the league). He also scored 119 times, producing 28 percent of the team's offense. He outslugged Henry Aaron of the pennant-winning Braves as well as his closest MVP competition, Willie Mays, who narrowly missed his

> ### *Winning for Losing*
>
> **Q.** Who are the only three players to win an MVP Award for a team that didn't have a winning record? Hint: They're all Cubs.
>
> **A.** Hank Sauer, Ernie Banks, and Andre Dawson

MVPs on Nonwinning Teams

YEAR	MVP	HR	RBI	BA	% OF OFFENSE*
1952	Sauer	**37**	**121**	.270	**28%**
1958	Banks	**47**	**129**	.313	**28%**
1959	Banks	45	**143**	.304	**29%**
1987	Dawson	**49**	**137**	.287	25%

*The percentage of runs a player either scores or knocks in—(R + RBI – HR)/Team Runs

Note: League-leading totals are in **bold**.

third consecutive 30/30 season while batting .347. Mays had no one on base to knock in, however, and the Giants finished third in their first season in San Francisco.

1959 Ernie Banks

In 1959, the Cubs finished fifth (again) and had a losing record (again), but Ernie Banks peaked as a major leaguer. His offense remained as potent as ever, with 45 home runs, a league-best and personal-best 143 RBIs, and a .304 batting average. He produced 29 percent of the Cubs' runs; without him, the team hit .243 with little speed and not so much as a 15-homer or 55-RBI bat in the lineup. He beat out Hank Aaron and Eddie Mathews—who did 39/123/.355 and 46/114/.306 for a Braves team that lost the pennant to the Dodgers in a play-off—and it was probably Banks's fielding that did it. Tightening it up dramatically from 1958, Banks set a record (since broken) with a fielding percentage of .985—only 12 errors in more than 800 chances.

1984 Ryne Sandberg

The only real competition for Sandberg for the MVP should have been from Rick Sutcliffe (who finished fourth behind Keith Hernandez and Tony Gwynn). Ryno simply had one of the greatest all-around seasons any player ever had. He hit for average: .314 with 200 hits. He hit for power: a .520 slugging average with 74 extra-base hits. He produced runs: 84 RBIs and 114 runs scored. He stole bases: 32 in 39 attempts. In the field, he handled 870 chances and booted only six of them.

1987 Andre Dawson

Dawson was the first player to win the MVP with a last-place team. In a bit of revenge for the MVP that light-hitting Cardinals shortstop Marty Marion took from slugging Cubs right-fielder Bill Nicholson in 1944 (see under "Near Misses"), The Hawk beat out Ozzie Smith for the award. Smith had no home runs and 70 RBIs, Dawson 49 and 137 (both league-leading totals). Dawson is one of only five players to lead the league in RBIs for a last-place team (the others are Wally Berger, Roy Sievers, Frank Howard, and Darren Daulton). He was the main reason the Cubs became the first last-place team to draw 2 million fans.

All this in his first year in town. He'd come to Chicago from Montreal in the midst of a collusion-warped free-agent market, finally handing the Cubs' heel-dragging front-office executives a blank contract and telling them to fill in the numbers. A look at the similar numbers (see chart on page 34) that Dawson, Banks, and Sauer put up for noncontenders should give you a good idea of what kind of numbers a losing team's superstar needs to put up to win the award.

Hawk always wanted that $100,000 from me.

Rick Sutcliffe, on the $100,000 of his own salary he offered to contribute to the signing of Andre Dawson in 1987

1998 Sammy Sosa

Mark McGwire might have hit more home runs, but Sammy Sosa was hitting his for a play-off contender. He led the league in runs scored with 134 and in RBIs with 158, producing 27 percent of Chicago's runs. While his stolen bases went down, his walks went up and his batting average ended up over .300 for the first time in his career (he hit an even .300 during the strike-shortened 1994 season). See "The Outfield," Chapter 10, for a breakdown of Sosa's home runs by game situation—only eight came in routs or blowouts.

The Unawarded

Hack Wilson had bad luck during much of his baseball career, and the fact that 1930 was the last season when no MVP was awarded was just another brick in the load. With a National League–record 56 home runs, a major-league-record 190 RBIs, a .356 batting average, and a .723 slugging average, he would have been a unanimous selection even though the Cubs didn't win the pennant.

Wilson isn't the only Cub who would have been honored had a Most Valuable Player Award of some kind been given from 1876 to 1910, from 1915 to 1924, and in 1930. Here's a list of worthy recipients; conservatively, Cap Anson could have won *seven* MVPs.

Near Misses

1932 Lon Warneke

The 1932 Philadelphia Phillies played in the Baker Bowl, which was the Coors Field of its day. The team's Dante Bichette was Chuck Klein, a player who never approached his lofty Phillies numbers when playing in any other park. Sportswriters didn't consider things like "park effects" back then—and barely do even now—so Klein's 36/137/.348 for a fourth-place team won him an MVP Award that rightfully belonged to Lon Warneke. Warneke went 22–6, leading the league in wins, winning percentage, shutouts (four), and ERA (2.37) for a first-place Cubs team that had a mediocre offense, at best.

1938 Bill Lee

Catcher Ernie Lombardi won the award in 1938, leading the league at .342 and knocking in 95 runs for the fourth-place Reds. It was an award that should have gone to Bill Lee, who went 22–9, leading the league in wins, winning percentage, shutouts (nine), and ERA (2.66) for a Cubs pennant-winner without so much as a 15-homer or 70-RBI hitter. Like Warneke in 1932, Lee had to settle for second place.

The snubs of Bill Lee and Lon Warneke were not a result of discrimination against pitchers. In fact, four starting pitchers won the MVP Award in the National League during the 1930s, and only five more have won since (the decline coincides with the establishment of the Cy Young Award in 1956). But the pitchers who won the MVP in the 1930s won on wins—30 by Dizzy Dean in 1934, 26 by Carl Hubbell in 1936, and 27 by Bucky Walters in 1939. Hubbell won it with 23 wins in 1933, but that was a year when Chuck Klein gave the voters an excuse *not* to vote for him; he won the Triple Crown while his team declined by 18 wins in the standings and dropped to seventh place.

Wins are less in a pitcher's control than just about any other statistic, but it's the standard by which they're judged. Evidently, 21 and 22 just weren't enough for these two Cubs.

MVP Would-Have-Beens

YEAR	PLAYER	Pos.	SEASON HIGHLIGHTS
1876	Ross Barnes	2B	**.429**; 59 RBIs in 66 games; league's best fielding percentage
1880	Cap Anson	1B	.337; **74** RBIs in 84 games; league's best fielding percentage
1881	Cap Anson	1B	**.399**; 82 RBIs in 84 games, league's best fielding percentage
1882	Cap Anson	1B	.362; 83 RBIs in 84 games
1885	Cap Anson	1B	.310; **114** RBIs in 112 games
1886	Cap Anson	1B	.371; **147** RBIs in 124 games
1888	Cap Anson	1B	**.344**; 84 RBIs in 135 games; league's best fielding percentage
1891	Cap Anson	1B	.291; **120** RBIs in 135 games
1906	Harry Steinfeldt	3B	.327; 83 RBIs; league's best fielding percentage
1918	Hippo Vaughn	P	22–10; **1.74** ERA; 148 strikeouts; 8 shutouts
1930	Hack Wilson	OF	.356; **56** home runs; **190** RBIs

Note: League-leading totals are in **bold**.

Imbalance of Power

Q. Who is the last National Leaguer to hit more than half of his team's home runs?

A. Bill Nicholson, 1943

1943, 1944 Bill Nicholson

Bill Nicholson was at his most fearsome in 1943, when he led the league in home runs (29 of the Cubs' 52) and RBIs (128) while hitting .309. The award went to Stan Musial, who led the league at .357 with 48 doubles and 20 triples, though he knocked in only 81 runs with 13 homers. Granted, Musial was the best hitter on a singles- and doubles-hitting pennant-winner, but how valuable was he? His team won by 18 games and had the league's best pitching staff; given the level of competition, it's quite possible they would have won it without him. Nicholson produced 31 percent of the Cubs' runs, while Musial produced *only* 26 percent of the Cardinals' runs. In 1943, without Nicholson, the Cubs would have lost at least 20 games in the standings and might have been the worst team in franchise history.

Nicholson had pretty much the same season in 1944 as he did in 1943, and so did the Cubs. He led the league in home runs (33 of the Cubs' 71) and RBIs (122) while batting .287. This time, the award went to the great-fielding shortstop Marty Marion, who hit .267 with six home runs and 63 RBIs. Nicholson lost by one vote in the closest MVP balloting until Keith Hernandez and Willie Stargell tied in 1979.

1955 Ernie Banks

Ernie Banks had one near miss before he won his two MVP Awards in 1958 and 1959. In 1955, his second full season in the majors, Banks put up eye-popping numbers for a shortstop, hitting 44 home runs while knocking in 117 runs, scoring 98, and batting .295 for the sixth-place Cubs. And this was a shortstop who could field, showing good range and leading the league in fielding percentage. He lost out to the catcher on the pennant-winning Brooklyn Dodgers, Roy Campanella, who did 32/107/.318. Banks produced 27 percent of the Cubs' runs, Campanella 18 percent of the Dodgers' runs. The criteria that elected him in 1958 and 1959 could easily have done the same in 1955.

1969 Ron Santo

If the Cubs had finished stronger in 1969 and taken the pennant, led by a strong September from Ron Santo, maybe the Cubs' captain and third baseman would have finished higher in the voting than a distant fifth behind Willie McCovey, Tom Seaver, Hank Aaron, and Pete Rose. As it was, Santo played a terrific third base and narrowly missed the RBI title by only three to Willie McCovey, while hitting .289 with 29 home runs. If only it were just 32 home runs, 135 RBIs, and .300 . . . if only . . . if only . . .

1970, 1972 Billy Williams

Billy Williams finished second to Johnny Bench in the MVP voting twice. It's hard to argue with the 1970 balloting. Williams hit 42 home runs, knocked in 129 runs, and batted .322 with a league-leading 205 hits and 137 runs, but Bench was spectacular behind the plate while hitting 45 home runs, knocking in 148 runs, and batting .293 for a pennant-winner. The 1972 outcome, however, is a different story. Williams won the batting title at .333 while hitting 37 home runs and knocking in 122 runs for a second-place team without much else, producing 26 percent of his team's runs. Bench hit three more home runs, knocked in five more runs, and batted 63 points lower for an easy pennant-winner that already had Tony Perez, Joe Morgan, and Pete Rose. Three home runs, two of them with a man on, and Williams would have had the Triple Crown.

1977 Bruce Sutter

Sutter is on this list for deserving to be more of a near miss than he actually was. It would be hard to deny the award to George Foster, who hit .320 with 52 home runs and 149 RBIs, but Sutter certainly deserved better than seventh place. He came out of nowhere to post 31 saves with a microscopic 1.35 ERA, and he had the mediocre-at-best Cubs in first place late into the summer before going on the disabled list for six weeks. With Sutter out of the lineup, the Cubs found their level and ended up in fourth place with a .500 record.

Cy Young Award—Winners

The Cy Young Award has been given to the best pitcher every year since 1956, and in both leagues since 1967. Four Cubs have won it, a number have just missed, and countless others would have taken it had the award been given for the years 1876 through 1955. In fact, it could just as easily have been called the Albert Spalding Award or simply the Chicago (19th-century slang for a shutout).

1971 Ferguson Jenkins

In his fifth consecutive 20-win season, Fergie Jenkins finally won a Cy Young Award, beating out Tom Seaver of the Mets and Al Downing of the Dodgers. He became the only pitcher in baseball history (and still is!) to strike out more than 250 batters while walking fewer than 40, one of the greatest performances that no one knows about.

Fergie had tremendous control. I could almost catch him with a pair of pliers.

Randy Hundley

1979 Bruce Sutter

By 1979, Bruce Sutter had proved he was no fluke while voters had come to terms with the concept of a relief pitcher's being the best pitcher in the league. Ironman Mike Marshall actually won the award for the Dodgers in 1974, while Sparky Lyle took it for the Yankees in 1977. Sutter's '79 season was every bit as dominant as his '77 campaign. He had a hand in 54 percent of the team's wins, the league hit .186 against him, and only 3 of the roughly 400 batters he faced were able to take him out of the yard. Basically, he turned the National League into a collective Mario Mendoza.

Cy Young Would-Have-Beens

YEAR	PLAYER	W	L	S	IP	SO	ShO	ERA
1876	Albert Spalding	**47**	13	0	529	39	8	1.75
1880	Larry Corcoran	43	14	2	536	**268**	4	1.95
1881	Larry Corcoran	**31**	14	0	397	150	4	2.31
1885	John Clarkson	**53**	16	0	**623**	**308**	**10**	1.85
1886	John Clarkson	35	17	0	467	313	3	2.41
1887	John Clarkson	**38**	21	0	**523**	**237**	2	3.08
1890	Bill Hutchison	**42**	25	**2**	**603**	289	5	2.70
1891	Bill Hutchison	**44**	19	1	**561**	261	4	2.81
1906	Mordecai Brown	26	6	3	277	144	**9**	**1.04**
1907	Orvie Overall	23	8	3	265	139	8	1.70
1909	Mordecai Brown	**27**	9	**7**	**343**	172	8	1.31
1910	Mordecai Brown	25	13	**7**	295	143	**6**	1.86
1918	Hippo Vaughn	**22**	10	0	**290**	**148**	8	**1.74**
1920	Grover Alexander	**27**	14	5	**363**	**173**	7	1.91
1927	Charlie Root	**26**	15	2	**309**	145	4	3.76
1929	Pat Malone	22	10	2	267	**166**	**5**	3.57
1930	Pat Malone	**20**	9	4	272	142	2	3.94
1932	Lon Warneke	**22**	6	0	277	106	**4**	**2.37**
1938	Bill Lee	**22**	9	2	291	121	**9**	**2.66**
1945	Hank Wyse	22	10	0	278	77	2	2.68

Note: League-leading totals are in **bold**.

1984 Rick Sutcliffe

When Sutcliffe was honored in 1984 for his miraculous 16–1 half season, he joined Sandy Koufax, Bob Gibson, and Steve Carlton as the only National Leaguers to have won the Cy Young Award by a unanimous vote. Maybe someday another pitcher will be that dominant in only 20 games of work, but don't hold your breath.

1992 Greg Maddux

The first of the four consecutive Cy Young Awards won by Greg Maddux came in his last season in Chicago. At 26, he came into his own, winning a league-leading 20 games with a microscopic 2.18 ERA, threw four shutouts, and fielded his position flawlessly. To say any more is simply too painful.

The Unawarded

Before the days of Hank Sauer, Ralph Kiner, Ernie Banks, Billy Williams, Dave Kingman, Andre Dawson, and Sammy Sosa, the Cubs were built on pitching and defense. *Especially* pitching. No fewer than 13 Cubs were the best pitchers in the National League for at least one season from 1876 to 1945.

Cy Young Award—Near Misses

1964 Larry Jackson

The Cy Young Award was in its ninth year before a Cub received a vote. Unfortunately, it was also still awarded to just one pitcher back then—the best in the majors. Jackson had the poor timing to win 24 games in the same season that Dean Chance went 20–9 with 11 shutouts and a 1.65 ERA for the Los Angeles Angels. The Cubs were 24–11 in Jackson's decisions, 42–75 in all other games, and he would have probably beaten out Sandy Koufax (19–5, 1.74) and Juan Marichal (21–8, 2.48) to take the National League award.

1967, 1970, 1972 Ferguson Jenkins

Fergie Jenkins received consideration for four additional Cy Young Awards, three during his time with the Cubs. In 1967—back when only one writer from each major-league city voted—Mike McCormick took 18 of 20 votes, with Jenkins and Jim Bunning each receiving a vote. By all rights, this should have been much closer. The Giants' McCormick earned his landslide on the basis of two more wins, two more shutouts, a higher ERA despite a much more favorable park, fewer innings, fewer complete games, more base runners allowed per game, and fewer strikeouts. With a better bullpen behind him, Jenkins might have taken the award or at least made it a much closer race.

In 1970, with writers allowed to list more than one pitcher on their ballots, Jenkins finished a distant third behind Bob Gibson and Gaylord Perry (whose brother Jim won the award in the AL). Gibson and Perry each won 23 games to Jenkins's 22. Gibson was a deserving winner who was more overpowering in his wins and toiled for an inferior club.

In 1972, Jenkins finished a distant third behind Steve Carlton and Steve Blass. Jenkins simply had the misfortune of winning 20 games in the same season that Carlton recorded 27 of his team's 59 victories.

1977 Bruce Sutter

Just as Bruce Sutter did not receive as much MVP consideration as he deserved, he was snubbed all the more so in the Cy Young voting—earning a mere five votes to finish sixth behind Steve Carlton, Tommy John, Tom Seaver, teammate Rick Reuschel, and John Candelaria. Some still viewed Sutter's performance as a fluke, while others held his six-week stint on the disabled list against him (though he still missed leading the majors in saves by only four!). True, he did break down, but the Cubs were on pace to use him in more than 80 games. Objectively, how could it be dismissed that Sutter had a hand in nearly half of the team's wins, back when saves were often two- or three-inning achievements? That his ERA was 1.35? That the league hit .183 against him? That he struck out 11 batters per nine innings while walking less than two? He was the most dominant pitcher in baseball—and, as we will see in much greater detail later, one of the most dominant in its history.

1987 Rick Sutcliffe

In the same season that Andre Dawson became the first player to win the MVP with a last-place club, Rick Sutcliffe came within two votes of doing the same in the Cy Young voting. In the closest balloting since voting was expanded in 1970, the Phillies' Steve Bedrosian received 57 votes to Sutcliffe's 55 and the Pirates/Giants' Rick Reuschel's 54. Voter confusion could be attributed to an absence of 20-game winners and two pennant-winners without so much as a 14-game winner between them. Bedrosian recorded a league-leading 40 saves, while Sutcliffe led the league with 18 wins. Sutcliffe's success was built mostly on guile and run support. His ERA was a high 3.68, and he recorded only one shutout. It was a year when the best pitcher in the NL went 8–16; Nolan Ryan posted that record despite leading the league in ERA and strikeouts and showing some of the best control of his career.

the dugout

One way out of the Cubs' clubhouse leads to a hallway to an elevator to a door and back out to the street. The other leads to a runway that takes you to the dugout, where 51 different men have run the Chicago Cubs during their 123 seasons. A few were legendary, others were forgettable—and there were a couple you wish you could forget but, try as you might, you just can't. Their won–loss records range from Frank Chance's spectacular 768–389 to the 0–1 of Roy "Hardrock" Johnson and Joe Altobelli, passing through Cap Anson's 1,283 wins along the way.

Some appointments were fortuitous, others disastrous. At times, management was rash (Rogers Hornsby in 1930), brash (Leo Durocher in 1966), or just plain silly (the College of Coaches in 1961). Ironically, the team's best managerial move was made by the players, who voted to name 27-year-old Frank Chance their manager in 1905 when his predecessor fell ill.

Anyone who doubts the impact a manager can have on a team need look no further than the history of the Chicago Cubs to be swayed. Consider:

- The 18 managerial changes that Ernie Banks endured, beginning with the first man to be fired during spring training
- The manager who said, "You do things my way or you meet me after the game," and whose response to a beanball was to acquire the pitcher who hit him, cut his salary, bury him on the bench, and eventually drive him into retirement; that makes charging the mound look positively sissy
- The manager who was fired for essentially *keeping* his players from making curfew
- Joe McCarthy's 10 Commandments and Rogers Hornsby's equally long list of neuroses
- When the Cubs traded their manager for a broadcaster
- Leo Durocher's thoughts on fair play and sportsmanship, Lee Elia's thoughts on unemployment, and Don Zimmer's thoughts on being Don Zimmer
- The first black manager—not Frank Robinson, but a Chicago Cub

So, lead, follow . . . or get out of the dugout.

ONE SHORT
OF A FULL DECK

Fifty-one men have managed the Chicago Cubs during their 123 seasons. Here they are, from best results to worst.

Managers, by Record

MANAGER	SERVICE	G	W	L	Pct.	1st PLACE FINISHES
Frank Chance	1905–12	1,157	768	389	.664	4
Albert Spalding	1876–77	125	78	47	.624	1
Joe McCarthy	1926–30	763	442	321	.5793	1
Cap Anson	1879–97	2,215	1,283	932	.5792	5
Frank Selee	1902–05	493	280	213	.568	
Rogers Hornsby	1930–32	257	141	116	.549	
Charlie Grimm	1932–38, 1944–49, 1960	1,728	946	782	.547	3
Tom Burns	1898–99	298	160	138	.537	
Gabby Hartnett	1938–40	379	203	176	.536	1
Fred Mitchell	1917–20	577	308	269	.534	1
Jim Frey	1984–86	378	196	182	.519	1
Johnny Evers	1913, 1921	249	129	120	.518	
Don Zimmer	1988–91	523	265	258	.507	1
Hank O'Day	1914	154	78	76	.5065	
Bill Killefer	1921–25	593	300	293	.5059	
Leo Durocher	1966–72	1,061	535	526	.504	
Jim Lefebvre	1992–93	324	162	162	.500	
Bob Ferguson	1878	60	30	30	.500	
John Vukovich	1986	2	1	1	.500	
Herman Franks	1977–79	479	238	241	.497	
Whitey Lockman	1972–74	319	157	162	.492	
Jim Riggleman	1995–	631	307	324	.487	1*
Jim Essian	1991	122	59	63	.484	
Gene Michael	1986–87	238	114	124	.4790	
Bob Kennedy	1963–65	380	182	198	.4789	
Roger Bresnahan	1915	153	73	80	.477	
George Gibson	1925	26	12	14	.462	
Jimmy Wilson	1941–44	471	213	258	.452	
Bob Scheffing	1957–59	462	208	254	.450	
Lee Elia	1982–83	285	127	158	.446	
Jim Marshall	1974–76	393	175	218	.445	
Phil Cavarretta	1951–53	382	169	213	.4424	
Lou Klein	1961, 1962, 1965	147	65	82	.4422	
Joe Tinker	1916	153	67	86	.4379	
Harry Craft	1961	16	7	9	.4375	
Charlie Fox	1983	39	17	22	.436	
Rabbit Maranville	1925	53	23	30	.4340	
Tom Trebelhorn	1994	113	49	64	.4336	

continued

*Wild card

Ernie's Managers

Ernie Banks's managers, in order: Phil Cavarretta, Stan Hack, Bob Scheffing, Charlie Grimm, Lou Boudreau, Vedie Himsl, Harry Craft, Vedie Himsl, El Tappe, Harry Craft, Vedie Himsl, El Tappe, Lou Klein, El Tappe, Lou Klein, Charlie Metro, Bob Kennedy, Lou Klein, Leo Durocher.

MANAGER	SERVICE	G	W	L	Pct.	1st PLACE FINISHES
Stan Hack	1954–56	461	196	265	.425	
Tom Loftus	1900–01	279	118	161	.423	
Preston Gomez	1980	90	38	52	.422	
Frankie Frisch	1949–51	337	141	196	.418	
El Tappe	1961, 1962	116	46	70	.397	
Lou Boudreau	1960	137	54	83	.394	
Charlie Metro	1962	112	43	69	.384	
Joey Amalfitano	1979, 1980–81	182	66	116	.363	
Vedie Himsl	1961	31	10	21	.323	
Frank Lucchesi	1987	25	8	17	.320	
Silver Flint	1879	17	5	12	.294	
Roy Johnson	1944	1	0	1	.000	
Joe Altobelli	1991	1	0	1	.000	

THE CHRONOLOGY: HIGHLIGHTS

Cap Anson 1879–97

Round up the strongest men who can hit a baseball the farthest the most often, put yourself on first base, and win.   —Cap Anson, on how to be a managerial genius

As a hitter, Cap Anson was the first to reach 3,000 hits and to hit five home runs in two games. His résumé as a manager is even more impressive. Anson introduced platooning, the hit-and-run, the third-base coach, and the pitching rotation. He was so popular he even had candy named after him nearly 100 years before Reggie Jackson.

Anson was forced out as manager after the 1897 season in a bitter power struggle with club president and part-owner James Hart.

Frank Selee 1902–05

I do not believe that men who are engaged in such exhilarating exercise should be kept in strait-jackets all the time, but I expect them to be in condition to play. I do not want a man who cannot appreciate such treatment.   —Frank Selee

Selee managed in street clothes, like Connie Mack. He had his biggest success with the Boston Beaneaters of the 1890s. As a Cub, his greatest contribution was laying the groundwork for the 1906–10 dynasty. He put the Tinker-to-Evers-to-Chance infield in place by moving Tinker from third, Evers from short, and Chance from behind the plate.

Frank Chance 1905–12

You do things my way or you meet me after the game.   —*Frank Chance*

When Frank Selee fell ill during the 1905 season, he allowed his successor to be elected by his players. To his surprise, they chose 27-year-old Frank "Husk" Chance, who went on to be the team's greatest manager and the only player-manager to win two World Series. He came to be known as "the Peerless Leader" and was a hardnose to say the least (he would fine his players for shaking hands with opponents). Physically imposing, he was viewed by some as "the greatest amateur brawler in the world," a quote attributed to both John L. Sullivan and Jim Corbett. He furthered his reputation by provoking a riot at the Polo Grounds when he decked Giants pitcher Joe McGinnity; he responded to bottle-throwing fans in Brooklyn by heaving the bottles back into the stands (he needed an armed escort to leave that game).

> *He asked no man to take any chance he would not take himself.*
>
> *New York Giants manager John McGraw, on Frank Chance*

Chance was one of the headiest players in the game. His teams won on pitching, defense, and smart play. He was a smart trader, handpicking the players before the 1906 season; his team then going from 92 wins to 116. He could also be a ruthless dealer. When a pitcher named Jack Harper beaned him once too often for his liking, he traded for him, cut his salary by two-thirds, refused to pitch him, and drove him into retirement at the age of 28.

Frequent beanings cost Chance his hearing in one ear and led to blood clots in his brain and brutal headaches. He demanded a four-year deal from odious club owner Charlie Murphy but was fired while in the hospital recovering from brain surgery. Chance died at 47 in 1924 before he could accept a job as manager of the Chicago White Sox.

Most Wins with One Franchise

Connie Mack	Philadelphia Athletics	3,637
John McGraw	New York Giants	2,658
Walter Alston	Brooklyn–Los Angeles Dodgers	2,040
Fred Clarke	Louisville Grays/Pittsburgh Pirates	1,602
Tommy Lasorda	Los Angeles Dodgers	1,599
Earl Weaver	Baltimore Orioles	1,480
Joe McCarthy	New York Yankees	1,460
Wilbert Robinson	Brooklyn Dodgers	1,375
Bucky Harris	Washington Senators	1,336
Sparky Anderson	Detroit Tigers	1,331
Cap Anson	**Chicago White Stockings**	**1,283**

Johnny Evers 1913, 1921

My favorite umpire is a dead one.   —*Johnny "the Crab" Evers*

Evers got the four-year deal that Chance wanted, but he lasted only one season as Cubs manager. The Crab was tossed from countless games during 1913 and was fired at the end of the season after losing the City Championship Series to the White Sox. The following year, he went on to play for the Miracle Braves of 1914, leading them to the pennant. He returned to manage the Cubs again in 1921.

> **Q.** Who is the only man to manage both the Cubs and the White Sox?
>
> **A.** Johnny Evers

Fred Mitchell 1917–20

The manager of those same Miracle Braves took over the Cubs in 1917, the sixth manager in six years—a group that included Tinker, Evers, and Chance, as well as Hank O'Day, the umpire who called Fred Merkle out in the boner game of 1908. Mitchell stabilized the situation for a while, lasting four seasons and leading the club to the World Series in 1918.

Rabbit Maranville 1925

There will be no sleeping on this club under Maranville management.   —*Rabbit Maranville*

Possibly the worst manager in club history was Rabbit Maranville, a self-described "rum hound." Acquired during the 1925 season—the first year the Cubs ever finished last—he replaced Bill Killefer as manager and lasted only 53 games. On the team's first road trip, he barged into his players' Pullman berths to splash cold water in their faces from a spittoon.

Joe McCarthy 1926–30

A manager shouldn't play unless he's better than anybody else on the team.
—Joe McCarthy

Joe McCarthy hadn't played in the big leagues, uncommon for managers at the time. The 15-year minor leaguer was considered a risky hire, but he had the Cubs back in the World Series in four years. An astute judge of talent, he directed the Cubs' front office to acquire Charlie Root, Guy Bush, and Hack Wilson. Though he had a well-deserved reputation for being a strict disciplinarian, he turned out to be the only one who could manage the hard-drinking Hack Wilson, which he did by *not* trying to make him toe the line. "What am I supposed to do?" McCarthy said during Wilson's 190-RBI season in 1930. "Tell him to live a clean life and he'll hit better?"

McCarthy resigned with four games to go in the 1930 season, knowing that he was about to be fired. The Cubs have had some great firings (simply because they've had quite a few lousy hirings), but replacing McCarthy with Rogers Hornsby was a disaster. McCarthy went on to manage the Yankees to eight pennants and seven championships and ended his career with 24 seasons at the helm, *none* of them with a losing team.

Rogers Hornsby 1930–32

He was frank to the point of being cruel and subtle as a belch. **—Lee Allen, sportswriter,** *on Rogers Hornsby*

I'm a tough guy, a gambler on horses, a slave driver, and in general a disgrace to the game. I wish I knew why. I only wanted to win. **—Rogers Hornsby**

McCarthy may have been a disciplinarian, but Hornsby was a psychopath. He banned reading, movies, and soda pop, forebade smoking or eating in the clubhouse, and rarely instructed his players. He was a perfectionist who expected others to achieve his standards. Hornsby ruined Hack Wilson by forcing him to take too many pitches and by cracking down hard on his lifestyle, while alienating most of his other players, too. He was eventually fired on August 2, 1932, because of his gambling, having borrowed $11,000 from his players to pay his debts. He was so despised by his players that he wasn't voted a single cent of the team's World Series money in 1932 despite spending four months with the team.

Charlie Grimm 1932–38, 1944–49, 1960

Every time we call on Charlie, we win a pennant. **—Philip Wrigley, after the 1959 season** *(Grimm lasted 17 games before switching jobs with one of the team's announcers, Lou Boudreau.)*

Replacing Hornsby with a jokester like Charlie Grimm was an inspired choice. The players loosened up under banjo-playing Jolly Cholly immediately, winning their first game 12–1 against the Phillies. Two weeks later, the Cubs scored four in the bottom of the ninth to beat the Braves 4–3 at Wrigley Field on Charlie Grimm Day, and they were well on their way to steamrolling to the pennant. He managed the Cubs during their 21-game winning streak of 1935, returned in 1944 to bring Stan Hack out of retirement and lead them to the World Series in 1945, and took the helm for a third time briefly, in 1960, eventually trading places with Lou Boudreau, who'd been in the broadcast booth. He became the second of only four men to manage the same team three times (Bucky Harris, Danny Murtaugh, and Billy Martin share the record).

After leaving the Cubs the first time, Grimm became the manager of Bill Veeck's Milwaukee Brewers team in the American Association, where he was tossed from games for protesting the playing conditions in colorful ways. When it was raining, he'd walk out to the umpire with a beach umbrella; when it was dark, he'd carry a railroad lantern. When he died, his ashes were scattered on Wrigley Field by his widow.

Gabby Hartnett 1938–40

Philip Wrigley changed managers again during the 1938 season, and once again it worked. Under Gabby Hartnett, the Cubs hunted down the Pirates and effectively took the pennant on September 28 when Hartnett hit his famous "homer in the gloamin'" (see "Home Plate," Chapter 8). Like Chance and Grimm before him, the Cubs had another manager taking the pennant in his rookie season (and, after Grimm, only the second manager to take over in midseason and lead his team to the World Series). But when the outmanned Cubs were wiped out by the Yankees in four games, Hartnett blew up at his players on the train ride home from New York. Congenial as a player, Hartnett proved difficult and occasionally arbitrary as manager, burying Phil Cavarretta on the bench for the next two seasons and losing the respect of many of his players.

Frankie Frisch 1949–51

I've got one ballplayer on the team, and the rest are minor leaguers. —Frankie Frisch in 1949 *(referring to a team that included Andy Pafko, Phil Cavarretta, Hank Sauer, Bob Rush, and Dutch Leonard)*

Frankie Frisch was a great player-manager with the Gas House Gang, but he went from genius to idiot upon taking over the Cubs. If the true test of a manager is what he can do without great players, then Frisch failed—finishing eighth, seventh, and eighth in parts of three uninspired seasons. His heart was never really in the job, he didn't get along with his players, and he used to encourage them to get games in the Polo Grounds over with quickly so he could go home to New Rochelle and his garden. He should have been fired in 1951 for not using a fixed pitching rotation, but instead it was the sight of him reading a novel in the dugout in the Polo Grounds that ended his tenure.

Phil Cavarretta 1951–53

Phil, I'm a member of your club. . . . Mr. Finley just fired me, too, in spring training. —Alvin Dark in 1976

The highlights of Phil Cavarretta's tenure were closing the center-field bleachers in 1951 to make a better (and safer) backdrop for hitters and guiding the team to a .500 record in 1952. He was fired *before the season even started* when he was too candid with Philip Wrigley during spring training in 1954 about the team's (lack of) talent. Stan Hack replaced him, and the team finished exactly where Cavarretta had said they would.

The College of Coaches 1961–65

If Mr. Wrigley wants to hire eight coaches and no manager, that's strictly his business. My only concern is that he has nine men on the field. —Baseball Commissioner Ford Frick

The Cubs have been playing without players for years. Now they're going to try it without a manager. —Anonymous critic

At first, I didn't like it because it wasn't traditional. Then I became disenchanted when it didn't work.   —Dick Ellsworth

Every few weeks, they'd have a new head coach. It was weird. They assured us there was no competition between the coaches, but I couldn't see how there wasn't. Nobody knew who was playing until after you got to the ballpark and they had their meeting. They had the ballplayers so screwed up because nobody knew what was going on. . . . The year was a complete waste.
—*Ed Bouchee*

This coaching system is killing one of their best prospects, Ron Santo.   —Don Zimmer in a 1961 radio interview

It was a nutty idea.   —Richie Ashburn

All El Tappe wanted to do was to have a set group of coaches and a set manual for instruction at all levels, rather than firing all the coaches every time the Cubs changed managers. Members of this "brain trust" would rotate between the major leagues and minor leagues, making certain that a "Cubs way" of doing things was being taught. Philip Wrigley had the idea of making one of the rotating coaches the manager (along with hiring the 63-year-old Colonel Whitlow as "athletic director" to run spring training like a military camp). The original eight coaches were: Bobby Adams, Rip Collins, Harry Craft, Charlie Grimm, Vedie Himsl, Goldie Holt, El Tappe, and Verlon Walker. They later added Lou Klein, Fred Martin, and Charlie Metro to the College of Coaches.

The unfortunate experiment lasted from 1961 to 1965. The problems were numerous. When coaches changed, the status of players changed. Rules changed, too; Charlie Metro blamed losing on shaving in the clubhouse and banned the practice. And the head coach didn't change on a fixed basis—no one knew when or why a new head man would be established. The coaches wouldn't help each other—in fact, one just hit his son fungoes while he waited his turn to manage.

The 1961 team, with Ernie Banks, Ron Santo, rookie star Billy Williams, and budding star George Altman, managed to lose 90 games and finish seventh. The 1962 team, with Ken Hubbs and Lou Brock added to the cast, lost 103 games and finished behind the expansion Colt .45s. Bob Kennedy was named head coach in 1963, the revolving stopped, and the team won 82 games and finished seventh. But the experiment wasn't officially terminated until after the 1965 season, when the Cubs hired the first and only headstrong manager of Philip Wrigley's tenure: Leo Durocher.

Leo Durocher 1966–72

Somebody had to wake (the players) up.   —Philip Wrigley, on hiring Leo Durocher

They already had Billy, Ernie, and Ron. But it was Leo's leadership that put the team together.
—*Glenn Beckert*

Leo liked veterans, didn't have patience with rookies, couldn't stand mediocrity.   —Gene Oliver

When Leo touched his nose, it meant the hit-and-run was on. But there was a problem. He was always picking his nose.   —Herman Franks

Leo Durocher is a man with an infantile capacity for immediately making a bad thing worse.
—*Branch Rickey*

In those early days, he was an SOB, but he was a sharp SOB. But by the time he was finished in Chicago, he was just an old SOB.   —Jack Brickhouse

It took the United States 35 years to get revenge for Pearl Harbor.   —Vin Scully, on Leo Durocher's being hired by a Japanese baseball team

In hiring Leo Durocher, Philip Wrigley hired himself a man who once gave Babe Ruth a black eye. Who was suspended for a season for associating with gangsters. Who was thrown at by Cubs pitchers—*when he was in the dugout*. Durocher's time in Chicago was just about as chaotic. He built the Cubs into contenders, thanks not just to his leadership but also to the input he had on personnel decisions. But he also went out of his way to hit just about every bump in the road.

Reacting to Astrodome cartoons of him on the scoreboard, he ripped the phone out of the dugout and threw it onto the field. When players underperformed, he ranted and raved and threatened to "back up the truck." Jealous of Ernie Banks, he kept trying to find a rookie to replace him at first base (Clarence Jones, John Boccabella, John Herrnstein), but none could. He was so abrasive that his third-base coach, Pete Reiser, walked out on him in the middle of a game. He left the team in June of 1969 for his fourth bachelor party, then was nearly fired during the season for blowing off two games to visit his newest wife's kids at Camp Ojibwa in Wisconsin.

He called his veteran pitchers gutless and gave up on his young ones quickly, having several potentially reliable fourth starters traded away. He burned out his starters in 1969 and let his reserves rust on the bench. Taking the '69 collapse hard, by 1970 he was on radio station WIND announcing managerial decisions on the air: "Santo is playing like he's in a fog. Let him sit down." On August 30, 1971, the players finally rebelled. When Durocher accused Ron Santo of requesting that a day be given in his honor—like those honoring Williams and Banks—the third baseman had to be physically restrained from attacking him. Wrigley took out ads to defend his manager's authority, and disgruntled players such as Ken Holtzman were dealt away. Somehow, Durocher lasted until July 24, 1972, with the Cubs having seen both his best and his absolute worst.

Herman Franks 1977–79

I've got my own problems. I've got a couple of players I don't talk to.   —*Herman Franks, to reporters complaining about players not speaking to the press*

The Cubs of 1977, 1978, and 1979 were some of the most entertaining teams the franchise has ever seen. Despite the departure of Bill Madlock before the season, Franks had the Cubs in first place on August 4, 1977, but the team collapsed when Bruce Sutter and Rick Reuschel both went down to injury. While the team was being torn down around him in 1978 and 1979, Franks—a Durocher henchman for many years—dribbled tobacco juice on his uniform, called for Sutter out of the bullpen, and kept the Cubs competitive.

Lee Elia 1982–83

Eighty-five percent of the people in this country work. The other 15 percent come here and boo my players. They oughta go out and get a #@$%ing job and find out what it's like to go out and earn a #@$%ing living.   —*Lee Elia*

Just Leo Being Leo

This is definitely not an eighth-place club. [He was right; in 1966 they finished 10th.]

Look, I'm playing third base. My mother's on second. The ball's hit out to short center. As she goes by me on the way to third, I'll accidentally trip her up. I'll help her up, brush her off, tell her I'm sorry. But Mother don't make it to third.

I was just a guy who wanted to win, and I would have taken your teeth to do it.

Win any way you can as long as you can get away with it.

You never save a pitcher for tomorrow. Tomorrow it may rain.

Show me a good loser in professional sports, and I'll show you an idiot. Show me a sportsman, and I'll show you a player I'm looking to trade.

Nice guys finish last.

Leo Durocher

The First Black Manager

On May 8, 1973, Whitey Lockman was ejected from the game. His two lieutenants were unavailable, so Ernie Banks took over the team—two years before Frank Robinson broke the managerial color line in Cleveland in 1975.

The foregoing comments came after the Cubs fell to 5–14, losing to the Dodgers at Wrigley Field on a Lee Smith wild pitch in April 1983 and prompting some hostile fans to douse Keith Moreland with beer on his way to the clubhouse. It was a tribute to the loyalty of new GM Dallas Green that his handpicked manager wasn't dismissed until four months later.

Jim Frey 1984–86

With Gooden and Strawberry playing the roles of Seaver and Agee, the Mets had delusions of another last-to-first miracle pennant. But this time the veteran Cubs beat them back. Their fiery leader (Dallas Green) was up in the front office, while Leo Durocher's polar opposite, Jim Frey, kept things calm in the clubhouse. Frey was the club's first Manager of the Year, but his team fell precipitously in 1985 when his entire starting rotation went on the disabled list.

Gene Michael 1986–87

> *He's a big buffoon with a big mouth. He didn't make a mistake hiring me. His mistake was not listening to me.* —**Manager Gene Michael, on GM Dallas Green in 1987 as he announced his resignation on the radio**

The highlight of Gene Michael's time at the helm was how he chose to go out: live on the radio. At the time of the quoted announcement, what would become the greatest last-place team in the history of baseball—featuring the league leader in wins, the home-run champ and MVP, the best second baseman in baseball, the league's most dominant closer, a powerful young rookie named Rafael Palmeiro, and a struggling young pitcher named Greg Maddux—was 68–68 and watching the St. Louis Cardinals growing smaller on the horizon. Dallas Green resigned a few weeks later, having accused his team of "quitting with a capital *Q.*"

Don Zimmer 1988–91

> *The weather's cold. My club's bad. My knee hurts. I can't putt no more. I'm off my diet. My wife is nagging me. Other than that, everything's great.* —**Don Zimmer in 1990**

It all came together for Zimmer in 1989, as every move he made—most going against "the book"—paid off. Every pinch hitter he selected seemed to come up with the big hit, every spot starter seemed to throw a gem, and he came away with the club's second Manager of the Year Award. Things changed quickly in 1990 when every one of his starting outfielders went on the disabled list at the same time and both Rick Sutcliffe and Mitch Williams were lost for significant periods of time. In 1991, he was one of three managers to leave within the same week in mid-May.

Tom Trebelhorn 1994

Tom Trebelhorn's tenure was brief and undistinguished, but he did win points for guts. At the start of a season in which the Cubs didn't win a game at Wrigley Field until May 4, Trebelhorn faced a mob of angry Cubs fans in front of Engine Company 78 on Waveland Avenue after yet another brutal loss. "Not since Daniel went into the lions' den," wrote Joseph Reaves of the *Chicago Tribune,* "has anybody taken such a chance and lived to tell about it."

Jim Riggleman 1995–

Through 1998, Jim Riggleman managed more games than all but five Cubs managers: Cap Anson, Charlie Grimm, Frank Chance, Leo Durocher, and Joe McCarthy. For a while, it didn't look as if he'd even make it to sixth on the list. Riggleman's job was on the line going into the 1998 season, and his team responded with inspired play all year. Though the Cubs suffered many wrenching defeats during the wild-card race, to Riggleman's credit the team never folded. But perhaps his greatest managerial move was confronting Sammy Sosa for "selfish play" during the final days of the 1997 season, challenging him to raise his game and play for the team. Sosa responded as no one else ever has.

the lineup card

Posted on the wall of the dugout is the lineup card, listing who's playing where and when they're batting, who's available to pinch-hit, and who's down in the bullpen. Thousands of these cards have been posted in Chicago's dugouts, and here are a few more—though the methods used to choose up sides here are a bit different from most:

- The All-Name Teams of 1900–49, 1950–98, and the 19th century. A chance for Malachi Jeddidah Kittridge, Zeriah Zequiel Hagerman, and Facundo Barragan to stand alongside stars like Adrian Constantine Anson, William Jennings Bryan Herman, and Miltiades Stergios Papastegios.

- The All-Nickname Teams of 1900–39, 1940–98, and the 19th century. A chance for The Hawk to stand in against Hippo or, in a bit more obscure of a matchup, Bear Tracks to stare down Bunions. Meanwhile, down in the bullpen, Grandmother and Prunes are warming up Grasshopper and Fido.

- The Odds and Evens Teams. The Cubs first wore uniform numbers on July 1, 1932. More than 60 years later, you can fill two All-Star rosters with Cubs who've worn each number from 1 through 50.

- The Rookies and Flashes Teams. Who'd you rather have on your side: the greatest Cubs in their rookie seasons or the team's hottest-burning flashes in the pan? Take the flashes, since it's always 1957 for the all-too-briefly brilliant Dick Drott, and every day is May 1955 for Bob Speake.

- The Youth and Experience Teams. So, do you want the best Cubs at 21 or younger, or at 38 or older? Take the youngsters and get a pitcher who went 74–28 as a mere child. Take the oldsters and get the only 40-year-old to steal 40 bases. It's a tough call, but either way, you get Gabby Hartnett behind the plate.

- The Old and Modern Teams. The older era has half of its starting lineup from the 1929–30 seasons alone, and their "weak link" in the batting order is a .339 hitter. The modern era has Bruce Sutter in the bullpen and power hitters up and down the order, with the "lightweight" producing "only" 16 home runs and 51 doubles.

- The Geography Teams. What region of the country do you put your money on? The Northeast and Rhode Island's Gabby Hartnett? The South and Alabama's Billy Williams? The Midwest/Great Plains and Illinois's Phil Cavarretta and Iowa's Cap Anson? The West and Washington's Ryne Sandberg? The International Team and Canada's Ferguson Jenkins?

- The All-Decade Teams. The best from every decade, including a left-handed catcher, a palm-ball-throwing Cardinal-killer, and a pitching ace whose career took off after he broke his nose.

THE ALL-NAME TEAMS

Following are two squads, selected from two half centuries of Cubs baseball. Players merit inclusion based solely on the beauty, lyricism, historical significance, or sheer strangeness of their names. If these two teams ever do play—managed, of course, by El Tappe and Vedie Himsl—look for Fabian Kowalik and Porfi Altamarino to hook up in a pitchers' duel ultimately decided by a Facundo Barragan passed ball or an upper-deck blast off the bat of 129-pound Zebulon Terry.

The 20th-Century All-Name Squads

CHICAGO CUBS 1900–49		CHICAGO CUBS 1950–98	
PLAYER	**SERVICE**	**PLAYER**	**SERVICE**
Pitchers			
Jocko Menefee	1900–03	Luvern Fear	1952
Jeff Pfeffer	1905, 1910	Emory Nicholas	
Orval Overall	1906–10, 1913	"Bubba" Church	1953–55
Zeriah Zequiel "Rip" Hagerman	1909	Vincente Amor	1955
Irv Higginbotham	1909	Vito Valentinetti	1956–57
Grover Cleveland Lowdermilk	1912	Sterling Slaughter	1964
George Washington "Zip" Zabel	1913–15	Jophrey Brown	1968
Abraham Lincoln "Sweetbreads"		Miltiades Stergios Papastegios	
Bailey	1919–21	(Milt Pappas)	1970–73
Uel Eubanks	1922	Oscar Zamora	1974–76
Burleigh Grimes	1932–33	Porfi Altamarino	1984
Fabian Kowalik	1935–36	Heathcliff Slocumb	1991–92
JT Mooty	1940–43	Blaise Ilsey	1994
Calvin Coolidge Julius Caesar		Tanyon Sturtze	1995–96
Tuskahoma McLish	1949, 1951	Amaury Telemaco	1996–98
Catchers			
Elwood Wirts	1921–23	Facundo Barragan	1961–63
Thompson Orville "Mickey"		Steve Christmas	1986
Livingston	1943, 1945–47		
Infielders			
Harry Steinfeldt	1906–10	Joey Amalfitano	1964–67
Fritz Mollwitz	1913–16	Carmen Fanzone	1971–74
Otto Knabe	1916	Ralph Pierre "Pete" LaCock II	1972–76
Zebulon Alexander "Zeb" Terry	1920–22	Gonzalo Marquez	1973–74
William Jennings Bryan Herman	1931–41	Mike Tyson	1980–81
Willard Wayne Terwilliger	1949–51	Cleotha "Chico" Walker	1985–87, 1991–92
Outfielders			
Clarence "Ginger" Beaumont	1910	Ephesian "Ted" Savage	1967–68
Dutch Zwilling	1916	John Junior "Champ"	
Clarence "Babe" Twombly	1920–21	Summers II	1975–76
Denver Clarence Grigsby	1923–25	Rolando Audley Roomes	1988
Herman Coaker Triplett	1938	Candy Maldanado	1993
		Brooks Kieschnick	1996–97

THE ALL-NICKNAME TEAMS

Because modern players are at such a competitive disadvantage when it comes to nicknames, the dividing line between these two teams has been moved back to 1940. The early team would be managed by the Peerless Leader, of course, while the Lip would handle the chores for the more recent squad. Look for a high-scoring, seesaw game, with decisions going to relievers Tiny Osborne (all 6′5″ and 215 pounds of him) and the Monster (6′6″/230) or perhaps to Fidgety Phil and Jittery Joe.

The 20th-Century All-Nickname Squads

CHICAGO CUBS 1900–39		CHICAGO CUBS 1940–98	
PLAYER	**SERVICE**	**PLAYER**	**SERVICE**
Pitchers			
Brakeman Jack Taylor	1898–1903, 1906–07	Wimpy Quinn	1941
Carl "The Human Icicle" Lundgren	1902–09	Bear Tracks Schmitz	1941–42, 1946–51
Tornado Jake Weimer	1903–05	Jittery Joe Berry	1942
Three-Finger Brown	1904–12, 1916	Mad Monk Meyer	1946–48, 1956
Steam Engine in Boots Moore	1913		
Hippo Vaughn	1913–21	Riverboat Smith	1959
Sweetbreads Bailey	1919–21	The Monster (Dick Radatz)	1967
Tiny Osborne	1922–24	The Vulture (Phil Regan)	1968–72
Fidgety Phil Collins	1923	Big Daddy (Rick Reuschel)	1972–81, 1983-84
The Mississippi Mudcat (Guy Bush)	1923–34	Dirt (Dick Tidrow)	1979–82
The Arkansas Hummingbird (Lon Warneke)	1930–36, 1942–43, 1945	Rainbow Trout	1983–87
		Wild Thing (Mitch Williams)	1989–90
Catchers			
Bubbles Hargrave	1913–15	Heathcliff (Cliff Johnson)	1980
Pickles Dillhoefer	1917	Blue Berryhill	1987–91
Infielders			
Cupid Childs	1900–01	The Antelope (Emil Verban)	1948–50
The Crab (Johnny Evers)	1902–13	Catfish Metkovich	1953
Bunions Zeider	1916–18	Mr. Cub	1953–71
Jolly Cholly (Charlie Grimm)	1925–36	Popeye (Don Zimmer)	1960–61
Trolley Line Butler	1928	Mad Dog (Bill Madlock)	1974–76
Footsie Blair	1929–31	The Penguin (Ron Cey)	1983–86
Highpockets Kelly	1930		
Outfielders			
Kangaroo Davy Jones	1902–04	Swish (Bill Nicholson)	1939–48
Circus Solly Hofman	1904–12, 1916	The Mad Russian (Lou Novikoff)	1941–44
Wildfire Schulte	1904–16		
Hack Wilson	1926–31	Tarzan (Joe Wallis)	1975–78
Old Hoss Stephenson	1926–34	Sarge (Gary Matthews)	1984–87
		The Hawk (Andre Dawson)	1987–92
		Spider Man (Glenallen Hill)	1993–94, 1998

19th-Century Nicknames

Either of the 20th-century teams might have a hard time holding their own with these guys:

C—Silver Flint, Grandmother Powers, Prunes Moolic

1B—Baby/Cap/Pop Anson

2B—Dandelion Pfeffer

SS—Topsy Magoon, Death to Flying Things (Robert Vavasour Ferguson)

3B—Jiggs Parrott, Tacky Tom Parrott

OF—Little Eva (Bill Lange), Pony Ryan, King Kelly, Orator Shaffer, Terrible Sam Dungan, The Magnet (Bob Addy)

P—Grasshopper Mains, Bald Eagle Isbell, Peaceful Valley Dezner, Egyptian John Healy, Adonis Terry, Fido Baldwin

ODDS VERSUS EVENS

In case you're wondering about Tinker, Evers, and Chance, the Cubs didn't wear uniform numbers until July 1, 1932. An honorary member of the Evens team should be Bill Voiselle from Ninety-Six, South Carolina. One guess what number he wore.

The Odds have the edge in starting pitching, but the Evens bullpen is awfully tough. The Evens get the edge thanks to more Hall of Famers, a deeper bench, and a lineup in which Andre Dawson leads off and Phil Cavarretta bats eighth. (See following page.)

The Odds and Evens Teams

ODDS

UNIFORM NUMBER	PLAYER	YEARS WITH NUMBER
Starting Pitchers		
13	Claude Passeau	1939–47
15	Bill Lee	1935–36
31	Ferguson Jenkins	1966–73, 1982–83
33	Hank Wyse	1943–47
49	Bill Hands	1966–72
Relief Pitchers		
27	Phil Regan	1968–72
35	Turk Lown	1951–54
37	Dick Ellsworth	1960–66
41	Dick Tidrow	1979–82
45	Paul Assenmacher	1989–93
47	Rod Beck	1998–
Catchers		
7	Jody Davis	1981–88
9	Randy Hundley	1966–73
Infielders		
1	Woody English (UT)	1932–36
11	Don Kessinger (SS)	1964–75
17	Mark Grace (1B)	1988–
19	Manny Trillo (UT)	1975–78, 1986–88
23	Ryne Sandberg (2B)	1982–94, 1996–97
39	Stan Hack (3B)	1935–36
Outfielders		
3	Kiki Cuyler	1932–35
5	Riggs Stephenson	1933–34
21	Sammy Sosa	1992–
25	Rafael Palmeiro	1986–88
29	Doug Dascenzo	1988–92
43	Bill Nicholson	1943–48

Bear Tracks?

The origins of many nicknames are shrouded in mystery—often for the best. Here are some whose meanings are known:

As most Cubs fans know, Mordecai "Three-Finger" Brown had his right hand caught in a corn grinder as a seven-year-old. "Four-and-a-Third Finger" would have been more accurate but wouldn't quite trip off the tongue so easily. Most of his index finger was amputated, and his middle finger was mangled. Later his little finger was knocked askew by a shot back up the middle. With a devastating curveball released off the stub of his index finger, perhaps a few struggling pitchers might have looked twice at a corn grinder before thinking better of it.

"Death to Flying Things" was a term of endearment in the 19th century for extraordinary defensive players. "The Crab" and "Mad Dog" weren't so flattering, reflecting the sour dispositions of Johnny Evers and Bill Madlock—while "Jolly Cholly" did just the opposite for Charlie Grimm. Sandy Koufax hung the name "the Vulture" on Phil Regan after he picked up two relief wins within a week in games that Koufax took into the ninth inning with the score tied.

"Hippo" was given to Jim Vaughn for the way he walked, "the Penguin" for the way Ron Cey ran. "Bear Tracks" was an homage to Johnny Schmitz's size-14 shoes. Bill Nicholson got the name "Swish" for the sound of his powerful swings. "Hack" Wilson wasn't named after his hitting style but after Hack Miller, another Cubs outfielder who was also about as wide as he was tall and who was named after a pro wrestler named George Hackenschmidt.

"Sarge" was a tribute to Gary Matthews's leadership ability, "Brakeman" to Jack Taylor's penchant for halting losing streaks, "Sweetbreads" and "Prunes" to what Abe Bailey and George Moolic liked to eat, and "Big Daddy" to the sheer volume of what Rick Reuschel ate. Sometimes nicknames are simply a function of the sensitivity and understanding of teammates. "Catfish" wasn't a particular delicacy favored by George Metkovich but the type of fish from which he was trying to pull a hook when he injured himself. Rollie Zeider got his nickname after Ty Cobb's spikes sliced into his bunions and gave him blood poisoning. And while playing for the Blue Jays, Glenallen Hill had a nightmare so frightening that while still asleep, he jumped from bed, crashed through his apartment, broke a large glass coffee table, and crawled across the broken glass. His hands, feet, and face badly cut, he ended up on the 15-day disabled list. One guess what poisonous arachnid Spider Man dreamed he'd been covered with.

The Odds and Evens Teams

EVENS

UNIFORM NUMBER	PLAYER	YEARS WITH NUMBER
Starting Pitchers		
30	Ken Holtzman	1965–71, 1978–79
32	Milt Pappas	1970–73
34	Kerry Wood	1998–
36	Kevin Tapani	1997–
40	Rick Sutcliffe	1984–91
Relief Pitchers		
38	Willie Hernandez	1977–83
42	Bruce Sutter	1976–80
46	Lee Smith	1980–87
50	Les Lancaster	1987–91
Catchers		
2	Gabby Hartnett	1937–40
6	Keith Moreland	1982–87
Infielders		
4	Billy Herman (2B)	1937–40
10	Ron Santo (3B)	1960–73
12	Shawon Dunston (SS)	1985–95, 1997
14	Ernie Banks (SS)	1954–71
16	Ken Hubbs (2B)	1962–63
18	Glenn Beckert (2B)	1965–73
22	Bill Buckner (1B)	1977–84
44	Phil Cavarretta (1B)	1941–53
Outfielders		
8	Andre Dawson	1987–92
20	Bob Dernier	1984–87
24	Lou Brock	1962–64
26	Billy Williams	1959–74
28	Jim Hickman	1968–73
48	Andy Pafko	1944–51

Here's how they'd line up on Opening Day:

39—Stan Hack (3B)	8—Andre Dawson (RF)
23—Ryne Sandberg (2B)	4—Billy Herman (2B)
17—Mark Grace (1B)	26—Billy Williams (LF)
21—Sammy Sosa (RF)	14—Ernie Banks (SS)
3—Kiki Cuyler (CF)	10—Ron Santo (3B)
5—Riggs Stephenson (LF)	48—Andy Pafko (CF)
9—Randy Hundley (C)	2—Gabby Hartnett (C)
11—Don Kessinger (SS)	44—Phil Cavarretta (1B)
31—Ferguson Jenkins (P)	40—Rick Sutcliffe (P)

ROOKIES VERSUS FLASHES

A t first glance, this appears to be as lopsided a matchup as could be concocted: a team with four Hall of Famers and numerous others who will be or deserve to be inducted against a squad of journeymen. The first group comprises the best rookies the Cubs have produced—rookies who proved to be the real thing. The second group is composed of some much lesser known players who had monster seasons, months, or games before burning out or fading away. But at their best moments, frozen in time, they'd give the young immortals a run for their money.

> *His arm gave out while he was with us, and besides that, he got into fast company and, attempting to keep up the clip with his so-called friends, found the pace much too rapid for him and fell by the wayside.*
>
> *Manager Cap Anson, on Jocko Flynn*

Rookies

Pos.	PLAYER	YEAR	RESULTS
C	Randy Hundley	1966	Career-high 19 home runs with 63 RBIs and .236 BA
1B	Mark Grace	1988	His .296 BA and 57 RBIs runs Durham out of town
2B	Billy Herman	1932	206 hits and .314—one of the all-time great rookie seasons
SS	Ernie Banks	1954	19 home runs and 79 RBIs, and that's just the beginning
3B	Ryne Sandberg	1982	103 runs, 172 hits, 32 steals; moves to second base in September
OF	Billy Williams	1961	25/86/.278 in his first full campaign
OF	Bill Lange	1893	8/88/.281 while playing nearly every position
OF	Jimmy Ryan	1886	4/53/.306 for a pennant-winner
UT	Ken Hubbs	1962	Record-setting errorless streak and 172 hits
UT	Bill Madlock	1974	Hits .313 with 54 RBIs but loses Rookie of the Year to Bake McBride
SP	Larry Corcoran	1880	43 wins for a pennant-winner . . . not bad
SP	Ed Reulbach	1905	18–14 with a 1.42 ERA and 5 shutouts
SP	Larry Cheney	1912	League-leading 26 wins, first of 3 consecutive 20-win seasons
SP	Rick Reuschel	1972	10–8 with a 2.93 ERA and 4 shutouts
RP	Bruce Sutter	1976	10 saves, 2.71 ERA, with opponents batting .209 against him

Flashes

Pos.	PLAYER	YEAR	RESULTS
C	Rick Wilkins	1993	26 years old, 30 home runs, .303, and asking for "Piazza money"
1B	Vic Saier	1913	14/92/.288 at 22 and making them forget Frank Chance
1B	Ray Grimes	1922	14/99/.354, RBIs in 17 consecutive games; injures back in 1923
2B	Todd Haney	1995	Hits .411 in 25 games; falls all the way to .134 in 1996
SS	Alex Arias	1992	5-for-5 in his major-league debut, first to do it in 59 years
3B	Ross Barnes	1876	Hits .429 at 26 but plays only 3 more seasons; specialty was the fair-foul bunt hit—any ball landing in fair territory and rolling foul was considered a fair ball, until legislated away after '76 season
OF	Bob Speake	1955	10/31/.304 in May, somehow finishes at 12/43/.218
OF	Frank Ernaga	1957	Homers in first at bat off Warren Spahn, later triples, and is hitting .314 when he hurts himself crashing into the vines a few days later
OF	Lee Walls	1958	Fills the '50s outfield with 24/72/.304 in his only season as a regular
OF	Hack Miller	1922	5'9''/195 son of a circus strongman does 12/78/.352 but lasts only one more season as a regular; used a 47-ounce bat, pounded spikes into pieces of wood with his fist
OF	Jigger Statz	1923	10/70/.319 with 209 hits but is back in the minors 3 years later; racks up 3,356 minor-league hits, playing 18 years for L.A. Angels
OF	George Maisel	1921	Rounds out '20s outfield with .310 and 17 steals; then .190 and done in '22
SP	Jocko Flynn	1886	24–6 in his only big-league season, with a 2.24 ERA and a 14-game winning streak for the '86 pennant-winners

continued

Rookies of the Year

*The Rookie of the Year Award has been given out since 1947, with a Cub winning it four times. Here are the Cubs who have won it (in **bold**), came close, or would have won if the award were given.*

Year	Rookie	Results
1998	**Kerry Wood**	233 strikeouts, 13–6
1994	Steve Trachsel	Finishes fourth behind Mondesi, Hudek, and Klesko
1989	**Jerome Walton**	Wins the award ahead of Dwight Smith . . .
1989	Dwight Smith	. . . only the sixth time that teammates finished 1-2
1988	Mark Grace	A close second to Chris Sabo
1983	Mel Hall	Finishes third behind Strawberry and Craig McMurtry
1979	Scot Thompson	Receives 1 of 24 votes; Rick Sutcliffe wins
1975	Manny Trillo	Receives 1 of 24 votes; John Montefusco wins
1974	Bill Madlock	Receives only 1 vote behind Bake McBride and Greg Gross
1966	Randy Hundley	Receives 1 of 20 votes; Tommy Helms wins
1962	**Ken Hubbs**	Wins the award in a near-unanimous vote
1961	**Billy Williams**	Wins the award ahead of Joe Torre
1960	Ron Santo	Receives 2 of 22 votes; Frank Howard wins
1957	Dick Drott	Receives 3 of 24 votes; Jack Sanford wins
1954	Ernie Banks	Receives only 4 of 24 votes; Wally Moon wins
1950	Bill Serena	Receives 1 of 23 votes; Sam Jethroe wins
1932	Billy Herman	206 hits, 102 runs, .314
1922	Hack Miller	12 home runs, 78 RBIS, .352
1921	Ray Grimes	6 home runs, 79 RBIS, .321
1918	Charlie Hollocher	League-high 161 hits, .316, solid shortstop for a pennant-winner
1912	Larry Cheney	26–10, 2.85
1910	King Cole	20–4, 1.80
1906	Jack Pfiester	20–8, 1.56
1905	Ed Reulbach	18–14, 1.42
1903	Jake Weimer	20–8, 2.30

He can become a 20-game winner.

Manager Lou Boudreau, on Don Cardwell

Flashes

Pos.	PLAYER	YEAR	RESULTS
SP	Dick Drott	1957	Rookie fans 15 Braves (Aaron 4) and 14 Giants (Mays 2) with knee-buckling curveball; goes 15–11, then blows out arm
SP	Don Cardwell	1960	Throws no-hitter in Cubs debut, then goes 7–14
SP	Bert Humphries	1913	16–4 with a 2.69 ERA; 8–13 and done in '15
SP	King Cole	1910	Shutout in first game, 20–4 as rookie, but wins only 56 in career; dies in 1916 at 29
SP	Hi Bithorn	1943	18–12 with league-leading 7 shutouts; wins 7 more games in majors, then killed by police officer on New Year's Day 1952 in Mexico
SP	Buttons Briggs	1898, 1904	12–8 as a rookie, then goes 5–20 in his next 2 seasons and disappears; resurfaces in 1904 to go 19–11 with a 2.05 ERA, traded before 1906 season and never pitches again; dies in 1911 at 35
SP-RP	Clay Bryant	1938	19 of 32 career wins in pennant-winning season as he leads league in both walks and strikeouts

Batting 1.000, Slugging 4.000

At least after one at bat. Five Cubs have hit home runs in their first at bat, with pitcher Jim Bullinger doing it on the first pitch. Except for Carmelo Martinez, it hasn't been an indicator of much to come. Give Dee Fondy an honorable mention for a bases-clearing triple in his first at bat on April 17, 1951.

Debut HR	Batter	Opponent	Career HRS
September 11, 1942	Paul Gillespie	at New York Giants	6
May 24, 1957	Frank Ernaga	Milwaukee Braves	2
September 1, 1961	Facundo Barragan	San Francisco Giants	1
August 22, 1983	Carmelo Martinez	Cincinnati Reds	108
June 8, 1992	Jim Bullinger	at St. Louis Cardinals	4

Career ERA 0.00

. . . at least after one game. Eight Cubs have thrown shutouts in their major-league debuts:

Debut Shutout	Pitcher	Opponent	Career W–L
April 25, 1876	Albert Spalding	at Louisville Grays	48–13
May 31, 1884	John Hibbard	Detroit Wolverines	1–1
May 18, 1888	George Borchers	Boston Beaneaters	4–5
September 20, 1888	Frank Dwyer	Washington Statesmen	176–152
September 17, 1898	Bill Phyle	at Washington Senators	10–19
September 4, 1902	Alex Hardy	at Brooklyn Superbas	4–3
October 2, 1909	King Cole	Pittsburgh Pirates	56–27
May 31, 1988	Jeff Pico	Cincinnati Reds	13–12

YOUTH VERSUS EXPERIENCE

Youth or experience? Youngsters before they were established big leaguers, or veterans past their prime?

The Cubs have seen a number of youngsters thrive in the infield, but very few outfielders established themselves as stars as early as age 21. There's plenty more to choose from among the pitchers—Willie "the Kid" McGill not even making the cut, despite winning 17 games at the age of 19 in 1893 (on his fifth professional team, having been a 16-year-old pitcher in the Players League in 1890).

How Old Is Anson?

How old is Anson? No one knows.

I saw him playing when a kid

When I was wearing still short clothes.

And so my father's father did.

The oldest veterans of them all

As kids, saw Anson play baseball.

Hyder Ali, Sporting News, *1897*

Youth

Pos.	PLAYER	SEASON(S)	AGE	BORN	HIGHLIGHTS
C	Gabby Hartnett	1922	21	12/20/00	Hits .194 in 31 games
1B	Phil Cavarretta	1934–37	18–21	7/19/16	Hits .275 for a pennant-winner
2B	Ken Hubbs	1961–63	19–21	12/23/41	Rookie of the Year, defensive standout
SS	Woody English	1927–28	20–21	3/2/07	Hits .290 and .299 for contending teams
3B	Ron Santo	1960–61	20–21	2/25/40	23/83/.284 in his first full season
OF	Billy Williams	1959	21	6/15/38	Hits .152 in a brief trial
OF	Abner Dalrymple	1879	21	9/9/57	Hits .291 as a starter
OF	Wildfire Schulte	1904	21	9/17/82	Hits .286 with 2 home runs in 20 games
UT	Joe Tinker	1902	21	7/27/80	Hits .273 as starter
UT	Johnny Evers	1902–03	20–21	7/21/81	Hits .293 in '03 as a starter
UT	Frank Chance	1898–99	20–21	9/9/77	Solid-hitting, injury-prone catcher
SP	Dick Ellsworth	1958, 1960–61	18, 20–21	3/22/40	17–25 with a shutout in '61; 4-hits Sox 1–0 in a crosstown exhibition game at 18
SP	Ken Holtzman	1965–67	19–21	11/3/45	20–16, 9–0 in '67, beats Koufax 2–1 in '66
SP	Larry Corcoran	1880–81	20–21	8/10/59	74–28 in 2 seasons
SP	Kerry Wood	1998	21	6/16/77	Fans 20 Astros at 20, 233 for the season

Babes in the Woods

The youngest player to ever suit up for Chicago was 16-year-old Milton Scott. He played first base on September 30, 1882, the day after the pennant was clinched, and went 2-for-5 in a 6–5 victory over Buffalo at Lakefront Park. It was his only game with the Cubs, and he retired four years later, washed-up at the age of 20.

The youngest modern players were 17-year-olds: catcher Harry Chiti, third-baseman Jim Woods, and outfielder Danny Murphy (who stayed with the Cubs for three seasons, disappeared for six, then reappeared with the White Sox as a pitcher). At 18 years and 21 days, Murphy is the third-youngest player in the 20th century to hit a home run.

There have been several teenagers to play for the Cubs, but none who were as productive as Phil Cavarretta. He was 18 years and two months when he made his debut in 1934, and he ended up winning a 1–0 game with a home run in his first big-league start. He took over at first base for Charlie Grimm in 1935, knocking in 82 runs for the pennant-winners and playing in his first World Series at the age of 19.

Cavarretta's 14 home runs as a teenager are behind only Tony Conigliaro (24), Mel Ott (19), and Junior Griffey (16) and one ahead of Mickey Mantle.

Experience

Pos.	PLAYER	SEASON(S)	AGE	BORN	HIGHLIGHTS
C	Gabby Hartnett	1939–40	38–39	12/20/00	13 home runs in 134 games
1B	Ernie Banks	1969–71	38–40	1/31/31	23/106/.253 in '69
1B	Cap Anson	1890–97	38–45	4/11/52	827 hits after turning 40 (.318)
2B	Davey Lopes	1984–86	39–41	5/3/45	11/44/.284 in 275 at bats in '85, first to steal 40 bases at the age of 40
SS	Larry Bowa	1984–85	38–39	12/6/45	Steady play for pennant-winners, then whines about moving aside for Dunston
3B	Ron Cey	1986	38	2/15/48	13/36/.273 in half season
OF	Hank Sauer	1955	38	3/17/17	12/28/.211; played elsewhere until 42
OF	Dode Paskert	1920	38	8/28/81	5/71/.279 with 16 steals
OF	Andre Dawson	1992	38	7/10/54	22/90/.277; leaves town with 399 home runs
UT	Billy Jurges	1946–47	38–39	5/9/08	Solid .976 fielding average in 1946
SP	Grover Alexander	1925–26	38–39	2/26/87	15–11 with 20 complete games in 1925
SP	Ferguson Jenkins	1982–83	38–39	12/13/43	Wins 20 more and throws 2 shutouts
SP	Charlie Root	1937–41	38–42	3/17/99	39 wins and 18 saves as a swingman
RP	Elmer Singleton	1958–59	40–41	6/26/18	3–1 with a 2.44 ERA after turning 40
RP	Dutch Leonard	1949–53	40–44	3/25/09	18–11 with 28 saves as a reliever

40 and 0

Although Dutch Leonard was primarily a relief pitcher for the Cubs—the team's first "closer"—the knuckleballer threw a complete-game, three-hit shutout on June 2, 1949, at the Polo Grounds at 40 years of age. He wasn't the team's oldest pitcher, however. Another knuckleballer, Hoyt Wilhelm, pitched in 1970 at the age of 46.

"Rage, Rage, Against the Dying of the Light"

The best "old" player the Cubs have ever had was Cap Anson. Nevertheless, Anson was pretty sensitive about criticism that he was too old to play. At the age of 39 on September 4, 1891, at the tail end of his first sub-.300 season in the majors, Anson played a game in Boston wearing fake white whiskers and a long white wig. Legend has it that he informed the umpires: "If the ball so much as ruffles these whiskers, I'm claiming that I was hit by a pitched ball and taking my base."

Anson is the oldest player to hit a grand slam, doing it on August 1, 1894, at the age of 42. He's not the oldest player to hit a home run (pitcher Jack Quinn hit one for the Phillies in 1930 at the age of 46), though he is the oldest to go deep twice. He hit two home runs on October 3, 1897, in St. Louis, at the age of 45. It was his last day in the majors. Unlike Ted Williams, Anson didn't take the rest of the season off. He played the second game of the doubleheader and went 0-for-2.

From the ages of 41 through 44, Anson hit at least .314 (and as high as .395) and knocked in at least 90 runs each season. No one else has ever hit .300 four times after the age of 40, while Anson's run production puts him in another league entirely. Unlike Pete Rose, Cap Anson was a player-manager who had the right to pencil his own name into the lineup at first base and batting third.

OLD VERSUS MODERN

Here are the best seasons by position that any Cub has ever had. This team has been split in half at World War II to spur the debate of who would win a battle between the modern players and the old-timers. The pre–World War II squad certainly has the numbers, but the new-timers have the better glove men (especially in the infield) as well as Bruce Sutter coming out of the pen.

The most debatable selection: modern righty. You can't go wrong with the '84 Sutcliffe, the '71 Jenkins, or the '92 Maddux. Sutcliffe gets the nod for pitching the Cubs to the pennant.

Each team also has some flukes. Heinie Zimmerman was a good player, but he played out of his mind in 1912 and never approached these numbers again. The same holds true for Dick Ellsworth and Rick Wilkins, who weren't as good as Zimmerman but each of whom also had his one big year in Chicago. If not for these moments, Stan Hack, Ken Holtzman, and Jody Davis would be suiting up for the big game.

Best Seasons, by Position

YEAR	PLAYER	Pos.	G	AB	R	H	2B	3B	HR	RBI	BB	SO	SB	BA	SA
1876–1945															
1930	Gabby Hartnett	C	141	508	84	172	31	3	37	122	55	62	0	.339	.630
1886	Cap Anson	1B	125	504	117	187	35	11	10	147	55	19		.371	.544
1929	Rogers Hornsby	2B	156	602	156	229	47	8	39	149	87	65	2	.380	.679
1896	Bill Dahlen	SS	125	474	137	167	30	19	9	74	64	36		.352	.553
1912	Heinie Zimmerman	3B	145	557	95	207	41	14	14	103	38	60	23	.372	.571
1929	Riggs Stephenson	LF	136	495	91	179	36	6	17	110	67	21	10	.362	.562
1930	Hack Wilson	CF	155	585	146	208	35	6	56	190	105	84	3	.356	.723
1930	Kiki Cuyler	RF	156	642	155	228	50	17	13	134	72	49	37	.355	.547

YEAR	PLAYER	Pos.	W	L	S	G	GS	CG	IP	H	BB	SO	ShO	ERA	Pct.
1908	Mordecai Brown	RHP	29	9	5	44	31	27	312	214	49	123	9	1.47	.763
1918	Hippo Vaughn	LHP	22	10	0	35	33	27	290	216	76	148	8	1.74	.688

YEAR	PLAYER	Pos.	G	AB	R	H	2B	3B	HR	RBI	BB	SO	SB	BA	SA
1946–98															
1993	Rick Wilkins	C	136	446	78	135	23	1	30	73	50	99	2	.303	.561
1995	Mark Grace	1B	143	552	97	180	51	3	16	92	65	46	6	.326	.516
1984	Ryne Sandberg	2B	156	636	114	200	36	19	19	84	52	101	32	.314	.520
1959	Ernie Banks	SS	155	589	97	179	25	6	45	143	64	72	2	.304	.596
1964	Ron Santo	3B	161	592	94	185	33	13	30	114	86	96	3	.313	.564
1970	Billy Williams	LF	161	636	137	205	34	4	42	129	72	65	7	.322	.586
1950	Andy Pafko	CF	146	514	95	156	24	8	36	92	69	32	4	.304	.591
1998	Sammy Sosa	RF	159	643	134	198	20	0	66	158	73	171	18	.308	.647

YEAR	PLAYER	Pos.	W	L	S	G	GS	CG	IP	H	BB	SO	ShO	ERA	Pct.
1984	Rick Sutcliffe	RHP	16	1	0	20	20	7	150	123	39	155	3	2.69	.941
1963	Dick Ellsworth	LHP	22	10	0	37	37	19	291	223	75	185	4	2.11	.688
1977	Bruce Sutter	CL	7	3	31	62	0	0	107	69	23	129	0	1.35	.700

GEOGRAPHY

The rules are simple: Divide the country into regions, and form the best nine-man team you can with players hailing from each state (or large city if you're running short of states). The same can be done for international players, since the Cubs have attracted talent from Scotland, Poland, and points in between. Put these rosters in a five-team league, and watch the Midwest/Great Plains get off to a fast start. Maybe the Northeast and their 19th-century stars or the South and their strong offense could surprise.

Players from the South

Pos.	PLAYER	HOME STATE
C	Randy Hundley	Virginia
1B	Mark Grace	North Carolina
2B	Norm McMillan	South Carolina
SS	Barry McCormick	Kentucky
3B	Bill Madlock	Tennessee
OF	Billy Williams	Alabama
OF	Jerome Walton	Georgia
OF	Andre Dawson	Florida
P	Claude Passeau	Mississippi
P	Bill Lee	Louisiana
Bench		
C	Jody Davis	Georgia
IF	Fred Pfeffer	Kentucky
IF	Jim Hickman	Tennessee
OF	Riggs Stephenson	Alabama
OF	Brian McRae	Florida
OF	Jerry Martin	South Carolina
P	Guy Bush	Mississippi
P	Clay Bryant	Virginia
P	Lee Smith	Louisiana
P	Ted Abernathy	North Carolina

Strengths: Murderers' Row of Madlock, Williams, Dawson, and Grace, with Stephenson on the bench. Solid one-two punch of Passeau and Lee backed up by Lee Smith.
Weaknesses: Up the middle, with the exception of catching.

Players from the Midwest/Great Plains

Pos.	PLAYER	HOME STATE
C	Johnny Kling	Missouri
1B	Cap Anson	Iowa
2B	Billy Herman	Indiana
SS	Ernie Banks	Texas
3B	Woody English	Ohio
OF	Andy Pafko	Wisconsin
OF	Kiki Cuyler	Michigan
OF	Moose Moryn	Minnesota
P	Grover Alexander	Nebraska
Bench		
C	Scott Servais	Wisconsin
IF	Charlie Grimm	Missouri
IF	Joe Tinker	Kansas
1B	Phil Cavarretta	Illinois
OF	Bobby Murcer	Oklahoma
P	Hippo Vaughn	Texas
P	Mordecai Brown	Indiana
P	Ed Reulbach	Michigan
P	Lon Warneke	Arkansas

Strengths: Great staff, strong lineup.
Weaknesses: A moose in left, how Anson deals with Banks.

Players from the Northeast

Pos.	PLAYER	HOME STATE
C	Gabby Hartnett	Rhode Island
1B	King Kelly	New York
2B	Bump Wills	District of Columbia
SS	Shawon Dunston	New York
3B	Barney Friberg	New Hampshire
OF	Hack Wilson	Pennsylvania
OF	Jimmy Ryan	Massachusetts
OF	Bill Nicholson	Maryland
P	Bill Hutchison	Connecticut
Bench		
C	Steve Swisher	West Virginia
IF	Johnny Evers	New York
OF	George Gore	Maine
UT	Davey Lopes	Rhode Island
P	Fred Goldsmith	Connecticut
P	Lefty Tyler	New Hampshire
P	John Clarkson	Massachusetts
P	Bill Hands	New Jersey
RP	Bruce Sutter	Pennsylvania

Strengths: Nineteenth-century stars Gore, Ryan, Hutchison, Goldsmith, Clarkson, and the ever-versatile King Kelly.
Weaknesses: Composition requirements put Evers on the bench and Wills in the starting lineup.

Players from the West

Pos.	PLAYER	HOME STATE
C	Frank Chance	California
1B	Ed Bouchee	Montana
2B	Ryne Sandberg	Washington
SS	Vance Law	Idaho
3B	Ron Santo	Seattle
OF	Ralph Kiner	New Mexico
OF	Dave Kingman	Oregon
OF	Lou Novikoff	Arizona
P	Dick Ellsworth	Wyoming
Bench		
C	Damon Berryhill	California
IF	Jiggs Parrott	Oregon
IF	Ron Cey	Washington
IF	Mick Kelleher	Seattle
OF	Hank Leiber	Arizona
P	Rich Gossage	Colorado
P	Larry Jackson	Idaho
P	Elmer Singleton	Utah

Strengths: Sandberg and Santo.
Weaknesses: Players out of position, thin pitching staff, worst-fielding outfield ever assembled.

International Team

Pos.	PLAYER	COUNTRY
C	Hector Villanueva	Puerto Rico
1B	Dirty Jack Doyle	Ireland
2B	Manny Trillo	Venezuela
SS	Jose Vizcaino	Dominican Republic
3B	Marty Krug	Germany
OF	Robin Jennings	Singapore
OF	Bobby Thomson	Scotland
OF	Jose Cardenal	Cuba
P	Ferguson Jenkins	Canada
P	Moe Drabowsky	Poland
Bench		
C	Jimmy Archer	Ireland
IF	Jose Hernandez	Puerto Rico
IF	Luis Salazar	Venezuela
OF	Rafael Palmeiro	Cuba
OF	Sammy Sosa	Dominican Republic
P	Steve Wilson	Canada
P	Craig Lefferts	Germany
P	Jim McCormick	Scotland

Strengths: Bench.
Weaknesses: Starting lineup.

Q. Who is the only Cub to lead his state in home runs?

A. Ron Santo, Washington (Texas produced Frank Robinson and Eddie Mathews in addition to Ernie Banks, while Alabama produced Hank Aaron and Willie McCovey in addition to Billy Williams)

THE ALL-DECADE TEAMS

Here are the best teams the Cubs can field from each decade of the 20th century, as well as the All-1800s team. Players with a superscript number by their name are included in the "Trivial Matters" sidebar toward the end of this chapter.

The Centuries' Worth

Pos.	PLAYER	Pos.	PLAYER
19th Century		**1900–09**	
MGR	Cap Anson	MGR	Frank Chance
C	King Kelly	C	Johnny Kling
1B	Cap Anson	1B	Frank Chance
2B	Fred Pfeffer	2B	Johnny Evers
SS	Bill Dahlen	SS	Joe Tinker
3B	Ned Williamson	3B	Harry Steinfeldt
CF*	Bill Lange	LF	Jimmy Sheckard
CF*	Jimmy Ryan	CF	Jimmy Slagle
CF*	George Gore	RF	Wildfire Schulte
UT	Tommy Burns	UT	Solly Hofman
SP (R)	Larry Corcoran	SP (R)	Mordecai Brown
SP (R)	John Clarkson	SP (R)	Ed Reulbach
SP (R)	Wild Bill Hutchison	SP (R)	Orval Overall
SP (R)	Clark Griffith	SP (R)	Jack Taylor
		SP (L)	Jack Pfiester
		SP-RP	Carl Lundgren
		CL	Mordecai Brown
1910–19		**1920–29**	
MGR	Frank Chance	MGR	Joe McCarthy
C	Jimmy Archer	C	Gabby Hartnett
1B	Vic Saier	1B	Charlie Grimm
2B	Johnny Evers	2B	Rogers Hornsby
SS	Joe Tinker	SS	Charlie Hollocher
3B	Heinie Zimmerman	3B	Sparky Adams
LF	Les Mann/Max Flack	LF	Riggs Stephenson
CF	Cy Williams/Tommy Leach	CF	Hack Wilson
RF	Wildfire Schulte	RF	Kiki Cuyler
SP (L)	Hippo Vaughn	PH	Jigger Statz
SP (R)	Larry Cheney[1]	PH	Ray Grimes
SP (R)	Claude Hendrix	SP (R)	Grover Cleveland Alexander
SP (R)	Mordecai Brown	SP (R)	Charlie Root
SP (R)	King Cole	SP (R)	Pat Malone
SP-RP	Jimmy Lavender	SP (R)	Sheriff Blake
CL	Mordecai Brown	SP (L)	Percy Jones[2]
		SP-RP	Tony Kaufman
		SP-RP	Vic Aldridge
		CL	Guy Bush

continued

*Center fielders all—better let Anson decide who moves.

Pos.	PLAYER	Pos.	PLAYER
1930–39		**1940–49**	
MGR	Charlie Grimm	MGR	Charlie Grimm
C	Gabby Hartnett	C	Clyde McCullough
1B	Charlie Grimm	1B	Phil Cavarretta
2B	Billy Herman	2B	Don Johnson[4]
SS	Billy Jurges[3]	SS	Lennie Merullo
3B	Stan Hack	3B	Stan Hack
LF	Frank Demaree	LF	Peanuts Lowrey
CF	Hack Wilson	CF	Andy Pafko
RF	Kiki Cuyler	RF	Bill Nicholson
PH	Riggs Stephenson	PH	Eddie Waitkus
PR	Augie Galan	SP (R)	Claude Passeau
UT	Woody English	SP (R)	Hank Wyse
SP (R)	Bill Lee	SP (L)	Johnny Schmitz
SP (R)	Lon Warneke	SP (R)	Hank Borowy
SP (R)	Guy Bush	SP (R)	Paul Derringer
SP (L)	Larry French	SP-RP	Hi Bithorn
SP (R)	Pat Malone	RP (L)	Bob Chipman
SP-RP	Tex Carleton	RP (R)	Paul Erickson
RP	Jack Russell	RP (R)	Emil Kush
CL	Charlie Root		

continued

Trivial Matters

1. Larry Cheney had his thumb and nose broken by a Zack Wheat line drive in 1911. This forced him to change his delivery, and he responded with a 26–10 season in 1912.

2. Percy Jones broke his back in 1931 while in the minors, when he fell from a third-story window. He spent the rest of his life in a wheelchair.

3. Billy Jurges attended Richmond Hill High School in Brooklyn, the alma mater of Phil Rizzuto.

4. Don Johnson's father joined the White Sox's starting lineup when Black Sox shortstop Swede Risberg was banned from baseball.

5. The Cubs' catching was so weak in the 1950s that Dale Long takes the starting assignment on this all-decade team for being baseball's first left-handed catcher in 50 years.

6. Palm-baller Paul Minner owned the St. Louis Cardinals. He was 21–8 against them and 48–76 against the rest of the league in his career. He was 5–0 against St. Louis in a 9–9 1955 season with the Cubs.

7. Glen Hobbie threw a 1–0 one-hitter against the Cardinals on April 22, 1959, the lone hit and base runner a two-out double in the seventh by Stan Musial. His first major-league home run beat Vinegar Bend Mizell and the Pirates, 2–1, on August 25, 1960. Hobbie's career was short-circuited by back and shoulder problems.

8. George Altman also played for the Negro League Kansas City Monarchs. He hit 10 home runs in June 1961.

9. Dick Ellsworth went to the same high school as Jim Maloney and Tom Seaver.

10. Cal Koonce was 9–1 at one point in his rookie season in 1962 but finished 10–10 and never reached double figures again.

Pos.	PLAYER	Pos.	PLAYER
1950–59		**1960–69**	
MGR	Bob Scheffing	MGR	Leo Durocher
C	Dale Long[5]	C	Randy Hundley
1B	Dee Fondy	1B	Ernie Banks
2B	Gene Baker	2B	Glenn Beckert
SS	Ernie Banks	SS	Don Kessinger
3B	Randy Jackson	3B	Ron Santo
LF	Hank Sauer	LF	Billy Williams
CF	Frankie Baumholtz	CF	Lou Brock
RF	Walt Moryn	RF	George Altman[8]
UT	Eddie Miksis	PH	Adolfo Phillips
SP (R)	Bob Rush	UT	Andre Rodgers
SP (L)	Paul Minner[6]	SP (R)	Ferguson Jenkins
SP (R)	Warren Hacker	SP (L)	Ken Holtzman
SP (R)	Dick Drott	SP (R)	Bill Hands
SP (R)	Sad Sam Jones	SP (L)	Dick Ellsworth[9]
SP-RP	Glen Hobbie[7]	SP (R)	Larry Jackson/
RP (R)	Turk Lown		Bob Buhl
RP (R)	Don Elston	SP-RP (R/L)	Cal Koonce[10]/
RP (R)	Dutch Leonard		Rich Nye
RP (L)	Bill Henry	RP	Ted Abernathy
		RP	Don Elston
		RP	Lindy McDaniel
		RP	Phil Regan
1970–79		**1980–89**	
MGR	Herman Franks	MGR	Jim Frey/Don Zimmer
C	Barry Foote	C	Jody Davis
1B	Jim Hickman	1B	Bill Buckner/Leon Durham
2B	Manny Trillo	2B	Ryne Sandberg
SS	Don Kessinger	SS	Shawon Dunston
3B	Ron Santo/Bill Madlock	3B	Ron Cey
LF	Billy Williams	LF	Gary Matthews
CF	Rick Monday	CF	Bob Dernier
RF	Jose Cardenal	RF	Andre Dawson
PH	Dave Kingman	UT	Keith Moreland
PR	Ivan DeJesus	SP (R)	Rick Sutcliffe
SP (R)	Rick Reuschel	SP (R)	Greg Maddux
SP (R)	Ferguson Jenkins	SP (L)	Steve Trout
SP (R)	Ray Burris	SP (R)	Scott Sanderson
SP (R)	Bill Bonham	SP (R)	Mike Bielecki
SP (R)	Milt Pappas	RP (R)	Dick Tidrow
RP (R)	Oscar Zamora	RP (R)	Les Lancaster
RP (R)	Jack Aker	CL (L)	Mitch Williams
RP (L)	Darold Knowles	CL (R)	Lee Smith
RP (L)	Willie Hernandez		
CL	Bruce Sutter		

continued

Pos.	PLAYER
1990–98	
MGR	Jim Riggleman
C	Rick Wilkins
1B	Mark Grace
2B	Ryne Sandberg
SS	Shawon Dunston
3B	Jose Hernandez
LF	Henry Rodriguez
CF	Brian McRae
RF	Sammy Sosa
PH	Andre Dawson
UT	Rey Sanchez
SP (R)	Greg Maddux
SP (R)	Steve Trachsel
SP (R)	Frank Castillo
SP (R)	Kevin Tapani
SP (R)	Kerry Wood
RP (R)	Terry Adams
RP (L)	Paul Assenmacher
CL (L)	Randy Myers
CL (R)	Rod Beck

the batter's box

It's a short walk from the dugout to the batter's box. This chapter documents the results of those walks—for career, season, month, game, and inning, with streaks, hidden achievements, and dubious distinctions thrown in along the way.

Do you know:

- Which Cubs squad batted .309, which team *slugged* only two points higher, and which of the two won the pennant?
- The who, what, and when of every Cub to lead the league in an offensive category or reach milestones such as 200 hits, 30 home runs, or a .333 batting average?
- The three Cubs who've driven in more than 21 percent of their team's runs?
- Baseball's first home-run king, before McGwire, Sosa, Maris, and Ruth?
- The Cub who stole a batting title on the last day of the season?
- The Cub who was intentionally walked *five* times in one game?
- The who and when of every Cub who has won Player of the Month?
- Every record Sammy Sosa shattered during June 1998, when he took up residence in "the zone" for an entire month?
- The biggest days at the plate? Every Cub who has hit for the cycle? Hit safely six times? Hit three home runs? Knocked in eight runs?
- The Cubs teammates who hit grand slams in the same inning? Who went back-to-back *twice* in the same game? Who hit four home runs in the same inning in a *losing* cause?
- The only Cub to hit two home runs in the same inning?
- The Cub who hit game-winning, extra-inning home runs in consecutive games?
- The *pitcher* who hit the team's first grand slam?
- The Cub who hit 246 home runs before finally going deep with the bases full?
- The Cub whose last home run came while he was *manager*—a ninth-inning, pinch-hit, game-winner?
- The four Cubs pinch hitters who combined to bat .411 in 1989?
- The only Cub to hit in 30 consecutive games?
- The only *player* to knock in a run in 17 consecutive games?
- The first pitchers taken deep by Cubs legends such as Cap Anson, Ernie Banks, and Ryne Sandberg, to name just three?
- The only Cub to fan six times in one game? To go 0-for-9 in a game? To leave 12 men on base in one game?

If not, you're about to.

TEAM RESULTS

Year-by-Year Highlights

Here are the offensive highlights, including runs scored per game (R/G), home runs, batting average, and slugging average for every Cubs team since 1876. League-leading totals are in **bold**.

YEAR	W	L	R/G	HR	BA	SA
1876	52	14	**9.5**	7	**.337**	**.416**
1877	26	33	6.2	0	.278	.340
1878	30	30	**6.2**	3	**.290**	**.350**
1879	46	33	**5.5**	3	.259	.336
1880	67	17	**6.4**	4	**.279**	**.360**
1881	56	28	**6.5**	12	**.295**	**.380**
1882	55	29	**7.2**	15	**.277**	**.389**
1883	59	39	**6.9**	13	.273	.393
1884	62	50	**7.4**	**142**	**.281**	**.446**
1885	87	25	**7.4**	**55**	.264	**.385**
1886	90	34	**7.3**	53	.279	**.401**
1887	71	50	6.7	**80**	.271	.412
1888	77	58	**5.4**	**77**	.260	**.383**
1889	67	65	6.6	**79**	.263	.377
1890	84	53	6.2	**68**	.260	.356
1891	82	53	6.2	**60**	.253	.359
1892	70	76	4.3	26	.235	.316
1893	56	71	6.5	32	.279	.379
1894	57	75	7.9	65	.314	.441
1895	72	58	6.7	55	.298	.405
1896	71	57	6.4	34	.286	.390
1897	59	73	6.3	38	.282	.386
1898	85	65	5.5	19	.274	.350
1899	75	73	5.5	27	.277	.359
1900	65	75	4.5	33	.260	.342
1901	53	86	4.2	18	.258	.326
1902	68	69	3.9	6	.251	.299
1903	82	56	5.0	9	.275	.347
1904	93	60	3.9	22	.248	.315
1905	92	61	4.4	12	.245	.314
1906	116	36	**4.6**	20	**.262**	**.339**
1907	107	45	3.8	13	.250	.311
1908	99	55	4.1	19	.249	.321
1909	104	49	4.2	20	.245	.322
1910	104	50	4.6	**34**	.268	.366
1911	92	62	**4.9**	54	.260	.374
1912	91	59	5.0	43	.277	.387
1913	88	65	**4.7**	59	.257	.369
1914	78	76	3.9	42	.243	.337
1915	73	80	3.7	53	.244	**.342**
1916	67	86	3.4	**46**	.239	.325
1917	74	80	3.6	17	.239	.313
1918	84	45	**4.2**	21	.265	.342

continued

Pitching, Defense, Bunts, and Steals

The 1907 Cubs won it all despite a batting order that featured no more than two homers, 70 RBIs, or .293 from any of its batters. They scored 3.8 runs per game, good for second best in the league—but the fewest of any pennant-winner in history.

YEAR	W	L	R/G	HR	BA	SA
1919	75	65	3.2	21	.256	.332
1920	75	79	4.0	34	.264	.354
1921	64	89	4.4	37	.292	.378
1922	80	74	5.0	42	.293	.390
1923	83	71	4.9	90	.288	.406
1924	81	72	4.6	66	.276	.378
1925	68	86	4.7	85	.275	.396
1926	82	72	4.4	66	.278	.390
1927	85	68	4.9	74	.284	.400
1928	91	63	4.6	92	.278	.402
1929	98	54	**6.5**	140	.303	.452
1930	90	64	6.5	**171**	.309	**.481**
1931	84	70	**5.4**	83	**.289**	**.422**
1932	90	64	4.7	69	.278	.392
1933	86	68	4.2	72	.271	.380
1934	86	65	4.7	101	.279	.402
1935	100	54	**5.5**	88	**.288**	.414
1936	87	67	4.9	76	.286	.392
1937	93	61	**5.3**	96	**.287**	**.416**
1938	89	63	4.7	65	.269	.377
1939	84	70	4.7	91	.266	.391
1940	75	79	4.4	86	.267	.384
1941	70	84	4.3	99	.253	.365
1942	68	86	3.8	75	.254	.353
1943	74	79	4.1	52	.261	.351
1944	75	79	4.6	71	.261	.360
1945	98	56	4.8	57	**.277**	.372
1946	82	71	4.1	56	.254	.346
1947	69	85	3.7	71	.259	.361
1948	64	90	3.9	87	.262	.369
1949	61	93	3.9	97	.256	.373
1950	64	89	4.2	161	.248	.401
1951	62	92	4.0	103	.250	.364
1952	77	77	4.1	107	.264	.383
1953	65	89	4.1	137	.260	.399
1954	64	90	4.5	159	.263	.412
1955	72	81	4.1	164	.247	.398
1956	60	94	3.9	142	.244	.382
1957	62	92	4.1	147	.244	.380
1958	72	82	4.6	**182**	.265	**.426**
1959	74	80	4.4	163	.249	.398
1960	60	94	4.1	119	.243	.369
1961	64	90	4.5	176	.255	.418
1962	59	103	3.9	126	.253	.377
1963	82	80	3.5	127	.238	.363
1964	76	86	4.0	145	.251	.390
1965	72	90	3.9	134	.238	.358
1966	59	103	4.0	140	.254	.380
1967	87	74	**4.4**	128	.251	.378
1968	84	78	3.8	**130**	.242	.366
1969	92	70	4.4	142	.253	.384

continued

Entertaining, If Not Victorious

The 1958 Cubs finished 20 games out of first, but they were only the third National League team to have five players with 20 or more home runs: Ernie Banks 47, Walt Moryn 26, Lee Walls 24, Bobby Thomson 21, and Dale Long 20. Even now, only eight other NL teams have done it.

YEAR	W	L	R/G	HR	BA	SA
1970	84	78	5.0	179	.259	.415
1971	83	79	3.9	128	.258	.378
1972	85	70	4.4	133	.257	.387
1973	77	84	3.8	117	.247	.357
1974	66	96	4.1	110	.251	.365
1975	75	87	4.4	95	.259	.368
1976	75	87	3.8	105	.251	.356
1977	81	81	4.3	111	.266	.387
1978	79	83	4.1	72	**.264**	.361
1979	80	82	4.4	135	.269	.403
1980	64	98	3.8	107	.251	.365
1981	38	65	3.6	57	.236	.340
1982	73	89	4.2	102	.260	.375
1983	71	91	4.3	140	.261	**.401**
1984	96	65	**4.7**	136	.260	.397
1985	77	84	4.3	**150**	.254	**.390**
1986	70	90	4.3	**155**	.256	.397
1987	76	85	4.5	**209**	.264	.432
1988	77	85	4.1	113	**.261**	.383
1989	93	69	**4.3**	124	**.261**	.387
1990	77	85	4.3	136	.263	.392
1991	77	83	4.3	159	.253	.390
1992	78	84	3.7	104	.254	.364
1993	84	78	4.6	161	.270	.414
1994	49	64	4.4	109	.259	.404
1995	73	71	4.8	158	.265	.430
1996	76	86	4.8	175	.251	.401
1997	68	94	4.2	127	.263	.396
1998	90	73	5.1	212	.264	.433

Best & Worst, Most & Least, Highest & Lowest

Best offense:	9.5 runs per game, 1876
Best offense, 20th century:	6.5 runs per game, 1929–30
Worst offense:	3.2 runs per game, 1919
Most power, 154 games:	182 home runs, 1958
Most power, 162 games:	212 home runs, 1998
Least power, 154 games:	6 home runs, 1902
Least power, 162 games:	72 home runs, 1978
Highest batting average:	.337, 1876
Highest batting average, 20th century:	.309, 1930
Lowest batting average:	.235, 1892
Lowest batting average, 20th century:	.236, 1981
Highest slugging average:	.481, 1930
Lowest slugging average:	.311, 1907

Power Outage

The Cubs of the strike-shortened 1981 season featured the team's worst offense since the deadball days, batting .236 and scoring only 3.6 runs per game. But even this squad managed to hit more home runs per game than the 1978 squad. Dave Kingman hit 28 long balls but missed 43 games due to various injuries. Without him in the lineup, Bobby Murcer swung the big stick with nine home runs. No one else had more than five, as the Cubs were outhomered 125 to 72. But they did well without the long ball, leading the National League in hitting (.264) and finishing only 11 games off the pace.

10,000

On August 14, 1995, Sammy Sosa hit home run #10,000 for the Cubs off Tom Candiotti in Dodger Stadium—which means that Cubs hitters had trotted 682 miles in 120 seasons.

CAREER RECORDS

With 123 seasons and nearly 18,000 games played, Cubs hitters have piled up a massive amount of statistics. Here are the team's all-time leaders in everything from games played to walks drawn.

Games

1.	Ernie Banks	2,528
2.	Cap Anson	2,276
3.	Billy Williams	2,213
4.	Ryne Sandberg	2,151
5.	Ron Santo	2,126
6.	Phil Cavarretta	1,953
7.	Stan Hack	1,938
8.	Gabby Hartnett	1,926
9.	Jimmy Ryan	1,660
10.	Don Kessinger	1,648

At Bats

1.	Ernie Banks	9,421
2.	Cap Anson	9,108
3.	Billy Williams	8,479
4.	Ryne Sandberg	8,379
5.	Ron Santo	7,768
6.	Stan Hack	7,278
7.	Jimmy Ryan	6,757
8.	Phil Cavarretta	6,592
9.	Don Kessinger	6,355
10.	Gabby Hartnett	6,282

Hits

1.	Cap Anson	3,000
2.	Ernie Banks	2,583
3.	Billy Williams	2,510
4.	Ryne Sandberg	2,385
5.	Stan Hack	2,193
6.	Ron Santo	2,171
7.	Jimmy Ryan	2,073
8.	Phil Cavarretta	1,927
9.	Mark Grace	1,875
10.	Gabby Hartnett	1,867

Singles

1.	Cap Anson	2,252
2.	Stan Hack	1,692
3.	Billy Williams	1,629
4.	Ryne Sandberg	1,624
5.	Ernie Banks	1,574
6.	Jimmy Ryan	1,470
7.	Ron Santo	1,415
8.	Phil Cavarretta	1,395
9.	Mark Grace	1,346
10.	Don Kessinger	1,336

Doubles

1.	Cap Anson	528
2.	Ernie Banks	407
3.	Ryne Sandberg	403
4.	Billy Williams	402
5.	Gabby Hartnett	391
6.	Mark Grace	371
7.	Stan Hack	363
8.	Jimmy Ryan	362
9.	Ron Santo	353
10.	Billy Herman	346

Triples

1.	Jimmy Ryan	142
2.	Cap Anson	124
3.	Wildfire Schulte	117
4.	Bill Dahlen	106
5.	Phil Cavarretta	99
6.	Joe Tinker	93
7.	Ernie Banks	90
8.	Billy Williams	87
9.	Stan Hack	81
10.	Ned Williamson	80

Home Runs

1.	Ernie Banks	512
2.	Billy Williams	392
3.	Ron Santo	337
4.	Ryne Sandberg	282
5.	Sammy Sosa	244
6.	Gabby Hartnett	231
7.	Bill Nicholson	205
8.	Hank Sauer	198
9.	Hack Wilson	190
10.	Andre Dawson	174

Runs Batted In

1.	Cap Anson	1,715
2.	Ernie Banks	1,636
3.	Billy Williams	1,353
4.	Ron Santo	1,290
5.	Gabby Hartnett	1,153
6.	Ryne Sandberg	1,061
7.	Jimmy Ryan	914
8.	Phil Cavarretta	896
9.	Bill Nicholson	833
10.	Mark Grace	831

Runs

1.	Cap Anson	1,719
2.	Jimmy Ryan	1,409
3.	Ryne Sandberg	1,316
4.	Billy Williams	1,306
5.	Ernie Banks	1,305
6.	Stan Hack	1,239
7.	Ron Santo	1,109
8.	Phil Cavarretta	968
9.	Bill Dahlen	896
10.	Mark Grace	875
	Billy Herman	875

Batting Average
(minimum 1,000 at bats)

1.	Rogers Hornsby	.350
2.	Bill Madlock	.336
3.	Riggs Stephenson	.336
4.	Ray Grimes	.335
5.	Bill Lange	.330
6.	Cap Anson	.329
7.	Kiki Cuyler	.325
8.	Bill Everitt	.323
9.	Hack Wilson	.322
10.	King Kelly	.316

Home Runs per 500 At Bats
(minimum 1,000 at bats)

1.	Dave Kingman	40
2.	Sammy Sosa	34
3.	Hank Sauer	31
4.	Hack Wilson	30
5.	Ernie Banks	27
	Andre Dawson	27
7.	Rogers Hornsby	26
8.	Jim Hickman	24
9.	Dale Long	23
	Billy Williams	23

Runs Batted In per 500 At Bats
(minimum 1,000 at bats)

1.	Hack Wilson	122
2.	Rogers Hornsby	118
3.	Dave Kingman	106
4.	Cap Anson	94
	Sammy Sosa	94
6.	Hank Sauer	93
7.	Gabby Hartnett	92
8.	Andre Dawson	90
	Bill Lange	90
10.	Ernie Banks	87

Slugging Average
(minimum 1,000 at bats)

1.	Rogers Hornsby	.604
2.	Hack Wilson	.590
3.	Dave Kingman	.569
4.	Sammy Sosa	.526
5.	Hank Sauer	.512
6.	Andre Dawson	.507
7.	Billy Williams	.503
8.	Ernie Banks	.500
9.	Ray Grimes	.492
10.	Gabby Hartnett	.490

The Best Hitter Who Never Played

If the Batting Average roster went all the way down to 600 at bats, Mike Vail's name would be in the 10th slot. He played 2½ seasons with the Cubs from 1978 to 1980 without ever winning a full-time job. He was considered an inferior outfielder to Dave Kingman, if that's possible, and was a very free swinger. But he connected often enough with the bat, hitting safely in a then-record 23 straight games as a Mets rookie. His Cub totals amount to a full season's work—one of the best "hidden" seasons a Cub has ever had.

	AB	H	HR	RBI	BA
Mike Vail	671	213	17	115	.317

Walks

1.	Stan Hack	1,092
2.	Ron Santo	1,071
3.	Cap Anson	952
4.	Billy Williams	911
5.	Phil Cavarretta	794
6.	Mark Grace	768
7.	Ernie Banks	763
8.	Ryne Sandberg	761
9.	Bill Nicholson	696
10.	Gabby Hartnett	691

Strikeouts

1.	Ron Santo	1,271
2.	Ryne Sandberg	1,259
3.	Ernie Banks	1,236
4.	Billy Williams	934
5.	Sammy Sosa	903
6.	Shawon Dunston	770
7.	Bill Nicholson	684
8.	Gabby Hartnett	683
9.	Jody Davis	647
10.	Don Kessinger	629

SEASON RECORDS

For the key offensive categories, here are the Cubs' single-season leaders, league leaders, and those who've done it more than once. On the lists of single-season leaders—for example, Cubs who've had 200 hits—the first and last to do it are in **bold.**

Hits

League Leaders

1876	Ross Barnes	138
1880	Abner Dalrymple	126
1881	Cap Anson	137
1888	Jimmy Ryan	182
1906	Harry Steinfeldt	176
1912	Heinie Zimmerman	207
1918	Charlie Hollocher	161
1935	Billy Herman	227
1940	Stan Hack	191
1941	Stan Hack	186
1944	Phil Cavarretta	197
1970	Billy Williams	205

Multiple League Leaders

Stan Hack   2

Multiple 200-Hit Seasons

Billy Herman	3
Billy Williams	3
Kiki Cuyler	2
Woody English	2

200-Hit Seasons

Rogers Hornsby	1929	229
Kiki Cuyler	1930	228
Billy Herman	1935	227
Woody English	1930	214
Frank Demaree	1936	212
Billy Herman	1936	211
Jigger Statz	1923	209
Hack Wilson	1930	208
Heinie Zimmerman	**1912**	**207**
Billy Herman	1932	206
Billy Williams	1970	205
Augie Galan	1935	203
Billy Williams	1965	203
Kiki Cuyler	1931	202
Woody English	1931	202
Charlie Hollocher	1922	201
Billy Williams	1964	201
Bill Buckner	1982	201
Ryne Sandberg	**1984**	**200**

200 Hits in Each League

Q. What Cub went on to become the fourth player to get 200 hits in each league, joining Nap Lajoie, George Sisler, and Al Oliver?

A. Bill Buckner

Doubles

League Leaders

1876	Ross Barnes	21
1876	Paul Hines	21
1877	Cap Anson	19
1881	King Kelly	27
1882	King Kelly	37
1883	Ned Williamson	49
1885	Cap Anson	35
1888	Jimmy Ryan	33
1912	Heinie Zimmerman	41
1927	Riggs Stephenson	46
1934	Kiki Cuyler	42
1935	Billy Herman	57
1981	Bill Buckner	35
1983	Bill Buckner	38
1995	Mark Grace	51

Multiple League Leaders

Cap Anson	2
Bill Buckner	2
King Kelly	2

40-Double Seasons

Billy Herman	1935	57
Billy Herman	1936	57
Mark Grace	**1995**	**51**
Kiki Cuyler	1930	50
Ned Williamson	**1883**	**49**
Riggs Stephenson	1932	49
Rogers Hornsby	1929	47
Riggs Stephenson	1927	46
Walt Wilmot	1894	45
Ray Grimes	1922	45
Charlie Grimm	1932	42
Billy Herman	1932	42
Kiki Cuyler	1934	42
Heinie Zimmerman	1912	41
Augie Galan	1935	41
Bill Buckner	1980	41
Rafael Palmeiro	1988	41

Multiple 40-Double Seasons

Billy Herman	3
Kiki Cuyler	2
Riggs Stephenson	2

Triples

League Leaders

1876	Ross Barnes	14
1906	Wildfire Schulte	13
1913	Vic Saier	21
1939	Billy Herman	18
1961	George Altman	12
1964	Ron Santo	13
1984	Ryne Sandberg	19

Multiple 15-Triple Seasons

Bill Dahlen	3
Bill Lange	2
Jimmy Ryan	2
Wildfire Schulte	2

15-Triple Seasons

Wildfire Schulte	1911	21
Vic Saier	1913	21
Bill Dahlen	1892	19
Bill Dahlen	1896	19
Ryne Sandberg	**1984**	**19**
Billy Herman	1939	18
Jimmy Ryan	1897	17
Heinie Zimmerman	1911	17
Kiki Cuyler	1930	17
Woody English	1930	17
Bill Lange	1895	16
Bill Lange	1896	16
Topsy Hartsel	1901	16
Solly Hofman	1910	16
Jimmy Ryan	**1891**	**15**
Bill Dahlen	1893	15
Wildfire Schulte	1910	15
Phil Cavarretta	1944	15

Home Runs

League Leaders

1884	Ned Williamson	27
1885	Abner Dalrymple	11
1888	Jimmy Ryan	16
1890	Walt Wilmot	14
1911	Wildfire Schulte	21
1912	Heinie Zimmerman	14
1916	Cy Williams	12
1926	Hack Wilson	21
1927	Hack Wilson	30
1928	Hack Wilson	31
1930	Hack Wilson	56
1943	Bill Nicholson	29
1944	Bill Nicholson	33
1952	Hank Sauer	37
1958	Ernie Banks	47
1960	Ernie Banks	41
1979	Dave Kingman	48
1987	Andre Dawson	49
1990	Ryne Sandberg	40

Multiple League Leaders

Hack Wilson	4
Ernie Banks	2
Bill Nicholson	2

30-Homer Seasons

Sammy Sosa	**1998**	**66**		Sammy Sosa	1997	36
Hack Wilson	1930	56		Billy Williams	1965	34
Andre Dawson	1987	49		Bill Nicholson	1944	33
Dave Kingman	1979	48		Billy Williams	1964	33
Ernie Banks	1958	47		Ron Santo	1965	33
Ernie Banks	1959	45		Sammy Sosa	1993	33
Ernie Banks	1955	44		Hank Sauer	1950	32
Ernie Banks	1957	43		Ernie Banks	1968	32
Billy Williams	1970	42		Jim Hickman	1970	32
Hank Sauer	1954	41		Rick Monday	1976	32
Ernie Banks	1960	41		Hack Wilson	1928	31
Ryne Sandberg	1990	40		Ron Santo	1967	31
Sammy Sosa	1996	40		Andre Dawson	1991	31
Rogers Hornsby	1929	39		Henry Rodriguez	1998	31
Hack Wilson	1929	39		**Hack Wilson**	**1927**	**30**
Gabby Hartnett	1930	37		Hank Sauer	1951	30
Hank Sauer	1952	37		Ron Santo	1964	30
Ernie Banks	1962	37		Ron Santo	1966	30
Billy Williams	1972	37		Billy Williams	1968	30
Andy Pafko	1950	36		Ryne Sandberg	1989	30
Sammy Sosa	1995	36		Rick Wilkins	1993	30

Multiple 30-Homer Seasons

Ernie Banks	7		Hank Sauer	4
Sammy Sosa	5		Hack Wilson	4
Billy Williams	5		Andre Dawson	2
Ron Santo	4		Ryne Sandberg	2

Chasing Ruth

Before Sosa chased Maris, Banks chased Ruth. In 1958, Ernie Banks had 41 home runs on August 23, matching Ruth's 1927 output by that date. Banks finished the season with 47, catching Gehrig if not the Babe.

Teammates

The National League record for most home runs by teammates (93) set by Hack Wilson and Gabby Hartnett in 1930 stood for 68 years. In 1998, Mark McGwire and Ray Lankford combined for 101, while Sammy Sosa and Henry Rodriguez set a new Cubs record with 97.

"Babe" Williamson?

In 1884, Ned Williamson led the league with 27 dingers. The year before, Williamson hit two home runs, and he followed up his 27 with three in 1885. Turns out that a grounds rule had been in effect for only one season. Balls hit over the remarkably short fences at Lakefront Park were considered doubles in every season except 1884. But there was no official asterisk for Ned, and his record ended up standing longer than Babe Ruth's 60 in 1927.

Runs Batted In

League Leaders

1876	Deacon White	66
1881	Cap Anson	82
1886	Cap Anson	147
1888	Cap Anson	84
1891	Cap Anson	120
1906	Harry Steinfeldt	83
1911	Wildfire Schulte	107
1912	Heinie Zimmerman	103
1929	Hack Wilson	159
1930	Hack Wilson	190
1943	Bill Nicholson	128
1944	Bill Nicholson	122
1952	Hank Sauer	121
1958	Ernie Banks	129
1959	Ernie Banks	143
1987	Andre Dawson	137
1998	Sammy Sosa	158

Multiple League Leaders

Cap Anson	4
Ernie Banks	2
Bill Nicholson	2
Hack Wilson	2

120-RBI Seasons

Hack Wilson	1930	190	Ernie Banks	1958	129
Hack Wilson	1929	159	Billy Williams	1970	129
Sammy Sosa	**1998**	**158**	Bill Nicholson	1943	128
Rogers Hornsby	1929	149	Ron Santo	1969	123
Cap Anson	**1886**	**147**	Gabby Hartnett	1930	122
Ernie Banks	1959	143	Bill Nicholson	1944	122
Andre Dawson	1987	137	Billy Williams	1972	122
Kiki Cuyler	1930	134	Hank Sauer	1952	121
Walt Wilmot	1894	130	Cap Anson	1891	120
Hack Wilson	1927	129	Hack Wilson	1928	120

Multiple 120-RBI Seasons

Hack Wilson	4
Cap Anson	2
Ernie Banks	2
Bill Nicholson	2
Billy Williams	2

Sammy's Unfinished Symphony

Lost in all the excitement of Sammy Sosa's run at Roger Maris's major-league record and his shattering of Hack Wilson's Cubs record for home runs in a season in 1998 is what could have been in 1996. On August 20, 1996, Sosa's wrist was fractured by a Mark Hutton pitch. The Cubs were only 3½ games out of first but limped home losers of 14 of 16. Sosa's best year to date was finished seven weeks early. Compare his August 20 totals from 1998 and where he finished, and project the same sprint to the finish for Sammy's unfinished 1996 symphony.

	AB	H	HR	RBI	R
8/20/98	492	152	48	121	97
End of Season (Actual)	643	198	66	158	134
8/20/96	498	136	40	100	84
End of Season (Projected)	651	177	55	131	116

Pitching to Hack

I'll tell ya, son, the veteran said,

When ya see that sawed-off squirt,

Jes' pump one towards th' platter,

'N' take care ya don't get hurt.

L. H. Addington, *Sporting News,*
September 4, 1930

Carrying the Load

Only five National Leaguers have driven in more than 21 percent of their team's runs, and three of them are Cubs: Bill Nicholson (1943), Ernie Banks (1959), and Bill Buckner (1981). The only other NL players to do it are Wally Berger in 1935 and Nate Colbert in 1972.

Runs

League Leaders

1876	Ross Barnes	126
1880	Abner Dalrymple	91
1881	George Gore	86
1882	George Gore	99
1884	King Kelly	120
1885	King Kelly	124
1886	King Kelly	155
1906	Frank Chance	103
1911	Jimmy Sheckard	121
1913	Tommy Leach	99
1929	Rogers Hornsby	156
1935	Augie Galan	133
1944	Bill Nicholson	116
1968	Glenn Beckert	98
1970	Billy Williams	137
1978	Ivan DeJesus	104
1984	Ryne Sandberg	114
1989	Ryne Sandberg	104
1990	Ryne Sandberg	116
1998	Sammy Sosa	134

Multiple League Leaders

King Kelly	3
Ryne Sandberg	3
George Gore	2

120-Run Seasons

Rogers Hornsby	1929	156
King Kelly	1886	155
Kiki Cuyler	1930	155
Woody English	1930	152
George Gore	1886	150
Bill Dahlen	1894	149
Hack Wilson	1930	146
Jimmy Ryan	1889	140
Bill Dahlen	1896	137
Billy Williams	1970	137
Hack Wilson	1929	135
Walt Wilmot	1894	134
Sammy Sosa	**1998**	**134**
Augie Galan	1935	133
Jimmy Ryan	1894	132
Woody English	1929	131
Bill Everitt	1896	130
Bill Everitt	1895	129
Ross Barnes	**1876**	**126**
King Kelly	1885	124
Jimmy Ryan	1898	122
Jimmy Sheckard	1911	121
King Kelly	1884	120
Bill Lange	1895	120

Multiple 120-Run Seasons

King Kelly	3
Jimmy Ryan	3
Bill Dahlen	2
Woody English	2
Bill Everitt	2
Hack Wilson	2

I never saw a guy win games the way he did that year. We never lost a game all year if he came up in the late innings with a chance to get a hit that would win it for us. . . . No tougher player ever lived than Hack Wilson.
Manager Joe McCarthy, on Hack Wilson in 1930

The Element of Surprise

Cap Anson's RBI totals were impressive, but there was one advantage he had that modern players didn't. Until the early 1880s, lineups didn't need to be announced, so Anson wouldn't come to bat for the first time until there were runners on base to be driven in.

Batting Average

League Leaders

1876	Ross Barnes	.429
1879	Cap Anson	.317
1880	George Gore	.360
1881	Cap Anson	.399
1886	King Kelly	.388
1888	Cap Anson	.344
1912	Heinie Zimmerman	.372
1945	Phil Cavarretta	.355
1972	Billy Williams	.333
1975	Bill Madlock	.354
1976	Bill Madlock	.339
1980	Bill Buckner	.324

Multiple League Leaders

Cap Anson	3
Bill Madlock	2

.333 Seasons (minimum 500 plate appearances)

Bill Lange	1895	.389	Hack Wilson	1929	.345
King Kelly	1886	.388	Cap Anson	1888	.344
Rogers Hornsby	1929	.380	Riggs Stephenson	1927	.344
Heinie Zimmerman	1912	.372	Glenn Beckert	1971	.342
Cap Anson	1886	.371	Johnny Evers	1912	.341
Riggs Stephenson	1929	.362	Billy Herman	1935	.341
Jimmy Ryan	1894	.361	Bill Lange	1897	.340
Kiki Cuyler	1929	.360	Charlie Hollocher	1922	.340
Bill Everitt	1895	.358	Gabby Hartnett	1930	.339
Bill Dahlen	1894	.357	**Bill Madlock**	**1976**	**.339**
Hack Wilson	1930	.356	Kiki Cuyler	1934	.338
Kiki Cuyler	1930	.355	**Cap Anson**	**1884**	**.335**
Phil Cavarretta	1945	.355	Cap Anson	1895	.335
Ray Grimes	1922	.354	Topsy Hartsel	1901	.335
Bill Madlock	1975	.354	Woody English	1930	.335
Bill Dahlen	1896	.352	Billy Herman	1937	.335
Hack Miller	1922	.352	Billy Herman	1936	.334
Frank Demaree	1936	.350	Billy Williams	1972	.333
Cap Anson	1887	.347			

Multiple .333 Seasons

Cap Anson	5
Kiki Cuyler	3
Billy Herman	3
Bill Dahlen	2
Bill Lange	2
Bill Madlock	2
Riggs Stephenson	2
Hack Wilson	2

Slugging Average

League Leaders

1876	Ross Barnes	.590
1880	George Gore	.463
1888	Jimmy Ryan	.515
1911	Wildfire Schulte	.534
1912	Heinie Zimmerman	.571
1929	Rogers Hornsby	.679
1930	Hack Wilson	.723
1958	Ernie Banks	.614
1972	Billy Williams	.606
1979	Dave Kingman	.613

1-2 Punch

In 1880, 1886, and 1888, the White Stockings didn't have just the league leader in batting but also the runner-up: Cap Anson and Jimmy Ryan in 1888; King Kelly and Cap Anson in 1886; and George Gore and Cap Anson in 1880, with Abner Dalrymple and Tommy Burns finishing fourth and fifth. They didn't have the runner-up in 1876, so they had to settle for 1-3-4-5: Ross Barnes, Cap Anson, John Peters, and Cal McVey. The Cubs haven't taken both win and place since.

"Big Hitter, the Lama. Long."

Perhaps that's how Bill Murray's Karl from Caddyshack *would describe Glenallen Hill. If you're looking for another major leaguer with production like Glenallen Hill's in 1993 (87 at bats, 10 home runs, .345, .770 slugging), try Babe Ruth's average month in 1927 (90 at bats, 10 home runs, .356, .772 slugging). Hill is one of only three Cubs to have more extra-base hits than singles in a season (minimum 30 hits).*

		H	2B	3B	HR	SA
Glenallen Hill	1993	30	7	0	10	.770
Cliff Heathcote	1930	39	10	1	9	.520
Ned Williamson	1883	111	49	5	2	.438

Don't Count Your Titles . . .

In 1976, Ken Griffey Sr. looked as if he had a batting title locked up, so he took the day off in Montreal to protect his lead. After all, Bill Madlock would have to go 3-for-4 to edge him out. When word got to Griffey that Madlock was 3-for-3, he pinch-hit and made an out, and Madlock won it going away with a 4-for-4 day.

.550 Seasons (minimum 500 plate appearances)

Hack Wilson	1930	.723	Ernie Banks	1957	.579
Rogers Hornsby	1929	.679	Bill Lange	1895	.575
Sammy Sosa	**1998**	**.647**	Ray Grimes	1922	.572
Gabby Hartnett	1930	.630	Heinie Zimmerman	1912	.571
Hack Wilson	1929	.618	Andre Dawson	1987	.568
Ernie Banks	1958	.614	**Bill Dahlen**	**1894**	**.566**
Dave Kingman	1979	.613	Ron Santo	1964	.564
Billy Williams	1972	.606	Sammy Sosa	1996	.564
Ernie Banks	1955	.596	Hank Sauer	1954	.563
Ernie Banks	1959	.596	Riggs Stephenson	1929	.562
Andy Pafko	1950	.591	George Altman	1961	.560
Hack Wilson	1928	.588	Ryne Sandberg	1990	.559
Billy Williams	1970	.586	Ernie Banks	1960	.554
Jim Hickman	1970	.582	Bill Dahlen	1896	.553
Hack Wilson	1927	.579	Billy Williams	1965	.552

Multiple .550 Seasons

Ernie Banks	5
Hack Wilson	4
Billy Williams	3
Bill Dahlen	2
Sammy Sosa	2

Walks

League Leaders

1876	Ross Barnes	20
1882	George Gore	29
1884	George Gore	61
1885	Ned Williamson	75
1886	George Gore	102
1890	Cap Anson	113
1911	Jimmy Sheckard	147
1912	Jimmy Sheckard	122
1926	Hack Wilson	69
1930	Hack Wilson	105
1964	Ron Santo	86
1966	Ron Santo	95
1967	Ron Santo	96
1968	Ron Santo	96
1984	Gary Matthews	103

Multiple League Leaders

Ron Santo	4
George Gore	3
Jimmy Sheckard	2
Hack Wilson	2

90-Walk Seasons

Jimmy Sheckard	1911	147
Jimmy Sheckard	1912	122
Richie Ashburn	1960	116
Cap Anson	1890	113
Johnny Evers	1910	108
Hack Wilson	1930	105
Gary Matthews	1984	103
George Gore	**1886**	**102**
Woody English	1930	100
Stan Hack	1941	99
Stan Hack	1945	99
Jimmy Slagle	1905	97
Ron Santo	1967	96
Ron Santo	1968	96
Ron Santo	1969	96
Ron Santo	1966	95
Vic Saier	1914	94
Stan Hack	1938	94
Stan Hack	1942	94
Bill Nicholson	1944	93
Jim Hickman	1970	93
Mark Grace	**1998**	**93**
Eddie Stanky	1943	92
Bill Nicholson	1945	92
Ron Santo	1970	92
Rick Monday	1973	92

Multiple 90-Walk Seasons

Ron Santo	5
Stan Hack	4
Bill Nicholson	2
Jimmy Sheckard	2

Strikeouts

League Leaders

1882	Silver Flint	50
1917	Cy Williams	78
1918	Dode Paskert	49
1923	George Grantham	92
1924	George Grantham	63
1925	Gabby Hartnett	77
1927	Hack Wilson	70
1928	Hack Wilson	94
1929	Hack Wilson	83
1930	Hack Wilson	84
1947	Bill Nicholson	83
1950	Roy Smalley	114
1962	Ken Hubbs	129
1966	Byron Browne	143
1979	Dave Kingman	131
1997	Sammy Sosa	174
1998	Sammy Sosa	171

Multiple League Leaders

Hack Wilson	4
George Grantham	2
Sammy Sosa	2

Intentional Walks

Ernie Banks and Andre Dawson were two of the most aggressive hitters the Cubs have ever sent to the plate. Neither can be found on the list of walk leaders or 90-walk seasons. The most walks Banks received in a season was 71 in 1960, and a then-record 27 came intentionally. Thirty years later, Reds manager Lou Piniella decided he didn't want anything to do with Andre Dawson. He intentionally walked him a record five times in a 16-inning game.

100-Strikeout Seasons

Sammy Sosa	1997	174		Dave Kingman	1978	111
Sammy Sosa	**1998**	**171**		Jody Davis	1986	110
Byron Browne	1966	143		Ron Santo	1965	109
Adolfo Phillips	1966	135		Ron Santo	1970	108
Sammy Sosa	1993	135		Ron Cey	1984	108
Sammy Sosa	1995	134		Shawon Dunston	1988	108
Sammy Sosa	1996	134		Jerry Martin	1980	107
Dave Kingman	1979	131		Dee Fondy	1953	106
Ken Hubbs	1962	129		Ron Santo	1968	106
Billy Cowan	1964	128		Ron Cey	1985	106
Rick Monday	1976	125		Ron Santo	1967	103
Rick Monday	1973	124		Andre Dawson	1987	103
Lou Brock	1963	122		Rick Monday	1972	102
Ryne Sandberg	1996	116		Ernie Banks	1969	101
Roy Smalley	**1950**	**114**		Mel Hall	1983	101
Shawon Dunston	1986	114		Ryne Sandberg	1984	101
Randy Hundley	1966	113				

Multiple 100-Strikeout Seasons

Sammy Sosa	5
Ron Santo	4
Rick Monday	3
Ron Cey	2
Shawon Dunston	2
Dave Kingman	2
Ryne Sandberg	2

Whiffs Without Dingers

Q. What three players on the list of 100-strikeout seasons failed to hit at least 10 home runs?

A. Lou Brock, Ken Hubbs, and Shawon Dunston (1988)

BIGGEST MONTHS

Sammy's June

From now on, every big month for a Cub will be measured against what Sammy Sosa did in June 1998. He went 34-for-114 (.298), hit 20 home runs, knocked in 40, scored 25, and slugged an awesome .860. He had 12 multihit games and knocked in runs in 17 of 27 games.

Sammy smashed the Cubs' mark for home runs in June (14 by Ryne Sandberg in 1990), as well as the major-league mark (15, held by Pedro Guererro, Babe Ruth, Roger Maris, and Bob Johnson). He broke the Cubs' mark for home runs in a month (15 by Andre Dawson in August 1987), the National League mark (17 by Willie Mays in August 1965), and the major-league mark (18 by Rudy York in August 1937).

Sosa also set a new standard for home runs in a 30-day period (21 from May 25 to June 23), besting the previous mark of 20 set by Ralph Kiner in 1947 and Roger Maris in 1961. He set a Cubs record for RBIs in June with 40, previously held by Hack Wilson (29 in 1930). Wilson still holds the club record for RBIs in a month, with 53 in August 1930.

Sammy's month was made up of some pretty potent weeks. He tied a National League mark with eight home runs in a calendar week (June 14 to June 20) held by Ralph Kiner (1947), Ted Kluszewski (1956), and Nate Colbert (1972).

Finally, Sammy Sosa tied club records by homering in five straight games (June 3 through June 8), also done by Hack Wilson in 1928 and Ryne Sandberg in 1989. He hit five home runs over three games (June 19 through June 21), homering each game, which had been done by only Bill Nicholson in 1944 and Andre Dawson twice in 1987.

Finally, he set new standards for records no one even considered keeping by hitting 10 home runs in nine games. No Cub had ever been able to hit 10 homers in fewer than 13 games (Hack Wilson in 1928 and Sammy in August 1995). For good measure, Sammy did 10 home runs in nine games *twice* (May 25 through June 7 and June 13 through June 21).

Players of the Month

George Altman	June 1961	Leon Durham	May 1984
Billy Williams	May 1964	Ryne Sandberg	June 1984
Ron Santo	July 1964	Keith Moreland	August 1984
Ron Santo	June 1969	Andre Dawson	August 1987
Billy Williams	July 1972	Mark Grace	July 1989
Andre Thornton	September 1975	Andre Dawson	May 1990
Dave Kingman	April 1980	Sammy Sosa	July 1996
Bill Buckner	August 1982	Sammy Sosa	June 1998
Mel Hall	August 1983		

BIGGEST GAMES

As a team, the Cubs have had so many wild games (39 20-run games, a major-league record) that there is an entire chapter dedicated to them ("The Scoreboard," Chapter 11). Here are some impressive individual performances.

Six-Hit Games

DATE	PLAYER	H-AB	SCORE	LOCATION
July 22, 1876	Cal McVey	6-for-7	Chicago 30 Louisville 7	23rd Street Grounds
July 25, 1876	Cal McVey	6-for-7	Chicago 23 Cincinnati 3	23rd Street Grounds
July 27, 1876	Ross Barnes	6-for-6	Chicago 17 Cincinnati 3	23rd Street Grounds
May 7, 1880	George Gore	6-for-6	Chicago 20 Providence 7	Lakefront Park
June 29, 1897	Barry McCormick	6-for-8	Chicago 36 Louisville 7	West Side Grounds
July 5, 1937	Frank Demaree	6-for-8	Chicago 13 St. Louis 12 (14)	Wrigley Field
July 17, 1971	Don Kessinger	6-for-6	Chicago 7 St. Louis 6 (10)	Wrigley Field
July 26, 1975	Bill Madlock	6-for-6	Mets 9 Chicago 8 (10)	Wrigley Field
May 2, 1976	Jose Cardenal	6-for-7	Chicago 6 San Francisco 5 (14)	Candlestick Park
July 2, 1993	Sammy Sosa	6-for-6	Chicago 11 Colorado 8	Mile High Stadium

Home Runs

To many fans, Ron Santo and Billy Williams seem joined at the hip. They played together for 14 seasons, appearing in more games together than any other teammates (2,015) and hitting 711 of their 727 Cubs home runs while on the same team. They went deep in the same game 64 times, which places them fifth on the list of one-two punches behind Aaron and Mathews (75), Gehrig and Ruth (73), Mays and McCovey (68), and Hodges and Snider (67).

For the best years of his career, Ernie Banks had to be his own one-two punch. He had 42 multiple-homer games, the most of any Cub and good enough for 13th on the all-time list behind Ruth, Mays, Aaron, Foxx, Frank Robinson, Mathews, Ott, Killebrew, Mantle, McCovey, Schmidt, and Kingman. Banks is tied with Lou Gehrig and Reggie Jackson.

Multiple-Homer Games

Ernie Banks	42	Hack Wilson	24
Sammy Sosa	32	Andre Dawson	18
Billy Williams	29	Hank Sauer	18
Ryne Sandberg	25	Gabby Hartnett	14
Ron Santo	25	Bill Nicholson	13

The Cubs' record for multiple-homer games in the same season was 8, originally set by Hack Wilson in 1930 and tied by Andre Dawson in 1987, until Sammy Sosa obliterated the mark with 11 in 1998.

Only two Cubs have hit home runs from both sides of the plate in the same game. Augie Galan was the first National Leaguer to do it, on June 25, 1937, in an 11–2 win over the Dodgers at Wrigley. Ellis Burton is the only Cub to do it twice. He helped key a comeback from a six-run deficit to beat the Giants 12–11 in 10 innings at Wrigley on August 1, 1963. On September 7, 1964, he did it again, though the Cubs lost to the Braves, 10–9, at Wrigley.

Dave Kingman is the only Cub to go deep three times twice in the same season: May 17 and July 28, 1979. His July blasts (in a 6–4 loss to the Mets) came on the heels of a two-homer game, tying the major-league mark of five in two consecutive games also held by Cap Anson (August 5 and 6, 1884) and Billy Williams (September 8 and 10, 1968).

Kingman isn't the only Cub to hit three homers in a losing cause. Clyde McCullough, in a totally unexpected power outburst in 1942, accounted for the Cubs' only runs in a 4–3 loss to the Phillies in Philadelphia. Andy Pafko's big day in 1950 came in an 8–6 loss to the Giants at the Polo Grounds. Finally, there is Ernie Banks. Unfortunately, on some of his finest days, the Cubs still came up short. When he went deep three times in 1962—to go along with home runs by Billy Williams, George Altman, and Bob Will—the Braves still beat the Cubs, 11–9 in 10 at Wrigley. And in 1963, when he homered three times—twice off Sandy Koufax—the Dodgers still won, 11–8 at Wrigley.

On a happier note, there are the three-homer performances of Lee "Captain Midnight" Walls and Walt "Moose" Moryn in 1958. Walls's came in a 15–2 rout of the Dodgers at the Los Angeles Coliseum, giving Gene Fodge his first and last win as a pro. Moryn's came in the second game of a doubleheader sweep over the Dodgers in Wrigley—the first time his mother saw him play.

Finally, though no Cub has ever hit four home runs in a game, Billy Williams did hit four consecutive doubles on April 9, 1969—something only 17 players have done—in an 11–3 win over the Phillies at Wrigley. But it was George Gore who was the first major leaguer to get *five* extra-base hits in one game—a feat matched only five times since (by Larry Twitchell, Lou Boudreau, Joe Adcock, Willie Stargell, and Steve Garvey). Gore did it on July 9, 1885, against Providence. By hitting two triples and three doubles, he remains the only player of the six to get five extra-base hits in a game without hitting a home run.

Three-Homer Games

May 30, 1884	Ned Williamson	May 30, 1958	Walt Moryn
August 6, 1884	Cap Anson	May 29, 1962	Ernie Banks
July 26, 1930	Hack Wilson	June 9, 1963	Ernie Banks
April 24, 1931	Rogers Hornsby	June 11, 1967	Adolfo Phillips
July 20, 1933	Babe Herman	September 10, 1968	Billy Williams
July 4, 1939	Hank Leiber	May 16, 1972	Rick Monday
July 26, 1942	Clyde McCullough	April 17, 1974	George Mitterwald
July 23, 1944	Bill Nicholson	May 14, 1978	Dave Kingman
August 2, 1950	Andy Pafko	May 17, 1979	Dave Kingman
August 28, 1950	Hank Sauer	July 28, 1979	Dave Kingman
June 11, 1952	Hank Sauer	August 1, 1987	Andre Dawson
August 4, 1955	Ernie Banks	April 4, 1994	Tuffy Rhodes
September 14, 1957	Ernie Banks	June 5, 1996	Sammy Sosa
April 24, 1958	Lee Walls	June 15, 1998	Sammy Sosa

> *I'd rather hit home runs. You don't have to run as hard.*
>
> *Dave Kingman*

Let's Play Two

Bill Nicholson's four-home-run outburst in 1944 may be the best doubleheader performance in Cubs history, but he has plenty of competition for the honor. The nominees:

Best Doubleheader Performance

DATE	PLAYER	OPPONENT	HIGHLIGHTS
July 23, 1944	Bill Nicholson	at New York	4 home runs and a bases-loaded intentional walk
June 11, 1967	Adolfo Phillips	Mets	4 home runs, 6-for-9, 2 great catches, 6 standing ovations, and countless shouts of *"Olé!"*
July 6, 1970	Ron Santo	Expos	3 home runs (grand slam) and 10 RBIs
July 11, 1972	Billy Williams	Astros	2 home runs, 8-for-8

Cycles

Hitting a home run, triple, double, and single in the same game is even rarer than hitting three home runs in a game. Thirteen Cubs have done it, and only the underrated 19th-century star Jimmy Ryan did it twice. As for the unlikeliest, the nominees are: Ivan DeJesus (lifetime .254 with 21 home runs) and Randy Hundley (lifetime .236 with 13 triples). The Cardinals have been victimized four times, while the Braves and Pirates have managed to avoid it completely.

Hitting for the Cycle

DATE	CYCLIST	OPPONENT	. . . AND WHATNOT
July 28, 1888	Jimmy Ryan	Detroit	Cubs win 21–17
July 1, 1891	Jimmy Ryan	Cleveland	
September 16, 1894	George Decker	Brooklyn	2 home runs
June 13, 1904	Frank Chance	New York	Facing Christy Mathewson
July 20, 1911	Wildfire Schulte	Philadelphia	
June 23, 1930	Hack Wilson	Philadelphia	
September 30, 1933	Babe Herman	St. Louis	Facing Dizzy Dean
June 28, 1950	Roy Smalley	St. Louis	
July 2, 1957	Lee Walls	Cincinnati	Cubs lose 8–6 on a 10th-inning grand slam by Wally Post
July 17, 1966	Billy Williams	St. Louis	
August 11, 1966	Randy Hundley	Houston	Cubs win 9–8 in 11
April 22, 1980	Ivan DeJesus	St. Louis	
April 29, 1987	Andre Dawson	San Francisco	
May 9, 1993	Mark Grace	San Diego	

Runs Batted In

Heinie Zimmerman just missed a cycle on June 11, 1911, when he bashed two homers, a triple, and two singles in a 20–2 trashing of the Braves at West Side Grounds in Chicago. In the process, he set a Cubs record with nine RBIs in one game. Not a bad week's work.

Here are the Cubs who've knocked in eight or more runs in a game:

One-Man Wrecking Crews

DATE	PLAYER	SCORE	THE GORY DETAILS
June 11, 1911	Heinie Zimmerman	Boston 2 Cubs 20	2 three-run homers, 1 two-run triple, 1 single, 9 RBIs
April 24, 1931	Rogers Hornsby	Cubs 10 Pittsburgh 6	2 three-run homers, 1 two-run homer, 8 RBIs
July 20, 1933	Babe Herman	Philadelphia 1 Cubs 10	2 two-run homers, 1 grand slam, 8 RBIs
April 24, 1958	Lee Walls	Cubs 15 Los Angeles 1	2 three-run homers, 1 two-run homer, 8 RBIs
July 22, 1965	Ed Bailey	Philadelphia 6 Cubs 10	1 grand slam, 1 three-run homer, 1 single, 8 RBIs
July 6, 1970	Ron Santo	Expos 2 Cubs 14	1 grand slam, 1 three-run homer, 1 bases-loaded walk, 8 RBIs
April 17, 1974	George Mitterwald	Pirates 9 Cubs 18	1 grand slam, 1 two-run homer, 1 solo homer, 1 double, 8 RBIs
May 14, 1978	Dave Kingman	Cubs 10 Los Angeles 7 (15)	2 two-run homers, 1 three-run homer, force play, 8 RBIs
April 22, 1980	Barry Foote	Cubs 16 Cardinals 12	1 grand slam, 1 solo homer, 1 two-run double, 1 single, 8 RBIs

Note: Home team is listed second.

BIGGEST INNINGS

Chicago has had some big innings in 123 seasons, but none was bigger than the abuse heaped on the Detroit Wolverines at Lakefront Park on September 6, 1883. The White Stockings broke open a close game with a major-league-record 18 runs in the bottom of the seventh inning. Twenty-three batters came to the plate, 18 got hits, 8 for extra bases, scoring 13 runs before an out was made—all major-league records. Ned Williamson, Tommy Burns, and Fred Pfeffer each went 3-for-3, with Williamson and Burns scoring three times apiece—also major-league records.

Some of the team's most exciting moments have come in extra innings, with the bases full, or with pinch hitters at the plate.

Home Runs

The only thing better than a Cubs home run is another Cubs home run. Here are some big-home-run innings through the years.

August 16, 1890

The Cubs hit not one but two grand slams in a 13-run fifth inning against the Pittsburgh Pirates. Tommy Burns and Malachi Kittridge both clear the bases, the first time it happens in the same inning.

May 12, 1930

After falling behind to the Giants by two touchdowns at Wrigley, the Cubs mount a furious comeback that peaks in the seventh inning when Cliff Heathcote, Hack Wilson, Charlie Grimm, and Clyde Beck all go deep. Unfortunately, the Giants hold on for a 14–12 win.

August 11, 1941

The Cubs go back-to-back-to-back for the first time as they beat the Cardinals 7–5 in St. Louis, with Phil Cavarretta, Stan Hack, and Bill Nicholson all homering in the fifth inning.

April 16, 1955

Randy Jackson, Ernie Banks, and Dee Fondy go back-to-back-to-back in the second at St. Louis. Later, Banks and Fondy go back-to-back *again,* but the Cardinals win in 11 innings, 12–11. In 1955, the Cubs hit three home runs in an inning five times.

May 1, 1964

Billy Williams gets the Cubs off to a good start with a grand slam, a single, and five RBIs in a 10-run first inning in the Astrodome.

May 17, 1977

Not exactly Murderers' Row, but Larry Biittner, Bobby Murcer, and Jerry Morales go back-to-back-to-back in the fifth inning of a 23–6 brutalization of the San Diego Padres at Wrigley. Biittner, Steve Ontiveros, and Gene Clines have already homered in the third inning.

May 16, 1996

Sammy Sosa goes back-to-back with himself on May 16, 1996. In the seventh inning against the Houston Astros, Sammy leads off with a home run off Jeff Tabaka, then follows up with a two-run homer off Jim Dougherty. He is the only Cub to homer twice in the same inning.

Extra Innings

The Cubs' record for extra-inning home runs in a career is nine, shared by Ernie Banks and Billy Williams. Banks and Ron Santo hold the Cubs' record for extra-inning home runs in a season with three, Banks in 1955 and Santo in 1966. (Willie Mays shares the National League season record with 4 and owns the major-league record with 22.)

August 22, 1942

The Cubs beat the Reds 5–4 on a Bill Nicholson home run in the bottom of the 11th—after getting out of trouble in the top of the inning with a triple play.

June 8, 1965

The Milwaukee Braves hit a major-league-record four extra-inning home runs in Chicago. After being held hitless since the second inning, the Braves erupt in the 10th as Joe Torre, Felipe Alou, Hank Aaron, and Gene Oliver all go deep, scoring six runs off Lindy McDaniel and Bob Hendley.

May 28–29, 1966

Two of Santo's late blasts in 1966 come in consecutive games. On May 28, his three-run homer in the bottom of the 12th beats the Braves 8–5 in Wrigley. He does it again the next day, homering in the 10th to win the game 3–2.

August 11, 1968

Four Cubs have hit home runs in the 15th inning, including Vic Saier in 1915, Gene Baker in 1956, and Dave Kingman in 1978 (his third of the game). One of the most exciting extra-inning home runs in team history comes in the 15th inning at Crosley Field on August 11, 1968—a three-run, inside-the-park job by Billy Williams to defeat the Reds 8–5.

September 3, 1986

The "latest" home run hit by a Cub is Keith Moreland's 17th-inning bomb on September 3, 1986—the game began on September 2. It comes off Julio Solano and caps a three-run rally that ties the game back up at 7–7. Unfortunately, Billy Hatcher hits one even later than Moreland—in the top of the 18th inning off of a rookie call-up named Greg Maddux, who is making his major-league debut. The teams end up combining to use a major-league-record 53 players, including a National League–record 17 pitchers.

May 21, 1995

Sammy Sosa hits a home run in the top of the 13th inning in Dodger Stadium to beat Los Angeles 2–1 for the 9,000th win in club history.

Grand Slams

June 20, 1882

The first Cub to hit a grand slam is actually a pitcher, Larry Corcoran, who does it in Lakefront Park against the Worcester Ruby Legs. It comes in the ninth inning—back then, the home team has the option of batting first or second—and puts the finishing touches on a 13–3 victory. The first Cubs position player to hit a grand slam is Fred Pfeffer, two years and one day later.

May 18, 1950

Both teams hit grand slams in the same inning for the first time. Al Walker of the Cubs hits one in the top of the sixth at the Polo Grounds, and Monte Irvin of the Giants responds in the bottom of the frame. Rain then washes out the rest of the game, and the Giants win 10–4.

Nine in '29

The 1929 Cubs set a record with nine grand slams, a National League mark that they still share. Perhaps the 1955 Cubs should have broken it. That year, Ernie Banks set the major-league record for grand slams in a season with five in 1955, breaking the mark of four set by Wildfire Schulte for the Cubs in 1911. Banks's record lasted 32 years until Don Mattingly—who'd failed to deliver a grand slam in his first four seasons—hit six in 1987. He never hit another. The same held true for Schulte, both before and after 1911.

September 25, 1968

It isn't his first, it isn't a record-setter, and it's the only one of the game, but a grand slam during the Cubs' late-season push for third place is memorable nonetheless. The Dodgers' Bill Singer takes a 1–0 gem into the bottom of the ninth, only to load the bases and have Ron Santo ruin his day with a home run.

June 3, 1987

The Cubs combine with the Astros to set a National League mark for grand slams in a game with three, duplicating a feat accomplished only once in the American League. The Cubs hit two of them—Brian Dayett and Keith Moreland clearing the bases—as they maul Houston 22–7 at Wrigley.

July 27–28, 1998

Sammy Sosa is the active nonslam champion going into 1998, with 207 home runs but none with the bases full. He breaks Bob Horner's mark of 209 on April 15. After 246 career home runs, he finally hits his first grand slam against the Arizona Diamondbacks on July 27. Then he does it again the next night. A man who knows a little bit about streaks, Cal Ripken, has the record for consecutive home runs *between* grand slams: 266.

Cub Grand-Slam Leaders

Ernie Banks	12
Bill Nicholson	8
Billy Williams	8
Jody Davis	5
Gabby Hartnett	5
Andy Pafko	5
Ryne Sandberg	5
Ron Santo	5

Pinch Hitters

Pinch hitting is a difficult, if not impossible, art to master. The Cubs who have come the closest to doing just that are Dwight Smith and Thad Bosley. Smith has more pinch hits, 50, than any other Cub, while Thad Bosley is the only Cub with at least 35 pinch hits and a .300 average.

Neither Smith nor Bosley, however, can be found at the top of the list of pinch-hitting seasons. Though Bosley has the club record with 20 pinch hits in 1985, later tied by Dave Clark in 1997, Merritt Ranew holds the record for highest batting average: an amazing .415 in 1962, going 17-for-41, which tied Jim Bolger's then-record for Cubs pinch hits in a season,

Most Career Pinch Hits

PLAYER	AB	BA	H
Dwight Smith	167	.299	50
Larry Biittner	174	.264	46
Thad Bosley	152	.303	46
Phil Cavarretta	191	.241	46
Bob Will	199	.231	46
Dom Dallesandro	166	.271	45
Scot Thompson	143	.273	39

Q. Who is the only Cub to hit grand slams in three different decades?

A. Phil Cavarretta, 1936, 1945, and 1951

Multiple Pinch-Hit Home Runs

On August 13 and 14, 1959, Dale Long hit pinch-hit home runs in consecutive at bats. Fifteen years later, Carmen Fanzone—trumpet player in Johnny Carson's band and utility man extraordinaire—did it 41 days apart (July 31 and September 10). Darrin Jackson is the only other Cub to do it (August 14 and 16, 1988). Long had also hit pinch homers six days apart in 1958, two of seven the Cubs hit that year, including three by Chuck Tanner. Willie Smith tied that mark in 1969, including a heart-stopping, extra-inning game-winner on Opening Day 1969. Later Thad Bosley (1985), Kevin Roberson (1994), and Dave Clark (1997) joined the club—Clark's three homers and 20 hits helping him set a pinch-hit RBI record with 22.

set in 1957. Ranew's average surpassed Frankie Baumholtz's .405 performance in 1955 (15-for-37) and Babe Twombly's .395 in 1921 (15-for-38), his last in the majors. Chico Walker hit .406 (13-for-32) in 1991, but Ranew's mark still stands.

Perhaps the best collection of pinch hitters the Cubs have ever had was in 1989: Curtis Wilkerson (11-for-28), Dwight Smith (8-for-15), Lloyd McClendon (5-for-16), and Domingo Ramos (6-for-14). They weren't the team's only pinch hitters, but they were the most productive. As a group, they hit .411!

For one day, though, the 1927 Cubs couldn't be topped. On May 21, 1927, Cubs pinch hitters celebrated Charles Lindbergh's safe arrival in Paris by setting a major-league record with four hits in the ninth inning against the Brooklyn Dodgers. Pinch-hitter Pete Scott had two. The hits helped propel the Cubs to a nine-run inning, an 11–6 victory, and a double-header sweep.

June 19, 1913

The Cubs have no pinch-hit home runs until 1913, when they hit three. Wilbur B. Good hits the first off Grover Cleveland Alexander.

May 1, 1927

Chick Tolson hits the Cubs' first pinch-hit grand slam. It comes in the seventh inning at Forbes Field, but the Pirates bounce back to win the game 7–6 in the bottom of the ninth.

September 18, 1950

Ron Northey sets a record with the third pinch-hit grand slam of his career in a 9–7 victory over the Dodgers at Ebbets Field. His first two are hit with the St. Louis Cardinals.

August 18, 1952

Phil Cavarretta hits his last home run as a Cub. As manager, he calls his own number in the bottom of the ninth against the Pirates with a man on and the Cubs down 3–2. Cavarretta takes Murry Dickson out of the yard for a pinch-hit game-winner.

May 12, 1959

The Cubs mount an impressive rally against the Milwaukee Braves. Moose Moryn ties the game at 3–3 with a home run in the bottom of the ninth, then Earl Averill wins it with a pinch-hit grand slam off Lew Burdette. Every game counts, and many a Braves fan must think back on this one when they end the season tied with the Dodgers and lose the pennant in a play-off.

June 6, 1981

Perhaps no pinch-hit home run is more unlikely than the one Mike Tyson hits days before the strike. A three-run shot, it comes off Fernando Valenzuela during Fernando's phenomenal rookie season and propels the Cubs to an 11–5 win at Wrigley.

August 20, 1998

Pennant-drive-acquisition Glenallen Hill hits a pinch-hit grand slam against his former team to give the Cubs a big 7–3 victory over the San Francisco Giants at Wrigley Field.

September 17, 1998

For pressure pinch-hit home runs, there's none much better than one hit by another pennant-race pickup nearly a month later. Gary Gaetti's shot comes in the 10th inning of a crucial late-season series in San Diego off dominating closer Trevor Hoffman—one of only two he gave up all season—and it gives the Cubs a 4–3 victory.

Extra-Inning Pinch-Hit Grand Slams

Put it all together, and here's what you get. It's happened only four times in club history—and all at Wrigley Field. Oddly enough, Mike Vail did it in 1979 against the Mets and Dale Murray nearly a year to the day after Murray surrendered a pinch-hit grand slam to Dave Rader.

Date	Pinch Hitter	Inning	Final Score
September 13, 1931	Rogers Hornsby	11th	Cubs 11 Boston 7
July 23, 1933	Harvey Hendrick	10th	Cubs 9 Philadelphia 5
June 6, 1946	Frank Secory	12th	Cubs 10 New York 6
June 30, 1979	Mike Vail	11th	New York 9 Cubs 8

STREAKS

Cubs hitters have reeled off some impressive seasonal, game, and at-bat streaks. Here are the highlights.

Forty home runs in four straight seasons: Ernie Banks, 1957–60, one of only five players to do this.

Twenty home runs in 13 straight seasons: Billy Williams, 1961–73, one of only eight players to do this.

Eight consecutive hits: Sammy Strang in 1900, Wayne Terwilliger in 1949, Lee Walls in 1958, and Sammy Sosa (nine) in 1993.

Twenty-game hitting streaks: Thirteen Cubs have had hitting streaks of at least 20 games, including Bill Dahlen's streak of 42 games, the fourth longest in big-league history. Once his streak was snapped, he set off on a 28-game string—hitting safely in 70 of 71 games. Ron Santo's 28-game hitting streak was interrupted when Jack Fisher fractured Santo's left cheekbone with a pitch. Santo missed seven games, then picked up right where he left off.

Bill Buckner had a 19-game hitting streak going and always wore the same underwear. Of course, he had no friends.

Lenny Randle, 1980

20-Game Hitting Streaks

1894	Bill Dahlen	42	1937	Gabby Hartnett	24
1894	Bill Dahlen	28	1943	Bill Nicholson	21
1896	George Decker	26	1945	Stan Hack	24
1912	Heinie Zimmerman	23	1966	Ron Santo	28
1926	Hack Wilson	25	1966	Glenn Beckert	20
1927	Hack Wilson	25	1968	Glenn Beckert	27
1929	Hack Wilson	27	1973	Glenn Beckert	26
1929	Hack Wilson	20	1980	Lenny Randle	21
1930	Hack Wilson	22	1988	Rafael Palmeiro	20
1934	Billy Herman	20	1989	Jerome Walton	30

Multiple 20-Game Hitting Streaks

Hack Wilson	5
Glenn Beckert	3
Bill Dahlen	2

Jerome Walton's Hitting Streak

On July 20, 1989, the Cubs played a night game at Wrigley Field against the West-leading San Francisco Giants. The Cubs won 4–3 in 11 on a two-out double by pitcher Les Lancaster. In retrospect, the game was also noteworthy because it was the last time for the next four weeks that rookie center-fielder Jerome Walton went hitless.

When it started, the Cubs were in second place, just ½ game in front of the Mets and 2½ behind the Expos. When it ended—in another extra-inning night game at Wrigley—the Cubs were in first, 1½ games up on the Mets and 3 up on the Expos. Walton hit .338 during what proved to be the longest batting streak in modern Cubs history and the highlight of Walton's career.

The hits got bigger as the streak got longer, including back-to-back game-winners on the 16th and 17th of August, the second coming in the ninth inning off John Franco. Walton even managed a hit in a two-hitter thrown by Jose DeLeon and in a three-hitter by Ken Howell.

Walton ended up hitting in 30 consecutive games, breaking the Cubs' modern record of 28, set by Ron Santo in 1966.

Even after the streak was snapped, Walton kept going, hitting in 10 of his next 11 games. Here's how it went, game by game.

Walton's 1989 Streak, Game by Game

DATE	RESULT	AB	R	H	RBI	2B	3B	HR
July 21	**San Francisco 4** Cubs 3	5	0	1	1	0	0	0
July 22	San Francisco 2 **Cubs 5**	4	0	1	1	1	0	0
July 23	San Francisco 5 **Cubs 9**	5	1	1	0	0	0	0
July 24	**Cubs 3** St. Louis 2	4	0	1	1	0	0	0
July 25	**Cubs 4** St. Louis 2	4	0	1	0	1	0	0
July 26	Cubs 0 **St. Louis 2**	4	0	1	0	0	0	0
July 28	New York 5 **Cubs 6**	3	0	1	1	0	0	0
July 29	New York 3 **Cubs 10**	5	2	3	0	0	0	0
July 30	New York 4 **Cubs 6**	5	2	3	0	0	0	0
July 31	**Cubs 10** Philadelphia 2	5	0	1	1	0	0	0
	Cubs 4 **Philadelphia 7**	4	1	1	1	0	0	1
August 1	**Cubs 4** Philadelphia 1	5	0	2	2	0	1	0
August 2	Cubs 0 **Philadelphia 6**	3	0	1	0	0	0	0
August 3	**Cubs 2** Philadelphia 0	4	0	1	0	0	0	0
August 4	**Cubs 3** Pittsburgh 2	5	0	1	0	0	0	0
August 5	**Cubs 4** Pittsburgh 2	5	1	3	1	0	0	0
August 6	Cubs 4 **Pittsburgh 5**	7	1	3	0	1	0	0
August 7	Montreal 2 **Cubs 5**	4	2	3	0	0	1	0
August 8	Montreal 2 **Cubs 4**	4	1	1	1	0	0	1
August 9	Montreal 0 **Cubs 3**	4	1	1	0	0	0	0
August 10	**Philadelphia 16** Cubs 13	6	2	2	2	0	0	0
August 11	Philadelphia 2 **Cubs 9**	3	1	1	2	0	0	0
August 12	Philadelphia 7 **Cubs 9**	5	1	2	0	0	0	0
August 13	**Philadelphia 5** Cubs 3	3	1	1	1	1	0	0
August 15	**Cubs 5** Cincinnati 2	6	0	1	0	0	0	0
August 16	**Cubs 5** Cincinnati 1	5	1	3	2	1	0	0
August 17	**Cubs 3** Cincinnati 2	5	1	2	2	0	0	0
August 18	Cubs 5 **Houston 6**	4	1	1	1	0	0	0
August 19	Cubs 4 **Houston 8**	5	0	1	0	0	0	0
August 20	Cubs 4 **Houston 8**	5	0	1	0	0	0	0
Totals		136	20	46	20	5	2	2

Ray Grimes's RBI Streak

One of the lesser-known streaks in baseball history is Ray Grimes's RBI streak in June and July of 1922. In fact, at the time, no one even noticed. He knocked in a run in 17 consecutive games, despite sitting out a game with lumbago, injuring his back in the second game of a doubleheader, and having to sit out nine days. Grimes hit .424, slugged .727, and knocked in 27 runs along the way. He ended up falling short of 100 RBIs for the season by only one run.

Grimes's 1922 Streak, Game by Game

DATE	AB	R	H	RBI	2B	3B	HR
June 27 (2nd game)	5	1	1	1	0	0	0
June 30	4	1	2	1	0	0	0
July 1	4	0	2	3	1	0	0
July 2	4	0	1	1	1	0	0
July 3	4	0	1	1	0	0	0
July 4	4	0	1	1	0	0	0
	3	2	2	1	0	0	0
July 5	4	2	1	1	1	0	0
July 7	4	2	2	2	1	1	0
July 8	3	2	2	1	0	0	0
	1	0	1	1	0	0	0
July 18	4	1	4	2	1	0	1
July 19	5	0	1	1	1	0	0
July 20	5	2	2	3	0	0	1
July 21	4	0	1	1	1	0	0
July 22	5	1	3	4	1	1	0
July 23	3	1	1	2	0	0	1
Totals	66	15	28	27	8	2	3

HIDDEN ACHIEVEMENTS

Some noteworthy offensive accomplishments tend to be buried in a player's stat line.

Hardest to Strike Out
Strikeouts in Fewer than 1% of Plate Appearances, Season

PLAYER	YEAR	SO	PA	%
Cap Anson	1878	1	274	0.4
Emil Verban	1949	2	351	0.6
Charlie Hollocher	1922	5	650	0.8
Cap Anson	1879	2	229	0.9

One Too Many

Legend has it that in 1878, after fanning twice in an exhibition game, Cap Anson bet his White Stockings teammates $500 that he could go the entire regular season without striking out. It wasn't until well into the season that he was called out on strikes, on a pitch that even the opposing pitcher thought was a ball. Anson finished the season without striking out, and his teammates never made him fork over the $500.

Easiest to Strike Out
Strikeouts in More than 25% of Plate Appearances, Season

PLAYER	YEAR	SO	PA	%
Byron Browne	1966	143	459	31.2
Adolfo Phillips	1966	135	459	29.4
Jose Hernandez	1996	97	355	27.3
Jose Hernandez	1995	69	258	26.7
Jose Hernandez	1998	140	528	26.5
Rick Wilkins	1995	51	198	25.8
Dave Kingman	1978	111	434	25.6
Sammy Sosa	1997	174	687	25.3
Rick Wilkins	1991	56	222	25.2
Sammy Sosa	1996	134	532	25.2

Best Batting Eye
Walks in More than 20% of Plate Appearances, Season

PLAYER	YEAR	BB	PA	%
Jimmy Sheckard	1911	147	686	21.4
Stan Hack	1946	83	406	20.4
Johnny Evers	1910	108	541	20.0

Free Swingers
Walks in No More than 2% of Plate Appearances, Season (20th century)

PLAYER	YEAR	BB	PA	%
Bobby Sturgeon	1941	9	442	2.0
Jerry Kindall	1960	5	251	2.0
Shawon Dunston	1997	8	427	1.9
Mike Vail	1978	3	183	1.6

Earning Their Way On Base
More than 275 Hits and Walks in a Season

PLAYER	YEAR	TOTAL H & BB
Rogers Hornsby	1929	316
Woody English	1930	314
Hack Wilson	1930	313
Kiki Cuyler	1930	300
Jimmy Sheckard	1911	296
Stan Hack	1945	292
Augie Galan	1935	290
Stan Hack	1938	289
Stan Hack	1941	285
Billy Williams	1970	277
Hack Wilson	1929	276
Richie Ashburn	1960	275

Q. Who produced the *fewest* RBIs per hit for the Cubs? (Hint: It wasn't his fault. He batted .306 in the lead-off spot for a seventh-place team.)

A. Frankie Baumholtz in 1953, 159 hits and only 25 RBIs, or about 1 RBI for every 6.5 hits

Productivity
Nearly 1 RBI per Hit (minimum 100 hits)

PLAYER	YEAR	H	RBI	RATIO
Hack Wilson	1930	208	190	0.9
Hack Wilson	1929	198	159	0.8
Ron Cey	1984	121	97	0.8
Sammy Sosa	1998	198	158	0.8

COMBO PLATTERS

More RBIs than Games

In 1929, Hack Wilson became only the second National League player with more RBIs than games played (minimum 100 games). Rogers Hornsby had done it in 1925 and narrowly missed doing it again with the Cubs in 1929. In 1930, Wilson became the only NL player to accomplish this incredible feat twice. Sammy Sosa just missed in 1998, knocking in 158 runs in 159 games.

Some of baseball's rarest achievements can be uncovered when looking at what players did in two or more statistical categories in the same season. The best example of this is the Triple Crown, but here are some "Double Crowns" that are even rarer.

Two Hundred Hits and 40 Home Runs

Five National League players have won the Triple Crown, while only three non-Rockies have managed 200 hits and 40 home runs in the same season. The first two to do it were Cubs: Rogers Hornsby in 1929 and Billy Williams in 1970.

Two Hundred Hits and 100 Strikeouts

Almost as rare is 200 hits and 100 strikeouts. Only eight National Leaguers have done it, and none until Bill White in 1963. It was last done by a non-Rockie in 1984: Ryne Sandberg had 200 hits and 101 strikeouts, hitting .374 when putting the ball in play.

More Home Runs than Walks (minimum 40 homers)

Another rare "double" is 40 home runs with fewer walks than home runs—since most power hitters get pitched around. Only five non-Rockies have accomplished this feat in the National League, and three of them are Cubs: Dave Kingman in 1979, Andre Dawson in 1987, and Sammy Sosa in 1996.

More Home Runs than Strikeouts

Even less common is having more home runs than strikeouts. Only one 20th-century Cub has ever done it. In 1950, Andy Pafko hit 36 home runs while striking out only 32 times. He also did it for 49 games in 1951 before being dealt to the Dodgers. (Perspective check: Joe DiMaggio did this *seven* times and nearly did it for his entire career.) Cap Anson hit 21 home runs in 1884 with only 13 strikeouts, but he was aided by short fences, favorable grounds rules, and severely handicapped pitchers.

No Home Runs and 60 Strikeouts

How about the less flattering flip side? For example, have any Cubs struck out 60 times without hitting a single home run? Don Kessinger (80 in 1967) and Ivan DeJesus (61 in a wretched and mercifully strike-shortened 1981) accomplished the "anti-Maris." No National Leaguer topped Kessinger until Steve Jeltz blew by him in 1986 with a 97-whiff doughnut.

More Strikeouts than Hits

In the same spirit, only seven Cubs have had more strikeouts than hits (minimum 100 hits). Billy Cowan was the first to do it, in 1964. Adolfo Phillips and Byron Browne both did it in 1966, Sammy Sosa joined the club in 1997, and both Jose Hernandez and Henry Rodriguez did it in 1998. But the king was Dave Kingman. He did it five times, once with the Cubs, and when he retired, he was one of only three players (along with Reggie Jackson and Gorman Thomas) to have more strikeouts than hits for his entire career (minimum 1,000 hits).

ROOKIES

When Nomar Garciaparra reached 200 hits in 1997, he became only the 17th rookie to do so. Hall of Fame second-baseman Billy Herman was one of the handful, with 206 hits in 1932. Not bad, considering that in his first game in the majors late in 1931, he was plunked in the head with a pitch and carried off the field.

Rookie Seasons

Here's a list of Cubs who made a big noise in their rookie year. Rookie of the Year Award winners and Cubs rookie records are in **bold**. A number of these players—Cap Anson, Jimmy Ryan, Charlie Hollocher, Billy Herman, Phil Cavarretta, and Jerome Walton—made immediate contributions to pennant-winners.

PLAYER	Pos.	YEAR	AB	R	H	2B	3B	HR	RBI	BA	SA
Cap Anson	3B	1876	309	63	110	9	7	1	59	.356	.440
Jimmy Ryan	OF	1886	327	58	100	17	6	4	53	.306	.431
Wildfire Schulte	OF	1905	493	67	135	15	**14**	1	47	.274	.367
Charlie Hollocher	SS	1918	509	72	161	23	6	2	38	.316	.397
Ray Grimes	1B	1921	530	91	170	38	6	6	79	.321	.406
Hack Miller	OF	1922	466	61	164	28	5	12	78	**.352**	**.511**
Billy Herman	2B	1932	656	102	**206**	**42**	7	1	51	.314	.404
Phil Cavarretta	1B	1935	589	85	162	28	12	8	82	.275	.404
Ernie Banks	SS	1954	593	70	163	19	7	19	79	.275	.427
Billy Williams	OF	1961	529	75	147	20	7	**25**	86	.278	.484
Ken Hubbs	2B	1962	**661**	90	172	24	9	5	49	.260	.346
Randy Hundley	C	1966	526	50	124	22	3	19	63	.236	.397
Bill Madlock	3B	1974	453	65	142	21	5	9	54	.313	.442
Ryne Sandberg	2B	1982	635	**103**	172	33	5	7	54	.271	.372
Mark Grace	1B	1988	486	65	144	23	4	7	57	.296	.403
Jerome Walton	OF	1989	475	64	139	23	3	5	46	.293	.385

Andy Pafko debuted on September 24, 1943, with four RBIs in a 7–4 win over the Phillies. Rain halted the game, which was seen by a record low of 314 close friends and relatives at Wrigley.

More than a few tape-measure shots have been hit in Wrigley Field, but one of the most famous ones was hit in the Polo Grounds. On June 17, 1962, rookie outfielder Lou Brock hit a ball 475 feet into the center-field bleachers—only the second player ever to reach those seats (Joe Adcock did it for Milwaukee). It was Brock's first home run off of a lefty, serving notice that platooning wasn't in his cards.

Phil Cavarretta's first home run came at 17, in his first big-league start, and won the game 1–0. The following is a collection of Cubs stars and their first home-run victims.

May 2, 1876

Ross Barnes hit only one home run in his career, but it was a memorable one: the first home run ever hit in the National League. The Al Downing of 1876: Cherokee Fisher of the Cincinnati Red Stockings, who served it up.

First Dingers

HITTER	DATE	VICTIM
Cap Anson	August 26, 1876	George Bradley
Frank Chance	July 13, 1898	Cy Swaim
Joe Tinker	May 27, 1902	Ed Murphy
Johnny Evers	July 21, 1905	Chick Fraser
Gabby Hartnett	April 20, 1923	Earl Hamilton
Hack Wilson	April 20, 1926	Wit Reinhart
Stan Hack	May 3, 1932	Bill Swift
Billy Herman	May 24, 1932	Syl Johnson
Phil Cavarretta	September 25, 1934	Whitey Wistert
Bill Nicholson	August 1, 1939	Bill Kerksieck
Andy Pafko	May 30, 1944	Ewald Pyle
Ernie Banks	September 20, 1953	Gerry Staley
Ron Santo	July 3, 1960	Jim O'Toole
Billy Williams	October 1, 1960	Stan Williams
Glenn Beckert	May 9, 1965	Bob Bruce
Randy Hundley	April 19, 1966	Ron Herbel
Don Kessinger	May 14, 1966	Jim O'Toole
Jody Davis	June 11, 1981	Al Holland
Ryne Sandberg	April 23, 1982	Eddie Solomon
Shawon Dunston	May 4, 1985	Greg Booker
Mark Grace	May 4, 1988	Keith Comstock

OWNING PITCHERS

Cubs hitters have made lives miserable for more than a few opposing pitchers. Don Sutton, for example, was 0–13 across four seasons before he finally beat the Cubs in 1969. As a team, the Cubs owned Hall of Famer Warren Spahn in 1958, taking him deep 13 times—including Tony Taylor's first in the majors.

Two pitchers brought record-winning streaks into battle against Chicago and had them snapped. On July 8, 1912, the Cubs beat Rube Marquard 7–2 at West Side Grounds to end his 19-game winning streak. They'd done the same to another New York pitcher, Tim Keefe, beating him 4–2 on August 14, 1888, to end *his* 19-game winning streak. Both streaks are the longest in baseball history.

No one *owned* Giants ace Christy Mathewson, but the Cubs sure made his life difficult. Catcher Johnny Kling, a defensive standout, hit four home runs off of him, the most off any pitcher he faced. Frank Chance hit for the cycle against him in a 3–2 win at West Side Grounds. But it was Joe Tinker who Mathewson must have been seeing in his nightmares. Tinker hit 3 home runs off of him—not bad, considering that Mathewson yielded only 62 home runs during Tinker's career. Tinker also delivered a huge hit in the "play-off" game of 1908 (a replay of the "Merkle Boner" game, described in "The Pennants," Chapter 13). In fact, the Cubs shortstop considered his finest day as a pro an 8–6 win over the Giants at West Side Grounds on August 7, 1911, in which he went 4-for-4, scored three times, and stole home against the finest National League pitcher of his generation.

In addition to Joe Tinker, other individual Cubs have done quite well against Hall of Famers. On the list of Cubs legends and their favorite targets, you'll find Ernie Banks and Robin Roberts, Billy Williams and Bob Gibson, and Cap Anson and Old Hoss Radbourn.

Favorite Targets

CUB	PITCHER	HR
Ernie Banks	Robin Roberts	15
Billy Williams	Bob Gibson	10
Ron Santo	Dave Giusti, Ray Sadecki	8
Gabby Hartnett	Fat Freddie Fitzsimmons	7
Cap Anson	Charley Radbourn	7

Hank Sauer owned Curt Simmons, taking the Phillies' pitcher deep three times in a game *twice* (in 1950 and again in 1952). The second time it happened was on June 11, 1952, as Sauer accounted for all of the Cubs runs in a 3–0 victory. Sauer also owned the entire Pittsburgh Pirates staff in 1954, hitting a club-record 13 home runs against them. Sammy Sosa could say the same for Milwaukee's staff in 1998, as he hit 12 of his 66 home runs against the Brewers.

DUBIOUS DISTINCTIONS

Here's a collection of feats and firsts that aren't exactly sources of pride.

Frank Chance was hit by pitches three times in a game twice, and five times in a doubleheader against the Reds in Cincinnati on May 30, 1904. He suffered a black eye, a cut forehead, and briefly lost consciousness but never sat down and never backed up.

On September 17, 1928, the Cubs set a record with three hit batsmen in one inning against the Braves.

Don Hoak struck out six times in a 17-inning, 6–5 loss to the Giants at Wrigley on May 2, 1956. He "bested" Dee Fondy, who'd struck out five times in a game on July 22, 1953.

In a stretch of four games between June 7 and June 10, 1966, Adolfo Phillips struck out a record 12 times. In the process, he also set the mark for three games with 10 strikeouts. However, Adolfo didn't match Jerry Kindall's string of seven consecutive strikeouts, set in 1960.

They all went down together on July 30, 1933—down on strikes 17 times against Dizzy Dean in an 8–2 loss. The Cubs did themselves one better on April 24, 1962, when Sandy Koufax struck out 18 in a 10–2 victory. Finally, Chicago put a rookie in the record books

If I'd known I was anywhere near a record, I'da struck out 20 anyway.

Dizzy Dean, after fanning 17 Cubs

when the Cubs whiffed 18 times against the Expos' Bill Gullickson on September 10, 1980. At least Kerry Wood was able to take Gullickson's name out of the record books 18 years later.

In 1968, in a doubleheader on June 16 and games on June 19 and 20, the Cubs were shut out four times in a row. At its worst, the scoreless streak spanned 48 innings.

On September 16, 1972, Glenn Beckert left a record 12 men on base in one game.

Not only were the Cubs no-hit on August 19, 1965, by Jim Maloney—but they also were issued 10 walks in 10 innings and failed to score any of them.

On September 21, 1962, and on May 3, 1969, Cubs pinch hitters struck out four times against the Mets.

Cubs hitters have even managed to strike out four times in one inning—four times, to be exact.

1-2-3-4 *Innings and Their Perpetrators*

May 17, 1984	Mario Soto, Cincinnati Reds
September 3, 1986	Mike Scott, Houston Astros
June 7, 1995	Mark Wohlers, Atlanta Braves
July 25, 1996	Bruce Ruffin, Colorado Rockies

Infielder Sparky Adams went 1926 and 1927 without a home run, despite leading the league in at bats. He did it again in 1928 with the Pirates, and at one point went 3,104 at bats without a long ball (July 26, 1925, to June 30, 1931). Going without a home run in 500 at bats is a challenge—a challenge also met since the deadball era by Billy Herman (1933), Eddie Stanky (1943), Richie Ashburn (1960), and Don Kessinger (1967, 1973, and 1975).

Barry Foote went 0-for-1981. He came to bat 22 times without a hit.

It isn't in the books as a no-hitter or a perfect game, but the Phillies' Rick Wise retired 32 Cubs in a row in a 12-inning game in 1971.

Dave Kingman was a one-man perfect game on July 6, 1980, going 0-for-9 in a 5–4, 20-inning loss to the Pirates at Three Rivers.

In 1967, utility infielder Paul Popovich set a standard for hitting futilely that hadn't been matched since the deadball era and that still stands today. In 159 at bats, he knocked in two runs—putting him on pace for seven in a full season!

the pitcher's mound

Sixty feet six inches away and 10 inches up from the batter's box is the pitcher's mound. This chapter documents the results of both the kings and fools on the hill, those who blew batters away and those who chucked and ducked.

Do you know:

- Which Cub staff recorded 32 shutouts in one season, and which was touched up for 5.68 earned runs per game?
- Who was the only Cubs' pitcher to appear in more than 600 games? To record more than 2,000 strikeouts? To issue more than 1,000 walks?
- The who, what, and when of every Cub to lead the league in a pitching category or reach season milestones such as 200 strikeouts, 20 wins, or an ERA below 2?
- The four Cubs who've led the league in wins for a losing team?
- The four Cubs who've struck out four batters in an inning (including one who did it in the World Series)?
- The two Cubs who won 20 games in six consecutive seasons?
- The two Cubs teammates who won pitching's Triple Crown (wins, strikeouts, and ERA)?
- The Cub who went 15–1 for the *month*?
- The Cub who threw a *train*-shortened no-hitter? The Cub who threw a no-hitter and lost the game? The Cub obscurity who Sandy Koufax literally had to be perfect to beat?
- The who, what, when, and where of every no-hitter involving the Cubs?
- The only pitcher to ever throw two shutouts *on the same day*?
- The Cub who once threw 18 innings in an *exhibition game* and who once needed only 58 minutes to record a victory?
- The Cub starter who went 187 games and 1,727 innings without being relieved?
- Where Kerry Wood's 1998 season stands relative to the greatest rookie seasons any pitcher has ever had?
- The last Cub staff to lead the league in ERA?
- The Cub who gave up 17 hits and 14 runs and got the win?
- The pitcher who went 20–6 when the Cubs scored at least one run for him?
- The Cub who lost 13 consecutive games in his only big-league season?
- The "losingest" pitcher on a pennant-winner in the history of baseball?

And that's only scratching the surface of the pitcher's mound.

TEAM RESULTS

Year-by-Year Highlights

YEAR	W	L	BB	SO	ShO	ERA
1876	**52**	14	29	51	9	1.76
1877	26	33	58	92	3	3.37
1878	30	30	35	175	1	2.37
1879	46	33	57	211	6	2.46
1880	**67**	17	129	**367**	8	1.93
1881	**56**	28	122	228	9	2.43
1882	**55**	29	102	279	7	**2.22**
1883	59	39	123	299	5	2.78
1884	62	50	231	472	9	3.03
1885	**87**	25	202	458	14	2.23
1886	**90**	34	262	**647**	8	2.54
1887	71	50	338	**510**	4	**3.46**
1888	77	58	308	588	13	2.96
1889	67	65	408	434	6	3.73
1890	84	53	481	504	6	3.24
1891	82	53	475	477	6	3.47
1892	70	76	424	518	6	3.16
1893	56	71	553	273	4	4.81
1894	57	75	557	281	0	5.68
1895	72	58	432	297	3	4.67
1896	71	57	467	353	2	4.41
1897	59	73	433	361	2	4.53
1898	85	65	364	323	**13**	**2.83**
1899	75	73	330	313	8	3.37
1900	65	75	324	357	9	3.23
1901	53	86	324	**586**	2	3.33
1902	68	69	279	437	18	**2.21**
1903	82	56	**354**	451	6	**2.77**
1904	93	60	402	618	18	2.30
1905	92	61	385	627	**23**	**2.04**
1906	**116**	36	446	**702**	**31**	**1.76**
1907	**107**	45	402	586	**30**	**1.73**
1908	**99**	55	437	**668**	**28**	2.14
1909	104	49	364	680	**32**	**1.75**
1910	**104**	50	474	609	**27**	**2.51**
1911	92	62	525	582	12	2.90
1912	91	59	493	554	14	3.42
1913	88	65	478	556	12	3.13
1914	78	76	528	**651**	14	2.71
1915	73	80	480	**657**	18	3.11
1916	67	86	365	616	17	2.65
1917	74	80	374	**654**	15	2.62
1918	**84**	45	296	**472**	25	**2.18**
1919	75	65	294	**495**	21	**2.21**
1920	75	79	382	508	13	3.27
1921	64	89	409	441	7	4.39

continued

YEAR	W	L	BB	SO	ShO	ERA
1922	80	74	475	402	8	4.34
1923	83	71	435	408	8	3.82
1924	81	72	438	416	4	3.83
1925	68	**86**	485	435	5	4.41
1926	82	72	486	508	13	**3.26**
1927	85	68	514	465	11	3.65
1928	91	63	508	531	12	3.40
1929	**98**	54	537	548	**14**	4.16
1930	90	64	528	601	6	4.80
1931	84	70	524	541	8	3.97
1932	**90**	64	409	527	9	**3.44**
1933	86	68	413	488	16	2.93
1934	86	65	417	633	11	3.76
1935	**100**	54	400	589	12	**3.26**
1936	87	67	434	597	**18**	3.53
1937	93	61	502	596	11	3.97
1938	**89**	63	454	**583**	**16**	**3.37**
1939	84	70	430	584	8	3.80
1940	75	79	430	564	12	3.54
1941	70	84	449	548	8	3.72
1942	68	86	525	507	10	3.60
1943	74	79	394	513	12	3.24
1944	75	79	458	545	11	3.59
1945	**98**	56	385	541	15	**2.98**
1946	82	71	527	619	14	3.24
1947	69	85	618	571	8	4.10
1948	64	**90**	619	636	7	4.00
1949	61	**93**	575	544	8	4.50
1950	64	89	593	559	6	4.96
1951	62	**92**	572	544	10	4.34
1952	77	77	534	661	15	3.58
1953	65	89	554	623	3	4.79
1954	64	90	619	622	6	4.51
1955	72	81	601	686	10	4.17
1956	60	**94**	613	744	6	3.96
1957	62	**92**	601	859	5	4.13
1958	72	82	619	805	5	4.22
1959	74	80	519	765	11	4.01
1960	60	94	565	805	6	4.35
1961	64	90	465	755	6	4.48
1962	59	103	601	783	4	4.54
1963	82	80	400	851	15	3.08
1964	76	86	423	737	11	4.08
1965	72	90	481	855	9	3.78
1966	59	**103**	479	908	6	4.33
1967	87	74	463	888	7	3.48
1968	84	78	392	894	12	3.41
1969	92	70	475	1,017	22	3.34
1970	84	78	475	1,000	9	3.76
1971	83	79	411	900	17	3.61
1972	85	70	421	824	19	3.22
1973	77	84	438	885	13	3.66

continued

YEAR	W	L	BB	SO	ShO	ERA
1974	66	96	576	895	6	4.28
1975	75	87	551	850	8	4.57
1976	75	87	490	850	12	3.93
1977	81	81	489	**942**	10	4.01
1978	79	83	539	768	7	4.05
1979	80	82	521	**933**	11	3.88
1980	64	**98**	589	923	6	3.89
1981	38	65	388	532	2	4.01
1982	73	89	452	764	7	3.92
1983	71	91	498	807	10	4.07
1984	**96**	65	442	879	8	3.75
1985	77	84	519	820	8	4.16
1986	70	90	557	962	6	4.49
1987	76	85	628	1,024	4	4.55
1988	77	85	490	897	9	3.84
1989	**93**	69	532	918	5	3.43
1990	77	85	572	877	7	4.34
1991	77	83	542	927	4	4.03
1992	78	84	575	901	11	3.39
1993	84	78	470	905	5	4.18
1994	49	64	392	717	5	4.47
1995	73	71	518	926	12	4.13
1996	76	86	546	1,027	10	4.36
1997	68	**94**	590	1,072	4	4.44
1998	90	73	575	1,207	7	4.47

Note: League-leading totals are in **bold**.

Best & Worst, Most & Fewest, Highest & Lowest

Lowest ERA:	1.73, 1907
Highest ERA:	5.68, 1894
Highest ERA, 20th century:	4.96, 1950
Most shutouts:	32, 1909
Fewest shutouts:	0, 1894
Fewest shutouts, 20th century:	2, 1901, 1981
Fewest shutouts, 162 games:	4, 1962, 1987, 1991, 1997
Most strikeouts:	1,207, 1998
Fewest strikeouts:	51, 1876
Fewest strikeouts, 20th century:	357, 1900
Fewest strikeouts, 162 games:	737, 1964
Most strikeouts per game:	7.4, 1998
Fewest strikeouts per game:	.8, 1876
Fewest strikeouts per game, 20th century:	2.6, 1900
Most walks:	628, 1987
Fewest walks:	29, 1876
Fewest walks, 20th century:	279, 1902
Most walks per game:	4.4, 1893

Most walks per game, 20th century:	4.0, 1958
Fewest walks per game:	.4, 1876
Fewest walks per game, 20th century:	2.0, 1902
Highest strikeout/walk ratio:	5:1, 1878
Highest strikeout/walk ratio, 20th century:	2.3:1, 1968
Lowest strikeout/walk ratio:	.5:1, 1893
Lowest strikeout/walk ratio, 20th century:	.8:1, 1922

CAREER RECORDS

Games

1. Charlie Root — 605
2. Lee Smith — 458
3. Don Elston — 449
4. Guy Bush — 428
5. Ferguson Jenkins — 401
6. Bill Hutchison — 367
7. Bill Lee — 364
8. Rick Reuschel — 358
9. Mordecai Brown — 346
10. Bob Rush — 339

Games Started

1. Ferguson Jenkins — 347
2. Rick Reuschel — 343
3. Bill Hutchison — 339
   Charlie Root — 339
5. Bill Lee — 297
6. Bob Rush — 292
7. Hippo Vaughn — 270
8. Larry Corcoran — 262
9. Clark Griffith — 253
10. Guy Bush — 252

Complete Games

1. Bill Hutchison — 317
2. Larry Corcoran — 252
3. Clark Griffith — 240
4. Mordecai Brown — 206
5. Jack Taylor — 188
6. John Clarkson — 186
7. Charlie Root — 177
   Hippo Vaughn — 177
9. Fred Goldsmith — 164
10. Grover Alexander — 159

Innings

1. Charlie Root — 3,138
2. Bill Hutchison — 3,026
3. Ferguson Jenkins — 2,672
4. Larry Corcoran — 2,338
5. Mordecai Brown — 2,329
6. Rick Reuschel — 2,291
7. Bill Lee — 2,270
8. Hippo Vaughn — 2,216
9. Guy Bush — 2,201
10. Clark Griffith — 2,189

Hits Allowed

1. Charlie Root   3,184
2. Bill Hutchison   3,055
3. Clark Griffith   2,445
4. Ferguson Jenkins   2,402
5. Rick Reuschel   2,365
6. Guy Bush   2,354
7. Bill Lee   2,317
8. Larry Corcoran   2,084
9. Bob Rush   2,043
10. Hippo Vaughn   1,971

Hits per Nine Innings
(minimum 400 innings)

1. Bruce Sutter   6.79
2. Orvie Overall   6.86
3. Sam Jones   6.90
4. Ed Reulbach   7.04
5. Jack Pfiester   7.20
6. Mordecai Brown   7.26
7. Jake Weimer   7.32
8. Larry Cheney   7.63
9. Carl Lundgren   7.69
10. Lee Smith   7.80

Hits and Walks per Nine Innings
(minimum 400 innings)

1. Mordecai Brown   8.98
2. John Clarkson   9.48
3. Bruce Sutter   9.51
4. Jack Pfiester   9.62
5. Orvie Overall   9.71
6. Albert Spalding   9.76
7. Larry Corcoran   9.80
8. Ferguson Jenkins   10.11
9. Ed Reulbach   10.18
10. Jake Weimer   10.33

Walks

1. Bill Hutchison   1,106
2. Charlie Root   871
3. Guy Bush   734
4. Bob Rush   725
5. Bill Lee   704
6. Sheriff Blake   661
7. Ed Reulbach   650
8. Rick Reuschel   640
9. Hippo Vaughn   621
10. Ferguson Jenkins   600

Walks per Nine Innings
(minimum 400 innings)

1. Albert Spalding   0.43
2. Fred Goldsmith   1.00
3. Grover Alexander   1.28
4. John Clarkson   1.56
5. Dennis Eckersley   1.66
6. Mordecai Brown   1.72
7. Larry Corcoran   1.78
8. Jack Taylor   1.84
9. Larry Jackson   1.86
   Jocko Menefee   1.86

Strikeouts

1. Ferguson Jenkins   2,038
2. Charlie Root   1,432
3. Rick Reuschel   1,367
4. Bill Hutchison   1,226
5. Hippo Vaughn   1,138
6. Larry Corcoran   1,086
7. Bob Rush   1,076
8. Mordecai Brown   1,043
9. Ken Holtzman   988
10. John Clarkson   960

Control Freak

Grover Cleveland Alexander is one of the greatest control pitchers in baseball history. In 1923, he became one of only a handful of pitchers to walk less than one batter per nine innings (305 innings, 30 walks). He went the first 52 innings of the season before issuing his first walk.

#3,000

On May 25, 1982, Ferguson Jenkins fanned Garry Templeton in San Diego for the 3,000th strikeout of his career. He is the only pitcher to record 3,000 strikeouts while walking fewer than 1,000 batters.

Strikeouts per Nine Innings (minimum 400 innings)

1.	Bruce Sutter	9.04	6.	Rick Sutcliffe	6.46
2.	Lee Smith	8.50	7.	Willie Hernandez	6.36
3.	Sam Jones	7.82	8.	Bill Bonham	6.33
4.	Ferguson Jenkins	6.86	9.	Ken Holtzman	6.23
5.	Steve Trachsel	6.58	10.	Don Elston	6.18

Through 1998, Kerry Wood was 233⅓ innings away from vaulting to the top of the above list. In 1998, he struck out *12.58* batters per nine innings!

Strikeout/Walk Ratio (minimum 400 innings)

1.	Dennis Eckersley	3.4
	Ferguson Jenkins	3.4
3.	Bruce Sutter	3.3
4.	John Clarkson	3.2
5.	Scott Sanderson	2.8
6.	Larry Jackson	2.5
7.	Lee Smith	2.4
8.	Larry Corcoran	2.4
9.	Mordecai Brown	2.3
	Fred Goldsmith	2.3

Wins

1.	Charlie Root	201
2.	Mordecai Brown	188
3.	Bill Hutchison	182
4.	Larry Corcoran	175
5.	Ferguson Jenkins	167
6.	Guy Bush	152
	Clark Griffith	152
8.	Hippo Vaughn	151
9.	Bill Lee	139
10.	John Clarkson	136

300

No pitcher has won 300 games for the Cubs, but Grover Cleveland Alexander won his 300th as a Cub. On September 20, 1924, Alexander went 12 to beat the Giants 7–2, joining Christy Mathewson, Walter Johnson, and Eddie Plank as the first 20th-century pitchers in the 300 Club.

Losses

1.	Bill Hutchison	158
2.	Charlie Root	156
3.	Bob Rush	140
4.	Ferguson Jenkins	132
5.	Rick Reuschel	127
6.	Bill Lee	123
7.	Dick Ellsworth	110
8.	Hippo Vaughn	105
9.	Guy Bush	101
10.	Clark Griffith	96

Winning Percentage (minimum 400 innings)

1.	Albert Spalding	.787
2.	John Clarkson	.705
3.	Mordecai Brown	.694
4.	Ed Reulbach	.677
5.	Larry Corcoran	.673
6.	Orvie Overall	.662
7.	Jack Pfiester	.636
8.	Bob Wicker	.634
9.	Fred Goldsmith	.629
10.	Jake Weimer	.628

Shutouts

1.	Mordecai Brown	48	7.	Grover Alexander	24
2.	Hippo Vaughn	35	8.	Claude Passeau	23
3.	Ed Reulbach	31	9.	Larry Corcoran	22
4.	Ferguson Jenkins	29	10.	Larry French	21
5.	Orvie Overall	28		Bill Hutchison	21
6.	Bill Lee	25		Charlie Root	21

Shutouts per 30 Starts

1. Orvie Overall   6.3
2. Mordecai Brown   6.0
3. Ed Reulbach   4.3
4. Jack Pfiester   4.1
5. Albert Spalding   3.9
6. Hippo Vaughn   3.9
7. Carl Lundgren   3.8
8. Larry French   3.4
9. Grover Alexander   3.2
10. Bob Wicker   3.2

Earned Run Average (minimum 400 innings)

1. Albert Spalding   1.78
2. Mordecai Brown   1.80
3. Jack Pfiester   1.86
4. Orvie Overall   1.92
5. Jake Weimer   2.15
6. Ed Reulbach   2.24
7. Larry Corcoran   2.26
8. Hippo Vaughn   2.33
9. John Clarkson   2.39
10. Bruce Sutter   2.40

SEASON RECORDS

On the lists of single-season leaders, the first and last to do it are in bold.

Games

League Leaders

1885	John Clarkson	70	1929	Guy Bush	50
1887	John Clarkson	60	1958	Don Elston	69
1890	Bill Hutchison	71	1959	Don Elston	65
1891	Bill Hutchison	66	1959	Bill Henry	65
1892	Bill Hutchison	75	1965	Ted Abernathy	84
1911	Mordecai Brown	53	1980	Dick Tidrow	84
1913	Larry Cheney	54	1983	Bill Campbell	82
1914	Larry Cheney	50	1989	Mitch Williams	76
1917	Phil Douglas	51	1990	Paul Assenmacher	74
1927	Charlie Root	48	1998	Rod Beck	81

Multiple League Leaders

Bill Hutchison	3
Larry Cheney	2
John Clarkson	2
Don Elston	2

75-Game Seasons

Ted Abernathy	1965	84	Mitch Williams	1989	76
Dick Tidrow	1980	84	Bob Patterson	1997	76
Bill Campbell	1983	82	**Bill Hutchison**	**1892**	**75**
Rod Beck	**1998**	**81**	Willie Hernandez	1982	75
Bob Patterson	1996	79	Paul Assenmacher	1991	75

Multiple 75-Game Seasons

Bob Patterson 2

Complete Games

League Leaders

1885	John Clarkson	68	1912	Larry Cheney	28
1887	John Clarkson	56	1920	Grover Alexander	33
1890	Bill Hutchison	65	1930	Pat Malone	22
1891	Bill Hutchison	56	1933	Lon Warneke	26
1892	Bill Hutchison	67	1967	Ferguson Jenkins	20
1897	Clark Griffith	38	1970	Ferguson Jenkins	24
1909	Mordecai Brown	32	1971	Ferguson Jenkins	30
1910	Mordecai Brown	27			

Finishing What They Start

Grover Cleveland Alexander (1920) and Jack Taylor (1903) hold the modern club record for complete games in a season with 33. Alexander established the modern club record for innings in the process, with 363.

Multiple League Leaders

Bill Hutchison	3	Mordecai Brown	2
Ferguson Jenkins	3	John Clarkson	2

Innings

League Leaders

1885	John Clarkson	623	1919	Hippo Vaughn	307
1887	John Clarkson	523	1920	Grover Alexander	363
1890	Bill Hutchison	603	1927	Charlie Root	309
1891	Bill Hutchison	561	1971	Ferguson Jenkins	325
1892	Bill Hutchison	627	1991	Greg Maddux	263
1909	Mordecai Brown	343	1992	Greg Maddux	268
1918	Hippo Vaughn	290			

Multiple League Leaders

Bill Hutchison	3	Greg Maddux	2
John Clarkson	2	Hippo Vaughn	2

Strikeouts

League Leaders

1880	Larry Corcoran	268
1885	John Clarkson	308
1887	John Clarkson	237
1892	Bill Hutchison	316
1909	Orvie Overall	205
1918	Hippo Vaughn	148
1919	Hippo Vaughn	141
1920	Grover Alexander	173
1929	Pat Malone	166
1938	Clay Bryant	135
1946	Johnny Schmitz	135
1955	Sam Jones	198
1956	Sam Jones	176
1969	Ferguson Jenkins	273

Multiple League Leaders

John Clarkson	2
Sam Jones	2
Hippo Vaughn	2

200-Strikeout Seasons

Bill Hutchison	1892	316		Bill Hutchison	1891	261
John Clarkson	1886	313		Ferguson Jenkins	1968	260
John Clarkson	1885	308		John Clarkson	1887	237
Bill Hutchison	1890	289		Ferguson Jenkins	1967	236
Ferguson Jenkins	1970	274		**Kerry Wood**	**1998**	**233**
Ferguson Jenkins	1969	273		Tom Hughes	1901	225
Larry Corcoran	1884	272		Larry Corcoran	1883	216
Larry Corcoran	**1880**	**268**		Orvie Overall	1909	205
Ferguson Jenkins	1971	263		Ken Holtzman	1970	202

Multiple 200-Strikeout Seasons

Ferguson Jenkins	5
John Clarkson	3
Larry Corcoran	3
Bill Hutchison	3

Command

Command *is the word they use when a pitcher with great stuff can also control it. The statistical equivalent of this is the ratio of strikeouts to walks. A ratio of 2:1 is good, 3:1 is excellent, and 5:1 is frightening. Here are the five Cubs pitchers who've been that good.*

		BB	SO	SO/BB
Ferguson Jenkins	1971	37	263	7.1
Dennis Eckersley	1985	19	117	6.2
Bruce Sutter	1977	23	129	5.6
Terry Larkin	1878	31	163	5.3
Fred Goldsmith	1880	18	90	5.0

1-2-3-4 Innings for the Good Guys

Four Cubs have managed to strike out four batters in an inning. On May 27, 1956, Jim Davis did it to the Cardinals when Hobie Landrith dropped a third strike on Lindy McDaniel. History repeated itself on July 31, 1974, against the Expos, when Bill Bonham also fanned the opposing pitcher (Mike Torrez) only to have Dick Stelmaszek unable to handle the third strike.

And on October 14, 1908—the only time it's happened in the World Series—Orvie Overall struck out four Tigers in the first inning of the decisive game: Charley O'Leary, Ty Cobb, Claude Rossman, and with the bases loaded, Germany Schaefer.

Wins

League Leaders

1876	Albert Spalding	47		1920	Grover Alexander	27
1881	Larry Corcoran	31		1927	Charlie Root	26
1885	John Clarkson	53		1930	Pat Malone	20
1887	John Clarkson	38		1932	Lon Warneke	22
1890	Bill Hutchison	42		1938	Bill Lee	22
1891	Bill Hutchison	44		1964	Larry Jackson	24
1892	Bill Hutchison	37		1971	Ferguson Jenkins	24
1909	Mordecai Brown	27		1987	Rick Sutcliffe	18
1912	Larry Cheney	26		1992	Greg Maddux	20
1918	Hippo Vaughn	22				

Multiple League Leaders

Bill Hutchison   3
John Clarkson   2

30-Game Winners

John Clarkson	1885	53		Larry Corcoran	1884	35
Albert Spalding	**1876**	**47**		John Clarkson	1886	35
Bill Hutchison	1891	44		Larry Corcoran	1883	34
Larry Corcoran	1880	43		Terry Larkin	1879	31
Bill Hutchison	1890	42		Larry Corcoran	1881	31
John Clarkson	1887	38		Jim McCormick	1886	31
Bill Hutchison	**1892**	**37**				

20-Game Winners (20th century)

1902	Jack Taylor	23		1909	Orvie Overall	20
1903	Jack Taylor	21		1910	Mordecai Brown	25
1903	Jake Weimer	21		1910	King Cole	20
1904	Jake Weimer	20		1911	Mordecai Brown	21
1906	Mordecai Brown	26		1912	Larry Cheney	26
1906	Jack Pfiester	20		1913	Larry Cheney	21
1907	Orvie Overall	23		1914	Hippo Vaughn	21
1907	Mordecai Brown	20		1914	Larry Cheney	20
1908	Mordecai Brown	29		1915	Hippo Vaughn	20
1908	Ed Reulbach	24		1917	Hippo Vaughn	23
1909	Mordecai Brown	27		1918	Hippo Vaughn	22

1919	Hippo Vaughn	21
1920	Grover Alexander	27
1923	Grover Alexander	22
1927	Charlie Root	26
1929	Pat Malone	22
1930	Pat Malone	20
1932	Lon Warneke	22
1933	Guy Bush	20
1934	Lon Warneke	22
1935	Bill Lee	20
1935	Lon Warneke	20
1938	Bill Lee	22
1940	Claude Passeau	20
1945	Hank Wyse	22
1963	Dick Ellsworth	22
1964	Larry Jackson	24
1967	Ferguson Jenkins	20
1968	Ferguson Jenkins	20
1969	Ferguson Jenkins	21
1969	Bill Hands	20
1970	Ferguson Jenkins	22
1971	Ferguson Jenkins	24
1972	Ferguson Jenkins	20
1977	Rick Reuschel	20
1992	Greg Maddux	20

Winning the Hard Way

Four Cubs pitchers have led the league in victories while toiling for a losing team.

Year	Pitcher	W–L	Rest of Staff
1920	Grover Alexander	27–14	48–65
1964	Larry Jackson	24–11	52–75
1987	Rick Sutcliffe	18–10	58–75
1992	Greg Maddux	20–11	58–73

Better with Age

Grover Cleveland Alexander established a National League record when he won 22 games in 1923 at age 36. The record lasted for 59 years until Steve Carlton won 23 at the age of 37 in 1982.

Multiple 20- or 30-Game Winners

Mordecai Brown	6		Grover Alexander	2
Clark Griffith	6		Nixey Callahan	2
Ferguson Jenkins	6		Terry Larkin	2
Larry Corcoran	5		Bill Lee	2
Hippo Vaughn	5		Pat Malone	2
Fred Goldsmith	4		Jim McCormick	2
Larry Cheney	3		Orvie Overall	2
John Clarkson	3		Jack Taylor	2
Bill Hutchison	3		Jake Weimer	2
Lon Warneke	3			

120-Game Winners

Only eight pitchers of the modern era have won 20 games six seasons in a row. Along with Cy Young, Christy Mathewson, Walter Johnson, Lefty Grove, Robin Roberts, and Warren Spahn belong the names Mordecai Brown and Ferguson Jenkins.

Winning Percentage

League Leaders (minimum one inning pitched per scheduled game)

1876	Albert Spalding	47–13	.783
1880	Fred Goldsmith	21–3	.875
1882	Larry Corcoran	27–12	.692
1886	Jocko Flynn	24–6	.800
1906	Ed Reulbach	19–4	.826
1907	Ed Reulbach	17–4	.810
1908	Ed Reulbach	24–7	.774
1910	King Cole	20–4	.833

Third Time's the Charm

Ed Reulbach led the league in winning percentage for three straight years, a feat only Lefty Grove has been able to duplicate since.

1913	Bert Humphries	16–4	.800
1918	Claude Hendrix	19–7	.731
1929	Charlie Root	19–6	.760
1932	Lon Warneke	22–6	.786
1935	Bill Lee	20–6	.769
1938	Bill Lee	22–9	.710
1984	Rick Sutcliffe	16–1	.941
1989	Mike Bielecki	18–7	.720

Multiple League Leaders

Ed Reulbach	3
Bill Lee	2

.750 Seasons (minimum 10 wins)

Rick Sutcliffe	1984	16–1	.941
Fred Goldsmith	1880	21–3	.875
Hank Borowy	1945	11–2	.846
Jim McCormick	1885	20–4	.833
King Cole	1910	20–4	.833
Ed Reulbach	1906	19–4	.826
Mordecai Brown	1906	26–6	.813
Ed Reulbach	1907	17–4	.810
Jocko Flynn	1886	24–6	.800
Bert Humphries	1913	16–4	.800
Orvie Overall	1906	12–3	.800
Jack Taylor	1906	12–3	.800
Lon Warneke	1932	22–6	.786
Albert Spalding	**1876**	**47–13**	**.783**
Ed Reulbach	1908	24–7	.774
Mordecai Brown	1907	20–6	.769
Bill Lee	1935	20–6	.769
John Clarkson	1884	10–3	.769
Jose Bautista	**1993**	**10–3**	**.769**
John Clarkson	1885	53–16	.768
Mordecai Brown	1908	29–9	.763
Charlie Root	1929	19–6	.760
Larry Corcoran	1880	43–14	.754
Mordecai Brown	1909	27–9	.750

Multiple .750 Seasons

Mordecai Brown	4
Ed Reulbach	3
John Clarkson	2

Shutouts

League Leaders

1885	John Clarkson	10		1928	Sheriff Blake	4
1900	Clark Griffith	4		1929	Pat Malone	5
1902	Jack Taylor	8		1930	Charlie Root	4
1906	Mordecai Brown	9		1932	Lon Warneke	4
1907	Orvie Overall	8		1936	Tex Carleton	4
1909	Orvie Overall	9		1936	Bill Lee	4
1910	Mordecai Brown	6		1936	Lon Warneke	4
1918	Lefty Tyler	8		1938	Bill Lee	9
1918	Hippo Vaughn	8		1943	Hi Bithorn	7
1919	Grover Alexander	9		1945	Claude Passeau	5
1921	Grover Alexander	3		1971	Milt Pappas	5

Multiple League Leaders

Grover Alexander	2
Mordecai Brown	2
Bill Lee	2
Orvie Overall	2
Lon Warneke	2

Seven-Shutout Seasons

John Clarkson	1885	10		Mordecai Brown	1909	8
Mordecai Brown	1906	9		Lefty Tyler	1918	8
Mordecai Brown	1908	9		Hippo Vaughn	1918	8
Orvie Overall	1909	9		Larry Corcoran	1884	7
Grover Alexander	1919	9		Carl Lundgren	1907	7
Bill Lee	1938	9		Ed Reulbach	1908	7
Albert Spalding	**1876**	**8**		Grover Alexander	1920	7
Jack Taylor	1902	8		Hi Bithorn	1943	7
Orvie Overall	1907	8		**Ferguson Jenkins**	**1969**	**7**

Multiple Seven-Shutout Seasons

Mordecai Brown	3
Grover Alexander	2
Orvie Overall	2

Earned Run Average

League Leaders (minimum one inning pitched per scheduled game)

1882	Larry Corcoran	1.95	1919	Grover Alexander	1.72
1898	Clark Griffith	1.88	1920	Grover Alexander	1.91
1902	Jack Taylor	1.33	1932	Lon Warneke	2.37
1906	Mordecai Brown	1.04	1938	Bill Lee	2.66
1907	Jack Pfiester	1.15	1945	Ray Prim	2.40
1918	Hippo Vaughn	1.74			

Multiple League Leaders

Grover Alexander	2

ERA-Under-2 Seasons (minimum 100 innings)

Mordecai Brown	1906	1.04	Fred Goldsmith	1880	1.75
Jack Pfiester	1907	1.15	Ed Reulbach	1909	1.78
Carl Lundgren	1907	1.17	Hippo Vaughn	1919	1.79
Mordecai Brown	1909	1.31	Jack Pfiester	1910	1.79
Jack Taylor	1902	1.33	King Cole	1910	1.80
Bruce Sutter	1977	1.35	Jack Taylor	1906	1.83
Mordecai Brown	1907	1.39	John Clarkson	1885	1.85
Orvie Overall	1909	1.42	Mordecai Brown	1910	1.86
Ed Reulbach	1905	1.42	Mordecai Brown	1904	1.86
Mordecai Brown	1908	1.47	Clark Griffith	1898	1.88
Jack Pfiester	1906	1.56	Orvie Overall	1906	1.88
Ed Reulbach	1906	1.65	Grover Alexander	1920	1.91
Rube Kroh	1909	1.65	Jake Weimer	1904	1.91
Lee Smith	1983	1.65	Orvie Overall	1908	1.92
Ed Reulbach	1907	1.69	Larry Corcoran	1880	1.95
Orvie Overall	1907	1.70	Larry Corcoran	1882	1.95
Grover Alexander	1919	1.72	**Chuck McElroy**	**1991**	**1.95**
Hippo Vaughn	1918	1.74	Carl Lundgren	1902	1.97
Albert Spalding	**1876**	**1.75**			

Multiple ERA-Under-2 Seasons

Mordecai Brown	6		Larry Corcoran	2
Orvie Overall	4		Carl Lundgren	2
Ed Reulbach	4		Jack Taylor	2
Jack Pfiester	3		Hippo Vaughn	2
Grover Alexander	2			

BIGGEST MONTHS

Pitchers of the Month

Dick Ellsworth	May 1963	Rick Reuschel	July 1977
Ken Holtzman	May 1969	Dick Tidrow	July 1979
Ferguson Jenkins	July 1971	Rick Reuschel	August 1980
Ray Burris	August 1976	Rick Sutcliffe	August 1984
Bruce Sutter	May 1977	Greg Maddux	June 1988
Rick Reuschel	June 1977	Mike Morgan	May 1992

They didn't give Pitcher of the Month Awards back when Grover Cleveland Alexander played, but he would have been a lock in May 1920. He tied the National League mark set by Christy Mathewson in August 1903 and again in August 1904 by winning nine games in the month. Unlike Mathewson, Alexander went undefeated.

John Clarkson set the major-league record in June 1885 when he went 15–1.

BIGGEST GAMES

No-Hitters

There may be no other major-league team involved in as many wonderful and strange no-hitters. Consider:

Don Cardwell no-hits the Cardinals in his first game with the Cubs after being obtained in a trade with the Phillies. The last out is made when the lead-footed Moose Moryn makes a diving grab of a Joe Cunningham line drive. Cardwell induced ground ball after ground ball, with first-baseman Ed Bouchee (who came over from the Phillies in the same trade) racking up 17 assists and a putout, a record at the time. Touted as their next 20-game winner, Cardwell finished the season 8–14.

Sad Sam Jones—a.k.a. "Toothpick" for what he chewed while on the mound—was the first African American to throw a no-hitter in the major leagues. He was nearly pulled in the ninth inning. With a 4–0 lead, he lost control of his devastating breaking ball and walked the bases loaded—then proceeded to strike out Dick Groat, Roberto Clemente, and Frank Thomas on 12 pitches. Sad Sam is the last of only five pitchers to throw a no-hitter and lose 20 games in the same season.

Ken Holtzman no-hit the Atlanta Braves 3–0 in 1969 in front of 41,000 at Wrigley, perhaps the high point of that ill-fated season. Holtzman did it without the benefit of a single strikeout while throwing to not one but two backup catchers (in his last big-league game, Bill Heath broke his finger in the seventh on a foul tip and was replaced by Gene Oliver). Holtzman did have the benefit of a very stiff wind blowing in, holding up a sure home run by Hank Aaron in the seventh inning. The last out was another shot off the bat of Aaron,

So Close

In recent years, long since Milt Pappas threw the last Cubs no-hitter, a number of pitchers have come excruciatingly close. Jim Bullinger took a no-hitter into the eighth inning against San Francisco only to have it broken up by one of the weakest hitters in baseball, defensive standout Kirt Manwaring. On April 13, 1987, Jamie Moyer set a club record for strikeouts by a lefty with 12 against the Phillies but lost his no-hitter to Juan Samuel in the ninth. In his first start with the Cubs, on April 6, 1993, Jose Guzman went 8⅔ hitless innings before Otis Nixon of the Braves singled. On May 30, 1994, Willie Banks had a no-hitter broken up in the eighth by Kim Batiste of the Phillies. On September 25, 1995, Frank Castillo was one strike away from a no-hitter against the St. Louis Cardinals when Bernard Gilkey tripled. Since then, Steve Trachsel, Kevin Tapani, and Kerry Wood have also thrown one-hitters.

this one a line drive at Glenn Beckert at second base. Holtzman went on to become only the second Cub to throw more than one no-hitter; he notched his second in 1971 in a game in which he scored the only run.

Holtzman's follow-up no-hitter was the first of three in two seasons by three different Cubs pitchers in 1971–72 (a feat matched only by the 1904–05 and 1916–17 Boston Red Sox). Burt Hooton did it in one of his first professional games, under frigid conditions in April 1972. Milt Pappas followed up with a near-perfect game in September. After retiring 26 San Diego Padres in a row, he had a 1–2 count on pinch-hitter Larry Stahl before walking him. Pappas settled down to get the final out.

Bob Wicker threw 9⅓ innings of no-hit ball on June 11, 1904, against the Giants. He ended up pitching 12 innings of one-hit ball for a 1–0 victory as the Cubs snapped yet another winning streak belonging to a New York Giants pitcher—this time "Iron Man" Joe McGinnity at 12. On June 21, 1888, outfielder George Van Haltren pitched seven no-hit innings, but the game was rained out after six full, with the Cubs ahead of the Pirates 2–0.

It's not uncommon to find a rain-shortened no-hitter in the history books. It is uncommon to find any other reason for a truncated no-no. Perhaps the strangest of no-hitters the Cubs have seen took place on July 31, 1910, in the second game of a doubleheader in St. Louis. King Cole had thrown seven innings of no-hit ball when the game was called with the Cubs ahead 4–0. Both teams needed to catch trains.

No-Hitters—An Even Dozen, with Three for the Road

DATE	PITCHER	SCORE	OPPONENT	LOCATION
August 19, 1880	Larry Corcoran	6–0	Boston Beaneaters	Lakefront Park
September 20, 1882	Larry Corcoran	5–0	Worcester Ruby Legs	Lakefront Park
June 27, 1884	Larry Corcoran	6–0	Providence Grays	Lakefront Park
July 27, 1885	John Clarkson	4–0	Providence Grays	Messer Street Grounds
August 21, 1898	Walter Thornton	2–0	Brooklyn Bridegrooms	West Side Grounds
August 31, 1915	Jimmy Lavender	2–0	New York Giants	Polo Grounds
May 12, 1955	Sam Jones	4–0	Pittsburgh Pirates	Wrigley Field
May 15, 1960	Don Cardwell	4–0	St. Louis Cardinals	Wrigley Field
August 19, 1969	Ken Holtzman	3–0	Atlanta Braves	Wrigley Field
June 3, 1971	Ken Holtzman	1–0	Cincinnati Reds	Riverfront Stadium
April 16, 1972	Burt Hooton	1–0	Philadelphia Phillies	Wrigley Field
September 2, 1972	Milt Pappas	8–0	San Diego Padres	Wrigley Field

Pitching Duels

The Cubs have been involved in more than their share of slugfests, but there have been some great pitching duels along the way, too. The most famous is the Hippo Vaughn and Fred Toney double no-hitter.

On May 2, 1917, in front of only about 3,500 people at Weeghman Park in Chicago, Vaughn of the Cubs and Toney (once of the Cubs, then of the Reds) both threw nine-inning no-hitters, each walking only two. Vaughn faced a lineup stacked with righties—a lineup that got one ball out of the infield for the first nine innings, a bloop that Larry Doyle could have caught but that center-fielder Cy Williams took. Williams came into play in the 10th inning. After Larry Kopf hit a clean single into right center, Hal Chase hit what should have been the third out to Williams. Williams dropped it. Chase stole second, putting runners on second and third with a pinch hitter named Jim Thorpe at the plate. The Olympic gold medalist hit a swinging bunt right back to Vaughn. The pitcher could have just tagged Kopf running home, but he didn't see him. Hippo shoveled it toward his catcher, Art Wilson, instead. Wilson froze. The ball hit him in the chest and lay at his feet, and Kopf scored. Wilson eventually came out of his fog to tag Chase as he tried to score all the way from second.

Toney set the Cubs down in the bottom of the 10th for a 1–0 victory. Cubs owner Charlie Weeghman seemed to be taking it harder than anyone, berating his team in the locker room after the bitter defeat.

On August 19, 1965, the Cubs were on the wrong end of the only other 10-inning no-hitter in major-league history—again facing the Reds. Jim Maloney—a wild fireballer and high-school teammate of Cubs pitcher Dick Ellsworth—outdueled Larry Jackson. In a performance worthy of Nuke Laloosh, he struck out 12 and walked 10. Two months before, he'd taken a no-hitter into the 10th against the Mets only to lose in 11 on a home run by Johnny Lewis. This time, it was a teammate, Leo Cardenas, who went deep in extra innings, and Maloney had a 1–0 no-hit victory.

Turns out that 1–0 is a familiar score. Less than three weeks later, on September 9, 1965, in Dodger Stadium, the Cubs went 27 up, 27 down, against Sandy Koufax—the final 6 on strikes. The game saw a combined total of one man left on base, a major-league record. That's because Cubs pitcher Bob Hendley threw a one-hitter and lost—the one hit a soft, seventh-inning double down the line by former Cub Lou Johnson. Being no-hit twice in three weeks isn't even close to a record—the White Sox were blanked on consecutive days in 1917 by the Browns.

Hendley got his revenge five days later, beating Koufax in a rematch, 2–1, tossing a four-hitter and getting a Billy Williams home run with which to work. And a year later, on September 25, 1966, rookie Ken Holtzman—being touted as the next Sandy Koufax—nearly no-hit the first Sandy Koufax. Holtzman took a no-hitter into the ninth inning, settling for a two-hitter and a 2–1 victory at Wrigley Field. It was the only time the two hooked up, and the last time the Cubs faced Koufax.

Of the six no-hitters the Cubs have endured in the 20th century, four were lost 1–0. The first of the four came in an oft-repeated duel between Hall of Famers Christy Mathewson of the New York Giants and Mordecai "Three-Finger" Brown. Brown took a no-hitter of his own into the ninth before yielding two hits and the decisive run. Mathewson, the "Christian Gentleman," was considered the greatest pitcher of his day, but Brown was 12–10 in their 25 matchups. Brown won nine in a row after Mathewson's no-hitter, culminating in a 4–2 win in "sudden death"—the replay of the "Merkle Boner" game at the end of the 1908 season. On September 16, 1909, William Howard Taft became the first president to attend a major-league baseball game, heading out to West Side Grounds to watch Mathewson beat Brown 2–1. So famous were their showdowns that they were dusted off on September 4, 1916, at the end of their careers for one last duel. Mathewson, now with the Reds, won 10–8. Neither pitched in the big leagues again.

The Cubs haven't been no-hit since Koufax in 1965, the longest current streak in the National League and second only to the Yankees (1958). It took two ninth-inning hits off

Are you going to let him score, too?

Hippo Vaughn to a fogbound Art Wilson as Hal Chase tries to score the second unearned run of Vaughn's "no-hitter"

Brown and Mathewson

There is plenty of argument about the greatest pitching season in history, but the greatest consecutive seasons are a lot easier to pinpoint. Appropriately, they belong to Christy Mathewson and Mordecai Brown over the exact same period: 1908 and 1909. They are the only two pitchers in history to hold opposing batters to on-base percentages of less than .240 two years in a row. (In fact, Sandy Koufax is the only other modern pitcher to do it twice at all.)

20th-Century No-Hitters—The Wrong End

DATE	PITCHER	SCORE	OPPONENT	LOCATION
September 18, 1903	Chick Fraser	0–10	Philadelphia Phillies	West Side Grounds
June 13, 1905	Christy Mathewson	0–1	New York Giants	West Side Grounds
May 2, 1917	Fred Toney	0–1 (10)	Cincinnati Reds	Weeghman Park
June 19, 1952	Carl Erskine	0–5	Brooklyn Dodgers	Ebbets Field
August 19, 1965	Jim Maloney	0–1 (10)	Cincinnati Reds	Wrigley Field
September 9, 1965	Sandy Koufax	0–1	Los Angeles Dodgers	Dodger Stadium

Tom Seaver to keep that streak alive. On July 9, 1969, in front of 59,083 at Shea, Jimmy Qualls broke up Seaver's perfect game with a one-out single. On September 24, 1975, Seaver was down to the last strike of a no-hitter when Joe Wallis broke it up with a single.

Strikeouts

Going into 1998, the Cubs' record for strikeouts in a game was 17 by Jack Pfiester on May 30, 1906, against St. Louis, though it took him 15 innings to do it. The nine-inning record was established by Dick Drott on May 26, 1957, when he fanned the powerful Milwaukee Braves 15 times. Phil Wrigley was so impressed that he boosted Drott's salary from $6,000 to $15,000. Drott hung up another 14 strikeouts later in the season against the New York Giants, including Willie Mays twice. The previous record had been 13, set by Lon Warneke in 1934. Another rookie matched his 15 strikeouts 14 years later on September 15, 1971, when Burt Hooton and his knuckle-curve baffled the Mets in a 3–2 Cubs victory.

The 20-year-old Kerry Wood wiped all of them out of the record books on one May afternoon at Wrigley. Going into the game with the heavy-hitting Astros on May 6, 1998, many questioned whether Wood should even be in the majors. The Cubs were 16–15 and hardly appeared to be pennant contenders, while Wood was 2–2 with a 5.89 ERA.

He faced only 29 batters, yielding one scratch hit and hitting another batter, allowing only two balls to reach the outfield, and keeping both Jeff Bagwell and Moises Alou from even making contact. He struck out the side four times, ending up with a major-league-record 20 strikeouts (tying Roger Clemens) and a club-record seven in a row (tying Jamie Moyer).

It wasn't a no-hitter, but it was the most dominating pitching performance in major-league history. Here's what the scorecard looked like:

This is unfair.

Derek Bell to Mark Grace between innings, May 6, 1998

May 6, 1998

	1	2	3	4	5	6	7	8	9
Biggio, 2b	SO		GO			HBP			GO
Bell, cf	SO			FO		PO			SO
Bagwell, 1b	SO			SO			SO		
Howell, 3b		SO		SO			SO		
Alou, lf		SO			SO		SO		
Clark, rf		FO			SO			SO	
Gutierrez, ss			1B BK		SO			SO	
Ausmus, c			SO			GO		SO	
Reynolds, p			SH			SO			
Spiers, ph									SO

Wood fanned 13 in his next outing, surpassing Luis Tiant, Nolan Ryan, and Dwight Gooden and establishing a major-league record for strikeouts in consecutive games. After his next start in May, Wood's three-game pitching line looked like this:

IP	H	R	E	BB	SO
22	8	1	1	4	41

Shutouts

In the early days of the National League, the White Stockings' pitching was so dominant that shutouts were called "Chicagos"—and with Albert Spalding, Larry Corcoran, and John Clarkson pitching for the team, the reasons for that were obvious. Spalding is one of only eight pitchers to throw shutouts in his first two big-league games. The Cubs' star pitcher of the late 19th century, Clark Griffith—credited by some as inventing the screwball—chose not to follow in their footsteps. Believing that shutouts were bad luck, Griffith occasionally allowed the opposing team to score in the late innings to avoid blanking them.

Mordecai Brown recorded 39 shutouts from 1906 to 1910 as he won 20 games each season. Then, in 1911, he became the first National League pitcher of the modern era to win 20 without pitching a shutout. No Cub has done it since.

It's one thing to shut out the opposing team. In 1919, Grover Alexander shut out the league, blanking all seven teams for the third time in his career.

In the low-scoring, deadball era, pitchers occasionally had to work a little bit harder to get a shutout. On July 1, 1912, Jimmy Lavender had to go 12 innings at Pittsburgh until Wildfire Schulte homered off Marty O'Toole to give him the run he needed. On June 19, 1900, Clark Griffith did Lavender one better. He went 14 innings and drove in the winning run himself in a 1–0 victory over Hall of Famer Rube Waddell, then of the Pirates, at West Side Grounds. Appropriately enough, Long Tom Hughes holds the Cubs' record for longest shutout. On September 21, 1901, Hughes held off Boston at West Side Grounds until Cupid Childs finally singled home a run in the bottom of the 17th. Hughes struck out 13 in a game that featured no extra-base hits.

For one day's shutout work, however, no one can touch Ed Reulbach. He has a line all to himself in the major-league record books: most shutouts, day. On September 26, 1908, in the midst of a furious pennant race, Reulbach ran his season record against the Dodgers to 9–0 by shutting them out in both ends of a doubleheader. He beat them 5–0 on five hits, then 3–0 on three hits.

Some Cubs pitchers have given up far more than eight hits in far fewer than 18 innings in registering some sloppy shutouts. On April 30, 1899, Nixey Callahan fired a 12-hit shutout. Later that season, on September 22, Ned Garvin scattered 13 against Boston without allowing a run. Bill Lee matched him on September 17, 1938, against the Phillies at Shibe Park. But the Cubs—and major-league—record is held by Larry Cheney, who threw a 14-hit shutout against the New York Giants on September 14, 1913, at West Side Grounds.

The closest any Cub has come to this in recent years is Rick Reuschel. On June 20, 1974, Big Daddy blanked the Pirates 3–0 despite yielding 12 hits and putting men on base in each inning. Reuschel was involved in another famous shutout on August 21, 1975, a 7–0 whitewash of the Dodgers. He and his even bigger brother Paul were the only brothers in history to combine on a shutout.

Long Distance

Something you don't see too much anymore is the double complete game. Not both pitchers going the distance, but one—if not both—of the pitchers going 18 innings. Back in the deadball era, you were expected to finish what you started, no matter how long that took.

June 22, 1902

Jack Taylor has to go 19 innings to defeat Deacon Phillippe of the Pirates. He scatters 14 hits until Bobby Lowe can win it with a single in the bottom of the 19th.

File Under: Other Things We'll Never See Again

Two items from the Grover Cleveland Alexander file.

The Cubs and White Sox played a City Championship Series at the end of each season from 1903 to 1942 (except for seasons when one or the other had a date in the World Series). On October 7, 1925, in the first game of this essentially meaningless series between the fifth-place Sox and the last-place Cubs, the 38-year-old Grover Alexander pitched 18 innings, scattering 20 hits and stranding 16 runners in a 2–2 game called on account of darkness. That game lasted more than three hours. On September 21, 1919, Alexander beat the Boston Braves 3–0, holding them to five hits and disposing of them in 58 minutes—the shortest nine-inning game in Cubs history.

June 24 and August 24, 1905

Ed Reulbach goes long distance twice, exactly two months apart. In June, he beats ex-Cub Jack Taylor 2–1 in one of the greatest 14-hitters ever pitched. Then he outdoes himself two months later, throwing a 13-hitter in 20 innings to beat the Phillies and Tully Sparks 2–1.

July 17, 1918

The Cubs' record, though, belongs to Lefty Tyler, who goes 21 innings, holding the Phillies to 13 hits. Max Flack's fifth hit off Milt Watson finally wins the game. Tyler wins 19 games that season but is never the same again (see "Foul Territory," Chapter 16, for how desperate he got!).

May 14, 1927

Guy Bush becomes the last Cub to throw 18 innings in one game, winning by the unlikely score of 7–2. He holds the Braves to 11 hits until the Cubs erupt for five runs in the top of the 18th off Charlie Robertson, who lasts *only* 17⅓.

STREAKS

B ill Lee's 13-hit shutout of the Phillies on September 17, 1930, was his fourth in a row, helping him prolong a scoreless-inning streak that was extended to 39 innings on September 26, 1938. Greg Maddux took a run at that streak during the first half of 1988, one of the best half seasons a Cub has ever had. He went 26⅔ innings without giving up a run. He also won nine games in a row as he took a 15–3 mark into the All-Star break and finished the year with a victory over every National League team.

Bill Lee's four consecutive shutouts in 1938 tied Mordecai Brown and Ed Reulbach, who both threw four in a row in 1908. Reulbach's streak peaked during his doubleheader shutout of the Dodgers. Brown's finest moments came on the Fourth of July when he threw his second shutout in three days, and fourth consecutive, 2–0 over the Pirates at Pittsburgh.

Brown had two shutouts in three days, and Reulbach had two in one day. Ken Holtzman threw three in 10 days in 1968. Not bad, but in 1885, John Clarkson threw *three* shutouts in *five* days, on May 21, 22, and 25.

Eight Cubs pitchers have won 12 games in a row in the same season, but only one of them (Rick Sutcliffe) has done it since 1909.

Consecutive Victories (one season)

Pat Luby	1890	17
Jim McCormick	1886	16
Jim McCormick	1885	14
Ed Reulbach	1909	14
Rick Sutcliffe	1984	14
Larry Corcoran	1880	13
John Clarkson	1885	13
Ed Reulbach	1906	12

Pat Luby's 17 wins came in his rookie season in 1890, but not all of them were pretty. On September 5, Luby hit three batters in the sixth inning, four for the game, and issued seven walks. He had a better day at the plate, hitting a home run to help the Cubs beat Cincinnati 12–8 at West Side Park. Luby broke Jim McCormick's Cubs record on October 3, 1890, at West Side Park in a 3–2 victory over the Giants in a game called after seven innings on account of darkness. It remains a major-league record for rookies that no one has come close to breaking.

They weren't all wins or shutouts, but Brakeman Jack Taylor has a streak that no one will ever even approach: he started and completed 187 consecutive games stretching across six seasons and 1,727 innings.

ROOKIES

A rookie winning 20 is a rare event, with only 18 National League pitchers having done it in the 20th century. Four Cubs did it in the span of nine years: Jake Weimer in 1903, Jack Pfiester in 1906, King Cole in 1910, and Larry Cheney in 1912. Cheney's 26 wins are second only to Grover Cleveland Alexander's 28 for Philadelphia in 1911.

Here's a staff of the best rookie pitchers the Cubs have ever had (league-leading totals are in **bold**).

Best Rookie Pitchers

YEAR	ROOKIE	AGE	W	L	G	GS	CG	IP	H	BB	SO	ShO	ERA
1880	Larry Corcoran	20	43	14	63	60	57	536	404	**99**	**268**	4	1.95
1903	Jake Weimer	29	21	9	35	33	27	282	241	104	128	3	2.30
1905	Ed Reulbach	22	18	14	34	29	28	292	208	73	152	5	1.42
1906	Jack Pfiester	28	20	8	31	29	20	242	173	63	153	4	1.56
1910	King Cole	24	20	4	33	29	21	240	174	130	114	4	1.80
1912	Larry Cheney	26	**26**	10	42	37	**28**	303	262	111	140	4	2.85
1928	Pat Malone	25	18	13	42	25	16	251	218	99	155	2	2.84
1957	Dick Drott	21	15	11	38	32	7	229	200	**129**	170	3	3.58
1998	Kerry Wood	21	13	6	26	26	1	167	117	85	233	1	3.40

Rarer still are rookies who can blow batters away. Only 13 major-league pitchers have struck out 200 or more batters in their rookie season. Cubs rookie Long Tom Hughes (1901) was fifth on the list with 225, behind Dwight Gooden, Herb Score, Hideo Nomo, and Grover Cleveland Alexander—until Kerry Wood struck out 233 and took fourth place. Sad Sam Jones didn't strike out 200 in his first season in the majors, but he is one of 12 rookies to lead the league in strikeouts. He did it in 1955, but he was a bit overshadowed by Herb Score's brilliant season for the Cleveland Indians (see the following table). He was hardly a rookie, though; Jones was a 29-year-old veteran of the Negro Leagues.

Quick Learners—The All-Time Greatest Rookie Seasons

If Kerry Wood had been able to pitch in September, he'd have more wins, more strikeouts, and an even stronger claim to the most dominating season any rookie pitcher has ever had. It's rare enough for any pitcher to hold opponents to a batting average under .200 (OBA), but for a rookie to do it is extraordinary. *As for the strikeouts per nine innings, that's not just tops for a rookie but also tops for any starter in history!*

ROOKIE	YEAR	AGE	W–L	ERA	BB	SO	SO/9	OBA	LEAGUE BA
Herb Score	1955	22	16–10	2.85	154	245	9.71	.194	.258
Dwight Gooden	1984	19	17–9	2.60	73	276	11.39	.202	.255
Kerry Wood	**1998**	**21**	**13–6**	**3.40**	**85**	**233**	**12.58**	**.196**	**.262**

STAFFS

1905–10

It was an era of great pitching, perhaps best typified by a doubleheader on September 3, 1905, with the Pirates in which four three-hitters were thrown. The Giants may have had the greatest pitcher in Christy Mathewson, but the Cubs had by far the greatest staff—perhaps the best ever.

Yet, only one member of the staff, Mordecai Brown, is in the Hall of Fame, while the names of pitchers such as Ed Reulbach, Orvie Overall, Jake Weimer, Carl Lundgren, Bob Wicker, and Jack Pfiester remain known only to the most devoted of Cubs fans and the hardest of the hardcore baseball junkies. The staff was so good that Lundgren went 35–13 in 1906 and 1907 and didn't appear in either year's World Series.

In 1906, the Cubs allowed 379 runs, 2.5 per game, the fewest of any team in history. In 1907 and 1909, they established major-league marks with 32 shutouts. In 1906 and 1909, they established National League marks with four one-hitters. They led the league in shutouts each season—171 in only six years—and ERA five times.

Any doubt that this was the greatest pitching rotation in history? The core of the pennant-winning staffs—Brown, Reulbach, and Overall—can all be found in the top 10 in career ERA. You can find Brown's name two ahead of Mathewson's, and Reulbach's and Overall's just below Walter Johnson's. Among pitchers with at least 1,500 innings in the big leagues, Mordecai Brown's career ERA (2.06) is third all-time. He trails only Ed Walsh and Addie Joss. Eliminate his two seasons in the Federal League—considered a major league by the statistical authorities, if no one else—and his 1.80 mark would be the greatest of all time.

1918–19

It's rare enough for a Cubs team to have one dominant left-handed starter. The 1918 Cubs had an embarrassment of riches, with Hippo Vaughn and Lefty Tyler combining for 41 wins (the only time two Cubs lefties have ever combined for 40 wins). Claude Hendrix also won 19 games. Unfortunately, they met the Boston Red Sox and their left-handed ace, Babe Ruth, in a World Series that saw 19 runs scored in six games.

A Pair of Aces

In the 20th century, National League teammates have finished 1–2 in ERA 20 times. The Cubs have done it more times than any other team: 1906 (Brown, Pfiester, Reulbach), 1907 (Pfiester, Lundgren, Brown), 1918 (Vaughn, Tyler), 1919 (Alexander, Vaughn), and 1945 (Prim, Passeau).

Hendrix and Tyler fell apart in 1919, but Grover Alexander returned from the war, Hippo Vaughn won 21 games, and they almost "double-handedly" helped the Cubs lead the league in ERA again.

1929–38

The Cubs won four pennants in 10 years from 1929 to 1938, a period remembered best for Hack Wilson's offensive explosion in 1930. Most of the Cubs teams of this era were built on pitching, and their staff was usually the deepest in the league.

Lon Warneke used a hard curveball, a fastball with good movement, and a change-up to throw back-to-back no-hitters in his first two outings in 1934. Bill Lee had good control and owned the inside part of the plate. Guy Bush had a curveball and a screwball, both courtesy of Grover Alexander's tutelage. Bush was later traded for Larry French, a junk-throwing lefty with a screwball and a taste for practical jokes. Veteran Charlie Root was a hard-throwing sidearmer with a nasty disposition. Pat Malone might have been the best of the bunch if he hadn't closed down the bars with Hack Wilson every night. He started out 0–7 in his first season with the Cubs, then went on to go 18–6.

The Cubs had at least three 14-game winners 9 seasons out of 10.

Pitching Depth

1929	1930	1931	1932	1933
22–10 Malone	20–9 Malone	17–14 Root	22–6 Warneke	20–12 Bush
19–6 Root	18–14 Root	16–8 Bush	19–11 Bush	18–13 Warneke
18–7 Bush	15–10 Bush	16–9 Malone	15–10 Root	15–10 Root
14–13 Blake	11–4 Teachout	15–12 Smith	15–17 Malone	10–14 Malone

1934	1935	1936	1937	1938
22–10 Warneke	20–6 Lee	18–9 French	16–8 Carleton	22–9 Lee
18–10 Bush	20–13 Warneke	18–11 Lee	16–10 French	19–11 Bryant
14–7 Malone	17–10 French	16–13 Warneke	14–15 Lee	10–9 Carleton
13–14 Lee	15–8 Root	14–10 Carleton	13–5 Root	10–19 French

1945

Between 1938 and 1968, the Cubs only once had a staff as deep as those of the 1930s. In 1945, Hank Wyse was 22–10 and capably supported by the 36-year-old Claude Passeau (17–9), 38-year-old Paul Derringer (16–11), 38-year-old lefty Ray Prim (13–8), and midseason acquisition Hank Borowy (11–2). This staff, composed largely of pitchers too old or unfit for active duty in World War II, was the last to lead the league in ERA and the last to pitch the Cubs into the World Series.

1968–72

Leo Durocher's pitching rotations were never the best in the National League, but they were often the hardest worked (leading the league in complete games in both 1970 and 1971). With the emergence of the Big Three of Jenkins, Holtzman, and Hands, the Cubs became and remained contenders. Unfortunately, there was always that problem of the fourth starter. Durocher tried Joe Niekro (14–10) in 1968, then dealt him away in 1969 for Dick Selma (10–8), who was dealt away for an outfielder at the end of the season. In 1970, they brought in Milt Pappas in midseason, only to have Ken Holtzman fall apart in 1971 and demand to be traded. By 1972, the Cubs looked as if they might actually have five solid starters—with rookies Rick Reuschel and Burt Hooton beginning to establish themselves—just in time for Hands to be dealt away, Jenkins to falter, and Pappas to run out of gas. For more of the gory details of the Cubs chasing their own tail, see "The Front Office," Chapter 14.

The Cubs wouldn't truly have a Big Three again until 1989 when Greg Maddux won 19 games, Rick Sutcliffe stayed healthy and won 16, and Mike Bielecki had a career year with 18 wins.

Pitching and Defense

Doing It Themselves

Only a handful of pitchers have ever recorded three putouts in one inning. Three are Cubs: Rick Reuschel on April 25, 1975, Ed Lynch on July 22, 1986, and Mike Harkey on May 23, 1990.

Greg Maddux is the only Cubs pitcher to win a Gold Glove—three of them, to be exact, in 1990, 1991, and 1992. Among all of his other accomplishments, Greg Maddux may be the greatest defensive pitcher of all time as well. He's tied the National League record for putouts in a season (39) three times, twice while pitching for the Cubs (1990 and 1991). He holds the major-league record for putouts in a game with seven, set on April 29, 1990. And he's perennially at the top of the league in putouts, assists, chances, and double plays. Great reflexes, good hands, and befuddled hitters will do that!

Some other Cubs pitchers can lay claim to being among the great fielders. Lee Smith went a major-league-record 546 consecutive games without an error from July 5, 1982, to September 22, 1992. (Of course, it helps when all you have to do is flag down the ball coming back from the catcher after a strikeout.) Claude Passeau accepted a major-league-record 273 consecutive chances without an error from September 21, 1941, through May 20, 1946. During this stretch, he even turned his second unassisted double play, something only Tex Carleton—another Cub—has ever done. And reliever Ted Abernathy pitched in a National League–record 84 games without an error in 1965.

Perhaps the worst-fielding pitcher of all time is also a Cub: Hippo Vaughn. He has the most errors of any pitcher—74—a mark set in only 13 seasons. He led the league in errors five times, a distinction later equaled by Warren Spahn. One of the few errors records that the Hippo doesn't hold belongs to Cubs pitcher Jaime Navarro. Navarro tied a National League record established 98 years before when he committed three errors in the third inning of a game against the Mets on August 18, 1996.

DUBIOUS DISTINCTIONS

The highlight reel is over, and it's time to look at some of the ugly days the Cubs have had on the mound. Here are some of the more extreme cases.

Winning (and Losing) Ugly

The only win of Dave Wright's career came on September 28, 1897, when he held the Pirates to 17 hits and 14 runs in a 15–14 gem called after seven because of darkness. That he was around long enough to benefit from the Cubs' 11-run fifth inning was a tribute to 19th-century attitudes about relief pitching.

In 1887, George Van Haltren, the same man who went on to throw a rain-shortened no-hitter less than a year later, walked a major-league-record 16, hit two batters, and hurled a wild pitch for good measure in a 17–11 loss to Boston at West Side Park.

On August 5, 1975, Bill Bonham gave up a major-league-record seven hits to the first seven men he faced. He left without retiring a batter, and the Phillies greeted his replacement with another base hit.

Larry Corcoran's brother, Mike, didn't exactly swim in the same gene pool. In his only major-league game, on Bastille Day 1884, he threw five wild pitches in a 14–0 loss to Detroit.

On September 13, 1964, Cubs pitchers—aided and abetted by some porous defense—allowed the St. Louis Cardinals to put up crooked numbers on the Wrigley Field scoreboard every inning:

September 13, 1964

St. Louis	2	1	2	2	2	1	3	1	1	15	18	1
Chicago	1	0	0	0	0	1	0	0	0	2	8	7

It was only the second time in the 20th century that a team scored in every inning. The pitching lines:

September 13, 1964

	IP	H	R	E	BB	SO
Ellsworth L	3²/₃	7	7	6	2	2
F. Burdette	¹/₃	0	0	0	0	0
Elston	2	4	3	1	0	1
Slaughter	0	4	3	3	0	0
Flavin	2	2	1	1	0	3
Gregory	1	1	1	0	0	0

All for Naught

Addison Courtney Gumbert put in 20 innings of work on June 30, 1892, only to end up as one-half of a 7–7 tie with the Reds at South Side Park.

Ferguson Jenkins made an unfortunate habit out of losing 1–0 games, dropping 45 in his career. In 1968, he tied a major-league record by losing five 1–0 games in the same season, the final one coming on September 11 to the Mets' Jim McAndrew at Wrigley. He finished the season with nine shutout losses and a record of 20–6 when his team scored at least one run.

Warren Hacker ran into the same difficulties in 1953 when he went 12–19, two losses by 1–0 scores, two by 2–0 scores. So did Larry Jackson 10 years later when he went 14–18, three losses by 1–0, eight by one run. Bob Rush managed a 17–13 record in 1952 despite losing two 1–0 games, two 2–0, and another by 3–0. He took matters into his own hands by throwing three consecutive shutouts of his own at one point.

The Cubs' 1916 staff of Hippo Vaughn, Claude Hendrix, and Jimmy Lavender was victimized by similar nonsupport as the team dropped a major-league-record 10 games by a score of 1–0.

In 1980, the Cubs managed to give up two runs in 32 innings and fail to register a win. They lost 1–0 in 15 to the Giants on July 21, then lost 1–0 in 17 to the Astros on August 23.

Losses

One reason pitchers seem to achieve so many dubious distinctions is that so many pitching statistics are negative. Hits allowed, runs allowed, home runs given up, walks issued. Games lost.

In 1948, Dutch McCall set the Cubs record with 13 consecutive losses in his only big-league season. His efforts fall far short of those of former Cub Anthony Young, who lost 27 games in a row with the New York Mets. Later as a Cub—in a wonderful irony—it was AYo who recorded Chicago's first home victory on May 6, 1994, snapping the Cubs' record 14-game home losing streak.

As Young has proven, losing streaks are not a lost art. Losing 20 games, however, seems to be. No one's done it in the majors since Oakland's Brian Kingman in 1980 (who managed to go 8–20 for a *winning* team, the first pitcher to lose 20 games for a winning team since 1922!).

Larry Jackson won 24 games in 1964, then lost 21 games the next year. This very rare 20/20 has been done only twice in the National League since (by Jerry Koosman 1976–77 and Steve Carlton 1972–73).

Dick Ellsworth pulled the reverse 20/20, losing 20 in 1962 and winning 22 in 1963. Only Randy Jones has done that (1974–75) in the National League since (though Phil Niekro merits an honorable mention for both winning *and* losing 20 in 1979). Ellsworth also managed to counter his one 20-win season with another 20-loss season three years later. Moe Drabowsky practically lost 20 then won 20 *in the same season*. In a Jekyll-and-Hyde performance in his rookie year in 1957, Drabowsky went 2–13 in the first half and 11–2 in the second half.

Larry French didn't establish a club record when he lost 19 in 1938 (the modern club mark for losses belongs to Long Tom Hughes with 23 in 1901), but he did do something no one's done in the 60 years since: lose that many games for a pennant-winner! Don Drysdale (1963) and Ken Holtzman (1974) lost 17 for teams that won the World Series, but both those pitchers had winning records. French was 10–19; only Randy Lerch (4–14 for the 1980 Phillies) and Dennis Martinez (7–16 for the 1983 Orioles) have been able to match that kind of spirit in the face of success. Before French, you'd have to go back to George Mullin, who lost 20 for the 1907 Tigers (but he also won 20!). There were some big losers on 19th-century pennant-winners, but they always had even more wins. No pitcher with a losing record has ever lost as many games for a pennant-winner as Larry French managed to in 1938.

Wild Things

The Cubs had a long history of pitchers with control problems before Mitch Williams came along.

In addition to George Van Haltren's 16-walk performance in 1887, Cubs pitchers were able to combine for a National League–record 17-walk performance on May 30 against New York.

On August 9, 1942, the Cubs combined with the Cincinnati Reds for a National League–record 25 walks in an extra-inning game—the Cubs contributing 15 to the cause in an 18-inning affair. Chicago then worked with the Padres on June 17, 1974, to match that feat in only 13 innings, with the Cubs walking 12.

This kind of teamwork was also evident on April 24, 1957, when the Cubs issued a National League–record nine walks to the Reds in the fifth inning at Crosley Field. Moe Drabowsky walked four, Jack Collum three, and Jim Brosnan two in the 9–5 loss.

There are individual highlights as well. In 1955, not only did Sad Sam Jones throw a no-hitter and lose 20 games, but he also issued a 20th-century National League–record 185 walks in only 242 innings.

Terry Adams hadn't thrown a wild pitch all season when he heaved three in one inning against the Brewers on September 11, 1998—one short of the record shared by Hall of Famers Walter Johnson and Phil Niekro.

The Cubs staffs of the 1950s featured many of the team's wildest pitchers. On the team's top 10 list of most walks per nine innings, Sam Jones, Turk Lown, and Johnny Klippstein take the top four spots and six overall.

Most Walks per Nine Innings (minimum 80 innings)

	YEAR	IP	BB	BB/9
Sam Jones	1955	242	185	6.89
Turk Lown	1951	127	90	6.38
Turk Lown	1956	111	78	6.34
Johnny Klippstein	1954	148	96	5.84
Percy Jones	1927	113	72	5.75
Johnny Klippstein	1953	168	107	5.73
Jim Bullinger	1992	85	54	5.72
Mitch Williams	1989	82	52	5.71
Tim Stoddard	1984	92	57	5.58
Sam Jones	1956	189	115	5.49

Home Runs

Before taking the mound at Wrigley when the wind is blowing out, it's important to stretch those neck muscles—otherwise you're liable to pull something when you do that Linda Blair neck twist to follow the path of one of your pitches.

Ferguson Jenkins came within 16 wins of 300. He also came within 16 home runs of being only the second pitcher to give up 500 home runs in his career (Hall of Famer Robin Roberts gave up 505). Jenkins holds the major-league record for most seasons leading the league in home runs allowed (seven), as well as the National League record (five—1967, 1968, 1971, 1972, and 1973).

But many of the home runs Jenkins gave up came in Cubs victories. Another great Cubs tater-server wasn't so adept at winning games. In 1955, Warren Hacker allowed a Cubs-record 38 home runs in an 11–15 season. He improved to 28 home runs allowed in 1956, but a National League–record 13 were served up to the Brooklyn Dodgers as he went 3–13. In a disappointing but wonderfully appropriate moment on May 21, 1955, Hacker was two outs away from a no-hitter when it was broken up by, of course, a home run. George Crowe took him out of the yard, but Hacker held on to beat the Braves 2–1 in Milwaukee.

Hacker is tied for third on the Cubs all-time home-run list despite pitching only 6½ seasons (and parts of 3 others) with the team. Then again, a key to being a true home-run artist as a pitcher is to be successful enough to last long enough to serve up that many bombs.

Home Runs Allowed

1. Ferguson Jenkins — 271
2. Charlie Root — 183
3. Dick Ellsworth — 156
   Warren Hacker — 156
5. Bob Rush — 153
6. Ken Holtzman — 147
7. Rick Reuschel — 140
8. Steve Trachsel — 136
9. Bill Hands — 132
10. Guy Bush — 122

The Cubs' record for home runs allowed in a game is six, set by Frank Foreman on July 4, 1895. An asterisk needs to be hung on that one, however, since this holiday doubleheader featured the first 20,000+ crowd in Chicago history. These home runs were a function of the overflow crowd seated in the outfield. The Cubs beat the Reds 8–7, and Foreman gave up only five home runs in all of the other games he pitched that season. On August 3, 1967, against the Braves and on July 12, 1996, against the Cardinals, multiple Cubs pitchers gave up seven home runs in a game.

As a staff, few can touch the last-place 1966 Cubs, who allowed 184 home runs in the midst of a pitching era. At the time, the mark was third in the National League to only the 1955 Cardinals (185) and the 1962 Mets (192). The pitchers were paced by Dick Ellsworth (28), Ken Holtzman (27), and Ferguson Jenkins (24)—with the legendary Robin Roberts serving up 8 in 48 innings, the infamous Ernie Broglio 14 in his final 62 big-league innings, and the notorious Bill Faul (see "Foul Territory," Chapter 16) 12 in 51. The 1997 Cubs surpassed this mark when Steve Trachsel gave up home run #185 to Mark McGwire (the famous #62).

Along the way, Cubs pitchers have given up some famous home runs. On April 28, 1956, Paul Minner gave up Frank Robinson's first. Mel Ott, at the age of 18, hit his first home run off Hal Carlson on July 18, 1927. Lindy McDaniel served up Willie Stargell's first on May 8, 1963. Two years later *to the day*, he did the same for Joe Morgan.

The Dodgers hit back-to-back pinch-hit home runs on August 8, 1963, Frank Howard taking Bob Buhl deep, followed by Moose Skowron victimizing Don Elston.

Jocko Menefee served up grand slams to the Boston Braves in consecutive innings on August 12, 1903.

While no Cub has hit four home runs in a game, Cubs pitchers have been victimized by two opposing players. Adonis Terry gave up all four of Ed Delahanty's home runs on July 13, 1896, making him one of only four pitchers to give up four home runs to the same player in the same game.

Mike Schmidt hit four home runs against the Cubs in a wild 18–16 game on April 17, 1976. He hit two off Rick Reuschel, one off Darold Knowles, and the game-winner off Even Bigger Daddy, Paul Reuschel.

But easily the most ignominious gopher-ball performance has to be the three home runs served up to Jim "Abba Dabba" Tobin of the Braves on May 13, 1942. J T Mooty (that was his first name: J) and Hiram Gabriel Bithorn gave up the home runs in a 6–5 loss in Boston. The winning pitcher for the Braves: Jim Tobin.

the bullpen

The bullpen used to be where the ineffective pitchers were kept until they showed enough in mop-up duty to convince their managers they were ready to be starters again. In fact, the first great "closer" in the National League was a starter—Mordecai Brown. His saves record of 13 in 1911 lasted for 20 years, longer than any other in league history. The Cubs didn't get around to developing full-time relief specialists until 1950, when they finally figured out how best to use a 41-year-old knuckleballer named Dutch Leonard.

When the pitch is so fat that the ball hits the bat, that's Zamora.

Opposing players preparing to face Cubs bullpen "ace" Oscar Zamora

Cubs Closers

1950–53	Dutch Leonard	28		1976–80	Bruce Sutter	133
1954–55	Hal Jeffcoat	13		1981	Dick Tidrow	9
1956–57	Turk Lown	25		1982–87	Lee Smith	179
1957–62	Don Elston	58		1988	Rich Gossage	13
1963–64	Lindy McDaniel	37		1989–90	Mitch Williams	52
1965	Ted Abernathy	31		1990–91	Paul Assenmacher	25
1966	Help Wanted!			1991	Dave Smith	17
1967	Chuck Hartenstein	10		1992	Bob Scanlan	14
1968–71	Phil Regan	60		1993–95	Randy Myers	112
1972–73	Jack Aker	29		1996	Turk Wendell	18
1973	Bob Locker	18		1997	Terry Adams	18
1974–75	Oscar Zamora	20		1998	Rod Beck	51
1975	Darold Knowles	15				

Here are just some of the facts, feats, and firsts from the pitching mound:

- The career leaders for relief appearances and saves
- Every Cub who has led the league in saves or recorded at least 20 saves in a season
- A tribute to Mitch Williams's wild 1989 season, and to the unsung hero of that bullpen who went 19 games and more than six weeks without yielding an earned run
- A pitcher who went 18⅓ innings in *relief* for the win
- Two bullpens that should have traded places with the starting rotation
- The Cubs' reliever who was one of the most influential players in baseball history
- The greatest relief outing in baseball history

The call's been made. Stroll, sprint, or take the baseball-shaped golf cart.

CAREER RECORDS

Relief Appearances

1.	Lee Smith	452
2.	Don Elston	434
3.	Willie Hernandez	312
4.	Bruce Sutter	300
5.	Paul Assenmacher	278
6.	Charlie Root	266
7.	Dick Tidrow	263
8.	Phil Regan	245
9.	Terry Adams	224
10.	Turk Lown	211

Saves

1.	Lee Smith	180
2.	Bruce Sutter	133
3.	Randy Myers	112
4.	Phil Regan	60
5.	Mitch Williams	52
6.	Rod Beck	51
7.	Charlie Root	40
8.	Ted Abernathy	39
	Mordecai Brown	39
	Lindy McDaniel	39

SEASON RECORDS—SAVES

League Leaders

1877	Cal McVey	2		1929	Guy Bush	8
1887	Fido Baldwin	1		1963	Lindy McDaniel	22
1887	George Van Haltren	1		1965	Ted Abernathy	31
1890	Bill Hutchison	2		1968	Phil Regan	25
1903	Carl Lundgren	3		1979	Bruce Sutter	37
1908	Mordecai Brown	5		1980	Bruce Sutter	28
1909	Mordecai Brown	7		1983	Lee Smith	29
1910	Mordecai Brown	7		1993	Randy Myers	53
1911	Mordecai Brown	13		1995	Randy Myers	38
1913	Larry Cheney	11		1998	Rod Beck	51
1925	Guy Bush	4				

Multiple League Leaders

Mordecai Brown	4
Guy Bush	2
Randy Myers	2
Bruce Sutter	2

Guilty Until Proven Innocent

The umpires, convinced that he was throwing spitballs, nearly declared war on Cubs closer Phil Regan during the 1968 and 1969 seasons. Dave Davidson practically strip-searched him in Montreal, while Chris Pelekoudas took strikes away from him in a game against the Reds, forcing him to throw extra pitches to Alex Johnson and Pete Rose (with Rose getting a single after being retired on a pitch that moved too much for the umpire's liking). The league office eventually issued an apology to Phil Regan, declaring him a "fine Christian gentleman."

20-Save Seasons

The first and last to achieve this status are in **bold.**

Randy Myers	1993	53		Bruce Sutter	1977	31
Rod Beck	**1998**	**51**		Lee Smith	1986	31
Randy Myers	1995	38		Lee Smith	1983	29
Bruce Sutter	1979	37		Bruce Sutter	1980	28
Lee Smith	1987	36		Bruce Sutter	1978	27
Mitch Williams	1989	36		Phil Regan	1968	25
Lee Smith	1984	33		**Lindy McDaniel**	**1963**	**22**
Lee Smith	1985	33		Randy Myers	1994	21
Ted Abernathy	1965	31				

Multiple 20-Save Seasons

Lee Smith	5
Bruce Sutter	4
Randy Myers	3

BIGGEST GAMES

Long Distance

There weren't many closers before World War II, and certainly none who worked only one inning at a time. Here are some great relief moments from a different time.

June 17, 1915
Zip Zabel pitches the final 18⅓ innings of a 19-inning, 4–3 victory over Brooklyn at West Side Grounds, yielding 15 hits, two runs, and one walk, while striking out six. It's the longest relief outing in major-league history.

May 17, 1927
Bob Osborn pitches 14 innings in relief to beat Bob Smith of the Braves (who goes 22 innings, scattering 15 hits). The Cubs win 4–3 on a Charlie Grimm base hit, three days after Guy Bush pitches 18 innings against the Braves.

August 17, 1932
Bud Tinning goes 12⅔ shutout innings in relief, holding off the Braves until the Cubs can win it 3–2 in 19 innings at Wrigley. Frank Demaree's long fly with the bases loaded ends the game.

Double Duty

July 11, 1918

Not only does Shufflin' Phil Douglas do double duty as a starter and reliever, but he also occasionally does it on the same day. He beats the Boston Braves in the opener of a doubleheader at Wrigley, 4–3, in relief, then earns a complete-game, 3–2 victory in the second half of the bill.

August 28, 1937

Clay Bryant hits a grand slam in the top of the 10th in Boston to give himself the win in relief, 10–6.

May 13, 1962

Barney Schultz picks up relief wins in both ends of a doubleheader at Wrigley, 8–7 and 8–5 over the Phillies. Schultz is working in his eighth and ninth consecutive games.

June 6, 1963

In one of the great one-man shows in Cubs history, Lindy McDaniel extricates himself from a bases-loaded, one-out situation in the top of the 10th against the Giants by picking Willie Mays off second and then retiring Ed Bailey. If that weren't enough, McDaniel hits the game-winning homer in the bottom of the inning.

June 11, 1981

In the last games of the Wrigley regime, on the eve of the players' strike, Dick Tidrow saves both ends of a doubleheader, 2–1 and 7–4, against the Giants at Wrigley. Tidrow also nearly pitches a perfect game in relief in May of 1981, retiring 22 batters in a row over four games.

Mitch

I pitch like my hair is on fire.   —Mitch Williams

If everyone were like him, I wouldn't play. I'd find a safer way to make a living.
—Andy Van Slyke, on Mitch Williams, 1989

Of all the Cubs' relievers brought in to close out games, none managed to be as nerve-rattling about it as Mitch Williams. Here are the top 10 vintage Mitch pitching lines from his 36 heart-pounding saves and four wins in 1989—and remember, these are successful outings:

Date	Mitch	Opponent	Score	IP	H	R	ER	BB	SO	Other
April 4	s #1	Phillies	5–4	1⅔	3	0	0	2	3	Balk
May 5	s #9	Dodgers	4–2	1	0	0	0	2	2	
May 16	s #11	Braves	4–3	2	2	0	0	1	4	
May 30	s #13	Braves	3–2	1⅔	2	0	0	1	3	
June 8	w #1	Mets	5–4	2	2	1	1	0	2	HBP
June 17	s #16	Expos	3–2	1⅓	2	0	0	1	1	
July 25	s #25	Cards	4–2	2	2	1	0	1	0	
August 9	s #29	Expos	3–0	2	3	0	0	1	1	
August 27	w #4	Braves	3–2	2	1	0	0	2	4	
September 18	s #34	Mets	10–6	1⅔	3	2	2	1	2	HBP
Totals				17⅓	20	4	3	12	22	

Only Mitch could give up 20 hits, walk 12, hit two, and balk once in 17 innings yet be charged with only three earned runs while racking up eight saves and two wins.

STREAKS

It wasn't the 39 scoreless innings that Bill Lee threw in the heat of the 1938 pennant race or the 59 scoreless innings that Orel Hershiser threw in 1988, but it was impressive nonetheless. To go along with Jerome Walton's 30-game hitting streak during the 1989 pennant drive, relatively obscure reliever Les Lancaster threw 28⅔ consecutive scoreless innings, with only 17 hits and walking nine. Not bad, considering these were his first innings of that season and, on occasion, he'd be leaving games with men on base and relying on Mitch Williams not to usher them home.

Lancaster's string extended through 19 outings and more than six weeks. The streak began with Lancaster's pitching in blowouts and ended with his getting the ball in save situations. The Cubs were 14–5 in his appearances, 14–3 once they started using him in close games.

Les Lancaster's Scoreless-Innings Streak, 1989

DATE	OPPONENT	SCORE	IP	H	R	E	BB	SO	RESULT
June 24	Expos	0–5	3	2	0	0	1	2	
June 29	Giants	2–12	4⅔	2	0	0	2	2	
July 7	Dodgers	6–4	⅔	0	0	0	0	2	
July 9	Dodgers	11–4	1	0	0	0	0	0	
July 13	Padres	7–3	2⅓	0	0	0	1	2	Save
July 15	Padres	2–3	⅔	1	0	0	0	0	
July 16	Padres	3–4	⅔	1	0	0	0	1	
July 17	Dodgers	6–3	1⅓	0	0	0	0	0	Win
July 20	Giants	4–3	2	2	0	0	0	1	Win
July 22	Giants	5–2	2	2	0	0	0	2	Save
July 24	Cards	3–2	0	1	0	0	0	0	
July 25	Cards	4–2	⅓	0	0	0	2	0	
July 28	Mets	6–5	⅔	1	0	0	0	0	
July 30	Mets	6–4	2⅓	0	0	0	0	1	Win
August 1	Phillies	4–1	2⅓	2	0	0	1	2	
August 3	Phillies	2–0	1⅓	2	0	0	0	1	Save
August 5	Pirates	4–2	⅔	0	0	0	1	0	Save
August 6	Pirates	4–5	2	0	0	0	1	4	
August 8	Expos	4–2	⅔	1	0	0	0	0	Save
Totals			28⅔	17	0	0	9	20	

TEAM EFFORTS

The 1958 Cubs won 72 games despite having only one 10-game winner, while the 1986 Cubs won 70 without a single 10-game winner. The key: relief wins. (See table on page 136.)

The 1986 Cubs' bullpen won 32 games, with a winning percentage of .508, while their starters won only 38, with a winning percentage of .392. That's the difference between 82 and 63 wins over 162 games. The difference between rotation and bullpen was even more dramatic in 1958. The 12-man 1958 Cubs' bullpen won 29 games at a winning percentage of .558,

Bullpen Versus Rotation

1958			1986	
RELIEVERS	**W–L**		**RELIEVERS**	**W–L**
Don Elston	9–8		Lee Smith	9–9
Glen Hobbie	6–1		Guy Hoffman	4–0
Bill Henry	5–4		Ed Lynch	3–1
Marcelino Solis	3–1		Ray Fontenot	3–5
Ed Mayer	2–2		Dave Gumpert	2–0
John Buzhardt	1–0		Scott Sanderson	2–0
Taylor Phillips	1–0		Matt Keough	2–1
Elmer Singleton	1–0		Jay Baller	2–4
Moe Drabowsky	1–1		Frank DiPino	2–4
Hersh Freeman	0–1		George Frazier	2–4
Dave Hillman	0–1		Steve Trout	1–0
Dolan Nichols	0–4		Greg Maddux	0–1
			Ron Davis	0–2
Totals	29–23			32–31
STARTERS			**STARTERS**	
Moe Drabowsky	8–10		Jamie Moyer	7–4
Dick Drott	7–11		Scott Sanderson	7–11
Taylor Phillips	6–10		Dennis Eckersley	6–11
Johnny Briggs	5–5		Rick Sutcliffe	5–14
Glen Hobbie	4–5		Ed Lynch	4–4
Dave Hillman	4–7		Steve Trout	4–7
Bob Anderson	3–3		Guy Hoffman	2–2
Jim Brosnan	3–4		Greg Maddux	2–3
John Buzhardt	2–0		Drew Hall	1–2
Gene Fodge	1–1		Matt Keough	0–1
Dick Ellsworth	0–1			
Marcelino Solis	0–2			
Totals	43–59			38–59

while the 12-man rotation's winning percentage was only .422. That's the difference between 90 wins and 68 wins over a full season. It wasn't simply better pitchers in the bullpen, but also the same pitchers pitching better in the bullpen. The five pitchers who had decisions in both starting and relief were 11–4 as relievers and 14–19 as starters.

SUTTER AND THE SPLITTER

Most of the time, they'd be called balls if the batters would only leave 'em alone.
—*Bruce Sutter, on his split-fingered fastballs*

Not many players have changed the way the game is played. Babe Ruth did it when he started swinging for the fences—aided, in large part, by the banning of the spitball and the livening of the baseball. Jackie Robinson brought aggressive baserunning back to a game that had gotten slow, and Willie Mays took it even further with an unprecedented combination of power and speed. One player who doesn't get enough credit is Bruce Sutter.

First, some historical perspective. The period between 1969 and 1992 saw more significant rules changes than at any other time in the 20th century. It began in 1969, when, as a reaction to the low-scoring 1968 season, the changes made to increase the strike zone in 1963 were undone. More significantly, the pitcher's mound was lowered from 15″ to 10″. Both leagues expanded to 12 teams in 1969. If expansion did indeed dilute pitching, then this combination of changes would have been expected to usher in a hitting bonanza reminiscent of 1893 or 1920. The impact lasted exactly two years.

By 1972, runs per game in the American League were back to 1968's low levels, and home-run production had eroded even further. New stadiums with league-dictated minimum dimensions had something to do with this, too. Parks with short porches such as the Polo Grounds and Ebbets Field had given way to less hitter-friendly places like Shea Stadium, Candlestick Park, and Dodger Stadium—the latter two among the best pitchers' parks in baseball. Artificial turf was now in half of the parks in the National League. Teams such as the St. Louis Cardinals were building their offense around slap hitters with gap power and speed to take advantage of the fast track.

In 1977, the American League expanded to 14 teams, and this seemed to finally dilute pitching in the major leagues. Runs per game and home runs per game jumped in both leagues. In the middle of this suddenly hostile pitching environment, Bruce Sutter didn't just manage to survive, he *thrived*—despite an average fastball. How?

A roving pitching coach in the Cubs' system, Fred Martin, taught Bruce Sutter the splitter after Sutter injured his arm. The pitch was held like a forkball—an off-speed pitch whose invention is credited to Bert Hall of the 1911 Phillies and that was used effectively by Elroy Face, Tiny Bonham, and Lindy McDaniel—only, Sutter threw his forkball *hard*. To the hitter, it looked like a fastball, but it dropped sharply as it approached the plate. Many batters were unable to lay off, swinging and missing at balls that ended up in the dirt. On September 28, 1977, he struck out six consecutive batters, blowing through the ninth inning by fanning the side on nine pitches, nailing down a 3–2 win over the Expos at Wrigley. Sutter was, for all practical purposes, unhittable.

Consider, first, Sutter's ERA, which was well below the National League average every season he spent in Chicago.

Earned Run Average

	1976	1977	1978	1979	1980
Sutter	2.71	1.35	3.18	2.23	2.65
NL	3.51	3.91	3.57	3.73	3.60

Some might argue that relief pitchers' ERAs can be deceiving, so take a look at the batting average against him. It's even more impressive.

Opponents' Batting Average

	1976	1977	1978	1979	1980
Sutter	.209	.183	.220	.186	.242
NL	.255	.262	.254	.261	.259

His peers at the time—Sparky Lyle, Rollie Fingers, Kent Tekulve—were holding opponents to averages in the .220s in their best years. The number of pitchers who've held opponents to a .186 batting average for at least 80 innings couldn't fill a major-league locker room.

The Splitter's Effect in the National League

	1977	1978	1979	1980	1981	1982	1983	1984	1985	1986	1987	1988	1989
ERA	3.91	3.57	3.73	3.60	3.49	3.60	3.63	3.59	3.59	3.72	4.08	3.45	3.49
BA	.262	.254	.261	.259	.255	.258	.255	.255	.252	.253	.261	.248	.246
SO/G	10.8	10.2	10.2	10.1	9.8	10.6	11.0	11.3	11.0	12.0	12.0	11.4	11.7

Those who've done it *twice* are few and far between: Sutter and Nolan Ryan (1972 and 1991, 19 years apart!).

Few can imitate the fastballs of Nolan Ryan or Goose Gossage, who was an overpowering relief pitcher for a longer stretch than Sutter. Breaking balls *can* be imitated, but hitters eventually adjusted to Ron Guidry's slider and Fernando Valenzuela's screwball. They couldn't adjust to a splitter very easily, however, even one that was thrown "only" 90 miles per hour, so Sutter's innovation quickly became imitated (by those whose hands were big enough to hold the ball between their middle and index fingers). As a direct result of the proliferation of Sutter's pitch, the National League's ERA and batting average, having climbed from 3.45 and .248, steadily fell—despite the 1986–87 blips—to basically those same levels in 1989, while strikeouts per game climbed to new heights.

Though it's believed to place more strain on a pitcher's arm, more than 20 years later, Sutter's pitch remains one of the few reliable weapons that diluted pitching has against larger and quicker hitters and strike-zone-squeezing umpires.

MORDECAI BROWN: OCTOBER 8, 1908

When Manager Frank Chance led the Chicago Cubs team into New York the morning of October 8, 1908, to meet the Giants that afternoon to settle a tie for the National League pennant, I had a half dozen "black hand" letters in my coat pocket. "We'll kill you," these letters said, "if you pitch and beat the Giants." —*Mordecai Brown*

Mordecai Brown had started or relieved in 11 of the last 14 games in 1908, and 14 of the last 19, but he wasn't scheduled to start what was essentially the first one-game playoff in baseball history. He had to settle for the greatest relief outing in Cubs history—and, given the bizarre circumstances (see "The Pennants," Chapter 13), possibly in baseball history. He came on in the first with a run in, two on, two out, and the Giants on the verge of busting the game open immediately. Didn't happen, and 8⅓ innings of four-hit ball later, the Cubs had a 4–2 win and a trip to the World Series. Brown, himself, put it best: "I was about as good that day as I ever was in my life."

Cubs 4

CHICAGO	ab	r	h	bi
Sheckard lf	4	0	0	0
Evers 2b	3	1	1	0
Schulte rf	4	1	1	1
Chance 1b	4	0	3	2
Steinfeldt 3b	4	0	1	0
Hofman cf	4	0	0	0
Tinker ss	4	1	1	0
Kling c	3	1	1	1
Pfiester p	0	0	0	0
Brown p	2	0	0	0
Totals	**32**	**4**	**8**	**4**

Giants 2

NEW YORK	ab	r	h	bi
Tenney 1b	2	1	1	1
Herzog 3b	3	0	0	0
Bresnahan c	4	0	1	0
Donlin rf	4	0	1	1
Seymour cf	3	0	0	0
Devlin 3b	4	1	1	0
McCormick lf	4	0	1	0
Bridwell ss	3	0	0	0
Mathewson p	2	0	0	0
Doyle ph	1	0	0	0
Wiltse p	0	0	0	0
Totals	**30**	**2**	**5**	**2**

Chicago	0	0	4	0	0	0	0	0	0	4	8	0
New York	1	0	0	0	0	0	1	0	0	2	5	1

E—Tenney. DP—Chicago 1, New York 1. LOB—Chicago 4, New York 6. 2B—Donlin, Schulte, Chance, Evers. 3B—Tinker.

	IP	H	R	ER	BB	SO
Chicago						
Pfiester	⅔	1	1	1	2	1
Brown W	8⅓	4	1	1	1	1
New York						
Mathewson L	7	7	4	4	1	7
Wiltse	1	1	0	0	0	0

HBP—Pfiester (Tenney).

the base paths

The Cubs are known today for windblown fly balls, 15–12 slugfests, and furious comebacks. Yet, despite the fact that they've averaged a stolen base per game only once in the past 75 years, there have been a lot of baserunning heroics in Chicago. This chapter celebrates the greatest exploits that have taken place on the base paths, with more than a few tips of the cap to some great Cubs leadoff men through the years. Don't blink or you'll miss:

- The Cubs' career stolen-base leaders (since 1898, when the team's greatest base stealer debuted and the stolen base as we now know it first became recorded)
- Every Cub who has led the league in stolen bases, including the club leader at 67, the team's only three-time leader, and the last to lead the league (back in 1939!)
- Every Cub who has stolen 40 bases, including the only man to do it three times (a husky, brawling, player-manager at a traditionally lead-footed position)
- The Cub who stole only two bases in his career, with one a 10th-inning steal of home to win a game
- The juggler and violinist who brought the stolen base back into the team's offensive arsenal after a 40-year absence
- The only Cub to steal second, third, and home in the same inning
- The most audacious base runner in baseball history, celebrated in song and believed to be the inspiration for "Mighty Casey"
- The two Cubs to steal home more than 20 times in their career
- The four Cubs to hit 20 home runs and steal 20 bases in the same season
- The three Cubs to hit 100 home runs and steal 100 bases in their career
- The Cub who was hit by a batted ball twice in the same game, and the Cub who was caught stealing twice in the same *inning*
- An inside-the-park home run in which the owner's sleeping dog and a grown man named Buttercup featured prominently
- The six Cubs to hit inside-the-park grand slams
- The Cub who hit 17 leadoff home runs in only four seasons in Chicago
- Two great Cubs leadoff men who have been unfairly snubbed by Cooperstown

The 360-foot journey back home starts here.

CAREER RECORDS

Stolen Bases (since 1898)

1.	Frank Chance	404	6.	Jimmy Slagle	198
2.	Ryne Sandberg	344	7.	Shawon Dunston	175
3.	Joe Tinker	304	8.	Stan Hack	165
4.	Johnny Evers	291		Sammy Sosa	165
5.	Wildfire Schulte	214	10.	Jimmy Sheckard	163

SEASON RECORDS

Stolen Bases

League Leaders (since 1898)

1903	Frank Chance	67
1905	Billy Maloney	59
1906	Frank Chance	57
1928	Kiki Cuyler	37
1929	Kiki Cuyler	43
1930	Kiki Cuyler	37
1935	Augie Galan	22
1937	Augie Galan	23
1938	Stan Hack	16
1939	Stan Hack	17

Multiple League Leaders

Kiki Cuyler	3
Frank Chance	2
Augie Galan	2
Stan Hack	2

Power & Speed—20 Homers, 20 Steals

Year	Player	HR	SB
1911	Wildfire Schulte	21	23
1982	Bull Durham	22	28
1985	Ryne Sandberg	26	54
1991	Ryne Sandberg	26	22
1993	Sammy Sosa	33	36
1994	Sammy Sosa	25	22
1995	Sammy Sosa	36	34
1997	Sammy Sosa	36	22

Power & Speed—100 Homers, 100 Steals

	HR	SB
Ryne Sandberg	282	341
Shawon Dunston	107	175
Sammy Sosa	244	165

40-SB Seasons

The first and last to do it are in **bold.**

Frank Chance	1903	67		George Grantham	1923	43
Billy Maloney	1905	59		Kiki Cuyler	1929	43
Frank Chance	1906	57		Frank Chance	1904	42
Ryne Sandberg	**1985**	**54**		**Bill Lange**	**1899**	**41**
Johnny Evers	1906	49		Topsy Hartsel	1901	41
Davey Lopes	**1985**	**47**		Joe Tinker	1904	41
Johnny Evers	1907	46		Ivan DeJesus	1978	41
Bob Dernier	1984	45		Jimmy Slagle	1902	40
Ivan DeJesus	1980	44				

Multiple 40-SB Seasons

Frank Chance	3
Ivan DeJesus	2
Johnny Evers	2

PROFILES

Here's an alphabetical rundown on the Cubs' most noteworthy larcenists.

Marty Callaghan

In 1923, Marty Callaghan stole only two bases—but one came in the 10th inning of a game in St. Louis on May 4. He stole home with what proved to be the game-winning run in a 2–1 victory.

Jose Cardenal

A juggler and violinist, Jose Cardenal was also a great base stealer. When he stole 34 bases in 1975, it was the most by a Cubs player since 1930, when Kiki Cuyler led the league with 37.

Frank Chance

Chance was the Cubs' greatest base stealer—and possibly its greatest base runner—despite being one of the game's largest players at the time (6'/190 lbs.; his nickname was "Husk"). He once scored the winning run in a game by singling, stealing second, and scoring on a bunt. On April 28, 1906, he scored the only run of the game against the Reds by stealing home.

Wilbur Good

On April 18, 1915, Wilbur Good stole second, third, and home in the same inning against the Brooklyn Dodgers, the only Cub to ever do it.

King Kelly

Baseball's first superstar, King Kelly is considered the Babe Ruth of the 19th century—doing for baserunning what the Babe did for home runs. Kelly was sold to Boston for the jaw-dropping sum of $10,000 after the 1886 season. He lived hard and died young. On the base paths, he invented the "fadeaway slide" (a.k.a. the "hook slide"). He was also known for cutting the bases—not as in "hitting them at the proper angle," but as in "skipping them completely." Back in the days when one umpire was used, he once scored the winning run by advancing directly from second to home when the game's lone umpire wasn't looking.

Johnny Kling

Kling was a great catcher *and* a great base runner, who stole 23 bases *twice*—the only National League catcher to top 20 steals more than once.

Bill Lange

Even with the misleading stolen-base statistics prior to 1898, it's safe to say that Bill Lange was one of the game's greatest base runners. He led the league in 1897 with 73 after stealing 84 in 1896. In the final two seasons of his career in 1898 and 1899, he swiped 22 and 41 under the stricter scoring rules.

Davey Lopes

The 40 home runs and 40 stolen bases in the same season accomplished by Jose Canseco, Barry Bonds, and Alex Rodriguez is impressive, but let's see if any of them can match Lopes's 40/40. At the age of 40, Lopes stole 47 bases for the Cubs in 1985.

Wildfire Schulte

Wildfire Schulte holds the club record for stealing home, doing it 22 times in his career (Ty Cobb is the all-time leader with 35).

Sammy Sosa

Sammy Sosa was the last Cub to steal four bases in a game, doing it on September 29, 1993, at Dodger Stadium in his late-season drive to become the team's first 30-homer/30-steal man. But perhaps his most exciting steal of second came on August 1, 1992, against the Mets, when he scored from first on a pitchout after Mackey Sasser uncorked a two-base throwing error.

Joe Tinker

On June 28, 1910, Joe Tinker became the first and only Cub to steal home twice in one game. The Cubs beat the Reds 11–1 behind Mordecai Brown at West Side Grounds. On August 7, 1911, Tinker stole home against Christy Mathewson, one of 17 steals of home the Cubs had that season—a National League record.

Heinie Zimmerman

One of the most exciting and erratic players ever to wear a Cubs uniform, Zimmerman stole home almost as frequently as he was tossed from games. On June 5, 1916, he stole home against the Braves in Boston for the only run of the game. But his most exciting moment on the bases was on June 24, 1915, when he hit a two-run pinch-hit double in the bottom of the ninth to tie the Cardinals at 13–13, then stole home to win the game.

Believe It or Not

As the story goes, the White Stockings are tied 2–2 with Detroit in the ninth, back before runners were called out for passing one another on the bases. King Kelly beats out a bunt, and Ned Williamson walks. They engineer a double steal, though Kelly screams in pain and calls time-out. While directing Williamson to pull his "jammed" arm, Kelly whispers a plan to his teammate. Still faking his injury until the pitcher goes into his delivery, Kelly takes off for home. But he stops 10' short of the plate, with his legs spread wide. While the befuddled catcher walks up to him to make the tag, Williamson comes up behind Kelly and dives through his legs and past the catcher with the winning run.

Stealing Home

Wildfire Schulte	*22*
Johnny Evers	*21*
Jimmy Sheckard	*18*
Joe Tinker	*17*
Vic Saier	*14*
Heinie Zimmerman	*13*

Slide, Kelly, Slide

"Slide, Kelly, Slide" was the first song written about a baseball player, and fans sang it to King Kelly whenever he reached base. It was written by John W. Kelly in 1889, when King Kelly was playing for Boston, and made a star of its singer, Maggie Cline. It became one of the first "singles" in 1891.

Slide, Kelly, Slide

I played a game of baseball, I belong to Casey's Nine!
The crowd was feeling jolly, the weather it was fine
When the omnibuses landed that day upon the ground.
The game was quickly started, they sent me to the bat.
I made two strikes. Says Casey, "What are you striking at?"
I made the third, the catcher muffed, and to the ground it fell.
Then I ran like a devil to first base, when the gang began to yell . . .

Slide, Kelly, Slide,
Your running's a disgrace.
Slide, Kelly, Slide,
Stay there, hold your base.
If someone doesn't steal you,
And your batting doesn't fail you,
They'll take you to Australia.
Slide, Kelly, Slide.

'Twas in the second inning, they called me in, I think,
To take the catcher's place, while he went to get a drink.
But something was the matter, sure I couldn't see the ball,
And the second one that came in broke my muzzle, nose and all.
The crowd up in the grandstand, they yelled with all their might.
I ran towards the clubhouse, I thought there was a fight.
'Twas the most unpleasant feeling I ever felt before.
I knew they had me rattled, when the gang began to roar . . .

Slide, Kelly, Slide,
Your running's a disgrace.
Slide, Kelly, Slide,
Stay there, hold your base.
If someone doesn't steal you,
And your batting doesn't fail you,
They'll take you to Australia.
Slide, Kelly, Slide.

They sent me out to center field, I didn't want to go.
The way my nose was swelling up, I must have been a show!
They said on me depended victory or defeat.
If a blind man was to look at us, he'd know we were beat.
Sixty-four to nothing was the score when we got done,
And everybody there but me said they had lots of fun.
The news got home ahead of me, they heard I was knocked out.
The neighbors carried me in the house and then began to shout . . .

Slide, Kelly, Slide,
Your running's a disgrace.
Slide, Kelly, Slide,
Stay there, hold your base.
If someone doesn't steal you,
And your batting doesn't fail you,
They'll take you to Australia.
Slide, Kelly, Slide.

INSIDE-THE-PARK HOME RUNS

Perhaps the most exciting play in baseball is the inside-the-park home run.

May 2, 1876
The first home run in National League history is an inside job, hit by Ross Barnes off Cherokee Fisher.

May 14, 1881
Perhaps the strangest inside-the-park home run is hit by Tommy Burns at Lakefront Park. Burns's hit rolls up onto the clubhouse platform in the outfield, where owner William Hulbert's dog is sleeping. Buttercup Dickerson is afraid to go near it, and Burns circles the bases.

July 13, 1896
The Colts allow four inside-the-park home runs to Big Ed Delahanty in one game, but Chicago wins 9–8 at cavernous West Side Grounds.

August 5, 1901
Topsy Hartsel hits two inside-the-park home runs in the same game, the only Cub to do it other than Hugh Duffy on August 9, 1889.

June 23, 1946
Eddie Waitkus and Marv Rickert go back-to-back and inside-the-park at the Polo Grounds for the first time in major-league history. The Cubs lose 15–10.

Inside-the-Park Leaders

Totals for inside-the-park home runs are unofficial, but it appears that Wildfire Schulte is the club leader with 18, including 4 in 1906. Hugh Duffy had nine in only two seasons in Chicago, including five in 1889. Here are the Cubs who've pulled the most inside jobs.

Wildfire Schulte	18
Jimmy Ryan	12
Hugh Duffy	9
Cap Anson	6
Frank Chance	6
Johnny Evers	6
Bill Lange	6
Billy Williams	5
Ernie Banks	4

Inside-the-Park Grand Slams

Date	Hitter	Opponent	Location
July 15, 1923	Barney Friberg	New York Giants	Polo Grounds
August 9, 1924	Jigger Statz	Boston Braves	Braves Field
August 26, 1929	Norm McMillan	Cincinnati Reds	Wrigley Field
August 24, 1947	Eddie Waitkus	New York Giants	Polo Grounds
May 18, 1951	Jack Cusick	Philadelphia Phillies	Wrigley Field
August 28, 1991	Chico Walker	San Francisco Giants	Candlestick Park

LEADOFF HOMERS

Bobby Bonds created a stir in 1973 when he hit seven leadoff home runs for the San Francisco Giants. The major-league record he broke was set in 1889 by Jimmy Ryan, who hit 6 for the White Stockings and 20 in his career.

Rick Monday hit 17 leadoff home runs in only four seasons with the Cubs, including a club-record 8 in 1976. The 1976 team hit nine, a club record tied by the 1994 team (Tuffy Rhodes hit four, Dunston three, and Sosa two).

Sam Mertes hit only two leadoff home runs in his career, but the two came in back-to-back games (June 8 and 9, 1900, in Boston) for the only time in club history.

On September 27, 1995, Luis Gonzalez and Jose Hernandez hit back-to-back home runs leading off the game—also for the only time in club history.

SNUBBED BY COOPERSTOWN: STAN HACK AND JIMMY RYAN

The Cubs have had some great leadoff hitters, from Brian McRae to Bob Dernier to Rick Monday to Don Kessinger to Lou Brock to Tony Taylor to Frankie Baumholtz. Perhaps the greatest of all were Stan Hack and Jimmy Ryan, who each handled the duties for more than a decade. What they also have in common are snubs from Cooperstown.

Only one player has more than 2,600 hits and a .300 lifetime average without being in the Hall of Fame (Al Oliver). Every player with 2,000 hits and a .320 lifetime average has been inducted. That leaves 29 players with between 2,000 and 2,600 hits and a lifetime average between .300 and .320. Only one was a true power hitter: Johnny Mize, enshrined in 1981. That leaves 28 hitters much like Ryan and Hack. Who's in and who's out and why?

Of the 12 who are in, Joe Cronin, Billy Herman, Joe Sewell, and Arky Vaughan played second base and shortstop. Jim Bottomley and Roger Connor led the league in two Triple Crown categories at least once. Enos Slaughter played on three World Series–winning teams. Earl Averill had the most power of the group (238 home runs) and the highest batting average (.318). Richie Ashburn led the league in batting twice, hits three times, and walks four times, stole 234 bases, and was a great center fielder. This leaves Jim O'Rourke, Lloyd Waner, and George Kell—slap hitters with one batting title and 157 home runs between them.

Most likely to be inducted among the group is Kirby Puckett, whose career was shortened by an eye ailment. He won six Gold Gloves, was the key member of two championship teams, and led the league in hits four times, batting once, and RBIs once. Bill Madlock's four batting titles put him in elite company, and he was a member of the Pirates' 1979 championship team and two other pennant-winners. Perhaps it will be Madlock, not Ron Santo or Hack, who will be the first Cubs third baseman to enter the Hall of Fame; he could get in on the batting titles alone. After that, most of these players will never be enshrined.

The In Crowd

INDUCTION	HALL OF FAMER	H	BA	HR	TITLES	BIG YEARS	Pos.
1945	**Jim O'Rourke**	2,304	.310	51			OF
1956	Joe Cronin	2,285	.302	170			SS
1967	**Lloyd Waner**	2,459	.316	28			OF
1974	Jim Bottomley	2,313	.310	219	2	1926, 1928	1B
1975	Earl Averill	2,020	.318	238			OF
1975	Billy Herman	2,345	.304	47			2B
1976	Roger Connor	2,460	.318	137		1885, 1889	1B
1977	Joe Sewell	2,236	.312	49	2		SS
1983	**George Kell**	2,054	.306	78	1	1949	3B
1985	Enos Slaughter	2,383	.300	169	3	1946	OF
1985	Arky Vaughan	2,103	.318	96		1935	SS
1995	Richie Ashburn	2,574	.308	29		1955, 1958	OF

The Out Crowd

PLAYER	H	BA	HR	TITLES	BIG YEARS	Pos.
George Van Haltren	2,528	.319	69			OF
Jimmy Ryan	**2,500**	**.306**	**118**			**OF**
Stuffy McInnis	2,406	.308	20	2		1B
Jake Daubert	2,326	.303	56	1	1913–14	1B
Kirby Puckett	2,304	.318	207	2	1989	OF
Patsy Donovan	2,266	.304	16			OF
Stan Hack	**2,193**	**.301**	**57**			**3B**
Julio Franco	2,177	.301	141		1991	SS-2B
Don Mattingly	2,153	.307	222		1984–85	1B
Buddy Myer	2,131	.303	38		1935	2B
Harvey Kuenn	2,092	.303	87		1959	OF-SS
Ed McKean	2,079	.304	66			SS
Bobby Veach	2,064	.310	64		1915, 1917–18	OF
Dixie Walker	2,064	.306	105		1944–45	OF
George Burns	2,018	.307	72	1		1B
Bill Madlock	2,008	.305	163	1	1975–76, 1981, 1983	3B

The strongest case for the remaining 14 can be made for Chicago leadoff men Jimmy Ryan and Stan Hack. After all, if Jim O'Rourke and George Kell, why not Ryan and Hack?

Ryan Versus O'Rourke

	H	BB	R	HR	RBI	SB*	BA	SA	FA
Ryan	2,500	803	1,642	118	1,093	408	.306	.443	.910
O'Rourke	2,304	481	1,446	51	830	177	.310	.422	.907

*Though their stolen-base totals are inflated by 19th-century scoring, the numbers are still meaningful relative to each other.

O'Rourke played just about every position, including pitcher and catcher, from 1876 to 1893 but was primarily an outfielder for the New York Giants. Ryan was nearly as versatile and pitched even more games than O'Rourke during a career that lasted from 1885 to 1903. Ryan significantly outproduced O'Rourke at nearly every facet of the game.

Hack never received more than eight votes, while Ryan never received any. For now, Cubs fans will have to content themselves with knowing that they've got two third basemen, a shortstop, and the right fielder on the All-Snub Team.

Hack Versus Kell

	H	BB	R	HR	RBI	SB	BA	SA	FA
Hack	2,193	1,092	1,239	57	642	165	.301	.397	.959
Kell	2,054	620	881	78	870	51	.306	.414	.971

Hack played third base for the Cubs from 1932 to 1947; Kell played third for five teams from 1943 to 1957. Kell had a bit more punch and made fewer errors (though Hack's range was just as good). As the numbers show, Hack's batting eye was better, he accumulated more hits, and he was a base-stealing threat. And Hack played in four World Series, batting .348. If he had a "weakness," it was consistency. He never had a big year, his average never leaving the .280–.320 range from 1934 to 1944.

All-Snub Team

C—*Thurman Munson*
1B—*Tony Perez*
2B—*Buddy Myer*
SS—**Bill Dahlen**
3B—**Ron Santo/
        Stan Hack**
LF—*Tony Oliva*
CF—*Curt Flood*
RF—**Jimmy Ryan**
SP—*Tony Mullane*

home plate

Catchers toil in obscurity, their power and speed sapped by the most physically demanding of positions, while their defensive contributions are often the hardest to detect. Nearly all Cubs backstops have suffered this fate, so some light is cast their way in this chapter.

- The leaders in games caught are listed, along with Gold Glove and fielding-percentage winners and the backstops on the All-Glove Team.
- For all the major statistical categories, the best offensive seasons for catchers are shown—seven belonging to Gabby Hartnett alone. It's a different Cubs catcher who owns the mark for triples, though—one that has stood as a National League record for nearly a century.
- Memorable catchers through the years are profiled, including a bare-handed catcher from the first Chicago dynasty, the first to use signals, a pool shark, one blessed with an "industrial-strength" arm, a young .300 hitter shoved aside for an even younger Gabby Hartnett, a southpaw, and a one-handed catcher who was tough both on the field and in tax court—along with a list of the 47 catchers who tried to fill the job after Gabby Hartnett and before Randy Hundley.
- Gabby Hartnett's career is compared with those of the other Hall of Fame catchers, and his place on the all-time list is established. Hartnett's finest hour—the "homer in the gloamin'" of 1938—is recounted along with a box score.

Spit some tobacco juice on the batter's feet, straighten your mask, and settle in.

RECORDS

Games Caught—Career

1.	Gabby Hartnett	1,756		6.	Silver Flint	668
2.	Jody Davis	961		7.	Malachi Kittridge	567
3.	Johnny Kling	960		8.	Clyde McCullough	525
4.	Randy Hundley	939		9.	Rick Wilkins	432
5.	Jimmy Archer	681		10.	Scott Servais	408

Gold Gloves

1967	Randy Hundley
1986	Jody Davis

All-Glove Catcher

First Team: Gabby Hartnett. He led the league in fielding six times, and his mark of .996 in 1934 and 1937 went unmatched for 30 years and is yet to be topped by a Cub (Randy Hundley in 1967 and Rick Wilkins in 1993 also had .996 seasons).

Second Team: Johnny Kling. He was the secret weapon of the Cubs dynasty of 1906–10 (though in 1909 he held out for the season, and the Cubs finished second). A great handler of pitchers, he also had a terrific arm—posting a club-record 189 assists in 1903, when bunts and stolen bases were the key weapons of opposing offenses.

Honorable Mention: Randy Hundley. He was a workhorse, catching 149 games four seasons in a row and a jaw-dropping, major-league-record 160 in 1968. His lifetime fielding average of .992 is the highest in Cubs history.

Underrated: Bill Killefer. Reindeer Bill came over from Philadelphia in the Grover Cleveland Alexander trade. While Alexander went to Europe for World War I, the veteran Killefer led the Cubs staff to one of the great seasons in its history.

League Leaders—Fielding Percentage

1880	Silver Flint	.932		1930	Gabby Hartnett	.989
1885	Silver Flint	.927		1934	Gabby Hartnett	.996
1887	Tom Daly	.935		1935	Gabby Hartnett	.984
1906	Johnny Kling	.982		1936	Gabby Hartnett	.991
1907	Johnny Kling	.987		1937	Gabby Hartnett	.996
1918	Bill Killefer	.982		1972	Randy Hundley	.995
1928	Gabby Hartnett	.989				

Multiple League Leaders

Gabby Hartnett	6
Silver Flint	2
Johnny Kling	2

Better with Age

Gabby Hartnett set a National League record that no one is yet to equal when he led the league in fielding for four years in a row, from 1934 to 1937. He was 36 during his final season in the streak. Hartnett also established an NL record that he still holds by turning 163 double plays in his career.

Nearly Perfect

Randy Hundley had a fielding percentage of .996 in 1967, good enough to tie a Cubs record but just short of Tim McCarver's league-leading .997. Hundley did establish a major-league record, though, by committing only four errors while catching more than 150 games.

Catcher Season Records (minimum 100 games at position)

Games:	Randy Hundley	1968	160
At Bats:	Randy Hundley	1968	553
Hits:	Gabby Hartnett	1931	172
Doubles:	Gabby Hartnett	1927, 1931, 1935	32
Triples:	Johnny Kling	1903	13
Home Runs:	Gabby Hartnett	1930	37
RBIs:	Gabby Hartnett	1930	122
Runs:	Gabby Hartnett	1930	84
Walks:	Bob O'Farrell	1922	79
Strikeouts:	Randy Hundley	1966	113
Stolen Bases:	Johnny Kling	1902, 1903	12
Batting Average:	Gabby Hartnett	1937	.354
Slugging Average:	Gabby Hartnett	1930	.630

PROFILES

Silver Flint 1879–89

Flint was the bare-handed catcher of the five White Stockings pennant-winners of the 1880s. He broke every joint in all 10 of his fingers. He wasn't much of a hitter, though he did hit .310 in 1881. One of the team's heavy drinkers, Flint died at 36.

King Kelly 1880–86

King Kelly is the only Hall of Famer to play every position on the field, including catcher and pitcher. He shifted primarily between right field and catcher with the White Stockings, including 53 games behind the plate in 1886, when he hit .388 with 155 runs scored. Kelly was the first catcher to use signals, and he taught his pitchers how to signal to the infielders what pitch was being thrown. A notorious competitor, Kelly is also credited with being the first catcher to throw his mask into the path of incoming runners.

Johnny Kling 1900–08, 1910–11

Kling was a pool shark who also happened to be one of the most underrated catchers in baseball history. A terrific fielder, he hit .312 with the 1906 Cubs. He was credited with introducing the snap-throw to the majors, which he'd learned from Buddy Petway, a great Negro League catcher. He wore white gloves when catching Ed Reulbach, because the pitcher's eyesight was so poor that he couldn't see the signals otherwise.

Jimmy Archer 1909–17

The Irish-born Jimmy Archer was a rookie when he took over the catching duties for the holdout Kling. Legend has it that his arm strength came from an industrial accident in which his throwing arm was burned with hot tar. Archer caught for the Cubs until 1916, with his best

Catchers with 30 Homers, 100 RBIs, and .300 BA

YEAR	CATCHER	TEAM	G	HR	RBI	BA
1930	Gabby Hartnett	Cubs	141	37	122	.339
1947	Walker Cooper	Giants	132	35	122	.305
1951	Roy Campanella	Dodgers	140	33	108	.325
1953	Roy Campanella	Dodgers	140	41	142	.312
1993	Mike Piazza	Dodgers	146	35	112	.318
1996	Mike Piazza	Dodgers	146	36	105	.336
1997	Mike Piazza	Dodgers	139	40	124	.362
1998	Mike Piazza	Dodgers/Marlins/Mets	140	32	111	.329

Note: Minimum 100 games as catcher.

season in 1912, when he batted .283. He was the first catcher to set up in the now-familiar crouch behind the plate, rather than to stand, kneel, or hunch.

Bob O'Farrell 1915–25, 1934
O'Farrell came to the Cubs at the age of 18, serving as apprentice to Bill Killefer and others for seven seasons. He earned the starting job in 1922 and 1923; hit .324 and .314 with punch, plate discipline, and even some speed; then was promptly dealt away to make room for Gabby Hartnett. O'Farrell caught for 21 seasons, with one of his best seasons coming with the champion Cardinals of 1926.

Gabby Hartnett 1922–40
Hartnett was signed in 1921 by Worcester of the Eastern League as a favor to his father, who worked on the Worcester-Woonsocket trolley. Later that season, he went 6-for-6 in a 26–2 victory over Albany. He became the Cubs' starting catcher in 1924, hitting .299 with 16 home runs and 67 RBIs in two-thirds of a season. He proved to be a good-luck charm even when things seemed to be working out badly; in 1925, his dropped pop fly in the last game of the season put the Cubs in last place for the first time in their history, but it also gave them first pick in the annual minor-league draft. They came away with Hack Wilson for $5,000.

Hartnett missed almost all of the 1929 season with a sore arm but came back better than ever. In 1930, he hit 37 home runs while catching—a major-league record until Roy Campanella hit 40 for the Brooklyn Dodgers. That season, Hartnett also became the first catcher to hit 30 home runs, knock in 100 runs, and bat .300 in the same season. (Since then, Mike Piazza has made it an annual event—along with the accompanying crunch-time fold of his team—and if not for the strike-infected seasons of 1994–95, he'd have two more entries on what remains a very short list.)

Hartnett went on to win the MVP Award in 1935 when he hit .344 with 91 RBIs. His most famous moment came in 1938 in the heat of the pennant race; his "homer in the gloamin'" is described in detail at the end of the chapter.

Clyde McCullough 1941–43, 1946–48, 1953–56
The closest the Cubs came to replacing Gabby Hartnett prior to Randy Hundley's arrival was Clyde McCullough, who had three tours of duty with the team. McCullough produced more than a few oddities in his career. He was one of the last catchers to play without a chest protector. He is the only player to appear in the World Series without appearing in the regular season—in 1945, when he returned from the war. McCullough wasn't much of a power hitter, but he did hit three consecutive home runs in one game. Unfortunately, they accounted for all of the Cubs' runs in a 4–3 loss to the Phillies. Blessed with a strong throw-

Who's that gabby fellow I can hear no matter where I go on the island?

Chicago sportswriter, about Charles Leo Hartnett at spring training 1922 at Catalina Island

You gotta have a catcher or you're gonna have a lot of passed balls.

Mets manager Casey Stengel explaining the critical importance of their first selection in the Expansion Draft, ex-Cub catcher Hobie Landrith

Between Hartnett and Hundley

1941, 1943	Al Todd
1941–43, 1946–48, 1953–56	Clyde McCullough
1941–42, 1946–50	Bob Scheffing
1941	Greek George
1942, 1944	Jimmie Foxx
1942–43	Chico Hernandez
1942, 1944–45	Paul Gillespie
1942	Marv Felderman
1943, 1945–47	Mickey Livingston
1943–44	Billy Holm
1943–44	Mickey Kreitner
1944, 1946–47	Dewey Williams
1944	Roy Easterwood
1944	Joe Stephenson
1945	Len Rice
1946	Ted Pawelek
1948–51	Rube Walker
1949–51	Mickey Owen
1949, 1951	Smoky Burgess
1949	Rube Novotney
1950–52, 1955–56	Harry Chiti
1950–51, 1953	Carl Sawatski
1951–52	Bruce Edwards
1952–53	Toby Atwell
1952	Johnny Pramesa
1953–54	Joe Garagiola
1954–57	Jim Fanning
1954–55	Walker Cooper
1954–56, 1958, 1960, 1962	El Tappe
1956	Hobie Landrith
1957–60	Cal Neeman
1957	Gordon Massa
1957	Charlie Silvera
1958	Dale Long
1958–62	Sammy Taylor
1958, 1960–62	Moe Thacker
1959–60	Earl Averill
1960	Jim Hegan
1960	Del Rice
1960–65	Dick Bertell
1961–63	Facundo Barragan
1963–64	Merritt Ranew
1963–64	Jimmie Schaffer
1964–65	Leo Burke
1964–65	Vic Roznovsky
1965	Ed Bailey
1965	Chris Krug

ing arm, McCullough liked to show it off when throwing down to second on the pitcher's eighth warm-up toss—so, second-baseman Don Johnson got under his skin a bit one day by catching one of his rifle shots bare-handed.

Dale Long 1958

For 1⅔ innings on August 20 and September 11 in 1958, Dale Long became the first left-handed catcher since 1906—and no one else has done it since. With Moe Thacker in the hospital, Sammy Taylor pinch-hit for, and Cal Neeman ejected, Long and his first-baseman's mitt ended up behind the plate for the first time in a 4–2 loss to the Pirates at Wrigley Field.

Randy Hundley 1966–73, 1976–77

When Hundley retired, he took with him a .990 lifetime fielding average that was one of the highest in baseball history at the time. He was the first one-handed catcher, and he paid his father half of his signing bonus for teaching him how to do it. Hundley even wrote it off as a "business expense" and beat the IRS in tax court.

Jody Davis 1981–88

The Cubs were the third organization for Jody Davis before he ever made it to the majors, but he found a home in Chicago. He took over the starting role in 1982, had his best season in 1983 (24 home runs and .271), and knocked in 94 runs for the 1984 pennant-winners. He became a fan favorite at Wrigley in June 1984 when he hit three home runs and knocked in 10 runs in a crucial series with the Cardinals from June 22 to 24. The Cubs swept St. Louis, 9–3, 12–11, and 5–0.

Rick Wilkins 1991–95

One of the hottest-burning flashes in the pan the Cubs have ever experienced, Rick Wilkins hit .303 with 30 home runs in 1993. He wanted "Piazza money," the Cubs opted to wait and see, and he slumped to .227 in 1994 and .191 in 1995 before being traded to Houston for Scott Servais.

HARTNETT VERSUS THE HALL

Gabby Hartnett is one of what will soon be 12 catchers in the Hall of Fame. He stands out both in terms of seasons played as well as in his ability to hit for both average and power. Only Roy Campanella can better Hartnett's combination of hitting safely and hitting with punch.

Though it seems as if the Cubs have been forever trying to find a replacement for Hartnett, his shoes were very large to fill. Taking into account his superior defensive play and longevity, Hartnett is arguably the third-greatest catcher to ever play the game, behind only Johnny Bench and Yogi Berra.

Hall of Fame Catchers

HALL OF FAMER	YEARS	H	HR	R	RBI	BA	SA	SB
Johnny Bench	17	2,048	389	1,091	1,376	.267	.476	68
Yogi Berra	19	2,150	358	1,175	1,430	.285	.482	30
Roger Bresnahan	17	1,253	26	683	530	.280	.379	212
Roy Campanella	10	1,161	242	627	856	.276	.500	25
Mickey Cochrane	13	1,652	119	1,041	832	.320	.478	64
Bill Dickey	17	1,969	202	930	1,209	.313	.486	36
Buck Ewing	18	1,625	70	1,129	738	.303	.455	
Rick Ferrell	18	1,692	28	687	734	.281	.363	29
Carlton Fisk*	24	2,356	376	1,276	1,330	.269	.457	128
Gabby Hartnett	**20**	**1,912**	**236**	**867**	**1,179**	**.297**	**.489**	**28**
Ernie Lombardi	17	1,792	190	601	990	.306	.460	8
Ray Schalk	18	1,345	12	579	594	.253	.316	176
Hartnett's Ranking	**2nd**	**5th**	**5th**	**7th**	**5th**	**5th**	**2nd**	**9th**

*Soon to be inducted

SEPTEMBER 28, 1938

It's an overcast day in Chicago, and more than 34,000 are on hand for the game. The Cubs, having won 8 in a row and 18 of 21, now trail the first-place Pirates by a half game and are facing them at Wrigley in the second of a three-game series—with sore-armed Dizzy Dean pitching the Cubs to victory in the first game, 2–1, in a near-miraculous performance.

Today Clay Bryant, who is pitching his third game in seven days, walks the first three batters, then pitches out of it without letting a run score. The game is tied 3–3 in the top of the eighth, with Vance Page, the Cubs' third pitcher, on the mound. He walks Arky Vaughan and gives up a single to Gus Suhr, which prompts player-manager Gabby Hartnett to call on

False Alarms

More than any other position, catcher has provided false alarms for the Cubs and their fans. Some examples:
- *Paul Gillespie. Hit a home run in his first major-league at bat in 1942 and only five more in an 89-game career.*
- *Merritt Ranew. Hit .338 with 17 pinch hits for the 1963 Cubs, then proceeded to go 3-for-33 in 1964 and was traded to Milwaukee.*
- *Harry Chiti. A bonus baby, Chiti was in the big leagues at 17 and was 13-for-37 before turning 19. He didn't have the starting job until he turned 22, and he held it for only one season.*
- *Facundo Barragan. Hit a home run in his first at bat in 1961 and never hit another. At that time, he was only the third National League player to pull that off (the others: Ed Morgan of the '36 Cardinals and former Negro League pitcher Dan Bankhead, who briefly joined Jackie Robinson on the '47 Dodgers).*
- *Dick Bertell. Hit .302 in 1962, which helped him earn the starting job in 1963. He had five hits on May 24, 1963, in a 6–5 extra-inning loss to the Colt .45s at Wrigley. He finished the season at .233; by 1965 he'd been traded to the Giants in a deal that brought over . . .*
- *. . . Ed Bailey. Only nine Cubs have ever knocked in eight runs in one game. Three of them are catchers. The pride of Strawberry Plains, Tennessee, Bailey did it in a 66-game trial during 1965 in which he knocked in a total of only 23 runs.*
- *George Mitterwald and Barry Foote. Also knocked in eight runs in a game, nearly six years apart to the day. Both hit three home runs in the process and finished their seasons with 28 RBIs (Mitterwald hit four other home runs that season, Foote only three). Foote hit a grand slam during his outburst, his third within 12 months.*

one of his regular starters, Larry French, to relieve Page. Pinch-hitter Heinie Manush singles in Vaughan to put the Pirates up 4–3. Now Hartnett calls on another member of his rotation, Bill Lee, for his third appearance in three days. Lee doesn't fare much better, yielding a single to Jeep Handley that puts the Pirates up 5–3. That's all the Pirates manage, though, as Lee retires Al Todd and coaxes pitcher Bob Klinger—whom manager Pie Traynor has elected not to pinch-hit for—to hit into an inning-ending double play.

Traynor pulls Klinger in the bottom of the eighth after Ripper Collins singles to lead off the inning. Bill Swift comes in and walks Billy Jurges. Tony Lazzeri pinch-hits for Bill Lee and bunts through a pitch while Collins steals third. Swinging away now, the veteran Lazzeri doubles home Collins. Stan Hack is intentionally walked to load the bases, and Billy Herman singles home Jurges with the tying run. But the Cubs can do no better than tie the score, as pinch-runner Joe Marty is thrown out at the plate by right-fielder Paul Waner. Mace Brown comes in to face Frank Demaree, and he, too, bails himself out with a double-play ball.

It's 5:30, and the umpires meet to discuss the darkening conditions. They agree to play one more inning. Back in 1938, suspended games were not resumed. A tie would be played all over again as part of a doubleheader the next day. The more-rested Pirates staff would have a distinct advantage if that happens. And it looks as if that is exactly what will happen. After Charlie Root retires the Pirates in the ninth, Mace Brown quickly gets two outs in the bottom of the inning; Phil Cavarretta puts a scare into the Pirates with a fly to deep center, but then Carl Reynolds hits an easy grounder for the second out. The 37-year-old Gabby Hartnett comes to the plate and is quickly behind in the count 0-and-2. Then, instead of wasting a pitch, Brown throws a curveball over the plate. Only two people know it's gone the instant he hits it—Hartnett and Brown, who walks off the mound as soon as Hartnett makes contact. It lands in the left-field bleachers, barely clearing the fence.

The Cubs are in first for the first time since June 8 and go on to capture their fourth pennant in 10 years.

Well—I swung once—and missed; I swung again and got a piece of it, but that was all. A foul and strike two. I had one more chance. Mace Brown wound up and let fly; I swung with everything I had, and then I got that feeling I was talking about—the kind of feeling you get when the blood rushes out of your head and you get dizzy. A lot of people have told me they didn't know the ball was in the bleachers. Well, I did— maybe I was the only one in the park who did. I knew it the minute I hit it. When I got to second base, I couldn't see third for the players and fans there. I don't think I walked a step to the plate— I was carried in.

Gabby Hartnett

Pirates 5

PITTSBURGH	ab	r	h	bi
L. Waner cf	4	0	2	0
P. Waner rf	5	0	2	0
Rizzo lf	4	1	1	1
Vaughan ss	2	2	1	0
Suhr 1b	3	2	1	0
Young 2b	2	0	0	0
Thevenow 2b	0	0	0	0
Handley 3b	4	0	2	3
Todd c	4	0	0	0
Klinger p	4	0	0	0
Swift p	0	0	0	0
Brown p	0	0	0	0
Manush ph	1	0	1	1
Totals	**33**	**5**	**10**	**5**

Cubs 6

CHICAGO	ab	r	h	bi
Hack 3b	3	0	0	1
Herman 2b	5	0	3	1
Demaree lf	5	0	0	0
Cavarretta rf	5	0	0	0
Reynolds cf	5	0	1	0
Hartnett c	4	2	2	1
Collins 1b	4	3	3	1
Jurges ss	3	1	1	0
Bryant p	2	0	1	0
Russell p	0	0	0	0
Page p	0	0	0	0
French p	0	0	0	0
Lee p	0	0	0	0
Root p	0	0	0	0
O'Dea ph	1	0	0	0
Lazzeri ph	1	0	1	1
Marty pr	0	0	0	0
Totals	**38**	**6**	**12**	**5**

											R	H	E
Pittsburgh	0	0	0	0	0	3	0	2	0		5	10	4
Chicago	0	1	0	0	0	2	0	2	1		6	12	0

E—P. Waner, Vaughan, Handley, Todd. DP—Pittsburgh 1, Chicago 3. LOB—Pittsburgh 7, Chicago 10. 2B—L. Waner, Hartnett, Collins, Lazzeri. HR—Rizzo, Hartnett.

	IP	H	R	BB	SO
Pittsburgh					
Klinger	7	8	3	2	6
Swift	⅓	3	2	2	0
Brown L	1⅓	1	1	0	0
Chicago					
Bryant	5⅔	4	3	5	1
Russell	⅓	0	0	0	0
Page	1	3	2	1	1
French	0	1	0	0	0
Lee	1	1	0	0	0
Root W	1	1	0	0	0

WP—Lee. PB—Todd. T—2:37. A—34,465.

the infield

The Cubs have had a tradition of outstanding infielders through the years. Their fielding and hitting achievements from first to second to short to third will follow. Some detours on this trip around the infield include:

- Chicago's first-base jinx?
- The Mendoza Line middle infield of 1981
- Where Ryne Sandberg ranks among the greatest second basemen who ever played and perhaps his finest hour: June 23, 1984, in a pennant race, on national TV, against one of the game's greatest relief pitchers
- The Cubs' two Quintuple Crown winners: leading all at their position in home runs, RBIs, batting average, assists, and fielding average
- The one and only Roy Smalley Sr., who accomplished something no other player has ever seriously threatened to duplicate
- The immortal Ernie Banks and the all-too-mortal Charlie Hollocher
- The Shawon-o-Meter in 1989
- Why Ron Santo should have been in the Hall of Fame years ago

First stop, first base.

FIRST BASE

Games Played

1. Cap Anson	2,058
2. Mark Grace	1,591
3. Charlie Grimm	1,321
4. Ernie Banks	1,259
5. Phil Cavarretta	1,207
6. Frank Chance	989
7. Bill Buckner	855
8. Vic Saier	786
9. Dee Fondy	765
10. Bull Durham	575

Gold Gloves

1992	Mark Grace
1993	Mark Grace
1995	Mark Grace
1996	Mark Grace

All-Glove First Base

First Team: Mark Grace. Grace has four Gold Gloves to his credit and a lifetime fielding percentage of .995 (good for all-time top 10 status), including a club-record .998 campaign in 1992 in which he made only four errors while leading the league in putouts and assists.

The Stonewall Infield

In addition to their long line of great infielders, the Cubs have had a few outstanding infields as well. Perhaps the best ever was the Stonewall Infield of Cap Anson, Fred Pfeffer, Tom Burns, and Ned Williamson, which the White Stockings were able to keep together from 1883 to 1889. That's a mark that lasted until the Garvey-Lopes-Russell-Cey Dodgers of the '70s, and it remains the most stable the Cubs have ever had (though Burns and Williamson did switch positions in 1887, with Williamson moving to short and Burns to third). The Stonewall Infield was a unit known for its heady play—including the particularly shrewd tactic of getting the opposing pitcher in a rundown and keeping him in it until he was sufficiently tired out. Since the 1880s, the Cubs have managed to put together the same infield for two years in a row only 10 times.

Infield Stability

Years	1st Base	2nd Base	Short	3rd Base
1902–03	Frank Chance	Johnny Evers	Joe Tinker	Doc Casey
1906–08	Frank Chance	Johnny Evers	Joe Tinker	Harry Steinfeldt
1935–36	Phil Cavarretta	Billy Herman	Billy Jurges	Stan Hack
1937–38	Ripper Collins	Billy Herman	Billy Jurges	Stan Hack
1954–55	Dee Fondy	Gene Baker	Ernie Banks	Randy Jackson
1958–59	Dale Long	Tony Taylor	Ernie Banks	Alvin Dark
1962–63	Ernie Banks	Ken Hubbs	Andre Rodgers	Ron Santo
1965–69	Ernie Banks	Glenn Beckert	Don Kessinger	Ron Santo
1977–78	Bill Buckner	Manny Trillo	Ivan DeJesus	Steve Ontiveros
1985–86	Bull Durham	Ryne Sandberg	Shawon Dunston	Ron Cey

Note: Minimum 100 games for each member.

Tinker, Evers, Chance, and . . .

On September 15, 1902, the famous three turned their first double play, in front of a crowd of 260 at West Side Grounds. The Cubs beat the Reds 6–3. They played together until 1910, with Evers missing most of 1911 with a nervous breakdown, and a battered Chance coming to bat only five times in 1912. Ten Cubs manned third base during the days of Tinker, Evers, and Chance.

Harry Steinfeldt	729 games
Doc Casey	388 games
Heinie Zimmerman	23 games
Solly Hofman	20 games
John Kane	7 games
Otto Williams	7 games
Tommy Raub	4 games
George Moriarty	3 games
Bobby Lowe	1 game
Broadway Aleck Smith	1 game

Those ground balls ain't much different, and now I've got a bigger glove.

Ernie Banks, on moving to first base

Second Team: Charlie Grimm. Grimm was a slick fielder who would have won at least four Gold Gloves while a member of the Cubs and possibly double that number. He played more games at first base than any other National Leaguer of the modern era.

Honorable Mention: Cap Anson. He had the surest hands in the league six times and was one of the smartest players of his time. Anson led the league in fielding at age 27 and at 42, the longest stretch of any Cubs player (Ernie Banks did it at 24 and 38 at two different positions).

Underrated: Ernie Banks. Upon switching to first from shortstop, Banks became the model of consistency. In 1969, he led the league in fielding average (breaking a 31-year drought for Cubs first basemen), something no Cub first baseman—not even Mark Grace—has done since. When he retired, his fielding percentage of .994 was among the 10 highest of all time.

League Leaders—Fielding Percentage

1879	Cap Anson	.975	1928	Charlie Grimm	.993
1880	Cap Anson	.977	1930	Charlie Grimm	.995
1881	Cap Anson	.975	1931	Charlie Grimm	.993
1888	Cap Anson	.986	1933	Charlie Grimm	.996
1889	Cap Anson	.982	1938	Ripper Collins	.996
1894	Cap Anson	.990	1969	Ernie Banks	.997
1907	Frank Chance	.992			

Multiple League Leaders—Fielding Percentage

Cap Anson	6
Charlie Grimm	4

From what I've seen of you, the way you hustle and the way you give it your best . . . don't change.

Lou Gehrig to Phil Cavarretta during the 1938 World Series

Fielding Records

Cap Anson led the league in fielding percentage more than a few times, but he also set records for most errors in a season (58 in 108 games in 1884) and for most seasons leading the league in errors (five).

On May 9, 1963, with Dick Ellsworth two-hitting the Pirates 3–1 at Wrigley, Ernie Banks was kept busy at first base. He recorded a major-league-record 22 putouts.

Twenty-six years before, on June 29, 1937, Ripper Collins managed to go an entire game at first without a single putout. He'd also done this two years before while with the Cardinals, but this time he managed to go the entire game without an assist, either. The Cubs won 11–9 in St. Louis on 12 fly balls, eight strikeouts, two 4-6 force plays, and five other infield putouts.

Mark Grace has the National League record for assists in a season, with 180 in 1990, and he tied a major-league record with three in one inning on May 23 of that year. He fed three balls to pitcher Mike Harkey for all three outs. At the time, he was only the third National League first baseman to record three assists in an inning; the other two were also Cubs, Andre Thornton (August 22, 1975) and Leon Durham (July 22, 1986).

And on October 6, 1901, pitcher/outfielder/third baseman/second baseman/first baseman Jocko Menefee recorded four errors in one game, the first player of the modern era to do it.

First-Base Season Records (minimum 100 games at position)

Games:	Ernie Banks	1965	162
At Bats:	Bill Buckner	1982	657
Hits:	Bill Buckner	1982	201
Doubles:	Mark Grace	1995	51
Triples:	Vic Saier	1913	21
Home Runs:	Ernie Banks	1962	37
RBIs:	Cap Anson	1886	147
Runs:	Cap Anson	1886	117
Walks:	Cap Anson	1890	113
Strikeouts:	Dee Fondy	1953	106
Stolen Bases:	Frank Chance	1903	67
Batting Average:	Cap Anson	1886	.371
Slugging Average:	Ray Grimes	1922	.572

If at First You Don't Succeed

One position the Cubs have been able to fill consistently with talented players is first base. Yet, first base in Chicago, it seems, carries with it a curse.

Cap Anson was the biggest superstar of the 19th century but was forced out as both manager and player after the 1897 season in a power struggle. Frank Chance suffered from severe headaches and deafness as a result of all the beanings he endured and was fired from his managerial post while in the hospital recovering from brain surgery.

The unluckiest man on the face of the earth, Fred Merkle, ended up with the Cubs in 1918—just in time to lose his fifth World Series in five attempts. His bad luck perhaps replenished, he coached for the Yankees in 1926 and participated in another losing Series. As manager of Reading in the Eastern League in 1927, he presided over a 32-game losing streak in his first months on the job.

Heinie Zimmerman may have been touched by the virus, too, and he spent only 34 games at the position. Everyone knows about poor Bill Buckner's sorry fate in Game Six of the 1986 World Series, but Zimmerman also left Chicago and landed in the middle of a legendary Game Six fielding mishap. With Eddie Collins of the Chicago White Sox caught in a rundown between third and home in the 1917 World Series, Zimmerman of the Giants chased him all the way across the plate with the winning run in Game Six, bellowing, "Get out of the way. I'll get this monkey myself." Zimmerman was later banned for life after the 1919 season for trying to fix games.

First-baseman Eddie Waitkus, by then a Phillie, returned to Chicago to be shot in the chest by an obsessed groupie in the Edgewater Beach Hotel. The nearly indestructible Billy Williams spiked himself trying to play first base in 1974 and ended up on the disabled list.

In the Cubs' two NLCS appearances, each series revolved around first base. In 1984, the first baseman Dallas Green had aggressively tried to sign—the nauseating Steve Garvey—hit a game-winning home run in Game Four, knocked in seven runs, and batted .400. Meanwhile, the Cubs' first baseman, Bull Durham, let a ball go through his legs two years before Buckner to cost them the series. In 1989, while Mark Grace was hitting .647, the Giants' first baseman Will Clark—an obnoxious individual nearly as annoying as Garvey—hit .650, including the game-winner off Mitch Williams in Game Five.

SECOND BASE

Games Played

1.	Ryne Sandberg	1,994	6.	Manny Trillo	636
2.	Johnny Evers	1,368	7.	Don Johnson	495
3.	Billy Herman	1,340	8.	Gene Baker	434
4.	Glenn Beckert	1,206	9.	Eddie Miksis	391
5.	Fred Pfeffer	1,073	10.	Sparky Adams	370

Gold Gloves

1962	Ken Hubbs		1987	Ryne Sandberg
1968	Glenn Beckert		1988	Ryne Sandberg
1983	Ryne Sandberg		1989	Ryne Sandberg
1984	Ryne Sandberg		1990	Ryne Sandberg
1985	Ryne Sandberg		1991	Ryne Sandberg
1986	Ryne Sandberg			

All-Glove Second Base

The Cubs have had a very long tradition of excellent-fielding second basemen, so choosing only four is difficult.

First Team: Ryne Sandberg. The most sure-handed second baseman in baseball history, Sandberg was also the first player to win a Gold Glove at a new position. Having switched from third to second, he went on to win nine Gold Gloves and to record a lifetime fielding percentage of .989, including .995 in 1991. In 1983, he became one of only three Cubs second basemen to lead the league in both fielding percentage and chances per game.

Second Team: Billy Herman. The other Cub to lead the league in both surest hands and range, Herman did it in 1935. He would have been the hands-down winner of at least three Gold Gloves as a Cub and might easily have doubled that number.

Honorable Mention: Fred Pfeffer. Not only did he get to more balls than any other second baseman for most of the 1880s, but he did it bare-handed to boot. He was also known for his acrobatic throws, whether prone or on the run.

Taken Too Soon: Ken Hubbs. What might have been. Hubbs set a record for errorless games during his rookie season in 1962: 418 chances and 77 games from June 12 until a throwing error on September 5. Hubbs had been afraid of flying, so he decided to conquer the fear by getting his pilot's license. The plane he was piloting crashed in Utah before the 1964 season.

League Leaders—Fielding Percentage and Range (Chances per Game)

Players in **bold** led the league in both fielding percentage and chances per game.

Year	Player	Pct.	Range	Year	Player	Pct.	Range
1876	Ross Barnes	.910		1936	Billy Herman	.975	
1879	Joe Quest	.925		1937	Billy Herman		6.5
1884	Fred Pfeffer		8.1	1938	Billy Herman	.981	
1885	Fred Pfeffer		7.4	1940	Billy Herman		6.2
1887	Fred Pfeffer		7.0	1941	Lou Stringer		6.2
1888	Fred Pfeffer		7.0	1943	Eddie Stanky		6.1
1889	Fred Pfeffer		7.4	1956	Gene Baker		5.8
1891	Fred Pfeffer		7.2	1959	Tony Taylor		5.6
1902	Bobby Lowe		6.5	1977	Manny Trillo		5.5
1904	Johnny Evers		6.3	1978	Manny Trillo		5.9
1923	George Grantham		6.3	**1983**	**Ryne Sandberg**	**.986**	**5.8**
1925	**Sparky Adams**	**.983**	**6.4**	1984	Ryne Sandberg	.993	
1928	Freddie Maguire		6.9	1986	Ryne Sandberg	.994	
1932	Billy Herman		6.3	1991	Ryne Sandberg	.995	
1933	Billy Herman		6.7	1998	Mickey Morandini	.993	
1935	**Billy Herman**	**.964**	**6.3**				

Fielding Records

English to Maguire to Grimm? This double-play trio of 1928 was actually the Cubs' most prolific. The team turned a club-record 176 that season, with Freddie Maguire in the middle of 126 of them. Ryne Sandberg tied that mark in 1983, with Larry Bowa to one side and Bull Durham to the other.

Sandberg holds the record for consecutive errorless games at second base—123 from June 21, 1989, to May 17, 1990—handling 577 chances without an error. He shares the major-league records for most assists in a game—12 on June 12, 1983—and for most seasons with 500+ assists (1983, 1984, 1985, 1988, 1991, and 1992).

While Sandberg excelled at assists, Billy Herman racked up putouts. He holds the National League mark for putouts in a season, with 466 in 1933, and led the league in putouts

> *The best thing about baseball is that you can do something about yesterday tomorrow.*
>
> *Manny Trillo*

Tinker and Evers

Johnny Evers and Joe Tinker were the first double-play combination to switch off who would cover second base on a steal. They were also the first to decoy on hit-and-runs—pretending to field grounders when the ball was actually hit in the air, hoping to deceive the runner long enough for the outfielder to catch the fly ball and double the man off first. In fact, they did it to Sherwood Magee of the Phillies three times in one game. When he finally wised up, the outfielder dropped the fly ball and he was forced at second.

Evers and Tinker may have been a great double-play combination, but they weren't the best of friends. In fact, after the Crab took a cab to the park and left Joe Tinker waiting at the curb, the two came to blows during an exhibition game and didn't speak to each other for more than 25 years.

The Crab could be tough to take; his nervous and frenetic disposition resulted in two nervous breakdowns during his playing career. It also led some to claim that he was literally "electric." He did what he could to foster this legend by claiming that watches, once strapped to his wrist, would cease to work.

The Mendoza Line Middle Infield

George Brett named .200 the Mendoza Line, in honor of light-hitting shortstop Mario Mendoza, who could frequently be found below this line in the Sunday totals. During the strike year of 1981, the Cubs had four middle infielders below the Mendoza Line and another two who were too close for comfort. With 39 RBIs in 1½ years' worth of at bats and a .196 average, it is probably the least productive middle infield in baseball history.

Infielder	Pos.	AB	H	HR	RBI	BA
Ivan DeJesus	SS	403	78	0	13	.194
Steve Dillard	2B	119	26	2	11	.218
Pat Tabler	2B	101	19	1	5	.188
Mike Tyson	2B	92	17	2	8	.185
Joe Strain	2B	74	14	0	1	.189
Scott Fletcher	2B	46	10	0	1	.217
Total Mendoza		835	164	5	39	.196

Double Plays

On August 17, 1940, Billy Herman hit into three double plays in a game. Randy Jackson matched the feat on August 15, 1953. It remained a National League record until Joe Torre bounced into four in one game in 1975.

In 1935, second-baseman-turned-center-fielder Augie Galan set a record that will never be broken. He went the entire season without grounding into a double play—a mark later tied by catcher-turned-center-fielder-turned-second-baseman Craig Biggio. Unlike Biggio, Galan did hit into a triple play that season.

a National League–record seven times (tying Cubs second-baseman Fred Pfeffer). Herman also shares the NL mark for putouts in a game, with 11 on June 28, 1933, a mark later tied by Gene Baker on May 27, 1955.

Some Cubs entered the record book the wrong way. George Grantham made a modern-NL-record 55 errors in 1923, while Eddie Stanky made 3 errors in the eighth inning on June 20, 1943. Billy Herman and Glenn Beckert both led the league in errors four times (1932, 1933, 1937, and 1939 and 1966, 1967, 1969, and 1970, respectively).

Second-Base Season Records
(minimum 100 games at position)

Games:	Ken Hubbs	1962	159
At Bats:	Billy Herman	1935	666
Hits:	Rogers Hornsby	1929	229
Doubles:	Billy Herman	1935–36	57
Triples:	Ryne Sandberg	1984	19
Home Runs:	Ryne Sandberg	1990	40
RBIs:	Rogers Hornsby	1929	149
Runs:	Rogers Hornsby	1929	156
Walks:	Johnny Evers	1910	108
Strikeouts:	Ken Hubbs	1962	129
Stolen Bases:	Ryne Sandberg	1985	51
Batting Average:	Rogers Hornsby	1929	.380
Slugging Average:	Rogers Hornsby	1929	.679

Ryne Sandberg

There are currently 13 second basemen in the Hall of Fame. Should Ryne Sandberg be the lucky 14th? Here are their career totals:

Sandberg Versus the Hall

HALL OF FAMER	YEARS	H	HR	R	RBI	BA	SA	SB
Eddie Collins	25	3,311	47	1,818	1,299	.333	.418	743
Bobby Doerr	14	2,042	223	1,094	1,247	.288	.461	54
Johnny Evers	18	1,658	12	919	538	.270	.334	324
Nellie Fox	19	2,663	35	1,279	790	.288	.363	76
Frankie Frisch	19	2,880	105	1,532	1,244	.316	.432	419
Charlie Gehringer	19	2,839	184	1,774	1,427	.320	.480	182
Billy Herman	15	2,345	47	1,163	839	.304	.407	67
Rogers Hornsby	23	2,930	301	1,579	1,584	.358	.577	135
Napoleon Lajoie	21	3,244	83	1,503	1,599	.338	.466	382
Tony Lazzeri	14	1,840	178	986	1,191	.292	.467	148

continued

HALL OF FAMER	YEARS	H	HR	R	RBI	BA	SA	SB
Joe Morgan	22	2,517	268	1,650	1,133	.271	.427	689
Jackie Robinson	10	1,518	137	947	734	.311	.474	197
Red Schoendienst	19	2,449	84	1,223	773	.289	.387	346
[Ryne Sandberg]	16	2,386	282	1,318	1,061	.285	.452	344

Note: These are the career totals for Hall of Famers who played the majority of their games as a second baseman. Rod Carew played more games at first base than second.

Although ranking only 10th in years played, Sandberg is 9th in hits, 7th in runs, 6th in steals, and 2nd in home runs. An additional three years—which Sandberg could have easily done, if not for his own high personal standards—would have pushed him closer to the top of the career totals.

Recap: Sandberg Versus the Hall

	YEARS	H	HR	R	RBI	BA	SA	SB
Ryne Sandberg	10th	9th	2nd	7th	9th	12th	7th	6th

Since Sandberg didn't hang around to pad his stats, his list of *yearly* accomplishments is a more accurate reflection of his playing ability than are his *career* totals.

Sandberg's six seasons with 25+ home runs is a record that's unmatched. Among the Hall of Famers, only Rogers Hornsby hit more home runs in a season (42 in 1922) than Sandberg's 40 in 1990.

25-Home Run Seasons

Ryne Sandberg	6	Frankie Frisch	0
Rogers Hornsby	5	Charlie Gehringer	0
Bobby Doerr	2	Billy Herman	0
Joe Morgan	2	Napoleon Lajoie	0
Eddie Collins	0	Tony Lazzeri	0
Johnny Evers	0	Jackie Robinson	0
Nellie Fox	0	Red Schoendienst	0

His seven 100-run seasons are exceeded by only Joe Morgan and Charlie Gehringer. Like Morgan, Sandberg thrived in the demanding number-two spot in the batting order.

100-Run Seasons

Charlie Gehringer	12	Billy Herman	5
Joe Morgan	8	Nellie Fox	4
Eddie Collins	7	Napoleon Lajoie	3
Frankie Frisch	7	Tony Lazzeri	2
Ryne Sandberg	7	Red Schoendienst	2
Rogers Hornsby	6	Bobby Doerr	1
Jackie Robinson	6	Johnny Evers	0

Second to None

With 277, Ryne Sandberg hit more home runs while playing second base than any other player. On April 26, 1997, Sandberg took Steve Cooke of the Pirates deep for #267, passing Joe Morgan on the all-time list. Of Rogers Hornsby's 301, only 264 were hit while he was playing second base.

Second-Base Home Runs

Season

Rogers Hornsby	Cardinals	1922	42
Davey Johnson	Braves	1973	42
Ryne Sandberg	Cubs	1990	40
Rogers Hornsby	Cardinals	1925	39
Rogers Hornsby	Cubs	1929	39

Career

Ryne Sandberg	277
Joe Morgan	266
Rogers Hornsby	264
Joe Gordon	246
Lou Whitaker	239

Q. What Cub gave up
Ryne Sandberg's only
non-Cub base hit?

A. Mike Krukow in 1981

Slugging average is a better measure of a player's ability than batting average, for it separates the slap hitters from the contact-with-power hitters. Sandberg's four seasons slugging .500+ are bettered by only Rogers Hornsby, Charlie Gehringer, and Napoleon Lajoie.

.500-Slugging-Average Seasons

Rogers Hornsby	9	Joe Morgan	2
Charlie Gehringer	7	Frankie Frisch	1
Napoleon Lajoie	6	Red Schoendienst	1
Jackie Robinson	4	Eddie Collins	0
Ryne Sandberg	4	Johnny Evers	0
Bobby Doerr	3	Nellie Fox	0
Tony Lazzeri	2	Billy Herman	0

Ryno's seven 25+ stolen-base seasons are bested by only Joe Morgan and Eddie Collins. Only Joe Morgan was able to combine power and speed as well as Sandberg did.

Speed & Power

Player	25 SB	25 HR	Player	25 SB	25 HR
Eddie Collins	12	0	Charlie Gehringer	1	0
Joe Morgan	11	2	Red Schoendienst	1	0
Ryne Sandberg	7	6	Rogers Hornsby	0	5
Johnny Evers	7	0	Bobby Doerr	0	2
Frankie Frisch	7	0	Nellie Fox	0	0
Napoleon Lajoie	4	0	Billy Herman	0	0
Jackie Robinson	3	0	Tony Lazzeri	0	0

With the bat alone, Sandberg can keep pace with the best that baseball has seen. But his fielding sets him apart. His six seasons with a .990 fielding percentage are unparalleled. He won nine consecutive Gold Glove Awards and retired with the highest fielding percentage of any second baseman in history. With the glove, Sandberg was perhaps the best to ever play the position.

Quintuple Crown

Ryne Sandberg is one of only five players who have led all second basemen in home runs, RBIs, batting average, assists, and fielding percentage in the same season—and Sandberg is the only one to do it twice.

		HR	RBI	BA	A	FP
1909	Eddie Collins	3	56	.346	406	.967
1936	Charlie Gehringer	15	116	.354	524	.974
1951	Jackie Robinson	19	88	.338	435	.992
1984	Ryne Sandberg	19	84	.314	550	.993
1991	Ryne Sandberg	26	100	.291	515	.995

Fielding

Player	.990 Pct.	League Leader	Player	.990 Pct.	League Leader
Ryne Sandberg	**6**	**4**	Napoleon Lajoie	0	6
Joe Morgan	3	3	Frankie Frisch	0	3
Bobby Doerr	2	4	Billy Herman	0	3
Nellie Fox	1	6	Jackie Robinson	0	3
Red Schoendienst	1	5	Johnny Evers	0	1
Eddie Collins	0	9	Rogers Hornsby	0	1
Charlie Gehringer	0	7	Tony Lazzeri	0	0

> **Q.** Ryne Sandberg got off to a very slow start in Chicago, going 0-for-20, hitting a single, and then going 0-for-11. What less-than-stable Astros pitcher gave up his first Cubs hit?
>
> **A.** Joaquin Andujar (who was known for, among other things, challenging sportswriters to duels)

When one takes into account the complete package—run production, hitting, hitting for power, fielding, and speed—Sandberg moves up in the pack. And when one focuses on consistent yearly excellence rather than sheer length of career, only Rogers Hornsby (far and away the greatest-hitting second baseman of all time) and Charlie Gehringer are clearly superior to Ryne Sandberg.

Not only does Ryne Sandberg merit first-ballot induction into the Hall of Fame, but he also deserves to be mentioned in the same breath with Joe Morgan and Frankie Frisch as among the five greatest second basemen of all time.

Ryne Sandberg in All His Glory

YEAR	G	AB	R	H	2B	3B	HR	RBI	SB	BA	SA	FP	GAMES BY Pos.
1982	156	635	103	172	33	5	7	54	32	.271	.372	.977	3B—133, 2B—24
1983	158	633	94	165	25	4	8	48	37	.261	.351	**.986**	2B—157, SS—1
1984	156	636	**114**	200	36	**19**	19	84	32	.314	.520	**.993**	2B—156
1985	153	609	113	186	31	6	26	83	54	.305	.504	.986	2B—153, SS—1
1986	154	627	68	178	28	5	14	76	34	.284	.411	**.994**	2B—153
1987	132	523	81	154	25	2	16	59	21	.294	.442	.985	2B—131
1988	155	618	77	163	23	8	19	69	25	.264	.419	.987	2B—153
1989	157	606	**104**	176	25	5	30	76	15	.290	.497	.992	2B—155
1990	155	615	**116**	188	30	3	**40**	100	25	.306	.559	.989	2B—154
1991	158	585	104	170	32	2	26	100	22	.291	.485	**.995**	2B—157
1992	158	612	100	186	32	8	26	87	17	.304	.510	.990	2B—157
1993	117	456	67	141	20	0	9	45	9	.309	.412	.988	2B—115
1994	57	223	36	53	9	5	5	24	2	.238	.390	.987	2B—57
1996	150	554	85	135	28	4	25	92	12	.244	.444	.991	2B—146
1997	135	447	54	118	26	0	12	64	7	.264	.403	.984	2B—126
Totals	2,151	8,379	1,316	2,385	403	76	282	1,061	344	.285	.452	.989	2B—1,994, 3B—133, SS—2

Note: League-leading totals are in **bold**.

June 23, 1984

With this legendary, nationally televised, comeback-back-and-back-again victory, the Cubs rally from a 7–1 deficit and overcome a Willie McGee cycle to beat the Cardinals and stay within 1½ games of first place. Bruce Sutter gives up two game-tying home runs to Ryne Sandberg—one in the 9th and another in the 10th—when he will give up only nine all season. Sandberg goes 5-for-7 on the day, giving him 12 hits in his last 17 at bats. Cardinals manager Whitey Herzog revises his assessment that Sandberg is one of the best players in the league: "Now I think he's one of the greatest players I've ever seen."

Cardinals 11

ST. LOUIS	ab	r	h	bi
Lo. Smith lf	4	1	1	1
Sutter p	1	0	0	0
Ramsey ph	1	0	0	0
Rucker p	0	0	0	0
Lahti p	0	0	0	0
O. Smith ss	4	4	2	0
McGee cf	6	3	4	6
Hendrick rf	5	0	1	2
D. Green 1b	5	0	1	0
Braun ph	1	0	0	1
Jorgensen 1b	0	0	0	0
Herr 2b	6	1	3	0
A. Howe 3b	3	1	0	0
Allen p	0	0	0	0
Landrum lf	1	0	0	0
Salas lf	1	0	0	0
Porter c	4	0	0	0
Citarella p	3	1	1	1
Van Slyke 3b	1	0	0	0
Totals	**46**	**11**	**13**	**11**

Cubs 12

CHICAGO	ab	r	h	bi
Dernier cf	5	3	3	2
Sandberg 2b	6	2	5	7
Matthews lf	5	0	2	1
Durham 1b	5	2	1	0
Moreland rf	4	1	0	0
J. Davis c	3	0	0	0
Cey 3b	2	1	0	0
Stoddard p	0	0	0	0
Hassey ph	1	0	0	0
Frazier p	0	0	0	0
Woods ph	1	0	0	0
Le. Smith p	0	0	0	0
Owen ph	1	0	1	1
Bowa ss	4	1	0	0
Trout p	0	0	0	0
Bordi p	1	0	0	0
Johnstone ph	1	1	1	0
Noles p	0	0	0	0
Brusstar p	0	0	0	0
Hebner 3b	3	1	1	1
Totals	**42**	**12**	**14**	**12**

St. Louis	1	6	0	0	0	2	0	0	0	2	0	11	13	1
Chicago	1	0	0	0	2	5	0	0	1	2	1	12	14	2

E—Dernier, J. Davis, Porter. DP—St. Louis 1. LOB—St. Louis 11, Chicago 10. 2B—Matthews, Durham, Dernier, McGee. 3B—McGee. HR—McGee, Sandberg 2. SB—Dernier, O. Smith 2, Lo. Smith, Matthews, Van Slyke, Durham.

	IP	H	R	ER	BB	SO
St. Louis						
Citarella	5⅓	7	5	5	2	3
Allen	1⅓	3	3	3	2	2
Sutter	3⅓	3	3	3	2	0
Rucker L	0	0	1	1	1	0
Lahti	0	1	0	0	2	0

	IP	H	R	ER	BB	SO
Chicago						
Trout	1⅓	5	7	7	3	1
Bordi	3⅔	2	0	0	2	3
Noles	⅔	3	2	2	1	0
Brusstar	⅓	0	0	0	0	1
Stoddard	1	0	0	0	1	2
Frazier	2	1	0	0	1	2
Le. Smith W	2	2	2	2	1	0

HBP—Citarella (Cey). WP—Citarella. BK—Trout. T—3:53. A—38,079.

SHORTSTOP

Games Played

1. Don Kessinger   1,618
2. Joe Tinker   1,500
3. Shawon Dunston   1,228
4. Ernie Banks   1,125
5. Billy Jurges   965
6. Charlie Hollocher   751
7. Ivan DeJesus   736
8. Bill Dahlen   712
9. Woody English   707
10. Roy Smalley Sr.   643

Gold Gloves

1960   Ernie Banks
1969   Don Kessinger
1970   Don Kessinger

All-Glove Shortstop

First Team: Joe Tinker. He had sure hands and great range, and he was one of only two Cubs shortstops to lead the league in fielding percentage and chances per game in the same season. The best fielder on championship teams built on defense, Tinker would have been a perennial winner had Gold Gloves been awarded back then.

Second Team: Billy Jurges. The Cubs teams of the 1930s were nothing if not strong up the middle, with Gabby Hartnett, Billy Herman, and Billy Jurges manning the most crucial positions. Jurges is the only Cubs' second baseman, shortstop, or third baseman to *twice* lead the league in both surest hands and best range in the same season.

Honorable Mention: Don Kessinger. The anchor of the Chicago infield for 11 years, Kessinger won two Gold Gloves and played more games at shortstop than any other Cub.

Underrated: Ernie Banks. His hitting overshadowed the fact that he was one of the great fielding shortstops of his or any other day. His .969 lifetime fielding percentage is the highest in Cubs history, and his .985 in 1959 was a major-league record at the time and remains a club record.

The Greatest Shortstop No One Knows

In 1918, 22-year-old Cubs rookie shortstop Charlie Hollocher led Chicago's pennant-winning offense with a .316 batting average, a league-leading 161 hits (the season was cut to 140 games by World War I), and 26 stolen bases. After a solid albeit unspectacular season, he hit .319 with 20 stolen bases in an 80-game 1920 season that was cut in half by stomach miseries no doctor could diagnose. After a decent 1921 season, he batted .340 in 1922, with 69 RBIs and 19 steals, earning comparisons to Honus Wagner. But his stomach problems cut short a 1923 season in which he hit .342 in 66 games, and he retired at 28 after a lackluster 1924 season. An exceedingly nervous individual, he continued to be troubled by these mysterious stomach ailments and eventually killed himself in 1940.

League Leaders—Fielding Percentage and Range (Chances per Game)

Players in **bold** led the league in both fielding percentage and chances per game.

Year	Player	Pct.	Range	Year	Player	Pct.	Range
1876	Johnny Peters	.932		**1932**	**Billy Jurges**	**.964**	**6.2**
1877	Johnny Peters		6.4	**1935**	**Billy Jurges**	**.964**	**5.9**
1878	Bob Ferguson		5.9	1937	Billy Jurges	.975	
1890	Jimmy Cooney	.936		1949	Roy Smalley		5.6
1891	Jimmy Cooney	.917		1950	Roy Smalley		6.0
1893	Bill Dahlen		6.8	1955	Ernie Banks	.972	
1904	Joe Tinker		6.1	1959	Ernie Banks	.985	
1906	Joe Tinker	.944		1960	Ernie Banks	.977	
1908	Joe Tinker	.958		1961	Ernie Banks		5.3
1909	Joe Tinker	.940		1964	Andre Rodgers		5.4
1911	**Joe Tinker**	**.937**	**6.1**	1968	Don Kessinger		5.5
1912	Joe Tinker		6.2	1969	Don Kessinger	.976	
1921	Charlie Hollocher	.963		1983	Larry Bowa	.984	
1922	Charlie Hollocher	.965		1986	Shawon Dunston		5.5
1926	Jimmy Cooney	.972					

Shortstop Season Records (minimum 100 games at position)

Games:	Ivan DeJesus	1978, 1979	160
At Bats:	Don Kessinger	1969	664
Hits:	Woody English	1931	202
Doubles:	Woody English	1931	38
	Don Kessinger	1969	38
Triples:	Bill Dahlen	1896	19
Home Runs:	Ernie Banks	1958	47
RBIs:	Ernie Banks	1959	143
Runs:	Bill Dahlen	1896	137
Walks:	Ned Williamson	1886	80
Strikeouts:	Roy Smalley	1950	114
	Shawon Dunston	1986	114
Stolen Bases:	Ivan DeJesus	1980	44
Batting Average:	Bill Dahlen	1896	.352
Slugging Average:	Ernie Banks	1958	.614

Dubious Distinctions

On September 13, 1942, Cubs shortstop Lennie Merullo made four errors in the second inning. The Cubs won 12–8 anyway. It also happened to be the same day Merullo's first son was born. They named him Boots.

Merullo was ordinarily a good fielder, though not much of a hitter. In fact, legend has it that the Reds were convinced that veteran pitcher Paul Derringer was through and were willing to deal him to the Cubs because Merullo had hit a home run off of him (his first of seven lifetime).

It's the rare player who can be simultaneously behind and ahead of his time. And this is where a Cub stands astride every other player who ever took a called strike or heaved a ball into the third row. Forget the 30/30 Club. With 51 errors and 114 strikeouts in 1950—both major-league-leading totals—Roy Smalley Sr. became the only player in major-league history to do 50/100. Bill Almon came close in 1977 with 41 and 114, as did Jose Offerman (with 42 and 98 in 1992).

> Lennie Merullo was a good fielder, but as his roommate and best friend Phil Cavarretta frequently told him:
> You could live to be 89 and you'll never learn how to hit. Face it. You can't hit.

Ernie Banks

Gene Baker was the first black player signed by the Cubs, though he was kept buried for several years in the Pacific Coast League. Baker was to debut in September 1953, so Ernie Banks was signed because Baker needed a roommate. The second of 12 kids in Dallas, Banks played for the Kansas City Monarchs at the age of 19 with Satchel Paige, Josh Gibson, and Elston Howard. The Indians and Dodgers also wanted him, but Banks signed with the Cubs on September 7. He played his first game with a glove loaned to him by Eddie Miksis in an infield with Dee Fondy at first, Miksis at second, and Bill Serena at third—and he stayed in the lineup for 424 games, a record from the start of a career.

Banks was 6'1"/180 lbs., and he was even lighter when he first came to the big leagues. His power came from the snap of his wrists and his strong forearms, and he became a devastating power hitter despite using a thin-handled bat that was only 31 ounces at a time when sluggers were still using 40-ounce clubs. He stood slightly hunched over at the plate, his fingers gripping and relaxing on the bat as he waited for the pitch.

Banks established himself as a star in 1955 when he became the first major-league shortstop to hit 40 home runs in a season—his 40th coming on September 2. He also became the first shortstop to collect 80 extra-base hits in a season. Banks set another major-league record in 1955 when he fit five grand slams, breaking the mark set by Wildfire Schulte in 1911. The record-breaker came on September 19 in a game the Cubs lost 6–5 in 12 innings.

In 1958, Banks became the only shortstop other than Vern Stephens in 1945 to lead the league in home runs. He hit 47 while also leading the league with 129 RBIs and batting .313, earning his first MVP Award, the first given to a member of a losing team. As of August 23, he had hit 41 home runs, putting him on the same pace as Babe Ruth when he hit 60 in 1927.

Banks became the only shortstop to repeat as MVP in 1959, when he hit 45 home runs, knocked in 143, batted .304, and set a major-league record for fielding percentage. His share of the home-run title was taken from him by Eddie Mathews, who hit his 46th in a two-game play-off series with the Los Angeles Dodgers. Banks led the league in home runs in 1960 with 41 while also leading the league in fielding and winning his first Gold Glove but losing the MVP Award to Dick Groat.

Banks's streak of 717 consecutive games played, dating back to August 26, 1956, came to an end on June 23, 1961,

Mr. Cub

I saw right away that he was one of the nicest people in the game. And I could see that he could play.   **—Hank Sauer**

I was just two lockers away from him all those years, yet I never heard Ernie criticize anyone or openly express disgust at something bad that had happened. But I could see that he took defeats as hard as anyone.   **—Dick Ellsworth**

Without Ernie Banks, the Cubs would finish in Albuquerque. **—Veteran American League manager Jimmy Dykes**

You're hitting the home runs. Why am I spending the time in the dirt? **—Ron Santo, on batting behind Banks in 1961**

It was an American dream that one day I would wake up and be playing next to him.   **—Glenn Beckert**

I've only seen Ernie get mad once in my 13 years with him. . . . Jack Sanford hit him for the 12th time.   **—Ron Santo**

In 1957, Banks was knocked down four times by four different pitchers—Don Drysdale, Bob Purkey, Bob Friend, and Jack Sanford. And each time he was knocked down, Banks hit their next pitch out of the park.   **—Tom Gorman, umpire**

Ernie Banks: Let's Play 2,528

YEAR	G	AB	R	H	2B	3B	HR	RBI	SB	BA	SA	FP	GAMES BY Pos.
1953	10	35	3	11	1	1	2	6	0	.314	.571	.981	SS—10
1954	154	593	70	163	19	7	19	79	6	.275	.427	.959	SS—154
1955	154	596	98	176	29	9	44	117	9	.295	.596	.972	SS—154
1956	139	538	82	160	25	8	28	85	6	.297	.530	.962	SS—139
1957	156	594	113	169	34	6	43	102	8	.285	.579	.977	SS—100, 3B—58
1958	154	**617**	119	193	23	11	**47**	**129**	4	.313	**.614**	.960	SS—154
1959	155	589	97	179	25	6	45	**143**	2	.304	.596	**.985**	SS—154
1960	156	597	94	162	32	7	**41**	117	1	.271	.554	**.977**	SS—156
1961	138	511	75	142	22	4	29	80	1	.278	.507	.968	SS—104, OF—23, 1B—7
1962	154	610	87	164	20	6	37	104	5	.269	.503	.993	1B—149, 3B—3
1963	130	432	41	98	20	1	18	64	0	.227	.403	.993	1B—125
1964	157	591	67	156	29	6	23	95	1	.264	.450	.994	1B—157
1965	163	612	79	162	25	3	28	106	3	.265	.453	.992	1B—162
1966	141	511	52	139	23	7	15	75	0	.272	.432	.990	1B—130, 3B—8
1967	151	573	68	158	26	4	23	95	2	.276	.455	.993	1B—147
1968	150	552	71	136	27	0	32	83	2	.246	.469	.996	1B—147
1969	155	565	60	143	19	2	23	106	0	.253	.416	**.997**	1B—153
1970	72	222	25	56	6	2	12	44	0	.252	.459	.993	1B—62
1971	39	83	4	16	2	0	3	6	0	.193	.325	1.000	1B—20
Total	2,528	9,421	1,305	2,583	407	90	512	1,636	50	.274	.500	.986	1B—1,259, SS—1,125, 3B—69, OF—23

Note: League-leading totals are in **bold**.

when his aching knees forced him out of the lineup. Despite the bad wheels, Banks led the league in chances per game in his last season at shortstop. He moved to first in 1962 and joined Stan Musial as the first players to play 1,000 games at two different positions.

Ernie Banks had a rare off year in 1963 due to a case of subclinical mumps that limited him to 18 home runs, three after June 19. He also struggled with a left-eye depth-perception problem. When Leo Durocher arrived, he tried to get rid of Banks in 1966 and 1967, touting John Boccabella, John Herrnstein, and Clarence Jones in spring training as phenoms capable of taking the first-base job from Mr. Cub. Banks responded with 95 RBIs in 1967. On September 15, 1968, Banks played in his 2,254th game as a Cub, passing Cap Anson, as Ferguson Jenkins shut out the Phillies 4–0 in Shibe Park.

Banks hit his 500th home run in 1970 but played only 72 games. A knee injury limited him to 39 games in 1971, as he hit .193 with three home runs. He came out of retirement on August 14, 1972, as a pinch hitter in a charity game with the White Sox and got a standing ovation *in Comiskey Park*.

Ernie Banks entered the Hall of Fame in 1977 as Cooperstown's first power-hitting shortstop.

Q. Who replaced Ernie Banks as the Cubs' shortstop?

A. Elder White, though Andre Rodgers soon had the starting job

The Greatest

Every baseball fan has pondered the question: Who do you grab with the first pick when you're choosing up sides for nine innings on Mt. Olympus? Joe DiMaggio? Willie Mays? Griffey Junior? Would your selection change if you were choosing a player's best season, not his entire career? Would it be Babe Ruth in 1927 or Bob Gibson in 1968? Before you answer, keep in mind:

- The quality of play during his era
- Fielding skills and not just offensive prowess

- The inflating or deflating effect of the lineup on his stats
- Typical production at the position he plays

Take all that into account, and the 1959 Banks could be the top pick.

Quality of Play

The case can be made that baseball from 1958 to 1960 was the most challenging it has ever been: West Coast travel, a new pitch called a slider, night games, no expansion, integrated lineups, no dilution of pitching, and the beginning of relief specialists. Make it here, make it anywhere. During this three-year period, Ernie Banks won two MVP Awards and could have won three. In 1959 in particular, Ernie Banks was simply the best player in baseball—better than Mays, Aaron, Mantle, and Frank Robinson.

Fielding

The most important and demanding defensive position on the field is catcher or shortstop, depending on whom you ask. Catchers and shortstops can stay in the majors based solely on their defensive game. In 1959, not only was Ernie Banks the best defensive shortstop in baseball, but his .985 fielding percentage was the highest ever recorded at the time, a record that lasted 12 years. He did it with great range, too, leading the league in assists with 519. He was saving runs every inning, not just producing them four or five times a game.

Lineup

In 1959, Ernie Banks either knocked in or scored more than 30 percent of his team's runs. He knocked in 143 runs and scored 97 in a lineup that featured only one other player who hit as high as .280.

Typical Production

Before Ernie Banks, no shortstop had ever hit 40 home runs. Compare what baseball's best-fielding shortstop did with the bat in 1959 against the 15 other starting shortstops:

1959 Banks Versus the Competition

SHORTSTOP	TEAM	BA	HR	RBI
Ernie Banks	Cubs	.304	45	143
Woodie Held	Indians	.251	29	71
Don Buddin	Red Sox	.241	10	53
Tony Kubek	Yankees	.279	6	51
Dick Groat	Pirates	.275	5	51
Luis Aparicio	White Sox	.257	6	51
Johnny Logan	Braves	.291	13	50
Rocky Bridges	Tigers	.268	3	35
Joe DeMaestri	Athletics	.244	6	34
Eddie Kasko	Reds	.283	2	31
Alex Grammas	Cardinals	.269	3	30
Joe Koppe	Phillies	.261	7	28
Chico Carrasquel	Orioles	.223	4	28
Don Zimmer	Dodgers	.165	4	28
Ed Bressoud	Giants	.251	9	26
Billy Consolo	Senators	.213	0	10

The Gospel According to Ernie

At his Hall of Fame induction in 1977: There's sunshine, fresh air, and the team's behind us. Let's play two.

On awards: Awards mean a lot, but they don't say it all. The people in baseball mean more to me than statistics.

On his weight: I carry it in my toes. I've got very muscular toes.

On perseverance: Most of us fail. You must keep going.

On baseball: You know why it's the most unique game in the world? Because it ameliorates the classic polarization between self-motivated individuals and collective ideology.

Ernie's Second Basemen

Bill Serena	*1954*
Eddie Miksis	*1954, 1956*
Gene Baker	*1954–56*
Owen Friend	*1955*
Ed Winceniak	*1956–57*
Bobby Morgan	*1957*
Casey Wise	*1957*
Bobby Adams	*1957–58*
Jerry Kindall	*1957–58, 1960–61*
Johnny Goryl	*1958–59*
Tony Taylor	*1958–60*
Earl Averill	*1959*
Sammy Drake	*1960*
Grady Hatton	*1960*
Jim McKnight	*1960*
Don Zimmer	*1960–61*
Ken Hubbs	*1961*
Mel Roach	*1961*
Andre Rodgers	*1961*

Ernie's Milestones

Ernie Banks victimized 216 pitchers in his career. Here are seven of his most famous home runs.

Homer	Date	Victim	Location	Result
#1	September 20, 1953	Gerry Staley, St. Louis	Sportsman's Park	Cubs lose 11–6
#100	June 9, 1957	Robin Roberts, Philadelphia	Shibe Park	Cubs win 7–3
#200	June 14, 1959	Carlton Willey, Milwaukee	Wrigley Field	Cubs win 6–0
#300	April 18, 1962	Dick Farrell, Houston	Wrigley Field	Cubs win 3–2 in 10*
#400	September 2, 1965	Curt Simmons, St. Louis	Wrigley Field	Cubs win 5–3
#500	May 12, 1970	Pat Jarvis, Atlanta	Wrigley Field	Cubs win 4–3 in 11
#512	August 24, 1971	Jim McGlothlin, Cincinnati	Wrigley Field	Cubs win 5–4

*Game-winner

Taking it all into account, compare what Ernie Banks did in 1959 with the best seasons of any shortstop:

1959 Banks Versus the Best

YEAR	SHORTSTOP	HR	RBI	BA	SA	FP	TC/G
1998	Alex Rodriguez	42	124	.310	.560	.975	4.6
1998	Nomar Garciaparra	35	122	.323	.584	.962	4.6
1995	Barry Larkin	33	89	.298	.567	.975	4.5
1991	Cal Ripken	34	114	.323	.566	.986	5.0
1982	Robin Yount	29	114	.331	.578	.969	4.9
1969	Rico Petrocelli	40	97	.297	.589	.980	4.9
1959	**Ernie Banks**	**45**	**143**	**.304**	**.596**	**.985**	**5.2**
1949	Vern Stephens	39	159	.290	.539	.966	5.1
1948	Lou Boudreau	18	106	.355	.534	.975	5.3
1936	Luke Appling	6	128	.388	.508	.951	6.1
1935	Arky Vaughan	19	99	.385	.607	.950	5.2
1908	Honus Wagner	10	109	.354	.542	.943	5.8

Here's how Banks ranks in each category against the best any shortstop has ever done:

Recap: Banks Versus the Best

	HR	RBI	BA	SA	FA	TC/G
1959 Banks	1st	2nd	9th	2nd	2nd	4th

In summary, while playing superior defense at perhaps the most important position on the field, Ernie Banks hit for more power and more production—despite a wretched lineup around him during the most challenging era in baseball history—than any other shortstop before or since.

40-Homer Shortstops

Ernie Banks	1958	47
Ernie Banks	1959	45
Ernie Banks	1955	44
Alex Rodriguez	1998	42
Ernie Banks	1960	41
Rico Petrocelli	1969	40

Note: Banks hit 43 home runs in 1957 while splitting time between short and third.

Shortstop Home Runs

Cal Ripken	345		Vern Stephens	213
Ernie Banks	277		Alan Trammell	177

The Shawon-o-Meter

Cubs shortstop Shawon Dunston was a notoriously slow starter. It was never any slower for Shawon—or for just about anyone, really—than in 1989. He was 26, a former first overall pick in the Amateur Draft, and coming off a fourth consecutive season of decent production and higher expectations.

In April, he hit .160 with one RBI. After a game in Cincinnati on Sunday, May 21, in which he knocked in his second run of the season, he was 15-for-98 (.153). The team was 22–19, having already endured losing streaks of four, four, and five games, yet they trailed the first-place Mets by a half game.

The Cubs went to Houston, and Shawon started to wake up. He went 4-for-10, hit his first home run, and knocked in 4 of the Cubs' 13 runs as Chicago held off late charges by the Astros in all three games to sweep the series and take over first place. Dunston didn't go three games in a row without a hit for the rest of the season.

On May 28 in Wrigley, Dunston had a two-run single in a 6–1 win—raising his batting average at home to .140. They were 2½ games up, and Shawon went on to hit in the next six games, capped by a 3-for-4, two-home-run performance in Busch Stadium on June 4 against the Cardinals in an 11–3 romp.

When he came home with a seven-game hitting streak to face the Mets, one creative fan—knowing that Dunston's batting average rose with the temperature—welcomed him with a cardboard "Shawon-o-Meter," which read .203 on June 5. Dunston must have liked the sign—or maybe he wanted to put a more respectable number on display—because as the season wore on, the meter climbed steadily. It climbed most dramatically at Wrigley, where he hit .346 the rest of the way. Here are some big games for Dunston and what the Shawon-o-Meter read (in **bold**) in Wrigley at the time:

June 8—**.213** as he goes 5-for-17 in helping the Cubs take three of four from the Mets and move three games up on the Expos.

July 6—**.236** as he breaks up a close game with a late home run against the Padres to pull the Cubs to within 1½ games of Montreal.

July 20–23—**.242** as he goes 5-for-11 in a four-game series with the front-running Giants, but the Cubs still trail the Expos—by 3½ games.

July 28–30—**.257** as he goes 6-for-11 in a three-game sweep from which the Mets never recover and that brings the Cubs to 1½ games behind Montreal.

August 12—**.268** as his three hits and 6 RBIs carry the Cubs to a 9–7 win over the Phillies that keeps Chicago 2½ games up on Montreal; over the past three games, he's gone 8-for-12 with 10 RBIs.

September 22—**.281** as he goes 1-for-3 in his final home games. He's hit in 13 consecutive games, a stretch during which he's batted .422, knocked in 11 runs, and helped the Cubs drive stakes through the hearts of both the Mets and Expos.

Dunston runs the streak to 14 on the 26th as the Cubs clinch the pennant in Montreal. He finishes the year at .278, playing his best when the games matter the most. His batting average against the Cubs' biggest Eastern rivals: .305 (Mets), .310 (Expos), and .325 (Cardinals).

THIRD BASE

Games Played

1. Ron Santo	2,102	6. Ned Williamson	601
2. Stan Hack	1,836	7. Heinie Zimmerman	535
3. Harry Steinfeldt	730	8. Ron Cey	518
4. Tom Burns	696	9. Bill Madlock	385
5. Randy Jackson	687	10. Woody English	379

Gold Gloves

1964	Ron Santo
1965	Ron Santo
1966	Ron Santo
1967	Ron Santo
1968	Ron Santo

All-Glove Third Base

First Team: Ron Santo. The winner of five consecutive Gold Gloves; when he was at his best, Santo's range was the equal of Brooks Robinson's.

Second Team: Stan Hack. Hack is the only Cubs' third baseman to lead the league in fielding percentage and range in the same season. His .975 in 1945 remains a Cubs record (though tied by Steve Buechele in 1993).

Honorable Mention: Charlie Deal. Deal led the league in fielding percentage three years in a row, and his .964 lifetime average is the highest of any Cubs third baseman.

Underrated: Ned Williamson. Williamson is best remembered for his 27 home runs in 1884, but he was also a key member of the White Stockings' "Stonewall Infield" of the 1880s. He had sure hands (by 19th-century standards) and was quick enough to make the switch from third base *to* shortstop later in his career.

Stan Hack has more friends than Leo Durocher has enemies.

Attributed to just about everyone who knew him

League Leaders—Fielding Percentage and Range (Chances per Game)

Players in **bold** led the league in both fielding percentage and chances per game.

Year	Player	Pct.	Range	Year	Player	Pct.	Range
1877	Cap Anson	.883		1933	Woody English	.973	
1878	Frank Hankinson		4.6	1938	Stan Hack		3.3
1879	Ned Williamson		4.5	1942	Stan Hack	.965	
1880	Ned Williamson	.893		**1945**	**Stan Hack**	**.975**	**3.6**
1881	Ned Williamson	.909		1948	Andy Pafko		3.4
1882	Ned Williamson	.881		1951	Randy Jackson		3.8
1883	Ned Williamson		4.6	1961	Ron Santo		3.2
1885	Ned Williamson	.892		1962	Ron Santo		3.3
1889	Tom Burns		4.4	1964	Ron Santo		3.4
1900	Bill Bradley		4.9	1965	Ron Santo		3.4
1905	Doc Casey	.949		1966	Ron Santo		3.7
1906	Harry Steinfeldt	.954		1967	Ron Santo		3.8
1907	Harry Steinfeldt	.967		1968	Ron Santo	.971	
1911	Jim Doyle		3.5	1981	Ken Reitz	.977	
1919	Charlie Deal	.973		1984	Ron Cey	.967	
1920	Charlie Deal	.973		1993	Steve Buechele	.975	
1921	Charlie Deal	.973		1996	Leo Gomez	.972	
1926	Howard Freigau	.966		1998	Gary Gaetti	.983	

Third-Base Season Records (minimum 100 games at position)

Games:	Ron Santo	1965	164
At Bats:	Ron Santo	1966	651
Hits:	Heinie Zimmerman	1912	207
Doubles:	Heinie Zimmerman	1912	41
Triples:	Heinie Zimmerman	1912	14
Home Runs:	Ron Santo	1965	33
RBIs:	Ron Santo	1969	123
Runs:	Stan Hack	1939	112
Walks:	Stan Hack	1941, 1945	99
Strikeouts:	Ron Santo	1965	109
Stolen Bases:	Ryne Sandberg	1982	32
Batting Average:	Heinie Zimmerman	1912	.372
Slugging Average:	Heinie Zimmerman	1912	.571

Fielding Records

Stan Hack set what was then a National League record for third basemen when he went 54 consecutive games without an error in 1942. His string came to an end on a bases-loaded grounder by Stan Musial in the second game of the July 4 doubleheader in St. Louis.

Stan Hack's Uniform Numbers

31—1932
49—1933
34—1934
39—1935–36
6—1937–42
20—1943
25—1944
6—1945–47, 1954–56

Ron Santo is known for his hitting (342 home runs, knocked out of the top 50 in 1997 by Jose Canseco), but he has set a number of records with the glove as well. Santo played in 364 consecutive games at third base, a National League record, which began on April 19, 1964, and lasted through May 31, 1966. In the process, he set the record in 1965 for most games played at third base—164, thanks to two suspended games.

Santo led the league in putouts seven times, a National League record, tying Pie Traynor and Puddin' Head Jones. Santo did it every season from 1962 through 1969, except 1968. He led the league in assists seven times, a National League record he holds by himself. Santo did that every season from 1962 through 1968. He led the league in chances nine times, a major-league record he has all to himself, doing it more times than even Brooks Robinson. Santo led the league in chances every season from 1961 through 1969. He led the league in double plays six times, a major-league record he shares with Heinie Groh and Mike Schmidt. Santo did it in 1961, 1964, 1966, 1967, 1968, and 1971.

And, on August 28, 1971—Ron Santo Day at Wrigley Field—he revealed for the first time that he'd done it all as a diabetic since the age of 18. Nearly 17 years to the day, in his final year of eligibility, the Baseball Writers' Association of America again refused to induct him into the Hall of Fame.

Dubious Distinctions

Stan Hack set the National League record for fewest assists by a third baseman appearing in at least 150 games. In 150 games in 1937, he earned only 247 assists. Still, it was enough to lead the league. For perspective, Graig Nettles has the record for most assists in a season, 412 in 1971—exactly one more assist per game—despite the fact that the pitchers on his Indians team were 50 percent more likely to strike out a batter than Hack's Cubs staff and only 5 percent more likely to put a runner on base.

Cubs pitchers kept Roy Hughes busy during the second game of an August doubleheader. On August 29, 1944, the Cubs' third baseman set a major-league record for chances with 13, only the fourth player this century to reach that level in a nine-inning game. Ironically, it's also a Cub who has the record for most innings played without accepting a chance at third base. On August 22, 1908, Harry Steinfeldt played 15 innings without touching the ball.

Many third basemen, and even a few Hall of Famers, have been moved off the hot corner late in their career when their range diminished, reflexes slowed, or arms weakened. Cap Anson was moved off third base at the tender age of 24, perhaps inspired by a sloppy performance on August 26, 1876. He made five errors in a game—a mark later eclipsed by Joe Mulvey in 1884. He also got four hits, including a home run, in a 23–3 thrashing of St. Louis in Chicago. Anson had 50 errors in 66 games at third base in 1876—still far off the pace of the league leader, who booted 73.

Bill Bradley matched Anson's five-error feat on May 30, 1900. It took him a doubleheader to do it, but by then, third basemen were wearing gloves.

Triples and Triple Plays

Two of the game's most exciting plays often end up involving third base: the triple and the triple play. Here are some noteworthy moments for both.

Triples

On May 14, 1904, and again on June 12, 1936, the Cubs hit bases-clearing triples twice in the same game. On May 27, 1922, the Cubs gave up a National League–record seven triples to the Cincinnati Reds. And on April 25, 1981, the Cubs hit back-to-back-to-back triples—Steve Henderson, Bull Durham, and Jerry Morales putting the Cubs in front of the Phillies 5–1 at Wrigley Field, only to lose 7–5 and fall to 1–12 on the season.

Triple Triples

On July 28, 1990, Shawon Dunston hit three of his eight triples for the season in the same game. It hadn't been done since Ernie Banks—bad knees and all—hit three of his seven triples for the season in an 8–2 Cubs win at the Astrodome on June 11, 1966. The trick has been turned only three times—appropriately enough—during the 20th century. Shortstop Charlie Hollocher did it on August 13, 1922, in a 16–5 rout of the Cardinals at Wrigley.

Triple triples were much more common in the 19th century, done three times—of course—in the White Stockings' 1885 championship season. Outfielder George "Piano Legs" Gore did it on May 6 and July 9, while Mike "not yet King" Kelly did it nine days later—one of the highlights of a disappointing season for him.

Nineteenth-century flash-in-the-pan outfielder Marty Sullivan did it on May 17, 1887, during a rookie season that saw him hit 16 of his 32 lifetime triples. Shortstop Bill Dahlen did it on May 3, 1896, benefiting from ground rules concerning balls hit into the overflow crowd at West Side Grounds in Chicago. He did it again on June 6, 1898. Dahlen is the only triples hitter of the group with a lifetime total of more than 160, which puts him in the top 30.

Triple Doubles

The baseball version of basketball's triple double is far more difficult: 20 doubles, triples, and homers in the same season. Only five players have done it, and the first was a Cub: Wildfire Schulte in 1911.

Triple Plays

The Cubs got Hall of Famer Roberto Clemente to go 0-for-6 in only two at bats. They actually turned *two* triple plays on him nearly two years apart to the day. The first came on July 21, 1963, in Pittsburgh. On July 25, 1965, in Wrigley, they did it to him again. The 1965 triple play was one of *three* turned by the Cubs that season. They tied the major-league record with their third on October 3 in a 6–3 loss to the Pirates at Forbes Field.

August 30, 1921

For the first time in baseball history, two triple plays are turned on the same day. Both teams that turn the triple plays actually lose—the Braves to the Reds 6–4, and the Cubs to the Giants 5–3 at the Polo Grounds.

May 30, 1927

Shortstop Jimmy Cooney becomes the only Cub to turn an unassisted triple play. He does the trick against the Pirates in Pittsburgh, retiring two Hall of Famers in the process: Paul Waner hits a line drive to him, which he catches, then he touches second to retire Lloyd Waner and tags Pittsburgh's remaining outfielder, Clyde Barnhart. In a bizarre irony, Jimmy Cooney had been the lead runner on the last unassisted triple play ever turned—by Glenn Wright in 1924, when Cooney was a Cardinal. Johnny Nuen of the Detroit Tigers also turns an unassisted triple play. Nuen has clearly been reading about Cooney's exploits in his morning paper. The first baseman catches a line drive in the top of the ninth, tags a runner between first and second, then sprints to second base to register the third out, all the while shouting some jibberish about immortality.

August 22, 1942

It's perhaps the most exciting triple play in Cubs history. Things look bleak at Wrigley in the top of the 11th, with Reds in scoring position and no one out. Someone somewhere is praying for a triple play—and gets it: 2-6-3, from catcher Clyde McCullough to shortstop Lennie Merullo to first-baseman Phil Cavarretta. Bill Nicholson proceeds to win the game in the bottom of the inning with a home run.

Q. What Cubs pitcher was on the mound for all three triple plays the Cubs turned during the 1965 season?

A. Bill Faul

June 6, 1962

Cubs shortstop Andre Rodgers blows an unassisted triple play. With Jim Davenport at second, Tom Haller at first, and the hit-and-run on, Jose Pagan hits a line drive right to him—the formula for most unassisted triple plays. Rodgers drops the ball.

Replacing Ron Santo (Or Is it Bill Madlock? . . .)

Ron Santo played third base for the Cubs from 1960 to 1973, before crossing town to finish his career with the White Sox. The Cubs have been trying to replace him ever since. Ironically, the closest they've come to a long-term solution was Bill Madlock, Santo's immediate successor. But after three .300 seasons and two consecutive batting titles, Madlock was traded away. Here is everyone the Cubs have put at third base since Ron Santo retired, from Mike Adams to Todd Zeile.

Mike Adams	1976	Junior Kennedy	1982–83	Angel Salazar	1988
Manny Alexander	1997–98	Don Kessinger	1975	Luis Salazar	1989–92
Bret Barberie	1996	Joe Kmak	1995	Rey Sanchez	1997
Steve Buechele	1992–95	Vance Law	1988–89	Ryne Sandberg	1982
Ron Cey	1983–86	Davey Lopes	1985–86	Gary Scott	1991–92
Fritz Connally	1983	Steve Macko	1979–80	Rodney Scott	1978
Heity Cruz	1978, 1981	Bill Madlock	1974–76	Mike Sember	1978
Steve Davis	1979	Dave Magadan	1996	Tommy Shields	1993
Steve Dillard	1979–81	Mike Maksudian	1994	Terry Shumpert	1996
Ron Dunn	1974–75	Carmelo Martinez	1983	Chris Speier	1985–86
Carmen Fanzone	1974	Lloyd McClendon	1989	Rob Sperring	1975–76
Scott Fletcher	1981	Dave Meier	1988	Doug Strange	1991–92
Matt Franco	1995	Rudy Meoli	1978	Pat Tabler	1982
Gary Gaetti	1998	Keith Moreland	1982–87	Andre Thornton	1974–75
Leo Gomez	1996	Paul Noce	1987	Manny Trillo	1986–88
Billy Grabarkewitz	1974	Steve Ontiveros	1977–80	Jim Tyrone	1974
Todd Haney	1994–96	Kevin Orie	1997–98	Wayne Tyrone	1976
Dave Hansen	1997	Dave Owen	1983–85	Mike Vail	1978–79
Vic Harris	1975	Ed Putnam	1978	Tom Veryzer	1983–84
Richie Hebner	1984–85	Luis Quinones	1987	Jose Vizcaino	1991–93
Jose Hernandez	1994–98	Domingo Ramos	1989–90	Chico Walker	1987, 1991–92
Tyler Houston	1996–98	Lenny Randle	1980	Tye Waller	1981–82
Mike Hubbard	1997	Ken Reitz	1981	Curtis Wilkerson	1989–90
Dave Johnson	1978	Dan Rohn	1984	Eric Yelding	1993
Howard Johnson	1995	Dave Rosello	1977	Eddie Zambrano	1994
Mick Kelleher	1976–80	Wade Rowdon	1987	Todd Zeile	1995

Ron Santo

One might expect that a breakdown of players in the Hall of Fame would fall out by position in equal proportions. After all, if voters were truly rewarding the best at each position, then for each eight everyday Hall of Famers, there should be one third baseman, more or less. This hasn't been the case, as the next table shows.

Hall of Fame Distribution

Pos.	EXPECTED % OF HALL OF FAMERS	ACTUAL % OF HALL OF FAMERS
Catcher	12.5	10 (13)
First Base	12.5	12.5 (16)
Second Base	12.5	11 (14)
Shortstop	12.5	14 (18)
Third Base	12.5	8.5 (11)
Outfield	37.5	44 (56)

Discounting for the somewhat erratic induction record of players from the Negro Leagues, the 19th century, and the deadball era of the early 20th century, here is the distribution of the 85 Hall of Famers who played all or most of their career in the major leagues after 1919.

Hall of Fame Distribution—Post-1919

Pos.	EXPECTED % OF MODERN MAJOR-LEAGUE HALL OF FAMERS	ACTUAL % OF MODERN MAJOR-LEAGUE HALL OF FAMERS
Catcher	12.5	10.5 (9)
First Base	12.5	12 (10)
Second Base	12.5	13 (11)
Shortstop	12.5	14 (12)
Third Base	12.5	8 (7)
Outfield	37.5	42.5 (36)

Outfielders and shortstops are overrepresented in the Hall? Why? Two explanations: (1) Offensive statistics are given the greatest importance, far and away, and are regularly used to excuse lousy, inconsistent, or disinterested defensive play (players typically hidden in the outfield, such as Ralph Kiner, Reggie Jackson, or Ted Williams). (2) Weak hitting is expected of shortstops and is excused for outstanding fielders and/or team leaders, such as Luis Aparicio, Lou Boudreau, Pee Wee Reese, or Phil Rizzuto. In fact, the only shortstops who could merit automatic induction on the basis of offensive production (i.e., 450 home runs, 2,800 hits, or a .320 lifetime average with 2,000 hits) are Ernie Banks and Robin Yount, and each played only half of his career at the position. Catchers Ray Schalk and Rick Ferrell and second-baseman Red Schoendienst were able to get into Cooperstown with their gloves, but it's a short list of players who are enshrined without gaudy offensive numbers, and the majority are shortstops.

Third basemen are the most *under*represented in the Hall of Fame. Why? Perhaps voters are not taking into account how difficult it is to play the position, where reflexes, a strong, accurate arm, and quick feet can regularly turn doubles into outs and singles into double plays. In short, the voters are not setting realistic offensive expectations for third basemen.

He was out there every day, hurt or not, he had marvelous instincts, and he could hit.

Billy Williams, on Ron Santo

Their voting record—of, namely, those players they've snubbed, as we'll see later—suggests that they expect numbers similar to those produced by more than a few lead-footed first basemen and outfielders.

Of the few modern third basemen enshrined, more than half have the automatic passes: 2,800 hits (George Brett, Brooks Robinson), 450 home runs (Mike Schmidt, Eddie Mathews), or .320 with 2,000 hits (Pie Traynor). The sixth is George Kell, a slick fielder who also happened to accumulate 2,000 hits and a .300 lifetime average.

The remaining inductee is the weak link: Fred Lindstrom, a .311 hitter with 1,747 hits, not much power, not much speed, and half of his career spent in the outfield. He was by no means an outstanding fielder. His selection by the Veterans' Committee in 1976 seems to have less to do with honoring a third baseman and more to do with inducting the entire mid-1920s New York Giants infield (which was finally completed in 1982, when shortstop Travis Jackson joined Lindstrom, first-basemen Bill Terry and Highpockets Kelly, and second-baseman Frankie Frisch).

Even with the undeserving Lindstrom, there are only seven third basemen among the modern major leaguers in the Hall of Fame, when a reasonable proportion would suggest that at least 11 belong. Wade Boggs will probably hang it up after the 1999 season when he finally wheezes home with 3,000 singles. His induction five years later will bring the number to eight. So, who should the other three be? Here's a list of possibilities:

Prospective Hall of Famers

THIRD BASEMAN	HR	H	BA	GOLD GLOVES
Buddy Bell	201	2,514	.279	1979–84
Ken Boyer	282	2,143	.287	1958–61, 1963
Ron Cey	316	1,868	.261	
Bob Elliott	170	2,061	.289	1947*
Darrell Evans	414	2,223	.248	
Stan Hack	57	2,193	.301	1938–39, 1942–43, 1945*
Carney Lansford	151	2,074	.290	
Bill Madlock	163	2,008	.305	
Graig Nettles	390	2,225	.248	1977–78
Ron Santo	342	2,254	.277	1964–68

*Gold Gloves were not awarded prior to 1957, but fielding statistics (double plays, chances per game, fielding average) suggest that Hack and Elliott deserved National League honors during these seasons.

Offensively, Darrell Evans, Graig Nettles, Ron Santo, Ron Cey, and Ken Boyer stand out as the power leaders (though Evans hit more than 100 of his home runs at positions other than third). Of these five, Santo, Nettles, and Boyer were defensive standouts, and only Santo and Boyer were consistent run-producers who could hit for average.

Bill Madlock and Stan Hack are the only two players with .300+ lifetime batting averages. Hack developed into a fine fielder, while Madlock was a liability with the glove for most of his career.

Ron Santo and Ken Boyer—two players who could hit for power, produce runs, and handle the glove—are the best third basemen not in the Hall of Fame. Arguably, it's another Cub, Stan Hack, who is third in line. So, in addition to being third basemen, are there other reasons why Santo and Hack haven't been inducted? For one thing, it's with whom they're being compared by the voters.

Ron Santo's numbers may be dwarfed by slugging third basemen such as Mike Schmidt and Eddie Mathews, but compare him with Brooks Robinson—both with the bat *and* with the glove—and he more than holds his own. Stan Hack may have been "cursed" with consistency—a level of performance that produced no batting titles—but he had few, if any, off years. His 2,000 hits and .300 lifetime average are levels that only 78 other players have achieved. Hack's role at the top of the order called for him to get into scoring position, but runs scored has never been given the same respect as runs batted in. Compare his consistent run-scoring with that of other Hall of Fame table-setters such as Richie Ashburn, Lloyd Waner, and Billy Herman, and he fits right in at Cooperstown.

Ron Santo and Brooks Robinson

Brooks Robinson goes into the Hall of Fame in his second year of eligibility. Ron Santo never comes close for 21 years and counting. Santo hits .300 four times; Robinson does it twice. Santo knocks in 100 runs four times (and 98 or 99 three times); Robinson does it twice. Santo hits 25 home runs eight times; Robinson does it once. What's going on?

Is it simply a matter of Robinson's playing for a number of great teams, ending up on the postseason stage six times, four times in the World Series? In part, but there's more to it than that. Here are five reasons.

Q. What position did Ron Santo sign to play for the Cubs?

A. Catcher

1. Defensive Reputation

Brooks Robinson is almost universally regarded as the greatest-fielding third baseman who ever lived. Ask people their basis for this assessment, however, and chances are they'll tell you about a spectacular backhanded play they saw him make on a remarkably slow runner in Game One of a one-sided 1970 World Series. (And if it all comes down to a battle of post-season highlight reels, then it's Graig Nettles who is the greatest ever. His Game Three in 1978, which kept the Yankees from going down three games to none to the Dodgers and turned the World Series completely around, may be the greatest single-game fielding performance in history.)

They may also tell you about Robinson's 16 consecutive Gold Glove Awards from 1960 to 1975. Few could tell you, however, that he led the league in total chances per game only twice during these 16 seasons. In this, the best measure of a fielder's range, he frequently took a back seat to Clete Boyer—easily the greatest fielder never to earn a Gold Glove. Robinson led the league in fielding percentage 11 times during these 16 years, the most subjective of fielding statistics (made all the more subjective later in his career by Baltimore official scorers who would sooner bungee jump out of the press box than give an error to one of their hometown defensive legends).

A comparison of Robinson's defensive performance with that of Ron Santo, considered a better-than-average but not great fielder, shows that the difference is nowhere near as large as you'd think. Rather than unfairly punish Robinson for the four extra years he spent hanging on at the end of his career or the five he spent at the beginning trying to earn a regular job, we'll use Robinson's best 14 seasons. These just happen to coincide with the 14 years Santo spent at third base: 1960–73.

162-Game Averages (1960–73)

	DPs	ERRORS	CHANCES
Santo	30	24	522
Robinson	34	14	522

During this 14-year period, Robinson made an average of 10 fewer errors per season and turned four more double plays than Santo. Most interesting, however, is the fact that Robinson and Santo got to the same number of balls each year. Some may point out the fact that Orioles pitchers were more likely than Cubs pitchers to strike out a batter rather than induce a ground ball. True, but only by 5 percent. At best, this translates to about 10 more chances per season for Robinson over this period.

Santo's defense was much less consistent than Robinson's and especially erratic at the beginning and end of his career. But when he was at his best—from 1963 through 1967—Santo's range was actually better than Robinson's, as he got to 50 more balls per 162 games. Even the superior Orioles pitching staff during this stretch and their greater likelihood of keeping a batter from putting the ball in play can account for no more than half of this difference. Perhaps the rest is due to Wrigley's notoriously tall infield grass. More likely it's due to Santo's quickness, at which Billy Williams would marvel while watching him from left field.

None of this is to suggest that Brooks Robinson was anything but a great-fielding third baseman. In fact, he may very well be the greatest to ever play the position—but not by as much as his reputation suggests. Not even close. He had the surest hands, perhaps, but chances per game reveal that his range wasn't as great as any number of third basemen: Mike Schmidt, Buddy Bell, Terry Pendleton, Clete Boyer, Graig Nettles—and, at his best, Ron Santo.

2. Padded Stats

Ron Santo broke in at age 20 on June 26, 1960, going 4–7 with five RBIs to spark the Cubs to a doubleheader sweep of the title-winning Pittsburgh Pirates and their two aces, Bob Friend and Vern Law. (For those of you scoring at home, Vern's kid Vance, one of the cast of thousands who've tried to replace Santo at third for the Cubs, was three at the time.) Santo went on to hit .251 for his rookie season. Brooks Robinson broke in at 18, hitting .232 from 1955 to 1958 as he struggled to win—and hold—a full-time job. Santo retired at 35 after his only bad season in the majors. Robinson hit .201 during his final three seasons, retiring at the age of 40. Simply put, there was very little downtime during Ron Santo's career.

Robinson wasn't the first nor will he be the last to put up surprisingly large offensive numbers simply by playing for a very long time—23 years in his case, compared with only 15 years for Santo. Playing as long as he did allowed Robinson to run his hit total all the way up to 2,848, 29th on the all-time list at the time of his induction into Cooperstown despite a career batting average of .267, which is lowest among the 2,800-Hit Club.

Getting that many hits is impressive no matter how long one plays, but Robinson was a productive offensive player for only 15 of his 23 years. These just happened to coincide with Santo's entire career: 1960–74. How did they fare side by side during this 15-year period?

1960–74

	AB	H	HR	R	RBI	BA	SA
Ron Santo	8,143	2,254	342	1,138	1,331	.277	.464
Brooks Robinson	8,948	2,459	248	1,085	1,217	.275	.418

During Robinson's best years, Santo hit for much more power and produced more runs. If he'd played until he was 40—for a team that didn't undermine his production by trying to convert him to a second baseman at 35—it's reasonable to expect that Santo would have accumulated 2,700 hits and 400 home runs. That combination, by the way, is another automatic Cooperstown invite.

3. Overlooked Walks

Judging just from these statistics, it would appear that Santo and Robinson were similar offensive players who were equally adept at getting on base. They were actually quite different. Robinson put the ball in play far more often, while Santo worked pitchers, striking out nearly twice as much but also drawing many more walks.

Ron Santo—Third and Long

YEAR	G	AB	R	H	2B	3B	HR	RBI	SB	BA	SA	FP	GAMES BY Pos.
1960	95	347	44	87	24	2	9	44	0	.251	.409	.945	3B—94
1961	154	578	84	164	32	6	23	83	2	.284	.479	.937	3B—153
1962	162	604	44	137	20	4	17	83	4	.227	.358	.955	3B—157, SS—8
1963	162	630	79	187	29	6	25	99	6	.297	.481	.951	3B—162
1964	161	592	94	185	33	**13**	30	114	3	.313	.564	.963	3B—161
1965	162	608	88	173	30	4	33	101	3	.285	.510	.957	3B—164
1966	155	651	93	175	21	8	30	94	4	.269	.464	.956	3B—152, SS—8
1967	161	586	107	176	23	4	31	98	1	.300	.512	.957	3B—161
1968	162	577	86	142	17	3	26	98	3	.246	.421	.971	3B—162
1969	160	575	97	166	18	4	29	123	1	.289	.485	.947	3B—160
1970	154	555	83	148	30	4	26	114	2	.267	.476	.945	3B—152, OF—1
1971	154	555	77	148	22	1	21	88	4	.267	.423	.957	3B—149, OF—6
1972	133	464	68	140	25	5	17	74	1	.302	.487	.948	3B—129, 2B—3, SS—1, OF—1
1973	149	536	65	143	29	2	20	77	1	.267	.440	.950	3B—146
Totals	2,124	7,768	1,109	2,171	353	66	337	1,290	35	.276	.467	.973	3B—2,102, SS—17, OF—8, 2B—3

Note: League-leading total in **bold**.

Santo drew 85 or more walks seven times, leading the league four times—including three consecutive seasons (1966–68), a major-league record since broken by Barry Bonds. As a result, he had on-base percentages of .400+ three times, and he led the league twice. For his career, he drew 1,108 walks for an on-base percentage of .366. Robinson never walked more than 63 times in a season and never had an on-base percentage higher than .354. He finished his career with 860 walks and an on-base percentage of .325. During 1960–74, Santo's hits and walks exceeded Robinson's by 155.

This ability to get on base is the main reason why his runs scored exceed Robinson's, though Robinson had an additional 100 games' worth of plate appearances.

4. The Wrigley Factor

Some will argue that Santo's statistics are inflated by playing in hitter-friendly Wrigley Field, while Robinson played in the more neutral Memorial Stadium. True, Santo hit more than 60 percent of his home runs at home, as Ernie Banks and Billy Williams also did. A 50-50 split is more common. With only 126 of his 342 home runs coming on the road, perhaps Santo would have hit only about 250 home runs if he'd played in Baltimore. But while his home runs may have declined significantly, it's reasonable to expect that his RBI and runs-scored totals would have gone up from his being in the far more productive Baltimore Orioles lineup of the 1960s and early 1970s.

From 1960 to 1974, Santo's team outscored Robinson's team only five times. While the Orioles scored more than 10,200 runs, the 1960–73 Cubs and 1974 White Sox scored only 9,900. Santo regularly produced more than 25 percent of the Cubs' runs, something Robinson did only once for the Orioles. If Santo had played for the Orioles, he would have had to shoulder less of the offensive burden, but his production would have gone up from having more protection in the lineup and more men on base.

5. The 350-Home-Run Jinx

More accurately, it's the 319-to-354-home-run jinx. Hitting that many is no small accomplishment, good enough for a slot somewhere between 49 and 67 on the all-time list. Yet, of this group of 18 players, only one has made the Hall of Fame—Hank Greenberg, who missed three prime years and, conservatively, 100 home runs due to World War II. It's a group

Guilt by Association?

PLAYER	HR	H	BA	Pos.
Lee May	354	2,031	.267	1B-DH
Gary Gaetti	351	2,223	.257	3B
Dick Allen	351	1,848	.292	1B-3B
Harold Baines	348	2,649	.291	DH
George Foster	348	1,925	.274	OF
Ron Santo	**342**	**2,254**	**.277**	**3B**
Jack Clark	340	1,826	.267	OF-1B
Dave Parker	339	2,712	.290	OF-DH
Boog Powell	339	1,776	.266	1B
Don Baylor	338	2,135	.260	DH
Joe Adcock	336	1,832	.277	1B
Bobby Bonds	332	1,886	.268	OF
Darryl Strawberry	332	1,385	.258	OF-DH
Chili Davis	331	2,252	.275	OF-DH
Willie Horton	325	1,993	.273	OF-DH
Gary Carter	324	2,092	.262	C
Lance Parrish	324	1,782	.252	C
Cecil Fielder	319	1,313	.255	1B-DH

Note: Andres Galarraga and Albert Belle apparently set up only temporary residence in this neighborhood in 1998, though both would fit right in—as Matt Williams quite likely will when all is said and done. By hitting 56 home runs, Griffey Junior nearly blew right through it without stopping.

bounded on both sides by Hall of Famers (Berra 358, Mize 359, DiMaggio 361, and Kiner 369 on the high side and Brett 317, Simmons 307, Hornsby 300, and Klein 300 on the low side). But once you throw out Greenberg, it's a group that is in large part composed of .260-hitting designated hitters and bad attitudes.

Only four players—Ron Santo, Gary Gaetti, Lance Parrish, and Gary Carter—aren't first basemen, outfielders, or designated hitters. Only Dick Allen, Harold Baines, and Dave Parker have a higher lifetime average than Santo, and through 1998 only Parker and Baines had more hits. Among that group, only Parker was ever much with the glove (for a while, anyway).

Perhaps Ron Santo is suffering from guilt by association with this mixed bag—rather than being more rightfully compared with his closest peer: Brooks Robinson.

the outfield

While Chicago's infield has been home to some of the team's most consistent players—from Cap Anson to Joe Tinker to Charlie Grimm to Billy Herman to Stan Hack to Ernie Banks to Ron Santo to Don Kessinger to Ryne Sandberg to Mark Grace—the grassy expanse behind the dirt has seen greater extremes and far more instability. In fact, in 123 seasons, the Cubs have kept their outfield together for three years only *twice*. This chapter celebrates the greatest extremes and those fleeting moments of stability:

- The defensive standouts—the Gold Glove winners; the best the team has seen in left, center, and right; the greatest throwing arms; the fielders who covered the most territory; and the record-holders
- The greatest offensive seasons by an outfielder—it's not Sammy Sosa, Hack Wilson, or Billy Williams who leads the way in three different statistical categories
- The 14 hardest-hitting outfields, from Abner Dalrymple, George Gore, and King Kelly in 1884 to Sammy Sosa, Henry Rodriguez, and the Brant Brown/Lance Johnson tandem in 1998
- The 22 center fielders who managed to keep the job for more than one season
- The seven most tragic fly balls in the team's history, from Brant Brown to Max Flack
- A tribute to the most consistent of all Cubs outfielders, Billy Williams
- A look back at Kiki Cuyler's greatest game—if only Harry Caray had been there to call that one!

And, oh, by the way, a look at a certain right fielder's home-run performance in 1998 from every conceivable angle:

- By inning
- By base runners
- By situation
- By opponent
- By month
- By result
- By Cubs pitcher

. . . and a list of all 66, by date, game situation, and opposing pitcher. In the immortal words of one-year Cubs center-fielder Richie Ashburn, "Yo la tengo."

RECORDS

Games Played

1.	Billy Williams	2,087	6.	Sammy Sosa	918
2.	Jimmy Ryan	1,591	7.	Riggs Stephenson	898
3.	Wildfire Schulte	1,540	8.	Jimmy Slagle	890
4.	Bill Nicholson	1,292	9.	Hack Wilson	837
5.	Jimmy Sheckard	999	10.	Andre Dawson	826

Gold Gloves

1984	Bob Dernier	CF
1987	Andre Dawson	RF
1988	Andre Dawson	RF

All-Glove Outfield

Right Field: Andre Dawson. Many weak-armed outfielders have racked up a lot of assists simply because base runners have given them plenty of opportunities. And many strong-armed outfielders have been equally as likely to heave the ball into the dugout as they have been to nail the runner at third. No one ran on the Hawk—and when he did throw the ball, he knew where it was going. The only Cubs' outfielder to win two Gold Gloves, the former center fielder recorded 51 assists to only 20 errors while patrolling right in Wrigley.

Center Field: Andy Pafko. No other Cubs outfielder has gotten to as many balls per game as Pafko regularly did during the 1940s. For an outfielder to reach the level of three chances per game is lofty territory—Ashburn did it nine times; Speaker, Maddox, and Mays five; and DiMaggio three. Blair did it only twice; Lofton, Rivers, and Flood only once; and Mantle never did it. Pafko did it in 1944—only one of two Cubs to do it since World War II—and was consistently at 2.5 or more during his days in Chicago.

Left Field: Hank Sauer. Hank Sauer? Great-fielding left fielders such as Barry Bonds are about as rare as a Barry Bonds base hit in October. The Cubs, like most other teams, have used left field as a home for severely flawed defensive players who can hit: Dave Kingman, Moose Moryn, Ralph Kiner, Riggs Stephenson. But prior to being moved out of position to right field to make room for Ralph Kiner, Hank Sauer was a very capable defensive player who got to more balls per game in 1951 and 1952 than any other left fielder in the league. During his 3½ seasons in left, the Mayor of Wrigley Field piled up 58 assists while making only 25 errors.

Honorable Mentions: Bob Dernier, Adolfo Phillips, Hal Jeffcoat, Peanuts Lowrey, Kiki Cuyler, and Bill Lange.

Multiple 15-Assist Seasons

Kiki Cuyler	4	1928–30, 1934	Frank Demaree	2	1936–37
Jigger Statz	3	1922–24	Peanuts Lowrey	2	1945–46
Bill Nicholson	3	1942–44	Hank Sauer	2	1951–52
Max Flack	2	1920–21	Billy Williams	2	1962, 1969
Hack Miller	2	1922–23	Sammy Sosa	2	1996–97
Cliff Heathcote	2	1925–26			

Fielding Leaders: Arms—15 Assists (since 1920)

Prior to the 1920s, base runners were much more aggressive and outfield assists that much more common. King Kelly often recorded assists by throwing runners out at first. Jimmy Sheckard had a modern-club-record 32 assists in 1911, while Orator Shaffer had 50 assists (and 37 errors!) in only 98 games in 1879. Since 1920, Jigger Statz has the club record for most outfield assists in a season, with 26 in 1923. Kiki Cuyler reached the 15-assist level four times, the most of any player since the deadball era ended. Players with a 3:1 ratio of assists to errors are in **bold**. Given the strength and accuracy of Hal Jeffcoat's arm in 1952, perhaps it should not come as a surprise that he became a pitcher.

YEAR	FIELDER	ASSISTS	ERRORS
1997	Sammy Sosa	16	8
1996	Sammy Sosa	15	10
1974	Jose Cardenal	15	10
1969	Billy Williams	15	12
1963	Lou Brock	17	8
1962	Billy Williams	18	10
1956	**Moose Moryn**	**18**	**5**
1952	**Hal Jeffcoat**	**16**	**1**
1952	Hank Sauer	17	6
1951	**Hank Sauer**	**19**	**6**
1946	Peanuts Lowrey	15	7
1945	**Peanuts Lowrey**	**17**	**4**
1944	**Andy Pafko**	**24**	**6**
1944	Bill Nicholson	18	7
1943	Bill Nicholson	16	8
1942	**Bill Nicholson**	**18**	**5**
1937	Frank Demaree	17	6
1936	Frank Demaree	16	10
1934	Kiki Cuyler	15	10
1930	Kiki Cuyler	21	8
1929	Kiki Cuyler	15	8
1928	**Kiki Cuyler**	**18**	**5**
1927	Riggs Stephenson	18	8
1926	**Cliff Heathcote**	**22**	**5**
1925	Cliff Heathcote	21	8
1924	Jigger Statz	22	16
1924	Denver Grigsby	16	7
1923	Jigger Statz	26	12
1923	Hack Miller	17	6
1922	Jigger Statz	16	14
1922	Hack Miller	15	10
1921	**Max Flack**	**19**	**3**
1921	Turner Barber	23	8
1920	Dode Paskert	23	15
1920	Max Flack	16	8

Multiple 2.6-Chance Seasons

Andy Pafko	4	1944–47	Hal Jeffcoat	2	1948–49
Jigger Statz	3	1922–24	Bob Dernier	2	1984–85
Hack Wilson	3	1926–27, 1929	Jerome Walton	2	1989–90
Peanuts Lowrey	2	1943, 1946			

Fielding Leaders: Range—2.6 Total Chances per Game (since 1920)

It was easier to reach 2.6 total chances per game after the deadball era—when players began uppercutting for the first time and before the strikeout rose to prominence after World War II—simply because more catchable balls were being hit into the outfield. Andy Pafko reached this level four times, more than any other outfielder since 1920 (Bill Lange did it five times in the 1890s). Players who averaged three total chances per game are in **bold**.

YEAR	FIELDER	TC/G
1995	Brian McRae	2.6
1990	Jerome Walton	2.6
1989	Jerome Walton	2.6
1985	Bob Dernier	2.8
1984	Bob Dernier	2.6
1976	Rick Monday	2.8
1967	Adolfo Phillips	2.6
1956	Pete Whisenant	2.7
1952	Frankie Baumholtz	2.6
1949	Hal Jeffcoat	2.7
1948	Hal Jeffcoat	2.7
1947	Andy Pafko	2.7
1946	Andy Pafko	2.8
1946	Peanuts Lowrey	2.6
1945	Andy Pafko	2.7
1944	**Andy Pafko**	**3.0**
1943	**Peanuts Lowrey**	**3.0**
1939	Hank Leiber	2.7
1938	Carl Reynolds	2.8
1936	Augie Galan	2.7
1933	Frank Demaree	2.6
1932	Johnny Moore	2.7
1930	Kiki Cuyler	2.6
1929	Hack Wilson	2.7
1927	Hack Wilson	2.9
1926	Hack Wilson	2.6
1925	**Mandy Brooks**	**3.0**
1924	**Jigger Statz**	**3.1**
1923	**Jigger Statz**	**3.1**
1922	**Jigger Statz**	**3.1**
1921	George Maisel	2.6

Fielding Records

Jimmy Ryan has the National League record for assists, piling up 356 in 15 years during the fast-and-loose days of the 19th century. But not even Ryan ever threw three runners out at the plate in one game, which Jack McCarthy did on April 26, 1905, as the Cubs beat the Pirates 2–1. On May 27, 1945, Andy Pafko threw out two runners in the same inning, a feat later matched by left-fielder Jim Hickman on May 4, 1970. It took an entire season for Brian McRae to record two assists, setting a National League–record low of two in 155 games in 1996, tying Len Dykstra of the Phillies.

Cubs outfielders have set records for both activity and inactivity. Topsy Hartsel recorded a major-league record for left fielders with 11 putouts in one game on September 10, 1901, and Bill Nicholson established the National League record for right fielders with 10 putouts on September 17, 1945. Wildfire Schulte set a National League record by going six consecutive games without recording a putout, an assist, or an error—from a doubleheader on June 25 to June 29, 1912.

Outfield Stability

When one thinks of Jose Cardenal, Rick Monday, and Jerry Morales, fifth place comes to mind. But these three players actually made up one of the most stable outfields in team history. After all, the Cubs have been able to keep the same outfield together for two years in a row only six times.

Back-to-Back Outfields

YEARS	LEFT	CENTER	RIGHT
1894–95	Walt Wilmot	Bill Lange	Jimmy Ryan
1909–11	Jimmy Sheckard	Solly Hofman	Wildfire Schulte
1916–17	Les Mann	Cy Williams	Max Flack
1928–29	Riggs Stephenson	Hack Wilson	Kiki Cuyler
1972–73	Billy Williams	Rick Monday	Jose Cardenal
1974–76	Jerry Morales (RF in '76)	Rick Monday	Jose Cardenal (LF in '76)

Note: Minimum 100 games by each outfielder.

Injuries kept the Stephenson/Wilson/Cuyler outfield from passing the 100-games test in 1930 and 1931. Injuries also kept the Sheckard/Slagle/Schulte outfield of 1906–08 from making the list. And the ability of King Kelly to play every position on the field kept him from playing enough games in the outfield to put the Dalrymple/Gore/Kelly unit of 1880 to 1886 on the list.

Outfield Season Records (minimum 100 games at position)

Games:	Billy Williams	1965	164
At Bats:	Jigger Statz	1923	655
Hits:	Kiki Cuyler	1930	228
Doubles:	Kiki Cuyler	1930	50
Triples:	Wildfire Schulte	1911	21
Home Runs:	Sammy Sosa	1998	66
RBIs:	Hack Wilson	1930	190
Runs:	Kiki Cuyler	1930	155
Walks:	Jimmy Sheckard	1911	147
Strikeouts:	Sammy Sosa	1998	174
Stolen Bases:	Billy Maloney	1905	59
Batting Average:	Bill Lange	1895	.389
Slugging Average:	Hack Wilson	1930	.723

OUTFIELDS

In chronological order, here are the 14 hardest-hitting outfields the Cubs have assembled. League-leading totals are in **bold.**

Dalrymple/Gore/Kelly 1884

These three played together as a unit on four pennant-winners, but their best statistical season was in 1884 when the team finished fourth.

	HR	RBI	BA
Abner Dalrymple, LF	22	69	.309
George Gore, CF	5	34	.318
King Kelly, RF	13	95	**.354**

Van Haltren/Ryan/Duffy 1889

There were wholesale defections from the National League to the Players League in 1890, though many White Stockings players returned to Chicago when the rival league folded after one season. Two players who defected and didn't return were George Van Haltren, who finished his career with more than 2,500 hits and a .316 average, and Hugh Duffy, who went on to a career .324 average while hitting .440 in 1894. This is what they did in 1889 while still in Chicago:

	HR	RBI	BA
George Van Haltren, LF	9	81	.309
Jimmy Ryan, CF	17	72	.307
Hugh Duffy, RF	12	89	.295

Wilmot/Lange/Ryan 1894

The Colts finished 18 games under .500 in 1894, 16 games off the pace, despite a huge season from Bill Dahlen at shortstop, a near-.400 season from Cap Anson at the age of 42, and a great offensive outfield. Then again, with the pitching distance pushed back to 60'6", the league hit .308 and the Philadelphia Phillies finished fourth with a *.400-hitting* outfield.

	HR	RBI	BA
Walt Wilmot, LF	5	130	.330
Bill Lange, CF	6	90	.328
Jimmy Ryan, RF	3	62	.361

Sheckard/Hofman/Schulte 1911

These three played together during the Cubs' dynasty of 1906–10, with Hofman splitting time with Jimmy Slagle, but they were their most productive during the livelier offensive season of 1911, when Chicago finished seven games behind the Giants. Sheckard scored a league-leading 121 runs as he walked 147 times, a National League record that stood for more than 80 years.

	HR	RBI	BA
Jimmy Sheckard, LF	4	50	.276
Solly Hofman, CF	2	70	.252
Wildfire Schulte, RF	**21**	**121**	.300

Stephenson/Wilson/Cuyler 1929

As a unit, the Cubs' outfield hit .350 in 1929, second only to the Detroit Tigers of 1925 (.367). Chicago's outfield also knocked in 371 runs, with 71 home runs, dwarfing Detroit's production. They weren't bad fielders, either. Hack Wilson may have been built like a fire hydrant—5´6˝/190 with a size-18 collar and size-5 feet—but he was a good enough outfielder that he could keep the speedy and graceful Kiki Cuyler in right. Wilson and Cuyler stepped it up a notch in 1930, and if not for an injury to Stephenson, the unit would have been even more impressive a year later.

	HR	RBI	BA
Riggs Stephenson, LF	17	110	.362
Hack Wilson, CF	39	**159**	.345
Kiki Cuyler, RF	15	102	.360

Kiner/Baumholtz/Sauer 1953

The Cubs' leadoff man, Frankie Baumholtz, got plenty of exercise playing center field between two lead-footed sluggers. Legend even has it that Baumholtz once ranged far enough to catch a ball in foul territory.

	HR	RBI	BA
Ralph Kiner, LF	28	87	.283
Frankie Baumholtz, CF	3	25	.306
Hank Sauer, RF	19	60	.263

Moryn/Thomson/Walls 1958

The first Cubs' outfield of 20-homer hitters helped Chicago climb to fifth place in 1958.

	HR	RBI	BA
Moose Moryn, LF	26	77	.264
Bobby Thomson, CF	21	82	.283
Lee Walls, RF	24	72	.304

Williams/Brock/Altman 1962

This young unit looked as though it might be the Cubs' outfield for the next 10 years, but Altman faded away, and Brock was given away.

	HR	RBI	BA
Billy Williams, LF	22	91	.298
Lou Brock, CF	9	35	.263
George Altman, RF	22	74	.318

Williams/Monday/Cardenal 1973

With better pitching, this outfield might have made it to the play-offs in place of the 82–79 Mets. It was Billy Williams's last big year.

	HR	RBI	BA
Billy Williams, LF	20	86	.288
Rick Monday, CF	26	56	.267
Jose Cardenal, RF	11	68	.303

Matthews/Dernier/Moreland 1984

This trio of former Phillies helped the Cubs reach the postseason for the first time in 39 years. Dernier stole 45 bases, and Matthews led the league with 103 walks.

	HR	RBI	BA
Gary Matthews, LF	14	82	.291
Bob Dernier, CF	3	32	.278
Keith Moreland, RF	16	80	.279

Mumphrey-Palmeiro/Martinez/Dawson 1987

The best last-place team in baseball history happened to have a very productive outfield.

	HR	RBI	BA
Jerry Mumphrey–Rafael Palmeiro, LF	27	74	.309
Dave Martinez, CF	8	36	.292
Andre Dawson, RF	49	137	.287

Smith/Walton/Dawson 1989

The Cubs put two rookies in their outfield next to Andre Dawson, and they finished 1-2 in the Rookie of the Year balloting.

	HR	RBI	BA
Dwight Smith, LF	9	52	.324
Jerome Walton, CF	5	46	.293
Andre Dawson, RF	21	77	.252

Gonzalez/McRae/Sosa 1996

This outfield built on three excellent trades helped the Cubs stay in the pennant race until Sammy Sosa's wrist was broken on August 20. They also combined to steal 64 bases.

	HR	RBI	BA
Luis Gonzalez, LF	15	79	.271
Brian McRae, CF	17	66	.276
Sammy Sosa, RF	40	100	.273

Rodriguez/Brown-Johnson/Sosa 1998

Sammy Sosa in 1998 was an outfield's worth of statistics on his own, but he had a home-run partner in Henry Rodriguez, while Brant Brown and later Lance Johnson were productive in center.

	HR	RBI	BA
Henry Rodriguez, LF	31	85	.251
Brant Brown–Lance Johnson, CF	16	69	.286
Sammy Sosa, RF	66	158	.308

Center Fielders

The Cubs have had a number of unsettled positions through the years: catcher between Gabby Hartnett and Randy Hundley, shortstop between Billy Jurges and Ernie Banks, third base since Ron Santo, and left field since Billy Williams. But center field is a position that no Cub has held down for seven years since Piano Legs Gore in the 1880s. They've even had a 14-year stretch, from 1953 to 1966, when they used a different center fielder each season.

Here are the Cubs center fielders who've kept the job for more than one season.

Center-Field Regimes

1997–98	Lance Johnson	1926–31	Hack Wilson
1995–97	Brian McRae	1922–24	Jigger Statz
1989–91	Jerome Walton	1918–20	Dode Paskert
1987–88	Dave Martinez	1915–17	Cy Williams
1984–86	Bob Dernier	1912–14	Tommy Leach
1979–80	Jerry Martin	1909–11	Solly Hofman
1972–76	Rick Monday	1905–08	Jimmy Slagle
1966–68	Adolfo Phillips	1900–01	Danny Green
1951–53	Frankie Baumholtz	1894–99	Bill Lange
1944–47, 1949–50	Andy Pafko	1887–89, 1891–93	Jimmy Ryan
1939–40	Hank Leiber	1879–1886	George Gore

Tragic Fly Balls

Long before Brant Brown dropped what should have been the final out of a crucial 7–5 victory with the bases loaded in the bottom of the ninth, the Cubs have had trouble with fly balls at the worst possible times. The less-than-magnificent seven, beginning with Brown:

7. **September 23, 1998.** Bases loaded, two out, bottom of the ninth in Milwaukee, left-fielder Brant Brown drops a fly ball to give the Brewers an 8–7 win, and the Cubs fall a half game behind the Mets.

6. **May 2, 1917.** Top of the 10th in Chicago, center-fielder Cy Williams drops what should have been the third out, giving the Reds the opportunity to push across the first run of the game. Hippo Vaughn loses the "double no-hitter" to Fred Toney, 1–0.

5. **July 8, 1969.** Ninth inning, Cubs up 3–1 at Shea, Ferguson Jenkins on the mound. Don Young plays two fly balls into doubles, and the Mets win 4–3.

4. **October 5, 1935.** Game Four of the 1935 World Series, tied 1–1 in the top of the sixth, with the Cubs fighting for their first postseason win at Wrigley in six attempts. With two down, left-fielder Augie Galan drops the third out, and a throwing error by Billy Jurges on the next play gives the Tigers what proves to be the winning run.

3. **October 12, 1929.** Game Four of the 1929 World Series, bottom of the seventh in Philadelphia, Cubs up 8–1. Center-fielder Hack Wilson loses a ball in the sun hit by Bing Miller for a single . . .

2. . . . and five batters later, Hack Wilson loses another ball in the sun, this one hit by Mule Haas, for a three-run homer that cuts the Cubs' lead to 8–7. The Athletics win 10–8 and take the Series in five.

1. **September 11, 1918.** World Series, Game Six, bottom of the third inning in Boston, no score, two men on. Right-fielder Max Flack drops a line drive hit by George Whiteman, and two runs score. The Red Sox win 2–1 and take the Series.

Sammy Sosa

From now on, every discussion of Cubs and home runs will begin with Sammy Sosa. Here is a breakdown of his 66 in '98.

Sosa hit 24 of his home runs in the first and fifth innings. Eight of his home runs came with two out and none on in the first. None came in extra innings, and none ended a game.

Home Runs by Inning

1st	2nd	3rd	4th	5th	6th	7th	8th	9th
12	2	8	5	12	8	6	9	4

Sosa had hit no grand slams going into the season, but he hit three in 1998. Thirty-seven of his home runs came with the bases empty.

Home Runs by Number of Base Runners

SOLO	2-RUN	3-RUN	GRAND SLAM
37	19	7	3

Nineteen of Sosa's home runs came with the score tied, and another 16 came with the Cubs within one or two runs of the lead.

Home Runs by Situation

UP 4+	UP 3	UP 2	UP 1	TIED	DOWN 1	DOWN 2	DOWN 3	DOWN 4	DOWN 5+
3	3	5	8	19	6	10	2	5	5

Twenty-two of Sosa's home runs put the Cubs in the lead, 7 tied the game, and 12 put the Cubs within one or two runs. Another 13 provided insurance runs in close games, 8 came in blowouts, 2 keyed comebacks, and 2 provided a comfortable cushion in a game the Cubs would blow (the 8–7 game in Milwaukee on September 23).

Sosa homered against every team he faced except the Cleveland Indians and Kansas City Royals, and he went deep in every ballpark in which he played except Kaufman Stadium (a total of 18 for the season, 3 more than McGwire). He homered in his final National League park when he took Jason Schmidt out of the yard in Three Rivers on September 4. By taking the Brewers deep 12 times, he came within 1 of the mark shared by Roger Maris and Hank Sauer.

Home Runs by Opponent

TEAM	HOME	AWAY
Arizona Diamondbacks	2	3
Atlanta Braves		3
Cincinnati Reds	2	2
Colorado Rockies	1	2
Florida Marlins	3	1
Houston Astros	2	2
Los Angeles Dodgers	0	1
Milwaukee Brewers	8	4
Montreal Expos	2	1
New York Mets	1	1
Philadelphia Phillies	7	1
Pittsburgh Pirates	0	2
St. Louis Cardinals	2	1
San Diego Padres	1	2
San Francisco Giants	1	2
Chicago White Sox	3	
Cleveland Indians	0	
Detroit Tigers		2
Kansas City Royals		0
Minnesota Twins		1
Total	35	31

Sosa's big home-run month was June, but he hit 33 more in July, August, and September.

Home Runs by Month

April	6
May	7
June	20
July	9
August	13
September	11

Home Runs by Result

	W	L	COMBINED
Comeback	1	1	2
Blowout	4	4	8
Big lead later blown	0	2	2
Insurance for 2-run lead	5	1	6
Insurance for 1-run lead	6	1	7
Puts Cubs in front	15	7	22
Ties game	1	6	7
Puts Cubs within 1	3	5	8
Puts Cubs within 2	2	2	4
Totals	37*	29	

*The Cubs were 30–24 when Sosa homered; 19 of Sosa's home runs proved to be the margin of victory in 15 of those wins.

Though Kerry Wood appeared in only 26 games, Sammy Sosa gave him 15 home runs to work with. Wins leader Kevin Tapani benefited only from nine.

Home Runs for Pitchers

Kerry Wood	15	Dave Stevens	2
Steve Trachsel	11	Rod Beck	1
Mark Clark	10	Kevin Foster	1
Kevin Tapani	9	Chris Haney	1
Terry Adams	5	Justin Speier	1
Terry Mulholland	4	Kennie Steenstra	1
Jeremi Gonzalez	2	Amaury Telemaco	1
Felix Heredia	2		

Here they are, all 66 of them, including the victimized pitchers. Cal Eldred and Jose Lima each yielded three, while Brett Tomko, Bronswell Patrick, Carlton Loewer, and Alan Embree were all touched twice. Only 12 of Sosa's home runs came against left-handers.

Sammy's 66 in '98

#	DATE	OPPONENT	INNING	OUTS	RBI	SCORE	FINAL	PITCHER
1	April 4	Expos	3	2	1	1–1	3–1	Marc Valdes
2	April 11	at Expos	7	1	1	3–4	4–5	Anthony Telford
3	April 15	at Mets	8	2	1	0–2	1–2	Dennis Cook*
4	April 23	Padres	9	0	1	0–4	1–4	Dan Miceli
5	April 24	at Dodgers	1	2	1	0–0	4–12	Ismael Valdes
6	April 27	at Padres	1	1	2	0–0	3–1	Joey Hamilton
7	May 3	Cardinals	1	2	1	0–0	5–8	Cliff Politte
8	May 16	at Reds	3	1	3	1–0	5–1	Scott Sullivan
9	May 22	at Braves	1	2	1	0–0	2–8	Greg Maddux
10	May 25	at Braves	4	0	1	1–1	5–9	Kevin Millwood
11	May 25	at Braves	8	2	3	2–6	5–9	Mike Cather
12	May 27	Phillies	8	0	1	2–10	5–10	Darrin Winston*
13	May 27	Phillies	9	2	2	3–10	5–10	Wayne Gomes
14	June 1	Marlins	1	1	2	0–0	10–2	Ryan Dempster
15	June 1	Marlins	8	2	3	7–2	10–2	Oscar Henriquez
16	June 3	Marlins	5	0	2	2–0	5–1	Livan Hernandez
17	June 5	White Sox	5	0	2	3–2	6–5	Jim Parque*
18	June 6	White Sox	7	2	1	6–5	7–6	Carlos Castillo
19	June 7	White Sox	5	1	3	10–2	13–7	James Baldwin
20	June 8	at Twins	3	1	1	1–0	8–1	LaTroy Hawkins
21	June 13	at Phillies	6	0	2	2–6	10–8	Mark Portugal
22	June 15	Brewers	1	2	1	0–0	6–5	Cal Eldred
23	June 15	Brewers	3	1	1	3–2	6–5	Cal Eldred
24	June 15	Brewers	7	2	1	5–5	6–5	Cal Eldred
25	June 17	Brewers	4	0	1	2–3	5–6	Bronswell Patrick
26	June 19	Phillies	1	2	1	0–0	8–9	Carlton Loewer
27	June 19	Phillies	5	1	2	3–5	8–9	Carlton Loewer
28	June 20	Phillies	3	2	2	1–4	9–4	Matt Beech*
29	June 20	Phillies	6	1	3	6–4	9–4	Toby Borland
30	June 21	Phillies	4	2	1	0–2	2–7	Tyler Green
31	June 24	at Tigers	1	1	1	1–0	6–7	Seth Greisinger

continued

Sammy's 66 in '98

#	DATE	OPPONENT	INNING	OUTS	RBI	SCORE	FINAL	PITCHER
32	June 25	at Tigers	7	0	1	1–3	4–6	Brian Moehler
33	June 30	Diamondbacks	8	1	1	3–5	4–5	Alan Embree*
34	July 9	at Brewers	2	2	2	3–4	9–12	Jeff Juden
35	July 10	at Brewers	2	0	1	0–1	5–6	Scott Karl*
36	July 17	at Marlins	6	2	2	4–1	6–1	Kirt Ojala*
37	July 22	Expos	8	2	3	5–3	9–5	Miguel Batista
38	July 26	Mets	6	1	2	0–1	3–1	Rick Reed
39	July 27	at Diamondbacks	6	2	2	0–2	6–2	Willie Blair
40	July 27	at Diamondbacks	8	0	4	2–2	6–2	Alan Embree*
41	July 28	at Diamondbacks	5	1	4	1–3	5–7	Bob Wolcott
42	July 31	Rockies	1	2	1	0–0	9–1	Jamey Wright
43	August 5	Diamondbacks	3	2	2	1–5	7–10	Andy Benes
44	August 8	at Cardinals	9	0	2	3–5	8–9	Rick Croushore
45	August 10	at Giants	5	2	1	3–5	8–5	Russ Ortiz
46	August 10	at Giants	7	2	1	5–5	8–5	Chris Brock
47	August 16	at Astros	4	1	1	0–0	2–1	Sean Bergman
48	August 19	Cardinals	5	2	2	4–2	6–8	Kent Bottenfield
49	August 21	Giants	5	1	2	2–1	6–5	Orel Hershiser
50	August 23	Astros	5	2	1	1–4	3–13	Jose Lima
51	August 23	Astros	8	0	1	2–13	3–13	Jose Lima
52	August 26	at Reds	3	2	1	3–1	9–2	Brett Tomko
53	August 28	at Rockies	1	2	1	0–0	10–5	John Thomson
54	August 30	at Rockies	1	1	2	0–0	4–3	Darryl Kile
55	August 31	Reds	3	2	2	0–4	5–4	Brett Tomko
56	September 2	Reds	6	0	1	0–0	4–2	Jason Bere
57	September 4	at Pirates	1	2	1	0–0	5–2	Jason Schmidt
58	September 5	at Pirates	6	0	1	3–2	8–4	Sean Lawrence*
59	September 11	Brewers	5	1	1	5–10	11–13	Bill Pulsipher*
60	September 12	Brewers	7	1	3	5–12	15–12	Valerio De Los Santos*
61	September 13	Brewers	5	0	2	6–3	11–10	Bronswell Patrick
62	September 13	Brewers	9	1	1	8–10	11–10	Eric Plunk
63	September 16	at Padres	8	2	4	2–2	6–3	Brian Boehringer
64	September 23	at Brewers	5	1	1	3–0	7–8	Rafael Roque*
65	September 23	at Brewers	6	2	1	6–0	7–8	Rod Henderson
66	September 25	at Astros	4	0	1	1–2	2–6	Jose Lima

*Left-hander

Billy Williams

Billy Williams was the greatest left-handed hitter who ever played for the Cubs. He grew up in Whistler, Alabama, overshadowed by other local heroes Hank Aaron, Willie McCovey, and Willie Mays. When the Cubs signed him, he didn't even receive a bonus. "There was no money involved," Williams said. "My father got a cigar, and I got a ticket to Ponca City."

He won the Rookie of the Year Award in 1961 after two brief trials in 1959 and 1960. He hit a grand slam on his 23rd birthday to beat the Giants on June 15 and never left the starting lineup again. In 1964 and 1965 he became only the fourth Cub to get 200 hits in consecutive seasons.

Billy Williams Day was celebrated at Wrigley Field on June 29, 1969, with the Cardinals in town for a doubleheader. Williams tied Stan Musial in Game One and passed him in Game Two for consecutive games played in the National League with 895 and 896. Williams

Billy Williams: The Cubs' Greatest Left-Hander

YEAR	G	AB	R	H	2B	3B	HR	RBI	SB	BA	SA	FP	GAMES BY Pos.
1959	18	33	0	5	0	1	0	2	0	.152	.212	1.000	OF—10
1960	12	47	4	13	0	2	2	7	0	.277	.489	.962	OF—12
1961	146	529	75	147	20	7	25	86	6	.278	.484	.954	OF—135
1962	159	618	94	184	22	8	22	91	9	.298	.466	.967	OF—159
1963	161	612	87	175	36	9	25	95	7	.286	.497	.987	OF—160
1964	162	645	100	201	39	2	33	98	10	.312	.532	.950	OF—162
1965	164	645	115	203	39	6	34	108	10	.315	.552	.968	OF—164
1966	162	648	100	179	23	5	29	91	6	.276	.461	.976	OF—162
1967	162	634	92	176	21	12	28	84	6	.278	.481	.989	OF—162
1968	163	642	91	185	30	8	30	98	4	.288	.500	.967	OF—163
1969	163	642	103	188	33	10	21	95	3	.293	.474	.957	OF—159
1970	161	636	**137**	**205**	34	4	42	129	7	.322	.586	.989	OF—160
1971	157	594	86	179	27	5	28	93	7	.301	.505	.977	OF—154
1972	150	574	95	191	34	6	37	122	3	**.333**	**.606**	.986	OF—144, 1B—5
1973	156	576	72	166	22	2	20	86	4	.288	.438	.987	OF—138, 1B—19
1974	117	404	55	113	22	0	16	68	4	.280	.453	.984	1B—65, OF—43
Totals	2,213	8,479	1,306	2,510	402	87	392	1,353	86	.296	.503	.976	OF—2,087, 1B—89

Note: League-leading totals are in **bold**.

collected five hits as the Cubs swept St. Louis 3–1 and 12–1. He was one of the few players to keep hitting during the September collapse of 1969, getting all four of his team's hits—two doubles and two home runs—on September 5 in a 9–2 loss to Steve Blass and the Pirates (Blass had four hits of his own in the game). It was Williams's second four-extra-base-hits game of the season, a record he shared with Joe Medwick, Jimmie Foxx, and George Burns.

Williams had the best year of his career in 1970, narrowly missing the Triple Crown as he hit 42 home runs, knocked in 129, and batted .322 with 205 hits. On April 30 in Atlanta, he became the third man to play in 1,000 consecutive games. The final game of his streak came on September 2 in a 17–2 drubbing of the Phillies at Wrigley. The MVP Award went to Johnny Bench, as it did again in 1972, when Williams won his first batting title (.333) while hitting 37 home runs and knocking in 122 runs.

He finally got to the postseason with the Oakland Athletics in 1975 after being traded from Chicago for Manny Trillo. He finished his career second only to Stan Musial for most home runs without ever leading the league and trailing only Willie Mays, Al Kaline, Jake Beckley, and Harry Heilmann for most RBIS without ever leading the league.

Billy Williams was inducted into the Hall of Fame in 1987.

Consecutive Games Played

Cal Ripken	2,632
Lou Gehrig	2,130
Everett Scott	1,307
Steve Garvey	1,207
Billy Williams	1,117

Sweet Swinging Billy Williams

Get that kid Williams up there as fast as you can. He's wasting his time here. —Minor-league instructor Rogers Hornsby to Cubs management in 1959

The first time you saw him, you said, "Here's a star." He had so much power. When he hit the ball, it was like a rifle shot. —Don Elston

He was already the best hitter on the team (in 1961). He's the best player I ever played with. —Ed Bouchee

Billy Williams had the best swing I ever saw in baseball. . . . He just went out and did his job day after day after day. —Ferguson Jenkins

It would have been like scratching Whirlaway from a big race. —Leo Durocher on why he never gave Billy Williams a day off

I'm tired. That's all it is.

Billy Williams taking a day off on September 3, 1970

Kiki Cuyler: August 31, 1932

When Rogers Hornsby is replaced as manager by Charlie Grimm, the Cubs loosen up and start winning. They win 20 of 21 games starting on August 16, including what is possibly Kiki Cuyler's finest game as a Cub. With Pittsburgh right on their heels, every game counts. This game, played in intermittent showers and with the Cubs down to their last out twice, puts a signature on their pennant-winning season just as much as Ryne Sandberg's two blasts off Bruce Sutter did to the 1984 campaign.

Lon Warneke doesn't have it. He starts for the Cubs and never records an out. Bud Tinning minimizes the damage in the first, but another Giants run in the second makes it 4–0. Kiki Cuyler gets the Cubs their first run with a triple over Fred Lindstrom's head in center that scores Billy Herman, and Cuyler scores when Riggs Stephenson doubles into the gap in left center.

The Giants score an unearned run in the fourth to make it 5–2, but then Bob Smith shuts them down for the next five innings. Scratching back with a run in the fourth and a run in the eighth, the Cubs are down 5–4 in the bottom of the ninth. Fat Freddie Fitzsimmons is still on the mound for the Giants. With one out, Frank Demaree pinch-hits for Smith and singles. Billy Herman flies out for the second out, but Woody English keeps the rally alive with a single. With Herman Bell warming in the bullpen, Bill Terry sticks with Fitzsimmons against Kiki Cuyler, who is 3-for-4 on the day and who promptly ties the game with a single to center. Bell comes in and walks Stephenson to fill the bases, and John Moore hits a sharp grounder to the right side, with Hughie Critz making a great play to send the game into extra innings.

With the rain coming down, Guy Bush comes in to pitch for the Cubs, but he doesn't have it, either. A walk, two consecutive hit batsmen, a single, and a wild pitch give the Giants a 7–5 lead. With runners on second and third and submariner LeRoy Herrmann not yet warmed up in the Cubs' bullpen, Critz singles in two more runs to give the Giants a 9–5 lead. Bill Terry singles to left off Herrmann, and Critz tries to score from second on Riggs Stephenson's notoriously weak arm, but Stephenson hits the cutoff man, and English throws out Critz at the plate.

Staked to a 9–5 lead, Sam Gibson retires the first two batters in the bottom of the 10th, but Mark Koenig homers to right. At this point, Herrmann is due to bat, but catcher Zack Taylor, an in-game substitute, goes to the plate instead. The Giants howl in protest, but umpire George Magerkurth lets Taylor hit even though he is batting out of order. With the rain coming down, the Giants relent, eager to simply get the final out and take the win. Big mistake.

Taylor singles. Billy Herman singles. Woody English singles in Taylor to make the score 9–7. Then Kiki Cuyler hits a three-run blast into the right-center bleachers to win the game 10–9, for his fifth hit and fifth RBI on the day.

We went out there that day feeling that this was the most important game of all—the biggest one of the season. A win here, and we'd show our heels to everybody.

Charlie Grimm, on the final game of a five-game series with the hated New York Giants. The Cubs had taken the first four in their first month under Grimm as manager.

Giants 9

NEW YORK	ab	r	h	bi
Joe Moore lf	5	2	1	1
Critz 2b	6	2	4	2
Terry 1b	6	1	5	3
Ott rf	6	0	2	1
Lindstrom cf	5	0	1	0
Hogan c	5	0	0	0
Marshall ss	4	1	1	0
Vergez 3b	4	2	2	0
Fitzsimmons p	2	0	0	0

Cubs 10

CHICAGO	ab	r	h	bi
Herman 2b	6	2	3	0
English 3b	6	1	2	1
Cuyler rf	6	2	5	5
Stephenson lf	3	1	1	1
John Moore cf	5	0	0	0
Grimm 1b	4	0	3	1
Hack pr	0	0	0	0
Taylor c	1	1	1	0
Hartnett c	2	0	0	0

Bell p	0	0	0	0	Koenig ss	5	2	2	1
O'Farrell ph	0	1	0	0	Warneke p	0	0	0	0
Gibson p	0	0	0	0	Tinning p	1	0	0	0
					Hemsley ph	1	0	0	1
					Smith p	1	0	1	0
					Demaree ph	1	1	1	0
					Bush p	0	0	0	0
					Herrmann p	0	0	0	0
					Jurges ph	1	0	0	0
Totals	43	9	16	7	**Totals**	43	10	19	10

New York	3	1	0	1	0	0	0	0	0	4		9	16	0
Chicago	0	0	2	1	0	0	0	1	1	5		10	19	2

E—Koenig, Tinning. DP—New York 3, Chicago 2. LOB—New York 10, Chicago 9. 2B—Critz, Stephenson, Grimm. 3B—Terry, Cuyler, Koenig. HR—Koenig, Cuyler. S—Fitzsimmons 2.

	IP	H	R	ER	BB	SO
New York						
Fitzsimmons	8⅔	14	5	5	2	3
Bell	⅓	0	0	0	1	0
Gibson L	⅔	5	5	5	0	0
Chicago						
Warneke	0	4	3	3	1	0
Tinning	4	4	2	1	0	0
Smith	5	5	0	0	0	1
Bush	0	2	4	4	1	0
Herrmann W	1	1	0	0	0	0

HBP—Bush (Vergez, O'Farrell). WP—Fitzsimmons, Bush. T—2:15.

the scoreboard

Since their inception in 1876—long before Wrigley Field was a gleam in an architect's eye—the Cubs have played some wild games. When a team has played about 18,000 games, choosing the wildest 100 is not an easy task. It boils down to 1 in 180, which is roughly equivalent to isolating the infinitesimal amount of impurities in $99^{44}/_{100}$-percent-pure Ivory Soap. Locating that $^{56}/_{100}$ percent is worth the trouble, for it includes:

- Twenty-three bloodbaths with the Philadelphia Phillies dating back to 1883, five in 1930 alone
- Eighteen runs in one *inning*
- Twenty opposition errors in one game
- A 32-hit, 36-run performance
- Nineteen runs off a pair of Hall of Famers
- Forty innings against one team in two consecutive games
- Sixteen runs scored by the infield alone
- Erasing a six-run lead with two outs and none on in the ninth
- Fifteen home runs in a doubleheader
- The out-of-body experiences of Adolfo Phillips in 1967, George Mitterwald in 1974, and Barry Foote in 1980
- Scoring five runs in the 11th inning . . . and *losing . . . twice*
- Coming back from deficits of 15–2 and 17–6 only to lose 17–15 and 23–22
- A famous debut in an 18-inning, two-day loss featuring the latest home run in Cub history
- Three grand slams in one game
- Six leads erased in one game
- Forty-nine runs in one game
- A 22–0 blanking and a blown 12–1 lead
- Coming back from 9–0 in the middle of a pennant race
- Back-to-back, last at-bat, 15–12 and 11–10, wild-card-race victories

Here are the Top 100—not necessarily the most significant and certainly not the best pitched, just the 100 most wonderful and strangest days at the ballpark. Ten of the best, with box scores, are included at the end of the chapter.

"Let's get some runs!"

THE TOP 100
WILDEST GAMES

1. **July 22, 1876.** With 31 hits off Louisville's John Ryan (and 10 Ryan wild pitches), the White Stockings score 10 in the first and plate a runner in every inning but the second as they romp 30–7 at 23rd Street Grounds. Cal McVey gets six hits. It's the first of a major-league record 39 20-run games for Chicago . . . and counting.

2. **July 25, 1876.** In their next game, the White Stockings pound out 26 hits in a 23–3 thrashing of the Reds in Chicago. Cal McVey gets six hits *again*—the only time that's been done in consecutive games. It gives them a major-league-record 53 runs in two games and 71 runs in three games.

3. **July 27, 1876.** The Reds hold Chicago to 17 runs—giving them 88 runs in their last four games—as the White Stockings rack up another 23 hits in a 17–3 win. This time, it's Ross Barnes who gets six hits.

4. **July 24, 1882.** Bored with 20-run games, the White Stockings pile up 35 in the most lopsided victory in club history—35–4 over the Cleveland Blues at Lakefront Park. A major-league-record seven players (Abner Dalrymple, King Kelly, George Gore, Ned Williamson, Tommy Burns, Silver Flint, and Hugh Nicol) get 4 hits as the club accumulates 29. Chicago sets two additional records when three different players score five runs and six different players score four runs.

5. **September 9, 1882.** The White Stockings dominate the Troy Trojans at the plate and on the mound, winning 24–1 as Larry Corcoran throws a three-hitter at Lakefront.

6. **May 30, 1883.** Chicago welcomes the Philadelphia Phillies to the National League with not one but two thumpings, 15–8 in Game One and 22–4 in Game Two at Philadelphia. The Phillies are well advised to get used to it.

7. **July 3, 1883.** The White Stockings put up four touchdowns and a field goal in beating the Buffalo Bisons 31–7 at Lakefront. In 1883, balls hit over the short fence at Lakefront were still just doubles and not home runs, or the carnage might have been worse. Chicago hits 14 doubles, including 4 by Cap Anson. He hits two more in the first game of the July 4 doubleheader, giving him a major-league-record six in two games. The White Stockings collect a record 32 hits along the way.

8. **September 6, 1883.** Five days after Chicago's 21–7 drubbing of the Cleveland Blues, the Detroit Wolverines would say Cleveland had it easy. In the greatest orgy of runs in any inning in major-league history, the White Stockings break up a close game with 18 in the seventh at Lakefront Park—13 scoring before Detroit records an out. Tommy Burns, Fred Pfeffer, and Ned Williamson become the first players to get three hits in one inning, a feat matched only once since. Burns racks up eight total bases in the inning, with two doubles and a home run. Burns and Williamson score three times in the seventh, the first to do that, a feat also matched only once since. In all, the White Stockings send a major-league-record 23 batters to the plate. For the game, Chicago sets another record when nine different players score three runs.

9. **July 4, 1884.** After beating the Phillies behind Larry Corcoran 3–1 in Game One at Lakefront Park, the White Stockings explode for 22 in the second game. Tommy Burns hits two homers in the 22–3 victory.

10. **September 16, 1884.** More superfluous run support for Larry Corcoran. The White Stockings throttle the Boston Beaneaters 17–0 at Lakefront Park behind two George Gore home runs and five hits by Fred Pfeffer in one of the more lopsided shutouts in big-league history.

11. **September 25, 1885.** Chicago capitalizes on *20 errors* by the Providence Grays in a 21–3 "home" victory in Milwaukee. With 26 hits to their credit, the White Stockings hardly need the defensive assistance.

12. **May 28, 1886.** Chicago scores 18 unearned runs against the Washington Statesmen in a 20–0 victory, the most one-sided shutout victory in Cubs history. After three innings, pitcher Jim McCormick and right-fielder John Flynn swap positions.

13. **July 20, 1886.** Chicago hits three home runs in an inning for the first time, as Cap Anson, Jimmy Ryan, and Abner Dalrymple circle the bases in the third at West Side Park. The White Stockings beat the St. Louis Maroons 20–4.

14. **July 28, 1888.** Not the Bears and the Lions, but a 21–17 White Stockings victory over the Wolverines at West Side Park. Among the 30 hits is one of each for Jimmy Ryan as he becomes the first Chicago player to hit for the cycle.

15. **May 8, 1890.** As with Wrigley, evidently no lead is safe at West Side Park, either. Down 9–4, the Colts erase the Reds' lead with a 12-run sixth and coast to an 18–9 triumph.

16. **August 16, 1890.** It's lucky 13 for the Colts as they score that many times in the fifth en route to an 18–5 victory over the Pittsburgh Pirates. Both Tommy Burns and Malachi Kittridge hit grand slams in the fifth-inning festivities.

17. **August 25, 1891.** The Colts pound the Brooklyn Bridegrooms 28–5 as pitcher Pat Luby hits two home runs at West Side Park.

18. **July 25, 1894.** The birth of the tape-measure home run. Legend has it that George Decker, dead ball and all, blasts a 520' home run at West Side Grounds. It is a matter of record that Jimmy Ryan scores a major-league-record six runs in a 24–6 defeat of the Pirates.

19. **August 1, 1894.** With three hits on the day, Bill Dahlen easily extends his hitting streak to 38 games as the Colts pummel the St. Louis Cardinals 26–8 at West Side Grounds.

20. **September 20, 1894.** For the second time in five years, Chicago puts up 10 runs in the first inning against the Phillies. The Colts take it easy the rest of the way, allowing seven innings to put up their next 10 as they beat Philadelphia 20–4 at West Side Grounds.

21. **May 20, 1895.** More from the friendly confines of West Side Grounds. When you put together 25 hits, an inside-the-park grand-slam home run by Asa Stewart, a 5-for-5 performance at the plate by Clark Griffith, and 13 Philadelphia errors, a 24–6 result makes it seem as if the Phillies got off light.

22. **July 17, 1895.** For the first time in club history, Chicago scores 10 or more runs in an inning and none the rest of the game. They put up 12 in the fourth in a 12–7 victory over Philadelphia at West Side Grounds. However, the Colts score another five in the bottom of the seventh and are still batting when the Phillies wave the white flag. They have a train to catch, and the runs don't count because the inning isn't finished.

23. **June 29, 1897.** It's the biggest scoring outburst in baseball history as the Colts annihilate the Louisville Grays 36–7 at West Side Grounds. Chicago scores in every inning,

tying the club record of 32 hits, including 5 by pitcher Jimmy Callahan and 6 by Barry McCormick (the last man to register eight at bats in a nine-inning game). Major-league records are set when 71 players come to bat for Chicago and 10 different players score two runs. They tie their own mark set 15 years earlier when four different players score six runs.

24. **June 7, 1906.** It's impressive enough to jump out on top with 11 runs in the first inning in your opponents' stadium. To do it to Christy Mathewson is one for the ages. The Cubs rough up yet another Hall of Famer, Joe McGinnity, as they pile up 19 runs on the New York Giants. Jack Pfiester throws a three-hit shutout for the Cubs.

25. **June 11, 1911.** Heinie Zimmerman just misses hitting for the cycle as he goes 5-for-5 with a club-record nine RBIs in leading the Cubs past Boston 20–2 at West Side Grounds. King Cole benefits from the run support.

26. **August 19, 1913.** If you think bombing Christy Mathewson in one-third of an inning is impressive, how about blowing open a tie game in Philadelphia against Grover Cleveland Alexander with nine consecutive hits and six runs in the ninth inning for a 10–4 victory?

27. **June 24, 1915.** In one of the great comebacks in club history, the Cubs erase a 13–10 deficit in the bottom of the ninth to beat the Cardinals at West Side Grounds. With a flair for the dramatic, pinch-hitter Heinie Zimmerman ties the game with a two-run pinch-hit double, then steals home to win it.

28. **August 25, 1922.** See "The Top 10 Strangest Games."

29. **July 23, 1923.** Stinging from having given up 12 runs in the sixth inning to the Phillies two days before, the Cubs take it out on the Pirates, 12–3. It's not often that you see a 12-inning game decided by nine runs, but the Cubs do just that, establishing a major-league record for runs scored in extra innings (broken five years later, when the Yankees beat the Tigers 11–0 in 12, and broken again in 1983, when the Texas Rangers say enough is enough and score 12 in the 15th against Oakland).

30. **May 14, 1927.** Guy Bush goes all the way to beat the Braves 7–2 in Boston as the Cubs erupt for five runs *in the 18th inning*. And then in their next game, three days later . . .

31. **May 17, 1927.** Chicago plays the longest game in its history (22 innings) and establishes a major-league record for most innings played in consecutive games by the same teams. The Cubs win again, 4–3, on a Charlie Grimm single, and Bob Osborn picks up the win with *14 innings of relief work*.

32. **May 4, 1929.** Pat Malone initiates a tradition of single-handedly beating the Phillies. His 2 RBIs are more than he needs, but the Cubs get him 14 more in a 16–0 rout at the Baker Bowl.

33. **May 12, 1930.** The Giants bomb Sheriff Blake in rolling up a 14–0 lead at Wrigley, but the Cubs nearly come back to win it. Chicago hits four home runs in the seventh inning (Cliff Heathcote, Hack Wilson, Charlie Grimm, Clyde Beck) for the only time in club history. Joe Genewich of the Giants pitches out of a jam in the ninth, leaving the tying runs on base.

34. **June 23, 1930.** Hack Wilson hits for the cycle and knocks in 6 of his 190 runs in a 21–8 win over the Phillies at Wrigley.

35. **June 25, 1930.** Two days later against the Phillies, Gabby Hartnett collects four hits, including two home runs, and knocks in seven runs. His final RBI wins the game in the bottom of the ninth, 13–12.

36. **July 24, 1930.** A month later, in one of the highest-scoring games in the team's history, the Cubs beat the Phillies 19–15. Chicago leaps out to a 13–3 lead after two innings at the Baker Bowl, then holds on for dear life as the Phillies close in to make it 18–15, with

seven in a wild eighth inning in which Bill Klem ejects Phillies right-fielder Chuck Klein, first-baseman Don Hurst, and pinch-hitter Fresco Thompson. In a box score that defies belief, 30 of the 34 hits are singles in a rout that lasts less than 2½ hours.

37. **July 26, 1930.** And two days later, Hack Wilson hits three home runs as the 1930 Cubs administer yet another beating to the Phillies (16–2), this time in Philadelphia. Pat Malone pitches a complete game and hits a home run.

38. **August 18, 1930.** And then three weeks after *that,* Pat Malone pitches another complete game and hits another home run, and the Cubs trounce the Phillies *again,* 17–3, at Wrigley. Hack Wilson pulls to within one of Chuck Klein's National League home-run record with #42. For the season, the Cubs score a record 218 runs against the Phillies, an *average* of 9 per game.

39. **September 6, 1930.** Down 12–8 to the Pirates after seven innings, the Cubs score four in the eighth and six in the ninth as Hack Wilson hits his 47th at Forbes Field. The Cubs win 18–14.

40. **September 28, 1930.** As is clear by now, no lead is safe in 1930. On the last day of the season, the Cubs overcome an 11–2 deficit to beat the Reds 13–11, with Hack Wilson knocking in runs #189 and #190.

41. **July 12, 1931.** See "The Top 10 Strangest Games."

42. **August 31, 1932.** The Cubs rally with a run in the 9th and five more in the 10th to beat the New York Giants 10–9 in a critical late-season game. Kiki Cuyler is the hitting star for Chicago (see "The Outfield," Chapter 10, for more details and a box score).

43. **June 12, 1935.** Manager Charlie Grimm evidently had a few things to get off his chest before this game in Philadelphia, and whatever he said worked. The Cubs gave Larry French a 15-run lead to protect, and he did just that, winning 15–0.

44. **August 21, 1935.** After hooking up with the Phillies in some of the most twisted games in history, the Cubs decide to do it twice. After losing 13–12 in the first game at Philadelphia, the Cubs score 12 times in the sixth inning as they cuff the Phillies around 19–5 in the second game. Billy Herman ties a major-league record by coming to bat 13 times in the doubleheader, while Chuck Klein ties a modern major-league mark by scoring eight runs in the two games.

45. **September 14, 1935.** The Cubs rely on great pitching to run off 21 consecutive wins in September 1935. They hold their opponents to three or fewer runs in every game . . . except this one. After 10 consecutive wins, the Brooklyn Dodgers come into Wrigley Field and put a scare into the Cubs. Down 8–0 in the fifth, Brooklyn cuts the lead to 8–4. So, the Cubs score *another* eight runs in the bottom of the sixth, only to have the Dodgers come back with five in the seventh. The Cubs make it 18–9 in the bottom of the seventh, only to have the Dodgers put up five more in the ninth until Fabian Kowalik finally strikes out Johnny McCarthy to end the game. Every Cubs starter knocks in at least one run in the contest.

46. **August 13, 1937.** Career backup catcher Ken O'Dea has his finest hour, getting four hits, scoring four runs, and knocking in four runs to lead the Cubs past the Reds 22–6 at Wrigley. In addition to the surprising production from O'Dea, the Cubs benefit from eight Reds errors.

47. **May 5, 1938.** With the game safely in hand, the Cubs pour it on against the Phillies with 12 runs in the eighth on the way to a 21–2 victory at Wrigley. This time, it's reserve outfielder Joe Marty who collects four hits, four runs, and four RBIs.

48. **May 17, 1939.** A long way to go for this one. The Cubs and Dodgers play a 19-inning, 9–9 tie at Wrigley. The Cubs are one out away from a victory in regulation when Pete Coscarart's double ties up the game.

49. **August 9, 1942.** The Reds don't die easy. The Cubs win 10–8 in 18 after the Reds rally to tie the game in the 9th, 10th, and 12th innings.

50. **July 23, 1944.** Having already seen Bill Nicholson hit four consecutive home runs in this doubleheader, Giants manager Mel Ott, his team up 12–9, intentionally walks him with the bases loaded in the seventh inning of a game at the Polo Grounds. The Giants hold on for a 12–10 win, and Ott remains tied with Nicholson in the home-run race at 21.

51. **September 26, 1944.** Yet another lopsided blanking of the Phillies—15–0 in Philadelphia—as Hank Wyse throws a four-hitter and the Mad Russian, Lou Novikoff, hits his last big-league home run.

52. **July 3, 1945.** The Cubs' infield establishes a major-league record by scoring 16 runs, 5 apiece by Phil Cavarretta, Don Johnson, and Stan Hack. Chicago collects 28 hits behind Claude Passeau en route to a 24–2 win over Boston at Braves Field. They set the 20th-century club record for margin of victory and hits (28).

53. **August 15, 1945.** Taking up where Ken O'Dea left off eight years before, catcher Paul Gillespie continues what would become a long-standing Cubs tradition of obscure catchers taking their moment in the sun. He gets three hits, including two home runs, and knocks in six runs in a 20–6 spanking of the Dodgers at Ebbets Field. Similar to Mitterwald and Foote after him, Gillespie manages to finish the season with only three home runs and 25 RBIs.

54. **May 5, 1946.** More late lightning for the Cubs as they break up a close game with the Phillies with 11 runs in the seventh, winning 13–1 at Wrigley. Hank Borowy drives in four with two doubles—one of only three National League pitchers, all Cubs, to get two extra-base hits in the same inning. Fred Goldsmith did it in 1883, and Adonis Bill Terry in 1895. The Cubs haven't scored that many runs in an inning since.

55. **July 2, 1950.** More Cubs-Reds weirdness. Monk Dubiel throws a four-hitter as the Cubs beat the Reds 16–0 at Crosley Field. Andy Pafko misses hitting for the cycle by going without a *single.*

56. **June 29, 1952.** If the list of all-time strangest games went all the way to 11, this would be the next in line. Bubba Church of the Reds scatters eight hits through the first eight innings and leads 8–2. He retires the first two in the ninth, at which point the Cubs have him right where they want him. The next nine batters reach base on five hits, two walks, an error, and a hit batsman. The Cubs push across seven—the game-tying and lead runs on a pinch-hit single by Johnny Pramesa—then call on 43-year-old Dutch Leonard to close out the Reds 9–8 in the bottom of the ninth in the greatest two-out, none-on, ninth-inning rally in National League history.

57. **April 17, 1954.** With the wind blowing out at Wrigley, Chicago outslugs the Cardinals 23–13, the 36 runs marking the third-highest-scoring Cubs game of the 20th century. Randy Jackson provides the game's highlight by hitting a home run off the third floor of a building on Waveland Avenue.

58. **April 16, 1955.** Nearly a year to the day later, the Cubs and Cardinals hook up in another wild one. This time, St. Louis prevails 12–11 in 11, despite three Cubs hitting two home runs apiece, Ernie Banks and Dee Fondy going back-to-back twice, and three consecutive home runs in the second inning.

59. **September 9, 1955.** Thirteen home runs are hit in a Wrigley Field doubleheader with the Dodgers. The Cubs take the opener 11–4 as Dee Fondy, Ernie Banks, and Eddie Miksis all go deep in the first inning. The Dodgers take the second game 16–9, though the Cubs hit three more home runs in the eighth inning—Dee Fondy, Gene Baker, and Ernie Banks this time.

60. **May 2, 1956.** The Cubs tie the Giants 5–5 in the bottom of the 8th, and the game goes scoreless through 10 relievers until the Giants score off Jim Brosnan in the 17th. Along the way, a major-league-record 14 pinch hitters are used. Other records set but since broken: eight pitchers used by the Giants, 25 players used by the Giants, and 48 players used by both teams. Cubs third-baseman Don Hoak strikes out six times against six different pitchers.

61. **May 30, 1956.** Thirteen home runs in a doubleheader is one thing, but 15 is a record. The Cubs beat the Braves 10–9 in the first game at Wrigley, then drop the second game 11–9. For the day, Bobby Thomson hits four home runs for the Braves, Hank Aaron and Eddie Mathews two, and Joe Adcock one; Gene Baker, Hobie Landrith, Monte Irvin, Harry Chiti, Ernie Banks, and pitcher Turk Lown homer for the Cubs. Fourteen pitchers are used—four of them twice—with Russ "Mad Monk" Meyer managing to get bombed in both ends of the doubleheader.

62. **June 1, 1957.** The Cubs give up a club-record seven home runs to the Reds in a 22–2 loss. Frank Robinson hits two, while Ed Bailey, Don Hoak, Wally Post, Gus Bell, and pitcher Hal Jeffcoat (a former Cubs outfielder) each hit one. This record is tied by the Cardinals on July 12, 1996, as Steve Trachsel establishes a tradition of being victimized by St. Louis hitters.

63. **September 2, 1957.** Frank Torre becomes only the third modern player to score six runs as the Milwaukee Braves pile up 26 hits against the Cubs, beating them 23–10 at Wrigley Field.

64. **May 2, 1958.** Down 7–0 after six, the Cubs rally to beat the eventual pennant-winning Braves 8–7 at Wrigley. Moose Moryn wins the game in the ninth with his second homer, this one off Dick Littlefield.

65. **August 13, 1959.** At the time, it's the longest nine-inning game ever played—three hours and 50 minutes. The Cubs beat the Giants 20–9 at Wrigley, with rookie George Altman going 5-for-6 with two home runs.

66. **September 13, 1964.** The Cardinals become only the second team in the 20th century to score runs in every inning as they beat the Cubs 15–2 at Wrigley. Only Freddie Burdette, who pitches just one-third of an inning, emerges unscathed. Every Cardinal player scores at least one run, and the recently acquired Lou Brock scores two and hits a home run.

67. **May 20, 1967.** In about as exciting a game as a 20–3 rout can be, the Cubs offer up for their fans a grand slam (Randy Hundley), a steal of home (Ted Savage), and an inside-the-park home run (Glenn Beckert). Adolfo Phillips knocks in six runs, and Don Drysdale waves a white flag from the Dodgers' dugout.

68. **June 11, 1967.** Another wild doubleheader at Wrigley. The Cubs win the first game over the Mets 5–3, with Ted Savage stealing home again. In the second game, the teams combine to hit a National League–record 11 home runs, including a club-record 7 by the Cubs and 3 by Adolfo Phillips, as the Cubs win 18–10.

69. **May 13, 1969.** The Cubs enjoy their most lopsided shutout of the 20th century—tying the mark set in 1906 against Christy Mathewson and the Giants—throttling the brand-new San Diego Padres 19–0 at Wrigley. Ernie Banks drives in 7 runs, including the 1,500th of his career.

70. **August 19, 1970.** The Cubs tie their club record of seven home runs as they administer some more punishment to the Padres. Chicago wins 12–2 as Jim Hickman (two), Glenn Beckert, Johnny Callison, Ferguson Jenkins, Joe Pepitone, and Billy Williams all leave the yard in San Diego.

71. **August 22, 1970.** Three days later in San Francisco, the Cubs pile up 15 runs for Ken Holtzman while he tosses a one-hitter. Hal Lanier's single with one out in the eighth is the Giants' only hit.

72. **September 16, 1972.** The Cubs deal Tom Seaver one of the worst defeats of his career, 18–5, at Wrigley. Chicago draws 15 walks against the Mets, including five by Elrod Hendricks, and pitcher Burt Hooton delivers a grand slam.

73. **May 31, 1973.** Of all the Cubs' 10-run first innings, this one may have been the messiest. With two out and none on at Wrigley, the Astros' third baseman, Doug Rader, makes an error, and when the dust clears, 10 unearned runs have been scored. The Cubs need all but one of them, holding on to win 16–8.

74. **April 17, 1974.** From the most unexpected of sources . . . Newly acquired catcher George Mitterwald introduces himself to the Wrigley faithful with a monster day, hitting a double and three home runs, including a first-inning grand slam, and knocks in eight runs as the Cubs crush the Pirates 18–9. Somehow he'll finish the season with only seven home runs and 28 RBIs.

75. **July 6, 1975.** The Pirates and Cubs combine to score in a record 14 of this game's 18 half innings, with the Pirates pulling away at the end for an 18–12 win. After being knocked around for three runs in the eighth inning, Darold Knowles closes the door on the Pirates in the top of the ninth to keep the Cubs from becoming the only team of the modern era to be scored upon in every inning *twice*. Despite the Lumber Company's 20 hits, the star of the game is pitcher Ramon Hernandez, who extricates the Pirates from a Cubs threat in the seventh on his way to three scoreless innings and the win.

76. **September 16, 1975.** See "The Top 10 Strangest Games."

77. **April 17, 1976.** See "The Top 10 Strangest Games."

78. **May 5, 1976.** Less than a year later, the Cubs and the Dodgers also combine to score in 14 of the game's 18 half innings. The Cubs come out on the short end yet again, 14–12, with Paul Reuschel saving the club's dignity by finally shutting the Dodgers out in the top of the ninth. The Dodgers hit seven home runs, helping Don Sutton get a rare win against the Cubs despite yielding 14 hits and six earned runs. Chicago wastes 21 hits, including two home runs and six RBIs from Rick Monday in the lead-off spot.

79. **May 17, 1977.** For the third time, the Cubs hit seven home runs as Chicago hammers the Padres 23–6 at Wrigley Field. They go deep three times in an inning *twice*—Larry Biittner, Steve Ontiveros, and Gene Clines in the third, while Biittner, Jerry Morales, and Bobby Murcer go back-to-back-to-back in the fifth. Dave Rosello adds the final blow in the eighth.

80. **July 28, 1977.** See "The Top 10 Strangest Games."

81. **September 5, 1978.** The Cubs and Expos combine to use 45 players—24 by the Cubs—in a nine-inning game at Wrigley Field. The Expos win 10–8 with four runs in the eighth, pushing the final two across against Bruce Sutter. The teams use 14 pitchers, eight pinch hitters, and 13 infielders. Sixteen days later, the Cubs set a National League mark by using 27 players in a 14-inning game against the Pirates.

82. **April 29, 1979.** Down 5–0 with two out in the ninth, the Cubs find a way to win. Larry McWilliams is tossing a one-hitter against the Cubs, the lone hit an Ivan DeJesus single, and he takes a comfortable five-run lead into the ninth at Atlanta. Dave Kingman and Steve Ontiveros single leading off the inning, but McWilliams retires Jerry Martin and pinch-hitter Gene Clines to put himself one out away from a complete-game shutout. When he walks Ted Sizemore to load the bases, Gene Garber is called in to close the door. Tim Blackwell singles in two runs, pinch-hitter Larry

Biittner singles to make it 5–3, and Bobby Murcer hits a three-run homer to put the Cubs on top 6–5. Bruce Sutter puts two on in the bottom of the inning but works out of it for the save.

83. **May 17, 1979.** See "The Top 10 Strangest Games."

84. **June 30, 1979.** The Mets and Cubs take a tight, 3–3 game into the 11th inning at Wrigley, and then things get crazy. The Mets score six runs, five charged to Dick Tidrow, four on two-run homers by Joel Youngblood and Lee Mazzilli. Steve Henderson adds a two-run triple off Donnie Moore, putting the Mets up 9–3 and sending most of the Cubs' fans home. In the bottom of the 11th, Dale Murray—a frequent victim of Chicago scoring barrages—yields one-out singles to Ken Henderson and Ivan DeJesus, a walk to Scot Thompson, a run-scoring single to Bill Buckner, and a pinch-hit grand slam to Mike Vail. Then Ed Glynn comes in to give up two long flies to center by Jerry Martin and Steve Ontiveros to seal the 9–8 victory.

85. **July 23, 1979.** A strange doubleheader sweep at Wrigley. In the first game, the Cubs complete a suspended game with the Reds, winning it 9–8 in 18. Steve Ontiveros ties the game in the 11th, then wins it in the 18th. In the "nightcap," the Cubs win 2–1 on a two-run home run by Dave Kingman in the bottom of the ninth.

86. **April 19, 1980.** The Cubs come storming back against the Mets to take them 12–9 at Wrigley. Ex-Met Dave Kingman hits a two-run homer in a four-run sixth, then adds a grand slam in a seven-run eighth when the Mets walk Bill Buckner to get to him. Carlos Lezcano adds his second major-league hit—both of them home runs—to the cause.

87. **April 22, 1980.** Three days later, the Cubs mount another extraordinary comeback as they fight back from a 12–6 hole to beat the Cardinals 16–12. Ivan DeJesus hits for the cycle, but catcher Barry Foote pulls a George Mitterwald to steal the show. Having already knocked in three runs with a single and a double, Foote hits a solo home run in the eighth inning off Roy Thomas to tie the game, then wins it in the bottom of the ninth with a two-out grand slam off Mark Littell. And, in another eerie similarity to Mr. April, George Mitterwald, Foote manages to finish the season with nearly identical numbers: six home runs and 28 RBIs.

88. **June 23, 1984.** Ryne Sandberg introduces himself to the United States in a nationally televised game with the St. Louis Cardinals. The improbable comeback win in front of a packed house features a cycle by Willie McGee in a losing cause and not one but two game-tying home runs by Sandberg (see "The Infield," Chapter 9, for more details and a box score).

89. **September 24, 1985.** How often does a team score 12 runs in the final three innings and lose? The Cubs come storming back from a 15–2 deficit, only to fall short 17–15 to the Expos at Wrigley. Andre Dawson knocks in 8 runs and hits three home runs, including two 3-run blasts in a 12-run fifth as Montreal unloads on Ray Fontenot and Jon Perlman (who allows 8 runs in one-third of an inning). Expos starter Bryn Smith leaves the game with a 15–3 lead and watches John Dopson and Randy St. Claire allow 12 runs in 2⅔ innings, forcing bullpen ace Jeff Reardon to come in to get the final out.

90. **June 23, 1986.** Two years to the day after Ryne Sandberg's coming-out party—on the same day that the Giants are pulverizing the Padres 18–1—the Phillies destroy the Cubs 19–1 in Philadelphia. Manager John Felske runs up the score, pulling only one of his regulars. In a box score that features only four doughnuts on the home side (Von Hayes and Glenn Wilson have no RBIs, while Steve Jeltz somehow avoids both RBIs and hits), the Phillies set a new National League record with 15 extra-base hits: 11 doubles and four home runs. Jamie Moyer, George Frazier, and Jay Baller are the Cubs' pitchers who get kicked around for a mercifully short 2½-hour game at the Vet.

91. **August 16, 1986.** The Pirates win a 17-inning game that began in April. The Cubs use 10 pitchers, the Pirates 7, in the 10–8 Pirates victory. Losing pitcher Frank DiPino was in Houston when the game started, while winning pitcher Barry Jones and game-winning hitter Barry Bonds were in the minors. A three-run rally in the bottom of the ninth by the Cubs is wasted.

92. **September 2–3, 1986.** Eight years after using 27 players in a 14-inning game with Pittsburgh, the Cubs use 27 (including eight pitchers) in an 18-inning game with the Astros. The teams combine to use a major-league-record 53 players in a game suspended for darkness after 14 innings and resumed the following day. After Lee Smith blows a save in the top of the ninth, Astros closer Dave Smith returns the favor in the bottom of the inning. Then, after the Astros score three times in the top of the 17th inning the following day, Keith Moreland hits the latest home run in club history—a three-run bomb off Julio Solano—to tie the game back up. The Astros end up with an 8–7 victory when Billy Hatcher homers in the 18th off a rookie named Greg Maddux who is pitching his first inning in the major leagues.

93. **June 3, 1987.** The Cubs and the Astros play another bizarre game, a 22–7 Cubs victory that features a major-league-record three grand slams. Brian Dayett and Keith Moreland strike with the bases loaded for the Cubs, while ex-Cub Billy Hatcher hits a slam for the Astros (and the notoriously antisocial Dickie Noles stretches the bounds of sportsmanship by plunking Hatcher in the eighth inning with a 15-run lead). Bob Knepper lasts only one inning for Houston, and Julio Solano returns to make another less-than-successful Wrigley Field appearance. Moreland knocks in seven runs, and Jody Davis goes 1-for-1 with five runs scored. The Cubs score in each of the first seven innings, but Larry Andersen sets them down in order in the eighth.

94. **August 16, 1987.** The Cubs score 10 against the Mets, but New York explodes for a club-record 23 runs at Wrigley. Greg Maddux is roughed up for seven runs in 3⅔, but Drew Hall is left out there to die: 10 runs in 1⅔. Darryl Strawberry goes 4-for-5 with five runs, five RBIs, a home run, a triple, and two doubles—a single from the cycle.

95. **August 29, 1989.** See "The Top 10 Strangest Games."

96. **April 21, 1991.** If you calculate the won–loss records of teams scoring five runs in the 11th inning, there won't be many in the loss column—but two of them will be the Cubs. At Three Rivers Stadium, Chicago blows 7–2 and 12–7 leads as the bullpen of Paul Assenmacher, Dave Smith, Heathcliff Slocumb, and Mike Bielecki give up 11 runs in 3⅓ innings. Andre Dawson hits a grand slam in the 11th—his second in three days—but the blow is wasted when Don Slaught doubles over Jerome Walton's head with the bases loaded to cap a six-run rally in the bottom of the inning.

Cubs and Phillies

When the three little words Cubs and Phillies *are put together, baseball fans know that anything is possible. Four of the five highest-scoring games in 20th-century Cubs history are between these two teams. In fact, of the 100 games just listed—by no means an exhaustive roster of every Chicago-Philly slugfest—23 involve the Phillies:*

Date	Score	Location
May 30, 1883 (1)	Chicago 15 Phillies 8	Recreation Park
May 30, 1883 (2)	Chicago 22 Phillies 4	Recreation Park
July 4, 1884 (2)	Chicago 22 Phillies 3	Lakefront Park
September 20, 1894	Chicago 20 Phillies 4	West Side Grounds
May 20, 1895	Chicago 24 Phillies 6	West Side Grounds
July 17, 1895	Chicago 12* Phillies 7	West Side Grounds
August 19, 1913	Chicago 10** Phillies 4	Baker Bowl
August 25, 1922	Chicago 26 Phillies 23	Wrigley Field
May 4, 1929	Chicago 16 Phillies 0	Baker Bowl
June 23, 1930	Chicago 21 Phillies 8	Wrigley Field
June 25, 1930	Chicago 13 Phillies 12	Wrigley Field
July 24, 1930	Chicago 19 Phillies 15	Baker Bowl
July 26, 1930	Chicago 16 Phillies 2	Baker Bowl
August 18, 1930	Chicago 17 Phillies 3	Wrigley Field
June 12, 1935	Chicago 15 Phillies 0	Baker Bowl
August 21, 1935 (1)	Phillies 13 Chicago 12	Baker Bowl
August 21, 1935 (2)	Chicago 19 Phillies 5	Baker Bowl
May 5, 1938	Chicago 21 Phillies 2	Wrigley Field
September 26, 1944	Chicago 15 Phillies 0	Shibe Park
May 5, 1946	Chicago 13*** Phillies 1	Wrigley Field
April 17, 1976	Phillies 18 Chicago 16	Wrigley Field
May 17, 1979	Phillies 23 Chicago 22	Wrigley Field
June 23, 1986	Phillies 19 Chicago 1	Veterans Stadium

*Chicago is in the process of scoring at least five more when the Phillies surrender.

**Six off Grover Cleveland Alexander in the ninth

***Eleven runs in the seventh

97. **August 18, 1995.** See "The Top 10 Strangest Games."

98. **September 28, 1995.** One game away from elimination in the wild-card race, the Cubs refuse to die against the play-off-contending Houston Astros. The Cubs win 12–11 in 11 despite seven steals in seven attempts by Houston. The two teams combine to use 18 pitchers and 45 players, leave 23 men on, pound out 36 hits, and draw 11 walks. Chicago erases *six* leads—down 1–0 in the 2nd, they score two; down 6–5 in the 6th, they score one; down 7–6 in the 7th, they score one; down 9–7 in the 8th, they score two; down 10–9 in the 10th, they score one; and down 11–10 in the 11th, they score two. The highlight of the game is the *fan* who charges the mound (see "The Park," Chapter 15) in the eighth after Randy Myers gives up a pinch-hit home run to James Mouton.

99. **September 12, 1998.** See "The Top 10 Strangest Games."

100. **September 13, 1998.** See "The Top 10 Strangest Games."

THE TOP 10 STRANGEST GAMES

Here they are: the 10 strangest Cubs games since box scores were being kept. Eight at Wrigley, three with the Phillies (of course), and a 6–4 record for the good guys.

August 25, 1922

There have been some incredible Cubs-Phillies slugfests through the years, but this one also happens to be the highest-scoring game in big-league history. Marty Callaghan becomes the first 20th-century player to come to bat three times in one inning. Cliff Heathcote sets a modern record by reaching base seven times, while Russell Wrightstone and Frank Parkinson of the Phillies become the first 20th-century players to come to bat eight times in a nine-inning game. The Phillies don't go quietly, storming back from a 25–6 deficit despite having subs in at several positions. They end up falling three runs short and leave the bases loaded in the ninth inning.

Phillies 23					*Cubs 26*			
PHILADELPHIA	ab	r	h		CHICAGO	ab	r	h
Wrightstone 3b	7	3	4		Heathcote cf	5	5	5
Parkinson 2b	4	1	2		Hollocher ss	5	2	3
Williams cf	3	1	0		Kelleher ss	1	0	0
LeBourveau cf	4	2	3		Terry 2b	5	2	2
Walker rf	6	2	4		Friberg 2b	1	0	1
Mokan lf	4	2	3		Grimes 1b	4	2	2
Fletcher ss	3	1	0		Callaghan rf	7	3	2
J. Smith ss	4	2	1		Miller lf	5	3	4
Leslie 1b	2	1	0		Krug 3b	5	4	4
Lee 1b	4	4	3		O'Farrell c	3	3	2

Henline c	2	1	2	Hartnett c	0	0	0
Withrow c	4	1	2	Kaufmann p	2	0	0
Ring p	2	0	1	Barber ph	1	2	0
Weinert p	4	2	1	Stueland p	1	0	0
Rapp ph	0	0	0	Maisel ph	1	0	0
				Eubanks p	0	0	0
				Morris p	0	0	0
				Osborne p	0	0	0
Totals	53	23	26	**Totals**	46	26	25

Philadelphia	0	3	2	1	3	0	0	8	6	23	26	4
Chicago	1	10	0	14	0	1	0	0	X	26	25	5

E—Wrightstone, Williams, Walker, Lee, Heathcote, Hollocher, Callaghan, Krug, Hartnett. DP—Philadelphia 3. LOB—Philadelphia 16, Chicago 9. 2B—Terry, Krug 2, Mokan, Hollocher, Heathcote 2, Grimes, Withrow, Friberg, Parkinson, Walker. 3B—Walker, Wrightstone. HR—Miller 2, O'Farrell. SB—Hollocher, Weinert. S—Leslie, O'Farrell, Hollocher.

	IP	H	R	BB	SO
Philadelphia					
Ring L	3⅓	12	14	5	2
Weinert	4⅔	13	12	5	2
Chicago					
Kaufmann W	4	9	6	3	0
Stueland	3	7	3	2	1
Eubanks	⅔	3	5	2	1
Morris	⅓	4	3	1	1
Osborne	1	3	6	2	0

HBP—Weinert (Grimes). WP—Stueland. T—3:01.

July 12, 1931

They have to seat the overflow doubleheader crowd in the Sportsman's Park outfield, and the result is more doubles (most of them of the crowd-necessitated grounds-rule variety) than in any other game in history—23. The Cardinals hit 13 of them in beating the Cubs 17–13.

SECOND GAME

Cubs 13   *Cardinals 17*

CHICAGO	ab	r	h	bi	ST. LOUIS	ab	r	h	bi
Blair 2b	6	3	3	4	Adams ss	4	3	1	0
English ss	6	1	3	2	Watkins rf	5	3	1	1
Cuyler rf	3	0	0	0	Frisch 2b	5	3	3	1
Wilson lf	6	0	1	0	Collins 1b	6	2	4	4
Hornsby 3b	4	1	2	0	Hafey lf	5	2	3	3
D. Taylor cf	4	1	0	0	Martin cf	6	1	3	3
Grimm 1b	5	2	1	0	High 3b	4	1	1	1
Hartnett c	5	3	5	1	Mancuso c	5	1	4	2
Malone p	0	1	0	0	Rhem p	1	0	0	0
Bush p	0	0	0	0	Orsatti ph	2	1	1	1
Bell ph	1	1	1	2	Stout p	0	0	0	0

Baecht p	0	0	0	0	Derringer p	3	0	0	0
Root p	0	0	0	0					
Sweetland ph	1	0	0	0					
Blake p	0	0	0	0					
Warneke p	0	0	0	0					
Stephenson ph	1	0	0	0					
Totals	**42**	**13**	**16**	**9**	**Totals**	**46**	**17**	**21**	**16**

Chicago	2	0	0	4	4	1	0	0	2	13	16	3
St. Louis	3	0	0	7	3	2	0	2	x	17	21	5

E—Blair, English, D. Taylor, Adams 4, Rhem. DP—Chicago 1, St. Louis 2. LOB—Chicago 9, St. Louis 13. 2B—Blair 2, Collins 3, Hafey 2, Hartnett 3, English 3, Mancuso 3, Orsatti, Frisch 2, High, Bell, Hornsby, Watkins. HR—Blair. S—Malone, Cuyler.

	IP	H	R	BB	SO
Chicago					
Malone	3⅓	10	7	0	3
Bush	⅔	4	3	1	0
Baecht L	0	0	2	2	0
Root	1	2	1	0	0
Blake	2	5	4	3	2
Warneke	1	0	0	1	0
St. Louis					
Rhem	4	7	6	3	5
Stout	0	2	3	1	0
Derringer W	5	7	4	1	6

HBP—Root (High). WP—Stout, Derringer 2, Blake. T—2:44. A—45,715.

September 16, 1975

The Pirates make an unfortunate habit out of throttling the Cubs: 18–0 in 1903, 15–0 in 1929, and 22–0 in 1975. This is the most lopsided shutout of the 20th century. The Pirates are led by Rennie Stennett, who goes 7-for-7 and twice has two hits in the same inning. Confident that the Cubs won't prolong the game with 22 runs in the bottom of the ninth, Danny Murtaugh gives Stennett the rest of the day off after his seventh hit and lets a rookie named Willie Randolph play. When one team hits .453 for the day and the other .100, this is what happens.

I was watching a spider crawl through the ivy. What else was there to do out there in a game like that?

Jose Cardenal

Pirates 22

PITTSBURGH	ab	r	h	bi
Stennett 2b	7	5	7	2
Randolph 2b	0	0	0	0
Hebner 3b	7	3	2	3
Oliver cf	4	2	1	1
Dilone cf	1	0	0	0
Stargell 1b	4	2	3	3
Robertson 1b	3	1	1	0
Parker rf	4	3	2	5
Zisk lf	5	2	2	1
Sanguillen c	5	2	2	1

Cubs 0

CHICAGO	ab	r	h	bi
Kessinger 3b	3	0	0	0
Dunn 3b	1	0	0	0
Tyrone lf	4	0	0	0
J. Morales cf	3	0	0	0
LaCock rf	1	0	0	0
Cardenal rf	2	0	1	0
Harris cf	1	0	0	0
Thornton 1b	3	0	1	0
P. Reuschel p	0	0	0	0
Trillo 2b	2	0	0	0

Brett p	1	0	0	0	Sperring 2b	1	0	0	0
Taveras ss	6	1	3	3	Mitterwald c	3	0	0	0
Candelaria p	5	1	1	2	Rosello ss	3	0	1	0
Ott ph	1	0	0	0	R. Reuschel p	0	0	0	0
					Dettore p	1	0	0	0
					Zamora p	0	0	0	0
					Hosley ph	1	0	0	0
					Schultz p	0	0	0	0
					Summers rf	1	0	0	0
Totals	53	22	24	21	Totals	30	0	3	0

Pittsburgh	9	0	2	1	6	2	2	0	0	22	24	0
Chicago	0	0	0	0	0	0	0	0	0	0	3	3

E—Dettore, Rosello, Dunn. LOB—Pittsburgh 12, Chicago 3. 2B—Stennett 2. 3B—Stennett. HR—Hebner, Parker. S—Parker.

	IP	H	R	ER	BB	SO
Pittsburgh						
Candelaria W	7	3	0	0	0	5
Brett	2	0	0	0	0	1
Chicago						
R. Reuschel L	1/3	6	8	8	2	0
Dettore	2 2/3	7	8	7	2	1
Zamora	1	4	2	2	0	2
Schultz	2	6	4	2	1	2
P. Reuschel	2	1	0	0	1	0

HBP—Dettore (Parker). WP—Dettore. T—2:35. A—4,932.

April 17, 1976

Here's one of the reasons they say that no lead is safe at Wrigley Field. The Cubs have the Phillies down 12–1, bombing Steve Carlton in a seven-run second inning. But Rick Reuschel can't hold the lead, and the Cubs fall behind 15–13 as the Phillies score 11 times in the seventh, eighth, and ninth innings. The Cubs rally to tie the game at 15–15 in the bottom of the 9th, only to see the Phillies score three more times in the top of the 10th on Mike Schmidt's fourth home run and eighth RBI. A rally in the bottom of the 10th falls short, the Phillies have an 18–16 victory, and the Cubs have a National League record for largest blown lead.

Phillies 18

Cubs 16

PHILADELPHIA	ab	r	h	bi	CHICAGO	ab	r	h	bi
Cash 2b	6	1	2	2	Monday cf	6	3	4	4
Bowa ss	6	3	3	1	Cardenal lf	5	1	1	0
Johnstone rf	5	2	4	2	Summers lf	0	0	0	0
Luzinski lf	5	0	1	1	Mitterwald ph	1	0	0	0
Brown lf	0	0	0	0	Wallis lf	1	0	0	0
Allen 1b	5	2	1	2	Madlock 3b	7	2	3	3
Schmidt 3b	6	4	5	8	Morales rf	5	2	1	0
Maddox cf	5	2	2	1	Thornton 1b	4	3	1	1
McGraw p	0	0	0	0	Trillo 2b	5	0	2	3
McCarver ph	1	1	1	0	Swisher c	6	1	3	4

	AB	R	H	RBI		AB	R	H	RBI
Underwood p	0	0	0	0	Rosello ss	4	1	2	1
Lonborg p	0	0	0	0	Kelleher ss	2	0	1	0
Boone c	6	1	3	1	R. Reuschel p	1	2	0	0
Carlton p	1	0	0	0	Garman p	0	0	0	0
Schueler p	0	0	0	0	Knowles p	0	0	0	0
Garber p	0	0	0	0	P. Reuschel p	0	0	0	0
Hutton ph	0	0	0	0	Schultz p	0	0	0	0
Reed p	0	0	0	0	Adams ph	1	1	1	0
Martin ph	1	0	0	0					
Twitchell p	0	0	0	0					
Tolan ph-cf	3	2	2	0					
Totals	50	18	24	18	Totals	48	16	19	16

												R	H	E
Philadelphia	0	1	0	1	2	0	3	5	3	3		18	24	0
Chicago	0	7	5	1	0	0	0	0	2	1		16	19	0

DP—Philadelphia 1, Chicago 1. LOB—Philadelphia 8, Chicago 12. 2B—Cardenal, Madlock 2, Thornton, Boone, Adams. 3B—Johnstone, Bowa. HR—Maddox, Swisher, Monday 2, Schmidt 4, Boone. S—R. Reuschel, Johnstone, Luzinski, Cash.

	IP	H	R	ER	BB	SO
Philadelphia						
Carlton	1⅔	7	7	7	2	1
Schueler	⅔	3	3	3	0	0
Garber	⅔	2	2	2	1	1
Reed	2	1	1	1	1	1
Twitchell	2	0	0	0	1	1
McGraw W	2	4	2	2	1	2
Underwood	⅔	2	1	1	0	1
Lonborg S	⅓	0	0	0	0	0
Chicago						
R. Reuschel	7	14	7	7	1	4
Garman	⅔	4	5	5	1	1
Knowles L	1⅓	3	4	4	1	0
P. Reuschel	0	3	2	2	1	0
Schultz	1	0	0	0	0	0

HBP—R. Reuschel (Schueler), Garber (Thornton), Twitchell (Monday). BK—Schultz. T—3:42. A—28,287.

July 28, 1977

The Cubs and Reds play a game that goes 13 innings, nearly five hours, and features 11 home runs by nine players—2 apiece by Bill Buckner and George Mitterwald—and a record 5 in the first inning alone. The Cubs rally from deficits of 6–0, 10–7, 14–10, and 15–14 to win the game. Dave Rosello is the hero in the 13th after his error gave the Reds the lead in the 12th. Rick Reuschel goes to 15–3, picking up the win in relief and scoring the winning run after singling with two out and none on. The Cubs are so short of players that Jose Cardenal has to play an inning at second, and later Bobby Murcer plays an inning switching between second and shortstop. Lost in the madness: Bruce Sutter pitches three shutout innings—the 9th, 10th, and 11th—striking out six.

Reds 15

CINCINNATI	ab	r	h	bi
Rose 3b	6	1	2	1
Griffey rf	8	2	5	4
Morgan 2b	8	1	2	0
Foster lf	6	2	3	0
Bench c	5	2	1	3
Geronimo cf	8	2	2	2
Lum 1b	5	3	2	2
Concepcion ss	6	2	2	2
Murray p	1	0	0	0
Borbon p	2	0	0	0
Armbrister ph	1	0	0	0
Sarmiento p	1	0	0	0
Hoerner p	0	0	0	0
Norman p	0	0	0	0
Summers ph	1	0	0	0
Billingham p	0	0	0	0
Totals	**58**	**15**	**19**	**14**

Cubs 16

CHICAGO	ab	r	h	bi
DeJesus ss	5	2	1	0
Cardenal rf-2b	2	0	0	0
Biittner lf	7	3	3	1
Buckner 1b	8	2	2	5
Murcer rf-2b-ss	8	3	3	2
Morales cf	6	1	2	1
R. Reuschel p	1	1	1	0
Ontiveros 3b	6	0	3	2
Trillo 2b	3	1	1	1
Hernandez p	0	0	0	0
Wallis ph	1	0	0	0
Rosello ss-2b	3	0	1	1
Mitterwald c	7	2	3	2
Burris p	1	1	1	0
Moore p	1	0	1	1
P. Reuschel p	1	0	0	0
Kelleher 2b	1	0	0	0
Gross ph	0	0	0	0
Sutter p	1	0	1	0
Clines cf	1	0	1	0
Totals	**63**	**16**	**24**	**16**

														R	H	E
Cincinnati	6	0	4	0	0	1	2	1	0	0	0	1	0	15	19	1
Chicago	4	3	1	2	0	0	0	3	1	0	0	1	1	16	24	3

E—Lum, Cardenal, Buckner, Rosello. DP—Chicago 2. LOB—Cincinnati 15, Chicago 16. 2B—DeJesus, Burris, Geronimo, Griffey 2, Mitterwald, Foster, Clines. 3B—Moore. HR—Rose, Bench, Lum, Buckner 2, Murcer, Mitterwald 2, Griffey, Geronimo, Morales. SB—Concepcion 3, Lum, Rose, Morgan. S—Rose.

	IP	H*	R	ER	BB	SO
Cincinnati						
Murray	1	5	6	6	1	1
Borbon	5	7	4	3	2	6
Sarmiento	2	4	3	3	2	2
Hoerner	2/3	1	1	1	0	1
Billingham L	1 2/3	5	2	2	0	0
Chicago						
Burris	2	7	8	8	1	2
Moore	1	5	2	2	1	0
P. Reuschel	3 1/3	3	3	3	2	1
Hernandez	1 2/3	2	1	1	2	2
Sutter	3	0	0	0	1	6
Broberg	1 1/3	2	1	0	3	2
R. Reuschel W	2/3	0	0	0	0	0

T—4:50. A—32,155.

*Official published box score is inaccurate. Fred Norman was not included in the pitching line for the Reds. He relieved Joe Hoerner, pitched 2⅓ innings, and gave up two hits and no runs. Even the official scorers lose count in this one!

May 17, 1979

Two years to the day after pounding the Padres 23–6, the Cubs score 22 . . . and lose. Chicago and Philadelphia hook up in yet another wild one as the Phillies get their revenge for the 26–23 thumping of 1922. Dave Kingman's three home runs go for naught when Mike Schmidt hits the game-winner off Bruce Sutter in the 10th inning. The Cubs have rallied from a 17–6 deficit to tie the game at 22–22 in the eighth inning but can't push any more runs across. Neither starter lasts more than a third of an inning, and Willie Hernandez manages to yield seven hits and seven walks, hit a batter, and have another reach base on an error in less than three innings but allow *only* eight runs.

Phillies 23   Cubs 22

PHILADELPHIA	ab	r	h	bi	CHICAGO	ab	r	h	bi
McBride rf	8	2	3	1	DeJesus ss	6	4	3	1
Bowa ss	8	4	5	1	Vail rf	5	2	3	1
Rose 1b	7	4	3	4	Burris p	0	0	0	0
Schmidt 3b	4	3	2	4	Thompson cf	2	1	1	0
Unser lf	7	1	1	2	Buckner 1b	7	3	4	7
Maddox cf	4	3	4	4	Kingman lf	6	4	3	6
Gross cf	2	1	1	1	Ontiveros 3b	7	1	1	1
Boone c	4	2	3	5	Martin cf	6	2	3	3
Meoli 2b	5	0	1	0	Sutter p	0	0	0	0
Lerch p	1	1	1	1	Foote c	6	1	3	1
Bird p	1	1	0	0	Sizemore 2b	4	2	2	1
Luzinski ph	0	0	0	0	Caudill p	0	0	0	0
Espinosa pr	1	1	0	0	Murcer rf	2	0	1	0
McGraw p	0	0	0	0	Lamp p	0	0	0	0
Reed p	0	0	0	0	Moore p	1	0	1	1
McCarver ph	1	0	0	0	W. Hernandez p	1	0	0	0
Eastwick p	0	0	0	0	Dillard 2b	1	2	1	0
					Biittner ph	1	0	0	0
					Kelleher 2b	1	0	0	0
Totals	**53**	**23**	**24**	**23**	**Totals**	**56**	**22**	**26**	**22**

Philadelphia	7	0	8	2	4	0	1	0	0	1	23	24	2
Chicago	6	0	0	3	7	3	0	3	0	0	22	26	2

E—Schmidt 2, Kingman, DeJesus. DP—Philadelphia 2. LOB—Philadelphia 15, Chicago 7. 2B—Bowa 2, Maddox 2, Rose 2, Foote, Martin, DeJesus, Boone. 3B—Moore, Gross. HR—Kingman 3, Schmidt 2, Boone, Lerch, Maddox, Ontiveros, Buckner, Martin. SB—Bowa, Meoli. S—Unser, Gross.

	IP	H	R	ER	BB	SO
Philadelphia						
Lerch	1/3	5	5	5	0	0
Bird	3 2/3	8	4	4	0	2
McGraw	2/3	4	7	4	3	1
Reed	3 1/3	9	6	6	0	0
Eastwick W	2	0	0	0	0	1
Chicago						
Lamp	1/3	6	6	6	0	0
Moore	2	6	7	7	2	1

W. Hernandez	2⅔	7	8	6	7	1
Caudill	1⅓	3	1	1	2	3
Burris	1⅔	1	0	0	0	1
Sutter L	2	1	1	1	1	0

HBP—W. Hernandez (Boone). T—4:03. A—14,952.

August 29, 1989

The Cubs have a 2½-game lead over the St. Louis Cardinals going into play on the 29th, but they've dropped 8 of their last 10. They appear to be on their way to nine losses in their last 11 when they fall behind 9–0 to the Astros. The Cubs fight back with two in the 6th, three in the 7th, four in the 8th, and the game-winner in the 10th—tying the team record for biggest comeback and sending Harry Caray into hysterics. Dwight Smith wins the game with a one-out, bases-loaded single off Dave Smith.

Astros 9

HOUSTON	ab	r	h	bi
Young cf	5	0	1	0
Doran 2b	4	1	0	0
Bass lf	4	1	1	0
Davis 1b	3	2	0	0
Wilson rf	5	0	1	0
Yelding pr	0	0	0	0
Da. Smith p	0	0	0	0
Caminiti 3b	4	2	1	0
Biggio c	3	2	1	0
Ramirez ss	5	1	3	7
Portugal p	3	0	0	0
Meyer p	0	0	0	0
Darwin p	0	0	0	0
Agosto p	0	0	0	0
Puhl rf	1	0	0	0
Totals	**37**	**9**	**8**	**7**

Cubs 10

CHICAGO	ab	r	h	bi
Walton cf	4	3	0	0
Sandberg 2b	5	1	3	1
McClendon lf	5	2	3	3
Grace 1b	4	2	2	1
Dawson rf	3	0	1	0
Dw. Smith rf	2	0	2	3
Dunston ss	5	1	2	0
Ramos 3b	4	0	2	1
Girardi c	4	1	3	0
Bielecki p	1	0	0	0
Wilkins p	0	0	0	0
Wilkerson ph	0	0	0	0
Schiraldi p	0	0	0	0
Webster ph	1	0	0	0
Sanderson p	0	0	0	0
Law ph	1	0	0	0
Lancaster p	0	0	0	0
Jackson ph	1	0	0	0
Assenmacher p	0	0	0	0
Totals	**40**	**10**	**18**	**9**

Houston	0	2	0	2	5	0	0	0	0	0	9	8	2
Chicago	0	0	0	0	0	2	3	4	0	1	10	18	1

E—Dunston, Portugal, Caminiti. DP—Houston 2. LOB—Houston 6, Chicago 12. 2B—Biggio, Ramirez, Dawson, Bass. HR—Ramirez, McClendon. S—Meyer, Ramos, Sandberg, Dw. Smith.

	IP	H	R	ER	BB	SO
Houston						
Portugal	6⅓	9	4	4	2	4
Meyer	1	4	4	2	0	0
Darwin	0	1	1	1	0	0
Agosto	⅔	1	0	0	0	0
Da. Smith L	1⅓	3	1	1	3	0

Chicago

Bielecki	4	3	6	5	5	5
Wilkins	1	1	3	3	2	1
Schiraldi	1	1	0	0	0	0
Sanderson	2	2	0	0	0	1
Lancaster	1	1	0	0	0	0
Assenmacher W	1	0	0	0	0	1

HBP—Portugal (McClendon, Walton). WP—Bielecki. BK—Meyer. PB—Girardi, Biggio 2. T—3:46. A—25,829.

August 18, 1995

The Cubs tie their 20th-century club record when they explode for 26 runs against the Colorado Rockies at Coors Field. With a major-league-record 14 players registering hits, the Cubs bat .500 for the game, .609 with runners in scoring position, and plate 76 percent of their base runners, a phenomenal rate of efficiency. When Bret Saberhagen takes 1996 off so that he can rehab his arm, perhaps this is the game on which he reflects to counteract any urges to suck it up and get back to Denver.

Cubs 26   *Rockies 7*

CHICAGO	ab	r	h	bi	COLORADO	ab	r	h	bi
McRae cf	5	2	3	1	E. Young 2b	4	0	0	0
Bullett cf	2	2	2	4	Burks cf-lf	4	0	0	0
Dunston ss	3	0	1	1	Bichette lf-rf	4	1	2	1
Hernandez ss	4	0	1	2	Walker rf	3	0	0	0
Grace 1b	6	3	1	2	Vander Wal rf-1b	2	0	0	0
Sosa rf	6	4	4	4	Galarraga 1b	3	1	1	1
Gonzalez lf	6	2	3	6	Kingery cf	2	1	1	1
Casian p	1	0	0	0	Castilla 3b	5	1	2	0
Myers p	0	0	0	0	Girardi c	3	1	1	0
Zeile 3b	4	2	3	3	Owens c	2	1	0	0
Johnson 3b	0	0	0	0	Weiss ss	2	0	0	0
Kmak ph-3b	2	1	1	0	Reed p	0	0	0	0
Sanchez 2b	4	1	1	0	Munoz p	0	0	0	0
Adams p	0	0	0	0	Hickerson ph-p	1	0	1	2
Timmons lf	1	0	0	0	Holmes p	1	0	0	0
Servais c	5	4	3	1	Saberhagen p	0	0	0	0
Foster p	2	1	1	2	Painter p	0	0	0	0
Perez p	0	0	0	0	Tatum ph	1	0	0	0
A. Young p	2	2	2	0	Nied p	0	0	0	0
Haney 2b	1	2	1	0	Bates ss	2	1	2	2
Totals	54	26	27	26	Totals	39	7	10	7

Chicago	7	0	2	0	6	3	4	4	0	26	27	3
Colorado	0	1	0	0	1	2	3	0	0	7	10	1

E—Zeile, Gonzalez, Haney, Bichette. DP—Chicago 1, Colorado 1. LOB—Chicago 7, Colorado 10. 2B—Grace, Gonzalez, Zeile, Servais 2, Foster, Bullett, Girardi, Bates. 3B—Bullett, Hickerson. HR—Sosa, Gonzalez, Zeile, Galarraga.

	IP	H	R	ER	BB	SO
Chicago						
Foster	3	1	1	1	2	2
Perez	⅔	0	0	0	0	1
A. Young W	1⅓	3	1	1	0	1
Adams	1⅔	6	5	4	2	1
Casian	1	0	0	0	0	0
Myers	1	0	0	0	0	0
Colorado						
Saberhagen L	⅓	5	7	7	2	0
Painter	2⅔	5	2	2	0	1
Nied	1⅓	6	5	5	1	1
Reed	1⅓	5	4	4	1	4
Munoz	1⅓	3	4	4	1	0
Hickerson	1	3	4	4	1	0
Holmes	1	0	0	0	0	2

T—3:22. A—48,082.

September 12, 1998

The Cubs are tied with the Mets for the wild-card play-off spot going into play and are one day removed from a disappointing 13–11 loss to the Milwaukee Brewers in which a late charge fell short. Chicago goes out on top 2–0, but eight runs off Mike Morgan and another two runs off Dave Stevens put the Brewers up 10–2. The Cubs hit six home runs in the course of their comeback, including Sammy Sosa's 60th and a pinch-hit shot by Tyler Houston in the eighth that cuts the lead to 12–10. The game is important enough that closer Rod Beck is brought into the ninth inning in a rare nonsave situation to get the last out. In the bottom of the ninth, Sosa—with a chance for 61—plays for the team and lines a single between short and third on the first pitch off Bob Wickman. Glenallen Hill follows with a single up the middle. Gary Gaetti bunts the runners along, then Mickey Morandini fouls off some tough pitches before drawing a walk to load the bases. Houston then hits a two-run seeing-eye single past second-baseman Fernando Vina into right field to tie the game. With only a long fly ball needed for a victory, newly acquired pinch-hitter Orlando Merced lofts a three-run homer into the right-field bleachers to win the game 15–12.

Brewers 12

MILWAUKEE	ab	r	h	bi
Vina 2b	5	1	2	3
Loretta ss-1b	5	1	3	0
Nilsson 1b	5	1	1	3
Fox p	0	0	0	0
Matheny c	0	0	0	0
Cirillo 3b	5	1	2	1
Burnitz rf	5	1	2	2
Grissom cf	4	0	0	0
Jenkins lf	3	3	2	1
Newfield ph	1	0	1	0
Jackson pr-lf	0	0	0	0
Hughes c	4	3	2	1

Cubs 15

CHICAGO	ab	r	h	bi
Johnson cf	4	1	0	0
Hernandez ss	5	1	2	1
Beck p	0	0	0	0
Grace 1b	5	1	2	0
Sosa rf	3	3	2	3
Hill lf	5	4	4	1
Gaetti 3b	4	1	2	2
Morandini 2b	4	1	1	2
Servais c	3	0	0	0
Houston ph-c	2	2	2	3
Morgan p	1	0	1	0
Stevens p	2	0	1	0

Wickman p	0	0	0	0	Heredia p	0	0	0	0
Roque p	1	0	0	0	Brown ph	1	0	0	0
Hamelin ph	1	0	1	0	Mulholland p	0	0	0	0
Belliard pr	0	1	0	0	Alexander ss	0	0	0	0
De Los Santos p	0	0	0	0	Merced ph	1	1	1	3
Valentin ss	0	0	0	0					
Totals	39	12	16	11	Totals	40	15	18	15

Milwaukee	0	0	8	0	2	0	2	0	0		12	16	0
Chicago	0	2	0	0	1	2	4	1	5		15	18	2

E—Sosa, Hernandez. DP—Milwaukee 2, Chicago 2. LOB—Milwaukee 5, Chicago 5. 2B—Cirillo, Burnitz, Hamelin, Grace. 3B—Nilsson. HR—Burnitz, Jenkins, Hughes, Hernandez, Sosa, Hill, Gaetti, Houston, Merced. S—Roque 2, Gaetti.

	IP	H	R	ER	BB	SO
Milwaukee						
Roque	6	9	5	5	2	3
De Los Santos	1	3	4	4	1	2
Fox	1	2	1	1	0	0
Wickman L	1/3	4	5	5	1	0
Chicago						
Morgan	3	8	8	5	1	1
Stevens	3 2/3	5	4	4	2	3
Heredia	1 1/3	2	0	0	0	1
Mulholland	2/3	0	0	0	0	0
Beck W	1/3	1	0	0	0	1

T—3:16. A—39,170.

September 13, 1998

It's a day later, the largest crowd of the year is on hand at Wrigley, and the Cubs look to be on the verge of extending their wild-card lead to two games. Ex-Cub Miguel Batista is pitching a gem in Montreal against the Mets while the Cubs are off to an 8–3 lead against the Brewers on Sammy Sosa's 61st home run. Ex-Cub Brian McRae single-handedly wins the game in Montreal for the Mets, making a game-saving catch, knocking in the lone run, then throwing the tying run out at the plate to end the contest 1–0. As the Mets celebrate their win, the Cubs are blowing their 8–3 lead. The Brewers score four in the eighth and add a run in the ninth to go up 10–8. With one down in the bottom of the ninth, Sammy hits another 480' bomb onto Waveland Avenue to cut the lead to 10–9, his 4th of the series and 10th off the Brewers for the year. After a six-minute delay as the fans call Sosa out of the dugout three times, pinch-hitter Henry Rodriguez doubles off Eric Plunk, and Gary Gaetti singles in pinch-runner Jason Maxwell to tie the game at 10–10 (giving the Cubs 10 runs in three consecutive games for the first time since June 1930!).

Rod Beck retires the Brewers in the top of the 10th, helped by a great diving tag at first base by Mark Grace on Gerald Martinez. Al Reyes is in the process of putting the Cubs down 1-2-3 when Grace lifts a home run into the right-field bleachers for the Cubs' second game-winning home run in two days. Grace, unable to keep from smiling as he rounds the bases, is mobbed at the plate and carried off the field by his teammates.

Brewers 10   Cubs 11

MILWAUKEE	ab	r	h	bi		CHICAGO	ab	r	h	bi
Vina 2b	5	0	2	0		Johnson cf	6	0	2	0
Loretta ss	4	1	1	2		Hernandez ss	6	1	1	1
Nilsson 1b	5	0	0	0		Grace 1b	6	3	3	2
Cirillo 3b	5	3	3	2		Sosa rf	4	3	2	3
Burnitz rf	4	2	2	2		Hill lf	3	0	2	1
Grissom cf	5	1	2	1		Brown pr-lf	0	0	0	0
Jenkins lf	3	0	0	0		Karchner p	0	0	0	0
Newfield ph	0	0	0	0		Heredia p	0	0	0	0
G. Martinez pr-lf	1	1	0	0		Wengert p	0	0	0	0
Hughes c	3	2	2	1		Haney p	0	0	0	0
Hamelin ph	0	0	0	0		Rodriguez ph	1	0	1	0
Belliard pr	0	0	0	0		Maxwell pr	0	1	0	0
Matheny c	1	0	0	0		S. Martinez c	0	0	0	0
Woodall p	0	0	0	0		Gaetti 3b	5	0	2	3
Patrick p	1	0	0	0		Morandini 2b	5	1	1	0
De Los Santos p	0	0	0	0		Servais c	3	1	1	0
Banks ph	1	0	0	0		Houston ph-c	1	0	1	0
Weathers p	0	0	0	0		Mieske ph-lf	0	0	0	0
Valentin ph	0	0	0	0		Trachsel p	3	1	1	1
Jackson ph	1	0	1	2		Mulholland p	0	0	0	0
Plunk p	0	0	0	0		Merced lf	1	0	0	0
Myers p	0	0	0	0		Alexander ph	1	0	0	0
Reyes p	1	0	0	0		Beck p	0	0	0	0
Totals	40	10	13	10		**Totals**	45	11	17	11

Milwaukee	1	0	1	1	0	1	1	4	1	0		10	13	0
Chicago	0	0	6	0	2	0	0	0	2	1		11	17	0

DP—Milwaukee 1. LOB—Milwaukee 5, Chicago 8. 2B—Vina, Burnitz, Grace, Trachsel, Rodriguez. 3B—Johnson. HR—Loretta, Burnitz, Sosa 2, Cirillo 2, Hughes, Grace. S—Woodall, Loretta.

	IP	H	R	ER	BB	SO
Milwaukee						
Woodall	2⅓	6	6	6	1	0
Patrick	3⅓	6	2	2	0	3
De Los Santos	⅓	0	0	0	0	0
Weathers	1	0	0	0	1	1
Plunk	1⅔	4	2	2	0	3
Myers	0	0	0	0	1	0
Reyes L	1	1	1	1	0	0
Chicago						
Trachsel	6	7	5	5	0	2
Mulholland	1⅓	3	4	4	1	3
Karchner	0	0	0	0	1	0
Heredia	⅓	2	0	0	0	0
Wengert	⅓	0	0	0	0	0
Haney	1	1	1	1	0	1
Beck W	1	0	0	0	0	2

T—3:52. A—40,846.

the bunting

There are those special days during the season when the stadium walls are draped in red, white, and blue bunting: Opening Day, interleague play with the White Sox, and the All-Star Game. This chapter is a celebration of these traditional days, which date back to 1876, 1997, and 1933, respectively, and it includes:

- Wrigley's firsts, back when it wasn't even Wrigley and the Cubs weren't the home team
- A snapshot of Opening Day third basemen, left fielders, and center fielders since 1976—a moving target, to say the least
- A near no-hitter followed by yet another near no-hitter
- Billy Herman's four extra-base hits and his eventual replacement's four errors
- Opening a season and a career with a bases-clearing triple
- A Hall of Fame pitchers' duel decided by a Hall of Fame hitter
- Larry Biittner's finest hour in front of a packed house
- Wild Thing's wild debut
- Tuffy Rhodes's mirage
- The Cubs' first designated hitter
- Sammy Sosa's vivid, firsthand reminder to the White Sox of just what they've been missing
- The year that five Cubs combined to single-handedly win the All-Star Game
- The Cubs' two greatest All-Stars
- The Cubs' All-Star starters and selections, by year and position
- All-Star home runs, game-winning hits, wins, and saves

Put me in, coach . . .

OPENING DAY

1876

Albert Spalding wins the franchise's first game 4–0, on April 25 at Louisville. Paul Hines scores the team's first run. On May 10, Spalding throws another shutout in Chicago's first National League home game, 6–0 over Cincinnati.

1880

King Kelly makes his White Stockings debut with a game-winning home run in the ninth at Cincinnati. Chicago wins 4–3 thanks to one of the team's four home runs of the year.

1914

The Federal League Chicago Whales beat the Kansas City Packers 9–1 in the first game played at what is now Wrigley Field. Art Wilson hits two home runs, including the first in the park's history.

1916

The first National League game at Weeghman Park is a 7–6 Cubs victory, as Vic Saier wins the game with a single in the 11th. Chicago forces extra innings with two in the eighth and one in the ninth.

1925

Grover Cleveland Alexander wins #301 by a score of 8–2 over the Pirates at Wrigley. He hits a single, a double, and a home run in the first regular-season Cubs game broadcast on radio.

1934

Lon Warneke takes a no-hitter into the ninth in Cincinnati on Opening Day, but Adam Comorosky singles with one out to break it up. Warneke finishes with 13 strikeouts and a 6–0 victory. He follows up this gem April 17 with another one-hitter on the 22nd as the Cubs bomb Dizzy and Daffy Dean 15–2 on 22 hits. The lone hit is a double by Ripper Collins in the fifth inning.

1935

As Fred Lindstrom hits a line drive off Dizzy Dean's shin in the first inning, the band strikes up "Happy Days Are Here Again." The Cubs go on to beat the Cardinals 4–3.

1936

Billy Herman hits three doubles and a home run for a record four extra-base hits on Opening Day. The Cubs beat Dizzy Dean and the Cardinals 12–7, with Frank Demaree contributing two home runs and Chuck Klein and Gabby Hartnett one apiece.

1941

Billy Herman's eventual replacement, Lou Stringer, makes four errors at shortstop on Opening Day in his major-league debut. The Cubs beat the Pirates 7–4 at Wrigley Field.

Getting Off to a Good Start

Opening Day	55–42–2	.567
Home Openers	58–39–2	.598

1945

The Cubs beat the Cardinals—the reigning National League champions of 1942, 1943, and 1944—3–2 at Wrigley Field, as Don Johnson singles home Bill Nicholson with the game-winning run.

1946

The Cubs beat the Reds 4–3 with four in the top of the ninth at Crosley Field. Bob Scheffing comes through with a two-run pinch-hit single in his first game back from the war.

1948

Johnny Schmitz tosses a two-hitter but loses to Harry Bleechen and the Cardinals 1–0 at Wrigley.

1951

Sam Snead becomes the first man to hit the center-field scoreboard—only he does it before the game with a golf ball teed up at home plate. The Cubs beat the Cardinals 8–3 as Dee Fondy clears the bases with a triple in his first major-league at bat.

1969

Ernie Banks homers twice as the Cubs beat the Phillies 7–6 in 11 in front of 40,796. Things look bleak in the top of the 11th as Don Money homers off Phil Regan. But in the bottom of the inning, Randy Hundley breaks Barry Lersch's streak of 10 consecutive batters retired when he singles, and pinch-hitter Willie Smith delivers a two-run, game-winning home run.

1971

Ferguson Jenkins outpitches Bob Gibson at Wrigley as Billy Williams's 10th-inning home run wins the game 2–1.

1973

The Cubs beat the Expos 3–2 at Wrigley Field as Mike Marshall walks Rick Monday with the bases loaded in the ninth, scoring a pinch runner named Tony LaRussa in his only game as a Cub and the last game of his major-league career. The Cubs beat the Expos again the following day in the 10th on a two-out Ron Santo single.

1976

The Cubs beat the Mets 5–4 at Wrigley as Rick Monday wins the game with a ninth-inning bloop single. Jerry Morales homers twice for the Cubs. The crowd of 44,818 is the largest to date for a Wrigley Field Opening Day.

1978

Coming off an exciting 1977 season, which saw Rick Reuschel and Bruce Sutter pitch the Cubs into first place for 69 days, and an off-season in which Dave Kingman was signed as a free agent, 45,777 pack themselves into Wrigley Field for the largest Opening Day crowd in club history. More late-game heroics as the Cubs win 5–4 on a first-pitch home run by Larry Biittner leading off the ninth inning.

Opening Uncertainty

One good way to check the stability of a team or a position is to look at Opening Day lineups over the course of several seasons. Doing so with the Cubs will tell you that it's not just third base that they're having trouble nailing down, as the following table shows. Streaks of four or more different players in four different lineups are in **bold**.

Third, Left, and Center on Opening Day

1976	Bill Madlock	Jose Cardenal	**Rick Monday**
1977	Steve Ontiveros	Jose Cardenal	**Jerry Morales**
1978	Steve Ontiveros	Dave Kingman	**Greg Gross**
1979	Steve Ontiveros	Dave Kingman	**Jerry Martin**
1980	**Steve Ontiveros**	Dave Kingman	**Carlos Lezcano**
1981	**Ken Reitz**	Steve Henderson	**Scot Thompson**
1982	**Ryne Sandberg**	Steve Henderson	**Tye Waller**
1983	**Ron Cey**	Mel Hall	**Bull Durham**
1984	Ron Cey	Gary Matthews	**Bob Dernier**
1985	**Ron Cey**	Gary Matthews	Bob Dernier
1986	**Manny Trillo**	Brian Dayett	Bob Dernier
1987	**Keith Moreland**	**Brian Dayett**	Bob Dernier
1988	**Vance Law**	Rafael Palmeiro	Dave Martinez
1989	Vance Law	**Mitch Webster**	Jerome Walton
1990	Luis Salazar	**Lloyd McClendon**	Jerome Walton
1991	Gary Scott	**George Bell**	**Jerome Walton**
1992	Gary Scott	**Luis Salazar**	**Sammy Sosa**
1993	Steve Buechele	**Candy Maldanado**	**Willie Wilson**
1994	Steve Buechele	**Derrick May**	**Tuffy Rhodes**
1995	Steve Buechele	**Scott Bullett**	**Brian McRae**
1996	Jose Hernandez	**Luis Gonzalez**	Brian McRae
1997	Kevin Orie	**Brant Brown**	Brian McRae
1998	Kevin Orie	**Henry Rodriguez**	Lance Johnson

1988

The Cubs and Braves tie a National League record set by the Mets and Expos two days before when they combine to hit seven home runs on Opening Day. Jody Davis, Bull Durham, and Shawon Dunston go deep for the Cubs, who win 10–9 in 13 innings in Atlanta. The Braves think they have it won in regulation, as Gerald Perry is hit on the helmet during a botched rundown between third and home, but he's called out for interfering with Vance Law.

1989

Wild Thing never does it the easy way, and certainly not in his Cubs debut. He has already walked two and balked once in a messy eighth inning in which the Phillies close to 5–4. In the ninth, he gives up three consecutive singles to load the bases, then with boos raining down, he strikes out Mike Schmidt. He then strikes out both Chris James and Mark Ryal for the save.

1994

Tuffy Rhodes becomes the second major leaguer and first National Leaguer to hit three home runs on Opening Day, taking Dwight Gooden deep three times at Wrigley Field. He goes 4-for-4, but the Mets beat the Cubs 12–8. Rhodes joins a bizarre Cubs club of April mirages.

George Mitterwald, 1974	April 17: 3 HRS, 8 RBIS	Season: 5 HRS, 28 RBIS, .215
Barry Foote, 1980	April 22: 2 HRS, 8 RBIS	Season: 6 HRS, 28 RBIS, .238
Tuffy Rhodes, 1994	April 4: 3 HRS, 3 RBIS	Season: 8 HRS, 19 RBIS, .234

1997

The Cubs lose 4–2 to Kevin Brown and the Florida Marlins at Joe Robbie Stadium, managing only three hits. A week later, they lose 5–3 to Al Leiter and the Marlins at the Wrigley home opener. They are well on their way to losing a club-record 14 in a row—a National League record from the start of a season—the first 10 to the Braves and the Marlins, the two best teams in the National League. They hit .174 as a team during the brutal stretch.

INTERLEAGUE PLAY

The Cubs played their first interleague game on June 13, 1997, at Wrigley Field, with Terry Mulholland losing to the Milwaukee Brewers and Jeff D'Amico 4–2. But that three-game series—in which the Cubs went on to take two of three—was just a warm-up for the crosstown showdown with the White Sox. It would be the first time since 1906 that the two teams met in a game that counted. And for those who doubted that they would ever live to see another Cubs-Sox World Series, it was a chance to see a reasonable facsimile of one, played out across two seasons. This section recaps the six meetings in 1997–98.

Game One
June 16, 1997, at Comiskey Park
The Cubs jump all over a former Cub, Jaime Navarro, for six runs in the first three innings and coast to an 8–3 victory. Brant Brown's first-inning triple scores Brian McRae, and Brown scores moments later on a Mark Grace sacrifice fly. McRae gets two more hits and knocks in two runs, while Sammy Sosa steals two bases against his former team and scores a run. Kevin Foster pitches six innings for the victory, with Ramon Tatis and Mel Rojas combining for three innings of scoreless relief. Lyle Mouton hits the first home run of the series for the White Sox.

Q. Who was the Cubs' first designated hitter?

A. Dave Clark, June 16, 1997, at Comiskey Park

Game Two
June 17, 1997, at Comiskey Park
The White Sox even the series at 1–1 with a 5–3 victory. Former Cub Dave Martinez hits a home run in the first off Jeremi Gonzalez as the White Sox jump out to an early 3–0 lead. Doug Drabek gets the win as Matt Karchner and Roberto Hernandez pitch three innings of scoreless relief. Sammy Sosa doubles twice and scores twice for the Cubs.

Game Three
June 18, 1997, at Comiskey Park
The White Sox now take a 2–1 lead in the series with a briskly played, two-hour, 3–0 shutout. Wilson Alvarez limits the Cubs to four hits as he outpitches Terry Mulholland. The key blow of the game comes in the first inning as Lyle Mouton hits a two-out, two-run double. Dave Martinez adds an insurance run in the seventh with his second home run of the series.

Game Four
June 5, 1998, at Wrigley Field
With the series shifting to Wrigley Field in 1998, the Cubs even it up at two games apiece with a 12-inning, 6–5 victory. The Cubs fall behind in the first after the White Sox score two runs after the first two batters are retired, but they score three times in the third when Henry Rodriguez hits a bases-loaded double, scoring Mickey Morandini, Sammy Sosa, and Jeff Blauser. Sosa adds a two-run home run in the fifth off Jim Parque to put the Cubs up 5–2, but a double by Magglio Ordonez and a single by Chad Kreuter cap a three-run rally by the White Sox in the sixth. The game remains scoreless until the 12th, when Brant Brown homers leading off against Tony Castillo. Terry Mulholland picks up the win in relief for the Cubs.

Game Five
June 6, 1998, at Wrigley Field
The Cubs move to within one game of winning the series, with a hard-fought, 7–6 victory. Down 1–0 in the third, the Cubs push three runs across, capped by a two-run, two-out single by Jeff Blauser, scoring Manny Alexander and Terrell Lowery. Jose Hernandez leads off the fourth with a home run, but the White Sox come back to take a 5–4 lead in the sixth. In the bottom of the sixth, pinch-hitter Derrick White delivers a two-out, two-run home run off starter Scott Eyre to put the Cubs back on top, and Sammy Sosa adds a two-out insurance blast in the seventh off Carlos Castillo to make it 7–5. Rod Beck pitches the ninth, yielding one run in closing out the victory for former-Sox pitcher Kevin Tapani.

Game Six
June 7, 1998, at Wrigley Field
The Cubs win the first June Classic of 1997–98 four games to two with a 13–7 pasting of Mike Sirotka and the White Sox. The Sox score once in the top of the first, but Sammy Sosa erases their lead with a two-run double in the bottom and later scores on a two-out, three-run homer by Jose Hernandez. Hernandez adds a two-run double, and the Cubs pull ahead to a 13–2 lead on a three-run home run by Sosa off James Baldwin in the fifth and coast home to a 13–7 victory. A total of 240,315 fans attend the six games and see Sammy Sosa put the hurt on his former team, going 9-for-23 (.391) and slugging .913, with three doubles, three homers, eight runs scored, eight RBIs, and two stolen bases.

ALL-STAR GAME

The first All-Star Game was played at Comiskey Park in 1933, and it's been a midsummer tradition ever since, with two games played each year from 1959 to 1962. While the fans and managers selected the squads for the first two seasons, selection subsequently became the sole responsibility of the prior year's pennant-winning managers until 1947. From 1947 to 1957, fans chose the starting position players. After Cincinnati fans stuffed the ballot boxes in 1957, the teams were chosen by major-league players, coaches, and managers until the fans got the vote back in 1970.

Here are the Cubs' All-Stars for every season since 1933, with starters in **bold** and those who did not appear in the game in *italics*. Following the rosters is a look at the ins and outs of the most memorable games through the years.

The All-Stars

1933

Woody English	SS
Gabby Hartnett	C
Lon Warneke	SP (R)

1934

Kiki Cuyler	RF
Gabby Hartnett	C
Billy Herman	2B
Chuck Klein	LF
Lon Warneke	SP (R)

1935

Gabby Hartnett	C
Billy Herman	2B

1936

Curt Davis	SP (R)
Frank Demaree	RF
Augie Galan	CF
Gabby Hartnett	C
Billy Herman	2B
Lon Warneke	SP (R)

1937

Ripper Collins	1B
Frank Demaree	CF
Gabby Hartnett	C
Billy Herman	2B
Billy Jurges	SS

1938

Stan Hack	3B
Gabby Hartnett	C
Billy Herman	2B
Bill Lee	SP (R)

1939

Stan Hack	3B
Billy Herman	2B
Bill Lee	SP (R)

1940

Larry French	SP (L)
Billy Herman	2B
Hank Leiber	CF
Bill Nicholson	RF

1941

Stan Hack	3B
Hank Leiber	CF
Bill Nicholson	RF
Claude Passeau	SP (R)

1942

Claude Passeau	SP (R)

1943

Stan Hack	3B
Bill Nicholson	RF
Claude Passeau	SP (R)

1944

Phil Cavarretta	1B
Don Johnson	2B
Bill Nicholson	RF

1945

Phil Cavarretta	1B
Stan Hack	3B
Don Johnson	2B
Bill Nicholson	RF
Andy Pafko	CF
Claude Passeau	SP (R)
Hank Wyse	SP (R)

1946

Phil Cavarretta	1B
Peanuts Lowrey	CF
Claude Passeau	SP (R)
Johnny Schmitz	*SP (L)*

1947

Phil Cavarretta	1B
Andy Pafko	CF

1948

Clyde McCullough	*C*
Andy Pafko	**3B**
Johnny Schmitz	SP (L)
Eddie Waitkus	1B

1949

Andy Pafko	CF

1950

Andy Pafko	CF
Bob Rush	*SP (R)*
Hank Sauer	**RF**

1951

Bruce Edwards	*C*
Dutch Leonard	*RP (R)*

1952

Toby Atwell	*C*
Bob Rush	SP (R)
Hank Sauer	**LF**

1953

Ralph Kiner	LF
Clyde McCullough	*C*

1954

Randy Jackson	3B

1955

Gene Baker	2B
Ernie Banks	**SS**
Randy Jackson	3B
Sam Jones	SP (R)

All-Stars by the Numbers

0: Number of All-Star Games in which Ken Holtzman, Rick Monday, Jose Cardenal, Ivan DeJesus, Keith Moreland, Bob Dernier, and Brian McRae represented the Cubs

1: Number of Cubs pitchers to start an All-Star Game (Claude Passeau, 1946) and number of All-Star at bats for Sammy Sosa through 1998

2: Number of different positions at which Ernie Banks and Andy Pafko appeared in All-Star Games

3: Number of Cubs left-handed starters to be named to an All-Star team (French, Schmitz, and Ellsworth)

4: Number of Cubs infielders appearing on the 1969 All-Star team

5: Number of Cubs relievers to appear in an All-Star Game (Elston, Sutter, Smith, Williams, and Myers)

6: Number of different Cubs to start in right field (Cuyler, Demaree, Nicholson, Sauer, Williams, and Dawson)

7: Number of different Cubs second basemen named to an All-Star team (Herman, Johnson, Baker, Zimmer, Beckert, Trillo, and Sandberg)

8: Number of All-Star games in which Ron Santo appeared

9: Club-record number of times Ryne Sandberg started an All-Star Game (1984, 1986–1993)

10: Longest gap in years that passed between appearances of a Cubs starting pitcher in an All-Star Game (Rick Reuschel, 1977, and Rick Sutcliffe, 1987)

1956

Ernie Banks	*SS*

1957

Ernie Banks	SS

1958

Ernie Banks	**SS**
Walt Moryn	*LF*
Lee Walls	RF

1959 *Game 1*

Ernie Banks	**SS**
Don Elston	RP (R)

1959 *Game 2*

Ernie Banks	**SS**

1960 *Game 1*

Ernie Banks	**SS**

1960 Game 2

Ernie Banks — SS

1961 Game 1

George Altman — RF
Don Zimmer — 2B

1961 Game 2

George Altman — RF
Ernie Banks — SS
Don Zimmer — 2B

1962 Game 1

Ernie Banks — 1B

1962 Game 2

George Altman — RF
Ernie Banks — 1B
Billy Williams — LF

1963

Larry Jackson — SP (R)
Ron Santo — 3B

1964

Dick Ellsworth — SP (L)
Ron Santo — 3B
Billy Williams — LF

1965

Ernie Banks — 1B
Ron Santo — 3B
Billy Williams — RF

1966

Ron Santo — 3B

1967

Ernie Banks — 1B
Ferguson Jenkins — SP (R)

1968

Don Kessinger — SS
Ron Santo — 3B
Billy Williams — LF

1969

Ernie Banks — 1B
Glenn Beckert — 2B
Randy Hundley — C
Don Kessinger — SS
Ron Santo — 3B

1970

Glenn Beckert — 2B
Jim Hickman — LF
Don Kessinger — SS

1971

Glenn Beckert — 2B
Ferguson Jenkins — SP (R)
Don Kessinger — SS
Ron Santo — 3B

1972

Glenn Beckert — 2B
Ferguson Jenkins — SP (R)
Don Kessinger — SS
Ron Santo — 3B
Billy Williams — LF

1973

Ron Santo — 3B
Billy Williams — RF

1974

Don Kessinger — SS

1975

Bill Madlock — 3B

1976

Steve Swisher — C

1977

Jerry Morales — CF
Rick Reuschel — SP (R)
Bruce Sutter — RP (R)
Manny Trillo — 2B

1978

Bruce Sutter — RP (R)

1979

| Dave Kingman | LF |
| Bruce Sutter | RP (R) |

1980

| **Dave Kingman** | LF |
| Bruce Sutter | RP (R) |

1981

| Bill Buckner | IB |

1982

| *Bull Durham* | CF |

1983

| Bull Durham | RF |
| Lee Smith | RP (R) |

1984

| Jody Davis | C |
| **Ryne Sandberg** | 2B |

1985

| Ryne Sandberg | 2B |

1986

| Jody Davis | C |
| **Ryne Sandberg** | 2B |

1987

Andre Dawson	RF
Ryne Sandberg	2B
Lee Smith	RP (R)
Rick Sutcliffe	SP (R)

1988

Andre Dawson	RF
Shawon Dunston	SS
Vance Law	3B
Greg Maddux	SP (R)
Rafael Palmeiro	LF
Ryne Sandberg	2B

All-Stars by Position

*(Players who started at least once in the position are in **bold**.)*

C	**Gabby Hartnett,** Clyde McCullough, Bruce Edwards, Toby Atwell, Randy Hundley, Steve Swisher, Jody Davis
IB	Ripper Collins, **Phil Cavarretta,** Eddie Waitkus, **Ernie Banks,** Bill Buckner, **Mark Grace**
2B	**Billy Herman,** Don Johnson, Gene Baker, Don Zimmer, **Glenn Beckert,** Manny Trillo, **Ryne Sandberg**
SS	Woody English, Billy Jurges, **Ernie Banks, Don Kessinger,** Shawon Dunston
3B	**Stan Hack, Andy Pafko,** Randy Jackson, **Ron Santo,** Bill Madlock, Vance Law
LF	Chuck Klein, **Hank Sauer,** Ralph Kiner, Walt Moryn, **Billy Williams,** Jim Hickman, **Dave Kingman,** Rafael Palmeiro, George Bell
CF	**Augie Galan, Frank Demaree,** Hank Leiber, Andy Pafko, Peanuts Lowrey, Jerry Morales, Bull Durham
RF	**Kiki Cuyler, Frank Demaree, Bill Nicholson, Hank Sauer,** Lee Walls, George Altman, **Billy Williams,** Bull Durham, **Andre Dawson,** Sammy Sosa
SP (R)	Lon Warneke, Curt Davis, Bill Lee, **Claude Passeau,** Hank Wyse, Bob Rush, Sam Jones, Larry Jackson, Ferguson Jenkins, Rick Reuschel, Rick Sutcliffe, Greg Maddux, Steve Trachsel
SP (L)	Larry French, Johnny Schmitz, Dick Ellsworth
RP	Dutch Leonard, Don Elston, Bruce Sutter, Lee Smith, Mitch Williams, Randy Myers

1989

Andre Dawson	RF
Ryne Sandberg	2B
Rick Sutcliffe	SP (R)
Mitch Williams	RP (L)

1990

Andre Dawson	RF
Shawon Dunston	SS
Ryne Sandberg	2B

1991

George Bell	LF
Andre Dawson	RF
Ryne Sandberg	2B

1992

| Greg Maddux | SP (R) |
| **Ryne Sandberg** | 2B |

1993

Mark Grace 1B
Ryne Sandberg 2B

1994

Randy Myers RP (L)

1995

Mark Grace 1B
Randy Myers RP (L)
Sammy Sosa RF

1996

Steve Trachsel SP (R)

1997

Mark Grace 1B

1998

Sammy Sosa *RF*

The Games

1933

Three Cubs are selected to the first NL All-Star team—Gabby Hartnett, Woody English, and Lon Warneke—with Warneke the first Cub to appear. He relieves Bill Hallahan in the third and pitches four innings, yielding only one run. The AL wins 4–2 at Comiskey Park.

1934

We gotta look at that all season.
—Gabby Hartnett, to the AL bench during Carl Hubbell's string of five consecutive strikeouts

The 1934 game at the Polo Grounds is famous for Carl Hubbell's magnificent performance. Few remember that his catcher was Gabby Hartnett. With men on first and second, Hubbell fans Babe Ruth, Lou Gehrig, and Jimmie Foxx in succession. He uses his screwball to ring up two more Hall of Famers in the second inning—Al Simmons and Joe Cronin—before Bill Dickey singles to break the string. Hubbell's sixth and final victim that day is pitcher Lefty Gomez. Hartnett greets the notoriously light-hitting Gomez at the plate: "You trying to insult Hubbell, coming up here with a bat in your hand?" The AL wins the game, however, 9–7.

1936

At Braves Field in 1936, the NL wins its first All-Star Game, thanks largely to the efforts of five Cubs—four of them starters. Gabby Hartnett knocks in Frank Demaree and later scores when he hits a triple in the second off Lefty Grove just out of the reach of a rookie right fielder named Joe DiMaggio who is trying to make a shoestring catch. With Billy Herman on first in the fifth, Augie Galan hits a home run off Schoolboy Rowe that ricochets off the right field foul pole, putting the NL up 4–0. Cubs pitcher Curt Davis nearly blows the lead when he yields four hits, one walk, and three runs in the seventh, but Lon Warneke bails him out by retiring DiMaggio on a wicked line drive to Leo Durocher at short. Warneke finishes the game for the save. Galan, Herman, Hartnett, and Demaree account for five of the nine NL hits in the 4–3 win.

1937

At Griffith Stadium in Washington, D.C., the starting lineup has Billy Herman hitting second and playing second, Frank Demaree playing center field and batting between Joe Medwick and Johnny Mize, and Gabby Hartnett batting seventh and catching Dizzy Dean. The AL wins 8–3, and as of 1998, the Cubs have yet to put another catcher or center fielder in the starting lineup of an All-Star Game.

Q. Who was the first Cubs player to be elected by fans to start in the All-Star Game?

A. Andy Pafko

1939

The NL loses 3–1 at Yankee Stadium, with Bill Lee taking the loss. He gives up all three runs, including a home run by Joe DiMaggio in the fifth.

1941

The 1941 game at Briggs (Tiger) Stadium is famous for Ted Williams's two-out, three-run home run to give the AL a 7–5 win. Claude Passeau serves it up and takes the loss.

1944

Phil Cavarretta sets an All-Star Game record when he reaches base five times on a triple, a single, and three walks. The NL wins 7–1 at Forbes Field, with Bill Nicholson contributing a big pinch-hit double off Tex Hughson that ties the game at 1–1 in the fifth.

1945

No game is played in 1945, though a club-record seven Cubs are named to the team.

1946

Claude Passeau becomes the first and, to date, the only Cubs' pitcher to start an All-Star Game. He takes the loss at Fenway Park in a 12–0 drubbing, though he fares much better than Kirby Higbe, Ewell Blackwell, and Rip Sewell, who pitch the final five innings of the game and give up 10 runs.

July 8, 1947

The first All-Star Game ever played at Wrigley Field ends up a 2–1 AL victory. Andy Pafko and Phil Cavarretta appear in front of the home crowd, with Pafko delivering a single after replacing Harry Walker in center field. Cavarretta strikes out for Bruce Edwards in the eighth and plays first base in the top of the ninth. Johnny Mize of the NL hits the first All-Star home run at Wrigley off Spec Shea in the fourth inning.

1948

The last time the Cubs have a lefty starter appear in the All-Star Game is at Sportsman's Park in St. Louis in 1948. And it's lefty Johnny Schmitz who takes the loss, yielding three runs in one-third of an inning, the big blow a two-run single by opposing pitcher Vic Raschi. The AL wins 5–2.

1952

It's a big day for the Cubs' All-Stars in 1952 at Shibe Park in Philadelphia. Though only Bob Rush and Hank Sauer appear in the rain-shortened game, Rush gets the win and Hank Sauer hits what proves to be the game-winning home run off Bob Lemon in the bottom of the fourth. The NL wins 3–2.

All-Star Home Runs

Year	Player	Pitcher	Location
1936	Augie Galan	Schoolboy Rowe	Braves Field
1952	Hank Sauer	Bob Lemon	Shibe Park
1960 (I)	Ernie Banks	Bill Monbouquette	Municipal Stadium, Kansas City
1961 (I)	George Altman	Mike Fornieles	Candlestick Park
1964	Billy Williams	Johnny Wyatt	Shea Stadium
1991	Andre Dawson	Roger Clemens	Skydome

1960 (Game One)

On a day when the temperature exceeds 100 degrees at Municipal Stadium in Kansas City, Ernie Banks is the star of the game when he hits a two-run first-inning homer off Bill Monbouquette. He doubles and later scores off Chuck Estrada in the third as the NL holds on to win 5–3.

1961 (Game One)

This is the game at Candlestick Park in San Francisco in which reliever Stu Miller is blown off the mound in the ninth inning. Just before that happens, George Altman pinch-hits for Mike McCormick in the bottom of the eighth and homers off Mike Fornieles to put the NL up 3–1. Altman is the fourth player to hit a home run in his first All-Star Game at bat. The NL eventually wins 5–4 in 10.

July 30, 1962 (Game Two)

Another All-Star Game at Wrigley and another AL victory. Ernie Banks replaces Orlando Cepeda at first, tripling off Hank Aguirre and scoring on a Billy Williams groundout. George Altman also appears in the game, flying out as a pinch hitter for Bill Mazeroski. The AL wins 9–4, thanks to home runs by Pete Runnels, Leon Wagner, and Rocky Colavito. John Roseboro homers for the Nationals.

1963

The NL wins 5–3 at Municipal Stadium in Cleveland, with Cubs pitcher Larry Jackson the second to earn a win. Ron Santo appears in his first All-Star Game, singling Bill White home with the NL's last run off Dick Radatz in the eighth.

1964

The 1964 game at Shea Stadium is remembered for Johnny Callison's two-out, three-run home run off Dick Radatz in the bottom of the ninth to give the NL a 7–4 win. Billy Williams ties the game at 1–1 in the fourth with a home run off Johnny Wyatt.

1965

Ron Santo's infield single off Sam McDowell knocks in Willie Mays with what proves to be the game-winning run in the seventh inning at Metropolitan Stadium. The NL wins 6–5 in the only All-Star Game in which Santo, Billy Williams, and Ernie Banks all appear.

1966

For the third time in his first three appearances, Ron Santo knocks in a run—and for the second year in a row, Santo scores Willie Mays with an infield single. It ties the game at 1–1 in the fourth at Busch Stadium, and the NL goes on to win 2–1 in 10 innings in 105-degree heat.

1967

Ferguson Jenkins ties the All-Star Game record with six strikeouts in the fourth, fifth, and sixth innings at Anaheim Stadium. He also yields the AL's only run—a home run by Brooks Robinson—in the NL's 2–1, 15-inning victory.

1969

The Cubs put their entire infield on the 1969 All-Star team along with catcher Randy Hundley for the game at RFK in Washington, D.C. The NL wins 9–3, though the Cubs' infield goes 0-for-8. Hundley becomes the first Cubs catcher to appear in an All-Star Game since 1937.

All-Star Game-Winning Hits

(Puts NL ahead to stay in seventh inning or later)

Year	Player	Victim	Hit	Location
1965	Ron Santo	Sam McDowell	Infield single in 7th	Metropolitan Stadium
1970	Jim Hickman	Clyde Wright	Single in 12th	Riverfront Stadium
1975	Bill Madlock	Rich Gossage	Single in 9th	County Stadium

1970

The 1970 game at Riverfront Stadium is remembered for Pete Rose's wrecking the career of Indians catcher Ray Fosse when he crashes into him to score the winning run in the 12th. Jim Hickman delivers the game-winning single off Clyde Wright in the NL's 5–4 victory.

1971

The 1971 game at Tiger Stadium sees home runs hit by six Hall of Famers: Reggie Jackson, Johnny Bench, Hank Aaron, Frank Robinson, Roberto Clemente, and Harmon Killebrew. Ferguson Jenkins serves up Killebrew's in the AL's 6–4 win.

1975

Ten years after a Cubs third baseman delivered the hit that proved to be the game-winner, Bill Madlock scores Reggie Smith and Al Oliver with a bases-loaded single in the ninth through a drawn-in infield off Rich Gossage. The hit puts the NL up 5–3, and they go on to win 6–3 at County Stadium, with Bill Madlock named co-MVP. Madlock is the first Cub to win the award, which has been given since 1962.

1976

It's a low point for the Cubs at Veterans Stadium in Philadelphia. For only the third time, and the first time since 1956, no Cub appears in the game, with catcher Steve Swisher the team's lone representative. The NL manages to overcome the lack of Cubs, winning 7–1.

1978

At Jack Murphy Stadium in San Diego, Bruce Sutter takes the win in a 7–3 victory as the NL rallies for four in the eighth off Sutter's AL counterpart, Rich Gossage.

1979

At the Kingdome in Seattle, Bruce Sutter pitches two scoreless innings and becomes only the second pitcher to win consecutive All-Star Games (Don Drysdale did it in 1967 and 1968) as the NL pulls out another late victory, 6–5.

1980

Finally given a lead to protect, Bruce Sutter records his first All-Star save with two scoreless innings in a 4–2 win at Dodger Stadium. Sutter will record another save as a representative of the Cardinals in the 1981 game.

All-Star Saves & Decisions

Year	Pitcher	Park
1936	Lon Warneke, S	Braves Field
1939	Bill Lee, L	Yankee Stadium
1941	Claude Passeau, L	Briggs (Tiger) Stadium
1946	Claude Passeau, L	Fenway Park
1948	Johnny Schmitz, L	Sportsman's Park
1952	Bob Rush, W	Shibe Park
1963	Larry Jackson, W	Municipal Stadium, Cleveland
1978	Bruce Sutter, W	Jack Murphy Stadium
1979	Bruce Sutter, W	Kingdome
1980	Bruce Sutter, S	Dodger Stadium
1987	Lee Smith, W	Oakland-Alameda County Stadium
1995	Randy Myers, S	the Ballpark at Arlington

1987

At Oakland-Alameda County Stadium, Lee Smith gets the win with three scoreless innings—the 10th, 11th, and 12th—in a 2–0, 13-inning victory. Rick Sutcliffe becomes the first Cubs' starting pitcher in 10 years to appear in an All-Star Game, throwing two scoreless innings in relief of starter Mike Scott.

1988

Six Cubs are named to the team—the most since 1945, when no game was played. Only four get into the game, falling short of the Cubs' top marks of five (1934, 1969) and six (1936). The AL wins 2–1 at Riverfront Stadium.

July 10, 1990

For the third time, an All-Star Game is played at Wrigley Field—though this time it's played at night. Yet again, the NL loses at the Friendly Confines, 2–0, with rain holding up play for more than an hour in the seventh.

1991

For the first time since 1964, a Cub homers in an All-Star Game as Andre Dawson takes Roger Clemens to deep center field in the fourth inning to pull the NL within one run, 3–2, at the SkyDome in Toronto. The AL holds on to win 4–2.

1992

Greg Maddux makes his only Cubs All-Star appearance, in a 13–6 loss at Jack Murphy Stadium, getting tagged for a home run by Junior Griffey in the third.

1995

At the Ballpark at Arlington, Randy Myers records the save in a 3–2 victory, and Sammy Sosa finally appears in an All-Star Game.

the pennants

An entire book could be written on the stories behind the pennant flags flying above the bleachers at Wrigley Field. This chapter looks at both the regular seasons and the postseasons of these pennant-winners, along with a painful but necessary review of some excruciating near misses. A small sampling of its ingredients:

- The month-by-month record of the 116–36 Cubs of 1906
- A case for Frank Chance as the game's greatest manager
- A pair of "threepeats" decades before Michael
- A day-by-day look at the 1908 pennant race, one of the strangest in baseball history, including Merkle's Boner, honorary Cub Harry Coveleski, early 20th-century trash talk, and the "replay-off" game
- A nonessential season and the threat of a players strike *during* the World Series
- The offensive juggernaut of 1929
- A 21-game winning streak in September
- Dizzy Dean's last stand and the "homer in the gloamin'"
- Avenging 1969 15 years later
- The 61 greatest games of a great 1998 season, including another play-off victory over the Giants 90 years after the "replay-off" of 1908
- The best offense in National League history, but no pennant and a disastrous change in the dugout
- The longest time spent in first place by any second-place team
- The lost pennant of . . . *1980?*
- The starting lineups and batting orders of the Cubs and their opponents in their 10 World Series appearances
- Line scores and a game summary of all 52 World Series games—and one tie—played by the Cubs
- Every World Series home run by a Cub and the victimized pitcher
- Cubs leaders in World Series games, at bats, hits, RBIs, runs, batting average, slugging average, appearances, innings, strikeouts, wins, and ERA
- A review of Chicago's last three trips to the postseason

It all starts in 1876.

REGULAR SEASON

The Cubs won 6 pennants during the 19th century and another 10 pennants and two division titles in the modern era of baseball. Here are some of the highlights from those regular seasons.

1876, 1880–82, 1885–86

The White Stockings championship teams, like those of many Cubs pennant-winners to come, were built on pitching. Albert Goodwill Spalding was the ace of the 1876 staff, winning 47 games and collecting 25 percent of the gate receipts for agreeing to jump to Chicago from the National Association's Boston team.

1876 Standings

TEAM	W	L	Pct.	GB
Chicago	52	14	.788	
St. Louis	45	19	.703	6
Hartford	47	21	.691	6
Boston	39	31	.557	15
Louisville	30	36	.455	22
New York	21	35	.375	26
Philadelphia	14	45	.237	34$\frac{1}{2}$
Cincinnati	9	56	.138	42$\frac{1}{2}$

Larry Corcoran was the pitching star of the 1880–82 teams, going 101–41 over three seasons. So deep was their pitching that when Corcoran blew his arm out in 1885 after winning 34 and 35 in 1883 and 1884, the White Stockings actually improved by 25 games in the standings and won the pennant.

1880 Standings

TEAM	W	L	Pct.	GB
Chicago	67	17	.798	
Providence	52	32	.619	15
Cleveland	47	37	.560	20
Troy	41	42	.494	25$\frac{1}{2}$
Worcester	40	43	.482	26$\frac{1}{2}$
Boston	40	44	.476	27
Buffalo	24	58	.293	42
Cincinnati	21	59	.263	44

Fred Goldsmith was part of baseball's first pitching rotation, going 73–32 alongside Corcoran from 1880 to 1882. Though Candy Cummings is credited with inventing the curveball, Fred Goldsmith was actually the first to do it, demonstrating his underhand bender for an audience in 1870 at the age of 18.

1881 Standings

TEAM	W	L	Pct.	GB
Chicago	56	28	.667	
Providence	47	37	.560	9
Buffalo	45	38	.542	10$\frac{1}{2}$
Detroit	41	43	.488	15
Troy	39	45	.464	17
Boston	38	45	.458	17$\frac{1}{2}$
Cleveland	36	48	.429	20
Worcester	32	50	.390	23

1882 Standings

TEAM	W	L	Pct.	GB
Chicago	55	29	.655	
Providence	52	32	.619	3
Buffalo	45	39	.536	10
Boston	45	39	.536	10
Cleveland	42	40	.512	12
Detroit	42	41	.506	12$\frac{1}{2}$
Troy	35	48	.422	19$\frac{1}{2}$
Worcester	18	66	.214	37

When Goldsmith broke down in 1884, John Clarkson stepped right into his place. One of the first overhand pitchers, Clarkson threw a change-up and great curve. He was one of the first to study hitters and wasn't above blinding batters on sunny days with his polished belt buckle.

The final great pitcher of the championship era was Jim McCormick, who went 51–15 in 1885 and 1886 after being brought over from Providence. The Scotsman was sold to Pittsburgh before the 1887 season as part of Spalding's cleanup efforts. He retired at 30 at the peak of his career after only one year with the Alleghenys, in protest of the way he was being treated financially, returning home to Paterson, New Jersey, to tend bar.

1885 Standings

TEAM	W	L	Pct.	GB
Chicago	87	25	.777	
New York	85	27	.759	2
Philadelphia	56	54	.509	30
Providence	53	57	.482	33
Boston	46	66	.411	41
Detroit	41	67	.380	44
Buffalo	38	74	.339	49
St. Louis	36	72	.333	49

1886 Standings

TEAM	W	L	Pct.	GB
Chicago	**90**	**34**	**.726**	
Detroit	87	36	.707	2$\frac{1}{2}$
New York	75	44	.630	12$\frac{1}{2}$
Philadelphia	71	43	.623	14
Boston	56	61	.479	30$\frac{1}{2}$
St. Louis	43	79	.352	46
Kansas City	30	91	.248	58$\frac{1}{2}$
Washington	28	92	.233	60

What was left of the championship teams after Spalding's temperance movement was decimated by player defections to the short-lived Players League in 1890, including their double-play combination and entire starting outfield. All that remained were two members of the Stonewall Infield—Tommy Burns and Cap Anson—though the Colts lost the pennant by only two games.

The Chicago Onions of the defunct Players League were incorporated into the Colts for the 1891 season, but Chicago was cheated out of the pennant when the New York Giants lay down for the Boston Beaneaters at the close of the season—so much was the enmity of rival players for Cap Anson and Albert Spalding after the Players League was forced into unconditional surrender by the National League. First-baseman Roger Connor (94 RBIs), 21-game winner Buck Ewing, and 33-game winner Amos Rusie all sat out decisive games against Boston in the season's final moments.

Chicago wouldn't come close to another pennant for 15 years.

1906–08, 1910

Manager and first-baseman Frank Chance insisted that his team play smart, one-run baseball. Hitters were to take of lot of pitches so that those batting behind them would benefit (one veteran was released simply for being a first-ball hitter). The team was adept at stealing signs. When they figured out that Giants manager John McGraw was using sign language to send signals to his team (one of his pitchers, Dummy Taylor, was deaf), the Cubs learned the system and intercepted the messages. The infielders were able to send signals of their own without anyone's stealing them—relaying the catcher's signs to each other so that they'd know where to play.

It worked. Consider what the Cubs' teams of 1906 through 1910 accomplished—no other team was this dominant for this long. In fact, of the 30 winningest teams in baseball history, four were Cubs squads from this five-year span. As the table above shows, they did it primarily on pitching and defense (the numbers in parentheses are the Cubs' rank within the league).

1906–10 Records

YEAR	W	L	Pct.	BA	SA	FA	ERA
1906	116	36	.763	.262 (1)	.339 (1)	.969 (1)	1.76 (1)
1907	107	45	.704	.250 (3)	.311 (4)	.967 (1)	1.73 (1)
1908	99	55	.643	.249 (2)	.321 (3)	.969 (1)	2.14 (3)
1909	104	49	.680	.245 (4)	.322 (4)	.961 (2)	1.75 (1)
1910	104	50	.675	.268 (2)	.366 (1)	.963 (2)	2.51 (1)
Totals	530	235	.693				

1906

The 1906 Cubs, the winningest team in history, led the league in batting, slugging, fielding, and pitching—something only four other teams have ever done. Due primarily to great pitching and defense, the Cubs gained steam as the season progressed, even winning 37 of 39 at one point. On the Fourth of July, they beat the Pirates in a doubleheader, 1–0 and 1–0, behind a one-hitter by Mordecai Brown and a five-hitter by Carl Lundgren. (This sweep came on the heels of a 1–0 victory over the Reds on July 2 and a 1–0 loss on July 3!) The Cubs could put up runs, too, including 19 off Hall of Famers Christy Mathewson and Joe McGinnity in a shutout drubbing of the Giants at the Polo Grounds. They clinched the pennant on September 19, with more than two weeks to go in the season, leaving a 96-win Giants team 20 games back.

116–36 in 1906

Month	W	L	Pct.
April	10	6	.625
May	19	9	.679
June	17	5	.773
July	20	8	.714
August	26	3	.897
September	21	5	.808
October	3	0	1.000

1906 Standings

TEAM	W	L	Pct.	GB
Chicago	**116**	**36**	**.763**	
New York	96	56	.632	20
Pittsburgh	93	60	.608	23$\frac{1}{2}$
Philadelphia	71	82	.464	45$\frac{1}{2}$
Brooklyn	66	86	.434	50
Cincinnati	64	87	.424	51$\frac{1}{2}$
St. Louis	52	98	.347	63
Boston	49	102	.325	66$\frac{1}{2}$

1907

The Giants-Cubs was one of the fiercest rivalries in baseball's history—even before passions were inflamed by the 1908 Merkle Game described in the next section. On May 21, 1907, yet another Cubs victory over Christy Mathewson at the Polo Grounds incited fans to riot, with policemen having to fire guns into the air to scatter the mob.

The 1907 team went on to win 107 games and another pennant despite scoring only 571 runs, a 19 percent decline from the year before and the lowest production of any pennant-winner ever (fewer runs per game than the lowly '62 Mets!). They had only 13 home runs, with no .300 hitters, and their RBI leader had 70. Their ERA, however, was 30 percent lower than the league average—which would be like having a staff ERA of 2.95 in 1998's high-scoring National League. They got off to a fast start—13–2, the best April winning percentage in 20th-century team history—and spent 151 days in first place, moving out in front of the Giants to stay on May 30.

If you didn't honestly and furiously hate the Giants, you weren't a real Cub.

Joe Tinker

Best Months

Year	W–L	Pct.
April 1907	13–2	.867
May 1904	19–6	.760
June 1936	21–5	.808
July 1945	26–5	.839
August 1906	26–3	.897
September/October 1935	23–3	.885

1907 Standings

TEAM	W	L	Pct.	GB
Chicago	**107**	**45**	**.704**	
Pittsburgh	91	63	.591	17
Philadelphia	83	64	.565	21$\frac{1}{2}$
New York	82	71	.536	25$\frac{1}{2}$
Brooklyn	65	83	.439	40
Cincinnati	66	87	.431	41$\frac{1}{2}$
Boston	58	90	.392	47
St. Louis	52	101	.340	55$\frac{1}{2}$

1908

The Cubs, Pirates, and Giants dominated the National League in the early years of the 20th century, taking the pennant every year until the Miracle Braves finally broke through in 1914. They often battled each other for the pennant, but never more fiercely or as closely as they did in 1908. It would be hard, if not impossible, to find three more closely matched teams than the 1908 Cubs, Giants, and Pirates. With virtually identical pitching results, the offensive numbers (see "1908 Leaders" sidebar) suggest that the Giants and Pirates should have been battling for the pennant, with the Cubs a few strides back.

The Giants made better contact and were on base more often, while the Pirates had more punch. The Giants had Turkey Mike Donlin (6/106/.334), and the Pirates had the great Honus Wagner (10/109/.354). The Cubs' most productive hitter was Joe Tinker (6/68/.266). So, how did they do it?

1908 Standings

TEAM	W	L	Pct.	GB
Chicago	**99**	**55**	**.643**	
New York	98	56	.636	1
Pittsburgh	98	56	.636	1
Philadelphia	83	71	.539	16
Cincinnati	73	81	.474	26
Boston	63	91	.409	36
Brooklyn	53	101	.344	46
St. Louis	49	105	.318	50

Fielding

The Cubs led the league in fielding, committing 21 fewer errors than the Pirates and 45 fewer than the Giants. Joe Tinker and Johnny Evers also had better range up the middle than either the Giants' or the Pirates' double-play combinations.

Baserunning

Though it's dangerous to draw conclusions from base-running data when caught-stealing information is not available, the Cubs did lead the league in stolen bases. They also led the league in doubles. Given all that's known about Frank Chance's smart and aggressive style of play, it's safe to assume that the Cubs were outstanding at taking the extra base.

Leadership

Each team was managed by a Hall of Famer, with the Pirates' Fred Clarke also a solid left fielder. Each had managed his team to pennants (Clarke in 1901 through 1903, John McGraw in 1904 and 1905, and Frank Chance in 1906 and 1907). The results suggest that Chance may have offered an edge to his team even against such strong competition.

The numbers might suggest that the 1908 team was the weakest of the 1906–10 squads, but the Cubs thrived under some of the most intense pressure any baseball team has had to endure. Here are some highlights from one of the most bizarre pennant races in history.

1908 Leaders

Team	W	L	BA	OBA	SA	ERA
Cubs	96	55	.249	.311	.321	2.14
Giants	98	56	.267	.342	.333	2.14
Pirates	98	56	.247	.309	.332	2.12

National League Pennant "Threepeats"

Only eight NL teams have won three consecutive pennants. Chicago did it first and in 1908 became the first to do it twice.

Chicago White Stockings	*1880–82*
Boston Beaneaters	*1891–93*
Baltimore Orioles	*1894–96*
Pittsburgh Pirates	*1901–03*
Chicago Cubs	*1906–08*
New York Giants	*1911–13*
New York Giants	*1921–24*
St. Louis Cardinals	*1942–44*

Luck or Chance?

Total Baseball uses fielding, pitching, and batting statistics to predict the number of wins that a team should have had, then compares this figure with their actual wins. Under this method, for example, the 1984 Cubs won 10 more games than they should have, whereas the 1961–62 Cubs of the College of Coaches won 15 fewer games than they should have. No team in baseball history even comes close to the sustained overachievement of the 1906–10 Cubs. Do it for one season, and call it luck. Do it for five, and call it Chance.

Year	W	Predicted W	Difference
1906	116	101	15
1907	107	91	16
1908	99	87	12
1909	104	92	12
1910	104	94	10
Totals	**530**	**465**	**65**

June 20.   The Cubs are playing the Giants in the Polo Grounds, and Laughing Larry Doyle twice tries to get hit with a pitch with the bases loaded. When he finally succeeds, umpire Bill Klem lets it go rather than—according to IE Sanborn of the *Sporting News*—let manager John McGraw "make a frantic demonstration and . . . infuriate the crowd, which already had once broken away from the helpless Pinkertons in an effort to get nearer the play. He knew that the crowd would attack him before or after the game, and he would have as much protection as the 25-cent bleachers in a cloudburst, and not half as good a chance to make a getaway. And McGraw knew that Klem knew it, and hence Doyle had only to get hit in order to win the game."

July 16.   At West Side Grounds, John McGraw is stalling the game in the bottom of the ninth inning to get Christy "Matty" Mathewson from the shower back into uniform to save the 4–3 game. As the *New York Evening Mail* reported, "His feet were wet and he couldn't get his baseball shoes on, so he grabbed a pair of street shoes, and, without a cap, raced out to see why his name was being yelled so persistently." Matty throws two warm-up pitches and puts out the fire.

July 17.   Mordecai Brown beats Christy Mathewson 1–0 the following day, with Matty's other nemesis, Joe Tinker, accounting for the only score with an inside-the-park home run.

July 22.   John McGraw's Giants cancel a doubleheader with St. Louis to be better rested for a crucial Pittsburgh game back East. That they can get away with this speaks volumes about McGraw's influence in league matters.

August 11.   John McGraw, having already been ejected, runs onto the field to argue another close play. An umpire named Hank O'Day is intimidated by McGraw and the howling fans into allowing a rain-soaked game to continue with the Cubs ahead 2–0. He finally calls it, giving the Cubs the win.

August 29.   After a 5–1 loss by the Giants to the Cubs in a showdown at West Side, the next game is deemed so critical that Christy Mathewson agrees to pitch on the Sabbath when rain appears likely to push Saturday's game back to Sunday. The rain holds off, but the Christian Gentleman loses 3–2 on Saturday to Mordecai Brown yet again. Crowds at Madison and Dearborn and another at the Illinois Central station at Randolph Street cheer the electronic scoreboards re-creating the game, as if the blinking lights are real players.

August 30.   The Cubs sweep the series 2–1, helped out by a big Tinker-to-Evers-to-Chance double play, and the Giants leave Chicago up by only a half game.

September 4.   The Cubs lose 1–0 to Pittsburgh in 10, though a base runner on first—backup first-baseman Doc Gill—leaves the field on the game-winning hit without touching second. This omission was the custom of the day. Johnny Evers takes the ball and steps on second for what is technically an inning-ending, run-nullifying force play, but umpire Hank O'Day refuses to call the runner out and the inning over. As the *Pittsburgh Post* reported the following day, "The final play of Friday's game between the Cubs and Pirates is one that does not come often, but next time it happens it is safe to predict that none who took part in the game will overlook the importance of touching the next base."

September 22. The Cubs sweep the Giants 4–3 and 2–1 at the Polo Grounds, with Orvie Overall and Mordecai Brown beating Red Ames and Doc Crandall. Brown gets the save in the first game, as a backup first baseman named Fred Merkle strikes out with the bases loaded in the seventh. More trickery from John McGraw, as he has 21-year-old rookie Rube Marquard warming up for both games—with Ames and Crandall hidden behind the grandstand—hoping to get a pitcher other than Overall or Brown.

September 23. The Merkle Game. It's the bottom of the ninth at the Polo Grounds, with two outs, and the score is tied at 1–1. Moose McCormick is on third base, and Fred Merkle is on first (playing for Fred Tenney, who is missing his only start of the season). Al Bridwell singles to center off Jack Pfiester to win the game, but Merkle doesn't touch second base, veering off halfway there to head for the clubhouse, with the fans streaming onto the field. Johnny Evers is screaming for the baseball, but center-fielder Solly Hofman heaves it over Evers's head. Giants pitcher Joe McGinnity, sensing what Evers is up to, retrieves the ball and heaves it into the crowd. Cubs pitcher Rube Kroh joins the melee; when he punches the fan who has the ball, Harry Steinfeldt picks it up and throws it to Joe Tinker, who throws it to Evers on second. Umpire Hank O'Day—a Chicago native who later managed the Cubs—doesn't render a decision on the field but later tells a *New York Herald* reporter in the clubhouse that Merkle is out and the game is a tie. He will later claim that it was too dark to resume the game, but truth be told, he is probably frightened for his life should he use the fans' presence on the field as cause for forfeiting the game to the Cubs.

September 24. The Cubs show up early the next day hoping to play two (a replay of yesterday's game and the regularly scheduled game), but the Giants aren't there to meet them until the regularly scheduled game time. There's been no official ruling by the league on whether or not to replay the game—and New York is still claiming victory. New York wins the regular game 5–4, with Hooks Wiltse beating Mordecai Brown. During the game, one hundred cops man the sidelines, and a swarm of gnats take over the field. The Giants nearly blow a 5–0 lead, with Christy Mathewson called on for yet another save.

September 26. Ed Reulbach shuts out the Brooklyn Dodgers in both ends of a doubleheader.

October 1. Ed Reulbach beats the Reds 6–0 for his fourth straight shutout.

October 4. In front of an overflow crowd of 30,247 fans on the last day of the regular season, the Cubs and Mordecai Brown beat the Pirates 5–2 for their 11th win in 12 games and take over first place. The players are carried on the shoulders of delirious fans for 15 minutes before they can get to the clubhouse. In yet another irony, it's umpire Hank O'Day who rules foul a long fly ball hit by Ed Abbaticchio down the left-field line into the crowd. If the ball had been ruled fair, the entire complexion of the game would have changed. During the off-season, a woman hit by the ball and suing for damages presents her ticket stub as evidence—a stub that shows she was sitting in fair territory.

I guess Miss Looker and I can wait. She's as anxious to have the Cubs win as I am.

Solly Hofman, after being forbidden by manager Frank Chance to marry his fiancée on September 7, 1908, as scheduled

The Merkle Aftermath

I don't know where Evers got the ball that he used to claim the force-out, but it wasn't the Bridwell hit because I flung that one out of sight. —**Joe McGinnity**

All our boys did rather well if Fred Merkle could gather the idea into his noodle that baseball custom does not permit a runner to take a shower and some light lunch in the clubhouse on the way to second. —**New York Herald**

If this game goes to Chicago by any trick of argument, you can take it from me that if we lose the pennant thereby, I will never play professional baseball again. —**Christy Mathewson**, **New York Evening Mail**

Outside of Manhattan Island, however, where baseball is considered a national pastime and not a form of paying tribute to New York, it is a recognized fact that the Giants lost that victory over the Cubs by a blunder more stupid than the rankest of fielding errors ever perpetrated. —**IE Sanborn**, **Chicago Tribune**

An Honorary Cub

On September 29, 1908, with every game precious, the Giants split a doubleheader with the fourth-place Phillies, losing to 22-year-old rookie Harry Coveleski. Two days later, they split another doubleheader with Philadelphia, again losing to Coveleski. On October 3, Coveleski beats Christy Mathewson. A year removed from pitching amateur ball in Wildwood, New Jersey, Harry Coveleski wins four games on the season, three within one week against the New York Giants. His lone loss in 1908 is a 14–2 pounding at the hands of the Giants earlier in the season. During the investigation of the 1919 World Series, it will come out that the Giants had attempted to bribe the Phillies and Coveleski to throw these games.

October 5–7.   Most of the National League's board of directors are praying that the Giants will drop one of their final three games to Boston, so New York won't end the season in a tie with the Cubs. If there is a tie, the tied Merkle Game will matter, and the directors will have to agree on whether to overrule the umpires and give the win to the Giants, declare a forfeit to the Cubs, or schedule a replay for October 8. Even a rainout would bail them out, since October 7 is the absolute last day of the season. But the Giants sweep the Braves, with Boston's manager, Joe Kelley, an old teammate of John McGraw's, accused of dumping the games. The decision is made to replay the tie game, setting up what is essentially the first play-off game in baseball history on October 8.

October 8.   Ticket holders are unable to get through crowds to the gate. It takes the umpires an hour to enter the stadium. The bluffs overlooking the Polo Grounds are crowded with people, as are housetops, telegraph poles, and elevated railroad tracks (though firefighters have turned their hoses on the crowds to try to drive them from the tracks). A mob sets fire to the left-field fence, trying to weaken it and burst through. Just before game time, another fence breaks, and mounted police have to beat back the crush of people. Inside the stadium, a steady roar of abuse pours down on the Cubs. John McGraw cuts the Cubs' warm-up time to five minutes, then instructs Mike Donlin, Joe McGinnity, and Cy Seymour to pick a fight with Frank Chance in the hopes of provoking a riot and a Cubs forfeit.

The game is a rematch between the starters in the Merkle Game: Jack Pfiester and Christy Mathewson. Pfiester struggles, hitting the leadoff batter, Fred Tenney, and walking Buzz Herzog on four pitches. He strikes out Roger Bresnahan, with Johnny Kling—in vintage, heads-up, Chance baseball—dropping the ball intentionally, knowing that the batter is not allowed to advance, but hoping that Herzog will take a few strides toward second. Herzog takes the bait, and Kling nails him. But Pfiester isn't out of the woods yet. Donlin doubles in a run, though Chance is screaming that the ball is foul. Meanwhile, a fan falls off a telegraph pole and breaks his neck. Seymour walks, and Chance calls for Mordecai Brown, who has to fight his way through the crowd on the outfield grass. Brown strikes Art Devlin out to end the inning.

In the top of the third, Christy Mathewson motions for Cy Seymour to back up in center field, but Seymour ignores him. Joe Tinker triples exactly where Mathewson has just motioned Seymour to go. Kling singles Tinker in, Brown bunts Kling to second, and Jimmy Sheckard flies to Seymour for what should have been the third out. Johnny Evers walks, then Wildfire Schulte and Chance double to put the Cubs up 4–1.

The Giants don't threaten again until the seventh, when Art Devlin and Moose McCormick single and Al Bridwell walks to load the bases. Larry Doyle bats for Mathewson and fouls to Kling, who has to dodge beer bottles to make the catch. Tenney hits a sacrifice fly, then Herzog grounds to short and is retired on a great play by Tinker. Brown closes out the Giants in the ninth on four pitches for a 4–2 victory.

The police have to draw their revolvers to get the Cubs' players off the field. Chance is sucker-punched in the neck. Harry Steinfeldt is punched in the face. Pfiester is hit in the jaw and slashed on the shoulder with a knife. Solly Hofman is hit in the face with a bottle. They race to the clubhouse in center field and barricade the door. Later, they ride to the hotel in a patrol wagon with six cops. Brown wanders out in his street clothes, unmolested, shunning the police escort as a dead giveaway.

And the newspapers report that seven men are carried away that day, raving mad, to the asylum. The final casualty is National League president Harry Pulliam, who is distraught over the pressure of having to make a ruling that helped decide the pennant. He kills himself during the off-season.

1910

Only six franchises have won four pennants in five years, with the Chicago Cubs the first. The Cubs did it in 1910 after winning 104 games in 1909 and finishing *second*. In 1910, Joe Tinker, Frank Chance, and Mordecai Brown turned in typically superb performances, but Orvie Overall and Ed Reulbach were troubled by injuries, Jack Pfiester was only a part-time performer, and Johnny Evers was lost late in the season with a broken leg. To compensate, key performances were turned in by rookie pitcher King Cole (20–4), midseason acquisition Lew Richie (11–4), emerging star Wildfire Schulte (.301), the no-longer-reserve Solly Hofman (.325 with 86 RBIs), the new super-reserve Heinie Zimmerman (.284 at all four infield positions as well as outfield), and catcher Johnny Kling, who returned from a one-year holdout spent shooting pool.

1910 Standings

TEAM	W	L	Pct.	GB
Chicago	**104**	**50**	**.675**	
New York	91	63	.591	13
Pittsburgh	86	67	.562	17$\frac{1}{2}$
Philadelphia	78	75	.510	25$\frac{1}{2}$
Cincinnati	75	79	.487	29
Brooklyn	64	90	.416	40
St. Louis	63	90	.412	40$\frac{1}{2}$
Boston	53	100	.346	50$\frac{1}{2}$

1918

It was the season when baseball was deemed nonessential.

Back in March, the players weren't even sure there'd be a season at all, what with the United States entering the Great War back in April 1917. The owners had staved off the forces of public opinion and the War Department throughout 1917 with spring training and pregame photo ops of drillmasters marching players with bats on their shoulders around playing fields.

In 1918, baseball's schedule was cut back from 154 to 140 games, with spring training shortened and held in closer locales to minimize travel. But the editorial pages of the *New York Times* kept the heat on, maintaining that baseball's nonessential nature was "perfectly evident to everyone whose common sense is not distorted by self-interest." The league put its best spin forward with parades, music, benefit games, real troops marching, and free admission for people in uniform (though the benefit games were really just an opportunistic ploy to hook fans on Sunday baseball, which wasn't yet a weekly occurrence).

These visible albeit token efforts weren't enough to further delay the inevitable. On May 23, 1918, the word came down from Provost Marshal Enoch Crowder: Every draft-eligible man, baseball players included, had until July 1 to find himself an "essential" job or face induction. Baseball asked for the deadline to be pushed back to October 15 but received only until September 1, with an additional two weeks for the members of the pennant-winners, allowing a September World Series to be played. The owners, in character to the end, pushed one day past the deadline in order to squeeze in some games on the Labor Day holiday.

When the order came down, 227 players entered the service in midseason, many in the reserves. Others took soft jobs in steel mills and shipyards and played baseball in the industrial leagues. Baseball itself hadn't been ordered to shut down and was left free to find replacements for its draft-eligible players. They could have played the season to its October conclusion, but they shut down early because the fans weren't showing up and they wanted to

This is a war of democracy against bureaucracy. And I tell you that baseball is the very watchword of democracy. There is no other sport or business or anything under heaven which exerts the leveling influence that baseball does. Neither the public school nor the church can approach it. Baseball is unique. England is a democratic country, but it lacks the finishing touch of baseball. . . . Simply because what baseball produces is intangible, I do not think it can be called non-essential or not productive.

National League president John Tener

cut their losses. One way they did that was by passing some of those losses on to the players: releasing all of their players on September 1, with a collusive agreement not to sign each other's "free agents," all to shave four weeks of salary off their players' final paychecks.

And that's how the Cubs clinched a pennant in August—August 29, to be exact, a 1–0 gem by Lefty Tyler (a left-hander, no less!) over the Reds at Wrigley. Only the shortened season kept the Cubs from having their first pair of 20-win lefties, as Tyler won 19 and Hippo Vaughn, in one of the great pitching seasons in Cubs history, 22. In a full season, Vaughn might have been able to earn the two additional shutouts to join the elite group of pitchers with 10 shutouts in a season. The Cubs hit only 21 home runs in one of the last of the deadball seasons, as rookie shortstop Charlie Hollocher led the offense with a .316 average and 26 stolen bases. Fred Merkle (!) was the team's top run-producer with 65 RBIs.

1918 Standings

TEAM	W	L	Pct.	GB
Chicago	84	45	.651	
New York	71	53	.573	10½
Cincinnati	68	60	.531	15½
Pittsburgh	65	60	.520	17
Brooklyn	57	69	.452	25½
Philadelphia	55	68	.447	26
Boston	53	71	.427	28½
St. Louis	51	78	.395	33

Offensive Juggernauts

Team	Runs per Game	Finish
1931 Yankees	6.97	2nd
1936 Yankees	6.96	1st
1930 Yankees	6.90	3rd
1950 Red Sox	6.67	3rd
1930 Cardinals	6.52	1st
1932 Yankees	6.51	1st
1930 Cubs	6.48	2nd
1929 Cubs	6.46	1st
1932 Athletics	6.37	2nd
1937 Yankees	6.36	1st

1929 Grand Slams

April 17	Rogers Hornsby
April 18	Charlie Grimm
May 17	Hack Wilson
June 15	Rogers Hornsby
June 18	Hack Wilson
June 29	Charlie Grimm
July 1	Riggs Stephenson
August 26	Norm McMillan
September 17	Kiki Cuyler

1929

The 1929 Cubs were another superb defensive team, but this time it was the offense that carried the pitching, as they took the flag by 10½ games over the Pirates. Four players had 100 RBIs, which has happened only three times in non-Colorado National League history. If not for a broken wrist suffered by Charlie Grimm, it would have been five players. As it was, Grimm and his replacement, Chick Tolson, combined for 110 RBIs in 151 games. This team would easily have been the highest-scoring squad in National League history if Gabby Hartnett hadn't been sidelined for most of the season with a sore arm.

The Cubs' offensive highlight reel for 1929 is a long one. They got 10 straight hits in the fourth inning in a 13–6 win over the Braves at Wrigley Field on September 4. They hit nine grand slams (at least one in each month), a National League record that still stands and that wasn't tied until 1995 by the San Diego Padres and 1996 by the Montreal Expos. The *team* hit .303 and scored 6.5 runs per game, placing it in the all-time top 10 of high-scoring teams. Ironically, only half of these teams actually won the pennant.

1929 Standings

TEAM	W	L	Pct.	GB
Chicago	98	54	.645	
Pittsburgh	88	65	.575	10½
New York	84	67	.556	13½
St. Louis	78	74	.513	20
Philadelphia	71	82	.464	27½
Brooklyn	70	83	.458	28½
Cincinnati	66	88	.429	33
Boston	56	98	.364	43

1932

Though only three years had passed since their last pennant, there were a lot of differences in the 1932 Cubs. They'd already gone through both Joe McCarthy and Rogers Hornsby before arriving at Charlie Grimm as manager. The offensive juggernaut was a thing of the past, with not even a 15-home-run or 90-RBI batter in the lineup. The strength of the team was pitching, though Pat Malone was no longer the ace of the deep staff, replaced by the league's best pitcher, 23-year-old Lon Warneke.

Billy Herman and Billy Jurges had replaced Hornsby and Woody English up the middle, with English moving over to third. Hack Wilson was gone, replaced by Johnny Moore in center field. Gabby Hartnett was back behind the plate. They won 14 games in a row down the stretch and clinched the pennant on September 20 against the Pirates, as ex-Pirate Kiki Cuyler cleared the bases in the seventh with a triple.

1932 Standings

TEAM	W	L	Pct.	GB
Chicago	**90**	**64**	**.584**	
Pittsburgh	86	68	.558	4
Brooklyn	81	73	.526	9
Philadelphia	78	76	.506	12
Boston	77	77	.500	13
St. Louis	72	82	.468	18
New York	72	82	.468	18
Cincinnati	60	94	.390	30

1935

> *They are a fine ball club, but the best I can see ahead of them is a second-place finish, with the Cubs first.* —Charlie Grimm, on the defending-champion Cardinals

After a disappointing 1934 season, 10 players were dealt away, including outfielder Babe Herman and pitchers Guy Bush and Pat Malone. Kiki Cuyler was dealt in midseason, while Charlie Grimm—coming off of an 0-for-43 spring training—handed the first-base job to 18-year-old Phil Cavarretta. Other changes since 1932 included 25-year-old Stan Hack at third; a new outfield of Chuck Klein, Frank Demaree, and Augie Galan; and lefty Larry French in the rotation and another new ace—Bill Lee, the league's best pitcher.

1935 Standings

TEAM	W	L	Pct.	GB
Chicago	**100**	**54**	**.649**	
St. Louis	96	58	.623	4
New York	91	62	.595	8$\frac{1}{2}$
Pittsburgh	86	67	.562	13$\frac{1}{2}$
Brooklyn	70	83	.458	29$\frac{1}{2}$
Cincinnati	68	85	.444	31$\frac{1}{2}$
Philadelphia	64	89	.418	35$\frac{1}{2}$
Boston	38	115	.248	61$\frac{1}{2}$

With all the changes, the Cubs underachieved early on. At the All-Star break, they were 40–32, 9½ games behind the Giants. North-South tensions permeated the team. On July 30, a dispute over the Civil War sparked a fight between Brooklyn's Billy Jurges and North Carolina's Tarzan Stephenson. The backup catcher, Stephenson, took the blame and was sent packing, but he had to return the next day when Gabby Hartnett fractured a bone in his ankle.

The tensions continued when a dropped pop fly by Jurges cost General Lee of Plaquemine, Louisiana, a game. Lee suggested that Jurges wear a Civil War helmet at shortstop: "It might keep you from getting killed by a pop fly." A few days later, another Jurges error cost the Arkansas Hummingbird, Lon Warneke, a game. In the second game of the doubleheader, Tarzan Stephenson got three hits and scored the winning run in a 4–3 victory over the Reds.

With such dissension as a prelude, few expected the Cubs to turn in the greatest September pennant drive in baseball history. Though the Cubs would have 21 games in a row at Wrigley Field, the Cardinals had 30 in a row at home to close out the season and a 2½-game lead. After splitting a doubleheader with the Reds, which ended a 14-game home winning streak, the Cubs won 18 in a row at Wrigley and 3 more in St. Louis. Their 20th consecutive victory clinched the pennant, while the 21st consecutive victory (tying a club mark set by the 1880 White Stockings) was their 100th of the season. They haven't won 100 games since.

The 1916 New York Giants won 17 in a row and 26 in a row in the same season *without winning the pennant!* However, their 26-game winning streak featured a tie between games 12 and 13. Taking that into account, the White Stockings and Cubs have the longest winning streaks in baseball history. Here's how it went in 1935.

> In all my 50 years in baseball, I never experienced a season to come close to 1935.
>
> *Charlie Grimm*

September 4

	1	2	3	4	5	6	7	8	9	R	H	E
Philadelphia	1	0	0	0	0	0	0	0	1	2	8	0
Chicago	0	0	0	2	0	1	0	5	x	8	8	1

W—French

Augie Galan hits two home runs, including a grand slam.

September 5

	1	2	3	4	5	6	7	8	9	10	11	R	H	E
Philadelphia	0	0	0	0	0	1	0	1	0	0	0	2	7	1
Chicago	0	2	0	0	0	0	0	0	0	0	1	3	7	3

W—Root

September 6

	1	2	3	4	5	6	7	8	9	10	R	H	E
Philadelphia	0	0	0	0	0	0	0	2	0	0	2	11	2
Chicago	1	0	0	0	0	0	0	1	0	1	3	6	1

W—Warneke

Galan hits a triple in the 8th for the tying run and a home run in the 10th to win it.

September 7

	1	2	3	4	5	6	7	8	9	R	H	E
Philadelphia	0	0	0	0	0	0	0	0	0	0	6	1
Chicago	0	0	0	0	2	1	0	1	x	4	9	1

W—Lee

September 9

	1	2	3	4	5	6	7	8	9	R	H	E
Boston	0	0	0	0	1	0	0	0	0	1	4	1
Chicago	0	0	0	3	1	1	0	0	x	5	10	2

W—Carleton

September 9

	1	2	3	4	5	6	7	8	9	R	H	E
Boston	0	0	0	0	1	0	0	0	0	1	9	1
Chicago	2	0	0	0	0	0	0	0	x	2	5	1

W—French

September 10

	1	2	3	4	5	6	7	8	9	R	H	E
Boston	0	0	0	0	0	0	0	0	0	0	6	0
Chicago	0	0	0	1	3	0	0	0	x	4	10	0

W—Root

September 11

	1	2	3	4	5	6	7	8	9	R	H	E
Boston	0	0	1	1	0	1	0	0	0	3	9	4
Chicago	1	0	0	0	6	0	0	8	x	15	19	3

W—Lee

September 12

	1	2	3	4	5	6	7	8	9	R	H	E
Brooklyn	0	2	0	0	0	0	0	1	0	3	8	1
Chicago	0	4	0	2	7	0	0	0	x	13	15	0

W—Warneke

Galan gets four hits, including a double and a home run, for five RBIs.

September 13

	1	2	3	4	5	6	7	8	9	R	H	E
Brooklyn	0	1	0	0	0	0	0	0	0	1	8	1
Chicago	0	0	0	3	1	0	0	0	x	4	10	0

W—French

21 and 0 in '35

The streak by the numbers:

- *The pitching staff threw 18 complete games, including the first 10 in a row.*
- *Other than the 18–14 slugfest, Cubs pitching held the opposition to three runs or fewer in every game.*
- *The Cubs actually trailed in 11 games and were tied late in another.*
- *The Cubs made 27 percent fewer errors, collected 42 percent more hits, and scored 174 percent more runs.*
- *Though 187 runs were scored by both teams, only 5 crossed the plate in the third inning.*
- *The Cubs outscored the opposition 27–2 in the fourth inning.*

September 14

	1	2	3	4	5	6	7	8	9	R	H	E
Brooklyn	0	0	0	0	2	2	5	0	5	14	15	4
Chicago	2	5	1	0	0	8	2	0	x	18	18	2
W—Root												

Cubs move into first place.

September 15

	1	2	3	4	5	6	7	8	9	R	H	E
Brooklyn	2	0	0	0	0	0	0	1	0	3	6	4
Chicago	2	2	0	1	0	0	1	0	x	6	8	0
W—Lee												

September 16

	1	2	3	4	5	6	7	8	9	R	H	E
New York	0	2	0	0	0	1	0	0	0	3	7	1
Chicago	1	0	0	6	1	0	0	0	x	8	12	0
W—Warneke												

September 17

	1	2	3	4	5	6	7	8	9	R	H	E
New York	0	0	0	0	2	0	0	1	0	3	11	4
Chicago	1	0	0	0	0	3	1	0	x	5	7	1
W—French												

It Wasn't All Pitching

Here's how the Cubs' regulars did at the plate during the 1935 streak:

Player		Avg
Billy Herman, 2B		*.400*
Augie Galan, LF		*.384*
Gabby Hartnett, C		*.356*
Fred Lindstrom, RF		*.354*
Stan Hack, 3B		*.343*
Frank Demaree, CF		*.341*
Phil Cavarretta, 1B		*.256*
Billy Jurges, SS		*.209*

September 18

	1	2	3	4	5	6	7	8	9	R	H	E
New York	0	0	1	1	0	0	1	0	0	3	9	4
Chicago	0	1	0	8	4	2	0	0	x	15	20	5
W—Root												

September 19

	1	2	3	4	5	6	7	8	9	R	H	E
New York	0	0	0	0	0	0	0	1	0	1	6	0
Chicago	2	0	0	0	0	1	2	1	x	6	13	1
W—Lee, L—Hubbell.												

September 21

	1	2	3	4	5	6	7	8	9	R	H	E
Pittsburgh	0	0	0	0	0	0	0	1	2	3	8	3
Chicago	0	0	0	0	2	2	0	0	x	4	8	1

W—Henshaw, S—Warneke.

September 22

	1	2	3	4	5	6	7	8	9	R	H	E
Pittsburgh	0	0	0	0	0	0	0	0	0	0	9	2
Chicago	1	0	0	0	0	0	0	1	x	2	7	1

W—French

September 25

	1	2	3	4	5	6	7	8	9	R	H	E
Chicago	0	1	0	0	0	0	0	0	0	1	7	0
St. Louis	0	0	0	0	0	0	0	0	0	0	2	0

W—Warneke

Phil Cavarretta homers after Paul Dean fans four of the first five batters.

September 27

	1	2	3	4	5	6	7	8	9	R	H	E
Chicago	0	0	2	1	0	0	1	1	1	6	13	2
St. Louis	2	0	0	0	0	0	0	0	0	2	6	3

W—Lee, L—Dean.

This is the pennant clincher.

September 27

	1	2	3	4	5	6	7	8	9	R	H	E
Chicago	0	0	0	0	0	0	3	0	2	5	13	2
St. Louis	0	0	0	0	0	3	0	0	0	3	4	0

W—Henshaw

September 4–27

	1	2	3	4	5	6	7	8	9	10	11	R	H	E
Opposition	5	5	2	2	6	8	6	8	8	0	0	50	159	37
Chicago	13	15	3	27	27	19	10	18	3	1	1	137	225	27

W—French 5–0; W—Lee 5–0; W—Root 4–0; W—Warneke 4–0; W—Henshaw 2–0;
W—Carleton 1–0

S—Root 1

1938

Well, Mr. Rickey, I predicted we'd win that flag right here in St. Louis, but now that I'm gone, we'll win it in Chicago. —Dizzy Dean in 1938

What have you done for me lately? Charlie Grimm was replaced as manager on July 20, 1938, with the Cubs on a seven-game winning streak and only 5½ games behind the Pittsburgh Pirates. The Pirates were pretty confident about their chances for postseason play; they'd enlarged their press box, put in more bleachers, and made arrangements for installing telegraph equipment in Forbes Field.

The Cubs dropped 15 of their first 29 games under Gabby Hartnett. To make matters worse, Hartnett fractured his right thumb on a Joe Medwick foul tip on August 15. The team bottomed out on August 20, making six errors in a loss to the Pirates and falling nine games behind.

Things began to turn around on August 21 as the Cubs swept a doubleheader from the Pirates in front of 40,000 at Wrigley. Then they had the second-greatest September in team history, going 21–4 down the stretch, including a Labor Day doubleheader sweep of the Pirates in Pittsburgh. With a hurricane pounding the East Coast, the Cubs and Pirates were forced to play five doubleheaders. Thanks to a deeper staff, the Cubs were able to win 7 of their 10 twin games, closing to within 1½ games by the time the Pirates came to Wrigley on September 27 in the final week of the season.

Knuckleballer Jim Tobin pitched the opener of the three-game series for the Pirates, while sore-armed Dizzy Dean and his self-proclaimed "nothingball" were dusted off for the Cubs. Dean hadn't started since August and hadn't pitched for two weeks, but he scattered six hits and held the Pirates scoreless into the ninth, with the Cubs clinging to a 2–0 lead.

Dean hit Arky Vaughan leading off the ninth. First-baseman Gus Suhr popped out, then Dean coaxed Woody Jensen to force Vaughan at second. But a double by Jeep Handley put the tying runs at second and third with two out. Due up was Al Todd—who'd once decked Dean after a beanball in the Texas League in 1931—and who already had two hits. Bill Lee came in, threw a wild pitch, scoring Jensen, then fanned Todd to save the game and put the Cubs down by a half game.

Chicago moved into first place to stay the next day on Gabby Hartnett's famous "homer in the gloamin'" (see "Home Plate," Chapter 8). It was their 9th win in a row, their 19th in 22 games, and it so demoralized the Pirates that the Cubs and Bill Lee beat them 10–1 in a walkover the following day and coasted home.

One Last Day in the Sun

Just a slow ball, control, and a world of heart. —Gabby Hartnett, on Dizzy Dean

You could see the man was suffering out there, and here we all were healthy, strong, and young. You'd say, "My God, let's go out and win it for Diz." —Phil Cavarretta

It was the Lord. He had his arms around me all the time, yes sir. Lik'd to choke me, he held me so tight. Whenever I was gonna go wild, he just patted me on the head, and the next guy popped up. It was a grand feeling. —Dizzy Dean

Homer in the Gloamin'

The mob started to gather around Gabby before he reached first base. By the time he reached second base, he couldn't have been recognized in the mass of Cub players, frenzied fans, and excited ushers except for the red face that shone out even in the gray shadows. After the skipper had finally struggled to the plate, things became worse. The ushers, who had fanned out to form the protective barrier around the field, forgot their constantly rehearsed maneuver and rushed to save Hartnett's life. They tugged and they shoved and finally they started swinging their fists before the players could carry their boss to safety.

Chicago Tribune, *September 29, 1938*

1938 Standings

TEAM	W	L	Pct.	GB
Chicago	89	63	.586	
Pittsburgh	86	64	.573	2
New York	83	67	.553	5
Cincinnati	82	68	.547	6
Boston	77	75	.507	12
St. Louis	71	80	.470	17½
Brooklyn	69	80	.463	18½
Philadelphia	45	105	.300	43

1945

The St. Louis Cardinals were the dominant team of the war years, winning the pennant in 1942, 1943, and 1944. The Cubs snapped that string in 1945, thanks to a lot of regulars who were too old, physically unfit, or otherwise unacceptable for military service. Though they were only 6–16 against St. Louis, they helped their cause by feasting on the Reds, winning 21 of 22. Phil Cavarretta led the league in hitting, and Andy Pafko blossomed into a star, off-setting the surprising power outage suffered by Bill Nicholson.

Hank Wyse was the workhorse of the pitching staff, winning 22 as he went to the mound in a corset because of a spine injury that kept him out of the army. The wins leader in the American League, Hank Borowy, was snuck through waivers at 11:55 P.M. on July 27 and sold to the Cubs for $97,000. Though several clubs howled in protest—the Cubs were already in the process of going 26–5 in July *without* Borowy—the deal with the Yankees was upheld. Borowy went 11–2 for the Cubs, beat the Cardinals four times, and nailed down the pennant against the Pirates on September 29, fanning Tommy O'Brien with two on, two out, and a one-run lead.

Charlie Grimm, back for his second tour of duty as Cubs manager, cut off all his players' ties at the victory party and had a quilt made.

1945 Standings

TEAM	W	L	Pct.	GB
Chicago	**98**	**56**	**.636**	
St. Louis	95	59	.617	3
Brooklyn	87	67	.565	11
Pittsburgh	82	72	.532	16
New York	78	74	.513	19
Boston	67	85	.441	30
Cincinnati	61	93	.396	37
Philadelphia	46	108	.299	52

1984

The Cubs were coming off consecutive fifth-place finishes under new GM Dallas Green; were 7–20 in spring training, the worst record in baseball; had released Ferguson Jenkins; and were loaded with veteran players and ex-Phillies. Sportswriters were calling for Green's head. But as one ever-optimistic fan put it, "We have the fewest Cubs in our lineup, and that's usually been an indicator of which team will win the pennant."

At the end of the season, the Cubs had the MVP, the manager of the year, the front-office executive of the year, and a Cy Young Award winner who wasn't even in the league until June. They established a club record with 10 consecutive errorless games from June 5 to June 14, and they went ahead to stay on August 1, ending a 39-year postseason drought, at the time the fourth longest in history. They spared themselves by one year the indignity of tying the Chicago White Sox, who were dry from 1919 to 1959.

If anyone offers you 100-to-1 odds on the Cubs' winning the NL East in 1984, then take them up on it. If I've ever seen a dead giveaway setup for a miracle, this is it.

Bill James

1984 Standings

TEAM	W	L	Pct.	GB
Chicago	**96**	**65**	**.596**	
New York	90	72	.556	6½
St. Louis	84	78	.519	12½
Philadelphia	81	81	.500	15½
Montreal	78	83	.484	18
Pittsburgh	75	87	.463	21½

It was June 13, time for the traditional swoon to begin, and the Cubs' starting rotation was injury riddled. This was the day that Dallas Green pulled the trigger on the Rick Sutcliffe deal, bringing the pitcher over from Cleveland for Joe Carter, Mel Hall, and Don Schulze. Lee Smith took an instant liking to this move, going 6–0 with 15 saves from the day the deal was made through the end of August. So did Ryne Sandberg, whose huge game against Bruce Sutter and the St. Louis Cardinals (see "The Infield," Chapter 9) took place 10 days later.

Sutcliffe liked the deal, too, for that matter, going 16–1 and slaying at least one dragon in the process. Fifteen years after a black cat appeared in front of the Cubs dugout at Shea Stadium in a critical late-season showdown with the Mets, a fan threw one at Sutcliffe while he warmed up in the bullpen. Pitching coach Phil Regan, the closer for the '69 Cubs, rolled his eyes in dismay. After all, Dwight Gooden had just shut down the Cubs on one hit the night before in a 10–0 blowout. Sutcliffe shook it off and threw a shutout of his own.

One could understand Regan's dismay. The similarities between the 1984 teams and the 1969 teams were striking. Chicago had the veteran team built largely on trades, while the Mets had improved dramatically after a stretch of wretched years, thanks largely to a pair of great young pitchers: Dwight Gooden and Ron Darling. But the Cubs weren't sticking to the script this season—making a deal for the extra pitcher they needed, while relying more heavily on their bullpen and bench—and time and again, it was Chicago that drove a stake through the hearts of the no-miracle-this-time Mets.

April 13–14

The Mets bring their 6–1 start into Wrigley and get beaten in both games, 11–2 and 5–2. In the first game, the Cubs rudely welcome rookie Dwight Gooden to Chicago with six runs in 3⅓ innings. The Cubs steal early and often on the rookie's high leg kick, scoring five runs in the fourth. Ron Cey, Jody Davis, and Gary Matthews all homer off Mets relievers while Steve Trout goes the distance for Chicago. The Cubs jump on Tim Leary for three runs in the first inning of the second game but nearly run themselves out of the ball game when two men are thrown out on the bases on one hit. Lee Smith pitches the final three innings to save the game for Dick Ruthven. Both teams finish the month at 12–8.

July 27–29

After a lackluster May and June, the Mets welcome the Cubs into Shea, having ridden a 20–4 July past the Cubs and into first place by 3½ games. The Mets win 2–1 in the opener on a Dwight Gooden gem, but the Cubs come back to thump New York 11–4 in the second game. Chicago gets the type of break the '69 Mets got on a bizarre strikeout in the first inning. On a 2–2 pitch from Rick Sutcliffe, Darryl Strawberry takes a half swing at a ball in the dirt that bounces away from catcher Jody Davis. While the home-plate umpire calls it a ball, third-base umpire Bruce Froemming punches Strawberry out without an appeal even being made. Meanwhile, Davis retrieves the wild pitch, exchanges the ball for a new one from the home-plate umpire, and hands it to Sutcliffe, who throws to first to officially retire Strawberry and prompt an argument that gets Mets manager Davey Johnson tossed.

The Cubs blow open a 3–3 game with eight runs in the eighth off Doug Sisk and Brent Gaff, thanks to a walk, a wild pitch, two singles, an error, a bases-loaded balk, an intentional walk, a single, another intentional walk, a two-run double by Ryne Sandberg (who'd led off the inning), and a two-run single by Henry Cotto.

The following day, the Cubs give up one run in taking two from the Mets, one of the turning points of the season. The Cubs win the first 3–0 as Steve Trout throws a complete-game shutout, using his sinker to induce 16 groundouts. They take the second 5–1 as Jody Davis breaks the game open in the fourth with a three-run homer. The Cubs are within 1½ games of first, and the Mets are on their way to a seven-game losing streak. On August 1, the Cubs beat the Phillies 5–4 while the Mets are losing 11–2 to the Cardinals, and Chicago moves into first place to stay.

August 6–8

When the Mets head into Wrigley, they've righted themselves a bit, having taken three close games in a row from the Pittsburgh Pirates. The Cubs have a 1½ game lead when New York comes in for a four-game series. The Cubs sweep them in a nasty series, the first four-game sweep of the Mets at Wrigley since 1964.

The Cubs pound Dwight Gooden again, 9–3, touching him up for six runs in four innings. Jody Davis does most of the damage with a run-scoring double, a two-run homer, and a sacrifice fly. Chicago takes a doubleheader the next day, 8–6 and 8–4. Rick Sutcliffe gets his ninth win in the first game despite being without his best stuff, thanks to a pair of home runs in a six-run fifth by Keith Moreland and Ron Cey. The two-run homer by Cey prompts Ron Darling to hit Dave Owen with a pitch. Scott Sanderson responds in the second game by throwing a pitch behind Keith Hernandez. The Cubs go up 5–0 on Ed Lynch in the fourth, but after a two-run double by Cey, Moreland is plunked in the back by a fastball. He charges the mound, tackling Lynch and triggering a bench-clearing brawl. Sanderson responds again by nailing Kelvin Chapman in the fifth and gets tossed after four innings of one-hit ball. Tim Stoddard gets the win in relief, and Lee Smith picks up his 25th save.

The Cubs finish off the Mets 7–6 in the finale. The Mets go up 5–3 with three runs in the top of the seventh, only to see Chicago respond with four in the bottom of the inning. Jay Johnstone leads off with a pinch-hit triple off Walt Terrell, who then hits Bob Dernier in the helmet and gets tossed along with manager Davey Johnson. As the Mets storm out to protest, fans behind the New York dugout give a beer shower to Keith Hernandez and coach Bill Robinson, who has to be restrained from going into the stands. When the game resumes, the Cubs greet rookie pitcher Wes Gardner with a run-scoring force play and a single. Gardner throws a wild pitch that allows Chicago to tie the game, Moreland singles to put the Cubs ahead with his fourth RBI of the game, and Thad Bosley adds another run with a single. With the loss, the Mets have dropped nine games in the standings in 12 days.

September 7–8

The Mets are down seven games when the Cubs head into Shea, with time left for one last run at first place. Dwight Gooden one-hits the Cubs in the opener of the three-game series, yielding only an infield single to Keith Moreland that doesn't even reach the third-base dirt. The next night, Rick Sutcliffe shrugs off the black cat hurled at him in the bullpen and shuts out the Mets in his finest performance of the season. He walks none, strikes out 12, and gives up only four hits. The Cubs pull away late for a 6–0 win. Sutcliffe knocks in two runs, raising his average to .240, and the Cubs leave town still up six games.

September 14–15

A week later, the Mets return to Wrigley and the Cubs deliver the knockout blow, beating them in the first two games of the series. On a gray Friday, the Cubs win 7–1 as Rick Sutcliffe wins his 15th, going the distance and scattering eight hits. Jody Davis continues to be a thorn in the side of his former team, hitting a grand slam in the sixth off Brent Gaff. On Saturday, the Cubs push their lead to 9½ games as they jump out to a 4–0 lead in the first off Sid Fernandez, then hold on for a 5–4 victory, with Lee Smith recording his 32nd save. With two out in the ninth and a runner on second, Ryne Sandberg makes a great backhanded play to his right on Mike Fitzgerald and throws him out to end the game.

When the final game between them is played on Sunday the 16th, the Cubs have taken 11 of 16, accounting for nearly all of their margin of victory in 1984. More like 1945 than 1969, the Cubs' midseason acquisition clinches the pennant against Pittsburgh. Rick Sutcliffe throws a two-hitter on September 24 at Three Rivers Stadium for his 14th win in a row.

When they're driving home tonight, they'll feel a helluva lot better than if they had lost. But it won't have any effect on us. Every Friday we come into Shea, Gooden beats us, and then we come back Saturday and win.

Cubs manager Jim Frey, after losing 10–0 to the Mets on a Dwight Gooden one-hitter on September 7

Now our lives are complete.

Harry Caray, 1984

1989

While the 1984 team was sparked by veteran outfielders Bob Dernier and Gary Matthews, the 1989 Cubs got their boost from two rookie outfielders: Dwight Smith and Jerome Walton. Their clutch play down the stretch helped wake up the offense and carry the Cubs home with an uncharacteristically strong second half.

1989 Standings

TEAM	W	L	Pct.	GB
Chicago	**93**	**69**	**.574**	
New York	87	75	.537	6
St. Louis	86	76	.531	7
Montreal	81	81	.500	12
Pittsburgh	74	88	.457	19
Philadelphia	67	95	.414	26

At the end of June, the Cubs were only four games above .500 and reeling from a seven-game losing streak that saw them outscored 37–9 and knocked from first place. The Montreal Expos had come to Wrigley and swept them 5–1, 5–0, and 5–0, and after the Cubs dropped three close games, the Giants trashed them 12–2. From this point forward, the Cubs played .624 baseball (53–32). Here are some highlights.

July 28–30

With many expecting them to fold, the Cubs hold their ground in July, going 18–9 to keep pace with the streaking Expos. The highlight of the month is a huge three-game sweep over the Mets in Wrigley Field. In the first game, on Friday, July 28, the Cubs score four in the seventh to erase a 5–2 deficit, with a two-run home run by Dwight Smith off Rick Aguilera putting the Cubs ahead. In the ninth, Shawon Dunston ends the game with an over-the-shoulder catch in short left followed by an outstanding throw to first to double off Juan Samuel. The Cubs blow out Wally Whitehurst and the Mets 10–3 on Saturday, then Mark Grace takes Randy Myers deep in the bottom of the ninth to win the finale 6–4.

August 6

The Cubs blow a chance to take over first place. The Expos lose to the Mets 2–1 in 14, but the Cubs lose to the Pirates 5–4 in 18 after four walks in the ninth force in the tying run for the Pirates. Scott Sanderson's eight innings of stellar relief are wasted when Jeff King homers leading off the 18th.

August 7–9

On the heels of this crushing defeat, the Expos come to town to try to repeat their 15–1 three-game sweep in June, providing a perfect opportunity for the Cubs to fold. Instead they sweep the Expos three straight, coming from behind in the first two games and blanking them 3–0 in the third. Greg Maddux outpitches Pascual Perez in the first game, with Mark Grace and Ryne Sandberg both homering. The Cubs hand Dennis Martinez only his second loss of the season as Mike Bielecki wins his 12th, with Sandberg and Grace homering again. To close it out, Rick Sutcliffe throws seven innings of one-hit ball to beat Bryn Smith, with Ryne Sandberg homering

Cardiac Cubs

In 1989, the Cubs won 17 games in their last at bat, 7 in August alone.

Date	Rally	Result
April 11	1 run in 8th	Cards 4 Cubs 5
May 1	1 run in 12th	Cubs 4 Giants 3
June 8	1 run in 10th	Mets 4 Cubs 5
June 20	1 run in 11th	Cubs 5 Pirates 4
June 21	1 run in 11th	Cubs 1 Pirates 0
July 20	1 run in 11th	Giants 3 Cubs 4
July 30	2 runs in 9th	Mets 4 Cubs 6
August 4	1 run in 9th	Cubs 3 Pirates 2
August 5	3 runs in 9th	Cubs 4 Pirates 2
August 15	3 runs in 12th	Cubs 5 Reds 2
August 17	2 runs in 9th	Cubs 3 Reds 2
August 25	1 run in 12th	Braves 3 Cubs 4
August 27	1 run in 10th	Braves 2 Cubs 3
August 29	1 run in 10th	Astros 9 Cubs 10
September 9	1 run in 10th	Cards 2 Cubs 3
September 23	1 run in 9th	Pirates 2 Cubs 3
September 30	2 runs in 9th	Cubs 6 Cards 4

in his third of five consecutive games. (The Chicago streak of seven consecutive well-pitched games is rudely interrupted by a vintage Cubs-Phillies game at Wrigley, a 16–13 Phillies victory featuring 35 hits.)

August 18–29

With a 4½ game lead going into play on August 18, the Cubs go into a tailspin. They drop three in a row to the Astros in Houston, and three more to Cincinnati in Chicago, before pulling out of it with a 12-inning victory over the Braves. Their lead is down to three on the 29th, when the Astros jump out to a 9–0 lead. The Cubs rally to win 10–9 in 10 (see "The Top 10 Strangest Games" in Chapter 11), while the Expos lose to the Padres 2–1 that night.

September 9

The Cardinals have pulled to within a half game of the Cubs after rallying from an 8–6 deficit to beat Chicago 11–8 in Wrigley the day before. St. Louis leads 2–1 in the 8th with a chance to take over first, but the Cubs rally for the tying run in the bottom of the inning and win it in the 10th off Ken Dayley. The Cubs beat them 4–1 the next day, with Steve Wilson striking out 10 in five innings and the bullpen pitching four innings of scoreless relief.

September 26

Chicago never looks back. Greg Maddux wraps up the division title with his 19th win in Montreal, outdueling Dennis Martinez 3–2.

1998

The Cubs established themselves as a play-off contender early on in 1998, winning six of their first seven (a decided improvement over their 0–14 start of 1997). Here are some memorable moments from the Cubs' gutty run to the wild-card spot.

April 4

Sammy Sosa hits his first home run of the year off Marc Valdes of the Expos, putting the Cubs ahead to stay in a 3–1 win at Wrigley.

April 12

The signal is clearly sent that the future is now. The top pitching prospect in baseball, Kerry Wood, makes his major-league debut against the Expos. He hadn't made the team out of spring training, but Chicago's fast start prompts the Cubs to recall him from Iowa almost immediately. He is wild in his debut and lasts only 4⅔ innings, losing 4–1 to Dustin Hermansen in Montreal. But half of the outs he records are on strikes.

April 18

Wood makes his Wrigley debut and dominates Hideo Nomo and the Dodgers for an 8–1 win. He yields four hits and no runs in five innings, fanning seven.

April 27

The Cubs' bats have gone silent, and the team is riding a five-game losing streak that has dropped them to 12–12 on the season. In San Diego, against the eventual Western Division winners, Sammy Sosa strikes early against Joey Hamilton. He hits his seventh home run, a two-run shot, in the first, and Kevin Tapani makes it stand up for a 3–1 win.

April 30

Having lasted only 1⅔ innings in his last start, Kerry Wood is 1–2 with an 8.74 ERA and 10 walks in 11⅓ innings. Another bad outing and Wood may be on his way back to Iowa for more seasoning. Instead, Wood throws seven innings of five-hit, one-run ball—striking out nine while walking only two—in an 8–3 win over the Cardinals.

May 2

The Cubs rally from a 3–0 deficit against the Cardinals at Wrigley as Jose Hernandez hits a three-run home run in the 5th and Sammy Sosa doubles in Mark Grace to win the game in the 11th. The bullpen throws 5⅔ innings of one-hit ball, with Terry Adams winning the game with two perfect innings.

May 6

Having staved off demotion, Kerry Wood responds with the most dominating pitching performance in major-league history. He strikes out 20, walks none, and yields only a single off Kevin Orie's glove against the best offensive team in the National League. Wood pitches his first shutout and first complete game, beating the Astros 2–0 at Wrigley (see "The Pitcher's Mound," Chapter 5, for a scorecard). The Cubs go on to win 10 of their next 13.

May 8

Rod Beck blows his first save of the season to his former team, the Giants, letting in the tying run in the top of the ninth at Wrigley. The game remains scoreless until the 14th, when the Giants push a run across on a two-out single by Charlie Hayes off Amaury Telemaco. In the bottom of the 14th, Manny Alexander and Brant Brown single off Julian Tavarez. After a groundout moves the runners up, Sammy Sosa is walked intentionally and Mark Grace delivers a game-winning two-run single off lefty Jim Poole for a 4–1 victory.

May 11

Kerry Wood sets a major-league record by fanning 33 batters in two consecutive games as he mows down the Diamondbacks, 4–2, in Arizona.

May 12

With the game tied at 6–6 in the top of the ninth in Arizona, Diamondbacks closer Felix Rodriguez retires the first two batters easily and then proceeds to walk Brant Brown, Mickey Morandini, Sammy Sosa, and Mark Grace to force in the eventual game-winner.

May 16

Sammy Sosa snaps a 43-at-bat homerless streak with a third-inning, three-run shot off Scott Sullivan to put the Cubs up 4–0 in Riverfront. They hold on for a 5–4 win over the Reds.

May 17

Kerry Wood's amazing May continues as he runs his record to 5–2 with six innings of two-hit ball against the Reds. His 8 strikeouts give him 66 in 40⅓ innings, or nearly 15 per 9 innings.

May 23

It takes 11 innings to do it, but the Cubs get their first victory at Turner Field with a 10–6 win over the Braves. They rally from a 6–2 deficit after seven with one in the 8th, three in the 9th, and four in the 11th. Mark Grace ties the game with a two-run double in the 9th, and the Cubs pull away in the 11th on two singles, two walks, a passed ball, a wild pitch, and an error.

May 25

Going into play, Sammy Sosa is on his way to a very solid albeit very un-Sammy season. He is hitting .333, but with nine home runs and 31 RBIS he is on pace for "only" 30 and 102. His two home runs in the 9–5 loss to the Braves at Turner Field are his first two of 57 home runs and a Hack Wilson–esque 127 RBIS in 110 games!

May 29

In Wrigley, the Cubs beat the Braves in 11 innings again, snapping a four-game losing streak. After blowing a 3–2 lead in the 9th, Brant Brown bails the Cubs out with a two-run homer in the bottom of the 11th. Kerry Wood strikes out 13 in seven innings but gets only a no-decision. The Cubs are now 7–2 in games that he starts.

June 1

For the third time in his last four games, Sammy Sosa hits two home runs. He knocks in five runs in a 10–2 thumping of the Marlins at Wrigley.

June 2

Brian Meadows, rookie pitcher for the Marlins, throws an eight-inning, two-hit gem against the Cubs at Wrigley, giving up only a sixth-inning game-tying home run to Brant Brown. Mark Clark and Terry Adams hold the Marlins to one run, then the Cubs load the bases in the bottom of the ninth against Felix Heredia, and Jason Hardtke's one-out single off Jay Powell scores Mickey Morandini with the winning run.

June 3

The Cubs run their Kerry Wood winning streak to seven games as the rookie goes to 6–2 with an eight-inning, five-hit, nine-strikeout gem against the Marlins in Wrigley. In Wood's first five outings at Wrigley, his pitching line looks like this:

	IP	H	R	ER	BB	SO
Wood 4–0	36	20	4	4	15	58

Sammy Sosa's two-run home run in the fifth—his 16th—blows open a close game.

June 5–7

For more details on Cubs–White Sox interleague play, see "The Bunting," Chapter 12. The bottom line: the Cubs sweep three at Wrigley as Sammy Sosa hits a home run in each game and knocks in eight runs against the team that traded him for George Bell.

June 8

Sammy Sosa ties a club record with a home run in five consecutive games as the Cubs beat the Twins at the Metrodome for their 10th in a row.

June 13

Nothing like a trip to Philadelphia to wake up the Cubs' bats. After dropping three in a row, managing only 13 hits and one run, the Cubs bomb the Phillies 10–8.

June 15

Sammy Sosa is a one-man wrecking crew, hitting three solo home runs off Cal Eldred in a 6–5 win at Wrigley Field. The third comes in the seventh and breaks a 5–5 tie. These are the first 3 of 12 home runs Sosa hits off Milwaukee in 1998, falling one short of the major-league mark for home runs off one team shared by Hank Sauer and Roger Maris.

June 18

The Cubs hit five home runs as they beat up on the Phillies 12–5 at Wrigley. It's their highest total for the season, though none comes off the bat of Sammy Sosa.

June 20

Sammy Sosa hits two home runs against the Phillies, his second off Toby Borland breaking the Cubs' mark for home runs in a month and the major-league mark for home runs in June. Kerry Wood fans 11 as the Cubs win 9–4.

June 24–25

In the Cubs' first trip to Tiger Stadium since 1945, Sammy Sosa breaks Willie Mays's National League record for home runs in a month and ties the major-league mark of 18 set by the Tigers' Rudy York. Unfortunately, Rod Beck yields a game-tying, two-out, two-run home run to Bobby Higginson, and they fall 7–6 in 11. Sosa breaks York's record the following day, but the Cubs fall again, 6–4.

June 30

Sammy Sosa hits his 20th home run and knocks in his 40th run, but the Cubs fall to 12–15 in June with a 5–4 loss to the Diamondbacks in Wrigley.

July 1

With the Cubs having dropped eight of nine, Kerry Wood halts the slide with an eight-inning, three-hit, 13-strikeout performance against the Diamondbacks. The Cubs hold on for a 6–4 win, their first of 14 out of their next 19.

July 4

The Cubs are down 3–1 in the bottom of the seventh against the Pirates at Wrigley, when Mickey Morandini ties the game with a two-run homer off Jason Schmidt, and Henry Rodriguez follows a few batters later with a two-run single, scoring Mark Grace and Sammy Sosa. The Cubs hold on for a 5–4 win.

July 5

Down 5–0 to the Pirates at Wrigley, the Cubs rally for two in the seventh and five in the eighth. Jose Hernandez delivers a two-run single in both innings, and Rod Beck holds on for a 7–6 win.

July 19

Jose Hernandez ties the game with the Marlins at 4–4 with a two-run home run in the 7th at Joe Robbie Stadium, and then the Cubs get three runs in the 12th on four walks and an error by Robby Stanifer. In the bottom of the 12th, Rod Beck yields four consecutive hits as the Marlins close the score to 7–6 with no outs, but he fans Craig Counsell and Gregg Zaun with the winning run on base.

July 21

In the first matchup of future and former Cubs aces, Kerry Wood outpitches Greg Maddux in Turner Field. He goes 7⅔ innings, yielding five hits and no runs while fanning 11 in a 3–0 victory over the Braves.

July 22

The Cubs break open a 3–3 game in the eighth as Sammy Sosa and Henry Rodriguez hit back-to-back two-out home runs off former Cub Miguel Batista. The Cubs beat the Expos 9–5 at Wrigley.

July 25

Having dropped a doubleheader to the Mets on July 24, the Cubs face their first crucial game of the season. They rally for a 3–2 win in the bottom of the eighth as Glenallen Hill hits a two-run pinch homer off Mets closer John Franco.

July 26

Kerry Wood pitches the Cubs to a series split with the Mets, as he goes seven innings yielding only four hits and one run. In his 19th start of the season, Wood fans fewer batters than innings pitched for the first time. Sammy Sosa gives the Cubs a 2–1 lead with a two-run home run off Rick Reed in the sixth, and Chicago goes on to win 3–1.

July 27

Sammy Sosa hits two home runs—his 39th and 40th—accounting for all six runs in the Cubs' 6–2 win in Arizona. Sosa ties the game at 2–2 in the sixth, then follows with his first career grand slam off Alan Embree in the eighth. Sosa's record run of home runs without a slam is halted at 246. Sosa hits another grand slam the next night, but the Cubs fall 7–5.

August 8

In a heartbreaking game in St. Louis, Sammy Sosa's game-tying two-run home run in the ninth goes for naught as Rod Beck serves up not one but two game-tying home runs of his own. In the 11th, Tyler Houston hits a two-run pinch home run to put the Cubs up 7–5, but Ray Lankford follows with a two-run, two-out, two-strike home run in the bottom of the inning. He had fanned his first five times at the plate. The Cubs push across another run in the 12th, but Eli Marrero ties it up again with a homer. In the 13th, Ray Lankford's bases-loaded single off Dave Stevens wins the game 9–8 for St. Louis.

August 10

Having dropped four in a row, including two consecutive one-run losses to the Cardinals, the Cubs face their second gut-check game of the year in San Francisco. They're down 5–2 with two out and none on in the fifth against Russ Ortiz, when Sammy Sosa, Mark Grace, and Henry Rodriguez hit back-to-back-to-back solo home runs to tie the game. Sosa puts the Cubs ahead to stay with a two-run shot in the seventh, and the Cubs go on to win 8–5.

August 16

After a brutal 5–4 loss in 11 at the Astrodome the day before, the Cubs respond with a thrilling 2–1, 11th-inning victory. Sammy Sosa hits his 47th home run off Sean Bergman, Kerry Wood fans 11 and yields only three hits in eight innings, and Manny Alexander's pinch-hit single scores Mickey Morandini with what proves to be the game-winning run.

August 19

For the first time, Sammy Sosa passes Mark McGwire in the home-run chase. He hits his 48th in the fifth to put the Cubs up 6–2, but two McGwire home runs key a St. Louis come-from-behind 8–6 win.

August 21

In one of their most remarkable come-from-behind wins all season, the Cubs rally for two against the Giants' dominating closer, Robb Nen, to win 6–5. Sammy Sosa's 49th in the fifth had put the Cubs up 4–1, but it took a one-out single by Sosa in the ninth followed by a walk to Mark Grace, a game-tying single by Henry Rodriguez, and a broken-bat flare to right by Jose Hernandez to win it.

August 26

It's up to Kerry Wood to yet again halt a Cubs slide, and he does so in grand style, snapping a four-game losing streak with a three-hit, 16-strikeout gem against the Reds at Riverfront. Sammy Sosa puts the Cubs up 4–1 in the third with his 52nd home run of the season.

August 27

The Cubs rally from a 9–3 deficit to the Rockies at Coors Field with five in the 7th, two in the 8th, and a run in the 10th to win 11–10. Highlights: Brant Brown brings the score to 9–7 with a three-run home run in the seventh, and Gary Gaetti puts the Cubs in front with a two-out, two-run double in the eighth. Lance Johnson steals second to put himself in scoring position in the 10th, and Mickey Morandini brings him in with a single.

August 30

Of all things, a pitchers' duel at Coors Field as Kevin Tapani outpitches Darryl Kile. Sammy Sosa hits his 54th to put the Cubs up 2–0, and Rod Beck pitches out of trouble in the ninth to save the 4–3 victory over the Rockies. Having walked the first two batters he faces, Beck fans John Vander Wal and retires Jeff Reed to end the game.

August 31

The Cubs run their record with Kerry Wood pitching to 18–8 with a 5–4 win over the Reds at Wrigley. With his team down 4–0 in the third, Sammy Sosa ignites the rally with his 55th home run, a two-run shot. Kerry Wood puts the Cubs in front to stay in the fourth with a two-run homer of his own. It's his last outing of the regular season.

September 1

Down 4–1 to the Reds at Wrigley, the Cubs rally for two in the sixth, one in the seventh, and two in the eighth to take the lead. Brant Brown, Lance Johnson, and Gary Gaetti deliver the big hits, and Rod Beck allows a run before sealing the 6–5 victory.

September 2

With Chicago down 2–1 to the Reds in the bottom of the eighth, Gary Gaetti's two-run home run off Gabe White puts the Cubs in front, and Scott Servais adds another home run to give them a 4–2 lead. Rod Beck records his 42nd save, his 4th in the Cubs' last four games. Sammy Sosa ties Hack Wilson in the sixth with his 56th home run, compliments of Jason Bere.

September 4

Despite going 1-for-14 with runners in scoring position, the Cubs beat the Pirates 5–2 with three in the ninth at Three Rivers. Sosa breaks Wilson's team mark with his 57th in the first off Jason Schmidt. Rod Beck saves his fifth in five games.

September 5

It looks as if Rod Beck will get the day off, but Terry Adams makes things interesting in the ninth, and Beck has to come in to fan Adrian Brown to close out an 8–4 Cubs win over the Pirates.

September 8

The day after Mike Morgan yields Mark McGwire's 61st home run in a 3–2 loss, Steve Trachsel serves up #62 in a 6–3 defeat at the hands of the Cardinals.

September 12

After their comeback falls short in a 13–11 loss to the Brewers at Wrigley the day before, the Cubs rally from a 12–5 deficit with four in the seventh, one in the eighth, and five in the ninth—capped by a game-winning three-run pinch homer by Orlando Merced off Bob Wickman. Sammy Sosa kicks off the comeback with his 60th home run, a three-run blast in the seventh to pull the Cubs within four.

September 13

The Cubs build an 8–2 lead over the Brewers, keyed in part by Sammy Sosa's 61st home run, which comes in the fifth. But Chicago has to rally for two in the ninth to tie it, the first coming on Sosa's 62nd home run. The Cubs win it in the bottom of the 10th on a home run by Mark Grace.

September 15

In a crucial series in San Diego with the Padres, the Cubs take the second game as Kevin Tapani outpitches Kevin Brown in a 4–2 victory. Brown is cruising until the seventh, when Mark Grace hits a two-run homer and Kevin Tapani singles in Gary Gaetti to put the Cubs ahead.

September 16

Sammy Sosa breaks open another close game against the Padres with his 63rd home run, a grand slam in the eighth off Brian Boehringer. The Cubs win 6–3.

September 17

The Cubs take three of four from the Padres with a 10-inning, 4–3 victory. The Cubs go ahead in the top of the 10th when Gary Gaetti hits a pinch homer off Trevor Hoffman. The game ends when Carlos Hernandez hits a shot up the middle off Rod Beck, which ricochets to Jose Hernandez at shortstop. With the tying run heading home from third, Carlos Hernandez is out at first on a controversial call.

September 23

The Cubs are rebounding from a devastating three-game sweep at Wrigley at the hands of the Reds. Sammy Sosa breaks his 0-for-21 slide with two home runs, as the Cubs pile up a 7–0 lead in the seventh against the Brewers in Milwaukee. On the 90th anniversary of Merkle's Boner, the Cubs find themselves clinging to a 7–5 lead with two out in the ninth and the bases loaded, when Rod Beck coaxes a routine fly to Brant Brown. Brown drops the ball, three runs score, and Expos manager Felipe Alou states that the Cubs will not win another game all season.

September 26

The Cubs rally for a 3–1 lead against the Astros in Houston, as Gary Gaetti hits a two-run double in the eighth inning. Jeff Bagwell homers off Rod Beck leading off the ninth to cut the Cubs lead to 3–2. Moises Alou doubles and goes to third on a groundout. Beck bears down and fans Tony Eusebio. The game ends with the tying run again steaming home from third as Rod Beck fields a grounder down the first-base line, sweeping a tag at Astros pinch-hitter Dave Clark and missing, then hitting him in the back with his throw. Clark is called out for running out of the baseline, and the Cubs win 3–2.

September 27

The Cubs and Giants are tied for the wild-card spot, and the collapsing New York Mets, a game back, are on their way to being eliminated by the Braves 7–2. The Cubs go up 3–1 on a two-run double by Terry Mulholland in the finale against Houston, but Chicago can't hold the lead as defensive replacements Jose Hernandez and Jeff Blauser both misplay balls in a two-run eighth (Jeff Bagwell scores all the way from first on a bloop single that drops between Blauser and Lance Johnson). Rod Beck pitches out of a bases-loaded, one-out jam in the 10th but can't do it again in the 11th. With one out, Carl Everett on third, and Craig Biggio on first, the Cubs bring Orlando Merced out of left field to stand on second base. Richard Hidalgo lofts a sacrifice fly to "left-center-fielder" Lance Johnson, and the Astros win 4–3. Meanwhile Neifi Perez is taking Robb Nen out of the yard in the bottom of the ninth for a 9–8 Rockies win over the Giants—in a game the Giants led 7–0 in the fifth.

September 28

I knew we would be better. We couldn't be any worse.

Mark Grace, on his expectations for 1998 after a 68–94 season in 1997

On the 60th anniversary of Gabby Hartnett's "homer in the gloamin'," the Cubs play the Giants in a one-game play-off at Wrigley Field. Ninety years ago, they'd done the same in the Polo Grounds in the replay of the Merkle Game, and the Cubs came out on top 4–2, with Mordecai Brown nearly pitching a complete game in relief. In 1998, the Cubs call on Michael Jordan to throw out the first ball and Bill Murray to sing "Take Me Out to the Ball Game" during the seventh-inning stretch. Fortunately for the Cubs, a wind blowing in from right also makes an appearance at the game.

Benefiting from the wind—which knocks down potential home runs by Brian Johnson and Charlie Hayes—the gopher-ball-prone Steve Trachsel pitches 6⅓ innings of one-hit ball. But Trachsel walks six batters and has to strike out Brian Johnson with the bases loaded in the fourth. Gary Gaetti breaks the scoreless tie with a two-run home run in the fifth off Mark Gardner that barely clears the wall just to the right of the left-field well. In the sixth, the Cubs push another two across when pinch-hitter Matt Mieske delivers a two-run single to right off Rich Rodriguez.

In the top of the seventh, Trachsel yields a single to Brent Mayne and walks pinch-hitter Armando Rios. Matt Karchner is called in to pitch, and Orlando Merced goes to left field in a double switch. Merced is tested immediately and makes a great catch in the Cubs' bullpen on a foul fly by Stan Javier. With Barry Bonds on deck, Karchner gives up an infield single to Shawon Dunston to load the bases, as Mickey Morandini makes a great play keeping the ball in the infield and saving a run. With the tying run at the plate, Felix Heredia coaxes Barry Bonds to hit an inning-ending grounder to first.

In the bottom of the eighth, the Cubs score another run when Sammy Sosa singles, Mark Grace doubles, and Jose Mesa uncorks a wild pitch. Kevin Tapani, who was brought in to close out the game in the eighth, yields two singles to start off the ninth, and Terry Mulholland—who'd pitched into the eighth the day before—is called in to face Stan Javier, who singles in a run on his first pitch. Ellis Burks pinch-hits and works the count to 3–2 before drawing a walk. Barry Bonds comes to the plate again as the tying run, and this time he delivers only a sacrifice fly to right to make the score 5–2. Rod Beck—who'd pitched 2⅓ innings the day before—is called in for the league-leading 81st time, to face Jeff Kent with runners on first and third. Kent hits what appears to be a double-play ball, but Mickey Morandini's throw to first is in the dirt. With the score 5–3 and Kent on first with two outs, Beck faces Joe Carter in the last at bat of the former Cub's career. The Shooter runs the count to 2–2, then retires him on a soft pop fly to Mark Grace, and the Cubs stagger into the postseason with a 5–3 victory.

National League Wildcard

TEAM	W	L	Pct.	GB
Chicago	**90**	**73**	**.552**	
San Francisco	89	74	.546	1
New York	88	74	.543	1½
St. Louis	83	79	.512	6½
Los Angeles	83	79	.512	6½

Near Misses

Easily the most painful near misses in club history are the September fades of 1930 and 1969.

1930

Despite one of the most devastating offenses in baseball history, the Cubs finished second in 1930, falling short of the Cardinals by two games (closing the gap after they were mathematically eliminated). What happened?

- **Injuries.** Rogers Hornsby broke his ankle, while third-baseman Les Bell hurt his arm, forcing the Cubs to field a makeshift, weak-hitting, weaker-fielding infield.
- **Pitching.** No one but Dazzy Vance and the ancient spitballer Burleigh Grimes pitched particularly well in the National League in 1930 (the entire Phillies staff had an ERA of 6.71!). The Cubs team ERA of 4.80 was the highest in team history. Guy Bush somehow went 15–10 despite a 6.20 ERA and turning every opposing batter into a .316 hitter. Hitting was so out of hand in 1930 that at midseason, John McGraw actually called for the distance from the mound to the plate to be reduced to 58′.
- **The Dodgers.** The Cubs were riding a nine-game winning streak heading into play on June 6, with a chance to move into first place with a victory over the Dodgers at Ebbets Field. After scoring at least 10 runs in five consecutive games, the Cubs scored only 9 and lost 12–9. The Cubs came into Ebbets Field in first place three months later on September 9, only to have Brooklyn throttle them in three straight. They lost 3–0 to Ray Phelps, 6–0 to Dolf "the Pitching Pearl of the Antilles" Luque, and 2–1 with 13 strikeouts to Dazzy Vance (the lone run a solo blast by Hack Wilson in the seventh inning).
- **The Cardinals.** Chicago hit .309 as a team, but that was five points below a pennant-winning Cardinals team that had a .300 hitter at each position and four more on the bench.
- **September.** The Cubs opened September in first place with a five-game lead but went 7–13 in their first 20 games. They finished with six wins in a row, but the Cardinals were safely ahead by then.

The aftermath of the 1930 season: the ground-rule double was established in the National League for balls bouncing over the fence, the stitches were raised on the ball, and a heavier cover and softer center helped take the jump out of the ball. Oh, and William Wrigley decided to fire Joe McCarthy and hire Rogers Hornsby—the worst managerial move in team history.

1969

In 1969, the Cubs started off 11–1 and were in first place for 155 days, only to fall short at the end, making them a reluctant member of baseball's Century Club. Painful as it was, the 1969 Cubs have plenty of company—23 other teams—even if they do have to reside at the top of the list. It could be worse; the Dodgers are on the list *six* times.

Everyone has a theory for why the Chicago Cubs could lead the National League East for five months, only to collapse in September. In fact, the collapse began immediately after Ken Holtzman's no-hitter on August 19 as they went 15–25 from that point forward and went from 7½ up to 8 down. Here are eight theories.

The First Juiced-Ball Controversy

It's not the pitching. It's that new jackrabbit ball. The pitchers have had their stuff. But with that jackrabbit ball, they haven't a chance. All a batter has to do is meet it, and if the ball is not hit right at somebody, it's a base hit. That ball travels like a bullet, and unless you are in front of it, you haven't a chance to stop it. Just tap it and it lands in the stands. It's making a joke of the game.

John McGraw, 1930

Pitchers are afraid to get off-balance . . . for fear that they'll get killed when the ball comes back at them. When they throw these days, they have to be prepared to duck.

Joe Tinker, on the state of pitching in 1930

---

10 × 5

The Cubs scored at least 10 runs in five consecutive games in June 1930.

June 1	Pirates 4 Cubs 16
June 3	Cubs 15 Braves 2
June 4	Cubs 18 Braves 10
June 5	Cubs 10 Braves 7
June 6	Cubs 13 Dodgers 0

Close But No Cigar

Twenty times in the 20th century, the Cubs have been in first place after June 1 without winning the pennant.

Year	Last Day in 1st	Days in 1st	Finish	GB
1930	September 12	40	2nd	2
1969	September 9	155	2nd	8
1937	September 1	75	2nd	3
1927	August 31	49	4th	8½
1911	August 24	53	2nd	7½
1936	August 11	31	2nd	5
1977	August 4	69	4th	20
1967	July 24	5	3rd	14
1973	July 21	80	5th	5
1915	July 12	45	4th	17½
1970	June 23	64	2nd	5
1978	June 23	29	3rd	11
1985	June 15	35	4th	23½
1924	June 14	5	5th	12
1947	June 14	13	6th	25
1963	June 6	1	7th	17
1903	June 5	11	3rd	8
1904	June 5	9	2nd	13
1975	June 5	51	5th	17½
1995	June 4	37	3rd	12

Month by Month

Month	W–L	GA
April	16–7	2
May	16–9	7½
June	17–11	7
July	15–14	6
August	18–11	4
September/ October	10–18	–8

We did everything we could. It didn't work out, but when you fill that bucket up and you put one more drop in it, and it overflows, that's 100 percent.

Randy Hundley

• **Leo Durocher.** From September 1 until the end of the season, the Cubs were the worst team in baseball (10–18) as the team went into a collective batting slump. Some suggested this was due to Leo Durocher's not using his bench. The 38-year-old Ernie Banks played 155 games, Don Kessinger 158, Randy Hundley caught 151 games, and the only time Glenn Beckert missed was due to a broken finger. The fielding of Beckert and Kessinger especially suffered. Here are the starters' batting averages in September—only Billy Williams and Jim Hickman raised their averages down the stretch.

	September	1969
Don Kessinger	.148	.273
Ernie Banks	.156	.253
Randy Hundley	.188	.255
Glenn Beckert	.203	.291
Jim Hickman	.246	.237
Ron Santo	.262	.289
Billy Williams	.329	.293
Chicago Cubs	**.219**	**.253**

• **Day games.** The theory goes that playing so many games in the heat of the day wore the Cubs out and led to the aforementioned collective batting slump.

• **Doubleheaders.** The Cubs' motto should have been "Let's *not* play two." Sportswriter Rick Talley's theory is that the Mets were younger, deeper, and better suited to playing doubleheaders (a much more common event on the schedule back then). The Mets went 30–14 in twin bills, the Cubs 13–17, which translates to a 10-game difference in the standings. The Mets won by only eight games.

• **Premature celebration.** Before the Cubs had the pennant, they had a theme song—"Hey Hey Holy Mackerel No Doubt About It The Cubs Are On Their Way"—and captain Ron Santo a tradition of clicking his heels after a win (which he first did after a two-out, three-run homer by Jim Hickman in the bottom of the ninth against the Expos). No doubt about it, the Cubs were doing their end-zone dance at the 20-yard line.

• **A curse.** The curse of Billy Goat Sianis? John McGraw? (See Chapter 16, "Foul Territory.") Perhaps it was the anonymous White Sox fan who hexed the Cubs for pulling six of their stars—Ernie Banks, Ron Santo, Glenn Beckert, Don Kessinger, Randy Hundley, and Billy Williams—out of a charity benefit game at Comiskey Park in July.

• **Underestimating the Mets.** The Mets had been the doormats of baseball since their inception in 1962. No one could believe that the Mets were for real. After two Mets errors opened the floodgates for a five-run inning in a 6–2 win by the Cubs at Shea in midseason, Leo Durocher was asked if those were the real Cubs. His response: "No, but those are the real Mets."

• **No fourth starter.** Throughout Durocher's tenure, he never could establish a solid four-man rotation. In 1969, Ferguson Jenkins, Bill Hands, and Ken Holtzman won 58 games while nine other starters combined for 12 wins. Meanwhile, ex-Cub Joe Niekro won 8 games for a wretched Padres team, and ex-Cub Ray Culp won 17 for the Boston Red Sox.

• **Divine intervention.** The signs that the gods were not on the Cubs' side began to appear in July and continued into September.

July

With Ferguson Jenkins up 3–1 on Jerry Koosman and the Mets in the ninth inning at Shea, center-fielder Don Young misplays two fly balls into doubles, and the Mets win 4–3. A week later, the Cubs drop two of three to the Mets at Wrigley as shortstop Al Weis hits two home runs.

August

L.A.'s Don Sutton snaps a 13-game losing streak against the Cubs, winning the first game of his career against Chicago. On the 15th and 16th, the Mets beat the Padres four times in 36 hours.

September 5

Billy Williams gets all four of the Cubs hits in a 9–2 loss to Steve Blass and the Pirates.

September 7

With a strong wind blowing in at Wrigley, Leo Durocher leaves righty closer Phil Regan in to face Willie Stargell rather than go to lefty Hank Aguirre. One strike away from a win, Willie Stargell hits a bomb onto Sheffield Avenue, and the Pirates go on to win in extra innings.

September 8

The Cubs lose 3–2 at Shea as a perfect throw from Jim Hickman nails Tommie Agee at home, but home-plate umpire Satch Davidson calls him safe.

September 9

A black cat walks in front of the Cubs dugout as Tom Seaver outpitches Ferguson Jenkins 7–1.

September 11

In Philadelphia, with a full count, two out, and runners at first and second going on the pitch, Dick Selma throws the ball into left field on a trick play that no one knew was on except Selma. The Phillies go on to win the game.

September 12

The Cubs finally win, but they still lose ground as the Mets sweep a doubleheader 1–0 and 1–0, with pitchers Don Cardwell and Jerry Koosman knocking in New York's only runs.

September 15

The Mets beat the Cardinals 4–3 despite 19 strikeouts by Steve Carlton.

Total Baseball uses fielding, batting, and pitching numbers to calculate how many games a team *should* win. In 1969, the Mets won *13* more games than they would be expected to—the biggest overachievement since the Miracle Braves of 1914. In fact, both the Mets *and* the Cubs were overachievers. According to the slide rules, *each* team should have only won 87 games. Unfortunately, the Cubs won "only" 92 to the Mets 100.

Giving It Away

Some claim that a 1969 pennant for the Cubs would have paved the way for a title in 1970 as well. There's another lost pennant buried in Cubs history: 1980. The numbers say that the Cubs finished last, 27 games behind the Phillies. The fact of the matter is, they had it won and traded it away. (After all, you knew there had to be a reason why the Phillies were actu-

100 *Days in First and No Pennant*

Team	Last Day in 1st	Days in 1st
1969 Chicago Cubs	September 9	155
1942 Brooklyn Dodgers	September 12	148
1951 Brooklyn Dodgers	October 2	147
1993 San Francisco Giants	October 2	144
1985 California Angels	October 2	142
1921 Pittsburgh Pirates	September 10	140
1964 Philadelphia Phillies	September 26	133
1991 Los Angeles Dodgers	October 3	132
1935 New York Giants	August 24	130
1979 Houston Astros	September 10	128
1934 New York Giants	September 28	127
1956 Milwaukee Braves	September 28	126
1995 California Angels	October 1	126
1946 Brooklyn Dodgers	September 30	122
1950 Detroit Tigers	September 21	120
1995 Los Angeles Dodgers	September 26	118
1989 Baltimore Orioles	August 31	117
1921 Cleveland Indians	September 19	115
1978 Boston Red Sox	October 1	115
1911 Detroit Tigers	August 3	112
1962 Los Angeles Dodgers	October 2	111
1987 Cincinnati Reds	August 20	111
1907 Chicago White Sox	August 25	102
1914 New York Giants	September 7	100

The Mets Before the Miracle

Year	W–L	Finish
1962	40–120	10th
1963	51–111	10th
1964	53–109	10th
1965	50–112	10th
1966	66–95	9th
1967	61–101	10th
1968	73–89	9th
1969	100–62	1st

I got my revenge. I beat the Mets in the seventh game of the 1973 World Series.

Ken Holtzman, the only member of the 1969 Cubs to go on to play in a World Series

ally able to win a World Series in 1980.) But for bad trades and holding the line on salaries, consider what the 1980 Cubs might have accomplished with a lineup like this:

CF—Miguel Dilone

Dilone hit .341 and stole 61 bases in a career year with the Indians. He'd been sold by the Cubs after a promising 1979 spent mostly as a pinch runner because he was trapped behind Jerry Martin, whom the Cubs had acquired for . . .

2B—Manny Trillo

Trillo played outstanding defense for the Phillies, raising the cutoff throw to an art form, while hitting .292.

3B—Bill Madlock

Mad Dog had an "off year" in Pittsburgh, hitting only .277 with 10 home runs and 16 stolen bases, but it's safe to say he would have beaten out Lenny Randle for the third-base job. As for the players they got for Madlock, Steve Ontiveros hit .208 and split for Japan while the 34-year-old Bobby Murcer was finishing up his career as a platoon player in New York.

1B—Bill Buckner

The National League's batting champion, Buckner hit .324 in Chicago.

LF—Dave Kingman

Perhaps Kingman would have come back a bit sooner from his shoulder injury had the aforementioned four guys been hitting in front of him. As it was, he hit 18 home runs and knocked in 57 runs in a half season.

RF—Oscar Gamble/Mike Vail

Remember this guy Gamble? He was given away after the 1969 season and developed into a dangerous left-handed slugger. In 1980, he had a broken toe, 14 home runs, and 50 RBIs in a half season. The other half of the platoon, Mike Vail, hit .298. Together they could have been Chicago's Lowenstein/Roenicke.

C—Tim Blackwell/Barry Foote

The Cubs haven't had a problem with dealing away catchers so much as finding them in the first place. As it was, Blackwell and Foote combined for 11 home runs, 58 RBIs, and a .259 average.

SS—Ivan DeJesus

DeJesus stole 44 bases, batted .259, and played solid defense for the Cubs.

With all the injuries and erratic gloves in the outfield, plenty of playing time would have been available for switch-hitting center-fielder Bill North, who was drawing walks and stealing bases (45) for the Giants.

Not a bad lineup, but here's the starting rotation:

SP—Steve Stone

Stone went 25–7 for the Orioles and won the Cy Young Award after being the first Cub lost to free agency.

SP—Larry Gura

Every rotation needs a solid left-hander, and Gura became just that after never really being given a chance in Chicago. He was 18–10 for Kansas City with a 2.96 ERA.

SP—Joe Niekro

Another young pitcher on whom Leo Durocher gave up too quickly, Niekro finally blossomed in the late '70s. He went 20–12 for the Astros in 1980.

SP—Burt Hooton

An unnecessary casualty when the Cubs were broken up in the early '70s, Hooton went 14–8 for the Dodgers.

SP—Rick Reuschel

The Cubs' workhorse, Reuschel went 11–13 for a bad team, with an ERA of 3.40. He could have won 20 as a fourth or fifth starter for a good team that didn't send him out against the other team's ace every five days.

Not that these pitchers would need much bullpen help, but backing them up would have been Bruce Sutter (the most dominating closer in baseball in 1977 and 1979 and still extremely effective in his last season in Chicago); Dick Tidrow (one of the first great setup men); a young future closer, Bill Caudill (2.18 ERA with 112 strikeouts in 128 innings); the erratic left-hander Willie Hernandez; and another lefty reliever the Cubs traded away, Dave LaRoche (who was being misused by Jim Fregosi in California).

Deal Lynn McGlothlen, Dennis Lamp, and Mike Krukow for a catcher or another outfielder with punch, and enjoy the show. After all, if not for the Cubs, the Orioles, Royals, Astros, and Dodgers would have all been in need of another starter!

POSTSEASON

World Series

1906

The Cubs are prohibitive favorites in their first World Series, coming off a 116–36 regular season and facing a Chicago White Sox team that hit .230 for the season and would be without their best hitter, George Davis, in the first three games. Lee Tannehill will move from third to short, and backup infielder George Rohe, a punchless .258 hitter, will enter the starting lineup in the role of Al Weis.

Q. What Cub is the only man to both pitch and umpire in a World Series?

A. Lon Warneke

Game One: October 9 at West Side Grounds

	1	2	3	4	5	6	7	8	9	R	H	E
White Sox	0	0	0	0	1	1	0	0	0	2	4	1
Cubs	0	0	0	0	0	1	0	0	0	1	4	2

W—Altrock, L—Brown. T—1:45. A—12,693.

Q. What three players have played the most games without appearing in a World Series?

A. Andre Dawson, Ernie Banks, and Billy Williams

Dodging snowflakes, Nick Altrock outpitches Mordecai Brown in the bitter cold. The big blow comes off the bat of George Rohe—a triple in the fifth that leads to the first Sox run. Brown fields a comebacker and throws home, but catcher Johnny Kling drops the ball, and Rohe scores.

Game Two: October 10 at South Side Park

	1	2	3	4	5	6	7	8	9	R	H	E
Cubs	0	3	1	0	0	1	0	2	0	7	10	2
White Sox	0	0	0	0	1	0	0	0	0	1	1	3

W—Reulbach, L—White. T—1:58. A—12,595.

Ed Reulbach throws the first one-hitter in World Series history and one of only five. The lone hit comes off the bat of Jiggs Donahue with no outs in the seventh. Having walked George Rohe leading off the inning, Reulbach bears down with runners on first and second and retires the next three batters. The Cubs score three in the second off Doc White while getting only one ball out of the infield—a single to left by Harry Steinfeldt. The Cubs manufacture the runs with two bunts, an infield hit, and an error. Their aggressive baserunning gets them two more runs, with Frank Chance stealing second and forcing a throwing error in the third, and Joe Tinker doing the same while stealing third in the sixth.

Game Three: October 11 at West Side Grounds

	1	2	3	4	5	6	7	8	9	R	H	E
White Sox	0	0	0	0	0	3	0	0	0	3	4	1
Cubs	0	0	0	0	0	0	0	0	0	0	2	2

W—Walsh, L—Pfiester. T—2:10. A—13,667.

Spitballer Ed Walsh answers Ed Reulbach's one-hitter with a two-hitter, both hits coming in the first and resulting in no runs because Solly Hofman is thrown out stealing ahead of Wildfire Schulte's double. The Sox score three in the sixth on a bases-clearing, two-out triple down the left-field line by George Rohe.

Game Four: October 12 at South Side Park

	1	2	3	4	5	6	7	8	9	R	H	E
Cubs	0	0	0	0	0	0	1	0	0	1	7	1
White Sox	0	0	0	0	0	0	0	0	0	0	2	1

W—Brown, L—Altrock. T—1:36. A—18,385.

Mordecai Brown answers Ed Walsh with his own two-hit shutout, holding the Sox hitless until two out in the sixth, when Eddie Hahn singles up the middle. The Cubs' lone run comes in the top of the seventh, when Hahn loses Frank Chance's fly ball in the sun and it falls for a single. In an example of true deadball, one-run strategy, the Cubs lay down not one but two sacrifice bunts, moving Chance to third. Johnny Evers then delivers the clutch, two-out single.

Game Five: October 13 at West Side Grounds

	1	2	3	4	5	6	7	8	9	R	H	E
White Sox	1	0	2	4	0	1	0	0	0	8	12	6
Cubs	3	0	0	1	0	2	0	0	0	6	6	0

W—Walsh, L—Pfiester, S—White. T—2:40. A—23,257.

The weather warms, and a large crowd and two live bear cubs are on hand to see the Cubs fall despite six errors by the White Sox, as Ed Reulbach can't hold an early 3–1 lead and Jack Pfiester is touched for four runs in 1⅔ innings of relief. The crowd spills over into the outfield, helping both teams combine for 11 doubles, including four by Frank Isbell of the Sox.

Game Six: October 14 at South Side Park

	1	2	3	4	5	6	7	8	9	R	H	E
Cubs	1	0	0	0	1	0	0	0	1	3	7	0
White Sox	3	4	0	0	0	0	0	1	x	8	14	3

W—White, L—Brown. T—1:55. A—19,249.

The Sox have a 3–2 advantage in the best-of-seven Series. Pitching on one day of rest, Mordecai Brown has one of the worst outings of his career: six runs and eight hits in 1⅔ innings. It doesn't help any that a policeman in right field kicks Wildfire Schulte in the seat of the pants as he tries to track down a George Davis fly ball in the first inning that falls for a double. The Cubs go down fighting, struggling back from a 7–1 deficit to cut it to 8–3 while loading the bases in the ninth. Schulte grounds to first to end the game, and the Sox have one of the greatest upsets in baseball history. The Hitless Wonders commit 15 errors and bat only .198 for the Series—two points higher than the Cubs—but their errors don't prove as costly, and their hits are much more timely.

1907

> To blazes to that crowd in Chicago tomorrow. I'll finish it today.
> —Mordecai Brown in Detroit before Game Five of the 1907 World Series, after owner Charlie Murphy dropped hints that a sixth game back in Chicago might prove more profitable than a decisive fifth-game victory in Detroit

Assuming nothing this time, the Cubs win 107 games, storm into the World Series, and throttle the Detroit Tigers, holding Ty Cobb to four hits in 20 at bats. The MVP of the Series, had one been chosen, would have been difficult to name, and the award could easily have gone to the entire pitching staff; four different Cubs pitchers each throw a complete-game victory. The Cubs steal 16 bases, 11 in the first two games alone.

> You're a fine bunch of stiffs. Maybe you &@#!%*s have learned your lesson in over-confidence and what happens when you underrate the other &@#!%*s.
>
> Frank Chance to his team after the 1906 World Series

World Series by the Numbers

0: Number of Tinker-to-Evers-to-Chance double plays turned in World Series play
1: Number of World Series games won by the Cubs at Comiskey Park
2: Number of World Series games won by the Cubs at Wrigley Field
3: Number of World Series home runs by Frank Demaree
4: Number of different Cubs pitchers yielding one run or less in complete-game victories in the 1907 World Series
5: Number of World Series wins by Mordecai Brown
6: Number of Jimmy Slagle stolen bases in 1907, a record broken by Lou Brock in 1967
7: Hits allowed by Mordecai Brown in the shutout victory that clinched the Cubs' first World Series championship in 1907
8: Size of the lead blown by the Cubs in 1929 Game Four
9: Number of World Series RBIs by Wildfire Schulte
10: Number of Cubs to hit a World Series home run

Game One: October 8 at West Side Grounds

	1	2	3	4	5	6	7	8	9	10	11	12	R	H	E
Tigers	0	0	0	0	0	0	0	3	0	0	0	0	3	9	3
Cubs	0	0	0	1	0	0	0	0	2	0	0	0	3	10	5

T—2:40. A—24,377.

The Cubs rally for two runs in the bottom of the 9th to tie Detroit at 3–3, and the game ends in a 12-inning tie. Chicago loads the bases on a single by Frank Chance, a hit batsman, and an error. Chance scores on a Wildfire Schulte groundout to make it 3–2, then Del Howard strikes out to end the game—only Boss Schmidt drops the third strike, and Harry

Starting Lineups: 1907

Detroit Tigers

LF	Davy Jones
2B	Germany Schaefer
CF	Sam Crawford
RF	Ty Cobb
1B	Claude Rossman
3B	Bill Coughlin
C	Boss Schmidt
SS	Charley O'Leary

Pitchers

SP	Wild Bill Donovan
SP	George Mullin
SP	Ed Siever
RP	Ed Killian

Chicago Cubs

CF	Jimmy Slagle
LF	Jimmy Sheckard
1B	Frank Chance
3B	Harry Steinfeldt
C	Johnny Kling
2B	Johnny Evers
RF	Wildfire Schulte
SS	Joe Tinker

Pitchers

SP	Orvie Overall
SP	Jack Pfiester
SP	Ed Reulbach
SP	Mordecai Brown

Steinfeldt scores the tying run. The final out of the inning comes as Johnny Evers tries unsuccessfully to steal home. The game is suspended due to darkness and called a tie. Schmidt is later accused of dropping the ball on purpose, since the winning and losing purses would be larger if more than four games were played. To this day, the World Series shares are now based on the first four games of the Series only, to remove any temptation to prolong matters artificially.

Game Two: October 9 at West Side Grounds

	1	2	3	4	5	6	7	8	9		R	H	E
Tigers	0	1	0	0	0	0	0	0	0		1	9	1
Cubs	0	1	0	2	0	0	0	0	x		3	9	1

W—Pfiester, L—Mullin. T—2:13. A—21,901.

Jack Pfiester works in and out of trouble all day as he scatters nine hits and benefits from some great Cubs defense. The first two batters he faces single, but he strikes out Hall of Famer Sam Crawford and gets Ty Cobb to hit into a double play. In the third, he's helped by Johnny Kling, who throws out Germany Schaefer trying to steal. In the fourth, Ty Cobb singles leading off the inning, and Claude Rossman follows with another single, but Wildfire Schulte throws him out trying to stretch it into a double. Pfiester then retires the next two batters, stranding Cobb at third. After a leadoff single by the Tigers in the fifth, Jimmy Sheckard helps protect the Cubs' 3–1 lead with a great catch against the left-field fence on a ball hit by pitcher George Mullin. Sheckard makes another great shoestring catch in the seventh, and Johnny Kling throws out Charley O'Leary trying to steal. With runners on first and second and two out in the eighth, Kling throws out Davy Jones trying to steal third. Finally, in the ninth, Claude Rossman singles to lead off the inning (the seventh time the Tigers put the leadoff man on), but Bill Coughlin lines into a back-breaking double play.

Game Three: October 10 at West Side Grounds

	1	2	3	4	5	6	7	8	9		R	H	E
Tigers	0	0	0	0	0	1	0	0	0		1	6	1
Cubs	0	1	0	3	1	0	0	0	x		5	10	1

W—Reulbach, L—Siever. T—1:35. A—13,114.

Ed Reulbach retires the first 10 batters he faces, until Germany Schaefer beats out a bunt in the fourth. Staked to a 4–0 lead, the defense helps Reulbach protect it. In the fifth, with runners on second and third and one out, Charley O'Leary lines to Joe Tinker for an unassisted double play. In the sixth, the first two runners reach safely again, but the Cubs turn a double play, Steinfeldt to Evers to Chance. Later in the inning, with two out and two on, Jimmy Slagle tracks down a Claude Rossman fly to deep center for the final out. And in the seventh, Joe Tinker fields a leadoff shot off Ed Reulbach's shin and gets Bill Coughlin at first. Reulbach coasts home from here with a six-hitter.

Game Four: October 11 at Bennett Park

	1	2	3	4	5	6	7	8	9		R	H	E
Cubs	0	0	0	0	2	0	3	0	1		6	7	2
Tigers	0	0	0	1	0	0	0	0	0		1	5	2

W—Overall, L—Donovan. T—1:45. A—11,306.

Tigers fans are so despondent that only about 11,000 show up for a rainy Game Four, though their team is down only two games to none. The Tigers jump out to a 1–0 lead in the fourth inning when Ty Cobb triples off Orvie Overall with two out and scores on a Claude Rossman single. The Tigers load the bases on a Bill Coughlin single and a Boss Schmidt walk, but with the game on the line, Orvie Overall fans Charley O'Leary. O'Leary compounds his failure with a bad throw on a Johnny Evers grounder leading off the next inning. After a brief rain delay, Wildfire Schulte walks, Joe Tinker bunts both runners along—with the pitcher coming up next!—and Overall singles them both home. The Tigers lose the Series in the seventh as their defense melts down and the Cubs score three runs without getting a ball out of the infield.

Game Five: October 12 at Bennett Park

	1	2	3	4	5	6	7	8	9	R	H	E
Cubs	1	1	0	0	0	0	0	0	0	2	7	1
Tigers	0	0	0	0	0	0	0	0	0	0	7	2

W—Brown, L—Mullin. T—1:42. A—7,370.

With the home team's dismal showing the day before fresh in their minds, only about 7,000 Tigers fans show up for the fifth game of the Series. The Cubs manufacture a run in the first, as Jimmy Slagle walks, steals his sixth base of the series, and scores on a Harry Steinfeldt single. Their other run comes on an error, a single, a double steal, a walk, and a groundout. Mordecai Brown shuts out the Tigers, though he retires the side in order only twice. He pitches out of big trouble in the fourth after Sam Crawford hits a leadoff double. He strikes out Ty Cobb, but a Claude Rossman single puts runners on first and third. Brown bears down and retires Bill Coughlin on a foul out and Jimmy Archer on a fly to left. Finishing with a flourish, Brown strikes out Cobb again leading off the ninth. The final out of the Cubs' first World Series championship is a Jimmy Archer bloop to Joe Tinker on the outfield grass.

1908

> *It was the most devastating pitch I ever faced.*   —Ty Cobb, on Mordecai Brown's curveball

The Detroit Tigers beat the Chicago White Sox on the last day of the season; otherwise the Cubs would have a chance to avenge 1906. They settle for facing just about the identical Tigers team they made short work of in 1907 and do the same in 1908, taking the Series in five games to become the first team to repeat as World Series champions. The MVP would have been Orvie Overall, who threw two complete-game victories in which he gave up only seven hits and one run.

Game One: October 10 at Bennett Park

	1	2	3	4	5	6	7	8	9	R	H	E
Cubs	0	0	4	0	0	0	1	0	5	10	14	2
Tigers	1	0	0	0	0	0	3	2	0	6	10	3

W—Brown, L—Summers. T—2:10. A—10,812.

Ed Reulbach and Ed Killian hook up on a rainy Saturday, but neither is around when the game is decided. Killian is knocked out in the third as the Cubs score four on a double, a bunt single, two singles, a walk, two force plays, and an error. There's more life in the 1908 Tigers, and they rally with three in the seventh off Ed Reulbach and take the lead with two in the eighth off Orvie Overall and Mordecai Brown. Down 6–5 in the ninth, the Cubs rally

---

Game Four, Seventh Inning

Three runs without leaving the infield; vintage deadball Cubs. Up 2–1, the Cubs put pressure on the defense, and the Tigers crack. Wildfire Schulte beats out a bunt leading off the seventh in Detroit. Joe Tinker bunts him along—for the second time with a .213-hitting pitcher up next!—and Wild Bill Donovan's throw to second is too late. Orvie Overall bunts both runners along. Jimmy Slagle grounds to short, but Schulte tries to score. Charley O'Leary's throw goes wild, and Tinker takes third. Jimmy Sheckard bunts to first and beats it out because no one covers the bag. Frank Chance hits into a 5–4 force play, putting runners on first and third with no one out. The final run crosses the plate when Chance intentionally gets himself caught in a run-down, allowing Jimmy Slagle to score.

Starting Lineups: 1908

Detroit Tigers

LF   *Matty McIntyre*
SS   *Charley O'Leary*
CF   *Sam Crawford*
RF   *Ty Cobb*
1B   *Claude Rossman*
2B   *Germany Schaefer*
C   *Boss Schmidt*
3B   *Bill Coughlin*
Pitchers
SP   *Ed Killian*
SP   *Wild Bill Donovan*
SP   *George Mullin*
SP   *Ed Summers*
RP   *George Winter*

Chicago Cubs

LF   *Jimmy Sheckard*
2B   *Johnny Evers*
RF   *Wildfire Schulte*
1B   *Frank Chance*
3B   *Harry Steinfeldt*
CF   *Solly Hofman*
SS   *Joe Tinker*
C   *Johnny Kling*
Pitchers
SP   *Ed Reulbach*
SP   *Jack Pfiester*
SP   *Orvie Overall*
SP   *Mordecai Brown*

for five runs off Ed Summers. Solly Hofman puts the Cubs ahead with a two-run, bases-loaded single, and Mordecai Brown retires Ty Cobb with two men on in the bottom of the ninth to end the game.

Game Two: October 11 at West Side Grounds

	1	2	3	4	5	6	7	8	9	R	H	E
Tigers	0	0	0	0	0	0	0	0	1	1	4	1
Cubs	0	0	0	0	0	0	0	6	x	6	7	0

W—Overall, L—Donovan. T—1:30. A—17,760.

With Cubs owner Charles Murphy quintupling ticket prices and releasing some to scalpers, only 17,760 fans show up for the first of Orvie Overall's two gems. The game is a scoreless tie in the bottom of the eighth, with the Cubs limited to a sixth-inning single by Overall. But after an infield single by Solly Hofman, Joe Tinker hits the first World Series home run in Cubs history into the right-field bleachers. After Johnny Kling doubles and Overall grounds out, the Cubs string together two singles, a Wildfire Schulte triple, and a wild pitch to take a 6–0 lead. Overall, who'd gone 4⅓ innings before giving up a hit, is touched for a run in the ninth on a walk and a single, then ends the game on a double-play grounder to Joe Tinker.

Game Three: October 12 at West Side Grounds

	1	2	3	4	5	6	7	8	9	R	H	E
Tigers	1	0	0	0	0	5	0	2	0	8	11	4
Cubs	0	0	0	3	0	0	0	0	0	3	7	1

W—Mullin, L—Pfiester. T—2:10. A—14,543.

Ty Cobb explodes for four hits, and the Tigers erase a 3–1 Cubs lead with five in the sixth off Jack Pfiester. The five runs come despite Solly Hofman's throwing Cobb out at the plate on a fly to center. Cobb also makes a spectacle of himself in the ninth when he steals second and third with an 8–3 lead. His attempt to steal home is thwarted.

Game Four: October 13 at Bennett Park

	1	2	3	4	5	6	7	8	9	R	H	E
Cubs	0	0	2	0	0	0	0	0	1	3	10	0
Tigers	0	0	0	0	0	0	0	0	0	0	4	1

W—Brown, L—Summers. T—1:35. A—12,907.

Q. Who hit the Cubs' first World Series home run?

A. Joe Tinker, 1908

The Cubs go up three games to one as Mordecai Brown extends his string of World Series innings without an earned run to 20 innings with a four-hit shutout of the Tigers. The Cubs go up 2–0 in the third on two walks and two run-scoring singles by Harry Steinfeldt and Solly Hofman. Brown and the Cubs' defense are both at the top of their games. In the first, Ty Cobb is retired with Sam Crawford at third. In the fifth, Joe Tinker makes a great play on Boss Schmidt. In the sixth, Brown snuffs out a Tigers threat by inducing Sam Crawford to bounce into a 1-6-3 double play. But there is no better example of great Cubs defense than the fourth inning, when the Tigers' first two batters single to put runners on first and second. Ty Cobb bunts, but Brown pounces on the ball and throws out Charley O'Leary at third. Johnny Kling then picks Sam Crawford off second, and Brown ends the threat by striking out Claude Rossman.

Closing It Out with Nine Zeros

Here are the 18 pitchers who pitched a complete-game shutout in the decisive game of a World Series. Overall's three-hitter has been matched by only Johnny Kucks and Sandy Koufax, with Koufax and Overall each having only two runs with which to work. Tom Glavine pitched an eight-inning, 1–0 one-hitter for the Atlanta Braves in 1995 but didn't finish the game.

Year	Pitcher	Team	Opponent	Result	
1903	Bill Dineen	Boston Pilgrims	Pittsburgh	3–0	4-hitter in Game 8
1905	Christy Mathewson	New York Giants	Philadelphia	2–0	6-hitter in Game 5
1907	**Mordecai Brown**	**Chicago Cubs**	**Detroit**	**2–0**	**7-hitter in Game 5**
1908	**Orvie Overall**	**Chicago Cubs**	**Detroit**	**2–0**	**3-hitter in Game 5**
1909	Babe Adams	Pittsburgh Pirates	Detroit	8–0	6-hitter in Game 7
1920	Stan Coveleski	Cleveland Indians	Brooklyn	3–0	5-hitter in Game 7
1921	Art Nehf	New York Giants	New York	1–0	4-hitter in Game 8
1934	Dizzy Dean	St. Louis Cardinals	Detroit	11–0	6-hitter in Game 7
1943	Spud Chandler	New York Yankees	St. Louis	2–0	10-hitter in Game 5
1955	Johnny Podres	Brooklyn Dodgers	New York	2–0	8-hitter in Game 7
1956	Johnny Kucks	New York Yankees	Brooklyn	9–0	3-hitter in Game 7
1957	Lew Burdette	Milwaukee Braves	New York	5–0	7-hitter in Game 7
1962	Ralph Terry	New York Yankees	San Francisco	1–0	4-hitter in Game 7
1965	Sandy Koufax	Los Angeles Dodgers	Minnesota	2–0	3-hitter in Game 7
1966	Dave McNally	Baltimore Orioles	Los Angeles	1–0	4-hitter in Game 4
1983	Scott McGregor	Baltimore Orioles	Philadelphia	5–0	5-hitter in Game 5
1985	Bret Saberhagen	Kansas City Royals	St. Louis	11–0	5-hitter in Game 7
1991	Jack Morris	Minnesota Twins	Atlanta	1–0	7-hitter in Game 7 (10)

Game Five: October 14 at Bennett Park

	1	2	3	4	5	6	7	8	9	R	H	E
Cubs	1	0	0	0	1	0	0	0	0	2	10	0
Tigers	0	0	0	0	0	0	0	0	0	0	3	0

W—Overall, L—Donovan. T—1:25. A—6,210.

After some rare defensive lapses in the eighth inning of Game One, the Cubs finish the Series with only one error in 37 innings. Orvie Overall follows up his four-hitter with a three-hit shutout, the fastest game in Series history, in front of the smallest crowd in Series history on a cold Wednesday afternoon. Johnny Evers, Wildfire Schulte, and Frank Chance give Overall all he needs when they string together three one-out singles. Johnny Evers doubles in Johnny Kling with an insurance run in the fifth, though the Cubs waste scoring chances all afternoon. Overall has a dicey moment in the first when he walks Matty McIntyre leading off and allows a one-out single to Sam Crawford. He strikes out Ty Cobb and appears to strike out Claude Rossman for his third of the inning, but the ball gets by Kling, and Rossman reaches first to load the bases. Overall then fans Germany Schaefer for his fourth strikeout of the inning. He strikes out 10 for the game, 9 through the first five innings. He closes out the series with a 1-2-3 ninth inning, retiring the side on groundouts.

1910

The Cubs come into the 1910 World Series as the favorites—especially with Philadelphia's star pitcher Eddie Plank out with an arm injury—but are done in by the Athletics' two-man staff of Chief Bender and Jack Coombs, uncharacteristically poor fielding and hittable pitching, and an inability to deliver timely hits. The Cubs lose in five, avoiding a sweep due only to a refusal to quit in Game Four, tying the game in the 9th and winning it in the 10th.

Game One: October 17 at Shibe Park

	1	2	3	4	5	6	7	8	9		R	H	E
Cubs	0	0	0	0	0	0	0	0	1		1	3	1
Athletics	0	2	1	0	0	0	0	1	x		4	7	2

W—Bender, L—Overall. T—1:54. A—26,891.

Orvie Overall is chased after yielding three runs in three innings, hurt by two doubles into the overflow crowd in the outfield and a bad-hop single by Chief Bender. Harry McIntire pitches five innings of one-hit relief, allowing only an unearned run in the eighth. The Cubs manage only a ninth-inning run off Bender, who yields his first hit since one out in the first inning. The Cubs pull to 4–1 when Johnny Kling singles in Joe Tinker. A Wildfire Schulte walk brings the tying run to the plate, but Solly Hofman grounds to third for the final out.

Game Two: October 18 at Shibe Park

	1	2	3	4	5	6	7	8	9		R	H	E
Cubs	1	0	0	0	0	0	1	0	1		3	8	3
Athletics	0	0	2	0	1	0	6	0	x		9	14	4

W—Coombs, L—Brown. T—2:25. A—24,597.

Mordecai Brown's scoreless streak is snapped at 24⅔ innings when the Athletics score an earned run in the fifth to go up 3–1. But the wheels come off in the seventh, when the Athletics hit four doubles off Brown and score six runs, breaking up a one-run game. The Cubs leave 14 runners on, as 31-game-winner Jack Coombs gives up eight hits and nine walks but only three runs.

Game Three: October 20 at West Side Grounds

	1	2	3	4	5	6	7	8	9		R	H	E
Athletics	1	2	5	0	0	0	4	0	0		12	15	1
Cubs	1	2	0	0	0	0	0	2	0		5	6	5

W—Coombs, L—McIntire. T—2:07. A—26,210.

A change of venue doesn't help Chicago, as Connie Mack starts Jack Coombs *again* on only one day of rest. The Cubs counter with Ed Reulbach, who lasts only two innings. Harry McIntire doesn't repeat his strong performance of Game One in relief, lasting only a third of an inning and giving up four runs—three on a home run by Danny Murphy that gets Frank Chance tossed, as he argues that it should have been a ground-rule double. Jack Pfiester finishes the game, giving up four runs in the seventh when Harry Steinfeldt commits an error on what should have been the third out of a 1-2-3 inning.

Game Four: October 22 at West Side Grounds

	1	2	3	4	5	6	7	8	9	10		R	H	E
Athletics	0	0	1	2	0	0	0	0	0	0		3	11	3
Cubs	1	0	0	1	0	0	0	0	1	1		4	9	1

W—Brown, L—Bender. T—2:14. A—19,150.

Of the 19 teams that have faced a 3–0 deficit in a World Series, only 3 have avoided the sweep—and only the Cubs have done so by rallying in the ninth and forcing extra innings. With Chicago down 3–2 in the ninth, Wildfire Schulte doubles off Chief Bender leading off the inning, and Frank Chance triples him home. But then with the winning run on third, Heinie Zimmerman—playing for Johnny Evers, who is out with a broken leg—pops out, and Harry Steinfeldt fouls out to end the inning. Mordecai Brown, pitching in relief of King Cole, works out of trouble in the 10th when Harry Davis doubles, but Joe Tinker throws him out at third on a Danny Murphy groundout. The Cubs win it in the bottom of the 10th when Jimmy Archer doubles and Jimmy Sheckard singles him home.

Game Five: October 23 at West Side Grounds

	1	2	3	4	5	6	7	8	9	R	H	E
Athletics	1	0	0	0	1	0	0	5	0	7	9	1
Cubs	0	1	0	0	0	0	0	1	0	2	9	2

W—Coombs, L—Brown. T—2:06. A—27,374.

Coming off two scoreless innings of relief in Game Four, in the follow-up, Mordecai Brown keeps the Cubs in a 2–1 game until the eighth inning, when the Athletics score five runs on four hits and two walks. Jack Coombs gets his third win of the Series thanks to 28 runs' worth of support in three games. In the 1907 and 1908 World Series, Cubs pitching gave up only 21 runs in 10 games.

1918

The Cubs and the Red Sox play in the World Series, and the world does not come to an end before it can be resolved—although a players strike nearly ends the series before Game Five. The Red Sox win their fourth championship since 1912 in six games, despite scoring only nine runs. The Cubs score only 10, only 1 for Hippo Vaughn in two complete-game losses. The game is played in September, as a work-or-fight order from the War Department shuts down the season immediately after Labor Day.

Game One: September 5 at Comiskey Park

	1	2	3	4	5	6	7	8	9	R	H	E
Red Sox	0	0	0	1	0	0	0	0	0	1	5	0
Cubs	0	0	0	0	0	0	0	0	0	0	6	0

W—Ruth, L—Vaughn. T—1:50. A—19,274.

Babe Ruth strands three Cubs runners at third en route to a six-hit shutout, working out of a bases-loaded jam in the second when he strikes out Charlie Pick to end the inning. The Red Sox score their lone run in the fourth, when Dave Shean walks, George Whiteman singles just out of reach of Charlie Hollocher at short, and Stuffy McInnis singles home Shean. The game is played at the larger Comiskey Park, but attendance is down as public attention is on matters overseas. A baseball tradition is born when "The Star-Spangled Banner" is played—during the seventh-inning stretch, rather than in its now-traditional "leadoff" spot.

Game Two: September 6 at Comiskey Park

	1	2	3	4	5	6	7	8	9	R	H	E
Red Sox	0	0	0	0	0	0	0	0	1	1	6	1
Cubs	0	3	0	0	0	0	0	0	x	3	7	1

W—Tyler, L—Bush. T—1:58. A—20,040.

Starting Lineups: 1918

Boston Red Sox

RF	Harry Hooper
2B	Dave Shean
CF	Amos Strunk
LF	George Whiteman
1B	Stuffy McInnis
SS	Everett Scott
3B	Fred Thomas
C	Wally Schang
	Pitchers
SP	Babe Ruth
SP	Joe Bush
SP	Carl Mays
SP	Sam Jones

Chicago Cubs

RF	Max Flack
SS	Charlie Hollocher
LF	Les Mann
CF	Dode Paskert
1B	Fred Merkle
2B	Charlie Pick
3B	Charlie Deal
C	Bill Killefer
	Pitchers
SP	Hippo Vaughn
SP	Lefty Tyler
RP	Phil Douglas
RP	Claude Hendrix

The Cubs even the Series at one game apiece as they score three runs in the second and Lefty Tyler makes them stand up. Chicago scores on a walk, a bunt single, a double by Bill Killefer, and a two-run single by Tyler. Tyler works out of trouble all day, finally yielding a run in the ninth on consecutive triples by Amos Strunk and George Whiteman leading off the inning. After a walk to Everett Scott with one out, Red Sox manager Ed Barrow uses a pitcher to pinch-hit—but instead of Babe Ruth, it's Jean Dubuc, who strikes out. Tyler ends the game by getting Wally Schang to pop out.

Game Three: September 7 at Comiskey Park

	1	2	3	4	5	6	7	8	9	R	H	E
Red Sox	0	0	0	2	0	0	0	0	0	2	7	0
Cubs	0	0	0	0	1	0	0	0	0	1	7	1

W—Mays, L,—Vaughn. T—1:57. A—27,054.

The Cubs waste another great outing by Hippo Vaughn as they can manage only one run off Carl Mays, a submariner with a nasty disposition. The Red Sox score two in the fourth on a hit batsman, two singles, and a bouncer back to the mound that Vaughn can't handle. Max Flack limits the damage when he throws out Wally Schang at the plate on a single to right. The Cubs score in the fifth on a double by Charlie Pick and a single by Bill Killefer. The game ends on one of the most exciting baserunning plays in Cubs history. With two out and none on, Charlie Pick beats out a slow roller and then steals second. A passed ball by Wally Schang sends Pick to third base, with Schang's throw then getting by Fred Thomas at third. Pick tries to score, but Thomas recovers and throws him out at the plate.

Game Four: September 9 at Fenway Park

	1	2	3	4	5	6	7	8	9	R	H	E
Cubs	0	0	0	0	0	0	0	2	0	2	7	1
Red Sox	0	0	0	2	0	0	0	1	x	3	4	0

W—Ruth, L—Douglas, S—Bush. T—1:50. A—22,183.

The Sox take a 3–1 lead in the series as Babe Ruth extends his record streak to 29⅔ scoreless innings. Ruth doesn't have his best stuff—he gives up seven hits and six walks while striking out none—but he's helped out by Max Flack's baserunning, as the Cubs' right fielder is picked off not once but twice. The Red Sox score twice in the fourth on two walks and a triple by Babe Ruth, who is batting sixth in the Boston lineup. The Cubs rally to tie the game in the eighth and end Ruth's streak. Bill Killefer walks, and Claude Hendrix—the pitcher pinch-hitting for starter Lefty Tyler—singles. The runners go to second and third on a Ruth wild pitch, but Max Flack's groundout doesn't advance the runners. Charlie Hollocher's grounder to second scores Killefer, and Les Mann ties the game with a single. The Cubs give the game away in the bottom of the inning on a single, a passed ball, and a throwing error. When Ruth gives up a single and a walk to the first two runners in the ninth, Joe Bush comes in to pitch, and the Babe goes to left. Bush works out of it on a force play and a 6-4-3 double play.

Game Five: September 10 at Fenway Park

	1	2	3	4	5	6	7	8	9	R	H	E
Cubs	0	0	1	0	0	0	0	2	0	3	7	0
Red Sox	0	0	0	0	0	0	0	0	0	0	5	0

W—Vaughn, L—Jones. T—1:42. A—24,694.

The game is delayed for nearly an hour as the players threaten not to play unless their trimmed World Series shares are increased. The powers that be call their bluff, and the players relent. The hard-luck Hippo Vaughn shuts out the Red Sox on five hits, and the Cubs finally get him some runs, sparked by three hits from rookie shortstop Charlie Hollocher.

Game Six: September 11 at Fenway Park

	1	2	3	4	5	6	7	8	9	R	H	E
Cubs	0	0	0	1	0	0	0	0	0	1	3	2
Red Sox	0	0	2	0	0	0	0	0	x	2	5	0

W—Mays, L—Tyler. T—1:46. A—15,238.

The Red Sox score two runs in the third without benefit of a hit as Lefty Tyler walks Carl Mays and Dave Shean, and then Max Flack drops a George Whiteman line drive for what should have been the third out. The Cubs respond with a run in the fourth, but the damage could have been worse had Les Mann not been picked off first by Wally Schang for the second out of the inning. The Cubs don't come close to scoring again, as the Red Sox make two great defensive plays to keep rallies from even starting. Put off by the threatened strike, attendance is down more than 9,000 for the last World Championship in Red Sox history.

1929

> *I like the way their batters whang the missile, and I think their pitching's good enough. I don't go in much for Mr. Wrigley's gum, but I think his ball team's pretty sweet.* —**Boston Post**, *on the Cubs' chances in the 1929 World Series*

The Cubs hit .303 as a team in 1929, and they face off against a Philadelphia Athletics team that hit .296 and ended the three-year reign of the New York Yankees atop the American League. Unfortunately, this Series becomes famous for the largest blown lead in World Series history as the Cubs fall in five.

Game One: October 8 at Wrigley Field

	1	2	3	4	5	6	7	8	9	R	H	E
Athletics	0	0	0	0	0	0	1	0	2	3	6	1
Cubs	0	0	0	0	0	0	0	0	1	1	8	2

W—Ehmke, L—Root. T—2:03. A—50,740.

A veteran sidearming righty, Howard Ehmke, with a 166–164 career record is the surprise starter in the Series opener, the first series game played in Wrigley Field. He's spent September scouting the Cubs and fits right in with Connie Mack's plan to avoid using lefties against Chicago's hard-hitting right-handed lineup. Ehmke pitches slowly and from the side, a type of pitcher the Cubs haven't seen much of that season, and he responds to the pressure with the game of his life: one run (unearned) and a record 13 strikeouts in a complete-game, 3–1 victory. The Cubs score their run in the ninth on a two-base error and a single by Riggs Stephenson. Charlie Grimm singles to put the tying run on first with one out, but Ehmke retires pinch-hitter Footsie Blair on a groundout and ends the game with a strikeout of pinch-hitter Chick Tolson.

My Kingdom for a Lefty!

Oh, no, not O'Doul again . . . my O'Doul.

William Wrigley watching Lefty O'Doul perform for the Philadelphia Phillies

Who knows where they would have played him, but the Cubs had—and gave away—the left-handed bat they needed to counteract Connie Mack's right-handed strategy in the 1929 World Series. His name was Lefty O'Doul, and he'd been signed personally by William Wrigley after a monster 1925 season in the Pacific Coast League, where at one point he went 19-for-21 with 16 hits in three games. But he was cut loose in spring training by Joe McCarthy because of his carefree attitude. O'Doul returned to the PCL to win the MVP in 1927, piling up 278 hits. At 32, he finally got a chance to play every day in the majors, and he batted .398 with 254 hits, 32 home runs, and 122 RBIs for the 1929 Phillies. He won another batting title in 1932 with Brooklyn, hitting .368 with 219 hits. O'Doul ended his career with a .349 lifetime batting average. Three times in four seasons, he pulled the feat of hitting more than 20 home runs while striking out fewer times than he homered.

Game Two: October 9 at Wrigley Field

	1	2	3	4	5	6	7	8	9		R	H	E
Athletics	0	0	3	3	0	0	1	2	0		9	12	0
Cubs	0	0	0	0	3	0	0	0	0		3	11	1

W—Earnshaw, L—Malone, S—Grove. T—2:29. A—49,987.

Nearly 50,000 pack Wrigley, and again go home disappointed. The Athletics knock Pat Malone out in the fourth as they move out in front 6–0. The Cubs fight back to 6–3, and Connie Mack goes to his bullpen for Hall of Famer Lefty Grove, who pitches $4\frac{1}{3}$ innings of shutout ball for the save. The Cubs again fan 13 times.

Game Three: October 11 at Shibe Park

	1	2	3	4	5	6	7	8	9		R	H	E
Cubs	0	0	0	0	0	3	0	0	0		3	6	1
Athletics	0	0	0	0	1	0	0	0	0		1	9	1

W—Bush, L—Earnshaw. T—2:09. A—29,921.

The Cubs fight their way back into the Series with a 3–1 victory over George Earnshaw, who starts again after only one day of rest. Guy Bush scatters nine hits, pitching out of first-and-third, bases-loaded, first-and-second, and second-and-third situations. He gives up the first run of the game in the fifth on a Bing Miller single, but the Cubs respond with three in the sixth on a walk, an error, a run-scoring single by Rogers Hornsby, and a two-run single by Kiki Cuyler. Bush finishes strongly, retiring the final eight batters he faces, as the Cubs win despite another 10 strikeouts.

Game Four: October 12 at Shibe Park

	1	2	3	4	5	6	7	8	9		R	H	E
Cubs	0	0	0	2	0	5	1	0	0		8	10	2
Athletics	0	0	0	0	0	0	10	0	x		10	15	2

W—Rommel, L—Blake, S—Grove. T—2:12. A—29,921.

For three innings, it's a pitchers' duel, for the next three a laugher, and for the final three a tragedy. The Cubs take a 2–0 lead on a two-run home run by Charlie Grimm, the first Cubs postseason home run since 1908. They pour on five more in the sixth on five consecutive singles and a two-base throwing error. But the Athletics rally for 10 runs against four pitchers in the seventh and steal a game that should have tied the Series at 2–2 for the Cubs. It all began with an Al Simmons home run, which prompted one Athletic to comment, "Well, we won't be shut out, anyway." Amid the carnage to follow, Hack Wilson loses two catchable fly balls in the sun—one for a single, the other for a three-run, game-tying home run—and Riggs Stephenson just misses catching the long Jimmy Dykes double that puts the Athletics in front. Lefty Grove records his second save of the Series with two innings of hitless relief, fanning four.

October 12, 1929

	1	2	3	4	5	6	7	8	9
Bishop, 2b	F7		3-3			F7	1B	1B	
Haas, cf	5-3			P2		4-3	HR	SH	
Cochrane, c	P6			2B		F8	BB	1B 7-2	
Simmons, lf		SO		5-4			HR 1B	SO	
Foxx, 1b		6-3		F8			1B 1B		
Miller, rf		5-3			1B CS		1B HBP		
Dykes, 3b			1B E9		E8		1B 2B		
Boley, ss			SH		F8		1B SO		
Quinn, p			SO		SO				
Walberg, p									
Rommel, p									
Burns, ph							P6 SO		
Grove, p									

Game Five: October 14 at Shibe Park

	1	2	3	4	5	6	7	8	9	R	H	E
Cubs	0	0	0	2	0	0	0	0	0	2	8	1
Athletics	0	0	0	0	0	0	0	0	3	3	6	0

W—Walberg, L—Malone. T—1:42. A—29,921.

Despite the train wreck of two days before, it looks as though the Cubs are going to send the Series back to Chicago for a sixth game. Two-out singles by Charlie Grimm and Zack Taylor score Kiki Cuyler and Riggs Stephenson and chase Howard Ehmke in the fourth. But Rube Walberg pitches 5⅓ innings of two-hit baseball, allowing no additional runs to cross the plate. Meanwhile Pat Malone is cruising, allowing only two hits and no runs through the first eight innings. He retires the first batter in the bottom of the ninth, then gives up a single to Max Bishop and a game-tying home run to Mule Haas. Malone retires Mickey Cochrane, then gives up a double to Al Simmons. The Cubs intentionally walk Jimmie Foxx to get to Bing Miller, who hits a Series-winning double, scoring Simmons. The Cubs lose, and the stock market collapses days later.

1932

The Cubs go up against a New York Yankees team stocked with Hall of Famers and irritated with Chicago for voting their former teammate Mark Koenig only a half share of the World Series money. The Cubs lead in three of the four games but can't keep pace with the powerful New York offense. To make matters worse, the legend is born that Babe Ruth "called his shot" in the fifth inning of Game Three.

Game One: September 28 at Yankee Stadium

	1	2	3	4	5	6	7	8	9	R	H	E
Cubs	2	0	0	0	0	0	2	2	0	6	10	1
Yankees	0	0	0	3	0	5	3	1	x	12	8	2

W—Ruffing, L—Bush. T—2:31. A—41,459.

Seventh-Inning Retch

Fifteen batters came to bat for the Athletics in the bottom of the seventh in Game Four of the 1929 World Series. It started with a home run by Al Simmons off Charlie Root, passed through five more hits off Root, a hit and a walk off Art Nehf, two more hits off Sheriff Blake, the game-winning hit off Pat Malone, and two strikeouts. Of their 15 hits, 10 came in one inning. Here's what the scorecard looked like— bizarre, to say the least.

When a kid asked Joe McCarthy for a ball before a game in 1930, McCarthy pointed to Hack Wilson and replied: Son, do you see that fat fella out there in the outfield? . . . Well, you just stand behind him and you'll get more balls than you know what to do with.

Connie taught me a lesson that time.

Cubs manager Joe McCarthy, on Connie Mack's decision to use right-handers throughout the 1929 World Series, relegating Lefty Grove to bullpen duty

The Yankees capitalize on six Cubs walks to score 12 runs on only eight hits off three Cubs pitchers. Lou Gehrig's homer puts New York ahead to stay in the fourth, wasting three hits and three RBIs by Riggs Stephenson. The Cubs fan 10 times and leave 11 runners on base.

Game Two: September 29 at Yankee Stadium

	1	2	3	4	5	6	7	8	9	R	H	E
Cubs	1	0	1	0	0	0	0	0	0	2	9	0
Yankees	2	0	2	0	1	0	0	0	x	5	10	1

W—Gomez, L—Warneke. T—1:46. A—50,709.

The Cubs jump out on top in the first on a leadoff double by Billy Herman and a sacrifice fly by Riggs Stephenson, but the Yankees respond with two in the bottom of the inning on run-scoring singles by Lou Gehrig and Bill Dickey. Lefty Gomez is touched for nine hits but walks only one and gives up only one earned run. Another good day at the plate by Riggs Stephenson is not enough.

Game Three: October 1 at Wrigley Field

	1	2	3	4	5	6	7	8	9	R	H	E
Yankees	3	0	1	0	2	0	0	0	1	7	8	1
Cubs	1	0	2	1	0	0	0	0	1	5	9	4

W—Pipgras, L—Root, S—Pennock. T—2:11. A—49,986.

The Cubs fall behind 3–0 in the first as Babe Ruth hits a three-run bomb, but they fight back to tie it at 4–4 as Kiki Cuyler doubles and homers. In the top of the fifth, Babe Ruth hits his 15th and final World Series home run—the "called shot"—and Lou Gehrig follows with another home run into the temporary bleachers built on Sheffield Avenue. The Cubs don't score again until Gabby Hartnett homers leading off the ninth.

The Truth Behind the Legend

With two strikes and Game Three of the 1932 World Series tied 4–4 in the fifth inning at Wrigley Field, Babe Ruth—being heaped with abuse from the Cubs' dugout—made some sort of gesture before hitting a home run into the center-field bleachers. Some say he was telling Charlie Root that he still had one more strike, while others claim that he was pointing at Guy Bush in the Cubs' dugout and reminding him that he'd be out there on the mound tomorrow. It made a great story to say that he was pointing to the center-field bleachers, but Babe Ruth never called his shot off Charlie Root. Consider these eyewitness accounts from those closest to the action, including Root and Ruth themselves.

Maybe I had a smug grin on my face after he took the second strike. Babe stepped out of the box again, pointed his finger in my direction, and yelled, "You still need one more, kid." I guess I should have wasted the next pitch, and I thought Ruth figured I would, too. I decided to try to cross him and came in with it. The ball was gone as soon as Ruth swung. It never occurred to me then that the people in the stands would think he had been pointing to the bleachers. —Charlie Root

If he'd pointed, he would never have got a chance to hit. Root would have had him with his feet up in the air. —Billy Herman

I'm going to point to the center-field bleachers with a barracuda like Root out there? On the next pitch, they'd be picking it out of my ear with a pair of tweezers. —Babe Ruth

Game Four: October 2 at Wrigley Field

	1	2	3	4	5	6	7	8	9		R	H	E
Yankees	1	0	2	0	0	2	4	0	4		13	19	4
Cubs	4	0	0	0	0	1	0	0	1		6	9	1

W—Moore, L—May, S—Pennock. T—2:27. A—49,844.

Neither starter survives the first inning, with the Yankees loading the bases on the first four pitches thrown by Guy Bush. Lou Gehrig is robbed of a grand slam on a great running catch by Frank Demaree, and Charlie Grimm calls on Lon Warneke. Warneke escapes the first without any further damage, and the Cubs go on to chase Yankees starter Johnny Allen in the bottom of the inning, scoring four runs, three on a Demaree home run. In the third, Warneke gives up a two-run home run to Tony Lazzeri, and he leaves the game in the fourth with a 4–3 lead. The Yankees get to Jakie May in the sixth, with Lou Gehrig singling in two runs—his ninth hit in 17 at bats—but the Cubs fight back to tie it in the bottom of the inning on two singles and a throwing error. The Yankees pull away for good with four in the seventh and another four in the ninth on Lazzeri's second homer as they rack up nine hits in the final three innings.

1935

The Cubs come into the World Series fresh off a 21-game winning streak in September. And with the Cubs leaving Tiger Stadium with a split in the first two games and an injury to Detroit slugger Hank Greenberg, things look very good for Chicago. Three one-run losses later, the Tigers have their first championship and the Cubs are waiting for next year again.

Game One: October 2 at Navin Field (Tiger Stadium)

	1	2	3	4	5	6	7	8	9		R	H	E
Cubs	2	0	0	0	0	0	0	0	1		3	7	0
Tigers	0	0	0	0	0	0	0	0	0		0	4	3

W—Warneke, L—Rowe. T—1:51. A—47,391.

Lon Warneke pitches a four-hit shutout and gets all of the offensive support he needs in the first inning, as an Augie Galan double, a Schoolboy Rowe throwing error, and a Gabby Hartnett single plate two. The Cubs add a run in the ninth with a Frank Demaree home run.

Game Two: October 3 at Navin Field (Tiger Stadium)

	1	2	3	4	5	6	7	8	9		R	H	E
Cubs	0	0	0	0	1	0	2	0	0		3	6	1
Tigers	4	0	0	3	0	0	1	0	x		8	9	2

W—Bridges, L—Root. T—1:59. A—46,742.

The Tigers send Charlie Root to the showers after the first four batters get hits, capped by a two-run Hank Greenberg home run. It's Greenberg's only hit of the series, however, his season finished by a broken wrist. The Tigers stake Tommy Bridges to a 7–0 lead that is never in jeopardy.

Game Three: October 4 at Wrigley Field

	1	2	3	4	5	6	7	8	9	10	11		R	H	E
Tigers	0	0	0	0	0	1	0	4	0	0	1		6	12	2
Cubs	0	2	0	0	1	0	0	0	2	0	0		5	10	3

W—Rowe, L—French. T—2:27. A—45,532.

With Marv Owen moving to first and reserve Flea Clifton taking over at third, the Tigers' offense is greatly weakened. The Cubs take a 3–1 lead into the top of the eighth and appear to be on their way to their first World Series win at Wrigley Field. Frank Demaree starts the scoring against Eldon Auker with his second home run of the Series. Bill Lee falters in the eighth, and Lon Warneke can't bail him out. In a painful irony, Detroit's fifth run scores when Billy Rogell takes a page out of Frank Chance's book, getting himself hung up in a rundown on an attempted steal of second while Pete Fox scores from third. The Cubs rally to tie the game against Schoolboy Rowe in the ninth, when Stan Hack, Chuck Klein, and pinch-hitter Ken O'Dea single and Augie Galan lifts a sacrifice fly to center. The Tigers get the game-winner in the 11th off Larry French, sandwiching two singles around an error by Fred Lindstrom at third base.

Game Four: October 5 at Wrigley Field

	1	2	3	4	5	6	7	8	9		R	H	E
Tigers	0	0	1	0	0	1	0	0	0		2	7	0
Cubs	0	1	0	0	0	0	0	0	0		1	5	2

W—Crowder, L—Carleton. T—2:28. A—49,350.

The Cubs get out on top in the second when Gabby Hartnett takes General Crowder deep, but they give the game away in the sixth on a pair of two-out errors, a dropped fly ball by Augie Galan followed by a Billy Jurges throwing error. In the bottom of the sixth, Billy Herman leads off with a double and tags up on a foul pop to Charlie Gehringer down the right-field line. Then Hartnett strikes out and Frank Demaree pops out. The Cubs rally in the ninth, with Demaree and Phil Cavarretta singling after Hartnett is robbed of a leadoff single by Billy Rogell. But the game ends when Stan Hack bounces into a 6-4-3 double play.

Game Five: October 6 at Wrigley Field

	1	2	3	4	5	6	7	8	9		R	H	E
Tigers	0	0	0	0	0	0	0	0	1		1	7	1
Cubs	0	0	2	0	0	0	1	0	x		3	8	0

W—Warneke, L—Rowe, S—Lee. T—1:49. A—49,237.

The Cubs finally get their first World Series win at Wrigley Field after six consecutive losses, as Bill Lee notches Chicago's first postseason save. A Billy Herman triple and a Chuck Klein home run give the Cubs a 2–0 lead in the third, and they add an insurance run in the seventh on a two-out Billy Herman double. Lee pitches the final three innings of the game after Lon Warneke hurts his shoulder, pitching out of trouble in each inning. An inning-ending double play erases a leadoff walk in the seventh. With runners on first and second and one out in the eighth, Lee strikes out Jo-Jo White and gets Mickey Cochrane to ground to

No Final Out

1924—Earl McNeely gets the Senators' second run-scoring, bad-hop single of the game over third-baseman Fred Lindstrom's head with one out in the 12th off Jack Bentley, and Washington beats the Giants 4–3 in Game Seven.

1929—Bing Miller's double off Pat Malone scores Al Simmons in the bottom of the ninth, capping a three-run rally that gives Philadelphia a 3–2 victory over the Cubs in Game Five.

1935—Goose Goslin's bloop single off Larry French scores Mickey Cochrane in the bottom of the ninth, giving Detroit a 4–3 victory over the Cubs in Game Six.

1953—Billy Martin's one-out single off Clem Labine in the bottom of the ninth scores Hank Bauer from second as the Yankees beat the Dodgers 4–3 in Game Five.

1960—Bill Mazeroski's leadoff home run off Ralph Terry in the bottom of the ninth gives the Pirates a 10–9 victory over the New York Yankees in Game Seven.

1991—Gene Larkin's pinch-hit single in the bottom of the 10th off Alejandro Pena scores Dan Gladden with the only run of Game Seven, sending the Minnesota Twins to victory over the Atlanta Braves.

1993—Joe Carter's three-run home run in the bottom of the ninth off Mitch Williams gives the Blue Jays an 8–6 win over the Phillies in Game Six.

1997—Edgar Renteria's single up the middle in the bottom of the 11th off Charles Nagy gives the Marlins a 3–2 win over the Indians in Game Seven.

Phil Cavarretta. In the ninth, three singles load the bases with no one out, but Lee gets Billy Rogell on a shallow fly, gives up a run on a groundout by Gee Walker, and gets Flea Clifton on a foul out with the tying runs on second and third.

Game Six: October 7 at Navin Field (Tiger Stadium)

	1	2	3	4	5	6	7	8	9	R	H	E
Cubs	0	0	1	0	2	0	0	0	0	3	12	0
Tigers	1	0	0	1	0	1	0	0	1	4	12	1

W—Bridges, L—French. T—1:57. A—48,420.

The Cubs and Tigers pile up 24 hits but leave 17 runners on as starters Larry French and Tommy Bridges pitch into and out of trouble all day. Billy Herman continues his spectacular Series, singling in Billy Jurges in the third to tie the game and hitting a two-out, two-run home run in the fifth to put the Cubs in front. The Tigers tie the game in the sixth with two out when the bottom of the lineup—Billy Rogell and Marv Owen—put together a ground-rule double and a run-scoring single. The Cubs struggle to get a fourth run, stranding Stan Hack at second in the sixth and hitting into a double play in the eighth after a leadoff single by Gabby Hartnett. In the ninth, Stan Hack triples over Gee Walker's head in center field leading off the inning. But Tommy Bridges strikes out Billy Jurges. The Cubs' bench has been ejected earlier in the game, so Larry French has to hit for himself, and he hits a comebacker to Bridges. Augie Galan then flies to Goose Goslin to end the inning. The Tigers win it in the bottom of the ninth when Mickey Cochrane singles off Herman's glove with one out, moves to second on a Charlie Gehringer groundout, and scores on a bloop single by Goslin, falling into the Bermuda Triangle between second, center, and right. When Stan Hack visits Tiger Stadium years later, he goes to third base "to see if I'm still there."

Starting Lineups: 1938

New York Yankees

SS   *Frankie Crosetti*
3B   *Red Rolfe*
RF   *Tommy Henrich*
CF   *Joe DiMaggio*
1B   *Lou Gehrig*
C   *Bill Dickey*
LF   *George Selkirk*
2B   *Joe Gordon*
    Pitchers
SP   *Red Ruffing*
SP   *Lefty Gomez*
SP   *Monte Pearson*
RP   *Johnny Murphy*

Chicago Cubs

3B   *Stan Hack*
2B   *Billy Herman*
RF   *Frank Demaree/*
    Phil Cavarretta
CF   *Joe Marty*
LF   *Carl Reynolds*
C   *Gabby Hartnett*
1B   *Ripper Collins*
SS   *Billy Jurges*
    Pitchers
SP   *Bill Lee*
SP   *Dizzy Dean*
SP   *Clay Bryant*
RP   *Jack Russell*
RP   *Larry French*
RP   *Charlie Root*
RP   *Vance Page*
RP   *Tex Carleton*

That was the lowest moment in my life. I knowed my arm was gone. I couldn't break a pane of glass. But Crosetti never was a powerful hitter, so I figured I had a chance.

Dizzy Dean, on his Game Two performance

1938

In a repeat of the 1932 whitewash, the Yankees sweep the fast-finishing Cubs, outscoring them 22–9.

Game One: October 5 at Wrigley Field

	1	2	3	4	5	6	7	8	9	R	H	E
Yankees	0	2	0	0	0	1	0	0	0	3	12	1
Cubs	0	0	1	0	0	0	0	0	0	1	9	1

W—Ruffing, L—Lee. T—1:53. A—43,642.

Red Ruffing earns his second Series-opening complete-game victory over the Cubs. Chicago's big chance comes in the third, as Ripper Collins singles leading off and moves to second with two outs. Stan Hack scores him with a single and moves to second on the throw. Hack's aggressive baserunning doesn't pay off, though, when Billy Herman singles off Red Rolfe's glove at third base and Hack is thrown out trying to score by shortstop Frankie Crosetti.

Game Two: October 6 at Wrigley Field

	1	2	3	4	5	6	7	8	9	R	H	E
Yankees	0	2	0	0	0	0	0	2	2	6	7	2
Cubs	1	0	2	0	0	0	0	0	0	3	11	0

W—Gomez, L—Dean, S—Murphy. T—1:53. A—42,108.

The Cubs continue to be snakebit in the postseason at Wrigley Field. The dead-armed Dizzy Dean nearly pitches his second miraculous game in a week, but his margin for error is erased in the second inning when, with runners on first and second and two out, Stan Hack and Billy Jurges collide in the infield on an easy grounder by Joe Gordon that rolls for a two-run double. The Cubs go back ahead on a two-run double by Joe Marty in the third, and Dean holds the lead until two outs in the eighth. With a runner on first, Dean is taken deep by the light-hitting Frankie Crosetti. As the Yankees' shortstop rounds the bases, Dean yells: "You'da never done that if I'da had my fastball." Crosetti can only nod in agreement. Joe DiMaggio adds two more in the ninth with another home run off Dizzy Dean. Johnny Murphy, one of the game's first firemen, nails down the victory with two on and two out in the bottom of the ninth when Stan Hack lines to short.

Game Three: October 8 at Yankee Stadium

	1	2	3	4	5	6	7	8	9	R	H	E
Cubs	0	0	0	0	1	0	0	1	0	2	5	1
Yankees	0	0	0	0	2	2	0	1	x	5	7	2

W—Pearson, L—Bryant. T—1:57. A—55,236.

The Cubs take the lead, briefly, for the last time in the Series on a fifth-inning ground-out, but the Yankees respond by breaking up Clay Bryant's no-hitter with a two-out, Joe Gordon home run in the bottom of the inning. Gordon adds a two-run single in the sixth to help the Yankees pull away.

Game Four: October 9 at Yankee Stadium

	1	2	3	4	5	6	7	8	9	R	H	E
Cubs	0	0	0	1	0	0	0	2	0	3	8	1
Yankees	0	3	0	0	0	1	0	4	x	8	11	1

W—Ruffing, L—Lee. T—2:11. A—59,847.

Red Ruffing stymies the Cubs again, and Frankie Crosetti hits a two-run triple in the second and a two-run bloop double in the eighth. It could have been worse, as Frank Demaree tracks down a Joe DiMaggio drive 415' away in left center in the third and robs Joe Gordon in the sixth with two men on and two out. When Billy Herman grounds out to end the game, the Yankees become the first team to "threepeat."

1945

The 98-win Cubs dethrone St. Louis and head into the World Series as favorites against the Tigers yet again, who win only 88 games in taking the American League pennant by 1½ games. The Cubs lose in seven, despite outhitting the Tigers .263 to .223, as a couple of key breaks go against them.

Game One: October 3 at Briggs (Tiger) Stadium

	1	2	3	4	5	6	7	8	9	R	H	E
Cubs	4	0	3	0	0	0	2	0	0	9	13	0
Tigers	0	0	0	0	0	0	0	0	0	0	6	0

W—Borowy, L—Newhouser. T—2:10. A—54,637.

The Cubs bomb the greatest pitcher of the war years, Hal Newhouser, who was 25–9 in the regular season. The big blow is a two-out triple in the first by Bill Nicholson after the Tigers intentionally walk Andy Pafko to get to him. Hank Borowy goes the distance, yielding six hits and no runs while stranding 10 base runners.

Game Two: October 4 at Briggs (Tiger) Stadium

	1	2	3	4	5	6	7	8	9	R	H	E
Cubs	0	0	0	1	0	0	0	0	0	1	7	0
Tigers	0	0	0	0	4	0	0	0	x	4	7	0

W—Trucks, L—Wyse. T—1:47. A—53,636.

Bill Nicholson puts the Cubs ahead with a two-out single after Phil Cavarretta's fly ball falls for a double as Doc Cramer and Roy Cullenbine both freeze. With the score tied at 1–1 and two out in the fifth, Hank Wyse hangs a curveball to Hank Greenberg that just barely clears the wall in left for a game-winning three-run home run.

Game Three: October 5 at Briggs (Tiger) Stadium

	1	2	3	4	5	6	7	8	9	R	H	E
Cubs	0	0	0	2	0	1	0	0	0	3	8	0
Tigers	0	0	0	0	0	0	0	0	0	0	1	2

W—Passeau, L—Overmire. T—1:55. A—55,500.

One of the first pitchers to throw a slider, Claude Passeau notches the second one-hitter in Cubs postseason history, yielding only a single to Rudy York in the second. Bill Nicholson knocks in his fifth run of the Series in the fourth to put the Cubs up 1–0, and Passeau brings home the final run in the sixth with a sacrifice fly. Passeau faces only 28 batters, retiring the last 11.

Game Four: October 6 at Wrigley Field

	1	2	3	4	5	6	7	8	9	R	H	E
Tigers	0	0	0	4	0	0	0	0	0	4	7	1
Cubs	0	0	0	0	0	1	0	0	0	1	5	1

W—Trout, L—Prim. T—2:00. A—42,923.

The Tigers even things up at 2–2 as the Series moves to Chicago. Ray Prim retires the first 10 batters he faces before unraveling in the fourth. He's pulled with one out after a walk, two singles, and a double. The Cubs score their only run on a Don Johnson triple and a grounder to short, when first-baseman Rudy York throws the ball away firing across the diamond trying to catch Johnson off third.

Game Five: October 7 at Wrigley Field

	1	2	3	4	5	6	7	8	9	R	H	E
Tigers	0	0	1	0	0	4	1	0	2	8	11	0
Cubs	0	0	1	0	0	0	2	0	1	4	7	2

W—Newhouser, L—Borowy. T—2:18. A—43,463.

The Cubs' World Series record at Wrigley falls to 1–10 as Hank Borowy struggles while Detroit's ace, Hal Newhouser, goes the route. Things look good for the Cubs in the third as Andy Pafko robs Hank Greenberg of a run-scoring extra-base hit and Borowy doubles in front of a Stan Hack single to tie the game at 1–1. The Tigers erupt for four in the sixth and two insurance runs in the ninth when Roy Cullenbine's drive is lost in the vines by Andy Pafko while Doc Cramer and Greenberg score.

Game Six: October 8 at Wrigley Field

	1	2	3	4	5	6	7	8	9	10	11	12	R	H	E
Tigers	0	1	0	0	0	0	2	4	0	0	0	0	7	13	1
Cubs	0	0	0	0	4	1	2	0	0	0	0	1	8	15	3

W—Borowy, L—Trout. T—3:28. A—41,708.

At nearly 3½ hours, it's the longest Series game ever played at the time and a rare Wrigley Field win, but a costly one. The Cubs register four runs in the fifth on a pair of run-scoring singles by Stan Hack and Phil Cavarretta to put them up 4–1. But with Claude Passeau cruising again, having yielded only one run in 5⅓ innings, a shot up the middle off his pitching hand tears the nail off his middle finger. He struggles from that point forward and is finally lifted with two outs in the seventh and a 5–2 lead. Hank Wyse allows another run on a Rudy York single before retiring the Tigers. The Cubs get both runs back in the seventh, going up 7–3 on a two-out, bases-loaded walk and an infield single by Roy Hughes. The Tigers fight back with four in the eighth, tying the game on a walk, a double, an error, a single, a sacrifice fly, and a home run by Hank Greenberg. The Cubs are forced to go to Hank Borowy in relief, who pitches four scoreless innings. The Cubs finally win it in the 12th on a two-out Stan Hack double.

Game Seven: October 10 at Wrigley Field

	1	2	3	4	5	6	7	8	9		R	H	E
Tigers	5	1	0	0	0	0	1	2	0		9	9	1
Cubs	1	0	0	1	0	0	0	1	0		3	10	0

W—Newhouser, L—Borowy. T—2:31. A—41,590.

The crucial at bat of a ball game does not always come in the late innings. Sometimes it's in the very first inning of a game that ends in a rout . . . but didn't have to. Such is the case in Game Seven of the 1945 World Series in Chicago. Hank Borowy is a seven-inning pitcher with blister problems who needs four days' rest between starts to be effective. He asks to go out for Game Seven on one day of rest and doesn't retire a batter. He gives up three consecutive singles, and Paul Derringer is called on to bail him out. Derringer retires cleanup hitter Hank Greenberg on a sacrifice bunt (!), then intentionally walks Roy Cullenbine to load the bases. Derringer breathes a sigh of relief when he retires Rudy York on a popup to Stan Hack at third, having moved past the dangerous part of the order. Light-hitting third-baseman Jimmy Outlaw is up. Derringer walks him to force in a run. Unnerved, the veteran yields a bases-clearing double to .256-hitting catcher Paul Richards. The Tigers coast to a 9–3 victory and the title. Hal Newhouser goes the distance for the win as the Cubs never bring the tying run to the plate.

Asking Borowy to pitch the seventh game was asking an awful lot from him. . . . You have to admire a guy for wanting to do it.

Don Johnson

World Series Leaders

Games

1. Johnny Kling — 21
   Wildfire Schulte — 21
   Jimmy Sheckard — 21
   Harry Steinfeldt — 21
   Joe Tinker — 21
6. Frank Chance — 20
7. Stan Hack — 18
8. Phil Cavarretta — 17
9. Johnny Evers — 16
   Gabby Hartnett — 16
   Solly Hofman — 16

At Bats

1. Wildfire Schulte — 81
2. Jimmy Sheckard — 77
3. Harry Steinfeldt — 73
4. Frank Chance — 71
5. Stan Hack — 69
6. Joe Tinker — 68
7. Johnny Kling — 65
8. Phil Cavarretta — 63
9. Johnny Evers — 60
10. Billy Herman — 58

Hits

1. Wildfire Schulte — 25
2. Stan Hack — 24
3. Frank Chance — 22
4. Phil Cavarretta — 20
5. Harry Steinfeldt — 19
6. Johnny Evers — 17
   Solly Hofman — 17
8. Joe Tinker — 16
9. Billy Herman — 15
10. Jimmy Sheckard — 14

Runs Batted In

1. Wildfire Schulte — 9
2. Solly Hofman — 8
   Bill Nicholson — 8
   Harry Steinfeldt — 8
5. Billy Herman — 7
   Riggs Stephenson — 7
   Joe Tinker — 7
8. Frank Chance — 6
   Kiki Cuyler — 6
   Frank Demaree — 6

continued

World Series Leaders

Runs

1.	Joe Tinker	12
2.	Frank Chance	11
	Wildfire Schulte	11
4.	Phil Cavarretta	9
	Johnny Evers	9
	Billy Herman	9
7.	Solly Hofman	7
	Jimmy Sheckard	7
	Harry Steinfeldt	7
10.	Kiki Cuyler	6
	Stan Hack	6
	Johnny Kling	6

Batting Average (minimum 25 at bats)

1.	Riggs Stephenson	.378
2.	Charlie Grimm	.364
3.	Stan Hack	.348
4.	Phil Cavarretta	.317
5.	Frank Chance	.310
	Peanuts Lowrey	.310
7.	Wildfire Schulte	.309
8.	Solly Hofman	.298
9.	Kiki Cuyler	.289
10.	Johnny Evers	.283

Slugging Average

1.	Charlie Grimm	.515
2.	Kiki Cuyler	.474
3.	Frank Demaree	.463
4.	Stan Hack	.449
5.	Riggs Stephenson	.432
6.	Gabby Hartnett	.426
7.	Phil Cavarretta	.413
8.	Billy Herman	.397
9.	Frank Chance	.380
10.	Wildfire Schulte	.370

Appearances

1.	Mordecai Brown	9
2.	Orvie Overall	8
3.	Ed Reulbach	7
4.	Charlie Root	6
5.	Larry French	5
	Jack Pfiester	5
	Lon Warneke	5
8.	Hank Borowy	4
	Guy Bush	4
	Bill Lee	4
	Pat Malone	4

Innings

1.	Mordecai Brown	$57^2/_3$
2.	Orvie Overall	$51^1/_3$
3.	Jack Pfiester	34
4.	Ed Reulbach	$32^2/_3$
5.	Lon Warneke	$27^1/_3$
6.	Hippo Vaughn	27
7.	Charlie Root	$25^2/_3$
8.	Lefty Tyler	23
9.	Bill Lee	$21^1/_3$
10.	Hank Borowy	18

Strikeouts

1.	Mordecai Brown	35
	Orvie Overall	35
3.	Hippo Vaughn	17
4.	Jack Pfiester	16
5.	Pat Malone	15
	Charlie Root	15
7.	Bill Lee	13
	Ed Reulbach	13
	Lon Warneke	13
10.	Larry French	10

Wins

1.	Mordecai Brown	5–4
2.	Orvie Overall	3–1
3.	Ed Reulbach	2–0
4.	Lon Warneke	2–1
5.	Hank Borowy	2–2
6.	Claude Passeau	1–0
7.	Guy Bush	1–1
	Lefty Tyler	1–1
9.	Hippo Vaughn	1–2
10.	Jack Pfiester	1–3

Earned Run Average (minimum 10 innings)

1.	Hippo Vaughn	1.00
2.	Lefty Tyler	1.17
3.	Orvie Overall	1.58
4.	Lon Warneke	2.63
5.	Claude Passeau	2.70
6.	Mordecai Brown	2.81
7.	Bill Lee	2.95
8.	Ed Reulbach	3.03
9.	Larry French	3.21
10.	Pat Malone	3.45

World Series Home Runs

Date	Hitter	Pitcher	Opponent	Situation
October 11, 1908	Joe Tinker	Bill Donovan	Detroit	8th inning, 1 on, 0–0
October 12, 1929	Charlie Grimm	Jack Quinn	at Philadelphia	4th inning, 1 on, 0–0
October 1, 1932	Kiki Cuyler	George Pipgras	New York	3rd inning, 0 on, 1–4
October 1, 1932	Gabby Hartnett	George Pipgras	New York	9th inning, 0 on, 4–7
October 2, 1932	Frank Demaree	Johnny Allen	New York	1st inning, 2 on, 0–1
October 2, 1935	Frank Demaree	Schoolboy Rowe	at Detroit	9th inning, 0 on, 2–0
October 4, 1935	Frank Demaree	Eldon Auker	Detroit	2nd inning, 0 on, 0–0
October 5, 1935	Gabby Hartnett	General Crowder	Detroit	2nd inning, 0 on, 0–0
October 6, 1935	Chuck Klein	Schoolboy Rowe	Detroit	3rd inning, 1 on, 0–0
October 7, 1935	Billy Herman	Tommy Bridges	at Detroit	5th inning, 1 on, 1–2
October 8, 1938	Joe Marty	Monte Pearson	at New York	8th inning, 0 on, 1–4
October 9, 1938	Ken O'Dea	Red Ruffing	at New York	8th inning, 1 on, 1–4
October 3, 1945	Phil Cavarretta	Jim Tobin	at Detroit	7th inning, 0 on, 7–0

Play-Offs

Since the National League split into divisions in 1969, the Cubs have gone to the play-offs three times.

1984

With Ernie Banks in uniform and on the bench as a coach, the favored Cubs bomb the Padres on October 2, 13–0, in the opener. At the time, it's as one-sided a game as any in post-season history, as the Cubs pound out 16 hits and five home runs, one by Bob Dernier leading off the game, two by left-fielder Gary Matthews, and one by pitcher Rick Sutcliffe. The Padres are limited to six hits, only two off Sutcliffe in seven innings. The Cubs will only hit .210 for the final four games of the series.

Chicago gets good pitching by Steve Trout to take the second game 4–2, with Lee Smith recording only the second save in Chicago's postseason history. In San Diego, Ed Whitson shuts the Cubs down on five hits, and Goose Gossage records the save in a 7–1 Padres victory. With Jody Davis and Bull Durham going deep in Game Four, the Cubs rally from deficits of 2–0 and 5–3, and the game is tied at 5–5 going into the bottom of the ninth. But Steve Garvey takes Lee Smith deep for the game-winner, forcing Game Five.

The Cubs jump on Eric Show early again, pulling out to a 3–0 lead after two innings. Dave Dravecky and Craig Lefferts shut Chicago down in relief, while the Padres rally for two against Rick Sutcliffe in the sixth and four in a tragic seventh in which a Tim Flannery ground ball goes right through Bull Durham's legs to tie the game. Tony Gwynn promptly doubles in a run and Garvey delivers the back-breaker moments later with a two-run single that puts the Padres ahead to stay, 6–3.

I have no idea how that happened. I've always swung hard, in case I hit it.

Rick Sutcliffe, on his Game One home run in 1984

Starting Lineups: 1984

San Diego Padres		Chicago Cubs	
2B	Alan Wiggins	CF	Bob Dernier
RF	Tony Gwynn	2B	Ryne Sandberg
1B	Steve Garvey	LF	Gary Matthews
3B	Graig Nettles	1B	Bull Durham
C	Terry Kennedy	RF	Keith Moreland
CF	Kevin McReynolds	3B	Ron Cey
LF	Carmelo Martinez	C	Jody Davis
SS	Garry Templeton	SS	Larry Bowa
Pitchers		**Pitchers**	
SP	Eric Show	SP	Rick Sutcliffe
SP	Mark Thurmond	SP	Steve Trout
SP	Ed Whitson	SP	Dennis Eckersley
SP	Tim Lollar	SP	Scott Sanderson
RP	Greg Harris	RP	Warren Brusstar
RP	Greg Booker	RP	Lee Smith
RP	Andy Hawkins	RP	George Frazier
RP	Dave Dravecky	RP	Tim Stoddard
RP	Craig Lefferts		
RP	Goose Gossage		

Starting Lineups: 1989

San Francisco Giants		Chicago Cubs	
CF	Brett Butler	CF	Jerome Walton
2B	Rob Thompson	2B	Ryne Sandberg
1B	Will Clark	LF	Dwight Smith
LF	Kevin Mitchell	1B	Mark Grace
3B	Matt Williams	RF	Andre Dawson
C	Terry Kennedy	3B	Luis Salazar
RF	Pat Sheridan	SS	Shawon Dunston
SS	Jose Uribe	C	Joe Girardi
Pitchers		**Pitchers**	
SP	Scott Garrelts	SP	Greg Maddux
SP	Rick Reuschel	SP	Mike Bielecki
SP	Mike LaCoss	SP	Rick Sutcliffe
RP	Jeff Brantley	RP	Paul Kilgus
RP	Atlee Hammaker	RP	Steve Wilson
RP	Kelly Downs	RP	Paul Assenmacher
RP	Craig Lefferts	RP	Les Lancaster
RP	Steve Bedrosian	RP	Scott Sanderson
RP	Jeff Robinson	RP	Mitch Williams

Starting Lineups: 1998

Atlanta Braves		Chicago Cubs	
SS	Walt Weiss	CF	Lance Johnson
2B	Keith Lockhart	2B	Mickey Morandini
3B	Chipper Jones	RF	Sammy Sosa
1B	Andres Galarraga	1B	Mark Grace
LF	Ryan Klesko	LF	Henry Rodriguez
C	Javy Lopez	3B	Gary Gaetti
CF	Andrew Jones	C	Tyler Houston
RF	Michael Tucker	SS	Jose Hernandez
Pitchers		**Pitchers**	
SP	John Smoltz	SP	Mark Clark
SP	Tom Glavine	SP	Kevin Tapani
SP	Greg Maddux	SP	Kerry Wood
RP	John Rocker	RP	Felix Heredia
RP	Rudy Seanez	RP	Matt Karchner
RP	Odaliz Perez	RP	Mike Morgan
RP	Kerry Ligtenberg	RP	Terry Mulholland
		RP	Rod Beck

1989

There are almost as many 1984 Padres on the San Francisco Giants' roster as there are 1984 Cubs on the 1989 squad. Just five years later, only Ryne Sandberg, Rick Sutcliffe, and Scott Sanderson remain. Not even the stadium is the same, as Wrigley Field now has lights. The first two games are played at night in Chicago, with the Giants bombing the Cubs 11–3 in Game One. Greg Maddux is tagged for three hits and six RBIs by Will Clark, as the Giants go out to an 8–3 lead. Mark Grace hits a two-run homer in the first inning, and Ryne Sandberg adds a solo shot off Scott Garrelts in the third, but that's it for Chicago's scoring.

Chicago comes back with six runs in the first in Game Two against former Cub Rick Reuschel. He lasts only two-thirds of an inning, giving up five runs on five hits. Mark Grace goes 3-for-4, knocking in four runs on two doubles, including a bases-clearing shot in the sixth. Les Lancaster pitches the final four innings to get the 9–5 win.

The Cubs let Game Three slip away in the bottom of the seventh, as Les Lancaster is called in to relieve Paul Assenmacher with a 4–3 lead, one on, and a 1–0 count on Rob Thompson. Lancaster throws a ball, but, thinking the count is now 3–0, he grooves a fastball that Thompson hits out for a two-run homer that proves to be the margin of victory (5–4) for the Giants.

In Game Four, Matt Williams puts the Giants in front 3–2 with a two-run single in the third and breaks a 4–4 tie in the fifth with a two-run homer off Steve Wilson. The Giants take the game 6–4. Maddux struggles again, while Kelly Downs pitches four innings of scoreless relief for the Giants.

The Giants close the Cubs out in Game Five in San Francisco when Will Clark delivers a two-run single in the eighth off Mitch Williams that puts them up 3–1. Rick Reuschel gets the win, redeeming himself for his Game Two performance with eight innings and no earned runs. The Cubs manage three hits and a run in the ninth, but their rally falls short.

1998

The Cubs are on empty by the time they reach the postseason, and they hit only .181 while scoring four runs in three games. They are in every game until the late innings, as the Cubs' starters allow only six runs in 18 innings. The staff holds the Braves to a .222 average, surrendering 8 of 15 runs on two swings.

In Game One, John Smoltz is nearly flawless, yielding only a solo home run by Tyler Houston leading off the eighth. The Braves win 7–1, pulling away with four in the bottom of the seventh when Ryan "Twinkletoes" Klesko hits a two-out grand slam off Felix Heredia while almost falling on his rear end.

In the second matchup, Kevin Tapani, nursing a 1–0 lead and two outs away from completing one of the great games in Cubs postseason history, is taken deep by Javy Lopez in the ninth to tie the score. The Braves win it in the 10th against Terry Mulholland when Chipper Jones singles home Walt Weiss.

Kerry Wood returns to the mound at Wrigley Field for Game Three for the first time since August 31. He throws 93 pitches, fanning five in five innings and giving up only one run on a double to Greg Maddux and a wild pitch. The Cubs threaten when Henry Rodriguez hits a fly to left that Twinkletoes Klesko plays into a double, but they strand him at third. The wheels come off in the seventh, as Rod Beck is brought in with the Braves threatening to break the game open and gives up a grand slam to Eddie Perez. Down 6–0, the Cubs score twice in the seventh as Mark Grace breaks an 0-for-11 skid. The Braves hold on to close out Chicago 6–2.

Despite the disappointing results, the fans call the Cubs out for one last curtain call after the final out is made. Not bad, considering that the Houston Astros and Atlanta Braves can each win 100 games and not even sell out their play-off games!

> ### *Amazing Grace*
> *Mark Grace delivers the greatest postseason performance in team history in a losing cause in 1989, hitting .647 (11-for-17) with a home run and eight RBIs. He slugs 1.118 and reaches bases 15 times in five games.*

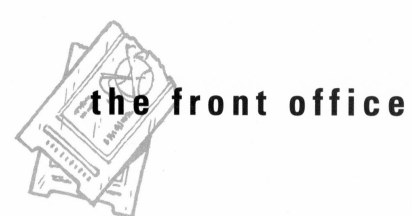

the front office

Baseball is too much of a sport to be a business and too much of a business to be a sport.
—Philip Wrigley

It is sadly appropriate that "The Front Office" follows "The Pennants," for herein lies the tale of why so few pennants have been run up Wrigley's flagpoles in the past half century. For those who scoff at the notion of curses, the solution to the riddle of the Cubs' woes can be found here. Where to begin?

- A brief profile of every Cubs owner
- A look at the team's general managers, including pearls of wisdom from these gentlemen and outsiders' assessments of their performance
- The Good, the Bad, and the Ugly of Cubs trading through the years, including a great trade that never happened . . . two players dealt between games of a doubleheader . . . the pitcher who was traded for himself . . . building a winner in *Brooklyn* . . . the eerie similarity of Billy Williams and Rafael Palmeiro . . . and the 1,656 saves recorded by former Cubs (who'd managed only 39 while in Chicago)
- A chart of free agents gained and lost since the reserve clause was abolished
- The farm system, or lack thereof, including the inability to develop *any* young pitching from 1948 to 1965 . . . trying to replace Ken Holtzman with everyone from Paul Assenmacher to Geoff Zahn . . . one 20-win left-hander in 79 years (and counting)—what the Cubs, Red Sox, Indians, Phillies, Angels, Padres, Expos, Rangers, and Astros all have in common other than one championship in the past 50 years (and counting)
- The Amateur Draft: do they call it that because amateurs are being drafted or because amateurs are doing the drafting? . . . Review the data and decide for yourself.

Come on in, but watch where you step.

THE OWNERS

William Hulbert	1876–82	Charles Weeghman	1916–18
Albert Goodwill Spalding	1882–1901	William Wrigley	1919–31
James Hart	1902–05	Philip Wrigley	1932–77
Charles Murphy	1906–14	William Wrigley	1977–81
Charles Taft	1914–15	The Tribune Company	1981–

Everything is possible to him who dares.

Albert Goodwill Spalding

William Hulbert 1876–82

One of the founding fathers of the National League (and its first president), William Hulbert took over the National Association's troubled Chicago White Stockings and promptly overhauled both the team and the league. He lured away the four best players of the Boston Red Stockings—Albert Goodwill Spalding, Ross Barnes, Deacon White, and Cal McVey—as well as a kid from Philadelphia's squad named Cap Anson. When the other owners complained about his raids, he rallied support for a new league run solely by the owners not in concert with the players, contrary to how the NA had been run. Hulbert put in place the foundation for a dynasty that lasted until 1886, well past his death on April 10, 1882, and for a league that is 123 years old and counting.

Albert Goodwill Spalding 1882–1901

Albert Goodwill Spalding retired as a player at the peak of his game in 1877 simply because he knew there was more money to be made in running the team than playing for it. As a player, Spalding had been a great pitcher and budding sporting-goods mogul who was one of the first major leaguers "sissy" enough to wear a glove (effectively popularizing them so that he could sell more of them). When later entrusted with recording and distributing the "official" rules of the game, he wrote the use of the Spalding baseball into the rule book.

He became Chicago's de facto general manager after the 1877 season and took over the team after William Hulbert's death. He was a man ahead of his time, building a private owner's box at Lakefront Park complete with a gong and a telephone, inventing spring training by taking his team to Hot Springs, Arkansas, in 1886, leading a team of all-stars on a tour of the world in 1887—all the way to the sphinx—and trying to institute night baseball as early as 1883.

He was also cheap. For example, when White Stockings shortstop Ned Williamson injured his knee on the world tour, Spalding left him in London to pay for his own hospitalization and return-trip home. He also helped institute a leaguewide salary cap. Ill treatment such as this prompted players to form their own league in 1890, which lasted only one season. After helping to quash this competitive uprising, Spalding stepped aside as the dominant force in the Chicago front office—though many accused him of running the team through a puppet president, James Hart.

James Hart 1902–05

James Hart had been club president since 1892 but did not become majority owner until 1902. The highlights of his tenure are a bitter feud with Cap Anson toward the end of the player-manager's career and the trading of ace pitcher Jack Taylor because of his poor pitching in an exhibition series. Hart was convinced that Taylor had been tanking games against the Chicago White Sox in the first City Championship Series of 1903.

Spring Training

In addition to Hot Springs, Arkansas, the Cubs trained in places such as Selma, Alabama; Champaign, Illinois; Los Angeles, Santa Monica, and Pasadena, California; West Baden, Indiana; and Shreveport and New Orleans, Louisiana.

It was William Wrigley who put an end to their preseason wandering, establishing a training site on Catalina Island—his own private island off the coast of southern California—in 1921. The Cubs trained there from 1921 to 1951 (though World War II travel restrictions kept them in French Lick, Indiana, from 1942 to 1945) before moving to Mesa, Arizona, in 1952. They trained in Long Beach, California, in 1966 before moving to Scottsdale, Arizona, in 1967 and back to Mesa in 1979.

Q. Though traditionally a member of the Cactus League, the Cubs spent four springs in Florida. Where did they train?

A. Tampa, 1913 to 1916

Charles Murphy 1906–14

Charlie Murphy was a blend of the worst elements of George Steinbrenner and Charlie Finley. He and his business partner, Charles Taft—half brother of William Howard Taft—bought the team after the 1905 season for $105,000. He presided over a dynasty despite alienating his players with his cheapness and his fellow owners with his obnoxiousness. During the Cubs' last World Series victory in 1908, Murphy gouged fans with inflated prices and was accused of colluding with scalpers. When the winning stopped and gouging was no longer an option, he lined his pockets by selling off his stars. Murphy goaded Orvie Overall into quitting baseball for two years in a salary dispute. He fired Frank Chance while Chance was in the hospital recovering from brain surgery. He even humiliated the great Mordecai Brown by farming him out to the minor leagues toward the end of his career. Murphy was finally ousted in February 1914 by his fellow owners, but he walked away with a $500,000 return on his $15,000 share of the initial investment.

Charles Taft 1914–15

Charles Taft merely held down the fort until the team was sold to Charles Weeghman, owner of the rival Federal League's Chicago Whales.

Charles Weeghman 1916–18

Charles Weeghman purchased the Cubs as part of a syndicate that included a fish wholesaler, a meat packer, and William Wrigley. He brought with him Weeghman Park at the corner of Clark and Addison—along with the novel ideas of permanent concession stands and allowing fans to keep foul balls. Financial difficulties in 1918 forced him to sell out his majority stake to Wrigley.

William Wrigley 1919–31

The club and the park stand as memorials to my father. I will never dispose of my holdings in the club as long as the chewing gum business remains profitable enough to retain it. —Philip Wrigley, 1933. The Cubs were the only direct bequest in his father's will.

I have outlived my usefulness. Everything has changed. —Philip Wrigley, 1977

Most Evil Eyes, I'm sure, are honest, tax-paying, respectable citizens. It's only that rotten 3 percent who don't give you an honest day's work for an honest day's pay who give the whole profession a bad name. —Young, front-office employee Bill Veeck on the hexer hired by Philip Wrigley to travel with the team

William Wrigley was one of the greatest owners major-league baseball has seen. He was one of the first to treat his employees as human beings, hiring full-time groundskeepers rather than laying them off during road trips, for example, because he wanted good people to take care of his stadium. Rather than chisel his players at salary time, he often used to hand them blank contracts. Wrigley paid Grover Cleveland Alexander's wife a stipend while the pitcher was away at war. Recognizing the untapped potential of the female market, Wrigley had the park kept sparkling clean and curtailed the rowdyism that deterred many women from attending games. In fact, the largest attendance for any Cubs game at Wrigley Field was Ladies Day in 1930 when 51,556 fans attended, 30,476 of them "guests." He assumed sole control of the team in 1921, and it stayed within the Wrigley family for the next 60 years. Wrigley died on January 26, 1932, at the age of 71, but not before making his son, Philip, promise never to sell the team.

Philip Wrigley 1932–77

Unfortunately, William Wrigley's only son wasn't much of a baseball fan. Philip Wrigley attended few games, even boasted of not being photographed during a Cubs World Series, and wasn't present at the 1962 All-Star Game on the Friendly Confines. His disinterest in the game did not keep him from meddling, however, in everything from trying to plant Chinese elm trees in the center-field bleachers, to having an expert study the players' reflexes, to having oxygen placed in the Cubs' dugout, to installing a rotating group of head coaches in 1961 and an athletic director soon after. He even spent $20,000 during the Depression to hire an "evil eye" to hex the opposing pitchers with furious gestures from behind home plate (on cold days the hexer would come inside and cast his spell over the Western Union ticker in the office). Philip Wrigley's lasting contribution may have been the tender loving care he lavished on "beautiful Wrigley Field." If not for him, the Cubs might not still be playing in the Friendly Confines today.

William Wrigley 1977–81

With a staggering estate-tax bill coming due at the same time that baseball's salary-curtailing reserve clause was being eliminated, the William Wrigley years saw many stars let go rather than be paid what they were now worth. The last act of his administration was dealing pitching ace Rick Reuschel to the Yankees for Doug Bird. The Cubs were sold to the Tribune Company for $20.5 million on June 16, 1981, a transaction announced during the players strike.

The Tribune Company 1981–

At times, the Tribune Company has been accused of milking the Cubs for profit rather than spending whatever it takes to build a winner, but such is the nature of corporate ownership. To a large extent, it's a competitive advantage to have a winning-obsessed lunatic like George Steinbrenner signing the checks rather than a roomful of bottom-line-conscious greedheads. But to be fair, the Cubs have brought in more free-agent talent than they've let go since the Tribune took over, with the one glaring error (Greg Maddux) less a function of the Tribune's tightness with the purse strings than of the bungling of GM Larry Himes.

Free Agents

SEASON	PLAYERS LOST	PLAYERS GAINED	NET IMPACT
1997–98	Kent Bottenfield Dave Clark Dave Hansen	Rod Beck Jeff Blauser Matt Mieske	**Cubs Win**
1996–97	Luis Gonzalez Dave Magadan Jaime Navarro	Shawon Dunston Terry Mulholland Mel Rojas Kevin Tapani	**Cubs Win**
1995–96	Shawon Dunston Randy Myers Mark Parent Anthony Young Todd Zeile	Doug Jones Dave Magadan Bob Patterson	Loss
1994–95	Dan Plesac	Jaime Navarro	**Cubs Win**
1993–94	Greg Hibbard Dwight Smith		Scoreless Tie
1992–93	Andre Dawson Greg Maddux	Jose Guzman Steve Lake Candy Maldanado Randy Myers Dan Plesac Willie Wilson	Loss
1991–92	Rick Sutcliffe	Mike Morgan	Tie
1990–91	Curtis Wilkerson	George Bell Danny Jackson Dave Smith	**Cubs Win**
1989–90	Scott Sanderson		Loss

continued

SEASON	PLAYERS LOST	PLAYERS GAINED	NET IMPACT
1988–89	Frank DiPino Manny Trillo		Scoreless Tie
1987–88		Vance Law	**Cubs Win**
1986–87	Chris Speier	Andre Dawson	**Cubs Win Big**
1985–86		Matt Keough	Scoreless Tie
1984–85	Rick Reuschel Tim Stoddard	Lary Sorensen Chris Speier	Loss
1983–84		Richie Hebner	**Cubs Win**
1982–83		Wayne Nordhagen	Scoreless Tie
1981–82	Tim Blackwell	Bill Campbell Ferguson Jenkins	**Cubs Win**
1980–81	Larry Biittner Lenny Randle		Scoreless Tie
1979–80			
1978–79			
1977–78		Dave Kingman	**Cubs Win**
1976–77	Steve Stone		Loss

GENERAL MANAGERS

There is a scene in *Apocalypse Now* in which Martin Sheen comes to a chaotic U.S. military outpost deep in the jungles of Vietnam. Jimi Hendrix is being played somewhere, interrupted by sporadic gunfire. Picking his way through dark, damp trenches lit only by flares and mortar fire in the night sky, he finds a GI and asks him, "Who's your commanding officer?" The soldier replies with frantic surprise, *"Ain't you?"*

Trying to determine the man primarily responsible for making trades with the Cubs is equally tricky business. Regardless of the title these men might have had, the individuals on the following list appear to have been the commanding officer. William Veeck Sr. was a former sportswriter who wrote under the name Bill Bailey. Jim Gallagher was another sportswriter with a lot less on the ball, who did as much to build the Dodgers as GM Branch Rickey. Salty Saltwell was promoted from head of concessions, while Larry Himes came over from the White Sox as, one can only conclude, a double agent and saboteur.

Wheelers, Dealers, & Empty Suits

William Veeck Sr.	1918–33	Salty Saltwell	1976
William Walker	1933–34	Bob Kennedy	1977–81
Boots Weber	1934–39	Dallas Green	1981–87
Jim Gallagher	1940–49	Jim Frey	1987–91
Wid Mathews	1950–56	Larry Himes	1991–94
John Holland	1957–75	Ed Lynch	1994–

Pearls of Wisdom

A collection of great quotes from the Cubs' front office over the past half century.

I've now got the starter to replace him. —GM **Larry Himes, having lost Cy Young Award–winner Greg Maddux to free agency, announcing the signing of Jose Guzman. Guzman is paid $14 million for four years to go 14–12 for the Cubs in 34 starts. Greg Maddux takes $28 million for five years—$500,000 more than the Cubs offered—to win three more Cy Young Awards.**

Either grow a beard or take the club to court. —GM **Bob Kennedy to sportswriter Karen Chaderjian in 1979 when she was barred entrance to the Cubs' locker room**

If they want to look like idiots, that's fine with me. —Beard-obsessed GM **Bob Kennedy on bearded Cubs players in 1978—a group that included his best player, Bruce Sutter**

No ballplayer is worth more than $100,000, and I'm not sure they're worth that much. —*Philip* **Wrigley in 1977 as the Cubs began to be dismantled, their stars unloaded rather than be paid the going rates**

The time is approaching when big-league clubs will have to be subsidized by local subscription in the manner of opera companies and symphony orchestras. —*Philip Wrigley in 1975*

If only we could find more team players like Ernie Banks. —*Philip Wrigley's ill-advised PS to* **his open letter to the team on September 3, 1971, addressing the "Dump Durocher Clique"**

They still do play a World Series, don't they? It's been so long, I don't remember. —*Philip* **Wrigley, May 14, 1966**

Baseball simply refused to accept his ideas. He was too far ahead of his time. —*Philip Wrigley* **on his athletic director, Colonel Whitlow, who resigned in 1965**

We're taking more than a shot at the pennant. We're cutting loose with both barrels. —GM **John Holland on June 15, 1964, announcing the trade of Lou Brock to the Cardinals**

When the bulldozer breaks down, you should hire a new driver. —*Philip Wrigley on* **managers, 1962**

Managers are expendable. I believe there should be relief managers just like relief pitchers. —*Philip Wrigley in 1959, on the verge of installing the College of Coaches*

He's the greatest player to hit the major leagues from a college campus since George Sisler. —**Wid Mathews, on Moe Drabowsky in 1957. Drabowsky was signed for $50,000 when he threw a no-hitter at Trinity College with Mathews in the stands.**

I am looking for the Cubs to crash into the first division. —GM **Wid Mathews in 1956**

This is the best-looking team I have ever seen in spring training, bar none. —VP **Clarence Rowland in 1955**

There has been only one team asking for you, and all they offered was an old ball, a caved-in catcher's mask, and a broken bat. —GM **Wid Mathews to reluctant-signee Randy Jackson before the 1952 season**

When I shake hands with a boy and he has a good grip, that's one of the essentials. Then I pat him on the shoulder to see how muscular he is. —*Newly hired* GM **Wid Mathews, explaining his science of talent assessment in 1950**

I think Charlie will live longer this way. —*Philip Wrigley in 1949, explaining why he was* **letting Charlie Grimm go as manager**

Our idea in advertising the game, and the fun, and the healthfulness of it, the sunshine and the relaxation, is to get the public to see ball games, win or lose. —*Philip Wrigley*

I have always wanted a World Championship team, and I am not sure that Joe McCarthy is the man to give me that kind of team. —**William Wrigley in 1930**

Comments from the Peanut Gallery

Those who've watched the Cubs' front-office struggles through the years have found it difficult to restrain themselves from commenting.

There is artistry in ineptitude, too, you know. —*Branch Rickey, on the Cubs*

The Cubs are into their 36th rebuilding year. —*Joe Goddard, sportswriter, 1981*

Any company that invests in the Chicago Cubs has a view of the future we cannot even begin to comprehend. —*Jeff MacNelly,* **Chicago Tribune** *cartoonist, on the Tribune Company, 1982*

Everybody said he should have stayed in the fish business. —*Woody English, on Cubs front-office executive and fishmonger William Walker*

During the 1948 season, when GM Jim Gallagher and manager Charlie Grimm were leading the Cubs to their first last-place finish since 1925 and only their second ever, Warren Brown of the *Chicago Herald-American* offered this "tribute":

Oh Mr. Gallagher, Oh Mr. Gallagher,
In another day we'll have to leave once more,
To play the Pirates, then the Cards,
In their very own backyards.
I hope it ain't what it was like before.

Oh Mr. Grimm, Oh Mr. Grimm,
These contenders may well tear us limb from limb.
We may emulate the dive
Of the Cubs of '25.
We ain't that bad, Mr. Gallagher.
That's what you think, Mr. Grimm.

TRADES

Of the most memorable trades the Cubs have made through the years, many were good, some were bad, and a few were just plain ugly. Making deals is how the Cubs acquired Hall of Fame pitchers such as Mordecai Brown, Grover Cleveland Alexander, and Ferguson Jenkins; batting champ Bill Madlock; Cy Young Award–winner Rick Sutcliffe; MVPs Hank Sauer and Ryne Sandberg; and slugger Sammy Sosa. It's also how they wasted huge sums on superstars in decline and how they lost 20-game-winners Joe Niekro and Curt Davis; batting-champ Bill Madlock; a host of future closers, including Cy Young Award–winners Dennis Eckersley and Willie Hernandez; the eerily Billy Williams–esque Rafael Palmeiro; and Hall of Famer Lou Brock.

The Good

December 12, 1903

Jack Taylor and Larry McLean to the St. Louis Cardinals for Mordecai "Three-Finger" Brown and Jack O'Neill.   The Cubs' dynasty of 1906–10 might never have been if not for the trade with the Cardinals in 1903 that brought over a young pitcher named Mordecai

"Three-Finger" Brown. The deal was prompted by anger, however, not rational thought. Jack Taylor's poor pitching in a postseason exhibition with the White Sox so infuriated the owner, James Hart, that he was determined to dump his 21-game winner. Taylor was in the midst of a record streak that will never be broken: 203 games and 1,727 innings without being relieved. Not surprisingly, Taylor lasted only four more seasons, finishing his career back with the Cubs. In return for Taylor, the Cubs got a 9–13 rookie with a mangled pitching hand. Brown went on to win at least 20 games every year from 1906 to 1911, closed out the 1907 World Series with a 2–0 shutout of the Tigers, retired with an ERA of 2.06 (third lowest in major-league history), and went into the Hall of Fame in 1949.

Taking Chance's Advice

Frank Chance took over the managerial reins during the 1905 season. After that season, ownership of the club changed hands from James Hart to Charles Murphy. Murphy asked what the Cubs needed, Chance told him—drawing on his player's "inside information"—and Murphy went out and got them: third-baseman Harry Steinfeldt, left-fielder Jimmy Sheckard, and pitcher Orvie Overall. The latter two trades appeared risky at the time but turned out to be especially lopsided in the Cubs' favor.

December 30, 1905

Billy Maloney, Buttons Briggs, Jack McCarthy, Doc Casey, and $2,000 to the Brooklyn Dodgers for Jimmy Sheckard. Brooklyn thought they were getting the Cubs' starting right-fielder and league-leading base stealer (Billy Maloney), a solid third baseman (Doc Casey), a young pitcher one year removed from a 19-win season (Buttons Briggs), and outfield depth (Jack McCarthy). None of these players lasted more than three seasons in the majors after leaving Chicago. Casey was a .230 hitter, Maloney .220; McCarthy had a solid half year left; Briggs never threw a pitch again. One can only assume that the check, at least, did not bounce. Jimmy Sheckard was the Cubs' right fielder for the next seven-plus seasons, setting what was then a record for walks with 147 in 1911.

June 2, 1906

Bob Wicker and $2,000 to the Cincinnati Reds for Orvie Overall. Bob Wicker had been 49–24 over the past three seasons for the Cubs but had struggled to a 3–5 record in 1906. In midseason, Chicago dealt him for a younger pitcher who was also 3–5—albeit for a much weaker team. Orvie Overall was in his second season, having lost 22 as a wild rookie. While Wicker struggled to a 6–14 mark and hung it up, Overall went 12–3 for the Cubs the rest of the way—and 70–36 from 1907 to 1910. Thus began the Cubs' tradition of midseason starting-pitching acquisitions during pennant-winning campaigns.

August 13, 1913

Lew Richie to Kansas City (American Association) for Hippo Vaughn. The date was a lucky 13. Though he'd won 13 as a 22-year-old rookie in 1910, the Yankees (Highlanders) soured on Hippo Vaughn after he struggled to a 2–8 mark in 1912. The Senators picked him up on waivers, but despite a 4–3 mark and a 2.89 ERA in 12 games, they had no room for him in 1913. Today, a team—not to mention *two* teams—wouldn't be so quick to give up on a big (6'4"/215), young, hard-throwing lefty. But in 1913, the Cubs were able to find Vaughn in the minor leagues and secured his services in exchange for a once-effective, now washed-up, veteran of eight big-league seasons (the inspiration for Ring Lardner's "Alibi Ike" baseball stories). Vaughn went on to become a much larger pitcher (close to 300 pounds at the end of his career) who also happened to be the best lefty starter the Cubs have ever had, racking up 151 wins, 35 shutouts, and five 20-win seasons in Chicago.

Unfair Trade Practices

In 1915, Federal Leaguer Mordecai Brown ended up in court testifying about abuse of players by owners. At the heart of his case: that on two separate occasions, players had been traded for dogs.

December 11, 1917

Mike Prendergast, Pickles Dillhoefer, and $55,000 to the Philadelphia Phillies for Grover Cleveland Alexander and Bill Killefer.   As World War I raged in Europe, the Cubs took advantage of a panic-stricken Phillies owner, prying away a 30-game winner for a 3-game winner, a .126-hitting catcher named Pickles, and $55,000. (It would have been a lopsided deal without Alexander, as the Cubs also received Reindeer Bill Killefer, a veteran catcher who later managed the team.) When Phillies owner Bill Baker got the word that Grover Cleveland Alexander would be called into military service imminently, he hurriedly dumped his ace for cash and two live bodies. Though Alexander returned from World War I shell-shocked, epileptic, and back on the bottle, he did manage to win 128 games for the Cubs from 1918 to 1926 and went into the Hall of Fame in 1938. Mike Prendergast won 13 games for Philadelphia, Pickles Dillhoefer hit .091, and the Phillies—who finished first, second, and second during Alexander's final three seasons with the club—didn't finish that high in the standings again for 33 years. They also didn't have a 20-game winner again until 1949, a record for futility. It wasn't the last time the Cubs fleeced the Phillies.

January 4, 1918

Larry Doyle, Art Wilson, and $15,000 to the Boston Braves for Lefty Tyler.   Larry Doyle and Art Wilson were part-time players for what was left of their careers, and Lefty Tyler had only one solid season left in his arm—but it was the best of his career. Tyler teamed with Hippo Vaughn as the best pair of lefties the Cubs have ever had—and anytime the Cubs can get 19 wins, eight shutouts, and a 2.00 ERA, they'll take it and run.

November 28, 1927

Sparky Adams and Pete Scott to the Pittsburgh Pirates for Kiki Cuyler.   The Cubs were able to draft a 27-year-old, good-hit/no-glove utility player named Riggs "Old Hoss" Stephenson out of the minors and away from the Cleveland Indians after the 1925 season, despite a .337 major-league batting average over five seasons. He was in Indianapolis learning how to play outfield. At the same time, a clerical error by the New York Giants allowed a funny-looking, 25-year-old imbiber named Hack Wilson to be plucked out of their farm system. He was in Toledo, learning the strike zone, though he'd known it well enough to hit two home runs in one inning with the Giants that season. When the Cubs stole Hall of Famer Hazen Shirley "Kiki" Cuyler from the Pirates' doghouse in 1927—Pirates manager Donie Bush was upset at the aloof pretty boy for not sliding at a key point in a game—for an aging, 5'5" 150-pound infielder (Adams) and a reserve outfielder (Scott), one of the greatest-hitting outfields in baseball history was complete.

November 7, 1928

Socks Seibold, Percy Jones, Lou Legett, Freddie Maguire, Bruce Cunningham, and $200,000 to the Boston Braves for Rogers Hornsby.   The final piece in the puzzle for the 1929 pennant-winners was second-baseman Rogers Hornsby, who came over from the financially strapped Boston Braves for five very mediocre players and $200,000. Hornsby had signed a six-year deal, with an annual salary of $40,000, only 10 weeks before. Rarely, if ever, has a five-for-one deal for an aging star proved to be so lopsided for the acquiring team. Hornsby lasted just four seasons with the Cubs, only one of which was up to his legendary standards, but it was one for the ages: 39 home runs, 149 RBIs, and a .380 batting average to lead the Cubs into the 1929 World Series.

November 22, 1934

Babe Herman, Guy Bush, and Jim Weaver to the Pittsburgh Pirates for Fred Lindstrom and Larry French. The Cubs appeared to be giving up two solid pitchers in Guy Bush—who had been a consistent winner for the Cubs from 1926 to 1934—and Jim Weaver—who had shown flashes of brilliance after coming over from the Browns during the '34 season. Not to mention the highly talented and enigmatic Floyd Caves "Babe" Herman, who'd put up some crooked numbers for the Brooklyn Dodgers before bouncing through Cincinnati to Chicago. Some suggested that Bush and Weaver were the price the Cubs had to pay to get the Pirates to *take* Herman off their hands. Still, the Cubs made out quite nicely. Weaver had two solid 14–8 seasons for Pittsburgh, but Bush went 24–35 in his final five seasons, and Herman went through three teams in three seasons before returning to Ebbets Field in 1945 at the age of 42 to take some curtain calls. Hall of Fame infielder Fred Lindstrom contributed to the 1935 pennant-winner, knocking in 62 runs in only 342 at bats, but was out of baseball in two years. Larry French, a 27-year-old lefty, was the key, winning 95 games for the Cubs from 1935 to 1941 and pitching well in losing postseason causes.

July 27, 1945

$97,000 to the New York Yankees for Hank Borowy. It wasn't really a trade, but like the Sutcliffe transaction 39 years later, it won the Cubs the pennant. Hank Borowy was the Yankees' best pitcher, 56–30 since he debuted in 1942. He was 10–5 at the time of the deal, one that had people scratching their heads and wondering whether Larry MacPhail was repaying the Cubs for previous deals that had benefited his team at Chicago's expense—or, more likely, whether he expected Borowy to be drafted imminently and was looking to make some money off his ace while he still could. MacPhail's motives may have been questionable, but Borowy's performance was not. He went 11–2 for the Cubs, beating the defending-champion Cardinals four times himself, including a clutch 6–5 win in Wrigley for his 20th that put the Cubs 2½ up with five to go. On the 29th of September, he pitched the pennant-clincher against the Pirates for his 21st win. At the time, only seven 20-game winners had pitched for two clubs in one season. The Cubs had acquired three of them: Borowy, Bob Wicker, and Jack Taylor. Rick Sutcliffe became the fourth.

June 15, 1949

Harry Walker and Peanuts Lowrey to the Cincinnati Reds for Hank Sauer and Frankie Baumholtz. In 1949, the Cubs brought veteran outfielder Hank Sauer over from the Reds in exchange for 1947 batting champion Harry Walker and small, contact-hitter Peanuts Lowrey. Lowrey was a reserve player for Cincinnati, then went to St. Louis, where he put together two fantastic pinch-hitting seasons, .481 in 1952 and .373 in 1953. Walker played only 165 games with the Reds before retiring; Sauer, though 32 at the time of the trade, had his best years ahead of him. In his first 39 games, he batted .367 with 15 home runs and 45 RBIs. He was with the Cubs until 1955, hitting 171 home runs, knocking in 100+ runs three times, and winning the MVP award in 1952. To sweeten the deal even further for the Cubs, reserve-outfielder and throw-in Frankie Baumholtz ended up playing a solid center field and hitting .300 over five seasons for Chicago.

Leo's Boys

The 1968–73 teams that competed for the National League East crown were led by home-grown talent such as Ernie Banks, Ron Santo, Billy Williams, and Ken Holtzman. But three key trades brought in a catcher, a slugger, two starters, and a closer to help push them almost over the top. Two of these were set up by a deal made before Leo Durocher arrived.

Borowy appears to have out-lived his usefulness with the Yankees.

Yankees GM Larry MacPhail, July 1945

Trading Places

The Cubs have been involved in two of the stranger trades in major-league history. On May 30, 1922, they traded Max Flack to the Cardinals for Cliff Heathcote between games of a doubleheader pitting St. Louis and Chicago. The change of scenery proved beneficial. Both outfielders, having gone hitless in the first game, got hits in the second game. And on September 22, 1987, Dickie Noles was traded to the Detroit Tigers for a player to be named later who turned out to be Dickie Noles.

October 17, 1962

George Altman, Don Cardwell, and Moe Thacker to the St. Louis Cardinals for Larry Jackson, Lindy McDaniel, and Jimmie Schaffer. The Cubs haven't gotten the best of the Cardinals very often, but this deal gave the Cubs a few good years and some great trade bait. George Altman was a star outfielder in Chicago, but he struggled in St. Louis and was a Met by 1964. The Cardinals used Don Cardwell to acquire Dick Groat from the Pirates. Larry Jackson won 24 games for the Cubs in 1964, while Lindy McDaniel led the league in saves in 1963. Soon after, both figured prominently in two of the best deals the Cubs have made.

December 2, 1965

Lindy McDaniel, Don Landrum, and Jim Rittwage to the San Francisco Giants for Randy Hundley and Bill Hands. In 1965, the Cubs sent veteran reliever Lindy McDaniel, outfielder Don Landrum, and a minor-league pitcher to the San Francisco Giants for two rookies: 23-year-old catcher Randy Hundley and 25-year-old pitcher Bill Hands. McDaniel had 10 more decent years left in his arm, but Landrum hit .186 and was done, and Jim Rittwage never played for the Giants. Hands, on the other hand, blossomed into a frontline pitcher, winning 92 games for the Cubs from 1966 to 1972, including 20 in 1969. Hundley turned in four consecutive solid seasons before succumbing to overwork, proving to be the best Cubs catcher since Gabby Hartnett, plugging the hole behind the plate that had been there since 1940.

April 23, 1968

Jim Ellis and Ted Savage to the Los Angeles Dodgers for Jim Hickman and Phil Regan. In 1968, the Cubs dealt veteran reserve-outfielder Ted Savage and young pitcher Jim Ellis to the Los Angeles Dodgers for first-baseman/outfielder Jim Hickman and reliever Phil Regan. Neither Savage nor Ellis contributed much of anything to the Dodgers. Both Hickman and Regan were 31, and their productive years in Chicago were brief, but the Cubs got four solid seasons out of Hickman, including a career year in 1970 (32 home runs, 115 RBIs, .315) and three good years out of Regan, including a 12-win, 17-save campaign in 1969.

April 21, 1966

Larry Jackson and Bob Buhl to the Philadelphia Phillies for Ferguson Jenkins, Adolfo Phillips, and John Herrnstein. The best of the three key trades that the Cubs made during the 1960s was the first one made after Leo Durocher arrived. Desperate for veteran pitching depth after the 1964 debacle in which a two-man rotation of Jim Bunning and Chris Short down the stretch cost them the pennant, Philadelphia sent 24-year-old outfielder Adolfo Phillips and a 22-year-old pitcher named Ferguson Jenkins to the Cubs for the 35-year-old Larry Jackson and the 37-year-old Bob Buhl. Phillips provided three productive seasons for the Cubs before being dealt to the Expos in early 1969. While Buhl and Jackson went 47–53 for the Phillies over the next three seasons and retired, Jenkins reeled off six consecutive 20-win seasons, racking up 147 wins in his first tour of duty with the Cubs, ending his career 17 years later with 284 victories and entering the Hall of Fame in 1991.

October 25, 1973

Ferguson Jenkins to the Texas Rangers for Bill Madlock and Vic Harris. Ironically, the Cubs made out quite handsomely when they dealt Ferguson Jenkins away, too. Paving the way for the deal that would send Ron Santo crosstown to the White Sox, the Cubs sent Jenkins to the Texas Rangers for a 22-year-old rookie third baseman named Bill Madlock. Though Jenkins had two big seasons left in his arm—winning 25 in 1974 and going 18–8 in 1978—he was pretty much a .500 pitcher after leaving Chicago. Madlock, however, was just getting started. He hit .313 as a rookie—losing the Rookie of the Year Award to Bake McBride in a questionable decision—then won two consecutive batting titles. The only other right-handed hitters to pull that off: Napoleon Lajoie, Honus Wagner, Rogers Hornsby, Al Simmons, Joe DiMaggio, and Roberto Clemente, Hall of Famers all. Unfortunately for the Cubs' faithful, Madlock was dealt away after the 1976 season in a trade discussed later in this chapter . . . under the heading "The Ugly."

Dallas Gets Busy

The biggest burst of trading in Cub history took place in the early 1980s, when Dallas Green took over the general manager responsibilities. Four deals over a 2½-year period helped the Cubs build the nucleus of their 1984 pennant-winner.

January 20, 1983

Vance Lovelace and Dan Cataline to the Los Angeles Dodgers for Ron Cey. In 1983, Dallas Green sent two minor leaguers to the Dodgers for veteran third-baseman Ron Cey. Cey was no Ron Santo or Bill Madlock, but the Penguin did provide four solid seasons at third base, hitting 84 home runs and holding down the position longer than anyone since Santo. Vance Lovelace and Dan Cataline never saw the light of day in Los Angeles.

March 26, 1984

Bill Campbell and Mike Diaz to the Philadelphia Phillies for Gary Matthews, Bob Dernier, and Porfi Altamarino. Dallas Green raided his old club quite effectively before the 1984 season, securing two-thirds of his starting outfield in exchange for an aging reliever (Campbell) and a rookie (Diaz) who never made it to the Phillies' major-league roster. Though neither Bob Dernier nor Gary Matthews could repeat his 1984 performance during four seasons in Chicago, they were critical contributors to the division-winner.

June 13, 1984

Joe Carter, Mel Hall, and Don Schulze to the Cleveland Indians for Rick Sutcliffe, George Frazier, and Ron Hassey. In the long run, the Cubs may have given away more than they got by sending away future World Series hero Joe Carter to the Indians for the frequently injured Rick Sutcliffe. But this deal won the Cubs the National League East in 1984, with Sutcliffe going 16–1 in the National League, winning the Cy Young Award, and tossing a shutout in the play-off opener while going deep in the third inning for good measure. Sutcliffe would be the fifth 20-game winner acquired in midseason. And if the parallels to Hank Borowy weren't enough, he too beat the Pirates to clinch a postseason berth. Sutcliffe also contributed 16 wins to the 1989 division-winner and provided veteran leadership to the Cubs for eight seasons.

January 27, 1982

Ivan DeJesus to the Philadelphia Phillies for Larry Bowa and Ryne Sandberg. They did it to the Phillies yet again. At the time this deal was made, it looked like a big win for the Phillies, who were getting a shortstop in Ivan DeJesus who was seven years younger than Larry Bowa. But the Cubs got a stabilizing force in Bowa . . . and a throw-in named Ryne Sandberg who went on to be an MVP, a Cubs legend, and one of the greatest second basemen in baseball history. DeJesus lasted three seasons with the Phillies, but his career was essentially over at 31 when he was run out of Philadelphia after Sandberg's magnificent 1984 season.

March 30, 1992

George Bell to the Chicago White Sox for Sammy Sosa and Ken Patterson. How sweet it is to find a deal with the hated White Sox on this list. Just before Opening Day 1992, the Cubs sent veteran slugger George Bell across town to the Sox in exchange for a free-swinging young outfielder named Sammy Sosa, who was nine years younger but already moving

Ugly for All Involved

One trade that was neither good nor bad for the Cubs but downright ugly for the New York Yankees and the player involved took place on July 12, 1987. "I just won you the pennant," Yankees owner George Steinbrenner said in a phone call to manager Lou Piniella. "I got you Steve Trout." Rainbow was a bit too tightly wrapped for New York, however, and he went 0–4 with a 6.60 ERA and countless errant pitches bouncing back to the screen. The Yankees finished fourth and shipped the frazzled pitcher off to Seattle at the end of the season, but the damage proved irreversible. A consistent winner until that point, Trout won only eight more games in his big-league career. In a wonderful irony, for the wild Trout, the Cubs received Bob Tewksbury, a pitcher who developed into one of the game's great control artists. Unfortunately, Tewksbury took three years to develop, and he ended up winning most of his games for the St. Louis Cardinals and none for the Cubs.

on to his third organization. The White Sox had finished second in 1991, despite Sosa's .203 batting average and frequent strikeouts, and were looking to win now. And at first, the Sox got the better of the deal, with Bell providing a 112-RBI season in 1992 while Sosa missed half the year with both a broken hand and a broken ankle. But Bell lost his power stroke during the 1993 pennant-winning campaign and proved to be a clubhouse distraction when he was benched during the play-offs. Ironically, the season Bell provided in 1993 was much like what Sosa had given them in 1991—some punch but a batting average down near the Mendoza Line. Had they kept Sosa, his 30/30 campaign with the Cubs and improved plate discipline might have been enough to get the Sox past the Blue Jays and into the World Series. Sosa blossomed into one of the most feared hitters in the National League, and this trade—already one of the best ever for the Cubs or any other team—just keeps getting better.

April 5, 1995

Geno Morones and Derek Wallace to the Kansas City Royals for Brian McRae. Like Bill Madlock, another Cubs standout whose stay in Chicago was brief was Brian McRae. Chicago gave up very little to land the center fielder before the strike-delayed 1995 season. Center field was an unsettled position in Chicago when he arrived, had been since the days of Andy Pafko, and continued to be when he left under something less than the best of terms 2½ years later. While he was there, however, he played hard and produced some of the best center-field numbers the Cubs had seen in 50 years: 12 homers, 27 steals, and .288 in 1995; 17 homers, 37 steals, and .276 in 1996. During the waning moments of the 1996 season, with the Cubs already mathematically eliminated from postseason play, McRae ran into the wall in Pittsburgh while making a great catch, then finished the season against the Pirates in Wrigley with another superb catch and a routine ground single up the middle that he stretched into a double. One of the streakiest hitters in the game and brutally honest, he slumped in 1997, was dealt to the Mets, and blasted the Cubs in the press on his way out.

December 12, 1997

Miguel Batista to the Montreal Expos for Henry Rodriguez. Like the Cubs of 20 years before, the Expos were in the position of having to shed high-priced talent before it left town as free agents with little compensation. The 27-year-old righty Miguel Batista, who had been winless in six starts with the Cubs in 1997, may turn out to be a capable major-league starter. Left-fielder Henry Rodriguez, however, paid immediate dividends. He hit 31 home runs in 1998, combining with Sammy Sosa for the most home runs by a pair of Cubs teammates, breaking the mark set by Hack Wilson and Gabby Hartnett in 1930.

The Bad

December 26, 1917

Cy Williams to the Philadelphia Phillies for Dode Paskert. Christmas comes a day late for the Phillies. Some might explain away this deal as an attack of conscience on the part of the Cubs after stealing Grover Cleveland Alexander from Philadelphia two weeks before. Dode Paskert played until 1920, Cy Williams until 1930, with Williams hitting 217 home runs and leading the league three times. Actually, it wasn't as bad a deal as it looks. Paskert, though 37, was a speedy center fielder and a better defensive player than Williams, and he helped the Cubs reach the World Series in 1918, when speed and defense ruled. Williams was already 30 at the time of the trade and assumed to be past his prime. His big numbers in Philadelphia were a function of his playing in the tiny Baker Bowl and getting to face livelier baseballs as the game changed to favor free-swinging sluggers in the 1920s. He was a dead-pull hitter, prompting Cubs manager Fred Mitchell to put on the Cy Williams shift—a forerunner of the Ted Williams shift.

October 8, 1936

Lon Warneke to the St. Louis Cardinals for Ripper Collins and Roy Parmelee.   The 1936 Cubs finished in a tie for second with the Cardinals, five games behind the New York Giants. A frustrated front office felt that another batter was necessary to put them over the top. Perhaps that strategy was sound, but its implementation was awful. They traded 27-year-old, three-time 20-game-winner Lon Warneke to the Cardinals for a 32-year-old backup first baseman (Ripper Collins) and a scatter-armed starter (Roy Parmelee). Quite simply, this deal cost the Cubs the pennant in 1937. The Cubs had plenty of offense in 1937 with Billy Herman hitting .335, Gabby Hartnett hitting .354, Frank Demaree hitting .324 with 115 RBIs, and Billy Jurges and Stan Hack pushing .300. With Phil Cavarretta's livelier bat in the lineup at first instead of Ripper Collins, it would have been an even more productive lineup. What the team lacked was a reliable fourth starter—starters other than Larry French, Tex Carleton, and Bill Lee going only 25–22 while Warneke went 18–11 for a fourth-place St. Louis team—and this kept the Cubs in second, three behind the Giants. Collins lasted only two seasons in Chicago, and Roy Parmelee one, while Warneke won 77 games for the Cardinals from 1937 to 1941.

Building a Winner . . . in Brooklyn

Four deals—three done directly with the Dodgers, twice with the woefully overmatched Jim Gallagher going up against Branch Rickey—helped build the Brooklyn Dodgers into a perennial pennant-contender.

June 11, 1934

Dolf Camilli to the Philadelphia Phillies for Don Hurst.   Philadelphia's Baker Bowl was the Coors Field of its day—dramatically inflating the numbers of moderately talented players—and Don Hurst was its Dante Bichette. Fixated on Baker Bowl superstars, the Cubs had already pried away Chuck Klein before the season, and now they wanted his hitting partner, Don Hurst. Klein had thus far shown very little in his brief stay in Chicago, while Hurst's numbers in 1933 had fallen off in a big way from his 1932 levels and had stayed there for the first 40 games of 1934. They brought him in, he hit .199 in 51 games and retired, and Dolf Camilli ended up hitting 239 home runs, winning an MVP Award, and leading the Dodgers into the 1941 World Series.

May 6, 1941

Billy Herman to the Brooklyn Dodgers for Charlie Gilbert, Johnny Hudson, and $65,000.   Hall of Famer Billy Herman had plenty of baseball left in him, hitting .291 for the pennant-winners of 1941, while Johnny Hudson hit .202 for the Cubs and was done. Dodgers GM Branch Rickey gave Jim Gallagher his choice of Charlie Gilbert or Pete Reiser, and Gallagher chose the slow-footed, punchless outfielder over the spectacular albeit injury-prone Reiser—though the 22-year-old Pistol Pete was already one month into a season in which he led the league in batting, slugging, doubles, triples, and runs!

June 6, 1944

Eddie Stanky to the Brooklyn Dodgers for Bob Chipman.   In 1944, the Cubs had to choose between two second basemen—having yet to find an adequate replacement for Billy Herman—and they selected Don Johnson. They traded away the loser in this battle, a scrappy 27-year-old named Eddie Stanky, to the Dodgers for lefty swingman Bob Chipman. While Chipman was going 26–25 over five seasons in Chicago, Stanky went on to spark the pennant-winning '47 Dodgers and '51 Giants while piling up 1,000 hits, 900 walks, and 700 runs.

June 15, 1951

Andy Pafko, Johnny Schmitz, Rube Walker, and Wayne Terwilliger to the Brooklyn Dodgers for Bruce Edwards, Joe Hatten, Gene Hermanski, and Eddie Miksis.   This deal was considered so lopsided at the time that a rumor went around that there was a player to be named later coming to the Cubs and that it would be Duke Snider. Andy Pafko played in the World Series for the 1952 Dodgers, then ended up contributing to the Milwaukee pennant-winners of 1957 and 1958. In return, the Cubs received a damaged backup catcher (Edwards) who played 105 games with the team, a 31-year-old, .250-hitting, reserve outfielder without power (Hermanski) who managed to last 174 games, a .250-hitting utility infielder (Miksis), and a 34-year-old lefty (Hatten) who went 6–10 and retired. The Cubs have been trying to find a long-term answer to the question mark left by Pafko in center field ever since.

June 4, 1953

Toby Atwell, Bob Schultz, Preston Ward, George Freese, Bob Addis, Gene Hermanski, and $150,000 to the Pittsburgh Pirates for Ralph Kiner, Joe Garagiola, Howie Pollett, and Catfish Metkovich.   Not many deals have involved this many mediocre players with funny-sounding names going from a last-place team to a second-to-last-place team. Strip it down to the bare essentials and you have $150,000 for Hall of Famer Ralph Kiner. This worked in 1928 with Rogers Hornsby, but Kiner—though only 30—had a lot less left than Hornsby. He hit 50 home runs in 264 games for the Cubs, but his days as a feared slugger—who led the league in home runs seven seasons in a row despite playing in cavernous Forbes Field—ended up coming to a sudden and ironic end once he finally got to play in a hitters' park.

May 13, 1960

Tony Taylor and Cal Neeman to the Philadelphia Phillies for Ed Bouchee and Don Cardwell.   It sure looked as though the Cubs made out in this deal when Don Cardwell threw a no-hitter in his first start. But Cardwell went only 30–44 in his 2½ seasons with the Cubs and bounced around the league before landing with the Mets in time to win his last five decisions in 1969. Ed Bouchee did little in his season-and-a-half in Chicago, ending up hitting .161 for the 1962 Mets. Tony Taylor, on the other hand, played 19 seasons in the majors, accumulating 2,007 hits and stealing 234 bases.

November 17, 1969

Oscar Gamble and Dick Selma to the Philadelphia Phillies for Johnny Callison.   After the 1969 season, the Cubs dealt Dick Selma and a 19-year-old outfielder named Oscar Gamble to the Philadelphia Phillies for 30-year-old outfielder Johnny Callison. Though the Phillies got the better of the Cubs, it was the Yankees and the crosstown White Sox who reaped the benefits. Callison had one mildly productive year left in him, while Gamble played until 1985, hitting most of his 200 home runs from 1973 on—once he escaped Philadelphia.

November 21, 1972

Bill North to the Oakland Athletics for Bob Locker.   Ken Holtzman to Oakland for Rick Monday had been a reasonable trade, though the Cubs should have expected even more in return for such a valuable commodity as a stud left-hander. But a year later, the Cubs sent a 25-year-old center fielder back to the Athletics—the speedy Bill North—for a 35-year-old reliever (Bob Locker) who would give the Cubs one good year and be dealt away for a mediocre relief pitcher named Horacio Pina. With North and Holtzman, the A's had a lead-off man and a frontline starter. With Monday and Locker/Pina, the Cubs had a power hitter trying to bat leadoff and a pair of back-line relievers.

May 17, 1976

Andre Thornton to the Montreal Expos for Steve Renko and Larry Biittner.   After stealing Andre Thornton from the Braves for an ancient Joe Pepitone, the Cubs wasted it by dealing him away. Thornton was a bust in Montreal, but he went on to put together seven productive seasons with the Cleveland Indians, hitting 30 home runs three times and knocking in 100 runs twice. Larry Biittner, the pride of Pocahontas, Iowa, managed 12 home runs and 62 RBIs in his only season as a Cubs regular. Steve Renko won 10 games for the Cubs in parts of two seasons before bouncing on to five other teams and retiring in 1983.

June 9, 1978
Woodie Fryman to the Montreal Expos for Jerry White.

December 14, 1978
Jerry White and Rodney Scott to the Montreal Expos for Sam Mejias. Jerry White proved to be a costly rental for the Cubs. They gave up reliever Woodie Fryman to acquire him—only to have the 38-year-old Fryman find the Fountain of Youth in Montreal, winning 29 games and saving 47 for Les Expos over 5½ seasons. The Cubs then returned White to Montreal, along with 25-year-old Rodney Scott, who went on to steal 102 bases for the Expos over the next three seasons. So, in exchange for a starting second baseman and a valuable reliever, the Cubs got 59 uneventful games out of Jerry White and a reserve outfielder named Sam Mejias who hit .182 in 31 games.

December 16, 1985
Billy Hatcher and Steve Engel to the Houston Astros for Jerry Mumphrey. Though he was only 25 and hadn't been given much of a chance to show the Cubs what he could do, Billy Hatcher was dealt to the Houston Astros for 33-year-old Jerry Mumphrey. A career .289 hitter, Mumphrey gave the Cubs two solid seasons in part-time duty and retired in 1988. Hatcher, though, was a productive player until 1993 with a knack for saving his best for big games. He hit a huge 14th-inning home run to prolong the sixth and deciding game of the 1986 NLCS for Houston, and he went 14-for-27 in the postseason for the world champion Reds in 1990.

December 5, 1988
Rafael Palmeiro, Jamie Moyer, and Drew Hall to the Texas Rangers for Mitch Williams, Paul Kilgus, Steve Wilson, Curtis Wilkerson, Luis Benitez, and Pablo Delgado. Andre Dawson expressed reservations about dealing Rafael Palmeiro, and he proved to be correct in his assessment. Wild Thing provided plenty of excitement in his two seasons in Wrigley, saving 36 games for the 1989 Cubs despite a fastball that was never really as fast as his chaotic pitching motion made it appear; Mitch Williams was later dealt for Bob Scanlan and Chuck McElroy, neither of whom developed into big-time pitchers. Paul Kilgus and Steve Wilson never developed into big-league pitchers at all, combining to win only 16 games for the Cubs. Jamie Moyer eventually developed into a consistent pitcher for Baltimore in 1993 and finally emerged as a frontline starter for Seattle in 1997. And after 12 seasons in the big leagues, Palmeiro was past 300 home runs and on his way to 2,000 hits. Ouch.

Sweet-Swinging Billy Palmeiro (the first 12 full seasons)

	HR	H	BA
Rafael Palmeiro	314	1,975	.294
Billy Williams	319	2,040	.295

Losing Winners

It wasn't just losing Rafael Palmeiro that made that 1988 deal so painful—it was also watching Jamie Moyer develop into a consistent left-handed winner in the American League. The Cubs have had to watch a lot of pitchers leave town and find success through the years. In addition to making the next four trades that are detailed in this section, Chicago let these 423 wins slip through their fingers:

Lefty **Fred Norman** went 104–98 in 11 seasons, primarily with the Reds, after a brief stay in Chicago. **Steve Stone** was the first Cub to be lost to free agency; he went 67–45 elsewhere, including a 25–7 Cy Young season in 1980. The Cubs gave up on **Rick Reuschel** *twice*. He was dealt to the Yankees in 1981, injured his arm, and returned to the Cubs in 1983. After Reuschel went 6–6 in two seasons, the Cubs let him leave as a free agent, and he pitched until he was 42, going 75–60 for the Pirates and Giants. The Cubs acquired **Milt Wilcox** from Cleveland in 1975, used him exclusively in relief, then released him. He went 97–83 and won a game for the Tigers in the 1984 World Series.

Perhaps most aggravating, however, was the case of **Russ "Mad Monk" Meyer.** Meyer, along with his hard screwball and notorious temper, was sold to Philadelphia at the end of a

1948 season in which he'd gone 10–10 for a last-place team. He won 79 games over the next seven seasons with three pennant-winners and went 24–3 against the Cubs before returning to Chicago in 1956 to win one game. For his career, he ended up 14–18 with the Cubs and 80–65 elsewhere, while the Cubs' record in games in which Meyer earned a decision was 17–42.

November 30, 1967
Ray Culp to the Boston Red Sox for Rudy Schlesinger.   Whatever position Rudy Schlesinger played is lost in the mists of time, because he only came to bat once in the majors, as a pinch hitter for the Boston Red Sox. Ray Culp, who'd been acquired from the Philadelphia Phillies for Dick Ellsworth, was dumped after one 8–11 season with Leo Durocher in 1967. He went on to win 71 games for the Boston Red Sox—including a 17–8 season in 1969, when the Cubs could have sure used him, and teaming up with Ellsworth of all people to win 32 games in 1968.

April 25, 1969
Joe Niekro, Gary Ross, and Francisco Libran to the San Diego Padres for Dick Selma.
Sometimes it takes a few years to truly gauge how a deal worked out. When Joe Niekro was dealt to the Padres for Dick Selma (who managed to get the Cubs coming and going), it looked for years like a minor transaction that got the Cubs a 10-game winner for the 1969 season and gave away nothing of value. Then, 10 years after the deal went down, Niekro—having bounced through four organizations since the Cubs, with much of his time spent in middle relief—suddenly learned how to pitch. At the age of 35, he had back-to-back 20-win seasons for the Houston Astros. He pitched until he was 44 and racked up 221 wins, calling it quits 14 years after Selma threw his last pitch.

August 31, 1973
Larry Gura to the Texas Rangers for Mike Paul.   Arizona State All-American Larry Gura was with the Cubs for four years, buried in Leo Durocher's bullpen, going 3–5 on the rare occasions when they let him start. He was traded to the Rangers (who promptly gave him away to the Yankees for catcher Duke Sims), and he ended up going 123–90, mostly with the Royals, and also contributed two play-off wins. In return for this valuable 100-win lefty, the Cubs received lefty Mike Paul, who went 0–2 and retired.

May 2, 1975
Burt Hooton to the Los Angeles Dodgers for Geoff Zahn and Eddie Solomon.
Knuckle-curve-artist Burt "Happy" Hooton is best known for serving up the first of Reggie Jackson's three home runs in Game Six of the 1977 World Series. But he was a solid starter who'd been 35–3 at the University of Texas, a three-time All-American, and the author of a 19-K performance in the Pacific Coast League. He went on to win 117 games over 11 seasons after leaving Chicago, including five postseason victories for the Dodgers. Geoff Zahn was no slouch either, piling up 111 victories in a 13-year career. He could have replaced Ken Holtzman, but, unfortunately, only two of Zahn's wins came in a Cubs uniform. He didn't become a consistent winner until he left Chicago, leaving the Cubs with nothing to show for a deal that solidified the starting rotation of a perennial pennant-contender.

Burning Firemen
Throughout their recent history, the Cubs have also shown an uncanny knack for dealing/giving away middle relievers who become top closers elsewhere—*three from the 1981 staff alone!* In the following *10* trades, spanning both "The Bad" and "The Ugly," the Cubs gave up *11* minor leaguers, middle relievers, or "washed-up" veterans who went on to record *1,550* saves elsewhere. Throw in the releases of 31-year-old Bill Landrum after the 1988 season and 38-year-old Doug Jones during the 1996 season, and the total goes up to 1,656 . . . and counting.

	Saves for the Cubs	*Saves Elsewhere*
Dennis Eckersley	0	390
Ron Perranoski	0	179
Jay Howell	0	155
Jim Brewer	0	132
Ron Davis	0	130
Willie Hernandez	20	127
Bill Caudill	1	105
Craig Lefferts	1	100
Dave LaRoche	9	94
Donnie Moore	5	84
Bill Landrum	0	56
Moe Drabowsky	1	54
Doug Jones	2	50
Totals	39	1,656

August 19, 1981

Bill Caudill and Jay Howell to the New York Yankees for Pat Tabler. Consider, for example, the deal in 1981 that sent two players to be named later to the Yankees for Pat Tabler. Tabler lasted two seasons with the Cubs, hitting .210 in limited infield duty. The players to be named turned out to be Jay Howell and Bill Caudill, who had combined for one save in their young careers but who went on to save 260 more games in the big leagues.

June 10, 1978

Ron Davis to the New York Yankees for Ken Holtzman. Jay Howell wasn't the first time the Yankees were able to pluck an unknown out of the Cubs' bullpen and turn him into a productive reliever. In 1978, the Cubs reacquired Ken Holtzman for a gangly minor-league pitcher named Ron Davis. Holtzman went 6–12 before retiring in 1979. Davis became baseball's first setup specialist, going 27–10 for the Yankees while getting the games from the starters to Rich Gossage. With the Twins, Davis became a closer, and he retired in 1988 with 130 saves.

February 25, 1975

Dave LaRoche and Brock Davis to the Cleveland Indians for Milt Wilcox. As desperate as the Cubs were to acquire Dave LaRoche, they sure gave up on him in a hurry. They traded Bill Hands and young, hard-throwing Joe Decker to the Minnesota Twins for him before the 1973 season. With the Cubs, LaRoche was 9–7 with nine saves in two seasons, setting up Bob Locker, Jack Aker, and Oscar Zamora, only to be dealt away for Milt Wilcox, who was released after one season to win 97 games elsewhere. LaRoche went on to become a stopper for the Indians and Angels, recording 94 more saves over the next nine seasons.

October 17, 1979

Donnie Moore to the St. Louis Cardinals for Mike Tyson. It took Donnie Moore six years and four organizations to establish himself as a top closer, but he eventually did in 1986 with the California Angels. Unfortunately, he was never the same after giving up a game-winning Dave Henderson home run in the '86 play-offs that kept the Red Sox alive and kept the Angels from their first World Series appearance. Still, he earned 84 saves in nine seasons after leaving Chicago, in return for which the Cubs got a .226-hitting utility infielder named Mike Tyson for 1½ seasons.

December 7, 1983

Craig Lefferts, Carmelo Martinez, and Fritz Connally to the San Diego Padres for Scott Sanderson. Craig Lefferts was coming off of a promising rookie season for the Cubs when he was dealt along with a 22-year-old rookie slugger (Martinez) to the Padres for Scott

Sanderson. The injury-plagued Sanderson managed only 42 wins in his six seasons with the Cubs. Carmelo Martinez had a few productive seasons with the Padres, while Lefferts blossomed into a dependable reliever who compiled 100 saves after leaving the Cubs. This deal came back to haunt the Cubs immediately, as Lefferts threw four scoreless innings in the play-offs against Chicago, winning both Game Four and Game Five of the NLCS in 1984. He followed that up with another six shutout innings in the World Series, allowing only three hits in the postseason.

May 22, 1983
Willie Hernandez to the Philadelphia Phillies for Dick Ruthven. Dick Ruthven won 22 games in his four injury-riddled years with the Cubs, while Willie Hernandez went on to register 127 saves over the next seven seasons. As with Oscar Gamble and Dolf Camilli before him, the Phillies mistakenly dealt away Hernandez to the Tigers for John Wockenfuss and Glenn Wilson after the 1983 season and watched him turn into the Cy Young Award winner who helped pitch Detroit to the 1984 World Championship.

April 8, 1960
Ron Perranoski, John Goryl, Lee Handley, and $25,000 to the Los Angeles Dodgers for Don Zimmer. The Cubs tradition of dealing away relievers to blossom elsewhere can actually be traced back all the way to 1960. Rather than give the third-base job to a hot rookie named Ron Santo who'd torn it up in spring training, the Cubs opened the vault to bring in Don Zimmer. Santo had the third-base job in a few months, anyway, and Zimmer was left exposed in the 1962 expansion draft after publicly criticizing the rotating-head-coach system and its effect on Santo's progress. Ron Perranoski became one of the first pure relievers, starting only one game while he went on to record 179 saves as a stopper for the Dodgers and Twins.

March 13, 1961
Moe Drabowsky and Seth Morehead to the Milwaukee Braves for Andre Rodgers and Daryl Robertson. Moe Drabowsky spent five seasons with the Cubs, primarily as a starter and a prankster, compiling a 32–41 record before being dealt for two shortstops. Andre Rodgers gave the Cubs four unspectacular seasons as Ernie Banks's replacement at shortstop while the pride of Cripple Creek, Colorado, Daryl Robertson, managed only 19 big-league at bats. Drabowsky went on to record 54 saves—not a bad total for the 1960s and early 1970s—for five different teams, with his finest hour coming in the Baltimore Orioles' sweep of the Los Angeles Dodgers in the 1966 World Series. Called on to relieve Dave McNally in the third inning of Game One, he finished the game, yielding only one hit and striking out 11 to get the win.

December 13, 1963
Jim Brewer and Facundo Barragan to the Los Angeles Dodgers for Dick Scott. The highlight of Jim Brewer's time with the Cubs was a sucker punch from Billy Martin that required three eye operations and resulted in a $100,000 judgment. He was 4–13 in four seasons as a Cub swingman. Warren Spahn taught him the screwball, and he lasted another 13 seasons, recording 132 saves along the way. Dick Scott gave up 10 hits and five runs in his only 4⅓ innings with the Cubs and retired.

The Ugly

April 3, 1987
Dennis Eckersley to the Oakland Athletics for David Wilder, Brian Guinn, and Mark Leonette. Of all the relief-pitcher trades the Cubs have made that came back to haunt them, none is more painful than the deal that sent Dennis Eckersley to the Athletics for three

minor leaguers. Apparently finished at 32, Eck resurrected his career in Oakland. He went on to become one of the most dominant relievers in the history of baseball, saving 390 games over the next 12 seasons and pitching himself right into first-ballot Hall of Fame consideration. Neither David Wilder, Brian Guinn, nor Mark Leonette ever appeared in a Cubs uniform.

December 9, 1980

Bruce Sutter to the St. Louis Cardinals for Leon Durham, Ken Reitz, and Tye Waller. The Cubs dealt relief-ace Bruce Sutter in one of a number of money-saving moves that were made by the Wrigley family toward the end of their reign. At the time of the deal, Sutter was arguably the top reliever in the game, leading the National League in saves in both 1979 and 1980, but he'd received what was then a jaw-dropping salary of $700,000 after going to arbitration during the 1979 off-season. In return for one of the greatest relievers in baseball history, the Cubs received a third baseman (Reitz) who lasted one season and hit .215, a utility player (Waller) who managed 92 at bats in a Cubs uniform, and a young prospect (Durham) who had five good seasons in Chicago but never really developed into the slugger he was billed to be. Sutter went on to lead the league three of the next four seasons for the Cardinals, tying Mordecai Brown's National League mark of four consecutive seasons as the saves leader, and to bring them a World Championship in 1982 before blowing out his arm four years later.

December 8, 1987

Lee Smith to the Boston Red Sox for Calvin Schiraldi and Al Nipper. Lee Smith put the finishing touches on his Hall of Fame career in Boston, St. Louis, New York, Baltimore, California, Cincinnati, and Montreal, recording nearly 300 saves for these seven teams and hanging it up in 1997 with an all-time-record 478. Calvin Schiraldi and Al Nipper combined to go 14–23 for the Cubs and were both gone inside of two years.

December 11, 1976

Bill Madlock and Rob Sperring to the San Francisco Giants for Bobby Murcer, Steve Ontiveros, and Andy Muhlstock. After his second consecutive batting title, the Cubs traded the 25-year-old Mad Dog to the Giants for the 30-year-old Bobby Murcer and a struggling young third baseman named Steve Ontiveros. Murcer lasted 2½ largely unproductive seasons in Chicago. Ontiveros managed only two full seasons in Chicago, putting up decent numbers in 1977 and 1979. Bill Madlock went on to win two more batting titles in 11 seasons—giving him four, which is more than anyone else in the National League except Honus Wagner, Rogers Hornsby, Stan Musial, Roberto Clemente, Pete Rose, and Tony Gwynn. He retired in 1987 with 2,008 hits and a .305 lifetime batting average. Madlock also became the only player since World War II to hit at least .340 for *two* teams.

April 16, 1938

Curt Davis, Clyde Shoun, Tuck Stainback, and $185,000 to the St. Louis Cardinals for Dizzy Dean. Ten years after buying Rogers Hornsby from the Boston Braves, the Cubs tried to turn the trick again with the 27-year-old Dizzy Dean. A broken toe suffered in 1937 had led to an altered pitching motion, a sore arm, and an uncustomarily average 13–10 record. Dean's arm woes continued with the Cubs in 1938. Brought in as a gate attraction, he managed only 16 wins in Chicago before retiring in 1941. Dean did win a crucial game in the 1938 pennant drive but had nothing left when he took the mound against the Yankees in Game Two of the World Series. Though Curt Davis was eight years older than Dean, he had a lot more innings left in his arm. He went on to win 100 more games in the big leagues, including 22 in 1939 as he helped lead the Cardinals past the Cubs in the standings.

June 15, 1964

Lou Brock, Jack Spring, and Paul Toth to the St. Louis Cardinals for Ernie Broglio, Bobby Shantz, and Doug Clemens. The Cardinals got the better of the Cubs in three of the worst deals in the franchise's history. Easily the most lopsided of these transactions—

The Cubs traded a horse and got two ponies.

Frank Robinson, on the deal that sent Lee Smith to Boston for Calvin Schiraldi and Al Nipper

We got Dizzy's spirit, courage, and enthusiasm— in addition to his arm.

Philip Wrigley

I ain't what I used to be, but who the hell is?

Dizzy Dean

arguably the worst trade in baseball history—was the midseason deal in 1964 that sent a 25-year-old outfielder named Lou Brock to the Cardinals. The Cardinals got a Hall of Famer and the catalyst of their two championship teams of 1964 and 1967. In return, the Cubs received a reserve outfielder (Clemens) who lasted 182 games, a classy albeit ancient pitcher (Shantz) who recorded no victories for the Cubs, and a once-capable starter (Broglio) they didn't really need and who broke down in Chicago, going 7–19 over the next three seasons before retiring. Brock played until 1979, finishing his career with 938 steals (second all-time), 3,023 hits, and a .391 average and a record 14 steals in his three World Series appearances. To add insult to ineptitude, he collected his 3,000th hit while playing against the Cubs in St. Louis on August 13, 1979.

THE FARM SYSTEM

It's no accident that the decline of the Cubs coincides with the rise of baseball's farm systems. No one has ever accused the Cubs' system of being a model of efficiency. Then again, like just about every other ball club except the Cardinals and the Yankees, they got a late start on establishing a system of farm clubs in the first place.

Prior to the 1920s, the minor leagues operated as independent entities. Their teams made some money by taking young players signed by big-league clubs and giving them a place to hone their skills, but the big money came from finding and signing their own talented amateurs and selling them to a big-league ball club at a huge profit. For example, Hall of Fame pitcher Lefty Grove was sold to the Philadelphia Athletics by the Baltimore Orioles of the International League for $100,000 before the 1925 season. Many teams couldn't afford to—or didn't want to—pay these prices. The St. Louis Cardinals, a team run by legendary baseball innovator Branch Rickey, did something about it. Once it became legal in 1921, they began buying minor-league teams at various levels and signing players to stock them, thereby establishing the first farm system. The best climbed the ladder to St. Louis; ones who didn't make the cut were sold to other major-league teams at a profit (Cubs star pitcher Bill Lee, for example).

By the 1930s—acting primarily in their own economic self-interest—the other major-league teams had followed the Cardinals' lead and began systematizing their own collection of farm teams. The Cubs didn't establish a formal system until the 1940s. They did have two of the more lucrative minor-league markets for their top minor-league teams: the Los Angeles Angels in the Pacific Coast League (a team that played its games in Los Angeles's Wrigley Field, first home of the major-league Los Angeles Angels) and the Milwaukee Brewers in the American Association. Unfortunately, Philip Wrigley had his own ideas about what his Los Angeles and Milwaukee teams were in business to do. Rather than exist to serve his Chicago Cubs, he wanted these teams to operate as independent, profit-driven organizations. As a result, when the farm system did produce a talented player, the minor-league club might have sold him to another major-league team willing to pay a higher price than the Cubs!

Consider pitcher Whitlow Wyatt. After nine years as a mediocre big-league pitcher with a nasty reputation as a headhunter, he found himself in the minors in 1938. While pitching for Milwaukee that season, he won the Triple Crown—wins, strikeouts, and ERA—in a league, incidentally, where Ted Williams was doing the hitting equivalent for Minneapolis. But rather than join the Cubs in 1939, he was sold to the Brooklyn Dodgers, where he reeled off five solid seasons, including a league-leading 22-win campaign for the 1941 pennant-winning team.

The Cubs could have used Wyatt, considering how little success they've had producing their own pitchers. Of the 11 Hall of Fame pitchers who've played for the Cubs at one time, none began his career in Chicago (a streak that Lee Smith and Greg Maddux will put to a bittersweet end once they become #12 and—appropriately, in Maddux's case—#13). Hall of Famers Mordecai Brown, Grover Cleveland Alexander, and Ferguson Jenkins have already appeared in this chapter under the heading "The Good"—along with Orvie Overall, Hippo Vaughn, Larry French, Hank Borowy, Larry Jackson, Bill Hands, and Rick Sutcliffe, as well as Claude Passeau and Milt Pappas.

The list of top starting pitchers produced by the Cubs' farm system is much shorter—and features a long and interesting gap between 1948 and 1965.

Developing Young Pitchers

This gap begins in 1948 when 22-year-old Bob Rush made his debut. Miscast as an ace out of necessity for most of his career, he was a good starter on lousy teams who went on to win 110 games for the Cubs. Due to bad luck, misuse, or sheer lack of talent, it didn't get any better than Rush for the Cubs until 1965, when 19-year-old Ken Holtzman came to the big leagues. It is no coincidence that the Cubs never finished higher than fifth between 1948 and 1965, came in last four times, and had a winning record (82–80 in 1963) only once. Nor is it a coincidence that Holtzman's arrival and development accompanied the team's return to contention.

Between Rush and Holtzman, the Cubs gave a first taste of the big leagues to countless pitchers—simply because the quality of the veteran pitchers on the staff offered them no reason not to try something new. There were 26 pitchers who were 22 or younger when pressed into action, 18 of whom were called on to start—with the game tied at zero and defeat not yet assured.

Often, making it to the big leagues by such a young age is a leading indicator of impressive performances to come (for example, Dwight Gooden, Bob Feller, Greg Maddux). More often than not, if you want to make it to Cooperstown, your odds will go up exponentially if you're in the majors before you turn 23.

The 1966 Orioles won a World Series with 20-year-old Jim Palmer and 21-year-old Wally Bunker in a rotation where Steve Barber was the grizzled veteran at 27. The Kansas City Royals duplicated the feat 19 years later with Bret Saberhagen and Mark Gubicza. While the Cubs struggled to improve on Bob Rush, every other major-league team (even three of the first four expansion teams of '61 and '62) could boast of a young pitcher who grew up to be a frontline starter. The Dodgers came up with five. The list is a virtual who's who of starting pitching during the '50s, '60s, and '70s:

Homegrown Pitching Talent

Angels	Dean Chance
Astros	Larry Dierker
Athletics	Catfish Hunter
Braves	Johnny Antonelli
Cardinals	Steve Carlton
Dodgers	Carl Erskine, Johnny Podres, Sandy Koufax, Don Drysdale, Bill Singer
Giants	Juan Marichal
Indians	Herb Score, Sam McDowell, Tommy John
Orioles	Milt Pappas, Dave McNally, Jim Palmer

Phillies	Robin Roberts, Curt Simmons, Rick Wise, Ferguson Jenkins
Pirates	Vern Law, Bob Friend, Steve Blass
Red Sox	Wilbur Wood
Reds	Claude Osteen, Mike Cuellar, Jim Maloney
Senators (Rangers)	Joe Coleman
Senators (Twins)	Camilio Pascual, Jim Kaat
Tigers	Mickey Lolich, Denny McLain
White Sox	Billy Pierce
Yankees	Whitey Ford, Mel Stottlemyre

This list doesn't include any of the top pitchers who happened to reach the majors after their 22nd birthday, such as Hall of Famers Bob Gibson, Jim Bunning, Phil Niekro, and Gaylord Perry, or 200-game winners Lew Burdette, Gary Peters, Larry Jackson, Frank Lary, Luis Tiant, and Jim Perry.

You won't find any names like those on the Cubs' lineup card. Here are the 18 sacrificial lambs that the Cubs sent out to the mound to start games between Rush and Holtzman:

Between Rush and Holtzman: Starters' Career Records

DEBUT	PITCHER	G	W–L
1958	Dick Ellsworth	310	108–132
1964	Fred Norman	268	98–98
1958	John Buzhardt	200	63–81
1957	Glen Hobbie	170	52–74
1956	Moe Drabowsky	154	43–73
1957	Dick Drott	101	24–43
1957	Bob Anderson	93	29–35
1962	Cal Koonce	90	29–34
1960	Jim Brewer	35	7–16
1955	Don Kaiser	35	6–15
1956	Johnny Briggs	21	6–8
1948	Dan Carlsen	7	2–4
1964	Sterling Slaughter	6	2–2
1962	Morrie Steevens	1	0–1
1964	John Flavin	1	0–1
1959	Joe Schaffernoth	1	0–0
1960	Dick Burwell	1	0–0
1962	George Gerberman	1	0–0

Not a winning record in the group.

Dick Drott possessed a devastating curveball, and he might have been one of the greats if his arm hadn't blown out. His rookie season in 1957 was the best for a Cubs pitcher until Kerry Wood and featured a club record that Wood eclipsed in stunning fashion 41 years later: 15 SOs in a game.

Don Kaiser was a bonus baby, signed for $50,000 out of East Central State Teachers College in Oklahoma. He'd been 49–1 in high school, with seven no-hitters and two perfect games. In his first start, he threw a two-hitter against the Dodgers in 1956 (in a game he didn't know he was to start until 20 minutes before showtime).

Fred Norman was a little left-hander on whom the Cubs, like many other teams, gave up too soon. He actually broke in with the Athletics in 1962. Before landing in Cincinnati, where he strung together seven consecutive seasons of 10+ wins, he passed from Chicago to Los Angeles to St. Louis to San Diego. The Cubs, however, have the right to kick themselves more than most. His 1967 stat line—his last season with the Cubs—is one of the more interesting you'll see. He pitched one inning and struck out the side. He didn't play in the majors again for three years.

Moe Drabowsky and Jim Brewer were converted to relievers, Drabowsky an infrequently spectacular one and Brewer a consistent performer.

Others may have been victims of the rotating-head-coaches experiment of 1961 and 1962, such as Glen Hobbie and Bob Anderson. At the time, Anderson was coming off a 12–13 season in 1960, his first as a full-time starter; it turned out to be his only 10-win season in the majors. Hobbie had won 16 in both 1959 and 1960; he went 12–27 in 1961 and 1962. A third was Dick Ellsworth, who was 21 and 22 during the worst years of the College of Coaches, going 19–31. Once Bob Kennedy was established in 1963, he won 22—only to go on to lose 22. Later with the Red Sox, he became the first player to win a second Comeback Player of the Year Award.

Big-Time Left-Handers

Dick Ellsworth leads us nicely into another topic: ace lefties, a rare and precious thing. Ellsworth is the only Cubs lefty to win 20 games since Hippo Vaughn in 1919. That's once in 79 seasons—and counting. Over that span, 81 lefties in the major leagues have had 150 20-win seasons—but only one Cub. It probably would have been two if the Cubs hadn't dealt away Holtzman (the only key member of the 1969 team to end up in a World Series) after the 1971 season.

Compare the Cubs' left-handed performance with that of other major-league teams:

Left-Handed 20-Game Winners (1920–98)

TEAM	20-W LEFTIES (SEASONS)	LONGEST DROUGHT	MOST RECENT
Yankees	8 (16)	23 years	1996 Andy Pettitte
Dodgers	8 (11)	19 years	1986 Fernando Valenzuela
White Sox	7 (12)	23 years	1975 Jim Kaat
Cardinals	7 (8)	27 years	1985 John Tudor
Giants	6 (12)	25 years	1973 Ron Bryant
Orioles	6 (12)	33 years	1980 Scott McGregor
Athletics	5 (14)	23 years	1975 Vida Blue
Reds	4 (6)	45 years	1988 Danny Jackson
Twins	4 (4)	33 years	1988 Frank Viola
Indians	4 (4)	38 years	1970 Sam McDowell
Braves	3 (19)	42 years	1998 Tom Glavine
Tigers	3 (7)	28 years	1972 Mickey Lolich
Pirates	3 (6)	53 years	1991 John Smiley
Phillies	2 (6)	50 years	1982 Steve Carlton
Red Sox	2 (3)	45 years	1953 Mel Parnell
Brewers	2 (2)	12 years	1986 Ted Higuera
Mets	2 (2)	14 years	1990 Frank Viola

continued

Lefty Corcoran?

Though Gus Krock is recognized as Chicago's first lefty, technically it was Hall of Famer Larry Corcoran. In the midst of a 20–9 drubbing at the hands of Providence on June 16, 1884, Corcoran pitched both right-handed and left-handed.

TEAM	20-W LEFTIES (SEASONS)	LONGEST DROUGHT	MOST RECENT
Padres	1 (2)	22 years	1976 Randy Jones
Expos	1 (1)	20 years	1978 Ross Grimsley
Mariners	1 (1)	20 years	1997 Randy Johnson
Royals	1 (1)	25 years	1973 Paul Splittorff
Angels	1 (1)	28 years	1970 Clyde Wright
Cubs	**1 (1)**	**44 years**	**1963 Dick Ellsworth**
Blue Jays	0 (0)	22 years	
Astros	0 (0)	37 years	
Rangers	0 (0)	38 years	

The Cubs are at the bottom among the original 16 and worse than most expansion teams. Let's not sugarcoat it. The Cubs haven't been particularly successful at developing starting pitching, but they've been one of the absolute worst at signing, keeping, and/or acquiring top left-handed starters.

This is not a good thing to be bad at. Only five teams have won a World Series without a left-handed starter in either their regular or postseason rotation: 1984 Tigers, 1947 Yankees, 1940 Reds, 1935 Tigers, and 1903 Red Sox. The 1984 Tigers had lefty Cy Young Award–winner Willie Hernandez in their bullpen, while the 1947 Yankees also had a lefty relief ace, Joe Page, who won a game and saved another in the World Series.

A brief digression may help explain the Cubs' postseason woes. Consider what some other long-suffering teams have in common.

Boston Red Sox

Two left-handed 20-game winners since Babe Ruth. The Sox are 2–5 in World Series games started by one of their rare lefties, including two of their Game Seven defeats. Perhaps the 1986 train wreck would have turned out differently if they hadn't traded away lefties John Tudor and Bob Ojeda (the Mets' starter in Boston's Game Six nightmare). Perhaps this has something to do with the fact that the best left-handed pitcher in team history is Babe Ruth.

Cleveland Indians

The Indians last won a World Series in 1948, paced by 20-game-winning lefty Gene Bearden. They've had two star-crossed ones since: Herb Score, whose brilliant career was ruined by a line drive to the eye, and Sam McDowell, who battled alcoholism. The 1995 and 1997 teams started four righties in the World Series and lost in six and seven.

Philadelphia Phillies

Philadelphia endured the second-longest drought in major-league history when the club went 50 years between 20-win lefties (Eppa Rixey and Chris Short). It's no coincidence that the Phillies' only title and their only consistent success came during the prime of Steve Carlton's career.

Anaheim Angels

One 20-win lefty in team history and no World Series appearances. A long, left-handed tradition of high-profile flameouts (Bo Belinsky), dead arms (Frank Tanana, Jim Abbott), and inconsistency (Mark Langston, Chuck Finley). Most of their successful seasons have featured staffs led by lefties, with two of their mere five postseason wins recorded by southpaws (Tommy John, John Candelaria).

San Diego Padres
Other than Randy Jones, the best it's gotten is 16 wins from Tim Lollar in 1982. Their first trip to the World Series (1984) was the only time they've featured three capable lefties in their rotation.

Montreal Expos
Other than Ross Grimsley, the best it's gotten is 16 wins from Bill Lee in 1979. What could have been their lone trip to the World Series (the 1994 strike season) was the only time they've featured three capable lefties in their rotation.

Texas Rangers
Never even so much as a left-handed 18-game winner. Perhaps things would have been different if they hadn't traded Claude Osteen for a thyroid condition with power (Frank Howard), rushed a high schooler to the majors to build attendance (David Clyde), given away Larry Gura and Dave Righetti to the Yankees, or packaged Wilson Alvarez with Sammy Sosa to rent Harold Baines for a few months. They tempted fate again in 1998 by dealing Darren Oliver. Best left-handed pitcher in team history? Kenny Rogers. Enough said.

Houston Astros
Another Texas team without so much as a left-handed 18-game winner. No coincidence that their best season came with the acquisition of Randy Johnson—though he may have brought some bad karma with him for the postseason after dogging it in Seattle for half the season.

Chicago White Sox
The exception. Their fans have gone longer without a title than the Red Sox, perhaps because throwing a World Series is even less forgivable than selling Babe Ruth. Yet, only the Yankees and Dodgers have had more 20-win lefties than the White Sox. The Sox have also been the only club to feature two different pairs of 20-win lefties: Wilbur Wood and Jim Kaat in 1974 and Dickie Kerr and Lefty Williams in 1920 (Williams had 22 wins at the time of his suspension-for-life in September). Perhaps this is the curse of Lefty Williams—that the White Sox will be destined to continually produce the vital ingredient for a World Championship, yet still be unable to attain it.

Replacing Ken Holtzman

If not for divine intervention in 1969, Ken Holtzman would probably have won 20 and perhaps repeated the feat in 1970 as the Cubs returned to the postseason to take on the Baltimore Orioles again. He didn't, the Cubs dumped him when he fell out of favor with Leo Durocher, it was the Oakland Athletics he helped to three consecutive titles, and the Cubs have been trying to replace him ever since. It's proven to be as thorny a problem as replacing Ron Santo . . . with even Ken Holtzman being brought back to try to do it. Their greatest success may have come during the 1994, 1995, and 1996 seasons—when they simply took the zero.

Here they are, from Paul Assenmacher to Geoff Zahn, with a little Mitch Williams along the way—choices ranging from inspired to desperate to foolhardy. As a whole, they came up with a record of 140–226, a percentage good enough for 100 losses in a 162-game schedule.

Pretenders to the Holtzman Throne

YEAR(S)	PITCHER	STARTS	W–L
1983–87	Steve Trout	123	41–37
1986–88	Jamie Moyer	79	26–34
1991–92	Danny Jackson	33	5–14
1993	Greg Hibbard	31	15–11
1978–79	Ken Holtzman	26	6–12
1977–78	Dave Roberts	26	1–1
1997–98	Terry Mulholland	25	9–12
1985	Ray Fontenot	23	6–9
1989	Paul Kilgus	23	6–10
1989–90	Steve Wilson	23	5–9
1974, 1976	Ken Frailing	19	5–9
1981–82	Ken Kravec	14	1–5
1979–80	Doug Capilla	12	1–9
1975–76	Geoff Zahn	12	0–7
1973, 1985	Larry Gura	11	2–6
1977, 1979–80, 1983	Willie Hernandez	11	0–8
1978	Woodie Fryman	9	1–4
1986	Guy Hoffman	8	2–2
1985	Steve Engel	8	1–5
1972	Juan Pizarro	7	1–5
1983	Craig Lefferts	5	1–1
1992	Jeff Robinson	5	1–1
1987	Mike Mason	4	2–1
1986	Drew Hall	4	1–2
1974	Dave LaRoche	4	1–1
1990	Lance Dickson	3	0–3
1975	Willie Prall	3	0–2
1978, 1981	Dave Geisel	3	0–0
1972	Dan McGinn	2	0–2
1974	Jim Kremmel	2	0–1
1990	Mitch Williams	2	0–1
1979	George Riley	1	0–1
1989	Joe Kraemer	1	0–1
1973	Mike Paul	1	0–0
1990	Paul Assenmacher	1	0–0
1992	Ken Patterson	1	0–0
1992	Dennis Rasmussen	1	0–0

THE AMATEUR DRAFT

Baseball's Amateur Draft was instituted in 1965 to stop the upward spiral of bonuses and to spread talent more evenly. Too many teams were like the Cubs: spending a lot of money (a then-record $130,000 on Danny Murphy in 1960, for example) while the Yankees and Dodgers were coming away with the talent.

The first pick of the draft was future Cub Rick Monday, to the Kansas City Athletics. Not bad, considering that other first picks included overrated players (Steve Chilcott, Danny Goodwin, Al Chambers, Shawn Abner) as well as the injury plagued, self-destructive, or unlucky (Ron Blomberg, David Clyde, Darryl Strawberry, Ben McDonald, Brien Taylor).

Coming away with talent at baseball's Amateur Draft is about as difficult as hitting a big-league fastball. Of the top 10 picks from 1965 to 1996, more than 25 percent never even made it to the major leagues. Of these 320 top picks, only 96 went on to become solid major leaguers—that's a .300 "batting average," for those of you scoring at home. Thirteen are (Reggie Jackson), will be (Robin Yount, Dave Winfield, Paul Molitor, Barry Bonds, Ken Griffey Jr.), should be (Thurman Munson, Dale Murphy, Joe Carter, Mark McGwire, Barry Larkin), or could be (Frank Thomas, Chipper Jones) Hall of Famers—with Derek Jeter and Alex Rodriguez threatening to join the latter group.

A team's draft position is determined by its finish the year before, with the worst going first. That's why the Cubs have had 16 top 10 picks in the draft's first 32 years—a total exceeded only by the Rangers/Senators (17), Padres (18), Indians (18), and Angels (19). Unfortunately, the Cubs have connected for "base hits" only three times through 1996—Joe Carter in 1981, Shawon Dunston in 1986, and Kerry Wood in 1994—for a batting average of .188. Only the Giants (.167), Tigers (.167), Blue Jays (.143), and Dodgers (.100) have done worse to date. How well they've done with Jon Garland in 1997 and Corey Patterson in 1998 remains to be seen.

With a crack at one of the 10 best amateurs in the country, here's how the Cubs have done:

1965 (6th)—Rick James, Pitcher

Superfreak appeared in three games for the Cubs in 1967, going 4⅔ innings for his only big-league experience. The Indians picked next and grabbed All-Star catcher Ray Fosse, who no doubt would have appreciated being a National League All-Star in 1970 rather than an American League tackling dummy for Pete Rose.

1966 (5th)—Dean Burke, Pitcher

Burke never made it past AAA.

1967 (2nd)—Terry Hughes, Shortstop

Hughes played in two games for the Cubs in 1970. He retired in 1974 after three big-league seasons, managing a .209 average in 89 at bats. The Mets took All-Star lefty Jon Matlack two picks later, the Astros grabbed All-Star slugger John Mayberry at number six, and the Cardinals ended up with All-Star catcher Ted Simmons with the 10th pick.

1974 (7th)—Scot Thompson, Outfielder

If only the Cubs had shown as much patience with Lou Brock as they did with Thompson. Perhaps inspired by his 6-for-12 performance as a rookie pinch hitter, the Cubs kept him around for six seasons. He hit anywhere from .165 to .417 in Chicago, retiring after the 1985 season with five home runs and a .262 lifetime batting average.

1975 (4th)—Brian Rosinski, Outfielder

Rosinski never made it past AAA. Yet another solid catcher, Rick Cerone, went to the Indians with the seventh pick.

1976 (7th)—Herman Segelke, Pitcher

Segelke pitched in three games for the Cubs in 1982, retiring with an 8.31 ERA. The White Sox followed the Cubs and grabbed Steve Trout.

1981 (2nd)—Joe Carter, Outfielder
Carter was traded to the Indians for Rick Sutcliffe in the 1984 season and went on to be one of the great RBI men in major-league history.

1982 (1st)—Shawon Dunston, Shortstop
Dunston was the first product of the farm system to become a Cubs regular since Don Kessinger in 1966. He attracted the Cubs' attention by hitting .790 at Thomas Jefferson High School in Brooklyn. To illustrate how inexact a science drafting is, the four picks that followed Dunston were Augie Schmidt, Jimmy Jones, Bryan Oelkers, and Dwight Gooden.

1983 (6th)—Jackie Davidson, Pitcher
Davidson never made it past AAA.

1984 (3rd)—Drew Hall, Pitcher
Hall lasted five seasons in the majors, going 9–12 and being included in the trade of Rafael Palmeiro and Jamie Moyer for Mitch Williams. The A's picked 10th and took Mark McGwire.

1985
Due to the Cubs' outstanding showing in 1984, they didn't get a top pick in one of the deepest drafts in history. The top four players taken were BJ Surhoff, Will Clark, Bobby Witt, and Barry Larkin. The White Sox selected a catcher named Kurt Brown with the fifth pick, just ahead of Barry Bonds. The Cubs had to "settle" for Rafael Palmeiro with the 22nd pick.

1986 (9th)—Derrick May, Outfielder
May was a career reserve outfielder, not quite up to the standards of the players taken just ahead of him: Jeff King, Greg Swindell, Matt Williams, Kevin Brown, Kent Mercker, and Gary Sheffield.

1987 (4th)—Mike Harkey, Pitcher
See Chapter 16, "Foul Territory," for Harkey's "finest hour" with the Cubs. The White Sox followed the Cubs and took Jack McDowell. Four picks later, the Royals took Kevin Appier.

1988 (9th)—Ty Griffin, Second Baseman
Griffin's dramatic home run pushed Team USA past Cuba in a stunning amateur baseball upset. He never pushed himself past AA. The White Sox—is this getting old yet?—followed the Cubs and took Robin Ventura.

1989 (8th)—Earl Cunningham, Outfielder
Cunningham never made it past A-ball. This time, the Cubs followed the White Sox, who'd taken Frank Thomas with the seventh pick. All-Star catcher—is this getting old yet, too?—Charles Johnson went to the Expos with the 10th pick.

1990
Due to another outstanding showing in 1989, the Cubs didn't get a top pick in what proved to be another very deep draft. Chipper Jones and Tony Clark were the top two picks. Two solid catchers, Mike Lieberthal and Dan Wilson, went third and seventh. The White Sox completed their unprecedented streak of four straight top 10 "base hits" by drafting Alex Fernandez. So, how come they never even made it to the World Series, much less won it? Something to do with trading Sammy Sosa, wasn't it? . . .

1993 (10th)—Brooks Kieschnick, Outfielder

After some brief, swing-and-a-miss-filled stints in Chicago, Kieschnick was left exposed in the 1997 Expansion Draft. Kieschnick was the Cubs' seventh consecutive top 10 "out," a hit-less streak exceeded only by the Angels (eight) and the Dodgers (their first nine top 10 picks, with 1993 second pick Darren Dreifort apparently having snapped the string).

1995 (4th)—Kerry Wood, Pitcher

Wood is the Cubs fans' reward for a miserable 1994 season, which saw the team lose its first 12 at Wrigley, lose its second baseman to retirement, and lose its August and September to the players strike.

Amateur Draft First-Round Picks

(Solid major leaguers in **bold**)

1965	6th	Rick James, RHP	1983	6th	Jackie Davidson, RHP
1966	5th	Dean Burke, RHP	1984	3rd	Drew Hall, LHP
1967	2nd	Terry Hughes, SS	1985	22nd	**Rafael Palmeiro,** OF
1968	15th	Ralph Rickey, OF		24th	Dave Masters, RHP
1969	16th	Roger Metzger, SS	1986	9th	Derrick May, OF
1970	19th	Gene Hiser, OF	1987	4th	Mike Harkey, RHP
1971	16th	Jeff Wehmeier, RHP	1988	9th	Ty Griffin, 2B
1972	15th	Brian Vernoy, LHP	1989	8th	Earl Cunningham, OF
1973	16th	Jerry Tabb, 1B	1990	23rd	Lance Dickson, LHP
1974	7th	Scot Thompson, OF	1991	12th	**Doug Glanville,** OF
1975	4th	Brian Rosinski, OF	1992	11th	Derek Wallace, RHP
1976	7th	Herman Segelke, RHP	1993	10th	Brooks Kieschnick, OF
1977	12th	Randy Martz, RHP		24th	Jon Ratliff, RHP
1978	13th	Bill Hayes, C	1994	15th	Jayson Peterson, RHP
1979	12th	Jon Perlman, RHP	1995	4th	**Kerry Wood,** RHP
1980	11th	Don Schulze, RHP	1996	17th	Todd Noel, RHP
1981	2nd	**Joe Carter,** OF	1997	10th	Jon Garland, RHP
1982	1st	**Shawon Dunston,** SS	1998	3rd	Corey Patterson, OF
	17th	Tony Woods, IF			
	27th	Stan Boderick, OF			

the park

It's time to take a step back and try to soak in the entire ballpark, all that Wrigley Field was and is. But doing that also means looking beyond Wrigley—for, prior to moving into the Friendly Confines of Weeghman Park in 1916, the Cubs won eight championships and two pennants during their first 41 years in five other ballparks. Taking it all means looking at:

- West Side Grounds, where the Cubs' dynasty of 1906–10 played; one of the great home teams of all time; and the absolute best *road* team that ever hopped a train
- The Cubs' record in every opposing stadium still in use today
- How Weeghman Park came to be Wrigley Field—the ivy, the scoreboard, the tape-measure blasts, and the ever-growing attendance marks
- The three Cubs among the handful of players to hit 200 home runs in one ball-park—and the visitors who enjoyed coming to Wrigley Field, too
- The night the lights went on in Chicago—and how the second-half slides have been reversed ever since
- The Bleacher Bums and the players who love them
- The men at the microphone, from presidents to men of far greater significance

Welcome to the Friendly Confines. Please don't interfere with balls in play.

BEFORE WRIGLEY

The White Stockings played their first National League home game and won their first pennant at 23rd Street Grounds. After two years, the team moved to larger accommodations at Lakefront Park, which was built on a dump—the former site of Lake Park, the home of the National Association's Chicago White Stockings until it burned in the Fire of 1871 in the middle of a pennant race.

Originally, enclosed stadiums were simply a means of making people pay their way in to see the game. Lakefront Park was the first stadium to be an attraction on its own. There were luxury boxes above the grandstand on the third-base side, with armchairs and curtains, while Albert Goodwill Spalding's owner's box had a phone and a gong. When its capacity was expanded to 10,000 in 1883, it became the largest park in the country.

As with many other parks of the day, it was long and narrow like the Polo Grounds. Left field was only 180' away, right field 196'. The White Stockings left after the home-run season of 1884 when the league established minimum distances for fences. They left behind the mark of 131 home homers in a season, which was a major-league record until broken by the 1970 Indians, and a National League record until broken by the 1995 Rockies (though the White Stockings hit their 131 in only 57 games!).

Their next home, West Side Park, was configured similarly to Lakefront, with the distances down the line pushed all the way back to 216'. In 1891, West Side was used for Monday, Wednesday, and Friday home games, while South Side Park (across the street from where Comiskey Park eventually was built) was used for Tuesday, Thursday, and Saturday games. Sunday games were not yet allowed.

South Side had been the home of the Players League's Chicago Pirates and was merely a temporary home while the Colts made plans to

Road Field Advantage

The Cubs have winning records at the BancOne Ballpark in Phoenix, Jack Murphy Stadium in San Diego, and Coors Field in Denver and are only seven games below .500 at Shea. Three Rivers has been their house of horrors.

Diamond	W	L	Pct.
BancOne Ballpark	4	2	.667
Jack Murphy Stadium	91	83	.523
Coors Field	13	12	.520
Shea Stadium	136	143	.487
Joe Robbie Stadium	15	17	.469
Candlestick Park	116	140	.453
Busch Stadium	124	153	.448
Riverfront Stadium	74	93	.443
Veterans Stadium	98	126	.438
Dodger Stadium	102	132	.436
Olympic Stadium	67	98	.406
County Stadium	56	85	.397
Astrodome	79	133	.373
Three Rivers	84	152	.356
Turner Field	3	9	.250

The Ballparks

Years	Park	1st Game	Last Game	W–L
1876–77	23rd Street Grounds 23rd and State	May 10, 1876 Chicago 6 Cincinnati 0	October 6, 1877 Chicago 4 Louisville 0	42–18
1878–84	Lakefront Park Randolph and Michigan	May 14, 1878 Indianapolis 5 Chicago 3	October 11, 1884 Chicago 12 Philadelphia 3	225–86
1885–91	West Side Park Congress and Throop	June 6, 1885 Chicago 9 St. Louis 2	October 2, 1891 Cincinnati 17 Chicago 16	288–131
1891–93	South Side Park 35th and Wentworth	May 5, 1891 Chicago 1 Pittsburgh 0	September 27, 1893 Chicago 7 New York 2	85–75
1893–1915	West Side Grounds Polk and Lincoln (Wolcott)	May 14, 1893 Cincinnati 13 Chicago 12	October 3, 1915 Chicago 7 St. Louis 2	1,018–639
1916–	Wrigley Field Clark and Addison	April 20, 1916 Chicago 7 Cincinnati 6	God forbid!	3,463–3,008

build a new home at Polk and what is now Wolcott. West Side Grounds was very spacious—340' to left, 560' to center, and 316' to right, leaving plenty of room for overflow crowds to be seated in the outfield. It made its debut in 1893 as the site for Sunday home games.

The stadium nearly burned down in only its second year when a discarded cigar ignited a blaze in the bleachers. Walt Wilmot, Jimmy Ryan, and George Decker had to free trapped fans by taking bats to the barbed-wire fence that had been put up to keep spectators from attacking the umpires. Given the large number of ballpark fires at Sunday games in 1894, arson by the Sunday Observance League was suspected.

West Side Grounds was the site of the Cubs' last championship and was the team's home during its best years: 1906 to 1910. The 1910 Cubs were the greatest home team in club history, playing .753 ball at West Side.

.750 Home Teams

YEAR	TEAM	Pct.	PACE
1932	New York Yankees	.805	130
1961	New York Yankees	.802	130
1931	Philadelphia Athletics	.800	130
1946	Boston Red Sox	.792	128
1949	Boston Red Sox	.792	128
1975	Cincinnati Reds	.790	128
1902	Philadelphia Athletics	.789	128
1902	Pittsburgh Pirates	.789	128
1929	Philadelphia Athletics	.781	127
1942	St. Louis Cardinals	.779	126
1953	Brooklyn Dodgers	.779	126
1954	Cleveland Indians	.766	124
1930	Philadelphia Athletics	.763	124
1998	New York Yankees	.765	124
1910	**Chicago Cubs**	**.753**	**122**
1942	New York Yankees	.753	122
1910	Philadelphia Athletics	.750	122
1927	New York Yankees	.750	122

As great as the 1906 Cubs were, winning 116 games, they also distinguished themselves that year by being the greatest road team of all time—playing .800 ball away from home, which translates to 130 wins in a 162-game season!

Only 18 teams have even played .670 ball on the road, and the Cubs did it four times—each year from 1906 through 1909. Only the 1908–09 Pirates have done it even two years in a row.

.670 Road Teams

YEAR	TEAM	Pct.	PACE
1906	Chicago Cubs	.800	130
1909	Chicago Cubs	.740	120
1939	New York Yankees	.730	118
1908	Pittsburgh Pirates	.727	118
1909	Pittsburgh Pirates	.720	117
1904	New York Giants	.704	114
1912	Pittsburgh Pirates	.701	114
1933	Washington Senators	.697	113

continued

YEAR	TEAM	Pct.	PACE
1902	Pittsburgh Pirates	.691	112
1931	St. Louis Cardinals	.688	111
1971	Oakland Athletics	.688	111
1923	New York Yankees	.684	111
1952	Brooklyn Dodgers	.680	110
1927	New York Yankees	.679	110
1972	Cincinnati Reds	.679	110
1908	Chicago Cubs	.675	109
1954	Cleveland Indians	.675	109
1907	Chicago Cubs	.671	109

By 1914 and 1915, attendance at Cubs games had dropped by two-thirds from its previous high of nearly 700,000 in 1908. The park was in bad shape, and the Cubs were facing competition from Joe Tinker's contending Chicago Whales in the Federal League, which featured Mordecai Brown as their pitching ace and a new ballpark in, of all places, the North Side of Chicago.

THE FRIENDLY CONFINES

The owner of the Chicago Whales, Charles Weeghman, bought a plot of vacant land from the Chicago Lutheran Theological Seminary and built a stadium. Designed by Zachary Taylor Davis, it took 500 workers, $250,000, and four acres of bluegrass to complete. Weeghman Park (a.k.a. North Side Ballpark and Whales Park) was the first stadium with permanent concession stands, and Weeghman was the first owner to allow fans to keep balls hit into the stands. On the last Sunday of the 1914 season, the Whales drew 34,361, compared with 3,500 for the White Sox at Comiskey and fewer than 2,000 for the Cubs at West Side Grounds.

When the Federal League collapsed after the 1915 season, Weeghman purchased the Cubs, bringing numerous Whales with him as well as his park. On April 20, 1916, the Cubs beat the Reds at the first National League game at the Friendly Confines, 7–6 in 11 innings. Thirty-four-year-old Cincinnati outfielder Johnny Beall hit the first home run at the park, his only homer of the season, and the third and final one of his career. The team's new mascot, Joa the Cubbie Bear—named after the initials of part-owner J. Ogden Armour—made his debut. He spent the summer of 1916 living in a cage on Addison (the bear, not the sausage magnate).

When William Wrigley became the owner of the team, keeping what was now called Cubs Park in pristine condition became a priority. Wrigley also funded numerous renovations and expansions. Between the 1922 and 1923 seasons, the grandstand and playing field were moved 60' to the southwest toward Clark and Addison, putting the mound where home plate had been. During the winter of 1926, the left-field bleachers were removed, the grandstand double-decked, the playing area lowered, and the park renamed: Wrigley Field. In the newly expanded stadium in 1927, the Cubs were the first franchise to draw more than 1 million fans. During the 1929, 1932, and 1935 World Series, the park's capacity was expanded further as extra bleachers were built over Waveland and Sheffield behind left field and right field.

If we all go to Chicago and play the ultimate baseball game in the sunshine of Wrigley Field, we will be able to be home by five, have a small barbecue, eat tofu burgers, and live in a perpetual state of grace.

The left-handed Bill Lee on helping players lead clean lives

Wrigley Field is a Peter Pan of a ballpark. It has never grown up and it has never grown old. Let the world race on—they'll still be playing day baseball in the Friendly Confines of Wrigley Field, outfielders will still leap up against the vines, and the Cubs . . . well, it's the season of hope. This could be the Cubbies' year.

EM Swift, sportswriter

Every player should be accorded the privilege of at least one season with the Chicago Cubs. That's baseball as it should be played—in God's own sunshine. And that's really living.

Alvin Dark

The Ivy

Bill Veeck—the son of the late William Veeck, the team's first general manager—planted the ivy on the outfield walls at Wrigley Field in 1937. Since then, it's provided more than its share of headaches for outfielders.

Lou Novikoff was afraid to touch the stuff. Andy Pafko lost a ball hit by Roy Cullenbine into the ivy near the left-field well during the 1945 World Series. Pirates right-fielder Roberto Clemente reached into the ivy for a baseball and came out firing an empty soda cup!

Bill Buckner got an inside-the-park home run against the Mets in 1982 when the ball was lost in the ivy. Outfielders are instructed to raise their hands when balls disappear, so a ground-rule double can be awarded. But outfielders aren't above a little trickery. On August 26, 1948, Braves left-fielder Jeff Heath pretended to lose a Phil Cavarretta drive in the vines when it was at his feet the whole time. Cavarretta's inside-the-park home run was waved off by umpire Jocko Conlan, who was showered with beer bottles after ruling it a ground-rule double.

Tape-Measure Blasts

The center-field scoreboard is an inviting target, but no one's hit it yet. Roberto Clemente just missed it to the left in 1959, Bill Nicholson to the right in 1948.

The longest home run ever hit at Wrigley Field was by Dave Kingman on April 14, 1976. Playing for the Mets, Kingman didn't just clear the bleachers; he hit it over Waveland Avenue, too. The ball traveled 550' and hit a house on the east side of Kenmore Avenue. Three more feet and it would have crashed through a window and smashed the television screen on which Naomi Martinez was watching the game.

On May 5, 1996, Sammy Sosa did smash a window across Waveland Avenue—with a game-winning home run off the Mets' Jerry DiPoto. Sosa displayed even more of a flair for the dramatic in 1998. On June 20 against the Phillies, his record-breaking 16th home run in June traveled 461' and landed in the middle of a rooftop shindig across the street. And on September 13 against the Brewers, Sosa hit not one but two 480' bombs onto Waveland—numbers 61 and 62 of the year—touching off a mad scramble for the ball reminiscent of the running of the bulls at Pamplona.

> *I'd play for half my salary if I could hit in this dump all the time.*
>
> **Babe Ruth,**
> **on Wrigley Field**

Attendance Extremes

- *July 27, 1930—51,556 (19,748 paid) on Ladies Day, with the Cubs winning 7–5 over the Dodgers on a 10th-inning Kiki Cuyler home run*
- *May 18, 1947—46,572 for a Cubs-Dodgers game*
- *May 31, 1948—46,965 paid for a Cubs-Pirates doubleheader (not bad for a last-place team!)*
- *September 21, 1966—440 for a Cubs-Reds game*
- *July 28, 1968—42,261, the largest Cubs crowd in 20 years, sees Chicago go over the .500 mark with a doubleheader sweep of the Dodgers, 8–3 and 1–0, behind Joe Niekro and Ken Holtzman*

When Philip Wrigley took over in 1932, he continued to refurbish the ballpark, at times placing more emphasis on the stadium than on the players it housed. He instructed a young Bill Veeck to plant Chinese elm trees in the newly constructed center-field bleachers in 1937, but wind kept blowing the leaves off. Undaunted, Veeck gave up on the trees and planted ivy on the outfield walls instead.

Just as much as the ivy, the new center-field scoreboard became the signature of Wrigley Field. It was also installed by Bill Veeck in 1937, with the 10' clock atop the scoreboard added in 1941. Team flags fly over the scoreboard, their daily placement dictated by the division standings. A flag bearing the number "14" flies from the left-field foul pole in honor of Ernie Banks, while a "26" flies from the right-field pole for Billy Williams.

The park's dimensions have changed through the years, with center field once being as deep as 447' from home plate in 1923, shortened to 400' in 1937 when the center-field bleachers were built. The distances can be a source of controversy. The sign in left center field reads "368," but those who've measured it insist that it is actually 357' from home plate. No one disputes the "495" on the roof of the house across Sheffield Avenue in deepest right center.

Wrigley Field was also the first park with an organ, which was installed April 26, 1941. As the Cubs began to decline after the 1938 season, "fun and sun" at "Beautiful Wrigley Field"—the phrase Philip Wrigley instructed his announcers to use as frequently as possible—was increasingly being offered as a substitute for wins.

Home Homers

Only Tiger Stadium has seen more home runs than Wrigley Field.

Ernie Banks hit 290 home runs at Wrigley Field, the second most in any park, behind Mel Ott's 323 at the Polo Grounds. Both Billy Williams and Ron Santo also hit 200 home runs at Wrigley; only Yankee Stadium has seen more 200-homer sluggers (Mantle, Ruth, Gehrig, Berra).

Only six players have hit 25 home runs in a season at Wrigley Field, with Sammy Sosa setting a new standard in 1998. Sosa also joined Hack Wilson and Ernie Banks as the only Cubs to do it more than once.

Much was made of the advantage that Sammy Sosa had over Mark McGwire in playing his home games at Wrigley Field. Sosa hit 31 home runs on the road, however, tying what had been George Foster's National League record and falling short by one of Babe Ruth's (and now Mark McGwire's) major-league record. Only nine Cubs have hit as many as 20 road home runs, with Banks the only one to do it twice.

The Cubs' modern club record of home homers is 114, set in 1987, which was approached by the Cubs in 1998 (111) but is still standing.

200 Home Runs in One Park

Mel Ott	Polo Grounds	323
Ernie Banks	**Wrigley Field**	**290**
Mickey Mantle	Yankee Stadium	266
Mike Schmidt	Veterans Stadium	265
Babe Ruth	Yankee Stadium	259
Lou Gehrig	Yankee Stadium	251
Ted Williams	Fenway Park	248
Carl Yastrzemski	Fenway Park	237
Willie McCovey	Candlestick Park	236
Billy Williams	**Wrigley Field**	**231**
Al Kaline	Tiger Stadium	226
Norm Cash	Tiger Stadium	212
Ron Santo	**Wrigley Field**	**212**
Eddie Mathews	County Stadium	211
Yogi Berra	Yankee Stadium	210
Jim Rice	Fenway Park	208
Dale Murphy	Fulton County Stadium	205
Willie Mays	Candlestick Park	203

20 Road Homers

1998	*Sammy Sosa*	31
1930	*Hack Wilson*	23
1960	*Ernie Banks*	23
1979	*Dave Kingman*	23
1987	*Andre Dawson*	22
1959	*Ernie Banks*	21
1930	*Gabby Hartnett*	20
1950	*Andy Pafko*	20
1954	*Hank Sauer*	20
1993	*Rick Wilkins*	20

25 Home Homers

1998	*Sammy Sosa*	35
1930	*Hack Wilson*	33
1958	*Ernie Banks*	28
1987	*Andre Dawson*	27
1955	*Ernie Banks*	26
1996	*Sammy Sosa*	26
1929	*Hack Wilson*	25
1957	*Ernie Banks*	25
1979	*Dave Kingman*	25
1990	*Ryne Sandberg*	25
1997	*Sammy Sosa*	25

Home Runs by Stadium

Tiger Stadium	10,879
Wrigley Field	**9,738***
Yankee Stadium	9,574
Fenway Park	9,256

*excludes Federal League play

Wrigley Field's Home-Run Leaders

Ernie Banks	290
Billy Williams	231
Ron Santo	212
Ryne Sandberg	164
Sammy Sosa	143
Gabby Hartnett	115

50 for the Visitors

Willie Mays	54
Hank Aaron	50
Mike Schmidt	50*

*Schmidt holds the single-season record with 8 in 1980, breaking the mark of 7, which he'd shared since 1976.

513 for Ernie?

A screen was erected on top of the center-field wall by the team's athletic director, Colonel Whitlow. It was there from June 18, 1963, to the end of the 1964 season. Intended to help the hitters' vision, it actually kept potential home runs by Ernie Banks and Willie McCovey—among others— in the field of play.

The Lights

A fad. Just a passing fad.   —Philip Wrigley, on night baseball in 1935

*Mayor Harold Washington
died in his office the day
before Thanksgiving 1987,
before an ordinance for lights
at Wrigley could be passed.
Eventually it was passed by
the city council, 29–19, on
February 25, 1988. And on
August 8, 1988, the lights
were turned on by Harry
Grossman, a lifelong Cubs
fan. The game with the
Phillies—in which Phil
Bradley homered in the top
of the first inning—was
called after 3½ with the
Cubs up 3–1. The next night,
the Cubs beat the Mets 6–4
in the first official night
game. The first night game
played at Wrigley was actually the All-American Girls
Professional Baseball League
All-Star game in July 1943
under temporary lights.*

*But what will go down
for now as the most memo-
rable night game in Wrigley
Field history was the play-off
game between the Cubs and
Giants on September 28, 1998
(see "The Pennants,"
Chapter 13).*

It's been said that the lack of lights at Wrigley Field contributed to the Cubs' fade in 1969 and numerous swoons that followed throughout the '70s. The theory is that Chicago's players wore down from playing so many day games, and that they were at a disadvantage when playing night games on the road as their body had to adjust to a different schedule. The evidence is compelling.

1978

On May 24, 1978, the Cubs move into first place for 30 days after Manny Trillo's 10th-inning dinger. The Cubs go 36–44 after the All-Star break and finish 11 games behind the Phillies.

1977

On June 28, 1977, the Cubs are 47–22—8½ games up. Injuries to Bruce Sutter and Rick Reuschel devastate the team, which loses 25 of its last 35 to finish .500, in fourth place, 20 games out.

1975

The Cubs are in first place from April 14 to May 30, but they finish in fifth place, 17½ games off the pace.

1973

On June 29, 1973, the Cubs are 46–31, eight games up. From June 30 to September 18, they go 25–48. They picked the wrong season for the wheels to come off, as the Mets win the division with a record of only 82–79.

1970

On June 3, 1970, the Cubs are in first place, and on September 4, they're only percentage points behind the Pirates. But the Cubs limp home 5 games back in a season in which the bullpen blew 15 of 17 games when called on with the tying run on base.

1969

The Cubs are 77–45 when Ken Holtzman no-hits the Braves on August 19, but they hit a wall, going 15–25 down the stretch as the Mets blow by and take the division by eight games.

Not Ready for Prime Time

August 8, 1988: Let There Be Lights

Putting lights in Wrigley Field is like putting aluminum siding on the Sistine Chapel.   —Roger Simon, sportswriter, 1988

The real litmus test for Cubs loyalty is the willingness to blow off the job and flirt with unemployment to attend a game starting in the early afternoon.   —Circuit Court Judge Richard Curry

On July 1, 1935, the Cubs won their first night game, 8–4, over the Reds at Crosley Field. Roy Henshaw got the win as Billy Herman racked up five hits. Philip Wrigley had plans to put lights in Wrigley for the 1942 season, having purchased the steel for towers and scheduled construction to begin on December 8, 1941. When the Japanese bombed Pearl Harbor on December 7, Wrigley donated the materials to the war effort.

By 1948, every team in the majors had lights except the Cubs, with Tiger Stadium the last holdout. When Peter Ueberroth replaced Bowie Kuhn as baseball's commissioner on October 1, 1984, his first actions were to bow to network pressures by stripping the Cubs of home-field advantage should they reach the World Series and letting it be known that future postseason contests involving the Cubs might have to be played in Busch Stadium, of all places.

Food for thought: from 1958 (back when every other team had lights and coast-to-coast travel came into play) to 1988 (when the Cubs played their first home night game in August), the Cubs' play deteriorated significantly after the All-Star break. Since 1989, the exact opposite has happened.

Day-and-Night Difference in Win–Loss Records

	BEFORE THE ALL-STAR BREAK	AFTER THE ALL-STAR BREAK
1958–88	1,261–1,334 (**.486**)	1,047–1,275 (**.451**)
1989–98	401–441 (**.476**)	364–346 (**.513**)

Translate these numbers to 162-game seasons, and, before lights, the Cubs are a 79-win team slumping to a 73-win pace after the break. Since lights are installed, the Cubs are a 77-win team that improves to an 83-win pace after the break.

The same trend holds true for night road games compared with day road games. The Cubs used to play 72-win baseball on the road during the day, while slumping to a 67-win pace on the road at night. Now that they also play night games at home, they play better at night on the road: up from a 75-win pace in road day games to an 80-win pace in road night games.

The Fans

It's rare to find Hillary Clinton and Ronald Reagan on the same side of an issue, but the Cubs are a unifying force. The fans at Wrigley Field have made their mark more so than those of any other team, whether it be from "salaam"-ing Andre Dawson to throwing opposition home-run balls back onto the field. Here are some other famous and infamous moments in the history of Cubs fandom.

Attendance
(first years at 500,000, 1 million, 1.5 million, 2 million, and 2.5 million are in bold)

YEAR	W	L	Pct.	GB	ATTENDANCE
1890	84	53	.613	6	102,536
1891	82	53	.607	3.5	201,188
1892	70	76	.479	29	109,067
1893	56	71	.441	29	223,500
1894	57	75	.432	34	239,000
1895	72	58	.554	15	382,300
1896	71	57	.555	18.5	317,500
1897	59	73	.447	34	327,160
1898	85	65	.567	17.5	424,352
1899	75	73	.507	26	352,130
1900	65	75	.464	19	248,577
1901	53	86	.381	37	205,071
1902	68	69	.496	34	263,700
1903	82	56	.594	8	386,205
1904	93	60	.608	13	439,100
1905	**92**	**61**	**.601**	**13**	**509,900**
1906	116	36	.763	+20	654,300
1907	107	45	.704	+17	422,550
1908	99	55	.643	+1	665,325

continued

The first time I tried it with the lights on, it was pretty much a washout, too.

David Letterman, after the first night game in Cubs history was rained out

The Cubs' involvement in the divisional race has built excitement, and that's great for their fans. But for the future, baseball must promptly find a clear-cut solution to the lights situation.

Commissioner Bowie Kuhn, 1984

If he throws another home run, I'm going to run out there and give him what for.

Twenty-seven-year-old bond trader John Murray to his brother shortly before Randy Myers served up an eighth-inning home run to James Mouton in 1995

YEAR	W	L	Pct.	GB	ATTENDANCE
1909	104	49	.680	6.5	633,480
1910	104	50	.675	+13	526,152
1911	92	62	.597	7.5	576,000
1912	91	59	.607	11.5	514,000
1913	88	65	.575	13.5	419,000
1914	78	76	.506	16.5	202,516
1915	73	80	.477	17.5	217,058
1916	67	86	.438	26.5	453,685
1917	74	80	.481	24	360,218
1918	84	45	.651	+10.5	337,256
1919	75	65	.536	21	424,430
1920	75	79	.487	18	480,783
1921	64	89	.418	30	410,107
1922	80	74	.519	13	542,283
1923	83	71	.539	12.5	703,705
1924	81	72	.529	12	716,922
1925	68	86	.442	27.5	622,610
1926	82	72	.532	7	885,063
1927	**85**	**68**	**.556**	**8.5**	**1,159,168**
1928	91	63	.591	4	1,143,740
1929	98	54	.645	+10.5	1,485,166
1930	90	64	.584	2	1,463,624
1931	84	70	.545	17	1,086,422
1932	90	64	.584	+4	974,688
1933	86	68	.558	6	594,112
1934	86	65	.570	8	707,525
1935	100	54	.649	+4	692,604
1936	87	67	.565	5	699,370
1937	93	61	.604	3	895,020
1938	89	63	.586	+2	951,640
1939	84	70	.545	13	726,663
1940	75	79	.487	25.5	534,878
1941	70	84	.455	30	545,159
1942	68	86	.442	38	590,972
1943	74	79	.484	30.5	508,247
1944	75	79	.487	30	640,110
1945	98	56	.636	+3	1,036,386
1946	82	71	.536	14.5	1,342,970
1947	69	85	.448	25	1,364,039
1948	64	90	.416	27.5	1,237,792
1949	61	93	.396	36	1,143,139
1950	64	89	.418	26.5	1,165,944
1951	62	92	.403	34.5	894,415
1952	77	77	.500	19.5	1,024,826
1953	65	89	.422	40	763,658
1954	64	90	.416	33	748,183
1955	72	81	.471	26	875,800
1956	60	94	.390	33	720,118
1957	62	92	.403	33	670,629
1958	72	82	.468	20	979,904
1959	74	80	.481	13	858,255
1960	60	94	.390	35	809,770

continued

YEAR	W	L	Pct.	GB	ATTENDANCE
1961	64	90	.416	29	673,057
1962	59	103	.364	42.5	609,802
1963	82	80	.506	17	979,551
1964	76	86	.469	17	751,647
1965	72	90	.444	25	641,361
1966	59	103	.364	36	635,891
1967	87	74	.540	14	977,226
1968	84	78	.519	13	1,043,409
1969	**92**	**70**	**.568**	**8**	**1,674,993**
1970	84	78	.519	5	1,642,705
1971	83	79	.512	14	1,653,007
1972	85	70	.548	11	1,299,163
1973	77	84	.478	5	1,351,705
1974	66	96	.407	22	1,015,378
1975	75	87	.463	17.5	1,034,819
1976	75	87	.463	26	1,026,217
1977	81	81	.500	20	1,439,834
1978	79	83	.488	11	1,525,311
1979	80	82	.494	18	1,648,587
1980	64	98	.395	27	1,206,776
1981	38	65	.369		565,637
1982	73	89	.451	19	1,249,278
1983	71	91	.438	19	1,479,717
1984	**96**	**65**	**.596**	**+6.5**	**2,107,655**
1985	77	84	.478	23.5	2,161,534
1986	70	90	.438	37	1,859,102
1987	76	85	.472	18.5	2,035,130
1988	77	85	.475	24	2,089,034
1989	93	69	.574	+6	2,491,942
1990	77	85	.475	18	2,243,791
1991	77	83	.481	20	2,314,250
1992	78	84	.481	18	2,126,720
1993	**84**	**78**	**.519**	**13**	**2,653,763**
1994	49	64	.434	16.5	1,845,208
1995	73	71	.507	12	1,918,265
1996	76	86	.469	12	2,219,110
1997	68	94	.420	16	2,190,308
1998	90	73	.552	12.5	2,622,800

Gabby Hartnett was reprimanded by baseball commissioner Kenesaw Mountain Landis for posing with Al Capone in a pregame photo before a charity exhibition with the White Sox. As Hartnett explained, "I go to his place of business. Why shouldn't he come to mine?" Valentine's Day Massacre victim Bugs Moran was also a Cubs fans. John Dillinger was one of the first bleacher bums, sitting in the right-field bleachers in a postal uniform.

The Bleacher Bums were born during the wild summer of 1969. They wore yellow helmets with "Bleacher Bums" emblazoned in red. William Wrigley took 100 of them with him on a charter flight for a three-game series in Atlanta (the Cubs swept). Leo Durocher even assigned Dick Selma to whip them into a frenzy.

They were not easily impressed, pouring beer on Hank Aaron's head after the 521st home run of his career and so aggravating Mudcat Grant that the pitcher threw baseballs at

Every time I go to town
The boys all kick my dog
around
Makes no difference if he's a
hound
You better stop kicking my
dog around.

Theme song of the Bleacher
Bums

Chicago Cubs fans are the greatest fans in baseball. They've got to be.

Herman Franks, 1978

One thing you learn as a Cubs fan: When you bought your ticket, you could bank on seeing the bottom of the ninth inning.

Joe Garagiola, on being a Cubs fan in the '50s

One thing about the Chicago Bears: When their season starts, it takes some heat off the Cubs.

Bill Madlock, 1975

them. This spirit still lives on; on July 13, 1996, still reeling from the seven home runs hit by the Cardinals the day before, frustrated fans in the bleachers brought some excitement to another lackluster Cubs performance by dumping beer on Brian Jordan and Ray Lankford on consecutive fly balls to the warning track. Not quite back-to-back home runs, but perhaps the next best thing.

Cubs fans have been known to throw more than beer and baseballs. They regularly showered Hank Sauer ("the Mayor of Wrigley Field") with bags of chewing tobacco after he hit a home run (what he couldn't fit in his pockets he stashed in the vines). They did the same on occasion to opposing outfielders, only without such good intentions. On June 9, 1962, right-field fans showered Frank Howard with peanuts, distracting him into missing a fly ball hit by Bob Lillis. The baskets along the outfield walls were put in place in 1970 not just to keep fans from dropping things onto the field, but also to keep the fans from throwing themselves onto the field.

Not just bleacher fans have been known to be knuckleheads. A fan jumped out of the box seats in 1946 to give Bill Nicholson a batting lesson, while a drunk yuppie charged the mound against Randy Myers after a home run in 1995 and got decked. He picked the wrong guy—Myers being 6'1"/230 lbs. with a weapons fetish and trained in martial arts. And in 1993, Reds pitcher Tom Browning was fined $500 for leaving the stadium to join a rooftop party on Sheffield Avenue.

Foolishness aside, Cubs fans are perhaps the most loyal in sports. The suits and bean counters may not have been able to appreciate this bond between fan and player, but many players have. Rick Sutcliffe's decision to take less than he could get on the free-agent market to stay with the Cubs after the 1984 season was a direct result of the way he was treated by the fans of Chicago. Here are some thoughts from Sutcliffe and others.

Rick Sutcliffe

The reason I went back to Chicago was because the people took me into their hearts. I know those fans deserved an opportunity to win. Sure, I could have gotten a lot more money than the Cubs gave me, and a couple more years, too, but it was more money than I was ever going to need the rest of my life. . . . Players don't get treated like that very often. But the Cubs' fans have been unbelievable to me. I don't know if any player was ever treated any better than I was. . . . You're like family to them, more than just a ballplayer.

Bruce Sutter

I'll always remember best the first time I stepped out on the mound. They gave me a standing ovation, which is what they do to every new player. They welcome you right in. . . . Everyone is cheering real loud and pulling for you.

Frankie Baumholtz

It was sad leaving fans who really liked me. I was never booed in Chicago. (Baumholtz was sold to the Phillies, where he was no doubt booed for so much as sticking his head out of the dugout.)

Hank Sauer

It was a great feeling. The loyalty went both ways. The best times of my career—my most fun and my best days—was with the Cubs.

Dick Ellsworth

We played for the fans, not for management. They were the ones who gauged our abilities and degrees of success.

The Broadcast Booth

The Cubs have put not one but three announcers into the Hall of Fame. Bob Elson was inducted in 1979, Jack Brickhouse followed in 1983, and Harry Caray went in during the magical summer of 1989. Caray had broadcast games for the Cubs' bitter rivals, the Cardinals and the White Sox, before joining WGN in 1982. In very little time at all, he was synonymous with the Cubs, even bringing over from Comiskey Park his traditional seventh-inning-stretch "singing" of "Take Me Out to the Ball Game" (a song first published in 1908, the year of the Cubs' last championship).

Ronald Reagan re-created Cubs games for WHO in Des Moines, and 50 years later, he called the broadcast booth to welcome Harry Caray back to work, explaining, "You know, in a few months, I'm going to be out of work, and I thought I might as well audition."

After Dutch Reagan and before Harry Caray, the Cubs actually traded their broadcaster for their manager. In 1960, Lou Boudreau came out of the broadcast booth to replace Charlie Grimm after only 17 games. At 24 in 1942, Boudreau had been the youngest manager to start a season in major-league history. Boudreau won a World Series in 1948, thanks in large part to a shortstop named Boudreau; with the Cubs, he had a shortstop named Banks, but no Bob Lemon, Bob Feller, Joe Gordon, Ken Keltner, or Larry Doby. The team finished a game out of last and 35 out of first, prompting Philip Wrigley to innovate yet again—the College of Coaches.

A manager for a broadcaster. Only with the Cubs.

Jack Brickhouse

Famous Phrases

I don't care who wins as long as it's the Cubs.
—Bert Wilson, radio broadcaster, 1944–55

Back back back. That's it. Hey-hey, hey-hey.
—Jack Brickhouse

It might be . . . it could be . . . it is.   —Harry Caray

Nothing beats fun at the old ballpark.
—Jack Brickhouse

Broadcast Firsts

- *October 1, 1924. The first Cubs game ever broadcast. WGN's Sen Kaney announces the 10–7 Cubs victory over the White Sox in the opening game of the City Championship Series at Wrigley.*
- *April 14, 1925. Quin Ryan and WGN broadcast the first regular-season game, as the Cubs beat the Pirates 8–2 on Opening Day.*
- *April 20, 1946. WBKB televises the first Cubs game, with Whispering Joe Wilson calling the play-by-play. The Cubs are blanked by Harry Brecheen 2–0 in their home opener.*
- *April 16, 1948. The Windy City Classic is the first game televised on WGN. Jack Brickhouse is at the mike for a 4–1 Sox win.*
- *July 17, 1964. The first baseball game to be broadcast on pay-TV has Don Drysdale beating the Cubs 3–2 in Los Angeles.*

foul territory

A ballpark without foul territory would be like . . . the Chicago Cubs without Lou Novikoff. The Cubs have enjoyed more than their share of strange days and twisted nights, wild men and knuckleheads, mutants and deviants, freaks and flakes and full-blown drunks, and always something vaguely supernatural hanging just outside the lines.

Submitted for your approval:

- Today's attendance: 12
- Game called on account of fire
- Game delayed on account of arrest
- Game suspended on account of blackout
- A doubleheader played against two different teams
- Players umpiring, Reds in White Sox uniforms, 220' home runs, and two balls in play
- And on the mound for the St. Louis Cardinals . . . *Stan Musial?*
- Now playing right field for the Los Angeles Dodgers . . . *Fernando Valenzuela?*
- Wrigley Field, California
- The Mad Russian
- St. Vrain, patron of the disoriented
- Hitters pitching, pitchers hitting, cats and dogs living together
- Wild at heart and weird on top: Eddie Solomon, Bill Faul, Babe Herman, the Gold Dust Twins, Billy Sunday, and Ruth Ann Steinhagen, to name but a few
- Lowball hitters and highball drinkers
- The curse of Fred Merkle—does John McGraw *still* have a meddlesome hand in the affairs of the National League?

What better way to close it out than with some of the weirdest moments, saddest stories, freakiest injuries, and strangest characters in Cubs history?

STRANGE DAYS

August 21, 1876

Chicago is the first team to forfeit a game. Down 7–6, they walk off the field in the ninth inning at St. Louis in protest of an umpire's call.

September 27, 1881

In a driving rain in Troy, NY, in front of *12 fans* (the lowest major-league attendance in history), the White Stockings wrap up their second consecutive pennant-winning season with a 10–8 win.

July 1, 1892

Jimmy Ryan is credited with being the first player to assault a sportswriter, George Bechel of the *Chicago Evening News*.

August 5, 1894

The game is called on account of fire. With the Colts up 8–1 behind Clark Griffith, a fire breaks out in the stands at West Side Grounds. Panicked fans try to tear through a barbed-wire fence put up to keep them from attacking the umpire. Bill Dahlen gets a hit in his 41st consecutive game, then manages to extend his streak to 42 the following day before going 0-for-6 in 10 innings against the Reds on the 7th.

> **"Respect the Streak"**
>
> . . . Crash Davis passed on these words of wisdom to Nuke Laloosh in Bull Durham, but the advice could just as easily have come from Cubs manager Charlie Grimm in September 1935. On September 4, the day the Cubs' 21-game winning streak began, a chubby 15-year-old named Paul Dominick was spotted outside the ballpark. The players joked that he looked like a miniature Gabby Hartnett, so they put him in a uniform and snuck him onto the bench. After winning the game 8–2 over the Phillies, they brought him back the next day. A trouper, Dominick had refused to attend school and jinx the club, but to avert such truancy, Grimm arranged for an auto shuttle from the school to the park. While this was going on, Grimm was also pegging tacks into his right shoe every day—a practice he'd started for no good reason on September 4—and which he continued to do in order to respect the streak.

June 23, 1895

The Colts are charged with "aiding and abetting the forming of a noisy crowd on a Sunday" by the Reverend W. W. Clark of the Sunday Observance League. Team president Jim Hart posts bail, the game is resumed, and Chicago goes on to beat the Cleveland Spiders 13–4. The Reverend is invited to join the 10,000 fans at West Side Grounds but declines.

October 8, 1899

In a wild doubleheader, Chicago plays Cleveland in the morning and Louisville in the afternoon at West Side Grounds. The Orphans sweep, 13–0 and 7–3, with Jack Taylor throwing his 39th complete game in the first (his first major-league shutout). In the second game, Bill Lange doubles, then steals third and home on Rube Waddell's next two pitches.

August 7, 1906

The New York Giants forfeit a game to the Cubs without a pitch being thrown. Manager John McGraw, upset over the umpiring in the previous day's game, refuses to allow umpire James Johnston to enter the Polo Grounds.

September 1, 1906

With the regular umpires laid up with food poisoning, Cubs pitcher Carl Lundgren and Cardinals catcher Peter Noonan are selected to umpire the game. Chicago wins 8–1 for its 14th in a row on a Mordecai Brown five-hitter.

April 29, 1913

The Cubs beat the White Sox 7–2 in baseball's first interleague game. Actually it just looks that way. The Reds forget their uniforms and have to wear those of the crosstown Sox.

"And an Eephus Ain't Nothin'"

In 1941, Rip Sewell debuted his high, arcing "eephus pitch" ("it's an eephus because it's a nothin' pitch, and an eephus ain't nothin'") against the Cubs. Sewell was protecting a 2–1 lead in the ninth inning with the bases loaded. He had a 3–2 count on Dom Dallesandro when he floated his eephus in for a called third strike. Pointing his bat at Sewell, Dallesandro said, "If this bat was a rifle, I'd shoot your @*#!in' head off."

Went to a Fight and a Cubs-Dodgers Game Broke Out

Many expressions of affection were exchanged between the Cubs and Dodgers during the 1940s. On July 19, 1940, Hugh Casey plunked Claude Passeau at Wrigley in an 11–4 Cubs blowout, and Passeau threw his bat at him. On July 15, 1942, Hi Bithorn threw at Leo Durocher—but Durocher was the Dodgers' manager and was sitting in the dugout at the time. Many of the combatants went to war, but things picked up right where they left off when they returned. On May 22, 1946, Lennie Merullo and former Cub Eddie Stanky duked it out at second base, triggering a 10th-inning brawl at Ebbets Field in which Passeau ripped off Durocher's jersey. Merullo had slid in hard at second trying to break up a double play only moments after Johnny Schmitz had spiked Pee Wee Reese on a play at short. The Dodgers went on to win 2–1 in 13. The following day, Merullo and Dixie Walker went at it during batting practice, and the Dodgers won another tense one, 2–1 in 11. The Dodgers sure weren't showing their gratitude for all the good players that had come their way courtesy of the Cubs.

July 27, 1930

Ken Ash throws one pitch, and Charlie Grimm lines into a triple play. When Ash is lifted and the Reds rally to win 6–5, Ash gets credit for the win in a one-pitch, one-inning performance.

April 30, 1949

Andy Pafko's great catch to end the game at Wrigley turns into a game-winning, two-run, inside-the-park home run when umpire Al Barlick rules it a trap. Rocky Nelson's home run, which gives the Cardinals a 4–3 victory, travels only 220' because he keeps running while Pafko is screaming at the umpire.

July 1, 1958

Tony Taylor is circling the bases while the Cubs' bullpen is giving Giants rookie outfielder Leon Wagner some lousy advice on where the ball went (it had rolled into a Wrigley Field gutter drain).

June 30, 1959

One of the strangest moments in baseball history. Pitching for the Cubs is Bob Anderson, while Stan Musial is the batter. Anderson delivers, and it's either a wild pitch or a foul tip. Catcher Sammy Taylor, thinking it's a foul ball, doesn't bother going after it. Third-baseman Alvin Dark isn't so sure, and he goes after it, but the ball boy has already tossed it to the field announcer. Musial thinks it's a wild pitch for ball four, and he's heading to first. Home-plate umpire Vic Delmore pulls out another ball and hands it to Anderson while the field announcer is giving the original ball to Dark. With Musial breaking for second, Dark and Anderson *both* throw to second. Ernie Banks catches Dark's toss, while Anderson's throw goes into center field. Ignoring Banks's tag, Musial heads for third. Cubs center-fielder Bobby Thomson retrieves the second ball and fires it past third base and into the Cubs' dugout. Meanwhile, home-plate umpire Vic Delmore is ruling Musial out at second while Al Barlick is calling Musial safe at first. Musial is eventually called out, and the Cards howl. St. Louis goes on to win 4–1, the Cardinals drop their protest, and Delmore's contract is not renewed at the end of the season.

August 26, 1966

Enraged by a cartoon of him on the Astrodome scoreboard, Cubs manager Leo Durocher calls the press box from the dugout to complain. Unsatisfied with the response, he rips the phone out of the dugout and and throws it onto the field in the middle of a 7–4 loss.

April 25, 1976

In Dodger Stadium, all the elements for a Norman Rockwell painting are in place as a father and son with an American flag take in the game. Except they also have a book of matches and a can of lighter fluid and are running out into left center to make a statement. Cubs center-fielder Rick Monday runs over, captures the flag, and instantly becomes a national celebrity.

July 13, 1977

The Cubs are up 2–1 in the sixth, with Ray Burris about to deliver a pitch to Lenny Randle when . . . the lights go out. New York City is in the middle of a massive blackout that suspends this game and postpones the following afternoon's game as well. Jerry Koosman has fanned 11 in six innings for the Mets, but he doesn't get a chance to take any further steps toward the record book. The Cubs end up winning 4–3 on September 16. To keep the fans entertained, Joel Youngblood and Craig Swan drive their cars onto the field to cast headlights on a phantom infield drill: Jackson Todd, Doug Flynn, Bud Harrelson, and Bobby Valentine fielding invisible "grounders" hit by Bob Apodaca.

I thought, "God, I'm gone." I thought for sure he was calling me. I thought it was my last at bat.

Lenny Randle's thoughts when the lights went out in Shea Stadium in 1977

August 8, 1980

The Cubs win a 15-inning game on a grand slam by a player not on the team at the beginning of the game. Cliff Johnson hits the blast when play resumes in the 11th inning of the suspended Cubs-Expos game. The game is won by a manager not managing the team at the beginning of the game: Joey Amalfitano, who replaces Preston Gomez.

August 17–18, 1982

There are 100 wild games in "The Scoreboard," Chapter 11, but possibly the weirdest game of them all is this 2–1, 21-inning affair. It's the longest game in terms of innings ever played at Wrigley Field, and the longest game in terms of time (six hours, 10 minutes) ever played by the Cubs. The score is tied at 1–1 in the second, and 17 scoreless innings follow, pitched by 14 different hurlers and managed by four different skippers as both Lee Elia and Tommy Lasorda are tossed. In the 20th inning, Dave Pallone tosses Lasorda and Dodgers third-baseman Ron Cey out of the game after Cey is picked off first. Cey does not appear to argue the call, and Lasorda later claims it was a deliberate attempt by Pallone to force a forfeit. With Cey gone, the Dodgers use their 25th player—Fernando Valenzuela—in left and right field (depending on the batter). Even the winning run is a strange one—a sacrifice fly by Dusty Baker to Keith Moreland in right field, with Eric Gregg first calling Steve Sax out at the plate and then reversing the call. Jerry Reuss gets the win with four scoreless innings, then pitches five in the regularly scheduled game for another win.

THROUGH THE LOOKING GLASS

The Other Wrigley Field

The top Cubs farm team in the 1930s, 1940s, and 1950s was the Los Angeles Angels. Some farmhands put up monster numbers down there that they could never reproduce in the big leagues.

Outfielder Jigger Statz did have one 200-hit season in the big leagues, but he set a minor-league record with 11 such campaigns.

Shortstop Gene Lillard hit 43 home runs for the Angels in 1933 and another 56 in 1935. With the Cubs in 1936, he hit .206 with no home runs. He tried it again as a pitcher but went 3–6 and didn't even hit particularly well for a pitcher.

Steve Bilko (6'1"/230) was bought from the Cardinals in 1954, but he hit only four home runs for the Cubs. He hit 37 home runs in 1955 for the Angels, including a 552' blast in

Oakland. He was just warming up. In 1956 and 1957, he hit 111 home runs and knocked in 304 runs for the Angels, including a Triple Crown in 1956 (55/164/.360 with 215 hits). His career minor-league numbers: 313 home runs and .312. His best season in the majors came in 1961 for the major-league version of the Los Angeles Angels, who just happened to play their games that year in Wrigley Field.

But Lou "the Mad Russian" Novikoff was perhaps the greatest minor leaguer to never stick in the majors. A harmonica virtuoso who spoke only Russian until he was 10, he won four consecutive minor-league batting titles: .367 for Moline of the Three-I League in 1938, .368 for Tulsa of the Texas League in 1939, a Triple Crown for Los Angeles of the Pacific Coast League in 1940 (41 home runs, 171 RBIS, and .363 with 259 hits), and .370 for Milwaukee of the American Association in 1941.

"I can't understand it," Novikoff said, as he struggled to hit in the big leagues. "I feel so strong, I could tear that ball in half."

Novikoff blamed losses on the new tight-fitting uniforms of the Cubs in 1942, complained that Wrigley's foul lines were crooked, played outfield in fear of touching the ivy, and caught line drives as if he were wrestling them into submission. He once stole third base with the bases loaded, explaining, "I got such a good jump on the pitcher." To try to get him to be more aggressive, he was fined for every called third strike he took—once prompting him to swing at a pitch over his head with the bases loaded. Oh, yeah, and he had a pet Russian wolfhound who ate only caviar while Novikoff feasted on ground meat wrapped in cabbage.

Novikoff retired after the 1946 season with a .282 lifetime average, took up softball, and became a Hall of Famer.

Pitchers Hitting

I enjoyed hitting—I just didn't make contact too often.   —Bob Buhl

Here are some of the greatest moments that Cubs pitchers have had in the batter's box.

The Magnificent Seven

DATE	HITTING PITCHER	THE GLORIOUS DETAILS
June 20, 1882	Larry Corcoran	It's not just the first Cubs grand slam by a pitcher, it's the Cubs' first grand slam period. Corcoran goes 4-for-4 with a slam and pitches the White Stockings past Worcester 13–3 at Lakefront.
May 27, 1884	Fred Goldsmith	The first Chicago pitcher to hit 2 home runs in a game, Goldsmith victimizes the Buffalo Bisons 14–6 in Buffalo.
May 31, 1920	Grover Alexander	Alexander beats the Reds for his 11th straight, 3–2 in 10 innings on his own dinger in the bottom of the 10th.
May 6, 1922	Vic Aldridge	Aldridge goes 5-for-5 and pitches the Cubs past the Pirates 11–7 at Pittsburgh.
August 28, 1937	Clay Bryant	Bryant hits a grand slam in the 10th in a 10–7 relief win over the Braves in Boston.
May 5, 1946	Hank Borowy	The Cubs win 13–1 over the Phillies at Wrigley thanks to Borowy's 4 RBIS in an 11-run 7th inning. He doubles twice in the frame, tying a mark held by 2 other Cubs pitchers: Adonis Terry and Fred Goldsmith.
August 11, 1972	Milt Pappas	Pappas knocks in 5 runs on 3 hits, including a home run, in a 7–2 win over the Mets at Wrigley.

Grand Slam Pitchers

June 20, 1882	Larry Corcoran	Worcester Ruby Legs
August 28, 1937	Clay Bryant	at Boston Braves
May 19, 1941	Claude Passeau	Brooklyn Dodgers
September 7, 1947	Ox Miller	at Pittsburgh Pirates
September 16, 1972	Burt Hooton	New York Mets
July 20, 1998	Kevin Tapani	at Atlanta Braves

Two-Homer Pitchers

May 27, 1884	Fred Goldsmith	at Buffalo Bisons
October 9, 1884	John Clarkson	Philadelphia Phillies
August 13, 1887	John Clarkson	Detroit Wolverines
July 27, 1894	Scott Stratton	at Cincinnati Reds
July 4, 1925	Tony Kaufman	St. Louis Cardinals
May 7, 1941	Bill Lee	at Philadelphia Phillies
September 2, 1960	Don Cardwell	at St. Louis Cardinals
July 2, 1961	Glen Hobbie	St. Louis Cardinals
September 1, 1971	Ferguson Jenkins	Montreal Expos

Pitchers Running

Only four Cubs pitchers have ever stolen home, and the group includes two fairly unlikely characters: a man named Hippo and all 6'7"215 of Rick Sutcliffe.

July 15, 1902	Jocko Menefee	Brooklyn Dodgers
June 23, 1916	Tom Seaton	Cincinnati Reds
August 9, 1919	Hippo Vaughn	New York Giants
July 29, 1988	Rick Sutcliffe	at Philadelphia Phillies

A Pitcher Neither Hitting Nor Running

In 1902, the Cubs had a lefty named Jim St. Vrain who couldn't hit (and he wasn't much of a pitcher either). Normally a right-handed batter, he was encouraged to try it left-handed. Sure enough, he hit the ball right to Honus Wagner at shortstop . . . but he ran to third instead of first. Wagner said he was so confused that he didn't know whether to throw it to first or third.

The Worst

Pitcher Bob Buhl went 0-for-1962. He came to bat 70 times without a hit that season, blowing by Bill Wight's major-league record of 61, set while he was with the 1950 White Sox, and Ernie Koob's 41 with the 1916 Browns. Prior to Buhl, no NL pitcher had gone even 30 at bats without a hit.

Buhl finally got a hit on May 8, 1963, after 87 straight outs because the infielder fell down on the play. Buhl: "They called time to give me the damn ball. I was embarrassed, but I had to take it."

Bill Hands also entered the record book for hitting futility when he struck out in 14 consecutive at bats (his streak included a walk and two sacrifice bunts) in 1968, a major-league record tied 12 years later by the Padres' Juan Tyrone Eichelberger.

But, for sheer surprise and importance, what happened on the night of September 18, 1989, can't be topped. The Cubs are 5½ up on the third-place Mets, who are in town for a two-game series. In the Monday-night opener, the Mets jump out to a 3–0 lead, chasing Paul Kilgus after three. Frank Viola surrenders the lead in the fifth, and the Cubs take a 6–3 lead into the top of the eighth. Les Lancaster runs into trouble, so Mitch Williams comes in to bail him out. It's 6–4 in the bottom of the eighth, when the Cubs push a run across on Jeff Musselman, who has given up singles to Doug Dascenzo, Ryne Sandberg, and Mark Grace. With one out, Mitch Williams's spot in the order comes up. Don Zimmer has already double-switched Marvell Wynne for Lloyd McClendon, used Dwight Smith, Vance Law, and Gary Varsho to pinch-hit for pitchers, and brought Dascenzo in to play center field. Zimmer lets Mitch bat, and Wild Thing takes Don Aase deep for a three-run dinger, his only career home run. The Cubs clinch the pennant eight days later.

Odds and Ends

Jim Bullinger hit the first pitch he saw in the big leagues for a home run against Rheal Cormier of the St. Louis Cardinals, the only Cub to ever do that.

The Cubs' record for home runs by a pitcher in one season is six, set by Wild Bill Hutchison in 1894 and tied by Ferguson Jenkins in 1971, one short of the National League record held by Don Newcombe and Don Drysdale.

The 1887 Cubs set a record with 16 home runs by the pitching staff. John Clarkson led the way with six.

Ken Holtzman, Rick Reuschel, and Lee Smith all took Phil Niekro deep for their first home run in the majors. Ferguson Jenkins's first homer also came off of a Hall of Famer: Don Sutton—making Jenkins one of only 16 Hall of Famers to victimize a Hall of Famer for his first home run.

Hitters Pitching

When things get out of hand, sometimes hitters are called on to pitch. Larry Biittner was called on in 1977 and struck out the side. Of course, he also gave up five hits, a walk, and six runs. Cap Anson tried his hand at it during the 1883 and 1884 seasons. After three scoreless innings in 1883, Anson may have been a bit overconfident. He put himself into a game in 1884 while the outcome was still in doubt and ended up taking the loss after one messy inning.

Many of Chicago's 19th-century stars took a turn on the mound—most impressively George Van Haltren, whose career totals of 2,500 hits, 40 wins, and a partial no-hitter are tough to match. Their Chicago pitching results aren't half bad.

The Not-Half-Bad Seven

HITTER/PITCHER	W–L	G	GS	IP	H	BB	SO	ERA
Cap Anson	0–1	3	0	4	4	2	1	4.50
Tommy Burns	0–0	1	0	1	2	2	1	0.00
King Kelly	0–1	4	0	9	16	3	2	4.82
Fred Pfeffer	2–1	6	2	33	29	9	13	2.76
Jimmy Ryan	6–1	24	5	117	133	44	43	3.62
George Van Haltren	24–20	50	42	407	440	126	215	3.65
Ned Williamson	1–1	12	1	35	38	5	7	3.34

The Cubs have turned a few minor-league hitters into pitchers, most recently Jim Bullinger and Kevin Foster. With outfielder Hal Jeffcoat, they turned a *major-league* hitter into a pitcher in 1954. And not just any pitcher: their *closer.* Jeffcoat recorded 13 saves for the Cubs in 1954 and 1955, then went on to have three productive seasons with the Reds, including an 8–2 mark in 1956.

Perhaps the greatest hitter/pitcher in the big leagues—at least since Babe Ruth—was Doug Dascenzo. In four appearances in 1990 and 1991, Dascenzo pitched five innings, yielding three hits and no runs. He appeared in a 19–8 loss to the Mets and Dwight Gooden, a 13–5 loss to the Dodgers and Ramon Martinez, a 14–6 loss to the Cardinals, and a 13–4 loss to the Pirates and Doug Drabek, all at Wrigley. Despite his impressive performances hooking up with these aces, Dascenzo was never used in a close game.

WILD AT HEART

The Cubs have had more than their share of flakes, freaks, free spirits, and other nefarious characters who could have stepped from the pages of a Barry Gifford novel or been right at home in a David Lynch movie.

Eddie Solomon

Deemed "incorrigible" by Cubs management, Eddie Solomon showed up in the Cubs' bullpen after being traded to the Braves, refusing to leave. Later, during spring training 1980, Solomon brandished a gun in a restaurant. He stuck around long enough in the majors to give up Ryne Sandberg's first home run.

Willie Hernandez

Responding to resounding boos from the fans at Wrigley on May 31, 1980, Willie Hernandez drop-kicked his glove into the stands. Later in the season, he punched a fan. The Cubs stuck with him for seven years, but he didn't fulfill his potential until 1984 with his third organization.

Dave Kingman

The large, moody slugger went AWOL in 1980 on Friday the 13th, after reportedly dogging it with a shoulder injury and refusing to travel with the team while disabled. Later in the season, he was booed on Dave Kingman T-Shirt Day. All this in a season that began with Kingman's dumping ice water on a reporter. Kingman was dealt to the Mets after the season, with the Cubs having to eat $200,000 of his $240,000 salary.

Joe Pepitone

The first major-league player to use a hair dryer in the clubhouse, Joe Pepitone played for the Cubs from 1970 to 1973. Depending on his mood, or where he'd woken up that morning, he might have shown up for a game in a limo or on a motorcycle—though he was once accused by Leo Durocher of messing up his hitting with the vibrations from his bike.

Adolfo Phillips

Adolfo Phillips had a wealth of talent and looked to be the solution to the Cubs' center-field situation for the next 15 years—especially after a monster doubleheader against the Mets in 1967 when he went 6-for-9 with four home runs, putting his average at .328. But he didn't want to bat leadoff, and he complained when pitchers began to throw at him, finishing up the 1967 season at .268. He was washed-up at 27, struggling through a 1968 season in Chicago and Montreal in which he had 16 extra-base hits in 248 at bats yet somehow only eight RBIS.

Bill Faul

Bill Faul was a bodybuilder and minister who pitched while under self-hypnosis and talked to his arm. Something was working, because he threw three shutouts for the 1965 Cubs in only 16 starts. Hip to the hypnosis, opposing players began to swing pocket watches in the dugout while chanting, "Tick! Tock! Tick! Tock!" Maybe it was the watches or maybe it was Leo Durocher, who didn't suffer flakes gladly, but he went 1–4 in 1966 and was turned loose.

> *It's like going to the dentist to get a tooth pulled. It's a great pain to lose a bat like that, but eventually the pain goes away and you feel a whole lot better.* —Bill Caudill, *on the trade of Dave Kingman after the 1980 season*

> *I'll be glad to throw at him.* —Lynn McGlothlen, *on the same trade*

> *He's got as much ability as Willie Mays, and he could make a fortune playing baseball—if he wanted to play baseball.*
>
> Leo Durocher, on Adolfo Phillips

> *Faul was a guy who used to prepare for games by ripping off the heads of live parakeets. With his teeth. Then he would put himself into a trance and go out to throw a shutout. When he wasn't decapitating birds, he was swallowing live toads, claiming they put an extra hop on his fastball. None of these tricks bothered anybody, and after a few performances, their novelty wore off. What did upset some people and help gain Faul undying notoriety was his habit of grabbing someone's attention by picking him up at the ankles and holding him upside-down . . . from outside the fourth-story window of his hotel room. . . . Bill was the craziest guy I ever met or heard of. With the possible exception of the Marquis de Sade, there was nobody else in his league.*
>
> The left-handed Bill Lee

The Gold Dust Twins

Moe Drabowsky and Dick Drott combined for 28 wins as 21-year-olds for the 1957 Cubs. Drott's career was cut short by injury, while Drabowsky lasted several seasons as a notorious bullpen flake. Though their time in Chicago was brief, they did have their moments. One of the most memorable was when Drabowsky was rolled to first base in a wheelchair by Drott after Moe was hit in the foot with a pitch.

Lefty Tyler

After going 19–9 in 1918, Lefty Tyler found himself in constant pain the following year. He was deemed a perfect physical specimen—with the exception of his teeth—by the Mayo Clinic. So, the desperate southpaw had all of his teeth extracted.

Babe Herman

I was due for a bad outing.

Bill Bonham in 1971, after failing to retire any of the four batters he faced in his major-league debut. The Cubs' first flower child, Bonham went on to set what was then a major-league record with eight balks in 1974.

A legend in Brooklyn, Floyd Caves "Babe" Herman once doubled into a double play when he and two other runners all ended up at third base. In Brooklyn, he made a habit of dawdling on the bases on home runs, being passed on the bases not once but twice in 1930 by hitters going deep. He was cut from his minor-league team while batting .416, for letting a pop fly hit him on the head. As the Omaha owner put it: "I don't care if he's hitting 4.000. I'm not going to have players who field the ball with their skulls." He was cut another time for responding to a fine by demanding a bonus. Brooklyn once tried to foist him off on a minor-league franchise in Minneapolis by sneaking him into a package with eight other players for one prospect. Minneapolis took the other eight but refused to take delivery on Herman. His stay in Chicago was brief, his numbers not large enough to make him worth the trouble, and he was traded before the 1934 season because he was holding out. Herman claimed he wasn't. "You got the wrong idea entirely. I am not holding out. I just don't want to sign this %&#*ing contract the Cubs have sent me because the dough ain't big enough."

Heinie Zimmerman

Heinie Zimmerman would make baseball's all-time all-erratic team. He was a lousy fielder, an inconsistent hitter, and an unpleasant person who constantly brawled with teammates. In the middle of the 1908 season, Zimmerman threw ammonia at teammate Jimmy Sheckard, nearly blinding him, and was beaten to a pulp by his manager, Frank Chance.

Zimmerman was also known to kick up a fuss with umpires, but he was truly "in the zone" in June 1913 when he was tossed from three games in five days. On June 13, Zimmerman argued with Malcolm Eason for calling Jake Daubert safe at third on a force; on June 15, it was William Brennan, for calling him out at home; and on June 17, he was ejected by Bill Klem for arguing balls and strikes on Roger Bresnahan from third base. All this prompted a letter to a Chicago newspaper from someone calling himself A. Split Century:

> Here's a $100 bill split in two. Go give half to Heinie, and if he stays in the game for two weeks— that is, if he doesn't get canned by an ump in that period of time—pass him the other half and a piece of sticking plaster to stick 'em together.

Bill Klem was given one half, and Zimmerman the other (which Joe Tinker ripped in two when it was shown to him, convinced it was a joke). Even with $100 riding on it—not an insignificant sum for ballplayers in those days—Zimmerman nearly got himself tossed by Hank O'Day on June 24 and again in the final game of the fortnight by Ernest Quigley, who called him out attempting to steal home.

Zimmerman was unofficially banned from baseball for life after the 1919 season—quietly and before the Black Sox scandal erupted—for allegedly conspiring to fix games.

Claude Hendrix

Rumors that Claude Hendrix had bet against his own team in a game he was scheduled to pitch (Grover Cleveland Alexander stepped in for him at the last minute) led to the investigation that eventually uncovered the Black Sox scandal. Hendrix was subsequently suspended from baseball for life.

Bob Ferguson

White Stockings manager and shortstop Death to Flying Things later became an umpire. In this new role, Robert Vavasour Ferguson didn't suffer whiners gladly. He once broke a player's arm with a bat to end an argument.

Marla Collins

In 1986, the Cubs' ball girl was fired after appearing nude in *Playboy*. It wasn't like she shot someone . . .

Violet Valli and Ruth Ann Steinhagen

Not one but *two* baseball players, a Cub and a former Cub, have been shot in Chicago. The more famous of the incidents involved then-Phillies first-baseman Eddie Waitkus and an obsessed, 19-year-old groupie named Ruth Ann Steinhagen, who shot him on June 14, 1949, at the Edgewater Beach Hotel. Waitkus recovered and played for the 1950 Whiz Kids, and Bernard Malamud incorporated the incident into his novel *The Natural*.

Before Waitkus was shot in the stomach, showgirl Violet Valli shot her boyfriend, Cubs shortstop Billy Jurges, in the hand with a .25-caliber handgun. It happened on July 6, 1932, in room 509 of the Carliss Hotel and was the reason the Cubs had to bring in shortstop Mark Koenig. Koenig was voted only a half share of the World Series money, prompting his former Yankees teammates to ridicule the Cubs as cheapskates and the Cubs to respond with trash talk of their own. This bench-jockeying led to Babe Ruth's gesturing before the alleged "called shot" in Game Three.

Dom Dallesandro

During World War II, Dom Dallesandro flunked his eye test and was rejected for military service. But when he hit .309 in 1944, the army decided that maybe his eyesight wasn't so bad after all and inducted him.

Joe Decker

The hard-throwing right-hander from Storm Lake, Iowa, was so wild that teammates refused to face him. Asked to explain his brief success with the Twins after being traded by the Cubs, Joe Decker said, "If I'm lethargic, I have better stuff."

Turk Wendell

Turk Wendell was a contrived Mark Fidrych without the 19-win season. He hopped over foul lines, chain-sucked licorice, and brushed his teeth every inning. Perhaps his most annoying trait, however, was briefly turning into a viable relief pitcher down the stretch for the '98 Mets.

Rube Waddell

Imagine Turk Wendell, only genuinely weirder and with a lot more talent. George Edward "Rube" Waddell of Punxsutawney, Pennsylvania, was a Cub only very briefly, released at age 25 despite 14 wins and one of the best fastballs any lefty has ever thrown. Connie Mack maintained he was the greatest pitcher who ever lived, and he might have been the greatest Cubs lefty ever—had they kept him and had Frank Chance been able to put up with him.

He poured ice water on his arm before he pitched to keep the catcher from "burning up." He turned cartwheels on the mound after victories. He was distracted by opponents

---

Who Says Baseball Isn't a Rough Sport?

Jose Cardenal was scratched from the Cubs' Opening Day lineup because one of his eyelids wouldn't open. A man described by a teammate as wearing his uniform like a tuxedo, waltz-champion Kiki Cuyler once ended up on the disabled list after infecting his hand while giving himself a manicure. And Cubs phenom Mike Harkey—finally putting it all together in 1992, with a 4–0 record and a 1.89 ERA—put himself on the disabled list when he tore up his knee turning cartwheels in the outfield.

Let's face it. Turk's not John Wetteland.

A "vote of confidence" for his temporary closer Turk Wendell, from manager Jim Riggleman

---

He often missed school, but I could always find him playing ball, fishing, or following a fire engine.

Rube Waddell's sister

who held up puppies or bright, shiny toys in the dugout. He had to be restrained by teammates from chasing fire engines during games. He played marbles with kids outside ballparks, holding up games he was supposed to start. Against Detroit, he waved his outfielders in and instructed them to have a seat, then struck out the side. He wrestled alligators in the off-season. His roommate with the A's—Ossee Schreckengost—insisted that Connie Mack insert a clause into Waddell's contract that forbade him from eating animal crackers in the bed they had to share on road trips.

Waddell's frequent marriages were followed by several jail terms for nonsupport. Waddell outpitched Cy Young, 4–2, in 20 innings, on the Fourth of July, 1905, and later traded countless copies of the "Cy Young game ball" to gullible bartenders from New York to Philadelphia. As hard as he threw, he drank even harder, and his teammates finally insisted he be let go in 1908. He died of tuberculosis on April Fools' Day 1914 at the age of 37.

THE WAGES OF SIN

Many a wiser man than Hack Wilson has drowned his sorrows in the flowing bowl. —**Baseball magazine 1934**

U nfortunately, the story of the Cubs cannot be told without consideration of the effect of alcoholism on major-league players.

Cubs pitching ace Pat Malone and slugging outfielder Hack Wilson were brawlers and drinking buddies. In 1928, Wilson—who fought in the off-season under the name "Battling Stouts"—hopped into the stands to punch a heckler, and he beat up two Reds pitchers on the Fourth of July in 1929 after a beanball incident. Malone knocked out the teeth of a Chicago writer in 1931. After going 76–41 in his first four seasons, Malone became a .500 pitcher. Wilson, the National League's answer to Babe Ruth, "a lowball hitter and a highball drinker," was undone in 1931 by a deadened ball and Rogers Hornsby's mismanagement. Malone died of pancreatitis at age 40, while Wilson died a pauper at 48, in Babe Ruth's hometown of Baltimore, just three months after Ruth's death. Hornsby didn't drink, but he was a heavy gambler, and he later was driven from managerial jobs because of it.

Dickie Ray Noles was known for bending the elbow a bit and picking a fight or two. He missed 1½ months after a Montreal street fight in which he tried to take on a half dozen guys. He tried to pitch the next day, but his first delivery ended up in the stands. Even more famous is an incident in Cincinnati. He kicked a bouncer in the groin, beat up a cop, and didn't remember any of it because he was in a blackout. In "subduing" him, the bouncer and cop tore up his knee ligaments, and it took two years for him to get the strength back in his knee. He ended up spending 180 days in jail, serving his time at the end of the season.

Shufflin' Phil Douglas was an alcoholic spitballer who was on and off the wagon on a semiregular basis and was eventually banned by Judge Landis for a vague offer to Les Mann to throw a game.

Shortly before his release by the Cubs on June 15, 1926, Grover Cleveland Alexander was suspended by new manager Joe McCarthy for showing up drunk six times in 10 days.

One hundred years before the 1986 Mets won it all and then collapsed under the weight of their own excesses, the 1886 White Stockings made New York's squad look like a team of altar boys. Many players from the great White Stockings dynasty of the 1880s literally drank themselves to death. Shortstop Ned Williamson and catcher Silver Flint were dead at 36, Larry Corcoran at 32. Pitching ace John Clarkson broke down, went into an asylum, and died of

I've never played drunk. Hungover, yes, but never drunk. —Hack Wilson

He was built along the lines of a beer keg and not unfamiliar with its contents. —Sportswriter Shirley Povich, on Hack Wilson

Mr. Wilson is a fine young man, and I know that Mr. Donohue deserved to be struck in the mouth. Otherwise Mr. Wilson would not have struck him there. —A Chicago alderman, on Hack Wilson's one-sided fight with Reds pitcher Tom Donohue in 1929

I could put away three cases of beer a night. Now I can't handle that much. If I have only 15 beers, I'm totally gone.

Dickie Noles

Billy Sunday

Avoid the hellish booze that makes a man's brain a mud puddle. —Evangelist and former Cubs outfielder Billy Sunday

Very few major leaguers have the distinction of being sung about in a rock and roll song. Joe DiMaggio is the most famous, though he reportedly bristled when hearing Paul Simon wondering where he went. Jonathan Richman gave Walter Johnson a much less ambiguous tribute. Bob Dylan sang of Catfish Hunter soon after the "million dollar man" moved on from "Mr. Finley's Farm" to the New York Yankees. Warren Zevon wrote a song called "Bill Lee" inspired not by the Cubs righty but by the Red Sox lefty and his famous quote: "In baseball you're supposed to sit on your ass, spit tobacco, and nod at stupid things." A band named Game Theory named their greatest-hits album Tinker to Evers to Chance, *though the album art featured Tinkertoys, pocket watches, and dice rather than bats, gloves, and balls.*

The Grateful Dead honored only one baseball player and did so unknowingly. No doubt knowing Billy Sunday better from his second career as a fierce temperance advocate, the intemperate Jerry Garcia sang of him in "Ramble On, Rose," lumping the evangelist and Cubs outfielder in with Wolfman Jack, Jack the Ripper, and Frankenstein.

Sunday was a much better evangelist than a ballplayer. As a fleet-footed Cubs outfielder from 1883 to 1887—Cap Anson said he was "the fastest man in the profession, and one who could run the bases like a scared deer"—he was a reserve who never came to bat 200 times in a season and never hit higher than .291. He went 0-for-4 with four whiffs in his first game with the Cubs in 1883. It was his glove, however, that probably drove him to seek spiritual guidance. Though he was reputedly a good fielder, his fielding average in his final season with Chicago was .766, as he booted 25 of his 107 chances. It was actually a marked improvement over his first two seasons with the team, when he managed to handle only 64 of 97 chances for a fielding percentage of .660, registering more errors than runs scored. That's lousy even by 19th-century standards.

Statistics weren't recorded in his second career, so his number of career saves can only be estimated. Certainly more than Oscar Zamora, maybe even more than Lee Smith, and possibly even more than the total recorded by the dozen-odd Cubs dealt away or given up on since the early '60s.

pneumonia at 47, unhinged by a rail accident in January 1894 when he watched catcher Charlie Bennett slide under a train, which severed his legs. Hall of Famer King Kelly's dazzling skills were shot by age 33. He had been too hungover to play a crucial game for Boston against Cleveland late in the 1889 season, and he was working vaudeville when he died of pneumonia on November 8, 1894.

Only a few weeks before Kelly passed, former White Stockings pitcher Terry Larkin died. A 31-game winner in 1879, he drank himself off the team and out of baseball by 1880. His remaining years included attempted murder of his wife and attempted suicide in jail.

While team owner Albert Goodwill Spalding was trying to market baseball as representing all that was decent about America, his incredibly successful team was composed largely of drunks. In fact, spring training was invented by Spalding in 1886 when he took his team to Hot Springs, Arkansas, intending to "boil out the alcoholic microbes." In an exhibition series between the National League champion White Stockings and the American Association pennant-winners the year before, Charles Comiskey's St. Louis Browns, Chicago's subpar showing was blamed in large part on key players' showing up drunk. George Gore was benched in favor of Billy Sunday for drinking before a game. John Clarkson was supposed to start Game Seven but was too drunk and was sent home, and Jim McCormick took the loss in his place.

He was a whole-souled, genial fellow with a host of friends and but one enemy, that one being himself. Time and again, I have heard him say that he would never be broke, but money slipped through Mike's fingers as water slips through the meshes of a fisherman's net, and he was as fond of whiskey as any representative of the Emerald Isle. —Cap Anson on King Kelly

It depends on the length of the game. —King Kelly, on drinking while playing

In a rematch the following season, it was McCormick who was in no condition to pitch Game Three and Clarkson who returned the favor. McCormick had already pitched poorly in Game Two, "so thoroughly soused, he could not have struck out the batboy," as Spalding put it. In a critical Game Five, Clarkson showed up too drunk to pitch, and shortstop Ned Williamson took the loss in his place.

In the understatement of the year, Cap Anson said, "We were beaten and fairly beaten, but had some of the players taken as good care of themselves prior to these games as they were in the habit of doing when the league season was in full swim, I am inclined to believe there might have been a different tale to tell."

His patience having run out, Spalding began dismantling the team, selling King Kelly and later John Clarkson to the Boston Beaneaters for the unprecedented sums of $10,000 apiece.

MERKLE'S CURSE?

My team merely lost something it had already won three weeks ago. The Cubs will be acknowledged as champions, but their title is tainted.   —*John McGraw, October 1908*

It's believed that the Cubs' failure to reach the World Series since 1945 is due to a curse put on the team by William "Billy Goat" Sianis, a tavern owner, who was forbidden to take his goat into a 1945 World Series game. His son, Sam, and his goat, were invited to a game at Wrigley in 1981 to lift the hex—then brought back in 1994 when the Cubs went into May without a win at Wrigley. But the goat doesn't explain the six World Series losses prior to 1945 and the strange run of bad luck that befell the Cubs soon after their last World Championship in 1908.

After winning 99 games in 1908—the 99th the replay of the "Merkle Boner" game in which Giants manager John McGraw believed his team was robbed of its rightful pennant—the Cubs won 104 in 1909 but finished second. It's a record for most wins by a second-place team that still stands, .680 being the highest winning percentage any team has ever achieved with nothing to show for it. Jack "the Giant Killer" Pfiester, the lefty who was pitching for the Cubs in the Merkle Game, had his last big season in 1909, washed up at 32.

The Cubs did win the pennant in 1910, but Johnny Evers—the brains behind the disputed force-out in the Merkle Game—had a miserable season. His friend was killed in a car accident while Evers was driving. His investments went sour, and he went broke. He broke his leg in a play at the plate late in the season at Cincinnati and missed the Series. After missing some time in 1909 with a nervous breakdown, the intense Evers missed most of the 1911 season with another nervous breakdown and did not return to glory until he left Chicago for Boston in 1914. As for the 1910 World Series, the Cubs lost to the Athletics as their league-leading pitching staff suffered through an uncharacteristically hittable five games.

Young pitching star King Cole was stricken by malaria during the 1911 season and was never the same again. Before the 1912 season, third-baseman Jimmy Doyle died of appendicitis in spring training. Frank Chance played his final games with the Cubs in 1912, severely damaged by the numerous beanings he suffered.

After Chance, the Cubs went through a procession of managers—including Hank O'Day, the umpire in the Merkle Game—before reaching the World Series again in 1918, with Fred Merkle at first base. It was the fifth and final Series in which Merkle played, on the losing end each time (he later coached for the Yankees in 1926, being on hand to lose a sixth Series). The 1918 Cubs lost to the Red Sox despite six consecutive pitching gems, losing the final game when sure-handed outfielder Max Flack dropped a line drive. The Cubs' rookie star of 1918 was Charlie Hollocher; throughout his shortened career, Hollocher was dogged by stomach problems that eluded diagnosis, and he eventually killed himself at 44.

The 1929 Cubs won the pennant but blew an 8–0 lead in Game Four of the World Series and were closed out in five games when they blew a 2–0 lead in the ninth. The great-hitting team of 1930 failed to win the pennant, as pitcher Hal Carlson died of a stomach ailment and Rogers Hornsby broke his ankle and was lost for most of the season. The Cubs won the pennant in 1932 and 1938 but were swept by the Yankees in both Series. Chicago also reached the Series in 1935 but lost in six to the Tigers when they left the tying run at third with none out in the ninth inning of Game Six.

In 1945, the Cubs reached the World Series one last time. They took it to seven games but lost to an overmatched Detroit team—with the turning point of the Series coming in the sixth game when the Cubs' starting pitcher had his fingernail torn off by a shot back through the box (see "The Pennants," Chapter 13).

Are the Cubs' troubles a result of a curse placed on them by John McGraw? And will it last 100 years until 2008? Or will it succumb to the Y2K bug and finally free the Cubs from their hex?

If you're looking for a sign that the curse has been lifted, keep your eyes peeled for a hard-throwing young left-hander joining Kerry Wood at Wrigley Field.

bibliography

Anson, Adrian. *A Ball Player's Career.*

Appel, Marty. *Slide, Kelly, Slide.*

Banks, Ernie, and Jim English. *Mr. Cub.*

Bartlett, Arthur. *Baseball and Mr. Spalding.*

The Baseball Encyclopedia.

Brown, Warren. *The Chicago Cubs.*

Caray, Harry, and Bob Verdi. *Holy Cow.*

Carmichael, John P., ed. *My Greatest Day in Baseball.*

Carter, Craig, ed. The Sporting News *Complete Baseball Record Book.*

Cohen, Richard M., and David S. Neft. *The Sports Encyclopedia: Baseball.*

———. *The World Series.*

Curran, William. *Big Sticks.*

Evers, John J., and Hugh Fullerton. *Touching Second.*

Fleming, G. H. *The Unforgettable Season.*

Gershman, Michael. *Diamonds.*

Gifford, Barry. *The Neighborhood of Baseball.*

Golenbock, Peter. *Wrigleyville.*

Grimm, Charlie, and Edward Prell. *Jolly Cholly's Story.*

Honig, Donald. *The Man in the Dugout.*

Lansche, Jerry. *Baseball's Forgotten Championships.*

Lee, Bill, with Dick Lally. *The Wrong Stuff.*

Lieb, Fred. *The Baseball Story.*

Lowry, Philip J. *Green Cathedrals.*

Mathewson, Christy. *Pitching in a Pinch.*

McConnell, Bob, and David Vincent, eds. *The Home Run Encyclopedia.*

McFarlane, Brian. *It Happened in Baseball.*

Mead, William B. *Two Spectacular Seasons.*

Nathan, David H. *Baseball Quotations.*

Peary, Danny, ed. *We Played the Game.*

Reichler, Joseph. *Baseball's Great Moments.*

———. *Great All-Time Baseball Record Book.*

Reidenbaugh, Lowell. *Baseball's 25 Greatest Pennant Races.*

Ritter, Lawrence. *The Glory of Their Times.*

Seymour, Harold. *Baseball: The Golden Age.*

Shatzkin, Mike, ed. *The Ballplayers.*

Smith, Curt. *Voices of the Game.*

Smith, Robert. *Baseball in the Afternoon.*

Spalding, Albert. *Baseball: America's National Game.*
Talley, Rick. *The Cubs of '69.*
Thorn, John, and Pete Palmer, eds. *Total Baseball.*
Veeck, Bill, with Ed Linn. *Veeck as in Wreck.*
Ward, Geoffrey C., and Ken Burns. *Baseball: An Illustrated History.*
Wheeler, Lonnie. *Bleachers.*
Wrigley, William. *The Man and His Business.*

index

Cast of characters: players, managers, and other notable personalities